THAT DEVIL FORREST

THAT DEVIL FORREST

Life of General Nathan Bedford Forrest

BY JOHN ALLAN WYETH

Foreword by Henry Steele Commager

Maps by Jean Tremblay

Original illustrations by T. de Thulstrup, Rogers,

Klepper, Redwood, Hitchcock, & Carlton

With a New Foreword by Albert Castel

LOUISIANA STATE UNIVERSITY PRESS

BATON ROUGE

Louisiana Paperback Edition, 1989
05 04 03 02 01 00   15 14

Library of Congress Cataloging-in-Publication Data

Wyeth, John A. (John Allan), 1845–1922
    That devil Forrest : the life of General Nathan Bedford Forrest /
by John A. Wyeth ; with a new foreword by Albert Castel.—
Louisiana pbk. ed.
     p. cm.
    Reprint. Originally published: New York : Harper, 1959.
    Bibliography: p.
    Includes index.
    ISBN 0-8071-1578-9
    1. Forrest, Nathan Bedford, 1821–1877.   2. Generals—United
States—Biography.   3. United States—History—Civil War, 1861–1865—
Biography.   4. Confederate States of America. Army—Biography.
I. Title.   II. Title: Life of General Nathan Bedford Forrest.
E467.1.F72W92   1989
973.7'3'092—dc20
[B]   89-8174
                                                  CIP

"That devil Forrest was down about Johnsonville, making havoc among the gunboats and transports."

—*General Sherman to General Grant, November 6, 1864*

CONTENTS

ILLUSTRATIONS

The illustrations in this book will be found in three groups facing pages 102, 262, and 486. In addition, there is a frontispiece of General Nathan Bedford Forrest.

The action drawings of the first and third groups were done by six well-known illustrators. of the late nineteenth century for the original edition of the book: T. de Thulstrup, Rogers, Klepper, Redwood, Hitchcock, and Carlton. In the first group the first six pictures describe events at Fort Donelson during Grant's successful siege and Forrest's ultimate escape; the last five pictures illustrate incidents during Forrest's pursuit of Streight's raiders. In the third group the first four pictures describe the storming of Fort Pillow; the next three illustrate highlights from the Battle of Brice's Crossroads; and the final picture depicts Forrest's raid on Memphis.

The central group of pictures are portraits, some by camera and some by pen or brush, of thirty-two of the men in Forrest's command.

MAPS

PUBLISHER'S NOTE

The *Life of General Nathan Bedford Forrest* was first published in 1899 and reissued in 1908, finally going out of print in 1924. Secondhand copies have been sought after by collectors for a long time.

The material for the book was carefully collected over many years. One of its unique features was the great body of firsthand, eyewitness testimony, much of it in the form of depositions, the rest based on the author's interviews and correspondence with men who served with and against Forrest. This firsthand material is responsible for many of the best anecdotes and bits of color about Forrest, and made the book the best primary source for other biographies and articles. But another important reason for taking so much trouble to check and recheck the accounts and reports was that Forrest was—and still remains—a very controversial figure.

There were several reasons for this, but the two factors which have done the most to damage his reputation were the charges that he was responsible for the massacre of Federal troops—about two-thirds of them Negroes—after the capture of Fort Pillow, and that he was the first leader of the Ku-Klux Klan after the war. The first of these charges is thoroughly explored and effectively answered in the book. The second is barely touched on, for at the time the book was written little was definitely known about this secret organization or Forrest's possible connection with it. The best evidence, based on his own testimony before Congress and some unverified statements by associates, was that Forrest was active in the Klan and probably served as its first Grand Wizard. However, it should be borne in mind in assessing this charge that the original Klan was born in the desperate year of 1867, and was officially disbanded in 1869, when it became evident that it could not be effectively controlled by its more responsible members. Its activities in this short time were not all terrorism and violence, and in many sections its aims were to maintain order and fill the void created by the collapse of local law enforcement.

There were other reasons that contributed to Forrest's tarnished reputation. The Northern press singled him out as the great evil bogey-man of the Confederacy, and added fabrication upon rumor till he became anathema to Northern sympathizers. Part of this was due to his background as onetime slave trader. Part of it was caused by his ferocious ultimatums to surrounded Federal garrisons to surrender or he would not be responsible for the lives of the defenders when the position was taken. That this was just bluff, almost always successful, was never understood, and Forrest was too wise in the ways of psychological warfare to give the bluff away. Part of it was due to rumors, completely untrue, as many of his foes testified, that he murdered or mistreated prisoners of war. And part of it was due simply to his fantastic success in bold raids into enemy territory. Forrest was no angel and he waged war to the hilt, but neither was he the monster that many made him out to be.

The original text of the book has not been altered for this new edition, other than to modernize spelling and punctuation, shorten some paragraphs, remove some of the flowery figures of speech popular in the nineteenth century, and to eliminate some of the repetitions and unnecessary details that slow the narrative. Some of the latter which have been deemed of interest to Civil War students and scholars have been preserved in notes in the back. The book has been completely reset, but the original illustrations have been retained. In addition, there are twenty-one new maps, an index, and a chronology of events.

John Allan Wyeth was born in Missionary Station, Alabama, in 1845, and lived in Guntersville at the southernmost loop of the Tennessee River. His father was Judge Louis Wyeth of Marshall County, who later became a district judge. His mother, Euphemia Allan, was the daughter of a Presbyterian minister in Huntsville, Alabama, who was active in the Southern abolition movement. When the Civil War broke out, John Wyeth was a sixteen-year-old student at La Grange Military Academy. The Academy closed in December, 1861, and he ran the family farm during the summer of 1862. In the late fall of that year he joined General Morgan's cavalry as a civilian "independent" and went along on their famous Christmas raid into Kentucky. It was decided on his return home that he would fare better if captured if he wore a uniform. He joined General Joseph Wheeler's command as a private in Colonel Russell's Fourth Alabama Cavalry and took part in the skirmishing and scouting in central Tennessee during the winter and spring of 1863 and in the hectic activities during the summer as Bragg retreated from Tennessee into Georgia before Rosecrans. On this campaign he was with Wheeler during the latter's rearguard fight at Shelbyville, and if his horse had not thrown him at a high fence he would have participated in the famous leap off the bluff into the Duck River. As it was, after the Union cavalry had ridden over him he escaped from the battlefield with his horse and made his way back to his unit.

At Chickamauga he carried a message through enemy lines and served under Wheeler on the Confederate left flank. Two weeks later, while raiding a Federal wagon train in the Sequatchie Valley, he got too far ahead and with two companions was cut off by a squad of Union troopers. Abandoning their horses, they took to the ridge and escaped.

Two days later, while making their way toward Confederate lines, they came face to face with the enemy at the top of a rise and were taken prisoner.

Wyeth was shipped to prison at Camp Morton, Indiana, where he spent sixteen months. Many years later he wrote an article describing the miseries and abuses of camp life that brought indignant denials from once-prominent Union figures. His rebuttal was effective, but the uproar forced the magazine to cancel a proposed sequel. Because of bad health he was among the first at Camp Morton to be exchanged. He was sent to Richmond and made his way by train and foot to southern Georgia, where his family had taken refuge after the burning of Guntersville. The sum total of his family's resources was the $15 young Wyeth had saved and hidden in the heel of his boot for many months.

It took several years of outdoor living, good food, and rest before Wyeth regained his health. In 1867 he began the study of medicine at the University of Louisville, and in 1869 opened his practice in Guntersville. Distressed over the death of his fourth patient, he took down his shingle and determined to earn the money to get clinical training. For three years he was a superintendent and river-boat pilot on the White and Red rivers in Arkansas for a contractor. In 1872 he matriculated at New York's Bellevue Medical College, and in the next forty years he became one of the most prominent surgeons of the country, author of a leading textbook, president of the A.M.A. and of the New York Medical Association, and founder of the first American post-graduate school of medicine, the Polyclinic Hospital. He married the daughter of Dr. J. Marion Sims, well-known gynecologist and founder of the Woman's Hospital, and was active in many causes. He died in 1922. The story of his life is told in his autobiography, *With Sabre and Scalpel.*

Foreword

Sherman called Nathan Bedford Forrest a "devil" and promised a brigadier general promotion to major general if he killed him. Two generations later the southern Agrarian writer Andrew Lytle described him as
the "spiritual comforter" of his people because during Reconstruction he
headed the Ku Klux Klan. Today blacks in Memphis regard the eques-
trian statue of him as an offense to their race and are demanding that it be
removed. On the other hand, to Civil War buffs, the vast majority of
whom are white, he is a hero with a status rivaling that of Lee, Grant,
and Stonewall Jackson. Hated and admired, feared and glorified when
alive, he remains more than a hundred years after his death a controversial figure and no doubt will continue to be.

About one thing, however, everybody always has agreed: he was a remarkable man and an outstanding military commander. The man was
born dirt poor in 1821 on a backwoods Tennessee farm. He had only a
few months of formal schooling, and though he learned to read with fair
facility, he never looked at a pen, as he once put it, "without thinking of
a snake." These educational deficiencies were not insuperable handicaps
in the semi-frontier society of his time and place, and by 1861 he had
made a fortune as a slave-trader, planter, and speculator. His appearance
reflected his background. In the words of one of his officers, "Without a
uniform, and this did not much change him, he looked like an old country farmer," and his "manner was mild, his speech rather low and slow."
Battle, or its approach, transformed him. "His face flushed," wrote another of his officers, "till it bore a striking resemblance to a painted Indian warrior," his eyes blazed "with the intense glare of a panther
springing upon his prey," and his voice became "shrill," "piercing,"

xv

and "electrifying." Perhaps no commander since the age of the armored knight killed more foes in personal encounters than he—at least thirty—or had more horses shot out from under him—twenty-nine. Yet he himself suffered, throughout the entire war, only two serious wounds—and one of those was inflicted by a disgruntled officer in his own command who shot him in the hip at point-blank range with a large-caliber pistol. Forrest's instantaneous reaction was to disembowel the officer with a pocketknife. Moreover, twelve days later he was back in action.

By all odds and all logic he should never have become a military leader, much less an outstanding one. Not only was he totally devoid of military training and experience, he had opposed secession until it took place, and when he joined the Confederate army in June, 1861, a month shy of his fortieth birthday, it was as a private. To be sure, he soon received a lieutenant colonel's commission and authorization to raise a cavalry battalion, but numerous other wealthy, upper-class Southerners started their war careers the same way, only to remain at their original rank, or close to it, and little known then and since. Forrest, in contrast, at once displayed a natural knack for warfare and did it, furthermore, in such a way and at such places as to make him famous quickly.

At Fort Donelson and Shiloh early in 1862 he distinguished himself for daring, skillful fighting, and enterprise. Starting in the summer of 1862, he made slashing raids through western Tennessee and Kentucky, harried the Federals in Middle Tennessee, and in northern Mississippi helped turn back Grant's first attempt to take Vicksburg. In the spring of 1863, now a brigadier general, he pursued Colonel Abel Streight's Yankee raiders through northern Alabama and captured them all, despite being outnumbered nearly three to one. Following the Battle of Chickamauga in September, 1863, when he again performed superbly, he became so disgusted with the petty-minded General Braxton Bragg that he refused to serve under him. Ordinarily such insubordination would have brought a court-martial, but in Forrest's case it resulted in his reassignment to Mississippi with the rank of major general, for even Bragg recognized his value to the Confederacy. There was, however, a catch to this transfer and promotion: he was permitted to take along fewer than three hundred veterans of his old command and thus would have to acquire a new one. In December, 1863, going into Union-occupied western Tennessee, he did exactly that, coming back with two thousand recruits.

Thus he made ready for 1864. Three times during that year he repulsed vastly superior Federal forces that set out from Memphis to destroy him, and on two of those occasions (Okolona and Brice's Cross Roads) he routed them. Then, faced by a fourth enemy expedition of overwhelming strength, he turned it back too by striking directly at Memphis itself. Following the defeat of the first invasion, he raided deep behind Union lines, penetrating all the way to the Ohio River, capturing forts, and in one case (Fort Pillow, Tennessee, April 12) wiping out most of an enemy garrison. In the autumn he swept northward twice more, each time to attack Sherman's supply line in Tennessee. But though he devastated an entire railroad, demolished depots, burned transport ships, and even captured and used Yankee gunboats, he was, through no fault of his own, too late to prevent what many believed then and believe now he could have prevented had he been unleashed sooner—Sherman's capture of Atlanta.

Finally, as a climax, in November he joined General John Bell Hood's army as it invaded Tennessee in a desperate attempt to undo the calamitous consequences of the fall of Atlanta by smashing Federal forces in that state before they could concentrate, seizing the immense military storehouse in Nashville, and then pushing on to the Ohio or to Virginia. At Spring Hill he gave Hood a chance of success, supposing he had any chance at all, only to have him muff it. At Franklin he gave Hood advice that would have enabled him to at least postpone failure, but Hood disregarded it and proceeded to murder his own troops. And after what was left of Hood's army was routed at Nashville on December 15–16, Forrest commanded the rear guard that prevented annihilation. Throughout the entire war no general, Northern or Southern, came close to matching, much less surpassing, the level of activity and intensity that Forrest achieved in 1864.

The spring of 1865 found him a lieutenant general in charge of the Alabama-Mississippi remnant of the Confederacy. On April 2 he fought his last battle and lost it—a hopeless defense of Selma against an immensely stronger force of Union cavalry armed with repeating rifles. Yet he remained in the field, undaunted and deadly, and Sherman worried that he would join John S. Mosby and Wade Hampton—both, like him, nonprofessionals who had fighting in their blood—in waging guerrilla warfare. When, following the surrenders of Lee and Johnston, Forrest obeyed the order of his departmental commander and also surrendered, Sherman and other Northern generals could feel much easier about the future.

No one illustrates better than Forrest the truth of what the Union general Jacob D. Cox, himself a civilian who became an excellent soldier during the Civil War, declared in his *Reminiscences,* namely, that "a bold heart, a cool head, and practical common sense were of much more importance than anything taught at school" in determining success as a commander. Or, as one of Forrest's veterans put it more succinctly and colorfully, Forrest's "commission as General was signed not only by Mr. Jefferson Davis, but by the Almighty as well."

What were the components of the spectacular success of what one author has called this "untutored military genius"? One, certainly, was his enormous energy, endurance, and determination. To quote another of his soldiers, "He never seemed to be satisfied with any amount of success so long as there remained anything else to do, and he never let a chance to strike the enemy go by if there was any possibility of defeating him or doing him damage, and never seemed to get tired or sleepy or discouraged." At Okolona in February, 1864, he routed a Union force that outnumbered his own three to one largely because, wrote one of his officers, he was able to "inspire every one with his terrible energy, more like that of a piece of powerful steam machinery than a human being." Four months later, following eight hours of fierce fighting against heavy odds at Brice's Cross Roads, he pursued the defeated Federals relentlessly for two days, not stopping until his troopers were falling out of their saddles and their horses collapsing from exhaustion.

He also possessed a talent for improvisation, an almost incredible ability to adapt to the unexpected, the element that Clausewitz terms the essence of war. Thus during an engagement near Franklin, Tennessee, in April, 1863, a courier galloped up to him with the alarming news that the enemy had gotten into his rear. Forrest instantly replied, "That's where I've been trying to get him all day, damn him! I'll be in *his* rear in about five minutes!"—and proceeded to do exactly that. Afterward he admitted that he had been taken totally by surprise and had thought his whole command had "gone up."

Yet he was no hell-for-leather berserker, wading into battle without foresight or forethought. On the contrary, he planned and prepared carefully whenever he had the opportunity. General Richard Taylor, a highly competent Confederate commander, relates in his memoirs, *Destruction and Reconstruction,* how he met Forrest for the first time in September, 1864, to plan the latter's raid into Tennessee against Sherman's supply line. To his surprise, Forrest "suggested many difficulties, and asked many questions"—so many that Taylor "began to think he had no stomach for the work." But then, "having isolated the chances of success from causes of failure, with the care of a chemist experimenting in a laboratory," Forrest's "whole manner" abruptly changed and in "a dozen sharp sentences" he outlined what he would do and how, then declared that he would "march with the dawn, and hoped to give an account of himself in Tennessee."

Last but far from least, Forrest had that power which all great commanders have and which, perhaps more than anything else, makes them great commanders—the ability, so to speak, to read the mind and sense the mood of an opponent and to act accordingly. The best, most telling example of this knack comes from the Okolona campaign of February, 1864. Brigadier General William Sooy Smith, at the head of a large and well-equipped Union cavalry expedition, moved deeper and deeper into Mississippi, encountering practically no resistance from Forrest's much smaller force. Suddenly—and correctly—he perceived that he was walking into a trap and was in danger of being destroyed. Therefore he sent several regiments to fake an attack on Forrest so as to conceal the retreat of his main body. Forrest was not deceived. "I think," he told one of his generals, "they are badly scared" and launched an all-out pursuit that overtook and routed Smith.

Complementing Forrest's personal strengths—indeed, making possible their full development—was the qualitative superiority of the Confederate cavalry. The Southern troopers were not braver than their Northern counterparts, certainly they did not surpass them in discipline, and—legend to the contrary—they were not necessarily better riders, at least in the West. There, a large portion of the Union cavalrymen were themselves Southerners from Kentucky and Tennessee, or else farm boys from the Midwest who by no means were strangers to either horses or the hunt. The Southerners, with their cavalier tradition and self-image, believed they were superior, and because this belief was not mere conceit, it helped make them so in actuality. More important, from the very beginning of the war the Confederates had a larger number of capable cavalry commanders than did the Federals, who failed to produce comparable leadership until much later, and the spectacular exploits of these commanders—notably Stuart, Ashby, Morgan, and Forrest himself—enhanced the Southern sense (and thus fact) of superiority. Likewise, the Confederate army organized and utilized its cavalry more effectively than did the Union forces, grouping them into large and centrally controlled units that performed important tactical and strategic missions. Northern horsesoldiers, in contrast, long remained scattered in small detachments engaged primarily in scout, picket, and police duties.

Finally, and also paradoxically, the one thing in which the Southerners were inferior—weapons—turned out to be yet another, sometimes decisive advantage. The Confederacy lacked the means to furnish its troopers with the breech-loading carbines that were standard for cavalry at the outbreak of the Civil War. Perforce, therefore, most of them, especially in the West, had to make do with the same long-barreled, muzzle-loading rifle issued to the infantry. Since they found aiming these rifles accurately and reloading rapidly to be virtual impossibilities while on horseback, out of necessity they dismounted to fight. They discovered that a man standing on the ground could shoot faster and truer than could one on horseback while at the same time offering a far less vulnerable target. Moreover, the rifle had a much longer killing range than did the carbine, not to mention revolver and saber. Besides, most of the time the terrain, being densely wooded and brush-covered, made classic cavalry tactics impractical. For example, prior to his ill-fated expedition against Forrest in 1864, William Sooy Smith proclaimed to his men that "on favorable ground a saber charge of our forces upon the enemy, who have laid aside their sabers, must result in most signal and decisive success, if resolutely made." Following his debacle at Okolona he complained that the Rebels were "better armed for fighting dismounted" and that saber attacks failed to "cut them to pieces because of the undergrowth to which they fled." Only in the closing months of the war, when they were armed with Spencer repeaters and themselves usually fought on foot, did the Union cavalrymen match their Confederate opponents in combat effectiveness—and even then their victories owed more to greater numbers than to anything else. Like Alexander the Great, like Napoleon, Forrest benefited from having at his disposal a superior military instrument, one that he improved even more by the skill and inspiration of his leadership.

But the ultimate explanation of Forrest's success lies in his realism—the ability to see things as they are and to do what needs be done. This ability can be found in his attitude toward war in general and the Civil War in particular. Despite all the rhetoric from the South's politicians and editors about "States Rights" and "Southern Nationalism," he had no illusions about its true purpose: "If we ain't fightin' to keep slavery, then what the hell are we fightin' for?" Following the failure to turn the hard-won victory at Chickamauga into a decisive one, he concluded that both the Confederacy and slavery were doomed, and accordingly he freed the forty-five slaves who were serving him as teamsters. Henceforth he fought only out of a sense of duty and honor—and, one suspects, for the sheer joy a master artist derives from doing what he does so well. After the military war was over he helped, as head of the Klan, the South to win what was still winnable—the political war—and thus get what it then wanted: "White Supremacy" and "Home Rule."

As for war per se, Forrest stripped it to its basics: "War means fighting, and fighting means killing." Victory goes to the side that does the best job of killing. The secret of victory is to "get there first with the most." To achieve that, he attacked whenever possible: "Fifteen minutes of *bulge* is worth a week of tactics." Yet he was an excellent tactician. Invariably he sought a weak spot in the enemy's line, supported his assaults with close-range artillery fire, and from his first skirmish onward sent part of his force to strike an opponent's flank or, as he put it, "hit 'em on the end." The detachment executing the flanking movement usually was mounted, an exception to his standard practice of fighting his troops on foot, and he himself rode into battle with his escort company, an elite band of fighters, if the issue trembled in the balance or when firepower had prepared the way for shock action. If at all possible, he endeavored not merely to drive back but to rout his foes: "The time to whip the enemy is when they are running." As a matter of policy he threatened fortified garrisons with extermination if he was forced to storm their works, with the result that they generally surrendered—especially after what happened at Fort Pillow. He could be equally harsh with his own men, shooting them down if they broke to the rear during combat and instructing his officers to do the same. Although he hacked down a large number of antagonists with his razor-sharp sword, thanks to his strength, size, and ferocity, he considered revolvers far more effective for hand-to-hand fighting and so retained sabers in his command only for officers as a badge of rank. In contrast, during the spring of 1864, by which time it should have been obvious that "cold steel" was about as obsolete as the crossbow, Major General Joseph Wheeler, head of the cavalry of the Confederate Army of Tennessee, West Pointer, and author of a manual on cavalry tactics, had his troopers practice saber attacks on straw dummies attired in Yankee uniforms because General Joseph Johnston, commander of that army, wanted "cavalry who can charge infantry." In the ensuing Atlanta Campaign, Wheeler's cavaliers did not make a single mounted charge against real Union infantry but did spend considerable time in the trenches serving as infantry themselves.

There can be no doubt that Forrest did everything that could be asked of a cavalry leader and did it supremely well: scout, screen, raid, and fight effectively both as part of an army and as head of an independent force. The only question that can be, and indeed has been, raised concerning his military talents is whether he could have successfully commanded a large, full-fledged army in major operations. On the negative side, his stormy temper would likely have provoked crippling conflicts with the high command in Richmond and with his subordinate generals. Further, his lack of formal education, intellectual sophistication, and military training would have handicapped him when it came to complex administrative, logical, and strategic matters. Last but far from least, the history of war is filled with generals who were brilliant so long as they, like Forrest throughout his career, headed a force small enough to direct and supervise personally, but who failed when placed in command of an army so big that they had to rely on others to implement their plans and who faltered under the awful responsibility of fighting a battle or waging a campaign that might determine the outcome of the whole war. On the positive side, Forrest obeyed orders even when, as at Harrisburg, Mississippi, on July 14, 1864, it would have been better had he not. His subordinates, fearing his wrath, would likely have done their best to carry out his instructions, no matter how much they might have disliked or disagreed with him. In addition, any technical or administrative deficiencies he had could have been supplied by competent staff officers, people he was adept at selecting. And, as another Confederate general observed after the war, "Forrest's capacity for war seemed only to be limited by the opportunities for its display." Which point of view is correct cannot, of course, be objectively determined. Furthermore, historically it is a moot question, for not once during the entire Civil War did Jefferson Davis give command of a major Confederate army to anyone who was not, as he himself was, a graduate of West Point. But at the very least it seems possible that the man who, unlike the West Pointer Simon Bolivar Buckner, refused to surrender at Fort Donelson when it was easy to escape; who at Chickamauga urged the West Pointer Bragg to go after the defeated Federals before they had time to recover; and who at Franklin tried to stop the West Pointer Hood from making an attack that was as unnecessary as it was doomed, had the potential of being a successful army commander, provided he had an army of sufficient strength to perform the mission assigned it. Certainly he could not have done worse than any of the commanders just named.

Forrest was bound to attract biographers. The first were Thomas Jordan and John P. Pryor, Memphis journalists and former Confederate officers. In 1868 they published *The Campaigns of Lieut. Gen. N. B. Forrest and of Forrest's Cavalry.* Based on Forrest's private papers, his personal testimony, and written under his supervision, it came close to being an autobiography. Containing much valuable information, the book presented Forrest's career as he saw it. Inevitably, however, it manifested a strong pro-Southern bias and either committed numerous factual errors or omitted important information. Thus it provided a good foundation for a biography of Forrest but not the complete structure.

To construct that was the task John Allan Wyeth set for himself. Born in 1845 at Missionary Station, Alabama, he was a cadet at La Grange Military Academy when the Civil War broke out. From the beginning of the conflict, he states in his autobiography, *With Sabre and Scalpel,* Forrest was "my hero, just as Marion was of the Revolution. I read with avidity of his great exploits, his hand-to-hand combat at Monterey, his refusal to surrender, and escape of his entire command at Fort Donelson." In the spring of 1863 he joined the 4th Alabama Cavalry, which had earlier formed part of Forrest's command, and was impressed by the outspoken admiration of its veterans for "Old Bedford." Following the war he studied medicine in both the United States and Europe, established his own clinic in New York, wrote a standard textbook on surgery, and became one of the nation's preeminent physicians. All the while, however, he retained a deep interest in Forrest and vowed that "should he not be placed right in history by the time I was fifty years old, I would undertake to do it." In 1895, a true biography of Forrest still lacking, he proceeded to keep his vow. First acquiring the *Official Records of the Union and Confederate Armies,* which was virtually complete by then, and other pertinent printed sources, he collected and collated a mass of written testimony from men who had ridden with Forrest, among them some of his closest associates. In 1899, Harper published his *Life of General Nathan Bedford Forrest.*

It far surpassed in breadth and depth of coverage, and in accuracy and analysis, Jordan and Pryor's book. Although also pro-Southern, it was less blatantly so, and it gave the Union version of events as well as the Confederate. It also revealed the harsher aspects of Forrest's character and career, such as his murderous temper and his tendency to be over-bearing and arrogant, as well as various personal altercations. Above all, through the accounts Wyeth had obtained from Forrest's veterans, it offered a great deal of new and valuable information about Forrest and his campaigns, and did so in highly readable fashion. In sum it was a major addition to the literature of Civil War history and at once became a classic in its field.

How well does Wyeth's work stand up after nearly a hundred years? In some places, frankly, it does not, or else is wobbly. Much more is known about Forrest's prewar life, thanks primarily to the researches of Captain J. Harvey Mathes of Memphis, who in 1902 published his findings in *General Forrest.* The story related in Chapter One, which Wyeth de-rived from Jordan and Pryor, of Forrest single-handedly holding off a would-be lynch mob with only a pocketknife, not only seems incredible but in fact is incredible: as contemporary newspapers make clear, the mob's intended victim was saved when his mother pleaded for his life. At Shiloh, Forrest did assault a Union battery but, contrary to the source that Wyeth used for his account (pp. 62–63), did not capture any of the artillery, as his regiment became bogged down in a marsh. Concerning the same battle, Wyeth (pp. 63–64) exaggerates both the precariousness of the Union situation at the end of the first day's fighting and the impor-tance of Forrest's reports that Grant was receiving reinforcements, thus contributing to the myth that the Confederates lost a great chance for a decisive victory when they did not continue their attack that day. By the same token, Longstreet's postwar statement, obtained and quoted by Wyeth (pp. 236–38), that Forrest's dispatch to Bragg on the day after Chickamauga, about the Federals' evacuating Chattanooga, "fixed the fate of the Confederacy" because Bragg then abandoned a plan to cut off their retreat. This observation, however, attributes too much to too little. In truth, Bragg received a number of reports to the same effect from others besides Forrest; and even had he not, he was physically and psychologically incapable of adopting any plan, much less the one alleged by Longstreet. With regard to the most controversial episode in Forrest's military career, the Fort Pillow slaughter of April 12, 1864, Wyeth does a persuasive job of absolving Forrest of direct personal blame, and he is honest enough to admit that "a number" of Union soldiers were "shot down who were trying to surrender and should have been spared," but he goes too far in asserting that there was no massacre in the usual sense of that term (pp. 337–38). The main basis for this claim is testimony presented in the 1890s by members of Forrest's command. This evidence, though valuable, comes from men who had strong motives for attempting to palliate what happened at Fort Pillow and therefore cannot be given the same weight as the statements of Federal survivors and the letters, diaries, and other reports written by Confederate participants immediately after the event. These make it clear that a very large number of the fort's garrison, particularly blacks, were killed after they ceased resisting or were incapable of resisting. Finally, Wyeth exaggerates the significance of the damage done by Forrest in September, 1864, to the railroad between Nashville and Decatur—this line never was of major importance to the supply of Sherman's army in Georgia—and his account of Forrest's participation in the Ku Klux Klan is as superficial as it is brief.

There are other weaknesses in the book but, like most of those mentioned earlier, they are either minor or else reflect the state of historical knowledge and the prevailing attitudes at the time Wyeth wrote—factors no historian can escape. Taken as a whole, it remains a superb work of history and biography. That is why during the ninety years since its original publication it has been reissued at least four times—in 1922 and (in abridged form) 1959 by Harper & Brothers, in 1975 by the Morningside Press, and now in this edition—and why it continues to be included on all lists entitled "One Hundred Best Civil War Books." That is why, too, of all the books about Forrest there is only one that bears comparison with it, and that is Robert Selph Henry's *"First with the Most" Forrest,* published in 1944. Henry was an excellent historian and writer, he had access to sources unavailable to Wyeth, he was able to approach Forrest and the Civil War from a longer perspective, and his interpretations are more objective and sophisticated. Yet factually he presents little of substance that cannot be found in Wyeth's work, from which he drew heavily, and his conclusions on most controversial events tend to be much the same. In sum, Henry supplements Wyeth but does not supplant him, and though there is need for a new study of Forrest, one embodying the vast amount of new information and fresh insights regarding the Civil War that have emerged since World War II, no such study has appeared or been announced as forthcoming.

It seems that when Wyeth wrote about Forrest he, like his hero, got there first with the most.

ALBERT CASTEL

Foreword

WHEN the Confederacy collapsed, it collapsed all over, and looking back at that prodigious disintegration we find it hard to imagine that the South ever had a chance to survive. Yet the doctrine of the inevitability of Union victory confronts us with one insuperable difficulty. If it was indeed clear from the beginning that the South must lose, how explain the readiness of upright and intelligent men like Davis, Benjamin, Yancey, Rhett, Cobb and others to lead their people to certain defeat? If defeat was inevitable these men must have known it, and their conduct takes on a sinister character. Were they so desperate that they preferred defeat to submission to the verdict of the 1860 election? Or were they so blinded by fanaticism and passion that they were guilty of massive self-delusion? Or was there another possibility: that the South did in fact have a very good chance to win—to win, if not the war, at least independence?

On the surface the prospects of the Confederacy were unpromising. The Union boasted three times the man power and more than three times the industrial and financial capacity of the South; what is more it had the ability—which the South did not—to replenish these resources when they were depleted. But clearly Davis and his colleagues read these statistics, too—read them and discounted them. Clearly they concluded that there were countervailing considerations that gave them the right to believe in a Confederate victory.

The South had, in fact, one categorical advantage, one which—had it been properly exploited—might have been decisive. It was this: that she did not need to win battles in order to win the war. If the Union was to win, it had to conquer the South—that is to invade and hold an area as large as all western Europe except Italy and Scandinavia—an achievement without parallel in modern history. But the Confederacy had a far less exacting task. She was under no obligation to carry the war to the North; she demanded neither territory nor tribute nor even terms, except the elementary term that she be left alone, to go her own way. Hence the paradox that the Confederacy might lose all the battles and campaigns and still emerge victorious. She had merely to hold the field long enough to weary the North with fighting; merely to persuade the North that she was unconquerable, or that the price of Northern victory was too high. There was, to be sure, no assurance that the North would tire of the war and give in. Yet it is sobering to recall how close a thing it was: as late as the summer of 1864, while Grant was hurling his army against Lee's thin gray line, the greenbacks fell to forty-seven cents on the dollar, draft riots swept New York, the Democratic party adopted a platform that declared the war a failure and that squinted toward peace, and Lincoln concluded that he could not be re-elected.

This fundamental consideration, that the South could win only by wearing out the North, should have dictated the grand strategy of the Confederacy, and off and on it did. Pretty clearly that strategy was to conserve resources, to avoid pitched battles and sieges, to take advantages of a vast terrain, a friendly population, and interior lines of communication; to spread the war as far as possible into the West—even into the trans-Mississippi West; to play for time—and for British intervention which might come with time; to exact a terrible price for every Union advance.

At times, and in some areas, the Confederacy adopted this strategy, but more often it did not. Confederate leadership was dazzled by the temptation of quick victory after First Bull Run; by the implicit belief in the superiority of the Confederate to the Union soldier; by the confident expectation that a successful invasion of the North would bring speedy recognition from abroad; by a fitful belief that it was possible to terrorize the North; by emotional commitment to the importance of a "capital" city and of some soil more "sacred" than other. Most of the Confederate leaders had been trained at West Point or other military academies, and in the regular army. They assumed that their job was to raise large armies, to hold fixed points like Richmond or Vicksburg or Atlanta, to fight pitched battles, and, if possible, to carry the war to the North. This was, on the whole, the dominant strategy of President Davis and his military advisers. They did create large armies; they did hold cities (until they lost them); they did fight pitched battles and won more than their fair share of them too; they did invade the North, with disastrous results.

It is against this background of competing strategies that the career of Nathan Forrest takes on significance. For Forrest, who had no military training whatsoever, seemed to know by instinct what was the right strategy for the Confederacy. He was not particularly articulate (he said that whenever he saw a pen he thought of a snake) and as far as we know he never formulated his own ideas of strategy in any systematic way. Instead he acted them. Who can doubt that of all Confederate generals he was the most successful practitioner of the strategy of dispersal, of harassment, of terror, of attrition, of what we now call irregular warfare. It was not, to be sure, his invention: after all Washington had practiced it, and Greene and Morgan in the South. Stonewall Jackson followed it, on occasion, in the Valley, and so too, Stuart and Early. Yet clearly it was not adapted to the Virginia theater of the war as it was to the West: the strategic possibilities of Virginia were too great, her soil too sacred, her capital too significant. If the Confederacy was to fight orthodox warfare anywhere it must be in Virginia. If she was to fight an unorthodox war, it would of necessity be in the expansive West.

Fighting almost always with inferior numbers, and even with inferior arms, General Forrest managed to disrupt, to delay, to destroy, and to defeat the enemy over an enormous territory. He tore up railroads, blew up bridges, burned warehouses, sank gunboats and supply boats, cut communications, raided deep into territory thought safely inside Union lines; he spread havoc over hundreds of miles from Memphis to the mountains, from Alabama to the heart of Kentucky. In all this he was more than a partisan leader, and more than a cavalry leader. Although he ended the war as a Lieutenant General, he was never given independent command in the West; nevertheless he operated independently, and we can trace, readily enough, the large pattern of his strategic concepts. His purpose was to wear down and disorganize the enemy, and to stimulate and maintain the spirit of Southern resistance, and this purpose he largely accomplished, and not by raids alone. He could fight battles—and win them; he could co-operate with larger armies—as at Chickamauga or later in the tragic weeks of the Nashville campaign. He depended on the cavalry for speed, but not for victory; he fought his men afoot, and he was, like Thomas, a master of artillery. He rarely had more than a few thousand effectives under his immediate command, but he proved capable of handling any number of men, of operating on almost any level of military effectiveness: he could conduct a raid, he could command a department.

It might be argued, to be sure, that the strategy of harassment was tried with the shift from Johnston to Hood, and that far from bringing victory, it brought disaster: after all disrupting communications had no effect on a soldier who cut himself loose from his communications and lived on the country! But a recognition of the effectiveness of Sherman and the ineffectiveness of Hood late in '64 is not conclusive on strategy. It should be pointed out that the Hood strategy came too late; that it was carried out with hopelessly inferior armies; that Hood himself was a sick man who first frittered away his army in futile attacks outside Atlanta, and then destroyed it by rashness at Franklin and Nashville. The strategy of harassment was never given a real chance.

Dr. Wyeth does not permit himself to be distracted by these larger strategical considerations. His biography of General Forrest is a straightforward military narrative. What he gives us is a stirring and brilliant picture of a *fighting* man—a man born to be a soldier. Dr. Wyeth—who entitled his own autobiography *With Sabre and Scalpel*—rejoices in the fact that Forrest loved fighting, that he loved the military life, life in the open, life on horseback, the pounding of the cavalry, the fluttering of banners, the smell of powder, the flash of the sabre, the life of heroism and of danger. And as Forrest was a born fighter, he was a born leader of men. He whipped them into shape—in his own image; he took care of them—of their physical comforts, of their weapons and their horses, of their honor; he asked of them nothing he was not himself prepared to do, from poling a boat to leading a charge.

Like most great fighters—like Lee, like Jackson, like Grant (but unlike Joe Johnston and Thomas)—he was an offensive fighter. From the first command at Ft. Donelson to the last rear-guard action defending Hood's retreating army, he seized the offensive. His principle of fighting was "to get there first with the most men," and that meant seizing and holding the initiative; actually he was quite ready to get there with the least men as long as he could get there first. He did not like to stand and receive the enemy, even when he had the advantage of position; on one occasion when the enemy charged he waited until they were within a few yards, and then charged in on them and cut them down with his sabres. He was an old-fashioned warrior, in the thick of every fight; he had twenty-nine horses shot from under him; he cut down at least thirty Yankees in hand-to-hand combat. Painfully wounded at Old Town Creek, after Harrisburg, the rumor spread that he was killed; hearing it he mounted his horse and galloped along the lines to show that he was not only alive but full of fight. He was master of the surprise raid, the lightning attack, the relentless pursuit, and he achieved one triumph after another over the most improbable odds: the pursuit and destruction of Streight is a classic case, and so, too, the defeat of Sooy Smith at Brice's Crossroads. He was, it seemed, everywhere. "His cavalry will travel one hundred miles in less time than ours will ten," said Sherman in disgust. He was equally effective in battle: at Donelson, at Shiloh, at Chickamauga, and in the end at Nashville and on the retreat.

No wonder the British Lord Wolseley thought him one of the great soldiers of the war: "Panic found no resting place in that calm brain of his, and no danger, no risk, appalled that dauntless spirit. Inspired with true military instincts, he was verily nature's soldier." No wonder Sherman and Joseph E. Johnston, who agreed on few matters, agreed on his genius. Sherman—it is reported—pronounced Forrest "the most remarkable man our civil war produced on either side. . . . He had a genius which was to me incomprehensible. . . . He always seemed to know what I was doing or intended to do, while I am free to confess I could never tell or form any satisfactory idea of what he was trying to accomplish." And General Johnston—it is another posthumous report we rely on—said that "had he had the advantages of a thorough military education and training he would have been the great central figure of the war."

Dr. Wyeth is, of course, an unabashed partisan. As a boy he fought in an Alabama regiment that had been part of Forrest's command, and he carried with him through a long life an uncritical admiration for the great commander. This admiration never flags, but it does not produce a wholly uncritical biography. Not for nothing was Wyeth a distinguished scientist. He worked up the evidence, and weighed it; he sounded out old veterans; he used the official records; he tried his best to be judicious. But his chief virtue is not judiciousness, nor is it analysis. There is little probing of character here, little exploration of background and motivation, and no psychological inquiry into the relation between middle-class origins and passionate devotion to the cause of the plantation South, or into the curious but not unusual combination of piety with reckless violence. Dr. Wyeth wrote in the age when the Confederate war was still The Lost Cause. Though he lived most of his life in New York City, and was entirely reconciled to the verdict of Appomattox, he threw an aura of romance over the war, and even over the dour and harsh figure of General Forrest. He brings him to life with startling clearness, and he brings to life, too, those romantic days, now almost as unreal as the Crusades, when Forrest's raiders stirred hope and fear throughout the West.

HENRY STEELE COMMAGER

CHRONOLOGY

Major Events in the East	Major Events in the West	Forrest's Activities
1861 Fort Sumter falls. Beauregard, Johnston, and Jackson rout McDowell at Bull Run. Union reorganization follows with McClellan named commander of Army of the Potomac.	Union and Confederate forces skirmish and prepare.	Enlists as private. Raises Kentucky and Tennessee volunteers. First Cavalry engagement, Sacramento (Ky.).
1862 *Monitor* defeats *Merrimac*. McClellan's Peninsular Campaign met by Lee at Gaines' Mill, White Oak Swamp, Malvern Hill, ends in withdrawal. Jackson and Longstreet drive off Pope at 2nd Bull Run. McClellan stops Lee at Antietam.	Grant pushes south, takes Forts Henry and Donelson, defeats Johnston and Beauregard at Shiloh and moves down on Vicksburg. Bragg invades Kentucky, retreats to Tennessee, and is pushed back at Murfreesboro by Rosecrans.	Escapes from Fort Donelson. On right flank at Shiloh, later wounded. Raids central Tennessee, captures Murfreesboro. Raids western Tennessee and eludes trap at Parker's Crossroads.

1863 Lee spars with Army of the Potomac; stops Hooker at Chancellorsville; invades the North and is defeated by Meade at Gettysburg, but retires south unopposed to lick his wounds.

Grant takes Vicksburg. Bragg retreats to Georgia before Rosecrans, turns on him at Chickamauga but fails to follow up his victory and is crushed by Thomas at Chattanooga.

Attacks Ft. Donelson. Assigned to Bragg's left flank in central Tennessee and to rear guard of retreat. Leads right flank at Chickamauga. Criticizes Bragg, is assigned to command in Mississippi. Raids western Tennessee.

1864 Grant, now in command of Army of the Potomac, pushes relentlessly south, meeting Lee at Wilderness, Spotsylvania, Yellow Tavern, Cold Harbor; invests Petersburg. Both sides dig in. Sheridan and Early spar in Shenandoah Valley.

Sherman advances on Atlanta, meets Johnston at Resaca, New Hope Church, Kenesaw Mt., defeats Hardee at Peach Tree Creek, Atlanta, and sweeps on to Savannah in march to the sea. Hood leads last Confederate offensive into Tennessee, is defeated at Nashville.

Routs invasion of Mississippi at West Point and Okolona. Raids western Tennessee and captures Ft. Pillow. Defeats Sturgis at Brice's Crossroads. Stops Smith at Harrisburg. Raids Memphis. Raids northern Alabama and central Tennessee. Raids western Tennessee, captures gunboats, and shells Johnsonville. Accompanies Hood to Nashville, covers rear guard in retreat.

1865 Sherman marches north, takes Charleston and Columbia. Grant takes Petersburg and Richmond. Lee and Johnston surrender at Appomatox and Durham.

Wilson invades Alabama and takes Selma, Montgomery. Confederate resistance collapses.

Opposes Wilson in Alabama and is routed at Selma. Surrenders his command at Gainesville.

Preface

For the last two years of the Civil War I was a private soldier in a regiment of Alabama cavalry which had formerly served under Forrest. Four companies of this regiment had formed a portion of the famous battalion which had distinguished itself in the engagement at Fort Donelson, and, refusing to surrender, had marched out with him through the gap in General Grant's lines. Although I was at no time directly under General Forrest, I was impressed by the enthusiastic devotion to him of these veterans, who had followed his banner for the first year of the war, and who seemed never to tire in speaking of his kind treatment of them, his sympathetic nature as a man, his great personal daring, and especially of his wonderful achievements as a commander. Of these achievements I was at that time not altogether ignorant. His escape from Fort Donelson; the desperate charge which saved Beauregard's army from Sherman's vigorous pursuit after Shiloh, in which he was severely wounded; the capture of Murfreesboro with its entire garrison of infantry and artillery, with his small brigade of cavalry without cannon; the charge on and capture of Coburn's infantry at Thompson's station; the capture of the garrison at Brentwood; and the relentless pursuit of Streight's raiders, which ended in the surrender of these gallant Union soldiers to Forrest with less than one-half of their number, had already attracted wide attention and had made him famous. The knowledge of these facts, together with a personal association with the men who had felt the influence of his immediate leadership, naturally interested me in his career, which I closely followed to the end of the great struggle. When the general government, with wise forethought, began to collect and to place at the disposal of its citizens the official reports and correspondence, and all the reliable literature of the war, I undertook in the light of these and other authentic papers, a closer analysis of his military record. The further my investigations proceeded, the more I became convinced that while Forrest was justly acknowledged to be one of the most famous fighters and leaders of mounted infantry or cavalry which the war produced on either side, he was more than this, and that a careful and unbiased statement of his achievements would place him in history not only as one of the most remarkable and romantic personalities of the Civil War, but as one of the ablest soldiers of the world. While I had hoped, as year after year slipped by since peace was declared, that someone abler than I would undertake the task of placing in readable shape the story of his life, I had determined if this were not done before I should pass into the "sere and yellow leaf" to pay this tribute to his memory myself. It has been a work of years to gather up from every available source the matter relating to this history—his early days, his civil and private life, and the accurate facts of his military record. In 1894 I wrote a condensed sketch, had it printed in single column upon the margin of wide sheets of paper, leaving a large blank space, and these I mailed to every surviving officer or soldier of his command whose address I could obtain, and to others personally acquainted with Forrest before or after the war. All were requested to return the sheet with corrections, and to add everything of interest, for the accuracy of which the sender could vouch. I also caused the publication of this sketch in various newspapers of wide circulation in the section of the South from which his troops were chiefly drawn, and asked as well for private letters of information. As a result of these efforts a great mass of material came into my possession, and an interest was aroused which encouraged me in the laborious task of sifting the reliable from the unreliable, and of making presentable to the reader the matter which was worthy of credence.

To each one of this long list of persons who so promptly and generously responded to my appeal I shall ever be grateful. I am also under great obligation to many officers and soldiers who served immediately with General Forrest, and to a number who served in the commands of the Union forces directly opposed to him, for much that is of interest, and that has enabled me to present a clearer history of this remarkable man than could otherwise have been obtained. It was my good fortune to become intimately acquainted with the late General Thomas Jordan, who, associated with Mr. J. B. Pryor, had immediately after the war written a book entitled *The Campaigns of Lieutenant-General N. B. Forrest,* a great portion of the manuscript of which book had been perused by Forrest, who had personally made important corrections and valuable suggestions. General Jordan had for a considerable period after the war been intimately associated with Forrest, and from him I received much that was of service to me in the work I had in hand. Naturally the volume he had written so soon after hostilities had ceased was pervaded by a bias or prejudice for the Southern side of the struggle which detracted from its value as an historical document, and many of the statements it contained I found were not accurate when tested by the official reports which came out later, and to which General Jordan and his associate could not have had access. I have endeavored to exclude from these pages everything bearing upon the civil or military life of Forrest that could not be substantiated. In the reports of battles and campaigns, when any material differences of opposing commanders were evident, I have analyzed the reports, in the effort to arrive at a fair and unbiased conclusion, making every allowance for the natural prejudice of the human mind under the influence of the excitement incident to war.

It has been suggested that certain portions of this book which bear testimony to Forrest's harshness and violent temper should not be made public, as they might detract from his reputation as a man; but it has been my endeavor to paint him exactly as he lived, so that posterity may form its own opinion of him from the evidence. To my mind it would be as inexcusable to hide any of his shortcomings as it would be to permit the assailants of his reputation to go unchallenged. He had his weaknesses, and was not an angel by any means, but he was very far from being a man who did not have a high sense of right and justice. Personally, nothing would please me more than to have left out of my book everything which could possibly awaken an unpleasant memory or cause the slightest irritation, but simple justice to Forrest requires a recitation of some of these unhappy incidents.

Happily for all, the bitterness engendered by that fratricidal struggle has passed away, and while Forrest took the Southern side and fought to the last with desperate energy and an intensity of purpose unsurpassed, his history and his fame are part of the glory of our common country. No spirit more loyal to its convictions ever animated a mortal frame than that which dominated his all too brief existence. When his blood-red sword was sheathed at last, he took on the modes of peace as earnestly and consistently as he had carried on the direful methods of war. From the day that his battle-flag was furled to the day of his death he labored for more than a political rehabilitation of the nation. He wished it a union heart to heart between the South and the North. This was the burden of his eloquent and pathetic addresses to the veterans of his command at the annual reunions; and when the hand of the Great Destroyer was laid upon him, in his last will he bequeathed his sword to his son with the expressed wish that, should occasion offer, he, as his father would have done, would use it under the Stars and Stripes with the same devotion and earnestness that it had been wielded for the Southern Confederacy.

JOHN A. WYETH.

THAT DEVIL FORREST

The Ancestry and Earlier Life of N. B. Forrest

Now and then there comes upon the stage of life, in the theater of this world, a man who so differs from the rest that he catches the eye and ear at once and, as long as he moves in the scene, holds the attention of his fellows. When his part in the drama is over, we who remain to fill the minor roles find time in moments of reflection to ask ourselves: What manner of man was this, and wherein did he differ from others of his kind? By what mysterious alchemy did the elements in him combine to lift him to the stars?

On the 13th day of July, in the year 1821, in a frontier cabin, amid surroundings which told of poverty, and in the obscurity of a remote backwoods settlement of middle Tennessee, there was born one of these rare beings. The light which first greeted his infant vision came through the cracks in the chinking between the logs of hewn cedar, or sent its penetrating rays beneath the riven boards of the roof which in overlapping rows were laid upon the rafters and held in place by heavy poles and blocks, in lieu of nails. The cabin, which was his mother's home, claimed no more than eighteen by twenty feet of earth to rest upon, with a single room below and a half-room or loft overhead. One end of this building was almost entirely given up to the broad fireplace, while near the middle of each side swung, on wooden hinges, a door. There was no need of a window, for light and air found ready access through the doorways and cracks, and down through the wide, squatty chimney. A pane of glass was a luxury as yet unknown to this primitive life.

Around and near the house was a cleared patch of land containing several acres enclosed with a straight stake fence of cedar rails, and by short cross fences divided into a yard immediately about the cabin; rearward of this a garden, and a young orchard of peach, apple, pear, and plum trees. The yard fence ran parallel with the public road so newly cut through the forest that stumps and roots of trees still showed above the level of the ground, waiting to be removed by the slow process of decay.

Across the highway, squatting among the giant cedars of the Duck River country, stood a log blacksmith shop, with bellows and forge, anvil, tongs, and hammer, and the other simple paraphernalia of an artisan in iron.

The owner of this shop was William Forrest, blacksmith, then twenty-one years of age, more than six feet in height, with the heavy, muscular development of a mechanic. He was an honorable man and a law-abiding citizen, sober and industrious. This I have from a perfectly reliable source—from one who lived a near neighbor and knew him well. He must have been this and more to have won the love and devotion of Mariam Beck, the woman of extraordinary character who on this day had borne him his first son and daughter.

For three generations the Forrests had belonged to that restless race of pioneers who in search of home and fortune had followed close upon the heels of the savages, as these were driven farther and farther toward the setting sun. While there was yet a narrow fringe of civilization along the Atlantic coast, they were content to dwell among the foothills of the eastern slope of the Alleghenies. But when the hardy Anglo-Saxon race began in earnest to cross the sea and establish more numerous settlements there, these bold and self-reliant frontiersmen, with wives and children, packing up their small store of household goods, gathered in little colonies, yoked their oxen to the wagons, turned their backs upon the Atlantic, and, cutting as they went a trail across the Eastern Divide, plunged into the vast wilderness of the valley of the Mississippi.

Among this class of men was Shadrach Forrest, who about 1740 moved from Virginia into the colony of North Carolina, settling in that section of country which afterward became Orange County when that state was admitted to the Union.

Here he lived many years, was married, and reared a large family of children. Among these children of Shadrach Forrest was Nathan, the second son, who had married in North Carolina a Miss Baugh, descended from an Irish family which had immigrated to that section of the New World. William Forrest, the blacksmith, and the father of the distinguished general, was the first-born child of this marriage, having seen the light of day about the year 1798.

When William was eight years of age, the family immigrated to Tennessee, and settled north of the Cumberland River, not far from the present town of Gallatin, in Sumner County. Not satisfied with their surroundings, two years later, pushing farther into the wilderness, they finally established themselves in the Duck River country in 1808, in what was then Bedford County, Tennessee. Here, as William Forrest grew to manhood, he learned the blacksmith's trade, which was his vocation when in 1820 he married Mariam Beck.

I obtained from Mr. J. B. Boyd, an aged and respected citizen of Holt's Corner, in this section of Tennessee, the following reliable information concerning the Forrest family a few years after their arrival in Bedford County:

The grandfather of General N. B. Forrest, whose first name was Nathan, lived within a half-mile of my father's house. In my early boyhood he had a small farm and nursery of fruit-trees. He was the father of eight children, five boys and three girls. William, the oldest son, and the father of General Forrest, was a blacksmith by trade. The other sons of Nathan Forrest were principally engaged as traders in live-stock; except one, who was a tailor. None followed farming as an occupation while living in this community. There are now none of the name living here. While I was yet quite a small boy, Nathan Forrest, the general's grandfather, sold his place and moved about five miles distant. Whether William Forrest, the general's father, continued to work at the blacksmith's trade after leaving our immediate neighborhood, I am unable to say. Nathan Bedford Forrest, who afterwards became so famous, was born in Bedford County, in that portion which was afterwards cut off to form in part the county of Marshall. The house in which he was born was a log cabin of the primitive kind, built by the early settlers in this then backwoods country. It stood a little less than a half-mile from where the village of Chapel Hill now stands, but at the time of which I write this country was very sparsely settled, and there was as yet no such place as Chapel Hill. This house was torn down many years ago. The Forrest family were all energetic, high-minded, straightforward people. I have never heard of any of them being dissipated or connected with anything that was disreputable.

Of William Forrest but little is known beyond the fact that he worked at his trade steadily and earnestly, in this sparsely settled backwoods country, to support a family which rapidly gathered about the fireside

as the years of his married life went swiftly by. He is said to have been
a man who possessed great determination and courage, and to have
exercised a considerable influence in the small community in which
he moved. In 1834, when Nathan Bedford Forrest was just thirteen
years of age, William Forrest, with his wife and children, moved from
middle Tennessee into northern Mississippi, to that portion of the
state which had been occupied by the Indians. The aborigines having
been transferred to reservations beyond the Mississippi, these lands
were opened to settlers, and thither he immigrated and entered a home-
stead on the banks of a small stream in Tippah County, not far from
the present village of Salem. Here, in 1837, when the subject of this
sketch was not quite sixteen years of age, his father died, leaving him
the "head of a family consisting of his widowed mother, six brothers,
and three sisters, and to these was added, four months later, his brother
Jeffrey, a posthumous child."[1]

General Forrest's mother was of Scotch extraction, her parents
having emigrated from South Carolina and settled near what is now
known as Caney Springs, not far from Duck River, in middle Tennessee, about the time of the admission of this state into the Union in
1796.

Mentally and physically Mariam Beck was a remarkable woman. In
stature she was almost six feet, of large muscular frame, and weighed
about one hundred and eighty pounds. Her hair was dark, her eyes a
bluish-gray, her expression gentle and kind; and yet no one who saw
the prominent cheekbones, the broad forehead, and the deep lines of
her face could doubt that she possessed great force of character, a
determination of will, and unusual courage. Hers was the ruling spirit
of the household and, although strict and severe with her children, it
may be said with perfect truthfulness that she won their affectionate
love and retained it throughout her life. Bedford Forrest's love for his
mother amounted to adoration, and was one of the noblest features of
this great man's character. It is said of this "Mother of the Gracchi,"
who gave eight sons to the service of her country, that she was in her
family, as well as in her neighborhood, self-willed and imperious to a
degree, and that, having undertaken any enterprise, she persisted in
it until it was accomplished. It is more than likely that this marked
trait in the character of her distinguished son was inherited chiefly

[1] *Campaigns of General N. B. Forrest.*

from the mother's side, for, once convinced that he was right, his determination to accomplish his end was characterized by a fixedness of purpose which brooked no opposition, and at times bore down with almost savage fierceness upon all who stood in his path. She bore eleven children to William Forrest, and six years after his death married Mr. Joseph Luxton, and to this union four children were born—three sons and a daughter.

John Forrest, the brother next to the general, volunteered in the American army and served in the Mexican War, and there received a gunshot wound through the lower part of the spinal cord which produced complete paralysis from that point downward. He could neither walk nor stand without the aid of crutches. He resided in Memphis, and was living at the Worsham House when the Federals occupied that city in 1862. A Union officer with a detachment of men had visited his mother's plantation, situated five or six miles in the country from Memphis, and had deported themselves in such manner as to arouse the indignation of the mother of the Forrests. All of her sons being absent in the army except John, she visited Memphis the next day and informed him of what had occurred.

A day or two later, as John Forrest was sitting in front of the hotel, this officer passed near him, when he stopped him, called his attention to his conduct in the presence of his mother, and told him that if ever he repeated the offense he would break his crutch over his head. The Federal officer resented this remark, and began to abuse not only John Forrest but all the family in severe terms. At this the cripple raised himself from his chair, and, leaning upon one crutch, tried to strike the officer with the other. His antagonist seized the crutch as it was raised in the air, and kicked the remaining one from underneath the paralyzed man, who immediately fell to the sidewalk. Having full use of his arms, he drew a derringer from his pocket and shot the officer, who for weeks lay at the point of death, but finally recovered. John Forrest was immediately arrested, placed in irons, and confined on board a gunboat anchored at the wharf or landing at Memphis. Here he remained in close confinement, isolated from all friends and acquaintances, for some time, and, the news of his arrest having come to General Forrest, he at once demanded of the general in command at Memphis the proper treatment or release of his brother, until he could be tried by law for shooting the officer. This demand was complied with at once, and John was set at liberty and afterward acquitted.

William Forrest, the next son, a captain of scouts, was an exceedingly handsome man of large build, big brown eyes, and brown curly hair, which in middle age was streaked with gray. He served with distinctiou in the Confederate cavalry, and was wounded on several occasions. He led the charge upon Streight's column at the battle on Sand Mountain, near Day's Gap, the last day of April, 1863, and was desperately wounded, his thigh having been shattered by a Minié ball. He had the reputation of being a headstrong, reckless, and dangerous character, but was neither reckless, high-tempered, nor violent. On the contrary, he was modest and reticent in his demeanor, yet possessed that quality of courage which did not seem to realize what fear meant. He was quick to resent an insult, and, following the rule which had prevailed in the frontier community where he was born and reared, he believed the only way to settle a dispute was to fight it out.

Aaron Forrest, the fourth son, became a lieutenant colonel of a Mississippi regiment of cavalry, and in the expedition to Paducah, Kentucky, in 1864, was taken ill with pneumonia, and died near Dresden, in west Tennessee.

Jesse Forrest served with the distinguished courage of the family, and became colonel of a regiment. He displayed exceptional ability and gallantry in the attack on Athens, Alabama, in 1864, where he was very severely wounded.

Jeffrey, the last son and child of William Forrest, born four months after the death of his father, was the pride and special care of his distinguished brother, who felt that he must be to this fatherless child not only an elder brother, but a father also. Having, by the time that Jeffrey was old enough to go to school, succeeded in amassing a considerable fortune, he determined to give him a thorough school and collegiate education, which he carried out up to the time the war came on, when Jeffrey, in common with all the Forrest brothers excepting John, enlisted. He exhibited military ability of an order which approached more nearly the genius of the great general, became colonel of cavalry, and was commanding a brigade in his brother's division when, at the battle near Okolona, in the pursuit of Sooy Smith, in 1863, while leading the charge, he was shot through the neck and instantly killed.

All of the daughters of William and Mariam Forrest died early in life. The sons, whose names have just been given, are now, in 1898, all dead.

Of the three sons by her second husband, the eldest two entered the Confederate service. The third was too young to be mustered in. After the war these children, one of whom became Sheriff of Uvalde County, accompanied by their mother, moved to Texas, where she died and was buried in Navasota, in 1867.

One or two incidents in the life of General Forrest's mother will serve to emphasize what has been said in regard to her physical prowess, as well as her strong and determined will. They are not the less interesting in the fact that the same characteristics belonged to her illustrious son, who at the period mentioned was but a boy fifteen years of age.

When the Forrests first settled in Mississippi, so sparsely peopled was this portion of the country, from which the Indians had but recently been removed, that it was some ten miles to their nearest neighbor. Roads were practically unknown, and those that existed were little better than bridle paths through the woods and canebrakes, and had to be traveled on foot or on horseback. On one occasion Mrs. Forrest and her sister, Fannie Beck, who lived with her, started out on horseback to pay a visit to this neighbor. When they were leaving for home late in the afternoon her hostess presented her with a basket containing several young chickens. Their return trip was without incident until they had arrived within a mile of their cabin. The sun had gone down, and it was beginning to grow quite dark.

At this moment they heard the yelp or scream of a panther in the dense woods, and only a few yards distant. They realized at once that the hungry beast had scented the chickens, and was bounding through the cane and undergrowth to secure its prey. At the first yelp of the animal the horses became frightened and broke into a run. Their riders, or at least one of them, was alarmed, and both urged their horses toward home as fast as they could go with safety over the narrow and rough trail. Mrs. Forrest's sister shouted to her from her position in front as they were galloping along to drop the basket and let the panther have the chickens, which would stop it, but Mariam Beck was not that sort of woman. There was too much determination and Scotch grit in her, and she declined to do as she was bid. She was "not going to let any varmint have her chickens," and on they sped, the horses holding the panther safely in their wake, until they approached the creek which ran near by their cabin.

On account of the high banks of this stream and the depth of the water, they were compelled, as they reached it, to slacken their speed almost to a standstill to prevent the horses from falling as they slid down the declivity and struck the water. This slowing up enabled their swift pursuer to gain on them rapidly, and, mad with hunger to such a desperate degree that it had lost the natural fear of human beings, the beast leaped from the top of the bank, striking Mrs. Forrest upon the shoulder and side of the neck with its front paws, while the claws of the hind feet sank deeply into the back of the animal she was riding. Smarting under the pain and wild with fright, the horse plunged forward so quickly that the hold of the panther was torn loose, and at the same time the rider's clothes were ripped from her back, and several deep, lacerated wounds were inflicted in the flesh of the shoulders as the beast fell into the water. The screams of the women brought the whole household out from the cabin, which was situated on the opposite bluff, and Bedford Forrest came running with his dogs to the rescue. The mother, still holding on to her basket of chickens, was lifted from the saddle and tenderly cared for by her eldest son and his aunt.

As soon as she was made as comfortable as possible, young Forrest took his flintlock rifle from the rack above the fireplace and started toward the door to call his dogs. His mother asked him what he was going to do. He said, "Mother, I am going to kill that beast if it stays on the earth." She tried to dissuade him from going into the woods at that hour, asking him to wait until daylight, when he could see what he was doing. The boy replied that by that time the trail would be so cold the dogs would not be able to follow it; that he was going now while the scent was fresh; the hounds would soon run it into a tree; and away he went into the darkness. The hounds soon picked up the trail, and followed it for miles through swamps and briers and canebrakes, until nearly midnight. After an hour or so of the chase, the boy perceived it would tax his strength sorely to keep up with the dogs, and fearing they would get out of hearing and reach of him he cut a small grapevine, tied it around the neck of one of the oldest hounds, and held fast to the other end of the tether. At times the other dogs would get out of hearing, but the captive hound followed unerringly upon the trail, and after a while, far in the distance, he heard the baying of the pack, which told him that they had at last treed the panther.

It was too dark when he arrived to see the beast, so he waited patiently until the day began to break, and then he saw it lying stretched at full length on a large limb, lashing its catlike tail from side to side and snarling with its white teeth at the dogs, which had never taken their eyes from it or given it a moment's peace. Putting a fresh primer in the pan of his flintlock, and taking steady aim, the young huntsman sent a bullet through its heart, when it fell limp and dead to the earth. Cutting off the scalp and ears, he started for home, where about nine o'clock the same morning he arrived to show his mother the trophy he had won.

That his unbending will came to him by direct inheritance is further borne out by the following incident:

Several years after the death of William Forrest, in 1837, his widow married Mr. Joseph Luxton, and when the Civil War broke out, in 1861, she resided upon her plantation some few miles out from Memphis on the Raleigh Road. The oldest son by this second marriage was then eighteen years of age, and had for some months been employed as a clerk in one of the stores in Memphis, and had enlisted in the Confederate army in one of the companies organized in that city. On a Friday afternoon he appeared at his mother's home clad in a neat-fitting new suit of Confederate gray, trimmed with gold lace and other fancy trappings, so much in fashion at the beginning of the war. His mother had some ideas of her own which the younger generation deemed old-fashioned, but to which, despite criticism, she tenaciously adhered. Some of her neighbors said she was "set in her ways." Among other eccentricities she maintained that no meal was so good as that which was ground from corn raised on her own farm and shelled under her personal supervision, where she could see that none of the small faulty grains near the point of the ear were used.

Every Saturday morning, bright and early, she would send one of her boys to mill with a sack of this corn to be ground. As her son retired to his room that night she said, "Joseph, I want you to get up early in the morning and go to mill with that sack of corn." She did not seem to take into consideration the fact that he was living "away from home," and was now a Confederate soldier. The young man did not respond to his mother's command, but went silently to bed none the less determined not to soil his new soldier clothes by riding on a sack of meal. The mother belonged to that robust and enterprising type of housewife who believed in getting up before daylight and having everything ready for work by the time it was light enough to see. On weekdays everybody on her farm had breakfast by candlelight.

The next morning, as usual, everyone was called early, and all appeared at the table excepting the devotee of Mars. The old lady said to the Negro servant who was waiting upon the table, "Tell Mr. Joseph to come to breakfast right away"; and continued, as the servant went on the errand, "I am not going to put up with any city airs on this place." She then occupied herself in pouring out the coffee for those at the table, and, while so doing, the Negro returned with a message from her impertinent offspring that "he did not intend to go to mill; she might as well send one of the niggers with the corn." One who was present on this occasion says:

> When this message was delivered, she was just in the act of pouring out a cup of coffee, with the cup and saucer in one hand and the pot in the other, lifted several inches from the table. For a moment she seemed dumfounded at such impertinence on the part of her son, and then, setting the half-filled cup and the coffee-pot down, she arose from the table, told us to go on with breakfast, and asked us to excuse her, as she would return in a few minutes. She marched out into the yard, broke off three or four long peach-tree switches, and went directly upstairs, pulled that eighteen-year-old warrior of hers out of bed, and gave him such a thrashing as to justify a remembrance of it for the remainder of his life. She made him get up and put on an old suit of farm clothes which he had left at home when he became a "city chap." The horse was already at the gate, and, accompanying the prodigal son that far, she picked up the two-bushel sack of corn, put it on the horse, and made him get up on top of it, and away he went to the mill. As she came back into the house, her eyes flashing and her face red with anger and the exertion which the chastisement had called for, she said, "Soldier or no soldier, my children will mind me as long as I live."

It is said that Joseph returned in due time with the meal, a wiser and probably a better son. Her influence over her children was great and unimpaired to the end. When her distinguished son was a lieutenant general, it is said that he was as docile in her presence and as obedient to her as if he were still a boy living under her roof, and no one could pacify him in his moments of anger or control him as could the mother whom he adored and the wife to whom he was always the loyal and devoted lover.

Of the boyhood life of General Forrest I have been able to obtain but little of interest which is reliable. Within recent years there was living at Chapel Hill an aged lady, a Mrs. Putnam, who was well acquainted with the family of William Forrest. She remembered Bedford when he was a mere child and young boy, and lived a near neighbor to his father. She says the only peculiarity she could recall in him as a child was that at play he could make more noise, and when his mother was whipping him could yell louder, than any other child in the neighborhood. All of which conveys the idea that he had considerable spirit and excellent lungs, and that his Calvinistic Scotch mother had not forgotten the Bible injunction that when the rod was spared the child was spoiled.

A playmate of Forrest in his earlier days, a Mr. McLaren, who died recently in Waco, Texas, says that, even as a very young boy, Bedford gave unmistakable evidence of the great physical courage and indomitable will which became such marked features of his character as shown later in life.

On one occasion a number of children were sent to gather blackberries, which grew wild and in profusion along the fence corners and hedges in the surrounding country. In the course of their rambling through the dense patches of briers they came suddenly upon a large rattlesnake, the rattling tail and angry hisses of which, as it was coiled to strike, frightened them so that they abandoned buckets and baskets and berries in a wild stampede for their homes. The panic, however, did not communicate itself to the future soldier. He shouted out to his companions to come back and help him kill it. This small detachment of young mankind did not seem to have confidence in his generalship on that occasion, and paid no attention to his orders. Single-handed (and, it might be added, left-handed, as he had in infancy developed this sinister preference) he undertook to battle with the enemy. The briers were so thick immediately about the venomous reptile that, as young Forrest approached, he could not from a safe distance attack it with stones. Procuring a stick long enough to enable him to hit the monster and still keep out of reach of its fangs as it would strike at him from the coiled position, he soon marched in triumph from the brier-patch with his dead enemy looped over the stick with which he had destroyed it.

Even at so young an age, he, in common with all boys brought up in a frontier settlement, became an adept at horseback riding. Neither saddle nor bridle was necessary to the urchins, who practically lived upon the backs of these noble animals, which they bestrode with the skill and security of seat of Comanches. To ride the horses and mules back and forth to the fields in plowing time, or to the pastures on Sundays, or to take them to water when required, or to go on errands to the doctor in the nearest town, were occasions in which the younger male members of the family, with great enjoyment to themselves, became useful members of a backwoods community.

On one of these trips McLaren, who was several years younger than Forrest, in leaning over to let his horse drink after he had ridden well out into the stream, lost his Barlow knife from his pocket, and to his great sorrow saw it disappear into the muddy water of the creek. To him, as to almost any boy in the country, this loss seemed irreparable, and he gave vent to his feelings in sobs and tears. His companion, touched by the grief of his playmate, attempted to comfort him by promising to get his knife for him. Riding to the shore, he dismounted, stripped off his clothes, and waded until he reached the point approximately near where the knife had fallen into the water, and then proceeded to search for the lost treasure. He would disappear beneath the water and remain out of sight as long as he could hold his breath, come up with both hands full of mud and gravel, which he would examine to see if he had been fortunate enough to include the knife; then he would repeat the performance, until finally, after fully a dozen efforts, he secured the trophy, greatly to the joy of the loser and the satisfaction of the finder.

On the road they usually took in riding the horses to water there lived a neighbor who owned two ferocious dogs, which on all occasions would rush from the yard and bark at and chase the youngsters on their fleet-footed horses a considerable distance from the house. This was great fun for the urchins, who felt perfectly safe from their point of vantage on horseback, and no doubt the ferocity of these animals had been cultivated by the natural proclivities of their two-legged tormentors to tease them by yelling and shouting and throwing stones as they rode by. On one occasion the cavalryman that was to be was riding a colt which was not yet broken and bridle-wise. As he approached the home of his natural enemies, hearing the shouts and the clatter of the colt's feet as it came in a swift run along the highway, the dogs rushed toward him, barking in such ferocious fashion that, as they came within a few feet of him, the horse bounded suddenly to one side and pitched his now terrified rider into, as he then fully believed, the jaws of death. Springing to his feet as he struck the earth, and proceeding to obey the first great impulse to run away, to his surprise he noticed that the dogs had fled and left him master of the field. The animals, accustomed to having stones and sticks shied at them, were evidently taken with panic at having such a thing as a boy of this size hurled at them through the air, and had sought safety in flight.

In after years General Forrest related this early experience, and said he had never in all his life had such a fright; that he sincerely believed the dogs would rend him in pieces by the time he struck the ground, and that he did not know which feeling was uppermost in his mind, surprise or joy, when he found that he was still living and the dogs were gone. He said also that it was a valuable lesson to him, which he turned to account in other ways later in life—that he had learned there the value of a bold attack, even when he knew he was inferior in strength to the enemy.

It may be said with truthfulness that at the age of sixteen years, when his father died, Bedford Forrest took up the burden of life, and unfortunate circumstances had made the load placed upon his young shoulders unusually heavy. He and the oldest of the brothers who came after him labored hard in clearing new land, and in cultivating that which had already been opened up while the father was still alive. They raised corn and wheat and oats and cotton, and gathered about them by thrift and industry, year after year, a drove of cattle and a goodly supply of horses and mules and other stock.

General Forrest told with pardonable pride to those to whom he was intimately attached in later years how, after being deprived of his father, and almost the sole dependence of his mother and the children, he would labor all day in the field and then at night sit up and work until it was late making buckskin leggings and shoes and coonskin caps for his younger brothers. In those primitive days everything was handmade. The mother and the maiden aunt and the older girls spun the yarn and cotton thread, wove the cloth on wooden looms, made the clothes, and knitted the socks. There was little brought from the outside world save the great luxury of an occasional supply of sugar and coffee, bought miles away at the nearest country storehouse. So much energy and tact had this young lad displayed in the management of his mother's affairs that by 1840, three years after his father's death, and when he was as yet only nineteen years of age, they were enjoying a degree of prosperity and plenty and comfort which at that time was new to the family.

By this time the country around was no longer so sparsely settled as when they came in there practically as pioneers. Other sections of land had been taken up, and near them had settled a family with the head of which young Forrest came in conflict. This neighbor had an ox, which was so enterprising and agile that he set at naught the fences around the Forrest farm, causing much annoyance and considerable loss by his depredations upon their fields of grain. Young Forrest called on his neighbor on several occasions, asked him earnestly and politely to put a yoke upon the steer, which would prevent him from jumping the fences; but to this request no heed was paid. Finally he said to his neighbor that if he ever again found the animal inside of his mother's place he would shoot it.

A few days later the ox was again seen inside the cornfield, and young Forrest, taking his flintlock as he had threatened, shot the animal dead. The owner, who was in a field of his own not far away, heard the report of the rifle, and, seizing his own gun—for in those days the farmers usually took their flintlocks to the field with them—hurried in the direction of his dead beast, with the seeming intention of doing harm to the determined youth. The latter, having quickly reloaded his gun, approached the partition fence between himself and his neighbor sufficiently near to be in range when his adversary should reach that point. As the man approached, Forrest told him that he did not wish to harm him, but if he climbed up on the fence or made any motion toward using his gun he would kill him, and accompanied this threat by bringing his gun down cocked and primed, and drawing a steady bead upon his neighbor. The man, by this time evidently appreciating the pluck and determination of the lad, remained upon his own ground and made no effort to do him harm.

In 1841, when the struggle for the independence of Texas was beginning to excite the sympathy and enlist the active aid of many citizens of the United States, Forrest, having bountifully provided for his mother and her family, joined in a company of volunteers which offered their service to the Lone Star Republic.

When this company arrived at New Orleans, the transportation which they expected to be furnished by steamer to Galveston was not forthcoming, which greatly discouraged a number of its members, and led to a partial disorganization. A good proportion of the volunteers returned home, but young Forrest, having started, would not turn back, and arrived safely at Houston, Texas. To the great disappointment of himself and those of his comrades who had stood by him, they found there was no need for their services in the army of Texas. They were forced to disband and make their way back home as best they could. Having by this time exhausted the funds which he had carried with him from home, Forrest sought occupation as a laborer upon a farm, and remained there diligently at work until he had earned sufficient money by days' wages to carry him back to Mississippi. He remained upon the farm with his mother until 1842, by which time he had demonstrated so much capacity for business, having been remarkably successful not only in the profitable working of the farm, but in speculation in horses and cattle, that an uncle residing in the town of Hernando, in northern Mississippi, offered him an interest in a well-established business there, which he was glad to accept. In this mercantile enterprise he was engaged until 1851, acquiring year after year a more comfortable fortune.

There occurred in 1845, in Hernando, an incident which severely tested the courage of Forrest, the result of which was to bring him prominently to the notice of the people in this section of Mississippi and Tennessee. An unfortunate personal dispute arose between Jonathan Forrest, his aged uncle, with whom he was associated in business, and four members of a family of planters who lived near by. The quarrel grew warmer, until at last, as was too common in those earlier days, a personal altercation took place, which ended in a bloody tragedy. Bedford Forrest had won the reputation of being a modest, sober, and energetic businessman. With the transaction which led to this fatal affair he had no interest or connection. When he saw that four men were preparing to attack his relative, he asserted that he was not a party to the controversy and did not want to engage in the quarrel, but he plainly told these persons that he would not stand quietly by and see his uncle unfairly assailed or maltreated; that if it was to be a fight it must be a fair one, not four against one. He had scarcely ceased speaking when one of the party drew a pistol and fired at him, but without effect, and this was the signal for a general fusillade. The older Forrest was shot down with a mortal wound.

Three of his opponents had pistols, which were turned upon the young man, who was wounded, but not seriously. With astonishing self-control and steady deliberation he had drawn a double-barrel pistol from his pocket and had disabled two of his assailants. A bystander, seeing him then practically helpless in the presence of his two remaining adversaries, ran out and handed him a bowie knife, with which Forrest rushed at one and then the other of these men, who fled at his approach and left the town. The sympathy of the community in which this occurred was so entirely with young Forrest that, in the arrests of all parties which followed, he was upon his statement released, while those who had attacked him were imprisoned without bail.

In this same year, on the 25th of April, 1845, when Forrest was not quite twenty-five years of age, he had the great good fortune to win the heart and hand of Mary Montgomery, a lady of excellent family, refined and educated, who devoted her life to her husband and family. It is said by one who knew her most intimately, and was in a position to judge her from her daily life, that she filled the measure of the Christian wife and mother. The great soldier simply worshiped her. His wife and his mother were the guiding stars of his mature life. It is said of Mary Montgomery that she was of those quiet, firm, yet sympathetic natures who seemed to take most pleasure in helping those in distress. It is a fact known only to a very few of the most intimate friends of General Forrest and his wife that, despite the loss of the great fortune he had acquired when the Civil War broke out, there was left to them a considerable income after peace was declared. As long as he lived, the greater portion of their income was spent by him and his wife in relieving the distress of wounded and impoverished Confederate soldiers, and the wives and orphans of those who had died in his command. This was kept up to the day of his death, and afterward by his wife as long as she lived. They belonged to that type that preferred not to parade their good works to the world.

From Mr. H. S. Halbert, of Newton County, Mississippi, I have received an interesting account of the manner in which Forrest first met the lady who afterwards became his wife. Riding along a country road one Sunday morning, he came upon a carriage stalled in a mudhole in the highway. As he approached, he saw that it contained two ladies, and that the horses were unable to move it. To his disgust, he also observed two men quietly sitting on their horses nearby and making no offer of help to the unfortunate women. Forrest dismounted, hitched his horse to the fence, waded through the mud and water to the carriage, and asked them to permit him to carry them from the wagon across the mud, which they did; and then, putting his shoulder to the wheel, he and the driver succeeded in extricating the vehicle. His indignation at the two men who had so lacked in gallantry as not to offer their services before he had arrived was so great that he did not take time to assist the ladies back into their wagon, but turned upon the men with the remark that he didn't see why they hadn't offered to help these ladies in their distress, adding, in a tone full of earnestness and anger, that if they didn't leave there at once he would give them both such a thrashing they would never forget it. They considered his advice timely, and immediately rode away.

The ladies thanked him earnestly for the kindness he had shown them, and were in the act of driving away when Forrest introduced himself and asked permission to call and make their acquaintance. His request, made so gallantly, was granted, and from this occasion sprang a lifelong and devoted friendship.

The period in which Forrest lived in Hernando was one which was marked by the rapid development of this section of the Mississippi Valley. The invention of the cotton gin by Eli Whitney and his co-workers had given a great incentive to the cultivation of cotton throughout the whole Southern country.

After the Indian reservations in Mississippi were declared open for settlers and had begun to fill up with white people, it was discovered that the land throughout this great basin was admirably adapted to the growth of cotton, yielding several times as much of this staple to the acre as the hill lands and the red-clay soils of the older states. It had also been discovered that the malarial diseases were extremely severe upon the early settlers, who were as yet unacclimated. This led to the introduction of Negro labor in order to work profitably at cotton raising, and brought about a great demand for slaves. Traffic in the selling and buying of Negroes was as common in the cotton belt of the South at this period as the buying and selling of horses or cattle, or any other merchantable live product. The exceptions were extremely rare to this statement that everybody bought and sold slaves, either for the profit that was in the transaction or for motives which appeared to them less selfish.

Into this business Bedford Forrest had entered, on as large a scale as his limited means would permit, while he was engaged in mercantile pursuits with his uncle at Hernando. As his capital accumulated under the energy and tact which he exercised, he closed out the business in Hernando, and, moving to Memphis, settled there, devoting his time as a broker in real estate in this rapidly growing young city, and as a speculator in slaves.

Colonel George W. Adair, now living (1898) in Atlanta, Georgia, was intimately associated with Bedford Forrest during this period of his career. He says:

Forrest was kind, humane, and extremely considerate of his slaves. He was overwhelmed with applications from a great many of this class, who begged him to purchase them. He seemed to exercise the same influence over these creatures that in a greater degree he exercised over the soldiers who in later years served him as devotedly as if there was between them a strong personal attachment. When a slave was purchased for him his first act was to turn him over to his Negro valet, Jerry, with instructions to wash him thoroughly and put clean clothes on him from head to foot. Forrest applied the rule of cleanliness and neatness to the slaves which he practised for himself. In his appearance, in those ante-bellum days, he was extremely neat and scrupulously clean. In fact, so particular was he in regard to his personal appearance that some were almost inclined to call him foppish. The slaves who were thus transformed were proud of belonging to him. He was always very careful when he purchased a married slave to use every effort to secure also the husband or wife, as the case might be, and unite them, and in handling children he would not permit the separation of a family.

Not a great while after he had established himself in Memphis there occurred a thrilling incident in which he took a part so prominent that it added to his reputation as a man of desperate courage. It may also serve to explain why, a few years later, when the call for arms was sounded, men naturally turned to him as a leader in those troublous days. There was living in Memphis a man of wealth and considerable influence who, in an unfortunate moment and, as it was then believed by a large majority of the citizens, without just provocation or cause, had taken an unfair advantage of and killed one of his neighbors in that city. So great was the indignation which was aroused by what was at the time deemed an outrageous murder that the slayer was taken to the county jail, locked up, and heavily guarded, in order to protect him from being hanged by a mob which soon surrounded the enclosure, and were preparing to overcome the guard and batter in the doors in order to reach their victim.

Hearing of what was transpiring at the jail, Forrest repaired thither, and arrived on the scene just in time to see the mob successful in effecting an entrance to the building. With no motive but to protect one who was helpless and who might suffer unjustly at the hands of an infuriated and unreasonable mob, wishing only to have the law take its course, without regard to his personal safety he made his way to the jail door, pushed those away who were nearest the prisoner, and, interposing himself between the victim and the leaders of the crowd, drew from his pocket a knife, and, holding it on high in that ready left hand which he always used by preference in moments of excitement, declared in earnest tones, which no one who heard him and saw the expression of his face could doubt, that he would kill any man or men that laid a hand upon the prisoner. He then addressed the people and their leaders in an impassioned speech, appealing to their calmer reasoning and better judgment, which with his desperate earnestness so swayed the mob that in half an hour they had left the premises. The prisoner was again turned over to the jailer, and the mob made no further effort to prosecute its unlawful undertaking.

Nathan Bedford Forrest had not resided long in Memphis before he had made a favorable impression upon the citizens of the new community in which he had cast his lot. He was, without opposition, nominated and elected a member of the Board of Aldermen of this thriving and rapidly growing city, was re-elected several times to the office, and finally resigned just before the outbreak of the Civil War, in order to attend more closely to the cultivation of cotton. Within the last ten years of his business career he had at various times invested in purchases of valuable uncleared cotton lands along the Mississippi River, and among these were two extensive plantations in Coahoma C unty, in Mississippi. In 1859 he closed out his real estate and slave business in Memphis and devoted his time entirely to looking after the interests of his plantations. On a scale of such magnitude did he now engage in this enterprise, and with such success, that from his various properties in 1861 there was yielded to him one thousand bales of cotton, or approximately $30,000, as an annual income.

The Mayor of Memphis said of Forrest: "While he was an official of the city he never offered a resolution in the board on any subject, no matter how unpopular it might be at first, that he did not stick to it and work at it until he carried it triumphantly through."[2]

[2] *Campaigns of General N. B. Forrest.*

Military Career

THE military career of N. B. Forrest began on the 14th of June, 1861, the date of his enlistment at Memphis as a private soldier in Captain Josiah White's Tennessee Mounted Rifles Company.[1] It constituted Company D in the Sixth Tennessee Battalion, which was organized September 7, 1861, and later became a part of the famous Seventh Tennessee Regiment of Cavalry, which surrendered under his command, at Gainesville, Alabama, in May, 1865. The first official record of Captain White's company on file is dated August 20, 1861, and the name of Nathan B. Forrest does not appear on the roster[2] for the reason that he had been transferred for other duty in July of that year.

Forrest's high character as a man of probity and courage, his success in business, and the position he had attained in Memphis were too well known to permit him to remain in the ranks. A few days after he had enlisted, influential citizens of that community visited Nashville to confer with Isham G. Harris, Governor of Tennessee, and General Leonidas Polk. Their representations obtained for him authority from the provisional government of the Confederacy at Montgomery to raise a battalion of cavalry for the volunteer service. Upon the receipt of this official authority, Forrest went to work to secure enlistments for the proposed command. There appeared in the Memphis *Daily Appeal* of this date the following notice:

A Chance for Active Service—Mounted Rangers

Having been authorized by Governor Harris to raise a battalion of mounted rangers for the war, I desire to enlist five hundred able-bodied men,

[1] *History of the Seventh Tennessee Cavalry,* by J. P. Young.
[2] War Office Records, Washington, D.C.

mounted and equipped with such arms as they can procure (shot-guns and pistols preferable), suitable to the service. Those who cannot entirely equip themselves will be furnished arms by the State. When mustered in, a valuation of the property in horses and arms will be made, and the amount credited to the volunteers. Those wishing to enlist are requested to report themselves at the Gayoso House, where quarters will be assigned until such time as the battalion is raised.   N. B. FORREST

Appreciating the inability of the new government to furnish suitable arms and equipment for his men, with characteristic foresight, scattering his agents through northern Alabama, middle and west Tennessee, and northern Mississippi to secure recruits, he supplied himself with ample funds from his private resources, and on horseback secretly made a trip to Kentucky and the Ohio River country, where proper material could be purchased. Although Kentucky had at this time not declared itself for or against the Union, and was practically neutral territory, in the section of this state bordering on the Ohio River the prevailing sentiment was strong in favor of the Union. Deeming it wise to refrain from any overt act which might attract attention at Frankfort, Lexington, and other large towns, he only made his presence and business known to Southern sympathizers, to whom he had confidential letters, and these he employed as agents. All the pistols, guns, saddles, blankets, and other cavalry equipment that could be purchased without attracting attention and carried south in wagons by unfrequented highways were gathered up and sent away. He visited Louisville, taking the precaution to remain at the house of a friend a few miles in the country, and day after day visited the city, where his agents secured a large supply of much-needed material. In small quantities this was carried in delivery wagons and stored in a large livery stable in the suburbs.

Mr. C. W. Button says: "At Louisville I was introduced to Forrest by my father. He had bought a large number of navy pistols, saddles, and other cavalry equipments, which had been stored in a livery-stable in Louisville. Six young volunteers, none of whom were over eighteen years of age, met him by appointment at the stable, and late in the night carried the articles in coffee sacks through the door into a back alley. Here wagons were ready to receive them, and when all were loaded we started out on the Elizabethtown turnpike."[3]

[3] Mr. C. W. Button, in the *Confederate Veteran*, p. 478, September, 1897.

While on this expedition, hearing that a company of mounted troops had been organized for the Confederate service by Captain Frank Overton in Meade and Breckenridge counties, Kentucky, Forrest repaired thither and induced this officer to join his forming battalion. He advised him to divide his company, which was well mounted but had no arms, into small detachments of from two to six men, which should start on different dates and by different routes, travel through portions of the country most remote from the larger settlements, and rendezvous in the neighborhood of Nolin, a station on the Louisville and Nashville Railroad, well toward the Tennessee border.

Here without molestation Forrest arrived with supplies, and in due time arms and equipment were furnished to Captain Overton's company, which was mustered in as the "Boone Rangers." At the head of this fine body he proceeded overland to Memphis, where he arrived the first week in August.

During his absence a splendid company had been recruited in Memphis by Captain Charles May, which, in honor of the future commander, had been named the "Forrest Rangers," and upon these two companies the future organization was effected. A few days later a company of Texans arrived, and an additional Tennessee company reported as ready to join, while several companies from northern Alabama had been gathered in.

As captain of one of these Alabama companies there came the Rev. David C. Kelley, a man of strong character and earnest convictions, who believed so earnestly in the cause of the South that he laid aside his pastoral duties, raised a company of mounted troops, and was now ready to enter the active service of the Confederacy. This shrewd observer and scholarly gentleman became intimately associated with Forrest, and served throughout the war under him as one of his most intimate friends. He says: "I had taken a company to Memphis for equipment. There were a number of companies of cavalry congregated there for the same purpose. In attempting to get my requisitions through the various departments I found that persistent watchfulness enabled me to accomplish what I desired ahead of any officer with whom I had to contend, except when I came in contact with the requisitions of N. B. Forrest."

The Alabama companies referred the question of joining the battalion to Captain Kelley, and this officer had the wisdom to recognize in

Forrest, even at this early date, a man of extraordinary ability, and one that could be relied upon as a leader.

By the first week of October, 1861, Forrest had succeeded in attracting to his standard eight companies of mounted volunteers, which were organized into a battalion: Company A, Captain Overton, from the vicinity of Brandenburg, Kentucky, about 90 strong; Company B, Captain Bacot, from southern Alabama, 80; Company C, Captain May, from Memphis, 90; Company D, Captain Gould, from Texas, about 90; Company E, Captain Trewhitt, from Gadsden, Alabama, 80; Company F, Captain Kelley, from Huntsville, Alabama, about 90; Company G, Captain Logan, from Harrodsburg, Kentucky, 45; Company H, Captain Milner, Marshall County, Alabama, 85—a complement of about 650, rank and file.

N. B. Forrest was elected lieutenant colonel, Captain D. C. Kelley was chosen as major, Lieutenant C. A. Schuyler was appointed adjutant, J. P. Strange sergeant major, and S. M. Van Wick surgeon of this battalion. Lieutenant Hambrick was elected captain to fill the vacancy made by the promotion of Major Kelley.[4]

Notwithstanding the great care Forrest had taken to secure suitable weapons for his men when the organization was effected, fully one-half of the troops had nothing better in the way of arms than double-barrel shotguns, which they had brought with them from their homes.

By the last week of October the battalion was ready for duty. Under Lieutenant Colonel Forrest it was ordered to proceed to Dover on the Cumberland River, and report there to Colonel A. Heiman, who was in command, and who was then beginning to throw up earthworks and fortify the point which afterward became famous as Fort Donelson.

In a spirit of prophecy, Colonel Sam Tate,[5] at that time president of the Memphis and Charleston Railroad, wrote on the 4th of November, 1861, to General Albert Sidney Johnston as follows: "Colonel Forrest's regiment of cavalry, as fine a body of men as ever went to the field, has gone to Fort Donelson. Give Forrest a chance and he will distinguish himself."

From Dover the new battalion was ordered to the headquarters of General Lloyd Tilghman, at Hopkinsville, and was placed in observation in the stretch of country between the Cumberland and Green rivers in

[4] *Campaigns of General N. B. Forrest.*
[5] *Official Records,* vol. iv, p. 513.

Kentucky. While engaged in this outpost duty a detachment under Major D. C. Kelley by a clever ruse captured a steam transport on the Ohio River, and, much to the delight of the Confederates, found it loaded with a rich booty of blankets and other army supplies, which were promptly appropriated. While at Princeton, Kentucky, at this time, Forrest received information that the gunboat *Conestoga,* of Admiral Foote's flotilla, had steamed up the Cumberland with the intention, as was believed, of destroying a storehouse of the Confederate commissary at Canton Landing. A rapid march brought the entire battalion on the ground early on the following morning.

The command had been reinforced by a small detachment of artillerists under Lieutenant Sullivan with one four-pounder gun. This was masked, and the troops concealed in the brush and timber and behind logs along the bank close to the point at which it was hoped the vessel would land. The commander of this craft, however, was too clever to be caught in such clumsy fashion, and, stopping short of the landing several hundred yards, dropped his anchor and proceeded to throw some shells into the timber, in order to be sure that no lurking enemy might take him unawares. Lieutenant Sullivan, of the artillery, under orders from Lieutenant Colonel Forrest, responded with his four-pounder, but by the time he had fired two rounds the broadsides from the heavy armament of the gunboat made his position untenable, and he withdrew his small gun to a position of safety some distance in the rear. Forrest's troopers, however, for the first time under fire, did not seem to be greatly disturbed by the tremendous noises which the Federal batteries and the screaming missiles were making, and stood their ground for several hours during this unequal combat.

The Federal commander, at last concluding that these men were not worth the ammunition he was wasting upon them, or that it was not safe for him to attempt to land to destroy the stores which had been the object of his expedition, closed his portholes and steamed away down the Cumberland. The lieutenant colonel of cavalry was well pleased with the manner in which his raw recruits had taken their baptism of fire. They may not have accomplished much in the killing and wounding of their enemies, but they had shown an eagerness for fighting which augured well for the future.

From Canton Landing the command marched to Hopkinsville, reaching there on the 21st of November, where they remained for the balance of this month. At this point the battalion was increased by two additional companies, one from Huntsville, Alabama, under Captain D. C. Davis, and another, known as "The McDonald Dragoons," under Captain

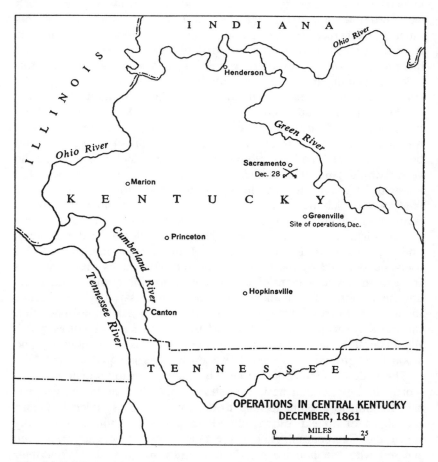

OPERATIONS IN CENTRAL KENTUCKY
DECEMBER, 1861

Charles McDonald, giving it a total of ten companies, and increasing the complement of effectives to about 790 men.

On November 24th, under orders from Brigadier General Charles Clark, in whose district Forrest was now stationed, he was directed to take some three hundred men and make a reconnaissance in the direction of the Ohio River. With these troops he marched to Greenville, where he was fortunate enough to make a capture of some arms and equipment which had been collected by the Union forces. Thence he proceeded to Caseyville, on the Ohio River, and on in the direction of Marion, in Crittenden County.

Approaching this village, Forrest was informed of the arrest of a prominent citizen, who had been thrown into prison upon the charge of being a "Southern sympathizer." On inquiry it was learned that two extreme Unionists had been the instigators of this arrest, and it was determined to hold them as hostages for the safety of the imprisoned Southerner, who, upon the approach of the Confederate cavalry, had been spirited away to a place of greater security. One of the prisoners it was intended to arrest was Jonathan Bells, and Forrest in person took charge of the detachment which had this particular duty in hand.

As he at the head of this small body of troopers was riding along the highway, side by side with Dr. Van Wick, the surgeon of the battalion, and as he approached the house of Mr. Bells, someone from within, mistaking the doctor, who was dressed in full uniform, for the officer in command of the squadron, selected him as his victim, and with deadly aim sent a bullet through his heart. The man who fired the shot ran out of the house through a rear door, and escaped in the woods. Had that missile been directed at the leader of this expedition with an aim as unerring, it would not be far from the truth to say that it would have been the cause of the Union the most valuable piece of metal fired from the Northern side.

Forrest reports that during the three weeks consumed in this expedition the troops were kept busy gathering up hogs, cattle, horses, and other supplies, which were driven south for the future needs of the army. "It is believed that the expedition has done great good in giving countenance to the Southern sympathizers in this region, and of disabusing the minds of the Union people, who expected every species of outrage at the hands of the Confederate soldiers. Not a few assured us that they would no longer use their influence against the cause of the South. Universal kindness was the part of the officers in command."[6]

On the return trip to Hopkinsville, a squadron of Federal cavalry, estimated at about four hundred in number, followed the Confederates for a part of one day, and, although Forrest turned on them and offered

[6] Official report.

battle, they showed no disposition to close with him.

Reporting to General Clark with the supplies he had gathered, on Thursday, December 26th, he was directed to make a tour of observation in the direction of Henderson, Kentucky. Taking a detail from Companies A, C, and D of his own battalion, which he placed respectively in charge of Lieutenant Crutcher and Captains May and Gould, and additional details from Companies E, F, and G, under Major D. C. Kelley, and an independent detachment of twenty-five Kentuckians under Captain Merriwether, Forrest started upon this expedition. On Saturday morning, December 28, 1861, a company of forty Tennesseeans, under the immediate command of Captain Starnes and Lieutenant McLemore, overtook Forrest and volunteered to accompany him. A few hours later on this same day a scout reported that a body of Federal cavalry, estimated at about five hundred in number, had crossed the road some eight miles distant and were moving at that time in the direction of a small village called Sacramento. These he determined if possible to overtake and attack, and the order to "move up" was given at once, and all pressed forward at a rapid gait.

Nearing this village the command was augmented by an unexpected volunteer in the person of a Kentucky belle, who, mounted on a magnificent horse, with more enthusiasm than discretion, galloped by his side and cheered him and his soldiers on to the conflict. The gallant *sabreur* so far forgot the strict business of his official report as to embody in that document the acknowledgment that "her untied tresses, floating in the breeze, infused nerve into my arm and kindled knightly chivalry in my heart."[7]

One mile from Sacramento, Forrest came in sight of the rear guard of the Union cavalry, which had halted, seemingly in doubt whether friends or foes were behind them. Seizing a rifle from the hands of one of his men, he settled all doubt in the minds of the enemy by firing the opening shot at them. Satisfied with this information, the Union vedettes immediately disappeared in the direction of their main column.

With seeming disregard for tactical formation, Forrest ordered his men to follow him, directing them not to fire until they were within close range. As they galloped along the road the enemy was soon in sight, deployed in line across and on either side of the highway in a heavy grove, and from this position they at once opened upon the

[7] *Official Records,* vol. vii, p. 65.

Confederate advance at a range of about two hundred yards. Recognizing the danger of moving directly upon them in column, Forrest for the first time (it was his first opportunity) put into execution the maneuver which he afterward practiced so frequently and with such signal success in nearly all of his encounters. Posting his men on horseback in a position of least exposure, he threw forward a certain number dismounted as skirmishers, with orders to keep the attention of the enemy in their front actively engaged.

As Starnes with his detachment and Kelley with a portion of the three companies under him came up, a hurried conference was held, and the famous movement by the flank and rear, and which preceded the charge from the front, was inaugurated. While Starnes took the left with thirty men, Kelley moved to the right with sixty more, all mounted, and starting from a point which could not be observed by the enemy. The dismounted troopers in front, behind trees and logs and in fence corners, were firing away and receiving volleys in return. As Kelley's column swung into view toward their right, and Starnes threatened the other flank, Forrest, with saber in hand and eye all strained to catch the first suggestion of confusion in the Union line, saw the moment had come, and, shouting in a manner which evinced the most intense excitement, "Charge! Charge!" was off at full speed in the direction of the enemy.

With no semblance of formation the troopers followed, each seemingly bent on keeping up with their leader, who, standing up in his stirrups, his saber in the left hand, looked a foot taller than any of his men. Threatened on both flanks, and assailed in such desperate fashion from the front, the Union cavalry, despite the gallant efforts of their officers to hold them to their work, broke and fled. For nearly one mile to and then through the village the pursuit and flight were little more than a horse race. The best mounted of the Confederates, among whom were Forrest, the impetuous Starnes,[8] and Captain Merriwether, soon began to overhaul the rear of the fleeing troopers, who either surrendered or went down at close range with saber thrust or pistol shot.

Beyond Sacramento the Union officers succeeded in rallying a squadron of the fugitives and turned upon their pursuers in a desperate

[8] Dr. J. W. Starnes became Colonel of the Fourth Tennessee Cavalry and won great distinction as a fighter. He was killed on the skirmish line in front of Tullahoma in 1863.

and bloody combat hand to hand. Forrest, still in advance, found himself confronted by this determined detachment of the Union cavalry, and at such headlong speed was he running toward them that before he could check his horse he was in their midst engaged in a desperate fight for his life. The Confederate Captain Merriwether, close at his heels, fell instantly dead from a pistol shot through the brain.

Assailed from all sides, Forrest's skillful left hand stood him in good need. Before they could strike him down a quick thrust from his saber brought Captain Bacon down mortally wounded. Private W. H. Terry, one of the foremost of the Southern troopers, was by Forrest's side, and in spurring his horse between his leader and the Federal Captain Davis, who was endeavoring to reach the Confederate chieftain, he received a fatal saber wound. Forrest rushed at Davis at full speed in the hope of saving Terry, but was a second too late. His horse collided with that of his plucky antagonist, and both animals with their riders fell in a heap. The Federal officer struck the ground with such velocity that his shoulder was dislocated, rendering him incapable of further resistance, whereupon he surrendered. Beyond the severe shock and several bruises received in this fall, Forrest escaped uninjured. Of the squadron which turned to offer battle none escaped. It was brave and brief work soon ended. Under the personal prowess of Forrest in this affair three of the enemy went down.

It was at this moment that Major Kelley rode up. He says: "Forrest seemed in desperate mood and very much excited. His face was flushed till it looked like a painted warrior, and his eyes, usually mild in expression, glared like those of a panther about to spring upon its prey. He looked as little like the Forrest of the mess-table as the storm of December resembles the quiet of June."

From the commencement of the affair Major Kelley had been alarmed for the safety of the command. It seemed to him that his senior, in the excitement of the moment and in the eagerness to close with the enemy, had lost his head, and he feared a well-concerted movement from the Federal side would result in the defeat and probably the destruction of the Confederate force. In order to be ready to counteract such a maneuver, should it occur after Forrest and Starnes had rushed pell-mell in the pursuit, he held his squadron in compact order and followed on at a gallop. When he came in sight of Forrest he saw him in mortal combat with Captains Bacon and Davis. Starnes, who had dashed through the first lines of Federals, was having a battle royal of his own just ahead in the road. Having fired the last shot from his pistol as the Union trooper turned and fled down the road, Starnes hurled the empty weapon at his back, where it struck and bounded off with no other effect than to speed the parting guest.

The pursuit and fight, which had now lasted for nearly three miles, were called off. The Confederates lost two killed and three privates wounded. The Union reports[9] show one officer (Captain Bacon) and eight soldiers killed; and Major Murray, commander of the unfortunate detachment, reports that "forty men are missing." The number of wounded must have been considerably more than this report would indicate. General T. T. Crittenden (Union), on December 30th, reports: "We have five or six men so badly wounded that we could not bring them in." The Federals he reported as numbering 168 men of Jackson's regiment.

Forrest does not give the number in his command. Fully 200 Confederates were present and took part in the affair. As he had moved at a gallop for nearly eight miles before the unsuspecting enemy were encountered, it is likely that at least another hundred fell out of the column and were coming toward the scene as fast as their tired horses could move, but these did not arrive in time to take part in the action. In any event, Forrest had demonstrated in this his first encounter one secret of his wonderful success in war. When asked in later years how he explained the success achieved in his many battles, he replied: "I do not know, unless it was because I generally got there first with the most men."

General Crittenden further reports:[10] "I regret to inform you that a command of 168 men under Major Murray, of Jackson's regiment, was surprised and pursued by rebel cavalry at Sacramento. Captains Bacon and Davis and Lieutenant Jouett are missing with forty men. I sent Colonel Jackson out with five hundred men to gather up the stragglers and wounded. Although attacked suddenly, they charged and drove back the rebels, who rallied, and a hand-to-hand conflict occurred. We lost eight soldiers and three officers—Captain A. G. Bacon killed, Captain A. N. Davis captured, and Lieutenant John L. Walters missing."

Brigadier General Charles Clark (Confederate) in an official report

[9] *Official Records,* vol. vii, p. 63.
[10] *Ibid.*

of this encounter to General A. S. Johnston, speaks of this as "Forrest's brilliant and dashing affair at Sacramento. It was one of the most brilliant and successful cavalry engagements that the present war has witnessed, and gives a favorable omen of what that arm of the service will do in the future on a more extended scale. For the skill, energy, and courage displayed by Colonel Forrest he is entitled to the highest praise, and I take great pleasure in calling the attention of the general commanding and of the government to his services."[11]

On December 30, 1861, Forrest reported that with over three hundred men, on December 26th, he moved on a scouting expedition in the direction of Sacramento. Hearing of the enemy, he pushed forward rapidly, and within one mile of the village struck their rear guard.

As only the advance guard of my command was seen, we came up to their main column. We halted, and seeing that they outnumbered me, I fell back a short distance. The enemy at once attempted to flank our left and began to move towards us, and apparently greatly animated, supposing we were retreating. They had moved down over one hundred yards and seemed to be forming for a charge, and began to move towards us, when the remainder of my men coming on the ground, I dismounted a number of them with long-range guns, directed a flank movement upon the part of Major Kelley and Colonel Starnes upon the right and left, and with the balance of my command, mounted, we charged into their ranks. The enemy broke in utter confusion, and in spite of the efforts of a few officers commenced a disorderly flight at full speed, in which the officers soon joined. We followed them closely, getting in an occasional shot, until we reached the village, when we began to catch up with them, and there commenced a promiscuous saber slaughter in their rear, which was continued for two miles beyond the village, leaving their wounded strewn along the route.

The month of January, 1862, was passed in scouting and other active duty, but without any incident of importance. On February 7th, Lieutenant Colonel Forrest received orders to report to the commander at Fort Donelson, where he arrived four days later.

Of the impression the Confederate leader had already made upon the men of his command, the Rev. D. C. Kelley, who was with him, writes: "In the short period since its organization, this command found that it was his single will, impervious to argument, appeal, or threat, which was ever to be the governing impulse in their movements.

[11] *Ibid.,* p. 64.

Everything necessary to supply their wants, to make them comfortable, he was quick to do, save to change his plans, to which everything had to bend. New men naturally grumbled, but when the work was done all were reconciled by the pride felt in the achievement."[12] In after years this scholarly soldier and Christian minister, probably the fairest and most competent critic and close personal observer of Forrest, wrote:

In his early battles he was so disregardful of the ordinary rules of tactics, so reckless in personal exposure, that I felt sure his career would be short. It seemed certain that whenever he should meet a skilful opponent his command would be utterly cut to pieces. So fierce did his passion become that he was almost equally dangerous to friend or foe, and, as it seemed to some of us, he was too wildly excitable to be capable of judicious command. Later we became aware that excitement neither paralyzed nor misled his magnificent military genius. What had seemed to us the most unreasonable command when given proved, both in its result and his after-explanation of the reasons on which he acted, consummate generalship. His genius in action rose to every emergency; he always did what the enemy least expected him to do, and when defeated, as others would have counted defeat, he was more fertile in resources, more energetic in attack, more resistless in his fiery onset than when the action began. While his desperate bravery and frequent charges were characteristic of his military career, they by no means exhausted his resources.

The manoeuvring of his forces in the presence of the enemy, his messages to opposing commanders, his matchless shrewdness in impressing them with the overwhelming superiority of his forces, and the necessity for surrender, were equally characteristic. The use of his artillery, often thrust forward to the skirmish-line, which would have been madness in an ordinary commander, was vindicated by the splendid results which he won. His common-sense led him at an early date to see that the day was past when a cavalry charge with sabers could be made effective in the presence of infantry.

After the battle of Shiloh he usually fought his cavalry on foot. The horses were used simply as a means of rapid transportation, which enabled him to throw his men on the enemy before they dreamed of his proximity. His pursuit of Streight, and his six hours of stubborn, unremitting, bulldog fighting at Brice's Crossroads, proved that his staying qualities were fully equal to the brilliancy of his rapid movements and the fierceness of his charges.

[12] Manuscript notes, Rev. D. C. Kelley.

THREE

Fort Donelson

THE struggle at Fort Donelson was the first decisive battle of the Civil War. In many respects it proved to be the most important engagement between the contending armies of the North and the South. There were to follow many more desperate encounters, where greater numbers were engaged, where the slaughter was more fearful, where day after day the murderous storm swept on with unabating fury, where the flash of musketry was more vivid and the thunder of artillery louder and caught more readily the eye and ear of the world at large. But in all probability the careful historian will yet decide that in shaping events, which step by step wrought the downfall of the Southern coalition, Fort Donelson stands pre-eminent. It was a blow which staggered the Confederacy, and from which it is safe to say it never wholly recovered. A disaster which led into captivity thousands of its best and bravest men, and thus early in the combat weakened the morale of one of its armies, in teaching it the bitter lesson of defeat. Above all, this monumental blunder made possible the career of a man who from that day until the end, with untiring energy and relentless hand, with giant blows struck down the Southern Cross.

Fort Donelson may, without successful contradiction, be asserted as the turning point in the career of Ulysses S. Grant, a man of tremendous courage and tenacity, and possessing a genius for war of a high order, and yet achieving by fortuitous circumstance in the dawn of his career the success which made this great career possible. Driven from the field at Belmont,[1] on which he had first been victor, and forced,

[1] So hurried was General Grant's retreat from Belmont that one of his regiments, the Twenty-seventh Illinois, failing to reach the transports in time, was left to the mercy of the Confederates. These, however, not pursuing with sufficient rapidity and spirit, permitted these men to escape.

in order to escape capture, to take refuge on his transports, himself the last man to quit the shore, riding his wounded horse with daredevil recklessness down the precipitous bank and along a single gang-plank to the steamer's deck, he there even in defeat gave evidence of that bulldog tenacity which was yet to stand him in good need on more successful scenes.

Signally failing in his next essay at Fort Henry, on February 6th, to throw his investing troops in overwhelming numbers around the garrison, in co-operation with the attack by Foote's flotilla, his soldiers by inexcusable miscalculation were four miles distant when the engagement opened. They did not reach the fort until it had been knocked to pieces and surrendered to Foote after a terrific cannonading of one hour and fifteen minutes. The garrison of 2610 men were by this blunder permitted to escape and march without hindrance to Fort Donelson, with a loss in sick, wounded, and captured of less than two hundred men.

At Fort Donelson, on the 15th of February, absent from his command and miles away on board a steamer of the Cumberland flotilla when his army was being knocked to pieces by the desperate onslaught of Pillow, Johnson, Buckner, and Forrest, arriving in the very crisis of defeat, when crowds of men in blue with anxious faces and empty cartridge boxes were running to the rear, and the cry, "All's lost! Save yourselves!"[2] was sweeping down the lines, and panic was in the air, just at this moment a halt was called along the Southern lines, and the troops thus far victorious were ordered back into the trenches, from which a few hours earlier they had sallied and fought with unequaled valor and persistence for this opening of escape. Had this army marched out then and there, as it might have done, or had it later in the night escaped, as we know and shall prove it could have done, Shiloh and Vicksburg would not be named on the pages of history, nor that majestic and matchless mausoleum now lift its marble dome from the banks of the Hudson in the heart of the metropolis of the Western World.

Had Nathan Bedford Forrest been in command of that gallant army of Southerners, no one who has read aright the story of his remarkable career can believe for a moment that he would have ever permitted a surrender. He might have died, and many more might have

[2] General Lew Wallace, *Battles and Leaders of the Civil War*, vol. i, p. 420.

died than fell there then, but there would have been no laying down of arms. When the final disaster came and the commanding general notified him of the capitulation, his answer was, "I cannot and will not surrender my command or myself."

Thirteen thousand men, the living and unwounded remnant of that heroic army, would have marched out of Fort Donelson to have swelled the ranks of Albert Sidney Johnston. Who can question the assertion that these additional veterans at Shiloh would have crushed the army which triumphed there? With defeat and flight at Belmont, and the escape of the garrison at Fort Henry, had the Confederate troops at Fort Donelson also escaped, can it be doubted that General Grant would have fallen short of that great career which was made possible by the capitulation of Generals Floyd and Buckner?[a]*

The campaign which ended in the surrender of the greater portion of the Confederate troops at Fort Donelson on the Cumberland River, on Sunday, the 16th of February, 1862, may properly be said to have begun with the bombardment and capture of Fort Henry on the Tennessee River by General Ulysses S. Grant, ten days earlier. Of the combined expedition by land and water against this stronghold, General Grant was in command. Landing his troops some few miles below the fort, they marched to invest it from the land side, in order to shut in and capture the garrison, which numbered 2610 men.[3]

The flotilla under Flag Officer Foote opened the fight at close range, firing the first guns at 12.30 P.M., and in one hour and fifteen minutes the fort, which was defended in most heroic fashion by General Lloyd Tilghman, was practically battered to the ground, three-fourths of its available guns dismounted or rendered useless, and nearly all of the artillerists placed *hors de combat.*

General Grant, in his *Memoirs,*[4] says: "Tilghman was captured with his staff and ninety men"; and adds, "the delay [in investing the fort] made no difference in the results."

This small number the advance of the Federal cavalry cut off from escape, and so close was Grant's infantry that the retreating Confederates came in contact with the advance regiments of the Union troops, who immediately gave pursuit, capturing about forty additional

* Superscript letters refer to notes which may be found beginning on page 579.
[3] *Official Records,* vol. vii, p. 140.
[4] *Memoirs of U. S. Grant,* vol. i, p. 292.

prisoners. The remainder escaped to give him battle within the next few days at Fort Donelson.[5] Although this occurrence took place on the 6th of February, it was not until the 12th that Grant put his army in motion for Donelson. On the 6th he had wired his chief, Major General Halleck: "I shall take and destroy Fort Donelson on the 8th and return to Fort Henry with the forces employed." Evidently he did not anticipate the character of the resistance that awaited him.

On the 12th, dividing his army into three divisions, of which the first two, numbering 15,000 men, Grant marched out on the two roads which run nearly parallel from Fort Henry to Fort Donelson, eleven miles distant; the third was loaded on transports and started for the same destination by water, some two hundred miles down the Tennessee and up the Ohio and Cumberland. When the advance guard of the Federal army reached within about three miles of Fort Donelson, their approach was for the first time contested by the cavalry of Forrest. This officer, acting under orders from Brigadier General Clark, had marched with his battalion to Fort Donelson, arriving on the 11th of February.

Scarcely had he reported at headquarters when he was ordered by General Pillow (then in command) to make a reconnaissance with three hundred of his troopers in the direction of Fort Henry. About three miles out from Donelson he came in sight of a detachment of Federal cavalry which he attacked with the same impetuosity that had carried everything before it in his first fight at Sacramento. The Union troopers were driven back in the direction of Fort Henry, losing two or three prisoners. Coming upon their infantry column, Forrest desisted from farther pursuit, returned, and reported to his commander.

On the following morning, Wednesday, the 12th, he was directed to advance over the same route, taking his own command and in addition three companies of Kentucky cavalry under Captains Williams, Wilcox, and Hewey, and a battalion of mounted Tennesseans under Lieutenant Colonel Gantt, a cavalry force present for duty of about thirteen hundred men, over which he was placed in command as acting brigadier.

[5] It was not until after ten o'clock of that morning that General Tilghman retired all of his troops excepting ninety men to a position beyond the breastworks on the land side of Fort Henry.—*Official Records,* vol. vii, p. 140.

As soon as Forrest came in sight of the advance guard of the Federal army he dismounted a portion of his command, took advantage of a ridge which was favorably situated, and from this position the Federal advance was checked. As additional troops from the Union column came up, an effort was made to turn the left of the Confederate line. As their cavalry made this essay a squadron of 200 Confederates under the gallant "fighting preacher," Major D. C. Kelley, dashed into them for close-quarter work, and the Federal troopers hastily retired upon the infantry. As these advanced, Forrest fell back, skirmishing steadily, until he was within the intrenchments about Dover, which by dark were well invested by the army of Grant.

General Buckner, in his official report, speaking of the thoroughness of the work done by Forrest, says: "During the morning of the 12th Forrest reported the enemy advancing in force with a view of enveloping our line of defence, and for a time he was engaged with his usual gallantry in heavy skirmishing with them, at one time driving one of their battalions back upon their artillery."[6]

Early in the morning of the 13th the skirmishing was resumed, the infantry of both sides taking part, the Confederates behind their intrenchments, the Federals being the aggressors. Meanwhile the commander of cavalry was not idle. Everywhere along the lines during the day he was attending closely to the duties of observation which devolved upon him. It was from the skirmish line that the movements of the enemy could best be observed, and throughout his military career he relied upon his unaided eyes rather than upon field glasses, which he very rarely employed.

Major J. P. Strange records the fact that while thus engaged, noticing one of Birge's sharpshooters well up in a tree and rather recklessly exposing himself, Forrest took a Maynard rifle from one of his men, and with the clear eye and steady aim of the backwoodsman fired at the unfortunate soldier, who tumbled headlong to the ground.

At 10 A.M. the Federals made a vigorous attack upon a portion of Buckner's and Heiman's lines, but were repulsed.[7] An hour later in the day quite a furious assault was made upon a Confederate battery by another portion of McClernand's division. This attack, made with great yet ill-advised gallantry and persistence, was repulsed with heavy

[6] *Official Records,* vol. vii, p. 330.
[7] *Ibid.*

loss to the assailants, while the Confederates, being protected by their intrenchments, suffered comparatively little.

Grant says:[8] "This general, without orders or authority, undertook to capture a battery of the enemy which was annoying his men. Of course the assault was a failure, and the loss on our side was great for the number of men engaged." No Confederate troops were engaged in these assaults on the 13th excepting Buckner's command, and these only for about two hours.

As dark came on, the weather, which had been mild for the preceding days, suddenly became bitter cold, with alternating snow and sleet throughout the night, which continued for the next forty-eight hours. Having waited for reinforcements to arrive before the attack, which it was intended should be made by the gunboats under Flag Officer Foote, and everything being now in readiness, Grant ordered the grand assault by the flotilla upon the water batteries of the Confederates. Beginning at three o'clock on the afternoon of the 14th of February, it lasted with unabated fury for an hour and a half.

It was probably one of the most spirited affairs of its kind which occurred during the war, and the result was entirely different from that which had been anticipated by Grant and Foote, who had learned to believe from the reduction of Fort Henry that Donelson would as easily fall captive to the Federal flotilla. The water batteries silenced, and the river above in possession of the fleet, the fate of the garrison was sealed. Although the gunboats steamed up to close range and sent a furious storm of well-directed shot and shell, which plowed through the Confederate earthworks and exploded in and around the narrow enclosure, dismounting or rendering unavailable all but one of the long-range guns of the fort, the boats were beaten off and so badly crippled that they drifted unmanageable from the scene, and never again became factors in the siege. The exultation of the Confederates over this result was as great as the victory was unexpected.

Captain Dixon, the commander of the water batteries, had been killed while bravely on duty. After his fall, Captain (afterward Brigadier General) Reuben R. Ross, of the Maury (Tennessee) Artillery, took personal charge of the only long-range rifled gun in the fort, and this gun, served with wonderful accuracy, without doubt saved the fort and entitled him to the honor of being the hero of the day. At a

[8] *Memoirs of U. S. Grant,* vol. i, p. 300.

distance of nearly two miles, such was the precision of the Confederate artillerists that "a 128-pounder struck our anchor, another cut away our boat-davits, another ripped up the iron plating, another struck the pilot-house, and still they came harder and faster, taking flag-staff and smokestacks, and tearing off the side-armor as lightning tears the bark from a tree."[9] Captain Ross reports: "One of the balls refused to go down, stopping half-way; our rammer was not sufficient; ten men left the battery, went out in front, cut a log of wood of size to fit, stood on the ramparts and coolly drove the shot home. They then deliberately scrubbed out the bore with warm water, and with the rifler cleaned the caked powder out of each of the six grooves, and all this while the air was full of shot and shell from the whole fleet of the enemy." Well might General Lew Wallace write: "The Confederates had behaved with astonishing valor."

There was probably no more interested witness of this thrilling scene than Forrest, who from that day on showed little respect for the Union gunboats. Riding along a small depression (now known as Forrest's Ravine) which concealed his person until it brought him out at a point where the fleet and battery were in plain view, he sat, by no means a calm spectator of the mighty duel. While it was at its height, the shells of the enemy exploding almost without cessation in and about the fort, and the issue yet in the balance, Rev. D. C. Kelley says, as he rode up to Forrest, who gave every indication of the most intense excitement, he shouted in earnest tones to his friend, "Parson! for God's sake, pray; nothing but God Almighty can save that fort!"

A few days later, in his official report,[10] Lieutenant Colonel Forrest says: "No one could do justice in description to the attack or the defence. More determination could not have been exhibited by the attacking party, while more coolness and bravery never were manifested than were seen in our artillerists. Never were men more jubilant than when victory crowned the steady bravery of our little force."

This affair seemed to have satisfied the warlike propensities of both armies for the day. General Grant had received reinforcements, which, as he states,[11] had brought his investing army to a total of 27,000 troops on the ground and ready for action, excepting a small contingent

[9] Report of the Rear Admiral of the U.S. gunboat *Carondelet.*
[10] *Official Records,* vol. vii, p. 384.
[11] *Memoirs of U. S. Grant,* vol. i, p. 315.

(probably the cavalry) used to guard the road four or five miles to his left and rear, over which all "our supplies had to be drawn on wagons." As these roads were immediately in the rear of the Federal army and covered by their gunboats, and as there was not a Confederate soldier in all that country excepting those penned up within the rifle pits at Fort Donelson, it may fairly be stated that this entire force of 27,000, ready for battle, confronted the 14,800 Confederates within the lines on the night of the 14th and on the 15th of February.

Despite the exultation of the Southern troops over the bloody repulse of McClernand on the 13th, and the confidence which the signal defeat of the flotilla on the following day had inspired in the rank and file of the army, the general in command and his immediate advisers were ill at ease. They were aware of the arrival on the 14th of heavy reinforcements for Grant, although, as usual under such circumstances, they greatly overestimated the number of the enemy. General Floyd said they were 50,000 strong, and that the Confederate army of 13,000 men were hopelessly unable to cope with their opponents. A council of war was called, and it was decided to attack the right wing and center of the Union line early on the following morning, beat this back, and if possible destroy it, and thus open the way of escape in the direction of Nashville. Unfortunately the plan of escape was not thoroughly understood by all, nor the details for its execution arranged.

The right wing of the Federal forces was commanded by General J. A. McClernand, the center by General Lew Wallace, the left by General C. F. Smith—in all, including the reserves as given by Grant, 27,000 strong. In order to mass a sufficient number of troops to make the attack on McClernand successful, Buckner's command was quietly, and before the dawn of day on the morning of Saturday the 15th, withdrawn from the intrenchments they had previously occupied on the extreme Confederate right, their places being taken by a single regiment of 450 effectives, the Thirtieth Tennessee, under Colonel Head. The brigades of Pillow, Floyd, and Johnston, and 1300 cavalry under Forrest, were to move out from Dover while it was yet dark, and at daylight attack McClernand. General John B. Floyd was in command over all, while the attacking column was led by the gallant soldier General Gideon J. Pillow. The understanding, as expressed in the official reports, was that Generals Pillow and Johnston and Lieutenant Colonel Forrest should attack vigorously on the Confederate

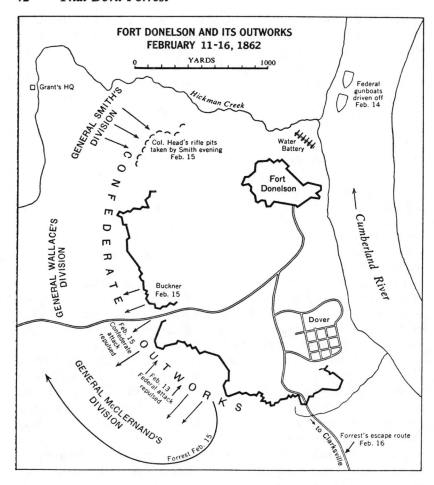

FORT DONELSON AND ITS OUTWORKS
FEBRUARY 11-16, 1862

YARDS
0 _____ 1000

Grant's HQ

Hickman Creek

Federal
gunboats
driven off
Feb. 14

GENERAL SMITH'S
DIVISION

Col. Head's rifle pits
taken by Smith evening
Feb. 15

Water
Battery

Fort
Donelson

C O N F E D E R A T E

GENERAL WALLACE'S
DIVISION

Cumberland River

Buckner
Feb. 15

Feb. 15
Confederate
attack
repulsed

O U T W O R K S

Dover

Feb. 13
Federal attack
repulsed

GENERAL McCLERNAND'S
DIVISION

to Clarksville

Forrest's escape route
Feb. 16

Forrest Feb. 15

left, and that as soon as they were well engaged, in order to prevent
any reinforcements from the Federal center and right under Wallace
and Smith, General S. B. Buckner should move out and hold Wallace
engaged until the proper moment, when a grand advance of the whole
line should be made and the defeat of McClernand assured.

Had General Grant known before daylight on the morning of the

15th, as he was mounting his horse to ride several miles[12] away down the Cumberland to hold a conference with Flag Officer Foote on one of his gunboats, the weakness of the Confederate right wing, that in fact only 450 men stood between Smith's division and the possession of Buckner's intrenchments, the probabilities are that the battle of Fort Donelson would have ended with the capture of the garrison before the sun was an hour above the eastern horizon. With 8000 infantry, General C. F. Smith, one of the ablest of Grant's lieutenants, was lying within short gunshot range of these intrenchments, at that time practically deserted, and could have captured the entire works of the Confederate right wing within thirty minutes. This accomplished, Fort Donelson was lost, and the Confederate army, at that time completely invested by twice their number, must have laid down their arms then and there. But the rumble of artillery, the tattoo of horses' hoofs, and the tramp of men over the frozen, snowy ground were unheard. The Union army was asleep, and their outpost pickets, instead of being keenly on the watch, were sheltering themselves from the fierce blasts of the winter's night. Their commander, famous and great in after years, had not the remotest idea of being attacked. He was in fact riding away, not to return until two o'clock, and never to the Southerners was moment more propitious.

At four o'clock on Saturday morning, the 15th of February, the Confederates were in motion. Forrest was in his glory, for it was he and his troops who led the advance of Pillow's attacking column.

Soldier by nature, from earliest boyhood at home on horseback, he rode at the head of the column, an ideal of the *beau sabreur*. From beneath the wide and slightly upturned brim of the soft felt hat, which bore no tawdry plumes, the large, deep-set blue eyes were peering with more than usual alertness. The look of kindliness which came in moments of repose or gentler mood was gone, and something hard and almost savage had replaced it. The broad, high forehead, the shaggy brows, prominent cheekbones, and bold, assertive nose told not only the story of his Gaelic origin, but the bulldog tenacity of the man. About the ears and neck heavy half-curling tufts of deep black hair hung so stiff and stubborn that they were scarcely swayed by the

[12] The distance from Flag Officer Foote's flagboat to McClernand's position was eight miles. (See *Memoirs of U. S. Grant.*)

strong, cold wind which swept the snowflakes in miniature clouds from the treetops and sent them scurrying to the ground. The dark mustache, and heavy, short chin beard were gray with frozen moisture of the expired air. The massive, firm-set jaw told of the strength of will which mastered all; the compressed lip and deep flush of the face bespoke the bloody business of the hour.[13] Six feet and two inches in stature, broad-shouldered and of athletic frame, well might one say there was in him

> A combination, and a form, indeed,
> Where every god did seem to set his seal,
> To give the world assurance of a man.

A plain caped overcoat of heavy gray, close-buttoned to the throat, reached amply beyond the knees. Above the waist, and buckled on the outside for quick and ready use, there was a broad black belt in which two "navy sixes" showed, and from which hung that famous saber, heavy and long, and, against all military rules, ground to a razor edge and swinging from the right side.[14] To his crude and earnest mind, "war means fighting, and fighting means killing."[15] He could cut or thrust deeper with a sharp than with a dull sword, and if in the melee he should happen to hit one of his own it was all intended for the good of the cause. He spoke not much, but when his thoughts were fashioned into words they came like pistol shots—short, quick, sharp, and sped right to the spot. Who heard them had no thought of answer-

---

[13] Lieutenant Colonel D. C. Kelley, who was intimately associated with Forrest, says that in the excitement of battle his commander became so transformed that it was difficult to believe him the same individual. Around the fireside of his home or at the mess table in camp he was kind, gentle, and considerate of all. His voice was soft and low in pitch, the words spoken slowly and deliberately. The expression of the face and the look from the large grayish-blue eyes were indicative of the generous and sympathetic nature which was his in times of calm and peace. When the storm broke, this picture vanished. The man became an intellectual fighting machine, seemingly intent on expending the great supply of pent-up energy in the destruction of the foe. The color of his face, which ordinarily was olive or sallow, became flushed and red, not unlike that of a painted Indian warrior; the eyes flashed with a look that suggested no mercy for any one who showed a disinclination to do promptly that which was bid.

[14] General Forrest was by nature left-handed, and although he cultivated his right upper extremity so thoroughly that he became ambidextrous, he used the pistol and saber in the left—the hand of preference.

[15] One of Forrest's maxims.

ing back, no dream of questioning, no argument, and, above all, no flickering. To his subordinates his order was, "Shoot any man who won't fight!" and he set the example.

At six o'clock the guns began to crackle at the front. McClernand says in his official report: "At early dawn the enemy were discovered rapidly moving in large masses on my extreme right. The battle opened at six."[16] It was no surprise to this vigilant officer, who was in line of battle before the attack began. Learning a lesson of caution on the 13th, he had thrown up earthworks for the protection of his batteries.[17] The overture of skirmishers was of brief duration. The Southerners, many of whom had only shotguns or squirrel rifles, rushed in for close work in order to make their weapons effective, and the fighting was at once severe and deadly. They pressed up to the Federal lines, but were met with stubborn resistance. With little advantage on either side, but with terrific carnage, the conflict raged for two hours. Then the Southerners began to gain and McClernand cried out for help. He was getting the worst of it, and sent hurriedly to Grant for troops, but Grant was not upon the field. He did not even know the battle was on.[18] The cry was unheeded and no help came. Oglesby's Illinois Brigade, the foremost in the Union line, was knocked to pieces, losing 836 men in this short cyclone of destruction.

Ever watchful for a place at which to strike from his position on the extreme Confederate left, Forrest had worked his way well around the Federal right flank and in their rear. His quick eye caught the first break in Oglesby's ranks, and shouting "Charge!" at the head of his men he rode into the wavering yet gallant Westerners. The pressure from the front and the rush of the horsemen on flank and rear were more than they could stand. Holding their empty cartridge boxes up to tell why they yielded, they broke and fled the field. Panic was in the air, and to the mind of Forrest the crisis of the battle had come. Galloping at full speed to General Bushrod Johnson, he pleaded with this officer to order an advance all along the line, but the West Pointer would not presume. General Pillow was over on the right, intent on urging Buckner to move out and attack, and the order for which Forrest was praying was not given.

[16] *Official Records,* vol. vii, p. 175.
[17] *Ibid.*
[18] *Memoirs of U. S. Grant.*

Observing a battery of the enemy comparatively unprotected, the lieutenant colonel of cavalry, this time not asking for orders, put himself at the head of his command and rode the gunners down before they could escape. The battery of six pieces was his. For the first time in the war he was able to show what cavalry could do. General Pillow, in his official report, says: "I found the command of General Buckner massed behind the ridge within the works, taking shelter from the enemy's artillery on the Wynn's Ferry road, having been forced to retire, as I learned from him. Our force was still slowly advancing, driving the enemy towards the battery, and I directed General Buckner immediately to move his command towards the rear of the battery, turning its left, keeping in the hollow, and to attack and carry it. Before the movement was executed, my force, forming the attacking party on the right, with Colonel Forrest's regiment of cavalry, had reached the position of the battery. Colonel Forrest's cavalry gallantly charged a large body of infantry supporting the battery, driving it, and taking six pieces of artillery—four brass pieces and two twenty-four-pounder iron pieces." Here fell a number of his men. His horse was shot, and that of his brother, Lieutenant Jeffrey Forrest, was killed, and in falling badly crushed his rider.

The lieutenant colonel of cavalry did not rest upon this feat, which won for him and his men the high commendation of his chief. Leaving the guns to be taken from the field by others, and under orders from General Pillow to leave Gantt's battalion to guard the left, he immediately moved his own regiment toward Buckner's position at the Confederate center. As General Buckner was advancing to the attack, General Pillow pointed out to Forrest two guns of the enemy which were doing considerable damage and greatly annoying the Confederate advance, and said, "They must be silenced; Forrest must do it." Leading the squadron in person, he asked General Pillow to give him the support of the nearest infantry. Roger Hanson's "Orphans," the Second Kentucky Regiment, stripped for the fray and moved up for the work.

With sabers out and bayonets fixed, horse and foot plunged through the tangled mass of undergrowth so thick that the infantry easily kept pace with the mounted troopers until reaching the edge of a narrow field or clearing. Here Hanson, shouting to his men, "Hold your fire until at close quarters!" and calling for the cavalry to go with him, rushed into the opening. With equal valor the Federals stood their ground. They swept the field with bullets, and crowds of Confederates went down. Riderless horses scurried from the scene, while the troopers yet mounted, yelling like demons, with guns discarded and pistols in hand, leaped over their fallen friends and went right on. Like a cane-brake on fire the Union muskets blazed and crackled right in the faces of the Southern men, and then it was hand to hand, bravely and briefly.

Under the pressure of this desperate onslaught the Federals finally gave way. Forrest's men, charging with the infantry, were first on the guns, but the glory was equally with the Kentuckians and their peerless leader, who later on, at Murfreesboro, slept "On Fame's eternal camping-ground." Among the gallant dead of the mounted troops in this charge was Captain Charles May of the "Forrest Rangers."

The commander of the cavalry found himself now on foot. Too fair a target, his horse, bleeding fatally from repeated wounds, fell beneath him. Securing another mount, he pushed on after the retiring Federals. Some distance in front of Buckner's infantry he halted his men, and with one or two members of his troop rode forward to reconnoiter. Pushing through the heavy undergrowth, he came suddenly upon a line of infantry and a battery, which made their presence known by a volley. As he turned to escape, the battery opened upon the group. A shell crashed through his horse's body, just behind his rider's leg, and tore the animal to pieces. Disentangling himself, Forrest ran on foot to the rear until he came up with his command. Here meeting with General Pillow, this officer gave him orders to employ his men in collecting the captured artillery and small arms and in removing the Confederate wounded from the field.

At the same time—for it was now about two o'clock in the afternoon—a general retrograde movement of the Confederate line in that part of the field which had been occupied by General Buckner had been ordered by General Pillow, and these troops retired within their in-trenchments. The left wing was also ordered to retire, and did this slowly, being followed only a short distance by McClernand's division, which had been heavily reinforced. The Federal line, however, occupied only a portion of the battlefield of the morning. The Confederates were busy until dark gathering up the wounded and the guns and accouter-ments scattered over the battlefield.

The official records show that between four thousand and five thousand stands of small arms and other military supplies were gathered up by the Confederates between the close of the fighting on the Federal right—about two o'clock—and sundown.

Colonel Forrest himself, in his official report made a few days after the battle, states distinctly that he was several times over the battle-field, from one end to the other, from the close of the fight until dark. About the time the retrograde movement of Buckner was ordered, and as he was retiring toward the center and right of the Confederate works, General Smith, commanding the Federal left wing, under orders from Grant, who had arrived upon the field of battle just as the Confederates were being withdrawn within their fortifications, made an assault upon the intrenchments which were immediately in front of him. The gallant Colonel John W. Head, with his 450 men, although assailed by over-whelming numbers, held the position with heroic obstinacy.

As soon as the firing in this direction was heard, the danger of the situation was appreciated by General Buckner, who hurried reinforcements to the scene. Unfortunately these did not reach there in time to prevent Smith from forcing an entrance into one of the outer angles of the Confederate intrenched position, beyond which, however, he was unable to advance. Assault after assault was made, but Buckner, arriving on the scene with reinforcements, had taken command and successfully held his ground until night put an end to the combat.

General Grant says:[19]

When I left to visit Foote I had no idea that there would be any engagement. From the 12th to the 14th we had but 15,000 men and no gunboats. Now we had been reinforced by a fleet of six more vessels, a large division of troops under General Lew Wallace, and 2500 from Fort Henry for Smith's division. The enemy, however, had taken the initiative. Just as I landed [from Foote's flagship] I met Captain Hillyer, of my staff, white with fear for the safety of the National troops. The enemy, he said, had scattered McClernand's division, which was in full retreat. In reaching the point where the disorder had occurred, I had to pass the divisions of Smith and Wallace. I saw no excitement on the portion of the line held by Smith. Wallace was nearer the conflict, and had taken part in it. When I came to the right, appearances were different. McClernand's division had to face the brunt of the attack. His men had stood up gallantly until the ammunition in their cartridge-boxes gave out. Then the division broke and a portion fled, but most of the men, as they were not pursued, only fell back out of range of the fire of the enemy. It must have been about this time

[19] *Memoirs of U. S. Grant,* vol. i, p. 305.

that Thayer pushed his brigade in between the enemy and those of our troops that were without ammunition. *At all events, the enemy fell back within his intrenchments, and was there when I got on the field.*[20]

The serious nature of the dilemma in which General Grant found himself upon arriving on the field is shown by his dispatch to Foote:

CAMP NEAR FORT DONELSON, *February* 15, 1862

ANDREW H. FOOTE, Commanding Officer Gunboat Flotilla—If all the gunboats that can will immediately make their appearance to the enemy it may secure us a victory. Otherwise all may be defeated. A terrible conflict ensued in my absence, which has demoralized a portion of my command, and I think the enemy is much more so. If the gunboats do not show themselves, it will reassure the enemy and still further demoralize our troops. I must order a charge to save appearances. I do not expect the gunboats to go into action, but to make appearance and throw a few shells at long range.

U. S. GRANT,
Brigadier-General Commanding.

It was toward the close of this memorable engagement that a young artillerist, just in his twentieth year, a lieutenant in Porter's battery, attracted the attention of Forrest. This company had been so badly cut up that he was the only unwounded officer left. As Porter was being carried from the field terribly wounded, he shouted, "Morton, don't let them have the guns!" This young man afterwards became famous as Forrest's chief of artillery, for in 1863, when the general was given a special command in the Department of Northern Mississippi, at his earnest request Captain John W. Morton went with him in command of his battery.

Having performed the duty which had been imposed upon him by General Pillow's last order, Forrest led his command within the intrenchments, where they were made as comfortable as the conditions would permit, and, weary with the hard work of the day, they were soon asleep.

At midnight a messenger came to awaken the lieutenant colonel. He was wanted immediately at headquarters. Arriving there he saw Generals Floyd, Pillow, and Buckner, and other officers in consultation. To his amazement they were discussing the surrender of the army. The generals said that the enemy had received heavy reinforcements

[20] Italics added.

since the fight and that they had returned to the position they had occupied when attacked that morning. Forrest protested that the army was not hemmed in and was not whipped. Of the three senior generals, two, Floyd and Buckner, thought the situation of the Confederates was hopeless. The other, the brave old warrior, Pillow, agreed with Forrest that the army was there to fight, not to surrender. These two had stood shoulder to shoulder through that bloody day, had hammered Mc-Clernand with terrific blows, and had beaten him back for nearly two miles, and still were full of fight. They knew the army was not whipped, and come what might they would not give up.

Not overgiven to speech, but rather a man of action, Forrest stalked out into the night. Arousing two of his most trusted men, he sent them out on the road to Clarksville to see if it was open. With these two men there went Dr. J. W. Smith, a practicing physician in Dover then, and at this day (1898) a venerable and respected man, living in retirement at his boyhood's home on the battlefield. The Clarksville road, the most-traveled route to and from Dover, crosses Lick Creek about one mile from town. The crossing is on the farm which Dr. Smith now owns, and upon which he was born and reared. Every bend in this stream, every tree on its banks, and every point where it can be crossed were as familiar to him then as now. As a boy he had waded and swum in it and fished along its banks. They reached one of the crossings and forded it. The water just touched the saddle skirts; the depth was three feet, the width here less than one hundred yards. There was not the sight or sound of an enemy. The way was open, and Dr. Smith so reported.[b] All claims to the contrary disappear before the overwhelming evidence obtained. They returned and reported to Forrest, and he to his superiors. Forrest says: "I returned to my quarters, and sent out two men, who, going by the road up the bank of the river, returned without seeing any of the enemy—only fires, which I believe to be the old camp-fires, and so stated to the general; the wind, being very high, had fanned them into a blaze."

In conclusion General Floyd said: "There were but two roads of escape. By one they would have to cut through the enemy in strong position, besides having to march over the battle-field strewn with corpses. If they retired by the lower road they would have to wade through water three feet deep, which latter ordeal the medical director stated would be death to more than half of the command, on account of the severity of the weather and their physical prostration."[21] How strange this would have sounded to the veterans of 1864, to that lion-hearted, half-famished, and barefoot rear guard which under Forrest and Walthall, day and night, through the ice and snow of December, stood off the victorious legions of Thomas and Wilson and saved the remnant of Hood's beaten army. How strange it reads now, after these many years! General Buckner, too, had weakened, and gave up the fight. He said his troops were so exhausted they could not make a march.[22] Their ammunition was nearly expended. There had been no regularly issued rations for a number of days. The Confederates were completely invested by a force with four times the strength of their own. An attempt to make a sortie would have been a virtual "massacre of the troops, more disheartening in its effects than a surrender."

It is true that the men had fought for a good part of the daylight of the 15th, but they were not so exhausted that they could not have marched away. Many of them on foot did march away, waded the eddy backwater of Lick Creek, or crossed on foot logs and escaped, and all could have followed. The fighting, as far as Pillow's division and Forrest's cavalry were concerned, ended at two o'clock, and from that time until dark these men were engaged in gathering up arms from the field of battle and in retiring within the intrenchments.

Buckner's division had not been as hard-worked or fought up to two o'clock as Pillow's command had, but later in the day were heavily engaged with Smith's assailing column. The fight, however, ceased at dark, which was between five and six o'clock at that season of the year. These troops had from that time until midnight to rest and make ready for the effort to escape. By this time they would have been fully able to march away, and as we know now, practically all could have made their escape. General Buckner claimed in extenuation of the surrender that the ammunition was expended.

A steamboat load of ammunition was coming from Clarksville for that garrison, the telegraph was working, and he and General Floyd knew, or should have known, that this vessel was coming, and that plenty of ammunition would be on the ground in time for distribution. This boat did arrive in the night and in time to distribute the ammunition had the fighting been continued on the 16th. These are facts of official

[21] *Official Records,* vol. vii, p. 273.
[22] *Ibid.,* p. 334.

record. Had these men started out at twelve o'clock, as they could have done under the offer of pilotage on the part of Forrest, they might have marched at least six miles by daylight, and have been free and beyond pursuit. Forrest pleaded for escape or an effort at it. He offered to cover the retreat, and guaranteed that the Federal cavalry would not bother the rear of the infantry. He had felt the caliber of the enemy's horse in front of Fort Henry, and he knew they did not bother him in the battle of Saturday. The records show that only one Federal cavalryman was wounded in the battle of the 15th of February.[23]

As to the failure to issue rations, none but the general in command was to blame for this. In his official report General Grant says: "The amount of supplies captured here is very large—sufficient, probably, for twenty days for all my army. Of rice I don't know that we will want any more during the war."[24]

General Buckner claimed that he could not hold his position after daylight, and in fairness to this officer it must be said that the position gained by Smith gave the Federal commander a great advantage; but since the Confederate general had maintained his second line from all the vigorous assaults of Smith's division on the afternoon of the 15th, it seems clear that, had further resistance been determined upon, by strengthening the line he had without breastworks so successfully held, the enemy could have been kept in check for a while on the morning of the 16th. General Pillow pleaded for further resistance, either to cut a way out if necessary with all the troops that could be gotten ready for a march, or to cross over to the opposite bank of the river in the boats that were nearing Dover at that hour.[25]

But no argument or protest of Pillow or Forrest wrought a change in the mind of Floyd or Buckner. The latter in his report of the surrender says: "Overton's cavalry, following after Forrest, was cut off from retreat by an infantry force of the enemy at the point where Forrest had crossed the stream on the river road." On the contrary, Overton's

[23] *Ibid.*
[24] *Ibid.*, p. 638.
[25] Colonel John McCausland testified that the boats arrived about daylight—were loaded one with corn and the other with ammunition and provisions. Captain Jack Davis testified: "Two boats could have taken the men and munitions of war in two hours [across the river]. The enemy did not come within gunshot distance of the fort until after the surrender. Had some five thousand men been kept in the intrenchments we could have transferred across the river ten thousand men."

company went out with Lieutenant Colonel Forrest and was not captured. Captain Overton, who did not accompany his command, and later in the day tried to escape, was taken prisoner. General Buckner does not state how long after Forrest had passed out the troops, if any, which followed were captured. In unanswerable proof of the fact that this army might have escaped, it is shown that a goodly number of the men on foot did escape, and some of them as late as an hour or two after the surrender was made.[c]

As soon as the conference ended, Forrest announced that he would not surrender himself nor his command, and strode out of the room. Arousing his sleeping troops, he gathered them about him and told them the situation of affairs, and that he would endeavor to take out all who would follow him; that he was going out if he went alone and died in the attempt. These brave men mounted their horses and rode out with their devoted commander; not a man was lost, not an enemy encountered.

As Forrest and those who followed him on horse and foot were marching away, before the day had yet dawned, a Confederate bugler from the parapets of Fort Donelson sounded a truce. The echo brought an answer from the lines of Grant, and there was sent a message from General S. B. Buckner to General U. S. Grant, with offers of capitulation and asking for terms. The gruff soldier had no time to talk of terms. With him it was "unconditional surrender or I will storm your works." That was all. Buckner laid down his arms and accepted the humiliating conditions. Thus fell the curtain upon the opening scene in the bloody drama of the ill-fated Army of Tennessee.

From Fort Donelson to Nashville, almost without surcease, the clouds of disaster gathered over this army. The annals of warfare will in vain be searched for an equal record of persistent courage, of heroic self-sacrifice, of valor that availed naught by reason of unfortunate leadership. What a tragedy of errors! The unnecessary surrender at Fort Donelson; the delayed attack at Shiloh, and the lamentable failure to reap the full benefit of the first day's victory; Corinth, where a thousand gallant spirits laid down their lives in vain assault against impregnable intrenchments; the trap at Vicksburg; then Perryville and the retreat from Kentucky; Murfreesboro, with the loss of Tennessee; Chickamauga's bloody and bootless victory; the defeat at Knoxville, and the wild stampede from Missionary Ridge. Only for a little space of time the clouds rolled back and the sunlight of hope shone through. From Dalton to Atlanta the mighty genius of defensive warfare guided this army and made it stronger and even victorious in retreat under that great leader of brave men, General Joseph E. Johnston. But the strategy of Fabius, which alone bore promise of success, was not to be permitted.[d]

The mad policy of aggression prevailed, and then the meteoric campaign of Hood, Atlanta, Peach Tree Creek, Jonesborough, Altoona, Franklin, and Nashville, in quick and bloody succession, and the Army of Tennessee vanished in air.

Ten thousand men, armed and ready for battle, should have marched out that night, and, with the boats which arrived in the early morning, three thousand more could have escaped across the river. Grant would have arrived to find the bird had flown. The empty fort and the artillery only would have been his. How changed would have been the pages of history if the plea of Nathan Bedford Forrest had been heeded by Generals Floyd and Buckner!

In Forrest's report, written immediately after the battle, he says:

February, 1862

The fight ended about 2.30 P.M., without any change in our relative positions. We were employed the remainder of the evening in gathering up the arms and assisting in getting off the wounded. I was three times over the battle-field, and, late in the evening, was two miles up the river, on the road to the forge. There were none of the enemy in sight when dark came on. Saturday night our troops slept, flushed with victory and confident they could drive the enemy back to the Tennessee River the next morning.

About twelve o'clock at night I was called in council with the generals, who had under discussion the surrender of the fort. They reported that the enemy had received 11,000 reinforcements since the fight. They supposed the enemy had returned to the positions they had occupied the day before.

I returned to my quarters, and sent out two men, who, going by a road up the bank of the river, returned without seeing any of the enemy, only fires, which I believed to be the old camp-fires, and so stated to the generals; the wind, being very high, had fanned them into a blaze.

When I returned, General Buckner declared that he could not hold his position. Generals Floyd and Pillow gave up the responsibility of the command to him, and I told them that I neither could nor would surrender my command. General Pillow then said I could cut my way out if I chose to do so, and he and General Floyd agreed to come out with me. I got my command ready and reported at headquarters. General Floyd informed me that General Pillow had left, and that he would go by boat.

I moved out by the road we had gone out the morning before. When about a mile out, crossed a deep slough from the river, saddle-skirt deep, and filed into the road to Cumberland Iron Works. I ordered Major Kelley and Adjutant Schuyler to remain at the point where we entered this road, with one company, where the enemy's cavalry would attack if they attempted to follow us. They remained until day was dawning. Over five hundred cavalry had passed, a company of artillery horses had followed, and a number of men from different regiments, passing over hard-frozen ground. More than two hours had been occupied in passing. Not a gun had been fired at us, not an enemy had been seen or heard.

The enemy could not have reinvested their former position without travelling a considerable distance and camping upon the dead and dying, as there had been great slaughter upon that portion of the field, and I am clearly of the opinion that two-thirds of our army could have marched out without loss, and that, had we continued the fight the next day, we should have whipped them. The roads through which we came were open as late as eight o'clock Sunday morning, as many of my men who came out afterwards report. . . .

My regiment charged two batteries, taking nine pieces of artillery, which, with near four thousand stands of arms, I had taken inside of our lines.

The long controversy over the comparative numbers of Federal and Confederate troops at Fort Donelson can now be practically settled. In his *Memoirs,* written after all the official records were printed, General Grant says that on the 15th, the day of the battle, he had 27,000 troops. He claims that there were on that day in the Confederate lines 21,000 men, which estimate cannot be sustained by the records. Generals Floyd, Pillow, and Buckner all state 13,000 as the total of the Southern troops. General A. S. Johnston on March 17th says he ordered troops enough there to make the force 17,000. As he was not there, he could not say with any degree of accuracy how many of these reached there and were present for duty. Nevertheless, an informed estimate, based on a search of the *Official Records,* reveals that, including infantry, cavalry, and artillery, there were in all a grand total of 14,805 Confederate troops at Fort Donelson.[e]

In regard to the number of prisoners surrendered, it is a matter of very great surprise that no accurate report was submitted by General Grant or his staff, or if such report were made it has never found a place in the published official records. There can be no possible excuse for this failure. The men were there cooped up within the intrench-ments, and a list of their names should have been made. Rations had to be issued to these men and transportation secured to the various prisons, and yet no record exists. General Grant claimed 15,000 prisoners, and says General Buckner told him that there would not be less than 12,000; but the records show specifically that 1134 wounded Confederates were shipped from Dover up the river to Clarksville and other points before the surrender. Grant says that fully 1000 went out with Forrest. He also says: "It is now known that Floyd and Pillow escaped during the night, taking with them not less than 3000 men."[26] The testimony of a number of men who escaped on this route shows that at least 1500 went out with the cavalry leader.

The official records do not bear out this statement of General Grant as to the number with Generals Floyd and Pillow.

A careful search shows that when these regiments which escaped with Floyd reached Murfreesboro they numbered about 1286 officers and men. General Floyd reports that he saved only a portion of each regiment.

Thirty-sixth Virginia	243
Fiftieth Virginia	285
Fifty-first Virginia	274
Fifty-sixth Virginia	184
Twentieth Mississippi	300
Total	1286

These troops maintained their organization, and were held together from Fort Donelson to Murfreesboro.

In addition to these a sufficient number escaped by crossing the Cumberland from Dover, or walked out by Forrest's route, to make the total of Floyd's brigade escaping fully 1500. General Floyd says: "These reports were made before those who had been ferried over the river at Donelson had come up. A great many who were left effected their escape," etc.[27]

Of the Confederates killed no report is made. I have arrived at the estimate of the Confederate dead as follows:

[26] *Memoirs of U. S. Grant,* vol. i, p. 314.
[27] *Official Records,* vol. vii, p. 275.

An accurate list of the Federals killed and wounded shows that they had 500 men killed and 2100 wounded. In the two different assaults made on the 13th, the Federals suffered a very much larger proportion of killed and wounded than the Confederates, for the reason that the Confederates were sheltered behind their breastworks. As far as the battle of the 15th is concerned, General C. F. Smith's division of necessity suffered a larger proportion of casualties than Buckner's division, for the reason that Smith advanced over open ground and had to work his way through an abattis, which exposed his men to a destructive fire from the Confederates who were then behind the earthworks. In the open fight with McClernand and Lew Wallace's portions of the Union line, where the Confederates were the aggressors, it is safe to assume that the killed and wounded on the two sides were about equal. It will therefore be fair to estimate that the number of the Confederates killed were about one hundred less than the Federals, or four hundred in all, and that the Confederates wounded amounted to about fifteen hundred, all of whom escaped by being sent away, as above shown, excepting about 366 who were left upon the battlefield or were in the hospitals in Dover when Buckner surrendered.

This gives as being absent and not surrendered: with Floyd and Pillow, 1500; Forrest, 1500; wounded sent away, 1134; dead on the battlefield, 400; total not surrendered, 4534.

FOUR

Nashville and Shiloh

AFTER the escape from Fort Donelson, Forrest and his command encamped for the night twenty miles from the field of battle. There was no thought of following him or the infantry that escaped with him on the part of the Federal general, notwithstanding the fact that the Union cavalry had taken little or no part in the action of the 15th, and was therefore in excellent condition for pursuit, if such had been deemed safe. On Monday the march was continued, and on Tuesday, the 18th of February, at 10 A.M., Forrest reached Nashville and reported to General Floyd, who was then commanding the city.

The wildest condition of disorder prevailed in the capital of Tennessee. Panic was not confined to the citizens, women, and children, but soldiers and officers alike seemed to have lost their heads as the result of the disaster at Fort Donelson and the approach of Buell's army, which was reported to be advancing from the direction of Bowling Green. The enormous and exceedingly valuable quantity of supplies which had been gathered for the future use of the Confederate army was left behind in the hurry and confusion attending the general stampede to get away from the city before the Federals arrived. No intelligent or energetic effort was being made to have these supplies shipped to the South.

Into this scene of disorder and alarm Forrest brought the influence of his cool head, clear judgment, and personal courage. He was authorized by General Floyd to take command of the city, which at that time was in the possession of a plundering and violent mob. Neither private nor public property nor human life was safe. The government stores were being broken open and pillaged in broad daylight. Wagonloads of material were being carted away to the country without

58

authority and for private use. The government officials were gone. The president of one of the largest railroads, with more discretion than valor or patriotism, appropriating an engine and a great train of cars for the removal of his personal property, had steamed away for the far South.

Forrest's first order was to detail his men to take possession of and place guards over the public commissary. The rabble refused at first to disperse as ordered. When this was reported to Forrest he rode with his troops directly into the plundering crowd, belaboring the more obstinate members over the heads and shoulders with their sabers until they yielded. In one instance a fire engine was brought up and a stream of cold water played upon the mob with great and immediate success. One man, a ringleader of the motley crowd, evidently under the influence of liquor, rushed at Forrest, and was in the act of striking him when the butt of the cavalryman's six-shooter came down upon his head, felling him unconscious to the ground. The conquest over the leader had the happy effect of inducing his followers to desist from further attempts at violence or robbery.

The impressment of every available wagon, horse, and mule in and about Nashville, for removal of the stores, was ordered. Several hundred large boxes of clothing were sent to the Nashville and Chattanooga depot, and rolling stock ordered to return there to carry these supplies away. One hundred bales of Osnaburgs, large quantities of other military supplies from the quartermaster's department, and nearly a thousand wagonloads of meat, were hauled to the depot of the Tennessee and Alabama Railroad.

Finding that supplies were gathering at these two depots in such quantities that they might not be able to load all on the cars, he had all the ammunition hauled some eight miles on the line of the railroad leading to Decatur, from which point it was shipped by train farther south after the enemy had occupied the city.

Forrest remained in Nashville with forty men twenty-four hours after the arrival of the enemy at Edgefield, upon the opposite bank of the Cumberland. He said in his report that with proper diligence all the public stores could have been transported to places of safety. He finally left the city as the Federals entered, and marched to Murfreesboro, reaching there on Sunday night, February 23, 1862, where he reported to General Albert Sidney Johnston. He was on the following day ordered to proceed with his regiment to Huntsville, Alabama, to rest and recruit his men, where they arrived on February 25th. The entire command was immediately disbanded by furlough, to reassemble on the 10th of March.

Without exception the men reported back on the date given, newly clad and fitted out for the rough and trying campaign which they well knew was in store for them under their vigorous and earnest leader. At this place they were joined by a new company (D), which had been raised by a brother of the lieutenant colonel, Captain Jesse A. Forrest. The command had scarcely reassembled when orders came to proceed at once to Burnsville, Mississippi, seven miles west of Iuka, which place was reached on the 16th of March. Here another company, under Captain C. H. Schuyler, raised in Fayette and Hardeman counties, Tennessee, was added to the command, which was now organized as a full regiment. N. B. Forrest was elected colonel; D. C. Kelley was promoted to the grade of lieutenant colonel, and Private R. N. Balch elected major; J. P. Strange was made adjutant of the regiment. At Burnsville the command went into camp with daily drill and post and picket duty.

Until the forward movement to the battlefield at Shiloh on the 2nd of April, nothing of interest transpired as far as the cavalry of Colonel Forrest is concerned, with the exception of dispatching a scout of twenty men from McDonald's company, who were sent to the neighborhood of Marr's Landing, on the Tennessee River, to watch and report the movements of the enemy, who were supposed to be moving at that time under the command of General Buell to Pittsburg Landing. The full corroboration of this movement was reported back to Forrest, who immediately informed General A. S. Johnston that a large force was moving in the direction of Shiloh to reinforce General Grant. It was the knowledge of these heavy reinforcements which caused the Confederate commander to hurry forward his army in order to strike and crush his antagonist before Buell could reach him.

When the movement toward Shiloh began, Forrest's regiment was attached to Breckinridge's division, and marched with it as far as Monterey. At this point he was directed to advance along the south side of Lick Creek, to throw out a strong picket force, and closely observe any movement on the part of the enemy; and on the night of Friday, April 4th, his men were disposed on this part of the field as ordered. On Saturday, April 5th, some slight skirmishing occurred between the Federal outposts and his pickets, and on the afternoon of that day Colonel Forrest rode to the headquarters of General Johnston to inquire what duty he was expected to perform in the impending battle. He returned to his command by dark, and slept with his troops in such close proximity to the Federal encampments that the music from the various bands along the Union lines was distinctly heard.

Major G. V. Rambaut, in his reminiscences of Forrest at Shiloh, states an amusing incident which occurred during the night before the first day's battle. About midnight the camp was awakened by the lieutenant in command of the outpost with orders to " 'make no noise, and get to your horses as fast as you can.' We could distinctly hear the steady tramp of feet (as we then supposed) of the enemy's infantry moving along the banks of the creek. Our vedettes and outposts had been withdrawn, and our men stood ready to fire at command. Gradually and steadily the advancing tramp grew nearer until it reached the side of the creek just opposite to us, and as each man stood peering through the darkness to catch a glimpse of the supposed enemy, imagine our relief when we saw it was only an escaped artillery horse which had strayed away from one of the Union batteries."

Early on the morning of the 6th the heavy firing rolled in from the left of the Confederate line, and told that the fight had commenced. As soon as the sound of battle was heard, Forrest led his regiment across Lick Creek and sent one of his staff to his commander in chief for instructions, but no answer was received from General Johnston. The firing grew heavier, and, judging from the changing directions in the sound, the Federals were evidently being driven back. It was now about eleven o'clock. Forrest rode out in the front of his command in the direction of the enemy, and, finding that they were giving way toward the river, he came back, and, waiting no longer for orders, marched in the direction of the firing. Failing to find General Breckinridge or any other commander to whom he could report, he advanced his command at a gallop to the point where the infantry seemed to be most desperately engaged. As the cavalry came up they were met by the men of Cheatham's division, which had just been repulsed.

Major Rambaut says: "We passed to the front of them at a point where there was just ahead an open field, and beyond that a black-jack thicket. On the left of the field was a skirt of timberland with considerable underbrush and to the right a small peach orchard, and farther back another thicket of black-jack. Across this field two or more batteries were planted, and one in the edge of the peach orchard. As we came in sight, the guns from one of these batteries were turned upon us. Forrest rode up tò General Cheatham and asked him if he would

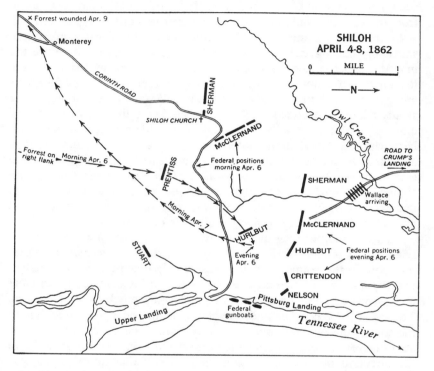

give him orders to charge the battery, saying, 'I cannot permit my men to remain here under fire; I will have either to move forward or backward.' Cheatham replied, 'I cannot give you orders; if you make the charge, it will be on your own responsibility.' Forrest's answer was, 'Then I'll do it.' "[1] He at once ordered his regiment to move forward. Reaching the open field, they received a volley from the battery. By this discharge three men and four horses were killed. The bugle sounded the charge, and the cavalry moved down upon them at full speed. They did

[1] *With Forrest at Shiloh.*

not have time to fire a second round, as the troopers rushed on the gunners, running over and through the battery. The guns to the right escaped, as they were protected by a thick undergrowth through which the horses could not pass. The infantry came up and took possession of the guns, and the mounted men again fell back behind them.

Shortly after this episode an order came to Forrest to move to that portion of the field where Prentiss was being sorely pressed. Marching at a rapid gait, they arrived just in time to witness the disorganization of this Union division. The cavalry regiment rode at the flying infantry, passed entirely through their ranks, and cut them off from the river by taking position between the troops of Prentiss and the reserves near Pittsburg Landing. Here occurred the surrender of General Prentiss and about three thousand of Grant's army.

Keeping on the right flank of the infantry as it still pushed on, Colonel Forrest came upon the battery planted in the last stand by the Federals on the ridge near Pittsburg Landing. Throwing forward his skirmishers, dismounted, the colonel, who advanced with them, soon discovered the great confusion in the ranks of the enemy, and immediately dispatched a courier to General Polk, acquainting him with the condition of affairs, and venturing the suggestion that if the infantry were at once vigorously thrown forward the Union army would be driven into the river. But other counsel prevailed, and between four and five o'clock in the afternoon Forrest received orders to fall back with Chalmers's brigade and camp upon the battlefield. During the night the enemy's gunboats kept up an almost constant shelling of the woods, in which the Confederates were trying to sleep. Soon after dark the colonel of cavalry went to the front, and, creeping along the riverbank, reached a position where he could distinctly see the lights from arriving steamers and hear the commands given in the disembarking of reinforcements. He hastened to convey this information to General Chalmers. This officer says:

I was awakened by one of my staff, who told me that Colonel N. B. Forrest desired to see me. I got up and went out in the darkness and asked him what he wanted. He said: "I want to know if you could tell me where I could find the commanding officer of the army?" I replied I did not know, and upon my inquiry as to what news he had, if any, he said: "I have been way down along the river-bank, close to the enemy. I could see the lights on the steamboats and hear distinctly the orders given in the disembarkation of the troops. They are receiving reinforcements by the thousands, and if this army does not move and attack them between this and daylight, and before other reinforcements arrive, it will be whipped like hell before ten o'clock to-morrow." Forrest rode away and found the commander-in-chief, told him what he had heard and seen, and the unlettered colonel was told to go back to his regiment.[2]

Late on Sunday afternoon, and all night, Buell's troops were landing. Early on Monday morning the enemy, with more than 25,000 fresh soldiers, advanced full of fight and swept the Confederates away. Forrest, ordered to protect the right flank, was soon heavily engaged, and when the order for the retreat of the army was issued Breckinridge covered the movement, with Forrest's regiment between him and the enemy. At night, when about four and one-half miles from Pittsburg Landing, he moved with a portion of his command in the direction of Lick Creek, to guard against any advance from that direction. The retreat toward Corinth was resumed the next morning, with Colonel Forrest covering the Confederate rear.

Near Monterey, General Sherman advanced with two brigades of infantry and the Fourth Illinois Cavalry under Colonel Dickey, the cavalry in front. Reaching the fork of the road leading to Corinth, the infantry, under General Wood, was ordered by Sherman to advance cautiously along one road, while he took the third brigade of his division along the other route, which led to the right. One-half mile beyond the forks of this road was an open field, through which the highway passed, and beyond this field a clearing of fallen timber several hundred yards wide. The Confederate camps could be seen from this point, from one-half to three-fourths of a mile in the distance. Sherman immediately pushed forward a strong line of infantry skirmishers, and advanced his entire command in the direction of the encampment. He did not know until later that Forrest was a close observer of his movements and was ready to contest his advance.

Major Thomas Harrison, then in command of the gallant "Texas Rangers," had reported to Forrest with 220 of his men, and, in addition, a company from Wirt Adams's regiment and two companies of Morgan's Kentucky cavalry; and these, together with his own men, this commander had carefully concealed behind a wooded ridge which ran nearly parallel with the road upon which Sherman was advancing.

[2] *Southern Historical Society Papers.*

Following his usual custom, he had dismounted a certain number of his men, and these were offering slight resistance to the advance of the line of Federal skirmishers. Behind the Union skirmishers and about two hundred yards in front of the brigade under Sherman, in line of battle, came the Illinois cavalry under Colonel Dickey.

After passing through the fallen timber a short distance, and while crossing a small stream, Dickey's cavalry was thrown into temporary confusion, and just as this was observed by Forrest he shouted "Charge!" and at the head of his command, about eight hundred in all, rode right over the line of infantry skirmishers, and closed in with Dickey's cavalry. Being in confusion when the assault was made, their resistance was feeble, and they gave way in a wild stampede, running roughshod over their comrades in Sherman's first line of infantry. The Federal and Confederate cavalry became mixed up in a wild melee. The infantry were thrown into a panic, threw down their guns, and also broke for the rear, suffering considerable damage from the pistols and sabers of the Confederate cavalry. As they approached the second line of Sherman's reserves, a brigade in line of battle, the more cautious of the Confederate troopers pulled up their horses in time, and under the direction of their officers made their way safely back to the rear.

Unfortunately for Forrest, his horse had carried him so far into the line of Union reserves before he could check the animal and turn to retreat that the soldiers rushed forward and attempted to surround and capture or kill him. They fired at him from all sides, shouting, "Shoot that man!" "Knock him off his horse!" So close were they that one infantryman pushed his musket almost against the colonel's side and discharged it, the ball entering just above the left hip, traversing the large muscles of the back, and lodging against the spinal column. He was barely able to maintain his seat, and, to add to the peril of the situation, his horse was wounded severely in two places. Though mortally shot, the plucky animal leaped from his rider's assailants, while Forrest, with pistol in hand, opened an avenue of escape through which he spurred his horse, and found safety in flight.

As shown in General Sherman's official report, this desperate and successful attack by Colonel Forrest checked all pursuit of the flying Confederate army, which, badly beaten at Shiloh on the second day, was retreating toward Corinth, in no shape to resist a vigorous pursuit such as Sherman was capable of.

From this severe wound Forrest did not entirely recover for many weeks, during which period it gave him much pain and annoyance. The noble steed that had done him such great service in this trying experience lived to reach Corinth, but died from his wounds the day after.

Sherman, in speaking of this episode, says:

HEADQUARTERS FIFTH DIVISION, *Tuesday, April* 8, 1862

With the cavalry placed at my command and two brigades of my fatigued troops I went this morning out on the Corinth road. One after another of the abandoned camps of the enemy lined the roads, with hospital flags for their protection; at all we found more or less wounded and dead men. At the forks of the road I found the head of General T. J. Wood's division of Buell's army. I ordered cavalry to examine both roads leading towards Corinth, and found the enemy on both. Colonel Dickey, of the Fourth Illinois Cavalry, asking for reinforcements, I ordered General Wood to advance the head of his column cautiously on the left-hand road, while I conducted the head of the Third Brigade of my division up the right-hand road. About half a mile from the forks was a clear field through which the road passed, and, immediately beyond, a space of some two hundred yards of fallen timber, and beyond that an extensive rebel camp. The enemy's cavalry could be seen in this camp. After reconnaissance, I ordered the two advance companies of the Ohio Seventy-seventh, Colonel Hildebrand, to deploy forward as skirmishers, and the regiment itself forward into line, with an interval of one hundred yards. In this order we advanced cautiously until the skirmishers were engaged. Taking it for granted this disposition would clear the camp, I held Colonel Dickey's Fourth Illinois Cavalry ready for the charge. The enemy's cavalry came down boldly at a charge, led by General Forrest in person, breaking through our line of skirmishers; when the regiment of infantry, without cause, broke, threw away their muskets and fled. The ground was admirably adapted for a defence of infantry against cavalry, being miry and covered with fallen timber.

As the regiment of infantry broke, Dickey's cavalry began to discharge their carbines and fell into disorder. I instantly sent orders to the rear for the brigade to form line of battle, which was promptly executed. The broken infantry and cavalry rallied on this line, and, as the enemy's cavalry came to it, our cavalry in turn charged and drove them from the field. I advanced the entire brigade over the same ground, and sent Colonel Dickey's cavalry a mile farther on the road. On examining the ground which had been occupied by the Seventy-seventh Ohio, we found fifteen of our men dead and about twenty-five wounded. I sent for wagons, and had all the wounded carried back to camp and caused the dead to be buried, also the whole rebel camp to be destroyed.

Here we found much ammunition for field-pieces, which was destroyed; also two caissons, and a general hospital, with about two hundred and eighty Confederate wounded, and about fifty of our own wounded men. Not having the means of bringing them off, Colonel Dickey, by my orders, took a surrender, signed by the medical director (Lyle) and by all the attending surgeons, and a pledge to report themselves to you as prisoners of war; also a pledge that our wounded should be carefully attended to, and surrendered to us to-morrow as soon as ambulances could go out. I enclose this written document, and request that you cause wagons or ambulances for our wounded to be sent to-morrow, and that wagons be sent to bring in the many tents belonging to us which are pitched along the road for four miles out. I did not destroy them, because I knew the enemy could not move them. The roads are very bad, and are strewed with abandoned wagons, ambulances, and limber-boxes. The enemy has succeeded in carrying off the guns, but has crippled his batteries by abandoning the hind limber-boxes of at least twenty caissons. I am satisfied the enemy's infantry and artillery passed Lick Creek this morning, travelling all of last night, and then he left to his rear all his cavalry, which has protected his retreat; but signs of confusion and disorder mark the whole road. *The check sustained by us at the fallen timber delayed our advance, so that night came upon us before the wounded were provided for and the dead buried, and our troops being fagged out by three days' hard fighting, exposure, and privation, I ordered them back to their camps, where they now are.*

I have the honor to be, your obedient servant,

W. T. SHERMAN,

Brigadier-General Commanding Division

To Major-General Grant.[3]

The gallant part borne by Major Thomas Harrison and his Texas Rangers should not be forgotten. No braver soldiers ever fought under any flag than Terry's Rangers.

In addition to the fifteen men killed and twenty-five wounded in the desperate and brilliant charge, a number of prisoners were taken to the rear. Major Harrison reports forty-three taken by his own Rangers, and it is probable that others were captured. General Sherman admits that, as the result of this charge of Forrest, he did not push on any farther after the retreating army of Beauregard.

This was the first occasion in which this stern old warrior, one of the

[3] *Memoirs of Gen. W. T. Sherman,* vol. i, p. 243. Italics not in original.

greatest of all the Union generals, had men in battle and felt the prowess of the Confederate cavalry leader. From that day on he formed a high estimate of Forrest's ability as a soldier.

The wound received by Forrest was so severe that he was carried to his home in Memphis in order to submit to whatever surgical treatment was necessary for his recovery. He improved rapidly, and although very far from having sufficiently recovered to be back on duty, he left Memphis on the 29th of April (twenty-one days after he had been wounded) to rejoin his command.

He paid, however, the penalty of this indiscretion, for a few days after he had joined his command at Corinth the wound became exceedingly painful and swollen, and reopened, necessitating a second severe operation for the removal of the ball, which confined him to his bed for the next two weeks.

FIVE

The Capture of Murfreesboro, July 13, 1862

O<small>N THE</small> 13th of July, 1862, on his forty-first birthday, Forrest, in the capture of Murfreesboro, with its entire garrison, a brigade of infantry and cavalry, Brigadier General T. T. Crittenden, and Colonel, acting Brigadier, W. W. Duffield, performed what General Wolseley, commander in chief of the British army, considers one of the most remarkable achievements of his career. "His operations that day showed a rare mixture of military skill and what is known by our American cousins as '*bluff*,' and led to the surrender of the various camps attacked. It was a brilliant success, and as it was Forrest's first great foray, it at once established his reputation as a daring cavalry leader, to be dreaded by all Federal commanders of posts and stations within his sphere of action."

The advance of this cavalry expedition into middle Tennessee was in accordance with the plan of campaign which had been determined upon by the Confederate leaders, Beauregard and Bragg, shortly after the defeat of the Southern army at Shiloh and the retreat to Corinth, and thence to Tupelo, Mississippi. The chief feature of this aggressive movement was the advance of the army under Bragg from the neighborhood of Chattanooga into middle Tennessee and thence on to Kentucky, and a similar movement on the part of General E. Kirby Smith, who from the vicinity of Knoxville, in east Tennessee, was to cross the Cumberland Mountains and co-operate with the movement of Bragg by a union of the two invading armies in time to confront Buell near the Ohio River.

It was not until the first week in June that Forrest had sufficiently recovered from the terrible wound received at Monterey on the 8th of April to again take the field. Reporting for duty to the commanding officer in northern Mississippi, he was on the 11th of June, 1862, ordered to proceed at once to Chattanooga to organize a brigade of cavalry, with which he was to operate in that department. To the great regret of his devoted troops and their leader, he was not permitted to take his already famous regiment with him. He was, however, allowed to select several of the officers and twenty picked men as his personal escort, and these he placed under the command of his brother, Captain William Forrest.

Arriving at Chattanooga on the 19th of June, it was his great good-fortune to find that the Eighth Texas Cavalry, better known as Terry's Rangers, was to form a part of his small brigade. Entering the service in the early months of the war, this command, made up of hardy rough riders from the cattle ranches of Texas, men who from their earliest boyhood were accustomed to the horse and the ready use of the gun and pistol, sustained to the close of hostilities the reputation for gallantry which they achieved under the brave Terry, their first colonel, who fell in a skirmish near Green River, Kentucky, in 1861. Colonel, afterward Major General, John A. Wharton succeeded to the command of this body of cavalry, and was then at the head of the regiment when it came under Forrest. In addition there were the Second Georgia regiment of cavalry under Colonel J. K. Lawton, the Second Georgia battalion, commanded by Colonel Morrison, and 100 Kentuckians formerly belonging to Helm's regiment, who, having re-enlisted, and having elected as their commander Lieutenant Colonel Woodward, were mounted and assigned to the brigade of acting Brigadier General Forrest.

With his wonted energy, Forrest applied himself at once to the organization and equipment of his new command. By the 6th of July he had everything in readiness for the advance into middle Tennessee. In the meantime he had sent several of his most reliable scouts into this section, and these had returned with accurate information as to the location of various Federal commands in that region. He learned that at Murfreesboro there were two regiments of infantry—the Ninth Michigan and Third Minnesota—a portion of the Seventh Pennsylvania Cavalry, and a battery of four guns. The capture of these troops he determined to undertake.

Crossing the Tennessee River on the 9th of July, his command moved rapidly by two different routes to McMinnville, forty miles from Murfreesboro, where all the troops arrived on the 11th of July. At McMinnville he received accessions to his command in two com-

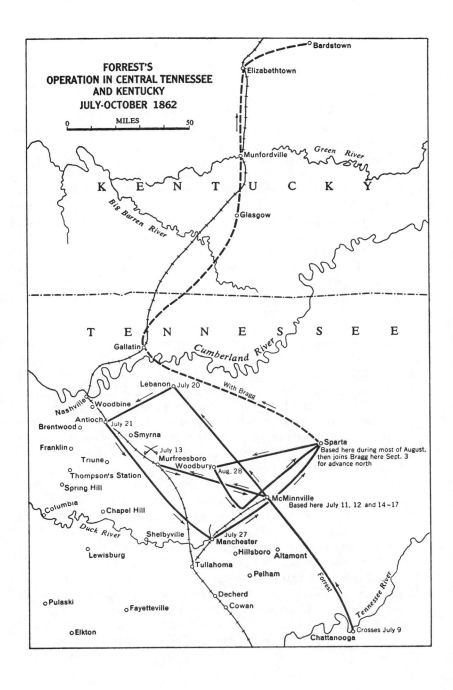

FORREST'S
OPERATION IN CENTRAL TENNESSEE
AND KENTUCKY
JULY-OCTOBER 1862

MILES
0   50

Bardstown
Elizabethtown
Munfordville
Green River
K E N T U C K Y
Big Barren River
Glasgow
T E N N E S S E E
Gallatin
Cumberland River
With Bragg
Lebanon July 20
Nashville
Woodbine
Antioch   July 21
Brentwood
Smyrna
Franklin
July 13
Triune
Murfreesboro
Woodbury
Thompson's Station
Aug. 28
Spring Hill
Sparta
Based here during most of August,
then joins Bragg here Sept. 3
for advance north
Columbia
Chapel Hill
Duck River
McMinnville
Based here July 11, 12 and 14–17
Shelbyville
July 27
Lewisburg
Manchester
Hillsboro   Altamont
Tullahoma
Pelham
Forrest
Tennessee River
Pulaski
Decherd
Fayetteville
Cowan
Elkton
Crosses July 9
Chattanooga

panies of Spiller's battalion, commanded by Major Smith, and two independent companies under Captains Taylor and Waltham, bringing the entire force in this expedition to 1500 men.

At noon of July 12th he moved from McMinnville, and early on the morning of the 13th, while it was as yet not quite daylight, the advance of the column reached the suburbs of Murfreesboro. A company of Wharton's Texans was sent forward, and was soon halted by the Federal outposts. In answer to the challenge, "Who goes there?" they replied that they were a company of the Seventh Pennsylvania Cavalry marching to join their command in Murfreesboro. The Federal sentinels were not aware of their mistake until they were surrounded by the Rangers, who with pistols drawn captured the entire picket force without firing a gun to arouse the sleeping garrison. From these prisoners Forrest learned that Colonel Duffield had been superseded in command by Brigadier General Thomas T. Crittenden of Indiana, who had arrived on the 12th of July. He also learned, to his great satisfaction, that there had been no concentration of the different Federal commands in Murfreesboro; that the Ninth Michigan Infantry and two companies of the Seventh Pennsylvania Cavalry were camped near each other just within the edge of the village; the Third Minnesota and Hewett's battery occupied a second camp one mile and a half beyond the town; while two other companies of the Eighth Kentucky Cavalry and one company of the Ninth Michigan, and other small detachments, were doing provost duty at the jail, in which a number of Confederate soldiers and citizens were imprisoned, as well as guarding the headquarters of General Crittenden in the principal hotel.

Quickly forming his plans, his command was divided into three sections. The Texas Rangers, under Colonel John A. Wharton, were to take the advance and assail the camp of the five companies of the Ninth Michigan Infantry and two companies of the Seventh Pennsylvania Cavalry, situated to the right of the pike as they entered Murfreesboro, and either to capture them at once or, failing in this, to hold them engaged until the other detachments could be disposed of. Colonel Morrison's battalion, under Forrest's personal leadership, was to advance immediately to the center of the town, divided into three squadrons, one of which was to assail the courthouse, another the jail, while the third detachment was to surround the hotel in which General Crittenden was known to be sleeping, and to capture this officer.

The First Georgia Cavalry, under Colonel Lawton, with Woodward's Kentuckians, and the independent Tennessee companies, under the command of Colonel Lawton, were to charge immediately through the village without halting for any purpose, and to throw themselves between the Third Minnesota and Hewett's battery and the village, in order to prevent their junction with the Federals that were being assaulted in Murfreesboro. The command was then formed in columns of fours upon the pike, and advanced slowly and cautiously until, just as the day was dawning, they were in sight of the tents of the Federal encampment. The command to charge was then given, and away Wharton sped down the pike at the head of the Texans. The roar and clatter of the horses' hoofs upon the macadamized turnpike, and the wild yells of the entire Confederate command as they swept onward, aroused the sleeping Federals from their beds.

Before the Pennsylvania cavalrymen could get to their horses the Texans were among them, and those not captured or killed rushed over to the camp of the Ninth Michigan, which by this time was in wild confusion as the result of the surprise. The plucky Michiganders, however suddenly and unexpectedly assailed, were not to be taken without a fight. Acting Brigadier General W. W. Duffield, running out of his tent, called to his men to get their arms and stand their ground. He had scarcely given this command before the Texans were riding in among them, firing at them, as the gallant Duffield said in his official report, at close range with *"shotguns and pistols."* A pistol shot from Wharton himself seriously wounded Duffield, who was forced to relinquish the command of the infantry to Lieutenant Colonel John G. Parkhurst.

By this time the Federals had rallied, and under Parkhurst's command poured a heavy fusillade into the Confederates, who had lost their organization and were scattered in all directions through the camp. Here Colonel Wharton was badly wounded, and, being unable to take further part in the melee, the Texans were thrown into temporary confusion and driven back some two hundred yards from the Federal position. The Union commander, with great judgment, rapidly rallied his troops in an enclosure or lot fenced with heavy cedar pickets or posts set on end in the ground, and by the use of a number of wagons which were loaded with hay and other army supplies within a few minutes had extemporized a formidable stockade, and now held a strong position. Lieutenant Colonel Walker, who took command of the Rangers after Wharton was disabled, recognizing the great loss of life which would follow any attempt to take Parkhurst's position by storm, deployed his men around it in order to hold them penned up until Forrest could come to him with aid. Meanwhile the firing was severe, and from every point of vantage the Texans kept the Federals within the stockade busy.

While this was transpiring, Forrest, who was in command of the second detachment, charged straight to the center of the village, and surrounded the jail, courthouse, and inn, which served as the head-quarters of General Crittenden, his staff, and the provost guards, all of whom were made prisoners. As they reached the jail they found this building on fire, it having been ignited by a Federal soldier, who immediately, with the other troops, rushed into the courthouse, to form part of the garrison defending that position. About one hour was occupied in the search of the houses throughout the central portion of the village for the various parties of Federals who were quartered there, resulting in a number of captures. In the meantime the Federal troops who had taken refuge in the courthouse were pouring volleys into all Confederates who came within their range. In order to silence these, Forrest organized an assault which was to move upon the building from all sides, batter down the doors, and immediately close with the garrison. Under a galling and effective fire, at a word from Forrest they made short work of it. The doors yielded to the hastily improvised battering ram. An entrance was effected, then hand to hand for a few minutes, and the Union troops, who had defended the position with great gallantry, threw down their arms.

As soon as this was accomplished, a portion of the troops immediately under Forrest's supervision were detailed to reinforce the Texans, who were still engaging Parkhurst, while Forrest, with the remainder, moved rapidly in the direction of the second camp, which meanwhile had been attacked by Colonel Lawton's troops—the Georgians and Tennesseeans. Upon hearing the uproar in the village, Colonel Lester had aroused his camp and thrown his men into line of battle. As Forrest's attacking column was advancing in that direction, they came into contact with the Third Minnesota and Hewett's battery moving toward Murfrees-boro, to unite with their comrades there. They had proceeded only about four hundred yards from their camp when they met Lawton, who checked their progress in this direction.

When Forrest reached the scene the troops were engaged at long range, but on account of the artillery which the Federals possessed the Confederates were at great disadvantage. He immediately led in person a detachment of his command to the Federal rear, and charged into the camp which Colonel Lester had occupied previous to the attack. This camp had been left in charge of about one hundred soldiers, and, rushing upon them suddenly from the rear, they offered little resistance. As the men were in the act of surrendering, one, more combative than his comrades, from behind a wagon not more than thirty feet from Forrest, blazed away at him with a musket, but fortunately missed his mark, and he was instantly shot down by the Confederate leader, who was almost unerring in his practice with the repeating pistol.

Having captured the camp, and satisfied now that the Minnesota troops under Colonel Lester could neither advance nor retreat from their present position, by a wide detour Forrest hastened with the troops under him to give his attention to that part of the fighting which had been undertaken by the Texas Rangers in the first assault of the morning. It was about eleven o'clock when Forrest arrived in front of the Michigan and Pennsylvania troops, who were gallantly defending their stockade. He immediately sent a flag of truce to Colonels Duffield and Parkhurst, stating that he had succeeded in capturing all the other troops and had concentrated his entire command upon their position, and to avoid a further effusion of blood he demanded their immediate and unconditional surrender. This demand was accentuated with Forrest's usual threat—that if he was compelled to carry their position by assault, he would give no quarter to those who resisted. Colonel Duffield and Lieutenant Colonel Parkhurst had been shot down, and this detachment had already lost eleven killed and eighty-six wounded.

Colonel Parkhurst says "that as General Forrest had concentrated his entire force save one squadron, and was preparing to make a charge upon us, and evidently intending to execute the threat contained in his demand for surrender, the officers of the regiment voted unanimously to surrender. At twelve o'clock, eight hours after the battle had begun, I surrendered my command as prisoners of war." Of course all the other Union troops had not been captured, nor had Forrest any idea of giving "no quarter" had Duffield not surrendered; but with him "everything was fair in war," and he saved his men by causing the enemy to believe he would. Leaving a sufficient number of troops to guard the prisoners thus made, he hastened with the remainder of his soldiers to the position beyond Murfreesboro, where Colonel Lester with the Minnesota troops and artillery were being held at bay. Here he practiced successfully the same ruse which had been so effectual in inducing the surrender of the Michiganders. A flag of truce was sent forward with the following message:

MURFREESBORO, *July* 13, 1862

COLONEL—I must demand an unconditional surrender of your force as prisoners of war, or I will have every man put to the sword. You are aware of the overpowering force I have at my command, and this demand is made to prevent the effusion of blood. I am, Colonel, very respectfully, your obedient servant,   N. B. FORREST,
To Colonel Lester   Brigadier-General of Cavalry, C. S. A.

Upon the receipt of this message Colonel Lester asked permission to consult with Colonel Duffield. As Duffield was wounded and a prisoner, Lester was immediately taken to the village under an escort, and, finding that all the other troops had surrendered, he immediately capitulated, turning over, as he said in his official report, about 450 infantry, along with Captain John N. Hewett's Battery B, Kentucky light artillery, three six-pounder smoothbores, and one ten-pounder Parrott gun. Pluck and bluff had won the day.

While all this was transpiring, among the many unhappy and anxious prisoners crowded in the county jail there were two who had every reason to be thankful that fate had led the great cavalryman into Murfreesboro at that particular hour. One of these was a spy, under tne assumed name of James Paul; the other was Captain William Richardson, at this date (1898) a prominent lawyer in Huntsville, Alabama. These two men had been informed that they had been condemned to death as spies, and would be executed at sunrise on the following day. Having spent the early part of the night with their minister, the Rev. D. T. Hensley, and then later on talked of their unhappy fate, it was not until a late hour that tired nature asserted itself and they fell asleep. Judge Richardson says:

Just about daylight on the morning of the 13th I was aroused from sleep by my companion Paul, who had caught me by the arm and was shaking me, saying, "Listen, listen!" I started up, hearing a strange noise like the roar of an approaching storm. We both leaped to our feet and stood upon an empty box, which had been given us in lieu of a chair, and looked out through the small grating of our prison window. The roar grew louder and came nearer, and in a very few seconds we were sure we could discern the clatter of horses' feet upon the hard turnpike. In a moment more there could be no doubt as to the riders of these horses, for on the morning air there came to our ears with heartfelt welcome the famous rebel yell, the battle-cry of the Confederate soldiers. Almost before we could speak the advance-guard of the charging troopers came into sight and rushed by us on the street, some halting in front of the jail.

Within the prison-yard one company of Federal troops had been stationed, and, seeing they were about to be surrounded by the Confederates and that our rescue was sure, several of these soldiers in wicked mood rushed into the passage-way in front of our cell and attempted to shoot us before they ran from the building. We only saved ourselves by running forward and crouching in the corner of the cell by the door, a position upon which they could not bring their guns to bear. Before leaving the jail one of the Federal guards struck a match, and, lighting a bundle of papers, shoved this beneath the flooring of the hall-way where the planks were loose, and to our horror we realized that he was determined to burn us to death before the rescuing-party could break open the door. When the Southern riders reached us the fire was already under good headway, and the jailer had fled with the keys. It seemed as if we were still doomed. The metal doors were heavy, and it was not until some of our men came in with a heavy iron bar that the grating was bent back sufficiently at the lower corner to permit us to be dragged through as we laid flat upon the floor.

At this moment Forrest dashed up and inquired of the officer in charge if he had rescued the prisoners. He said that they were safe, but added that the jail had been set on fire in order to burn them up, and the guard had taken refuge in the courthouse. Forrest said, "Never mind, we'll get them." I shall never forget the appearance of General Forrest on that occasion; his eyes were flashing as if on fire, his face was deeply flushed, and he seemed in a condition of great excitement. To me he was the ideal of a warrior. While I was talking to him he turned to a crowd of ladies who, frightened almost out of their wits by the terrible uproar that had so suddenly sprung upon them, had rushed out of their homes and into the streets, many of them in their night-clothes. In most respectful yet very earnest terms he told them they must go back to their homes to save themselves from personal injury.

After the fighting had ceased and the Federal prisoners were all brought together, General Forrest came to me and said: "They tell me these men treated you inhumanly while in jail. Point them out to me." I told him there was but one man I wished to call his attention to, and that was the one who had set fire to the jail in order to burn us up. Forrest asked me to go along the line with him and point that man out. I did so. A few hours later, when the list of the private soldiers were being called, the name of this man was heard and no one answered; Forrest said, "Pass on, it's all right."

Captain Richardson had been wounded at the battle of Shiloh, where he was captured and forwarded to a Federal prison in Indiana. Having recovered from his wound, he made his escape and found his way back to Nashville, then in possession of the Federal army. Friends in that city, in the hope of aiding him to return to the South, placed him in company with a man who was said to be familiar with the routes leading out of Nashville between the Federal pickets. By some unfortunate error, near Black's shop on the Murfreesboro turnpike, they ran into the Federal outposts and were made prisoners.

At Murfreesboro the captain, who was in citizen's clothes, was informed, to his horror, that the person who was with him was a Confederate spy, and that strong incriminating evidence had been found upon his person. This sealed the doom of both captives before any court-martial. On Saturday evening, July 12th, he was informed that if he had any preparations to make it would be advisable to make them, as he and Paul were to be executed on the next morning. The Rev. D. T. Hensley came to the prison and offered his services to the condemned men, but before the fatal hour could strike Captain Richardson and the spy, as well as others incarcerated with them, had found their freedom in a manner entirely unexpected. The hand of fate and Forrest had rescued them.

In his official report Forrest states that there were captured between eleven and twelve hundred privates and noncommissioned officers. "I captured four pieces of artillery, which are still in my possession, with harness and ammunition, some fifty or sixty large wagons and teams, a number of cavalry horses, saddles, small arms, and ammunition." All the material which could not be removed was destroyed. As Forrest immediately left with his command in the direction of McMinnville, he was unable to make an exact list of his killed and wounded. He states about twenty-five killed and sixty wounded. There can be but little doubt, however, that this estimate falls short of his actual loss. Wharton's command must have suffered severely in their encounter with the five companies of the Ninth Michigan and two companies of the Seventh Pennsylvania Cavalry, which detachment, commanded by two very gallant officers, resisted strongly and fought with pluck, as shown by their losses. Eleven killed and eighty-six wounded in the five Michigan companies, and five killed and twenty wounded, as reported by Major James J. Seibert of the Seventh Pennsylvania Cavalry, out of the eighty duty men present at the time of the attack, all attest the bravery of the soldiers. In Hewett's battery the casualties were one killed, three wounded, and seventy-one additional captured. The Michigan company in the courthouse lost three wounded and one not accounted for. The losses in the Third Minnesota were two killed and eight wounded. As Forrest was the assailant, it would be a fair estimate to place his killed at twenty-five to thirty and wounded at one hundred. Colonel Duffield says that "he buried more Confederates than Union dead."[1]

General Crittenden claims his total effective force was 814, but a careful study of the report shows that this does not include the Seventh Pennsylvania troops and others on detached duty at Murfreesboro, and is therefore considerably less than the actual number engaged.

The court of inquiry appointed to examine into the cause of this disaster, in their report of January 24, 1863, stated that "their estimate of the Federal troops present on the 13th of July, 1862, was 1040"; to which, if one adds the teamsters connected with the wagon trains, and others on detached duty, the number would correspond to Forrest's report, which is eleven or twelve hundred. Major General J. P. McCown, C.S.A., on July 17, 1862, from Chattanooga, telegraphed to General Bragg that "Forrest attacked Murfreesboro at five o'clock Sunday morning, July 13th, and captured two brigadier-generals, staff and field officers, and 1200 men; burned $200,000 worth of stores; captured sufficient stores with those burned to amount to $500,000; 60 wagons; 300 mules; 150 or 200 horses, and field-battery of four pieces; destroyed the railroad and depot at Murfreesboro. Had to retreat to McMinnville owing to large number of prisoners to be guarded. Loss 16 or 18 killed, 25 or 30 wounded."

Immediately upon the surrender of the last detachment of the Federals, between three and four o'clock, Forrest gathered his prisoners and captured property together, and started at once in the direction of

[1] *Official Records,* vol. xvi, part i, p. 809.

McMinnville, camping for the night nine miles east of Murfreesboro. Before leaving he destroyed the depots containing all government supplies which could not be transported and the railroad bridges in this immediate vicinity. On the following day, the 14th, the prisoners were placed in charge of an escort commanded by Colonel Wharton, who, although suffering from the wound received in the action of the 13th, was still able to keep his saddle and attend to the lighter duties assigned him. On the night of the 14th the entire command reached McMinnville. Here the prisoners and noncommissioned officers were paroled, while the commissioned officers were sent to Knoxville to be held for exchange.

Naturally the sudden advent of the Confederates in middle Tennessee and the capture of such a formidable garrison as that at Murfreesboro, by a command in general badly armed and equipped, *and without artillery,* created considerable excitement throughout the country, and a very general consternation and anxiety among the Federal commanders of neighboring posts and their troops. It is a matter of surprise that no greater precautions were taken on the part of the Federals to prevent this disaster. It will, however, be remembered that this event took place comparatively early in the war and was the first great foray made by any Confederate commander within the Union lines. Later on the lesson of misfortune bore fruit, and it came to be a rare occurrence for a camp, however small, to be taken unawares.

That the possibility of such invasion had been in the minds of some of the Federal officers is evident from the dispatches about this date which may be found in the official records.[2] On June 8, 1862, Major General O. M. Mitchel, from Huntsville, Alabama, dispatched General Buell that Colonel Lester at Murfreesboro had informed him that 1000 of the enemy were eight miles south of McMinnville and might attack him. Mitchel adds: "I do not know what reliance ought to be placed on these reports. One thing is certain, that region ought now to be strongly occupied"; and this careful officer again emphasized his apprehension of attack on June 24th in a dispatch to General Buell in which he says: "It is possible the enemy's cavalry crossing opposite Chattanooga might pass the mountains to McMinnville for a raid on Wartrace and Murfreesboro. I have directed the commanding officer to be ready."[3]

[2] *Ibid.,* vol. x, part ii, p. 275.
[3] *Ibid.,* vol. xvi, part ii, p. 58.

From the manner in which the surprise was effected it is evident that the warning of his superior was not fully appreciated by acting Brigadier General Duffield. Moreover, as late as the 12th of July, the day preceding the attack, Buell wired Halleck that a heavy cavalry force was being thrown across the Tennessee River to operate in middle Tennessee.[4] Duffield was advised again to take every precaution, and to build a stockade for the protection of every bridge in his jurisdiction.[5]

Three days prior to the attack the Federal authorities were the recipients of a rather mysterious telegram signed by Stanley Matthews, but sent in a spirit of sheer bravado by another bold raider. The guilty person in this instance was none other than the distinguished Colonel John H. Morgan, who about the time that Forrest was starting for middle Tennessee had gone on a raid of his own into his native land of Kentucky. Morgan carried with him a very daring and expert telegraph operator, George A. Elsworth, who bore the fitting nickname of "Lightning." On the 10th of July, Elsworth cut the wire about one and a half miles below Horse Cave, on the Louisville and Nashville Railroad, inserted his instrument, and began to inform his commander of the various events which were passing over the wire. When about to close, Morgan, who was sitting at his side, dictated to him and he immediately sent the following prophetic dispatch:

NASHVILLE, TENNESSEE, *July* 10, 1862.
To HENRY DENT, Provost Marshal, Louisville, Kentucky—General Forrest attacked Murfreesboro, routing our forces, and is now moving on Nashville. Inform general commanding.
STANLEY MATTHEWS, Provost Marshal[6]

As had been expected, one of the immediate results of Forrest's raid was a rapid concentration of troops in this direction to protect the various Federal stations and at the same time to drive him back across the Tennessee. This movement began at once and relieved the Confederate army in northern Mississippi of the great pressure which was being brought to bear on it at that time by the Federal commander. As soon as Buell, whose headquarters were at Huntsville, Alabama, received information of the disaster on the night of the 13th, he telegraphed to Major General McCook to move with his division at once to Colum-

[4] *Ibid.*, p. 127.
[5] *Ibid.*, p. 130.
[6] *Ibid.*, p. 775.

bia, adding that a large force of rebel cavalry had attacked Murfreesboro, and was threatening the Franklin and Columbia bridges.

Colonel Miller, commanding at Nashville, wired Buell that Murfreesboro was captured, and that he had recalled all the troops from Lebanon, had every man under arms, and had strong pickets out and patrols
on all the roads. Buell answered: "Reinforcements are moving forward
and will reach Nashville to-morrow." General Buell further dispatched
General William Nelson, at Athens, Alabama, that the troops had been
surprised and defeated, and Nelson's command was at once on the
march. On the 15th of July, Buell dispatched Halleck: "The worst
feature of Forrest's attack was the interruption of the Chattanooga railroad, just completed." He says: "I had taken the precaution to place
some twelve regiments on that route until it should be securely established. A large portion of the 50,000 rations of forage forwarded to
Murfreesboro have been captured or burned."

He regarded the whole affair as most disgraceful and demanding
prompt and vigorous treatment. "It has caused serious delay in the
means of supplying the army so that it can move on the Decatur route.
The force was more than sufficient to repel the attack. Take it in all its
features, few more disgraceful examples can be found in the history
of our war." He also wired General George H. Thomas, who was at
Tuscumbia, Alabama, "to move with all rapidity to Florence and Athens
and on to Murfreesboro. I deem it of very great importance that you
should get across the river at the earliest possible moment. Send one
of your brigades forward without delay to cross at Decatur. Cross everything you have at Eastport at once. Endeavor to get your trains across
at all points before Grant's troops come up, so that no time may be lost
after their arrival."[7]

Being well informed of the rapid concentration of heavy forces for
the purpose of destroying his command, a more timid leader than Forrest would have justified himself in resting upon his laurels and retiring
his command in safety to the neighborhood of Chattanooga, under the
protection of the infantry there. But the hardy cavalryman was on his
native heath, was born almost within sight of Murfreesboro, and he had
no notion of leaving Tennessee until he was driven out by main force.
In fact, that quality of caution born of timidity had neither lot nor part
in his sturdy nature. If it had been otherwise the chances are that the

[7] *Ibid.,* vol. xvi, part ii, p. 175.

success at Murfreesboro would have been only partial. To have captured a brigadier general and the troops forming his guards in sight of two large bodies of well-equipped infantry, and liberated a large number of imprisoned Confederates, might have satisfied a less energetic soldier, but there was so much of the bulldog in this man's nature that he would not let loose and was not satisfied until everything was his.

And so at Murfreesboro he refused to listen to the suggestions of his officers to leave the infantry alone and retire with the property and the prisoners they had already captured. He said: "I did not come here to make half a job of it; I'm going to have them all." While resting at McMinnville, the trusted scouts sent out in various directions for the purpose of obtaining the necessary information for his future enterprises returned, and on the 18th of July he started at the head of a detachment of his command in the direction of Lebanon. On the 20th, arriving near this town, he found the quarry had been flushed, for, apprised of his advance, the Federals had scurried away for shelter behind the ramparts of Nashville. From Lebanon he followed them as they retired in this direction.

Four miles from Nashville he came upon a detachment, about twenty in number, who, protected by a strong stockade, were guarding a railroad bridge over Mill Creek. This time he was not without cannon, and stockades, however well constructed, could soon be battered down by artillery. He so convinced the garrison that this would be the result that they surrendered, and the bridge was forthwith destroyed. Moving still farther around the city and in sight of the capitol on this same date, his advance guard, composed of the Eighth Texas, had a lively encounter with a second detachment of the Union troops at Antioch station. These also surrendered after some resistance, and the depot, filled with government supplies, was destroyed and all the rolling stock there burned. Farther down on the road toward Murfreesboro on this same day another bridge was destroyed.

Major General Nelson had already informed General Buell that "Forrest had returned, but in three days he would take the field and try to clear him out of the country." On July 22nd Colonel John F. Miller, commanding at Nashville, telegraphed Buell that "Colonel Forrest, with a force variously reported from twelve hundred to four thousand strong, advanced yesterday from Lebanon within eight miles of this city, marched across the Mill Creek, destroyed three bridges, took eighty prisoners, killed two and wounded one of the Second Kentucky Volunteers. Enemy's loss reported, twenty killed and wounded. He took the prisoners on Murfreesboro road twelve miles from this place, camped, paroled the prisoners this morning, and then marched to Murfreesboro to capture wagon-trains with 360 of the Thirty-sixth Indiana, who left here yesterday morning."

So desirous was our new brigadier general (for his commission was dated July 21st) to let Colonel Miller know he was still in the country, he sent him a polite note to this effect, adding that if he didn't believe it and would come out he would give him a warm reception. Colonel Miller was not afraid, but he had orders to hold Nashville, and he stayed there and held it. General Nelson, on the 24th of July, from Murfreesboro, reported that on the 21st Forrest was within five miles of Nashville burning bridges and trestlework. "I determined to cut off Forrest's retreat, but before marching a courier came to me from Franklin, bringing a dispatch that Forrest with twenty-five hundred or three thousand men was at Nashville. Forrest escaped. The eighty men that were guarding the bridge that was burned are lost, three of them killed and the rest taken. They were of the Second Kentucky. That regiment is much reduced since leaving Athens; three were killed and forty-eight wounded on the railroad, eighty-one taken prisoners, making a loss of six killed and one hundred and twenty-nine lost by death and prisoners. I will have about twelve hundred cavalry, and Mr. Forrest shall have no rest. I will hunt him myself."[8]

Instead of permitting himself to be cut off or whipped by General Nelson, "Mr. Forrest," leaving the main road as the Union commander approached, hastened across the country with his troops, and paid his respects on the 27th of July to General W. Sooy Smith, who was then in command at Manchester. He wired General Buell from Manchester that day: "Forrest appeared before me and made a successful dash on one of my reconnoitring parties, killed three and captured fifteen men." Later on, in the campaign of 1864, in Mississippi, Forrest and Smith met again, to the great and lasting discomfiture of the latter. Under the persistent prodding of his superior, General Buell, Nelson was kept busy in the effort to hunt Forrest down. It was a game of hide-and-seek, in which the cavalry leader was hard to beat. Buell reiterated his dispatch: "Destroy Forrest if you can."

[8] *Ibid.*, vol. xvi, part i, p. 815.

"In spite of the hot weather and the seeming hopelessness of his task, Nelson, with commendable persistence, chased to and fro across middle Tennessee in a vain effort to come up with the Confederates. On July 30th he gave it up. He telegraphed to Buell on this date that "with infantry in this hot weather it is a hopeless task to chase Forrest's command mounted on race-horses." Still came from Buell the watchword, "Destroy him if you can," and still the clouds of disappointment hung over Nelson. In a dispatch from McMinnville he says: "The condition of the country is as bad as possible. It is in arms almost to a man. Bragg's army is expected. Three wagons have been cut off close to camp; patrol fired on, four killed; two other sentries shot. Forrest himself is here at Sparta with twenty-five hundred men. Sent a regiment of cavalry out yesterday to attract his attention."

And promptly, on the 15th of August, Forrest was attracted for he moved out from Sparta, swooped around his pursuers, and went in the direction of Murfreesboro, which place was now again heavily garrisoned by the Union forces. Turning toward McMinnville, he followed the branch of the railroad leading to this place, destroying all the bridges and tearing up the track. Once more the Federal post commanders in the region round about had the wires hot with dispatches. Some inquired where Forrest was when last heard from, and others contained the information that "Forrest may be expected." In doleful vein General Buell dispatched to Miller at Nashville: "Our guards are gathered up by the enemy as easily as he would herd cattle. One resolute company properly stockaded could defy Forrest's whole force."[9]

On the 18th of August, Buell wired that "Forrest is certainly at Nashville. Troops cannot safely cross." On the 26th he wired General Hazen: "Endeavor to assure yourself whether Forrest has any infantry with him." On August 27th, General Thomas had heard that "the train of the Fourth Division was captured by Forrest yesterday," and on the 28th he wired Buell: "I have sent a brigade after Forrest, who is at Woodbury with something over one thousand men."

In the meantime, Forrest, duly informed of the various columns marching to hem him in, and knowing also that General Bragg with a heavy infantry force had already crossed the Tennessee River at Chattanooga and was moving toward Altamont, determined without delay to proceed to this latter place and there await the advance guard of the

[9] *Ibid.,* vol. xvi, part ii, p. 340.

infantry column. Although he moved with his usual celerity, he was too late to escape an additional body of Union troops who, under the active leadership of General McCook, had headed him off and was then in possession of Altamont. However difficult and dangerous the predicament in which he found himself, Forrest was not slow in deciding what was to be done. He knew that a brigade which had been rushed forward by General Thomas was close behind him, coming from the direction of Murfreesboro. There was but one route left for escape; this he followed.

Throwing his scouts well in advance, and with flankers on either side to prevent the possibility of a surprise by ambush or collision with an enemy too large for him to engage in battle, he had advanced only a few miles when his vedettes came rushing back with the information that they had just encountered a considerable force of infantry not more than half a mile ahead, and that these were advancing immediately upon them. Fortunately he received this information before the main body of his command had been discovered by the Federals. If the roads were all filled with soldiers in pursuit of him, Forrest concluded, there was plenty of room in the woods, and straightway he took to the brush with his entire command, successfully concealing them within a half-mile of the route along which the Federal infantry soon passed, little suspecting that their wily adversary was closely observing them at such short range. The rear guard of this column had scarcely passed his place of concealment when he again led his men into the road and resumed the march which had been so unceremoniously interrupted.

Forrest was, however, not yet out of danger. Being compelled to pass near McMinnville, it was his intention to make a detour around this heavily garrisoned town. To accomplish this, when about eight miles from the village he turned from the main thoroughfare into a byway or country road which was ordinarily but little traveled. Unfortunately he had not cleared the main road when a heavy column of Federal infantry came in sight, which, deploying, at once opened upon his troops with artillery and small arms as they were moving with all possible rapidity. No effort at resistance was made by the Confederate commander, who promptly put his troops in rapid retreat. He, with one-half of the command, had already passed from the main road, and these continued at full speed in that direction. That portion which had been cut off by the Federal attack turned about, scampered away in the opposite direction, and was soon out of danger. Cutting across the country, before sundown these had rejoined the main column under Forrest. Not a man was captured or even wounded in this attack, the only loss the Confederates suffered being one light spring wagon and some dozen horses and mules, which were being led with the command.

General Thomas, speaking of this affair, said: "Yesterday I learned that Forrest's command was three miles west of my camp, going northward. I sent our three regiments to cut him off. About one-half of his command had passed when we arrived. Fyffe opened with shell and musketry, and captured a number of horses and mules and a light spring-wagon. His force numbered between fourteen and fifteen hundred men."[10]

It will be observed that this official report does not mention the capture of one of Forrest's troopers.

On the 3rd of September, Forrest reached the advance guard of General Bragg's army of invasion at Sparta, bringing with him in safety his "pets"—the four pieces of artillery he had captured at Murfreesboro—and his entire command, excepting those lost in battle or broken down and rendered unfit for service by the long and arduous marches.

At Sparta our cavalryman was greatly pleased to know that the four Alabama companies of his old regiment under Captain Bacot had been permitted to rejoin his command, and that he was to be allowed also to keep a section of the artillery he had captured. Reporting here to Major General Braxton Bragg, then in command of the Confederate army of invasion, he was directed to move forward in the line of advance of the Union army under General Buell, and to harass and impede his progress as much as possible. Moving again toward Murfreesboro, the Federals rapidly retreated, and the place was once more occupied by the Southern troops. Pressing after them toward Nashville, Forrest crossed the Cumberland River a few miles from this city, and was in almost constant conflict with the rear guard and flankers of Buell's army.

Finding that his section of artillery would be of great service in retarding Buell's advance, with his usual audacity he pushed his guns in such proximity to the Federal infantry that they were often compelled to deploy in line of battle and advance in order to drive him away. This was exactly what Forrest wished to accomplish, for the more they formed in line, the greater would be the delay in their march toward

[10] *Ibid.*, vol. xvi, part i, p. 900.

Louisville, and Bragg would have that much the better start in the race. By the 8th of September his army had advanced into southern Kentucky, and on the 10th of that month Forrest arrived at Glasgow with his cavalry.

At this place he was temporarily attached to the division of the Confederate army commanded by General Leonidas Polk, and, under orders of this officer, pushed his command beyond Munfordville on the Elizabethtown and Bardstown road. In this movement he threw himself between the Federals in Munfordville and their only avenue of escape, and, together with the rapid advance of the Confederate infantry converging toward this stronghold, contributed largely to the capture of a brigade of infantry which surrendered on the 17th of September. This accomplished, Forrest proceeded along the line of the Louisville and Nashville Railroad, destroying bridges, capturing Federal outposts, and reporting ultimately at Bardstown to General Polk.

At this place he received a letter asking him to report immediately in person to the headquarters of General Bragg. And here, on the last day of September, he was directed to turn over the brigade which he had organized at Chattanooga, and had thoroughly armed and equipped by captures from the enemy, to Colonel John A. Wharton, of the Texas Rangers, and to proceed at once and establish headquarters at Murfreesboro and undertake the organization of another brigade for his own service. At his earnest entreaty he was allowed to take with him the four Alabama companies of the "Old Regiment," which had served with him at Sacramento, Fort Donelson, and Shiloh. With these and his staff he marched away to his recruiting camp.

SIX

The Raid into West Tennessee, December, 1862

Dᴜʀɪɴɢ the first week of October, 1862, General Forrest established the headquarters of his recruiting bureau at Murfreesboro, the scene of his recent brilliant exploit. Concealing the disappointment and indignation which he keenly felt at having the brigade he had recently organized and equipped, and by a severe and successful campaign had transformed into veterans full of confidence in their chief and ready to follow him in any enterprise, taken from him and given to another officer, he applied himself with diligence to the task in hand.

The ruling spirit in this man was devotion to the cause of the South in its struggle to establish an independent confederation. With absolute unselfishness and with earnestness of purpose he gave not only his private fortune but untiring energy, and for the ultimate success he would have cheerfully given the life which he risked on so many notable occasions. He was now so well known as a dashing cavalry leader, and so popular with all classes in the middle Southern states, that he had little difficulty in gathering about him within six weeks of the time he had located at Murfreesboro a very formidable body of mounted men. Many of these were Tennesseans, enlisting from the middle counties of that state, and not a few were natives of Bedford and Marshall counties, almost in sight of the spot where Forrest was born and had spent his boyhood.

Among others there joined him here a man of great ability and courage who earlier in the war, quitting the peaceful practice of medicine, had organized a company of Tennesseans and had volunteered to accompany him in the scouting expedition which culminated in the brilliant affair at Sacramento, Kentucky, in December, 1861. This man was James W. Starnes, who had signally distinguished himself on that occasion and had won the lasting regard and friendship of Forrest, a friendship which endured until at Tullahoma, in 1863, death brought to an untimely end a career full of the promise of great deeds in war.

A new regiment was now organized with Starnes as colonel, and took its place with Forrest as the Fourth Tennessee Cavalry; it was destined to become famous and to sustain throughout the war the reputation it was soon to win west of the Tennessee, ending its career in a blaze of glory in a brilliant charge at Bentonville, North Carolina, in the last pitched battle of the Civil War. Scarcely less famous were two other regiments of Tennessee troops organized at this time—the Eighth, under Colonel George G. Dibrell, of which Jeffrey E. Forrest, the youngest brother of the general, was elected major, and the Ninth, under Colonel J. B. Biffle.

These three regiments of Tennessee troops, with the Fourth Alabama Cavalry, under Colonel A. A. Russell, with one battery of artillery, under Captain Freeman and Lieutenant John W. Morton, were organized into a brigade, to which Forrest was assigned as commanding officer. At this time General Joseph Wheeler had been promoted to the chief command of the cavalry in that department, and Forrest, being thus relieved, was ordered to march to Columbia, in Murray County, preparatory to being sent to break up the enemy's communications and to make a diversion in the rear of Grant's army in northern Mississippi and west Tennessee.

Russell's Fourth Alabama,[1] as it was afterward known, was a mixed organization of veterans and new troops. Four companies of this regiment had volunteered early in the war and had formed a part of Forrest's original battalion, had served with him at Sacramento, had escaped with him at Fort Donelson, and were with him at Shiloh and Monterey. After persistent entreaty they had been permitted to join their old commander again, and now formed the nucleus to which six other companies of recent Alabama volunteers were added. This regiment greatly distinguished itself under their brave colonel, and was especially complimented in the official report of General Forrest after his return from the arduous campaign in the winter of 1862-63.

About one-half of the men of this command, which took position at Columbia the first week in December, 1862, had no other arms than shotguns and squirrel rifles which they had brought with them from home. Many of the army weapons issued to them were of ancient pat-

---

[1] As distinguished from Roddy's Fourth Alabama.

tern and not efficient as compared with those in the Union ranks. Dibrell's regiment alone had 400 flintlock muskets.[2] Forrest made application to Bragg for proper guns and equipment, but the Confederacy was too poor at that time to furnish them. The brigade which he organized earlier in this year at Chattanooga he had thoroughly equipped at the expense of the enemy, who even furnished his artillery, and now he was told that he must do practically the same thing with this, his third new command, and that in west Tennessee he would probably find the material he so much needed. Arms or no arms, General Bragg informed him, he was expected to march into that territory at a very early date, and must prepare for his expedition.

Though these difficulties embarrassed, they did not discourage him. Forrest appreciated fully the dangerous character of the work he was now called upon to perform. He was to cross a large river three-fourths of a mile in width, the fifth in magnitude in the United States. Its western shore was picketed by the cavalry of a brave and vigilant army. This river, the Tennessee, in its upward sweep from northern Alabama to pour its waters into the Ohio, flows nearly due north, cutting the State of Tennessee abruptly in twain. This fragment of the state has the Mississippi River as its westerly boundary and the Tennessee on the east. On the north is Kentucky and the Ohio, to the south, from Memphis to Corinth, stretched the mighty and victorious army of Grant. Once in this territory, swarming with the soldiers of the Union, well armed and equipped, there could be no escape except by recrossing the Tennessee. This navigable stream was being patrolled by a fleet of gunboats for no other purpose than to prevent incursions from the east, and in case any such were made, and the invaders once were in the trap, to prevent the possibility of escape.

On the 18th of December, 1862, General U. S. Grant[3] dispatched to Admiral Porter: "There is now four feet of water in the Tennessee River, and gunboats there would be of immense value." To this he received a reply signed by A. M. Pennock, that "five gunboats had gone into the Tennessee River service on the 15th inst. They draw three feet of water." On December 15th, General G. M. Dodge wired General J. C. Sullivan: "The Tennessee has risen two feet, and there is plenty of water there."

[2] *Official Records*, vol. xvii, part i, p. 598.
[3] *Ibid.*, vol. xvii, part ii, p. 426.

Once well inside of this isolated territory, with vigilance on the part of his adversary, Forrest knew full well that all his resources would be needed to extricate himself. On the 10th of December he received orders to move, and he again appealed to his commander for guns and ammunition. The same answer came back, that there were none for him, he must do the best he could and go on. He had already sent a detachment of his best troops, with some workmen, and had constructed two small flatboats for the purpose of ferrying his men and horses across. These were concealed in the neighborhood of Clifton, in a slough or narrow subdivision of the river on the east side of an island, and here, on the 15th of this month, he arrived with his command of 2100 men[4] and Freeman's battery of seven pieces.

The work of crossing the river was immediately begun. The command was kept well back from the banks, out of sight of any gunboats that might pass. A long line of sentries was placed up and down the river from this position at a sufficient distance to enable them to repeat the signals to each other and to notify their commander when any of the patrol gunboats were approaching. The work of crossing was done mostly at night. Each boat could carry not more than twenty-five men and horses at a single trip. When the gunboats were signaled, the ferryboats immediately put back to shore and ran in behind the island, where they could not be observed. By the 17th the command was successfully across the river, but not without the knowledge of the enemy. That wily soldier, Major General W. T. Sherman, on this date reported that "a boat from above, just in, reports a rebel force crossing the Tennessee from the east towards the west at Clifton," and with foresight adds, "I rather suspect it is the design to draw us back from our purpose of going to Vicksburg."[5]

General Grant telegraphed to the War Department at Washington: "I had timely notice of the advance of Forrest on the road, in the neighborhood of Jackson, and took every means to meet it. General Sullivan

[4] The troops under Forrest were Starnes's Fourth Tennessee, Dibrell's Eighth Tennessee, Biffle's Ninth Tennessee, and Russell's Fourth Alabama regiments; Cox's Tennessee battalion; Woodward's two Kentucky companies; Captain Bill Forrest's scouts; and General Forrest's escort, numbering in all 2100. Napier's battalion, 400 strong, joined at Union City. So poorly armed and equipped were the new recruits that his effective fighting force was not over 1500.

[5] *Official Records*, vol. xvii, part ii, p. 426.

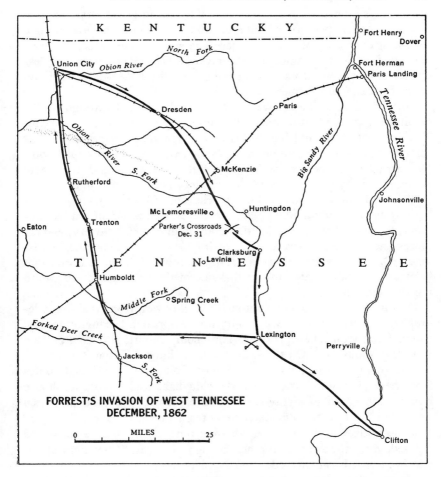

FORREST'S INVASION OF WEST TENNESSEE
DECEMBER, 1862

was reinforced from the army with me, and forces from Corinth, Forts Heiman, Henry, and Donelson sent to co-operate."[6]

Having consumed considerable time in crossing his men, horses, and artillery, carrying the horses over in the boats in order not to endanger their usefulness by the extra exposure which would result in swimming

[6] *Ibid.*, vol. xvii, part i, p. 477.

them across a wide stream, icy cold at this season of the year, the real business of the expedition was at once taken up. There was now no time for taking extra care of horses or men. The work in hand was dangerous and must be done quickly, and the more rapid the execution, the less danger of a concentration of troops in sufficient number to prevent him from recrossing the Tennessee.

Forrest's first stratagem was to cause to be spread throughout the country the rumor that he had with him a very large number of troops. The game of "brag and bluff" this crafty warrior often played, and it served him a good purpose on this as well as on many other expeditions. He carried a number of kettledrums with his troops, and kept them going, to convey the impression that infantry accompanied him.

Colonel Robert G. Ingersoll, of the Eleventh Illinois Cavalry, reporting through his commanding officer to General U. S. Grant, on December 18th, says: "At noon yesterday 3000 infantry, 800 cavalry, and six pieces had crossed and were still crossing the Tennessee at Wright's Island." On the same date General U. S. Grant wired Admiral Porter that "Forrest and Napier are now on this side of the river with from five to ten thousand men."

On this date also, General Jeremiah C. Sullivan, from Jackson, telegraphed General Grant: "My cavalry was whipped at Lexington to-day. Colonel Ingersoll taken prisoner. The enemy reported to be from ten to twenty thousand." On the next day he is informed that "the enemy are advancing in force, and the station on Columbus [road], eight miles from here [Jackson], was attacked at daylight and the station-house burned, the guard of eighty-seven men captured, and road at switch destroyed." A few moments later news from Corinth road was received that the bridges twelve miles south were burned and a large force had crossed, going toward the railroad leading to Bolivar. "Cheatham's brigade [infantry] is on this side, and Napier's also."

On the 19th of December the commander in chief says: "I have reinforced Sullivan to the full extent of the capacity of the road to carry troops, partly from Columbus, partly from Corinth, one brigade from here [Oxford], and troops from Jackson. Lowe is also moving from Heiman. I think the enemy must be annihilated, but it may trouble, and possibly lead to the necessity of sending further forces from here."[7]

January 9, 1863, Brigadier General Thomas A. Davies, commanding

[7] *Ibid.*, vol. xvii, part ii, p. 436.

at Columbus, telegraphed to Colonel John A. Rawlins: "I had what I supposed was reliable information that Forrest had 7000 men and ten pieces of artillery, and was backed by a heavy infantry force. I ordered General Curtis to send General Fisk's brigade to reinforce me at Columbus."

Here, in truth, were signs of concentration as well as relief for the sorely pressed Confederates in Mississippi. He says in this same dispatch: "Ingersoll's cavalry had an engagement with them yesterday at Lexington and were defeated. Two pieces of artillery fell into the hands of the enemy."[8] This engagement occurred on the morning of the 18th of December. Forrest, after crossing on the 17th, encamped eight miles west of the river that night. On the morning of the 18th, advancing in the direction of Lexington, when near that place the Confederates came in contact with some Union cavalry and a section of artillery.

This cavalry and artillery were under the command of our distinguished countryman, Colonel Robert G. Ingersoll, the famous lawyer and lecturer. He had arrived on the 17th at Lexington, where he was joined by Colonel Hawkins, of the Second West Tennessee Cavalry, with about 272 men. At noon he marched to Beech Creek, five miles from Lexington. Proceeding farther east, he was joined by Captain O'Hara with sixty-eight men additional, who reported that the Confederates, at least a thousand strong, were advancing upon them.[9] He at once ordered his advance guard to retire slowly, and at the same time withdrew his command to the crossing of Beech Creek, near Lexington. Here, just at night, he was joined by 200 troops of the Fifth Ohio, under Adjutant Harrison, and on the 18th, early in the morning, was attacked in this position.

At break of day Captain Frank B. Gurley, of the Fourth Alabama, was ordered by General Forrest to select twenty men of his company and take the advance on the Lexington road and drive in the enemy's pickets as soon as encountered, promising him that the remaining companies of this regiment would follow in close order and would reinforce him as might be necessary.

Advancing about two miles, Gurley found the enemy in line, and, after a slight skirmish, they fell back to the creek, leaving one or two of their wounded, who were captured. At Beech Creek the Second West

[8] *Ibid.*
[9] *Ibid.*, vol. vii, part i, p. 553.

Tennessee Cavalry was drawn up in line of battle upon the opposite bank. The bridge over this stream had been rendered impassable by the Federals, who had thrown the planks which formed the floor into the water. The advance of the Confederates, now reinforced by the other companies of Russell's regiment, dismounted and charged up to the creek, and by a heavy and well-directed fire drove back Colonel Hawkins and his Second West Tennessee regiment. Quickly relaying the floor of the bridge with fence rails which were near at hand, after a delay of not more than twenty minutes Gurley's command passed safely over. This short delay, however, gave Colonel Ingersoll time enough to form his troops where they were well protected in the edge of some timber just over the crest of a hill. Here the Federals fought stubbornly, but were finally driven back, with considerable loss on both sides. The Confederates, continuing to advance, and arriving in the immediate vicinity of Lexington, found a section of artillery so posted as to command the route by which they were approaching. Behind the guns was a strong body of cavalry. As the Fourth Alabama came up they were subjected to a sharp fire from the two guns in front as well as the small arms immediately defending the pieces. Seeing at a glance the folly of a direct assault from the front, Gurley quickly swung to the right, taking advantage of a depression or ravine which would enable his column to advance within one hundred yards of the pieces before they would be brought under fire. Giving the command, and with his squadron in advance, followed by the Fourth Alabama, Captain Gurley charged at full speed upon the two guns and the Second West Tennessee, the Eleventh Illinois, and the Fifth Ohio, which formed the bulk of the troops under Colonel Ingersoll.

Captain Gurley' says: "The gunners stood by their guns and died like soldiers. The last shot was fired just as we reached the battery, and my first sergeant, J. L. P. Kelly, and his horse were blown to atoms by the explosion. With the taking of the guns the cavalry gave way in a stampede, and many of them were captured in the chase from there to Jackson."

Colonel Ingersoll, in his report, says: "Learning that the enemy were in great force on the lower road, I ordered the guns to fall back with all possible despatch. When I gained my new position on the lower road they were pouring in on us from all directions. At this moment the Second West Tennessee came back on the full run, and it was impossible to stop them."

The Eleventh Illinois, under Colonel Ingersoll and Captain Burbridge, held their ground bravely until carried away by the Tennessee and Ohio cavalry, which fled, and then they were forced to yield.

The two steel Rodman guns of the Fourteenth Indiana battery, under Lieutenant McGuire, were the trophies of this affair, and remained with the "Old Brigade" until the war was ended. General Forrest, in his official report, claims he captured two guns, 140 prisoners, including Colonel Ingersoll and Major L. H. Kerr, also some seventy horses, which were badly needed, and immediately put in service in the batteries. Colonel Ingersoll reports eleven killed and eleven wounded, and, in addition to the wounded, 147 prisoners—a total capture of 158,[10] among which number were six officers. He further says that "the enemy were repulsed at first, but, coming again in overwhelming numbers, the third attack proved successful. The guns were taken, with every man but one. A moment after the guns were taken, I was taken prisoner with one hundred and twenty-four other captures." There were, in addition to the officers, 147 prisoners captured, as shown by a careful analysis of Colonel Ingersoll's report, and this agrees exactly with the official account of these captures given by Forrest. Ingersoll says: "From all the information I have received the belief is that the enemy were at least five thousand, with eight pieces of artillery (twelve-pounders)."

On the part of the Confederates the fighting was almost wholly done by one section of Freeman's guns and the companies of the Fourth Alabama Cavalry, which, under Gurley, captured the battery, while the remaining portion, under the personal leadership of Colonel A. A. Russell, drove the Federals from the field.[11] Forrest, in his report, says: "Colonel Russell and his men deserve especial notice for their gallantry at Lexington. Captain Gurley, of the Fourth Alabama Cavalry, captured the guns, losing his orderly by the fire of the gun when within fifteen feet of the muzzle."[12]

The Federal forces engaged, according to Colonel Ingersoll's report, were, in addition to the section of two guns of Captain Kidd's Fourteenth

[10] *Ibid.,* vol. xvii, part i, p. 563.
[11] *Ibid.,* p. 598.
[12] *Ibid.,* p. 594.

Indiana battery with 33 effectives under Lieutenant McGuire, 200 of the Eleventh Illinois, 272 of the Second West Tennessee, 200 of the Fifth Ohio, and 68 cavalrymen under Captain O'Hara—a total of 773.[13] The escaping Federals retreated precipitately in the direction of Jackson, and were pursued to within sight of this city on the evening of the 18th. The movement on Jackson was entirely a feint, as that town was heavily garrisoned and well fortified. Forrest was aware of the fact that his presence on the west shore of the Tennessee River had been known for at least forty-eight hours, and that General Grant was hurrying a concentration of troops to defend the several lines of railroad which traversed this section, as well as the immense government stores which were in the depots of this city.

As soon as he had reached the immediate vicinity of Jackson, and had driven the Union forces into this stronghold, the Eighth Tennessee, under Colonel G. G. Dibrell, was ordered to break the railroad to the north of the town. At ten o'clock on the night of the 18th, this officer moved rapidly to the north of this city, and by daylight reached the Mobile and Ohio Railroad at Carroll station just in time to fire a volley into a passing train. With his troops dismounted, Dibrell immediately charged the stockade and captured it after feeble resistance, taking 101 prisoners, a large amount of ammunition, stores, tents, etc.[14] His command at this time was very inefficiently armed, 400 of his men having no other than old-fashioned flintlock muskets; over 100 of these were exchanged for the better arms of the captured garrison. The stockade was burned, as were all supplies that could not be carried off, and the railroad track for a considerable distance was torn up. From this successful foray Dibrell returned and rejoined Forrest at Spring Creek on the morning of the 20th.

At the same time that Dibrell was ordered upon his raid to the north of Jackson, the Fourth Alabama and Second Tennessee battalion of cavalry were sent to the left and south of this city to destroy the bridges, culverts, and trestles on the two railroads leading from Jackson to Corinth and Bolivar. These troops, under Colonel Russell and Major Cox, rejoined Forrest at Spring Creek some twenty-four hours later. Deeming it essential to hold the Union forces engaged at Jackson until Dibrell, Russell, and Cox could accomplish the objects of these several expedi-

[13] *Ibid.*, p. 555.
[14] *Ibid.*, vol. xvii, part i, p. 598.

tions, Forrest made a great show of assault on this place on the morning of the 19th.

Colonel Adolph Engelmann, of the Forty-third Illinois Infantry, says:

> At daybreak of the 19th the enemy advanced with heavy columns of cavalry on either flank, when our cavalry retired slowly. They then brought their batteries into position and opened with a well-directed cross-fire upon our cavalry. Our position became untenable, and we fell back. The enemy's artillery also got range of this position, and its cavalry showing itself, our own again fell back. At this time information was received that a large body of the enemy's cavalry was passing at the distance of a mile to the south around my right flank (Fourth Alabama and Cox's battalion). A messenger was despatched to General Sullivan, requesting some troops to oppose this flank movement. At this time the cavalry both on my right and left flanks, weary from the hardships to which they had been exposed for the two preceding days, and now under fire from the enemy's battery, fell back about one mile towards Jackson without having first obtained any orders from me to that effect.[15] Soon after this a heavy column of the enemy charged upon our infantry and were repulsed.

From this position Colonel Engelmann again retired his troops: "As the enemy's artillery began to tell among my men, I determined to fall back out of the range of its shells."

In this affair the Federal troops engaged were the Forty-third, Sixty-first, and Eleventh Illinois, Fifth Ohio, and one company of the Second West Tennessee. The Confederates had only the regiments of Starnes and Biffle, and Major T. G. Woodward's two companies of Kentuckians —about one thousand strong. The losses were insignificant on both sides.

As soon as Forrest had seen the Union forces within their breastworks, where they were anticipating a general assault, leaving only a small line of skirmishers to keep up appearances, he withdrew the remnant of his command, and moved with great celerity to attack Trenton and Humboldt and a stockade which protected the railroad bridge at Forked Deer Creek. His troops encamped for the night of the 19th at Spring Creek, and here, early in the morning of the 20th, they were rejoined by Dibrell, Russell, and Cox, each of whom had, with complete success, performed the duties for which they had been sent out.

Very early on the morning of the 20th, the entire command, with the

---

[15] *Ibid.*, vol. xvii, part i, p. 555.

exception of the Fourth Alabama, which was left at Spring Creek to cover the rear, was in rapid motion to the north. There was now no time to be lost; the Confederate leader had much to accomplish. There was an extensive territory yet to cover and many pursuers to avoid before he turned his face eastward to more peaceful surroundings. Dibrell's regiment, with two pieces of artillery, under Captain John W. Morton, was ordered to march immediately and attack the stockade at Forked Deer Creek and destroy the bridge. To Colonel Starnes and his Fourth Tennessee was allotted the capture of Humboldt, while Forrest in person led a third detachment to Trenton.

Starnes arrived promptly at Humboldt, and, wasting no time for parley or flags of truce, charged in among the Federals, who surrendered almost as soon as the first gun was fired. He captured the stockade and over one hundred prisoners; burned the government supplies at this station, railroad depot, and a trestle bridge. Colonel Jacob Fry, commanding, did not give in his report the number of Federal troops at the time of the capture. He says: "The sick and convalescents blew up and burned the magazine, and then surrendered. The enemy burned the stores they could not carry away." General Forrest claims the capture of 200 prisoners, four caissons, with their horses, harness, etc., 500 stand of arms, and a large quantity of other valuable supplies.

The Confederate commander was equally successful at Trenton. About three o'clock on the afternoon of the 20th, according to the report of the Federal officer in command,[16] Forrest arrived in Trenton and immediately charged the Federal position. One detachment of the Union troops, as sharpshooters, had been placed in a brick building, which had been loopholed for better defense. Another detachment was placed in a second building, commanding the street leading from another direction. Other troops were stationed in the breastworks and in the depot. As Forrest's skirmishers advanced they were met with a sharp fusillade from these various points, which killed two and wounded seven of his men, and arrested his advance. Rather than expose his troops unnecessarily, he retired and proceeded immediately to surround the Federal position.

At this opportune moment, Biffle, with his command, came up in the rear and completed the investment. The artillery was immediately brought up and opened upon the stockade and houses in which the Fed-

[16] *Ibid.,* vol. xvii, part i, p. 561.

eral sharpshooters were concealed. At the third fire a white flag was run up, and the entire command immediately surrendered. The Federal commander admits a loss of one killed, and Forrest reported the capture of 700 prisoners, several hundred horses, and a large quantity of ammunition, government supplies, etc. Colonel Fry claims to have had "about two hundred and fifty men." He mentions a list of officers surrendered entirely disproportionate to so small a garrison, viz.: Colonel Jacob Fry, Sixty-first Illinois; Colonel Hawkins, Second West Tennessee; and nine officers of the One Hundred and Twenty-second Illinois Infantry and Fourth Illinois Cavalry.

The troops with Forrest at the time were Cox's battalion and his escort company under Captain Little, Freeman's battery, and Biffle's regiment. All during the night of the 20th Forrest was paroling the prisoners and destroying supplies. He says in his report: "On the morning of the 21st I fired the depot, burning up the remaining supplies, with about 600 bales of cotton, 200 barrels of pork, and a large lot of tobacco in hogsheads, used by the enemy for breastworks. Among the large quantity of supplies taken here were 20,000 rounds of artillery and 400,-000 rounds of small-arms ammunition, and 100,000 rations of subsistence."

After seeing everything destroyed which could not be removed, General Forrest, on December 21st, moved farther north in the direction of Union City. On this day, Russell, Starnes, and Dibrell rejoined their commander. The latter had failed on the 20th to capture the stockade on Forked Deer Creek or to destroy the bridge. Two companies of the One Hundred and Sixth Illinois held the fort valiantly until Colonel G. P. Ihrie, with about 400 infantry, came up and drove Dibrell off. Russell, acting as rear guard at Spring Creek, had acquitted himself with great satisfaction to his commander. Here on the 20th he had been attacked by an infantry column which had marched out from Jackson in pursuit of the Confederate raiders. He signally repulsed this infantry. In the official report Forrest says: "Russell's regiment, the Fourth Alabama, charged on horseback, and the enemy became panic-stricken and retreated hastily across Spring Creek, burning the bridge after them. We have heard nothing from them since in that direction."[17]

At Rutherford station two companies of Federals were captured and the trestles, bridges, and rails destroyed from Trenton to Kenton station,

[17] *Ibid.*, vol. xvii, part i, p. 568.

at which latter place Colonel Thomas J. Kinney, of the One Hundred and Nineteenth Illinois, with his command, was captured and, in addition, twenty-two men left sick in the hospital there who were paroled. The destruction of an extensive trestle and the crossing of the Obion River detained the Confederates here until noon of the 22nd. That afternoon and the next day, still pushing northward, at 4 P.M. of the 23rd Forrest reached Union City, charged into the town, and captured 106 Federal troops without firing a gun.

Captain Samuel B. Logan, in command, reports that the number of prisoners who surrendered was 94. He says: "The Confederate army under General Forrest, I judge to the number of 1500, surrounded my command in every direction but one, to within easy musket-range. Their cannon were shotted and sighted upon us, three of which were in full view. From the time their forces first appeared in sight three minutes did not transpire before we were thus surrounded. General Forrest sent a flag of truce forward. My men needing my attention for a moment, I sent sutler R. W. Jones to meet the flag. A demand was· made for an unconditional surrender of the post and forces. Deeming it to be extreme folly to fight so unequal a force, I surrendered my command of 94 men."[18]

Forrest had now reached the Kentucky border, which he crossed on December 23rd, and until the 25th the various detachments were engaged in destroying the railroad bridges over the bayou near Moscow and other bridges over the north and south fork of the Obion River, with several miles of wooden trestling in the bottoms between them and south of Moscow. In his report of December 24th, 1862, he says: "We have made a clean sweep of the Federals and roads north of Jackson. Reliable reports show that they are rapidly sending up troops from Memphis. One hundred and twenty-five transports passed down a few days ago, within ten hours, and daily they are passing up loaded with troops. General Grant must either be in a very critical condition or else affairs in Kentucky require the movement."[19]

By Christmas evening the "clean sweep," which meant the destruction of the Mobile and Ohio Railroad from Jackson, Tennessee, as far north as Moscow, Kentucky, was complete. With one exception there was not a bridge left on this line. Not a yard of trestlework was standing, not a

---

[18] *Ibid.*, p. 567.
[19] *Ibid.*, vol. xvii, part i, p. 594.

Lieutenant Colonel Forrest and Major D. C. Kelley at the bombardment of Fort Donelson by Foote's flotilla

Forrest at the **head** of the Confederate cavalry marching to attack the Federal right

Capture of the Federal battery by Forrest's cavalry

Forrest's horse killed by a shell

Confederate infantry escaping from Fort Donelson

The Confederate cavalry and the artillerists escaping across Lick Creek with Forrest

How Forrest crossed the river with his artillery

Colonel Streight capturing General Forrest's guns

General Forrest and Emma Sanson

Emma Sanson (From a photograph taken after the war)

The last stand of Streight's Raiders

culvert was left undestroyed, and the rails over much of this distance had been completely ruined for further use by building fires along the tracks, which, heating the metal, caused the rails to expand and buckle. The head of the column was now turned southward along the railroad leading from Union City to Dresden and McKenzie. On the 26th of December the bridge over the north fork of the Obion, on the branch railroad running to Paducah, was destroyed. Forrest had now concentrated his entire command, and, in addition to the force which had crossed with him when he advanced into west Tennessee, he had gained a battalion of 430 men under Lieutenant Colonel T. A. Napier, which had joined him soon after the capture of Trenton.

Having been informed that a heavy column of infantry was moving in pursuit from Trenton in the direction of Dresden, Colonel J. B. Biffle was at this time dispatched in that direction with his regiment to protect the Confederate leader from surprise from that quarter.

On the night of the 26th the main column arrived at Dresden, a distance of twenty-five miles, capturing that point and destroying all the government supplies and the railroad, and here the command encamped for the night. On the 27th Forrest moved forward as far as McKenzie, some fifteen miles beyond Dresden in the direction of Huntingdon and Lexington. Here he became informed of the fact that two brigades of infantry were moving in that direction to intercept him on his return toward the crossing of the Tennessee at Clifton, and now the first real difficulty of his enterprise confronted him. All the bridges across the Obion which lay immediately in front of him had been destroyed, and the crossings were guarded by the Union forces.

He learned, however, that a structure, which was considered so unsafe as to be impassable, and which was, moreover, in the line of a byway or country road but little used, had been overlooked by the enemy and might still be made available. This bridge, halfway between McKenzie and McLemoresville, and situated about five miles from either place, Forrest reached shortly after dark, and with his wonted energy soon had his men, already much fatigued, at work repairing the timbers and the long and narrow causeway which served as approaches and stretched out through the miry bottoms for nearly a quarter of a mile on either side of the stream. All through the night of the 27th and for a good part of the 28th they labored faithfully at this work and in conveying the troops, artillery, a long train of captured caissons loaded with ammunition, and wagons full of powder and ball over this formidable obstruction. The general made a "full hand" with his men, for the ax was a ready implement with him, and his enthusiasm and example stimulated all to the extra exertion which the emergency demanded. With his own hands he drove the first wagon over, keeping on the narrow, slippery causeway without accident, a success not altogether equaled by the teamsters who followed, for two loads of ammunition were upset.

While this was going on, just five miles farther south and directly in his path, through the sleepy little village of McLemoresville, a brigade of Federal infantry under Colonel Cyrus L. Dunham was passing from the direction of Trenton and marching to Huntingdon, where they arrived on the 29th of December. From his place of concealment in the Obion bottoms, Forrest waited until this command passed, and then moved forward to McLemoresville, arriving there a few hours after the rear guard of Dunham's brigade had defiled through. On this same night, only a few miles west of him, another brigade, composed of the Twenty-seventh, Thirty-ninth, and Sixty-third Ohio, under Colonel John W. Fuller, and with which were moving Generals J. C. Sullivan and I. N. Haynie, was marching from Trenton toward McLemoresville to unite with Dunham at Huntingdon.

Forrest was thus about halfway between two columns of infantry which might have overwhelmed him then and there had they known his whereabouts. In front and to the south of him, in full possession of the region between Corinth, Purdy, Lexington, and Clifton, and right in the line of his march for escape, was General G. M. Dodge, who under orders from General Grant had moved with "the First Brigade, made up of the Second, Seventh, and Fifty-second Illinois, the Third Brigade, composed of the Seventh, Fiftieth, and Fifty-seventh Illinois regiments, two batteries of the Missouri Light Artillery, the Fifth Ohio, and Stewart's cavalry. At Purdy these were joined by another section of artillery and the Forty-eighth Illinois regiment." A portion of these troops had been dispatched to Clifton and along the Tennessee River to destroy all the ferryboats, and to patrol the west bank of this stream in order to give timely notice of the presence of the Confederates in their effort to escape, and Brigadier General Dodge reported that all boats and rafts on the Tennessee were destroyed.

Northward, to retrace his steps, meant almost certain destruction.

There was a large force at Columbus, Kentucky, just behind him, and—although this did not much distress the Confederate leader—General Clinton B. Fisk was there, thirsting for glory and the opportunity of "doing up" the "brigand Forrest." On December 29th[20] he telegraphed to General S. R. Curtis a bloodcurdling message that "the brigand Forrest with about eight thousand mounted rebels and eight pieces of artillery undertook a raid on a large scale on the Mobile and Ohio railroad. He was rapidly accomplishing his purposes when reinforcements began to arrive from St. Louis. His bands are now scattering. His headquarters are about ten miles distant, where he is throwing up fortifications. I have been begging General Davies to let me take 4000 men and go out there and whip him, but the general will not allow the movement; is quite nervous about the post; but I am fully convinced that we could defeat or skedaddle the entire rebel horde. I know I am a young general, but I believe I am old enough to see through a millstone with so large a hole in it." What a different fate might have been in store for the "brigand" if this young general had been let loose upon him!

Forrest's entire force (with Biffle's regiment absent) at this time, confronting the powerful concentration which was being made against him, was 2000 men. Moreover, his troops and horses were now much exhausted by the terrible strain to which they had been subjected for the fortnight past. In the coldest season of mid-winter they had marched and fought almost without cessation for this period, with little time for rest and sleep.

Well might Brigadier General Jeremiah C. Sullivan, the man with "the genius for tardiness,"[21] as one of his subordinate officers in an official report said of him, wire General U. S. Grant, on this 29th of December, from Huntingdon: "I have Forrest in a tight place. The gunboats are up the river as far as Clifton, and have destroyed all the boats and ferries. My troops are moving on him in three directions, and I hope with success."

In this, as in every dilemma in which the fortunes of war placed him, the Confederate leader, as General Wolseley wrote of him, "showed that he was a man of quick resolves and prompt execution, of inexhaustible resource, and of ready and clever expedients. He had all the best instincts of the soldier, and his natural military genius was balanced by

[20] *Ibid.,* vol. xvii, part ii, p. 504.
[21] *Ibid.,* vol. xvii, part i, p. 587.

sound judgment. He always knew what he wanted, and consequently there was no weakness or uncertainty in his views or intentions, nor in the orders he gave to have these intentions carried out. There was never any languor in that determined heart, nor wearinesss in that iron body. Panic and fear fled and hid at his approach, and the sound of his cheer gave courage to the weakest heart."

At this juncture there were presented to the mind of Forrest two problems of importance to the complete success of his expedition. Should he now—having done so much damage to the enemy's communications and drawn off so many troops from Grant, and thus prevented any possibility of reinforcing Rosecrans at Murfreesboro, or the Union army moving on Vicksburg—make his run for the Tennessee and cross; or should he attempt the destruction of the two commands, now almost within sight of him, by getting between them, fighting and crushing the one before it could be relieved, and then turn upon the other? Even with Biffle and his regiment absent he was almost numerically equal to either of the infantry brigades. It was scarcely forty miles to the Tennessee, and were he to "run for it" these troops would undoubtedly push after him, and, with the slow ferriage of the two flatboats and the great probabilities of the gunboats taking a hand with the land forces while in the act of crossing, he must be in greater danger at the river than where he was. Moreover, he knew that at Bethel station, some thirty miles south of Jackson, there had been accumulated a large quantity of government stores, and, could he whip Sullivan's two brigades, he might destroy the rich supplies of Grant at that depot.

In any event, his mind reached the conclusion that he should fight even to secure a safe crossing of the Tennessee. On December 30th he dispatched his brother, Captain "Bill" Forrest, with his company of "Independents"[22] in the direction of Clarksburg, and here at dark this detachment collided with Dunham's troops, who were marching to Parker's Crossroads, and he determined to throw himself between Dunham and Fuller and try to beat them in detail.

[22] This organization was an independent company of about forty men, who served directly or indirectly with General Forrest in all his campaigns in Mississippi and west Tennessee. As they were not in the regular service, they drew no pay except from the enemy, and lived by foraging on foes when they could, and on friends when they could not find the foe. They early were baptized by their brother cavalrymen in the regular line "The Forty Thieves." Under a Forrest they always fought as well as they foraged, and as foragers they were not surpassed.

As soon as Colonel Dunham, at Clarksburg, had learned, on the night of the 30th of December, that Forrest was encamped within four miles of his position, he immediately notified his superiors, Brigadier Generals J. C. Sullivan and I. N. Haynie, at Huntingdon, suggesting that they move forward to his support with their commands. Before it was yet light, on the morning of the 31st, he moved his brigade and artillery with commendable rapidity the five miles from Clarksburg to Parker's Crossroads. Approaching the intersection of these two highways, his advance came in contact with the Confederate pickets, the latter retiring on the road from Parker's toward McLemoresville, on which route, about one mile north, Forrest's troops were halted. As soon as he was satisfied that Dunham's brigade was at the crossroads, he sent a detachment of four companies, with instructions to get in the rear of the Federals and take the road to Clarksburg and Huntingdon, to skirmish with and retard as far as possible every advance of Fuller's brigade, and to notify him in time of any advance from that direction to reinforce Dunham at Parker's. By an unfortunate blunder this detachment took the wrong road, and thus was left wide open a route for the march of Fuller and his men, who came up in Forrest's rear in the crisis of the fight, and without warning poured their volleys right into the backs of the Confederates, who up to that moment were victorious at every point.

The Confederate leader had now matured his plan. He had the two Federal brigades separated from each other a sufficient distance to permit him to interpose his command and destroy one before the other could come to the rescue. As he expected before the day was done to have to fight Fuller's brigade when it should come upon the scene, he determined to rely chiefly upon his artillery in fighting the Federals who were in his immediate front at the crossroads, and thus keep the greater portion of his troops fresh for the second encounter of the day. Marching rapidly southward, he soon had his men in line of battle, in such position that he was between Dunham and Fuller, thus preventing any communication between the two Federal detachments.

Lieutenant Nat Baxter, Jr.,[23] a member of Freeman's battery, who, as shown by the official records, did most effective work as an artillerist in this battle, says:

[23] *Official Records,* vol. xvii, part i, p. 598.

Very early on the morning of December 31st, 1862, General Forrest rode up to our battery and ordered me to hitch up my gun and come with him. Having gone about a half-mile in the direction of Parker's Crossroads, he ordered some cavalry that accompanied us to throw the fences down, and here we turned into a field with the piece. General Forrest dismounted and went ahead to the crest of a hill and selected a position for my gun. To my great surprise, as I reached the top of the hill I saw the Federals in heavy line of battle not more than four hundred yards away. With the exception of two or three hundred cavalry immediately behind my gun, and one or two hundred dismounted men, who were about one hundred yards in front, behind logs and trees and in fence corners skirmishing with the enemy, there were no other Confederate soldiers in sight. He told me to open immediately upon them, which I had no sooner done than three pieces of artillery from the Union side responded in lively fashion. I succeeded in dismounting one of the Federal guns, to the great satisfaction of General Forrest, who remained with me all through the duel, and was with my piece at frequent intervals throughout the day.

The fighting on our side was done almost entirely with our artillery. We drove the Federals back beyond the cross-roads, and had them corralled in a wooded lot, from which they made two or three charges to capture my battery, but failed. We were at such close quarters a good deal of the time that we used two charges of canister with a single charge of powder. We would cut the second charge of powder off, and as these fell upon the ground there had accumulated such a pile near the muzzle of the gun that at one time they became ignited and made a very considerable explosion. Seeing the flash and the momentary confusion which this caused in the battery, the Federals, thinking some great disaster had occurred, and that it was a propitious moment for a charge to take our guns, made a final desperate assault upon the battery, but were again repulsed.[24]

The Federal commander, with equal readiness, brought his artillery into play as a prelude to the spirited engagement which was to follow. He had, however, only three pieces, and the superior practice of Baxter's gun, aided as it was a half-hour later by seven additional guns under Freeman and Morton, soon told upon the Federal pieces and their line of infantry. Baxter had dismounted one of the enemy's guns before reinforcements arrived, and when the battery of eight guns opened their entire line fell back, in good order, however, toward the crossroads. As they retired, Forrest advanced his line until he

---

[24] Manuscript in possession of the author from Mr. Nat Baxter, Jr., in 1898 president of the Tennessee Coal and Iron Company of Birmingham, Alabama.

again came up with the enemy, now re-formed beyond Parker's house. The Union forces here made a stubborn fight, and on two occasions charged in gallant style to dislodge the Confederates. On each of these essays they were met with a withering fire of grape and canister, the Confederate troops being held well back out of range, yet close enough to support the guns should they be needed for this duty.

By twelve o'clock Dunham had been driven from his second position, and was retiring toward a heavy grove of timber in the direction of Lexington, when Forrest ordered Starnes' Fourth Tennessee and Russell's Fourth Alabama regiments to the right and left of the Federals, and thence to the rear, in order to cut off their retreat. At this propitious moment Biffle arrived[25] and took part in the general advance which Forrest now ordered, and which swept the Union forces precipitately from the field.

Of this particular advance of the Confederates Colonel H. J. B. Cumming (Thirty-ninth Iowa Infantry) says: "My command commenced breaking to the rear from near the right of the regiment, which, despite my efforts, became propagated along the whole line. I had done much towards re-forming when we were opened upon by a heavy fire of dismounted men, who had advanced within fifty feet of my troops. They then in more confusion fell back and received standing the fire from the enemy's artillery, and under it the confusion became worse. About half of my regiment broke and crossed the road into the corn-field."[26]

The piece which Baxter had dismounted in the first half-hour of the engagement had already fallen into Forrest's hands, and in this advance the Confederates captured the two remaining guns, leaving the beaten Federals without artillery. In desperate mood Dunham essayed to recapture the guns, but was repulsed with considerable slaughter, especially from the artillery of the Confederates, all of whose guns were still in action excepting one, which had exploded. It was at this moment that Colonel T. Alonzo Napier fell mortally wounded at the head of his battalion. In a moment of rashness, and without orders from his superior, this brave soldier advanced his battalion to a position of unnecessary exposure, and thus sacrificed his

[25] Near Trenton, on this scout, Biffle captured and paroled 150 prisoners, and was hastening to overtake his commander.
[26] *Official Records*, vol. xvii, part i, p. 589.

own life and a number of his troops.

Having lost his three guns, the disorder among the Iowa troops, as recorded by Colonel Cumming, compelled the Federal commander to retire in confusion from one-half to three-quarters of a mile south of Parker's, where his men were rallied for a final stand "in a grove of timber of about sixty acres, enclosed by a fence and surrounded by open fields." By this time Starnes and Russell had reached the rear of this position, had cut them off from escape, and captured their entire wagon and ammunition train, which had been driven to this point of supposed security. The Federals, now completely hemmed in, were at the mercy of Forrest, who, wishing to avoid the loss to which a final assault would expose him, sent forward a flag of truce asking for a conference with the commander of the Union forces. The firing on both sides immediately ceased, and at various points along the Union line white flags were noticed.

Lieutenant Baxter says: "It was after this charge that the white flags appeared all along the Union line. I was under the impression that they had surrendered, and had gone in front of my gun towards the Federal line to converse with one of their officers. Just at this moment a volley of small arms was heard immediately behind the location of our batteries and in our rear. I rushed back to my gun to see what had happened, and about this moment General Forrest came up to me, ordered me to limber up my piece and leave the field, pointing the direction we were to go."[27]

In his official report the Confederate general says:

At this time we occupied the battle-field, and were in possession of the enemy's dead and wounded and three pieces of artillery, and had demanded a surrender. Thirty minutes more would have given us the day, when, to my surprise and astonishment, a fire was opened on us in our rear, and the enemy in heavy force under General J. C. Sullivan advanced on us. Knowing that I had four companies at Clarksburg, on the Huntingdon road, I could not believe that they were Federals until I rode up myself into their lines. The heavy fire of their artillery, unexpected and unlooked for by all, caused a stampede of horses belonging to my dismounted men, who were following up and driving the enemy before them. Finding my men now exposed to fire from both front and rear, I was compelled to withdraw, which I did in good order, leaving behind our dead and wounded. We were

[27] Manuscript of Lieutenant Nat Baxter, in possession of the author.

able to bring off six pieces of artillery and two caissons. The balance, with the three guns we had captured, we were compelled to leave, as most of the horses were killed or crippled, which rendered it impossible to get them out under the heavy fire of the enemy from both front and rear. Our loss in artillery was three guns and eight caissons, and one piece which burst during the action. We brought off eighty-three prisoners.[28]

In all probability there was not in the history of the war a surprise more complete than that which was suffered by Forrest at the battle of Parker's Crossroads. There was certainly never such an opportunity as this for his complete discomfiture, and the fact that his entire command was not annihilated demonstrated his wonderful ability to meet any emergency, however great, with cool judgment and prompt action.

Despite the assertion of Colonel Dunham in his official report that he was not whipped when reinforcements came to the rescue, the reports of other Union officers present prove the correctness of General Forrest's claim.

Colonel John W. Fuller, commanding the brigade that came up in the rear, says in his official report:

We continued our march, and soon the sound of artillery in our front advised us that Colonel Dunham's brigade was engaging the enemy. The firing was first heard to the right of the point where the road from McLemoresville crosses that leading from Huntingdon to Lexington. In half an hour it was directly in our front. Half an hour later it was all to the left of the crossing, thereby rendering it certain that the enemy, who approached from McLemoresville, was rapidly driving Colonel Dunham's brigade before him. Very soon thereafter the rattle of musketry was distinct, and, thinking the hour a critical one, I urged my men to their utmost speed.

When the head of our column was within about two hundred yards of the hill which commanded a view of the enemy's position, and where our column was deployed, General Sullivan overtook me. The Twenty-seventh and Sixty-third regiments were at once formed on the left, and the Thirty-ninth regiment on the right of the road when we advanced upon the rear of the enemy's artillery, which was feebly supported, and abandoned (with but little fighting on his part) when we approached. Our artillery took position on the left (east) of the road, and, directly after opening fire, two pieces followed the infantry, until they occupied ground side by side with the rebel guns, while the other piece was moved to the west side of the road, where it was effectively used upon the rebels, who were escaping by breaking to the front and right of our lines.

[28] *Official Records,* vol. xvii, part i, p. 569.

Some hundreds of the enemy, who had dismounted and had been fighting as infantry, had left their horses in the orchard and yard near Parker's house. These horses were the first trophies which fell into our hands, and more than three hundred of their riders, thus rendered unable to get away, surrendered themselves as prisoners. A small train of wagons which the enemy had gained possession of was captured in the road a short distance south of Parker's house, and one at least of the guns belonging to Colonel Dunham's command was retaken from the enemy in this road.

When we reached the field, the enemy, who from the best evidence I could obtain were about double the number of Colonel Dunham's force, were in front and on both flanks of that brigade. A flag of truce, which had not returned to General Forrest when our guns opened, had, as Colonel Dunham informed me, demanded an unconditional surrender. Firing had ceased for some fifteen minutes prior to our arrival, nor did the command of Colonel Dunham fire a shot at the enemy as he moved past their flank to their rear.[29]

Colonel Edward F. Noyes, commanding the Thirty-ninth Ohio, reports: "At Parker's Crossroads we found Dunham's brigade surrounded on three sides by the enemy under General Forrest. Firing had ceased, flags of truce were passing, and, as we afterwards learned, General Forrest had demanded an unconditional surrender. A part, if not all, of Dunham's artillery, together with several hundred prisoners, had fallen into the hands of the enemy. The moment was a critical one, and the day seemed inevitably lost. We deployed and advanced upon the double-quick. The enemy, taken utterly by surprise by this sudden attack in the rear, were thrown into confusion, and were compelled to make a precipitate and irregular retreat."[30]

Although Colonel Dunham makes no mention of the loss of his artillery, only admitting the loss of his wagon train, Colonel John L. Rinaker, of the One Hundred and Twenty-ninth Illinois, in his report, says: "By this time our artillery was out of ammunition, and the guns were soon, from loss of horses, rendered useless, and were run into a ravine and temporarily abandoned."

The Federals claimed to have captured about 300 of Forrest's horses and troops, which claim seems to be authenticated. That they did not capture practically all of Forrest's command shows either a great lack of ability on the part of the Union commander or want of

[29] *Ibid.,* vol. xvii, part i, p. 569.
[30] *Ibid.,* p. 576.

concert of action between the two lines of battle, which had almost the entire force of the Confederates between them. The facts remain, however, that in the presence of overwhelming odds thus favorably placed for his discomfiture, General Forrest, with consummate ability, extricated his command from between the Union lines, carrying with him as many as six pieces of artillery, a number of caissons, a part of his wagon train, and all his troops, with the exception of about 150 killed and wounded, and 300 who were dismounted, and whose horses were captured before they were aware of the presence of the enemy in their rear.[31] The three guns captured in the battle by Forrest were left, with one other piece which exploded and two more of Freeman's guns, the horses for which were shot down by the volleys from Fuller's brigade, which marched up behind them and fired into them with great destruction before the men of the battery knew there were any Federals in that direction.

Notwithstanding Forrest's complete surprise and defeat here, the careful student of his military career will not find better evidence of his remarkable genius than the fight at Parker's Crossroads. He had taken every possible precaution to accomplish the work he had in hand, convinced that in order to recross the Tennessee with his booty he had to fight these pursuing columns. With keen discernment he had waited until the two columns of the enemy which he wished to destroy were at a sufficient distance from each other to enable him to strike and overwhelm one before it could be reached by the other. It was the analogue of Stonewall Jackson's brilliant movement in the valley of the Shenandoah, and the strategy of Jackson was the equal of that of Bonaparte in the great Italian campaign.

Although about equally matched with Dunham's brigade in small arms, Forrest more than doubled him in artillery, and all through the fight he made the artillery do the work, never exposing his soldiers unless it was absolutely necessary for the protection of the guns. He says: "I was whipping them badly with my artillery; had them entirely surrounded; was taking it leisurely, and was trying as much as possible to save my men"; and this policy accounts for the small losses he suffered in killed and wounded. In this way he had driven Dunham from the field, and had him finally hemmed up where his escape without

[31] Forrest's losses up to this fight since crossing the river were about fifty killed, wounded, and missing.

help was impossible. Relying upon the detachment he had sent out early in the morning to inform him of Fuller's approach from the direction of Huntingdon, and feeling in the absence of any such information that he had plenty of time to try his "old Murfreesboro game of bluff" upon the Federal commander, in the hope of saving his own troops from a final and bloody assault, he had sent to him a flag of truce demanding an immediate and unconditional surrender, with the usual threat and scare of "No quarter" if he had to storm his position. While the flags of truce were passing between the lines, and while not a gun had been fired for from fifteen to thirty minutes, Fuller's brigade, with small arms and artillery, opened upon the Confederate line of battle from the rear.

Colonel Dunham, in his official report, claims that he had no idea of surrendering; but no one who studies the situation from the official records can entertain a doubt that his position was extremely critical and that within an hour he would have been forced to have surrendered or had his command annihilated.

He states that he had in action 1554 men, rank and file, exclusive of the Seventh Tennessee, which was left at Huntingdon and probably came up with Fuller. This number does not include, however, a portion of the Eleventh Illinois Cavalry, which is mentioned incidentally further along in his report.

Up to the time of the arrival of Biffle's regiment, which was not present in the early part of the fight, Forrest had 1800 men on the field, and when Biffle arrived his entire force was 2250. This is exclusive of the four companies sent away on what turned out to be a wild-goose chase and which were cut off from rejoining their commander until they had recrossed the Tennessee River some days later, and two other detachments on scouting duty toward McLemoresville and Jackson.

Colonel Dunham reports 23 killed, 139 wounded, and 58 missing of his brigade. Among the prisoners were Captain Hungate and several other officers, and "Lieutenant D. S. Scott, of the Eleventh Illinois Cavalry, who was taken while zealously discharging his duties."[32] The corrected official list shows 2 officers and 25 enlisted men killed, 7 officers and 133 men wounded, 3 officers and 67 men captured. A total loss of 237.

[32] *Official Records*, vol. xvii, part i, p. 584.

General Jeremiah C. Sullivan, who came upon the battlefield with Fuller's brigade in time to see Forrest disappearing over the hills of west Tennessee in the direction of Lexington, lost no time in notifying General U. S. Grant of his great victory. He telegraphed from Parker's Crossroads as follows: "We have achieved a glorious victory. We met Forrest, 7000 strong, and after a contest of four hours completely routed him with great slaughter. We have captured six guns, over 300 prisoners, over 500 horses, and a large number of wagons and teams and a large quantity of small arms. Colonel Napier killed. Colonel Cox and Major Strange, Forrest's adjutant, and one aide-de-camp and a number of other officers captured. Colonel Rinaker slightly wounded. I will telegraph particulars of our loss."

He adds to this on the 2nd of January: "The rebel loss as estimated by Forrest is 1500 men killed and wounded and missing. Their dead I have good reason to believe is 200, their prisoners over 400. My loss will not exceed 100 killed and wounded, prisoners 63." The same date he says: "I have ordered Colonel Lawler with 3000 of the old troops and eight pieces of artillery to follow the retreating enemy to the river. Forrest's army is completely broken up. They are scattered over the country without ammunition. We need a good cavalry regiment to go through the country and pick them up."[33]

General Grant was quite pleased with the "wiping out" of Forrest. From Holly Springs, Mississippi, on January 1st, he wired: "Sullivan caught up with Forrest, and gave him a tremendous thrashing. The gunboats got up and destroyed all his ferries." And on the following day: "Sullivan has whipped Forrest, and entirely broken up his band, captured 400 prisoners, all their train, several wagon-loads of small arms, six pieces of artillery, over 500 horses, and recaptured much of the clothing and other property taken from our posts that surrendered."

Nor was Sullivan forgotten. On the same date he telegraphed the "Genius for Tardiness": "You have done a fine job—retrieved all lost at Trenton and north of you. I sent a fine regiment of cavalry to you. They left here on the 31st. Clear out west Tennessee of all roving cavalry. If it is necessary mount as much infantry as you think necessary. What do you estimate the loss on each side?" And closed

[33] *Ibid.*, p. 552.

by placing this final screw in the coffin lid of the bold raider: "Dodge is now out after Forrest's band."

While these despatches were flying over the wires, and General Sullivan was assuring his chieftain that there was "nothing left but to go through the country and pick Forrest and his command up," and notwithstanding the fact that "Dodge was now after him," the Confederate leader, with a number of his wounded, his wagons, artillery, horses, and men in compact organization and full of fight, was crossing the Tennessee River unmolested. By midnight of January 1st the ferriage was completed. Within less than thirty-six hours after the flight from Parker's Crossroads, these hardy riders had marched nearly forty miles and crossed this formidable barrier with no other means than two small ferryboats and some improvised rafts, and all this without loss of a man or a wheel!

When his quick ear caught the first round from the muskets of Sullivan's reinforcements, and he saw the horse-holders of Cox's dismounted battalion stampeded by this volley, General Forrest at once directed his dismounted men to mount their horses and gallop out between the double line of Federals and make for the road to Lexington. Placing himself at the head of his escort and Dibrell's regiment, he threw this command, as a rear guard, between his pet guns and Sullivan's advance. He was not going to give up his artillery without a desperate struggle. One of Fuller's regiments, more advanced than the rest, coming up too close to his pieces, which were being driven from the field, he rode at them just as recklessly and savagely as he did at Sherman's infantry at Monterey, and with the same result. Fuller's men went back in a hurry, and then they let him alone.

Lieutenant Baxter narrates that as he, on foot, was running across the field behind his gun, Forrest, who was halting every man that he could reach, ordered him to get into line with the others and advance upon the enemy that were coming up in his rear. He said: "General, I am entirely unarmed; have neither gun, pistol, nor sword." Forrest replied quickly: "That doesn't make any difference; get in line and advance on the enemy with the rest; I want to make as big a show as possible." There were a number of men in this charge who had no weapons, but Forrest led them with great boldness upon the advancing line of infantry. This show of force checked the Federal infantry and enabled him to escape.

The fire from Fuller's artillery had slaughtered the horses of six caissons and two of Freeman's guns, and these Forrest had to leave; the rest went galloping away and were saved. Sullivan threw one gun into play as they rode out, and with this piece he did considerable damage to Forrest's rear guard—thus accounting for the unusually large loss in Dibrell's regiment. It was at this crisis of affairs that Colonel Starnes again showed himself to possess the soldierly qualities which characterized him on so many occasions. It will be remembered that he and Russell had been sent on the flanks of Dunham, and when the flags of truce were passing they enclosed him on the south, or Lexington, side to prevent his escape. When the truce was interrupted, and the heavy firing from the direction of Huntingdon told him what had happened, Starnes saw immediately the predicament in which his chieftain was placed, and he and Russell at once attacked Dunham so viciously that they kept this brigade of Federals entirely engaged on their side of the field, and thus relieved Forrest from being attacked from this quarter as he rode away from the troops under Sullivan.

Dunham had all he could attend to, and, as the Federal reports show, he never fired a shot at Forrest as the Confederate cavalry and artillery escaped between him and Fuller's brigade.

General Sullivan seemed to be entirely satisfied with the result his timely arrival had achieved, for he held the field and made no effort to follow the retreating Confederates. With characteristic audacity, Forrest, after he had extricated his command and had his artillery and wagons well on the way to Lexington, turned on the Federals with such a show of force and fight that Sullivan took the defensive. Colonel Fuller says: "Two hours after Forrest had retired from Parker's Cross-roads, Sullivan informed me that Forrest was advancing upon his left and front. I remained in line of battle until daylight in the morning." It was this particular occasion that gave color to one of the many exaggerated stories concerning Forrest's original methods of warfare. When the troops of Sullivan advanced in line of battle and opened on Cox's horse-holders, Colonel Charles Carroll of his staff, in great perturbation, dashed up to his commander, shouting, "General Forrest, a heavy line of infantry is right in our rear; we are between two lines of battle. What shall we do?" Forrest, it is said, instantly replied: "We'll charge them both ways." He did charge both ways, but it was Starnes and Russell who did one side of the work.

The Confederate cavalry arrived at Lexington, twelve miles from the battlefield, on the night of the 31st, and here some few of the wounded, still able to travel, were cared for. The men and animals were fed and rested until about 2 A.M., when the command saddled up and again moved off in the direction of the Tennessee River, and by daylight of the 1st of January another halt was made ten miles east of Lexington. With the exception of a detachment of Dibrell's regiment, the entire command was allowed three hours of rest, and here the prisoners were paroled.

At this time Forrest ordered his brother, Major Jeffrey Forrest, with a detachment, to move immediately to the Tennessee River, and to have the ferryboats (which had been concealed by sinking them) bailed out and brought over to the west bank, ready for crossing. Between 9 and 10 A.M. the entire command followed at top speed in the wake of Major Forrest.

The Confederate leader had good cause for this rapid march toward Clifton. He had every reason to presume that the Federal infantry which fought him at Parker's Crossroads, on the day previous, would be relentless in their pursuit. He knew how greatly they had overmatched him in numbers, and he had also been informed by his scouts that a large body of troops under General G. M. Dodge was coming from the direction of Corinth and Purdy to interpose themselves between his command and the Tennessee. He had scarcely marched two miles from the point of starting on the 1st of January when his advance guards came back with the information that a heavy column of Federal cavalry was in his immediate front.

Nothing daunted, and not even taking time to determine their numbers by a reconnaissance in person, Dibrell's regiment, with Starnes's and Biffle's, were hurried in line of battle, and thus advanced until they came in sight of the Federal cavalry in battle array. The order to charge was given and the Union troopers were swept without ceremony from the field. Lieutenant Colonel W. K. M. Breckinridge, who commanded the Sixth Tennessee Cavalry (Union) on this occasion, reported to Brigadier General Dodge, to whose command he belonged:

On the morning of January 1st, near Clifton, a very short time after sunrise, our pickets were driven in by Forrest's advance. We first made an effort to form on a hill and then fell back to the foot of the hill. I then changed position, and would have been all right had it not been that one of the companies in the rear did not receive the order to fall back until they were very much exposed to the enemy's fire. In the mean time the enemy made an attempt to surround the company. We lost about six men as prisoners. We made our retreat and got in the rear of the enemy to annoy him all we could. We found that his rear was moving at a very rapid rate and followed them within a short distance of the river, and found that they had been advised that their rear was followed. I did not deem it prudent to follow farther.[34]

Colonel G. G. Dibrell, whose regiment led in this charge, says: "After skirmishing a few minutes we charged and routed them, killing or capturing fifteen or twenty of them."[35]

Being discreet as well as valorous, the Union troopers did not appear again upon the scene during the west Tennessee campaign.

After the defeat of Breckinridge's cavalry, Forrest left one regiment of his command to act as rear guard, and with these placed a section of artillery under Edwin H. Douglas, who was afterward first lieutenant in Huggins's battery, and was then serving under Freeman. He told him to fortify as best he could with rails, logs, and everything else at hand, and, with the aid of the detachment of cavalry he would leave with him, if attacked he was to fight to the last in order to give the remainder of the command time to ferry the other guns and the troops across the river.

Douglas threw his guns into position as his commander had directed, and was soon ready for the desperate effort.

That Forrest had not yet familiarized himself with the artillery manual is evident from the statement of Lieutenant Douglas:

When our section was ordered to take position and get ready for action, according to the manual of artillery drill we galloped up to the position, unlimbered, and the horses were moved obliquely to take their place in the rear of the guns and out of range. The general did not understand the rapid movement of the horses to the rear. Mistaking it for a cowardly runaway on the part of the drivers, he rode up to the man on the lead horse, and, as he struck him over the shoulders with the flat of his sabre, yelled: "Turn those horses around and get back where you belong, or by God I'll kill you!" The artilleryman answered: "General, I'm moving in accordance with tactics." Forrest yelled back at him: "No you are not; I know how to fight, and you can't run away with the ammunition-chest!"

[34] *Ibid.,* vol. xvii, part i, p. 590.
[35] *Ibid.,* p. 599.

A few days after I took my book of tactics to the general's tent and showed him that it was necessary for the horses to move off out of range, and offered to give him an exhibition-drill, so that he could see the reasons for such a manoeuvre. This was accepted, and he became greatly interested. In less than a week he had mastered the manual and become an expert among experts in placing a battery and in the use of the guns. I may also add that he was just as prompt and earnest in his apology to the soldier he had wronged as he was in the infliction of what he then believed to be a merited rebuke.

Between twelve meridian and one o'clock on January 1st the Confederates reached the Tennessee River. The two flatboats which had been left in charge of Captain J. M. Barnes and Lieutenant F. H. Daugherty, of the Eighth Tennessee, had been successfully concealed from the gunboats and the various scouting expeditions sent up and down the Tennessee to destroy all the facilities for Forrest's escape. As luck would have it, the gunboats also were not in sight at this important moment. Ever mindful of his artillery, the first thing Forrest did was to hurry four of his guns across the river on the first trip of the boat, taking the ammunition chests and artillerists with a few of his men. The boats were propelled by two oars near the bow and by poles up the riverbank close to shore, where the current was less swift for about a half-mile, and then across the river, drifting down with the current and landing opposite the place of starting. Going and coming, this process was rapidly repeated.

As soon as the cannon and artillerists reached the east shore, the horses were hitched on and the pieces hauled up the bank and immediately thrown into position, two at the point of crossing to command the approach from behind the troops still on the west shore. One was sent up and another down the stream to keep off any craft that might be steaming from either direction and hold them at safe distance from the mass of men and animals that were working their way across the river. Scouts had already been dispatched up and down the river to give timely notice of any approach of the gunboats.

Company after company were made to unsaddle their horses and pile their saddles, blankets, guns, and other equipment in the boats, and these were carried immediately over with as many men as the boats would hold. Others of the troops rapidly constructed rafts of fence rails and logs that would hold from five to ten men each, and on these frail floats the hardy troopers would launch themselves into the current and paddle across, leaping ashore when the bank was touched, and letting the abandoned craft float away on the swift current.

There was now no time to ferry the horses across, and they were forced to swim. Two men would man a canoe or skiff, while a third, holding the bridle of a horse, would strike out with the animal swimming by the side of the boat. When this piloted horse was a short distance from the shore, the other animals, stripped for the plunge, were led to where the bank was perpendicular from the edge of the water, the bridles taken off, and one after another pushed into the stream. They could do nothing but swim, and naturally struck out to follow the lead of the horse already in the river. Fully one thousand of these faithful creatures were thus at the same moment struggling in the swift-flowing water.

Such was the ready method by which this remarkable man conveyed a force of about two thousand men and horses, six pieces of artillery, and a train of wagons and captured stores across a river nearly three-quarters of a mile in width, accomplishing the wonderful feat in the short period of ten hours.

To his commanding officer he writes: "After the fight, and knowing that we were followed by the Federals in heavy column from Trenton and Huntingdon, I deemed it advisable to cross the Tennessee, which I accomplished yesterday and last night in safety."[36]

Meanwhile his Federal antagonists were floundering through the mud, sleet, and rain in a cold and hopeless stern chase after the swift-moving Confederates. They had rested upon the laurels won on the battlefield of Parker's Crossroads, and upon their arms for the balance of the day and the entire night of the 31st of December, in hourly anticipation of attack from the command which General Grant had been informed were "scattered over the country." It was not until the next morning, January 1st, as Colonel J. W. Fuller reports, that

we marched to Lexington. On the 2d my brigade and Colonel Lawler's brigade from Jackson marched towards the Tennessee River—five or six miles east of Lexington. Here we learned that Forrest's command (prisoners and stragglers excepted) had crossed the river. On the 3d we moved to Clifton. Learning the road ran along stream for two miles near Clifton, and fearing the enemy would use his artillery from the opposite bank, we

[36] *Ibid.*, vol. xvii, part i, pp. 571, 598.

halted. We found a small picket of about fifteen men, with which we exchanged fire and retired. As soon as our cavalry appeared opposite the town the enemy began to shell them from batteries on the bluff. A wagonload of ammunition was twice struck, and so disabled that we were compelled to abandon it. The march of this day was more severe on the men of my command than any I have witnessed. The road was horrible, and the rain, which fell steadily, made it more so.

Colonel M. K. Lawler says: "On the 1st I marched towards the Tennessee River in pursuit of the rebels under General Forrest. The second day we reached Mr. Sparks's house, nine miles on this side of Clifton, and on the 3d of January marched with our brigade to the river. The rebels had all crossed the river the evening previous at Clifton and other points below. My adjutant-general, Joseph B. Thorp, was wounded in the leg by a rifle-ball."

And, last of all, on January 3, 1863, Brigadier General G. M. Dodge brought up the rear guard of the procession in the following dispatch to Major General Grant: "Forrest escaped across the river at Clifton at 7 A.M., January 1st, having travelled all the time since his fight, and immediately attacked my cavalry. They kept him from the river until night, when they found they were surrounded by a heavy force and two pieces of artillery. Forrest commenced crossing that night, his men on rafts; his horses swam. The cavalry attacked again on the 2d, and this morning he had everything across by ten o'clock. I could not reach him with my forces, but sent forward all the mounted men I could raise, with one section of artillery. Our cavalry have lost considerably in killed and wounded, but not many prisoners. They took several of Forrest's men."[37]

The actual work of the west Tennessee campaign consumed fifteen days, from the 17th of December, the date Forrest completed the passage of the Tennessee, to January 1st, when he recrossed this stream to the eastern shore. In midwinter, and for nearly one week of this time, there was a heavy fall of rain or sleet and snow, and in a section of the country notorious for bad roads, which were rendered practically impassable in wet weather, he had marched with artillery and wagons about three hundred miles, had fought one pitched battle lasting five hours, two other well-contested engagements, and from one to two or more skirmishes daily. When not fighting the men were

[37] *Ibid.,* p. 551.

hard at work destroying railroads, bridges, trestles, culverts, depots, and rails, and all captured supplies which could not be removed. Two important lines of communication had been wiped out, and the work of destruction had been thorough, as is attested by General Grant, who says:

At the same time, Forrest got on our line of railroad between Jackson, Tennessee, and Columbus, Kentucky, doing much damage to it. This cut me off from all communication with the North for more than a week, and it was more than two weeks before rations or forage could be issued from stores obtained in the regular way. This demonstrated the impossibility of maintaining so long a line of road over which to draw supplies for an army moving in an enemy's country. I determined, therefore, to abandon my campaign into the interior with Columbus as a base, and returned to La Grange and Grand Junction, destroying the road to my front and repairing the road to Memphis, making the Mississippi River the line over which to draw supplies.[38]

Not for a single night had these rough riders or their horses had undisturbed repose. Of the Union troops they had killed and wounded and captured some fifteen hundred, and among the officers were four colonels of regiments. They had captured in battle five pieces of artillery (three of which were afterward retaken), eleven caissons, and thirty-eight wagons and teams. When Forrest entered west Tennessee more than one-half of his men were without serviceable arms. In one regiment alone four hundred men had nothing but flintlock muskets, and one-half of the troops had no other arms than shotguns and squirrel rifles, which would not carry a bullet with fatal effect over one hundred yards. When he came out from this expedition every soldier of his command had a modern and effective weapon, with abundant ammunition, and was well supplied with blankets and other equipment furnished by the enemy.

The largest number of troops at any time under his command in the west Tennessee raid was 2500, but at no time were they wholly concentrated. When he entered west Tennessee he had two thousand, and on the expedition he was joined by Napier with about four hundred men, and from the best information I can obtain he picked up about one hundred additional troops during the two weeks of the campaign. Detachments on scouting duty were always out in various directions,

[38] *Memoirs of U. S. Grant,* vol. i, p. 432.

and when the Tennessee was recrossed, on the 1st of January, a number of these detachments made their way into middle Tennessee at points from fifty to one hundred miles distant from Clifton, where Forrest crossed with the main command. He carried seven pieces of artillery into west Tennessee, and brought out six, having lost only one gun, which exploded in the battle of Parker's Crossroads and was abandoned.

His entire loss, it is safe to say, would not reach more than five hundred. He estimated his killed and wounded and captured at considerably less than this number, but when Forrest made his report he could not have had access to the facts which are now on record. The chief loss was at Parker's Crossroads, and it fell most heavily on Dibrell's regiment and the battalions of Cox and Napier. Cox's battalion happened to be dismounted and about at the center of the Federal line of battle which advanced in the rear of Forrest at the crossroads. Before they knew the enemy were coming from that direction, their horses, which were back about a quarter of a mile from their line, had been taken possession of by the Union troops, and about two hundred of these men failed to make their escape on foot. Napier's battalion lost very few if any prisoners, except their wounded, but the rash advance of this command by its leader into a position of great exposure caused considerable loss in killed and wounded before it was retired to a place of greater safety. Dibrell's regiment suffered from the fact that it was immediately under Forrest's eye when the crisis of the battle came, and followed him in the desperate assault on Fuller's advance. Here this regiment lost 4 killed, 27 wounded, and 122 captured, and in the entire campaign it lost 173 men in killed, wounded, and missing.

That the results of this expedition were eminently satisfactory to its commander and to the government at Richmond is evident from the vote of thanks which was made by the Congress of the Confederate States to Brigadier General Forrest and his troops, and the following report from General Braxton Bragg, at Winchester, Tennessee, January 8th, 1863, to General S. Cooper, at Richmond, Virginia:

General Forrest proceeded with his brigade of cavalry to west Tennessee. His command was composed chiefly of new men, imperfectly armed and equipped, and in his route lay the Tennessee River, which had to be crossed by such means as could be hastily improvised. The result of his expedition has been most brilliant and decisive. The enemy, in consequence of this vigorous assault in a quarter vital to their self-preservation, have been compelled to throw back a large force from the Mississippi, and virtually to abandon a campaign which so seriously threatened our safety. The loss of Forrest, though considerable, is small in comparison with the results achieved and the loss of the enemy. He has received my thanks, and deserves the applause of his government.

The number of prisoners taken by General Forrest amounted to fifteen hundred.[39]

That he had accomplished the chief purpose intended by his expedition—namely, to weaken Grant's army of invasion in Mississippi, and to prevent any possible reinforcement of Rosecrans at Murfreesboro or of the army then moving upon Vicksburg—is shown from a dispatch from General in Chief H. W. Halleck to Major General Grant on December 27th: "I think no more troops at present should be sent against Vicksburg. I fear you have already too much weakened your own force. Concentrate and hold only the more important points."[40]

And, finally, the great importance to the Union cause of keeping Forrest out of this territory in the future is shown from the following dispatch sent on January 2nd by Major General Grant to General H. W. Halleck: "I will make a dash at the enemy's lines of communication that, if successful, will leave west Tennessee easily held, so as to be able to send large reinforcements to Vicksburg if necessary."

[39] *Official Records*, vol. xvii, part i, p. 592.
[40] *Ibid.*, p. 478.

SEVEN

Fort Donelson Again

O<small>NCE</small> more in safety upon the eastern bank of the Tennessee, General Forrest moved with his command leisurely to Mount Pleasant, and later, under orders from the commander in chief, to Columbia, where his men and horses found the rest they had so well earned. Here for three weeks there was little for them to do beyond the routine of camp life and the care of the animals in the effort to restore them to serviceable condition. Their chief military duty for the remainder of the month of January, 1863, was to picket and protect the army of General Bragg from surprise from the right wing of the Federal army, which was then stationed in the neighborhood of Franklin, Tennessee.

About the last of this month General Forrest was ordered by his immediate commander, Major General Joseph Wheeler, who had been promoted to be chief of cavalry, to take eight hundred men and proceed to the Cumberland River, at whatever point he thought his force would be most effective in accomplishing the object of the expedition, which was to interrupt, as far as practicable, the navigation of that stream. He moved out promptly under these instructions, and was soon heard from not far from the scene of an earlier and famous exploit.

Colonel A. C. Harding, of the Eighty-third Illinois Infantry, who was commanding at Dover (Fort Donelson), in a dispatch dated February 6, 1863, says: "On the 2d inst. I was led to believe that Forrest, with about nine hundred men and several pieces of artillery, had taken a position on the river at Palmyra for the purpose of obstructing the navigation of the Cumberland."[1] This officer proposed to move in that direction on the 3rd to stir Forrest up, but before he started he received information that the Confederates were advancing upon Donel-

[1] *Official Records,* vol. xxiii, part i, p. 34.

son by the road leading down the river. He therefore wisely abandoned the idea of a reconnaissance in the open country.

Near Palmyra, Forrest, who had masked his guns and ambushed his men, and was all ready for a bout with any passing craft, was overtaken by the chief of cavalry, who brought with him a portion of Wharton's brigade. General Wheeler, having concluded that the Federals had become apprised of the Confederate position along the river and would not, for the present, send any more boats on that stream, and having nothing else in hand, determined upon an expedition for the capture of the Federal garrison at Dover. In his official report he says: "After maturely considering the matter, we concluded that nothing could be lost by an attack upon the garrison at Dover, and from the information that we had there was good reason to believe that this post could easily be captured."

In the *Campaigns of General Forrest,* which was edited under his personal supervision, it is stated that some difference of opinion existed as to the propriety of this attack upon the fort at Dover, and that General Forrest submitted to his chief that he was not only poorly supplied with ammunition, but that the effort did not promise results commensurate with the losses that an assault upon such a formidable position would entail, and earnestly advised that the effort be abandoned.

The premonition of disaster weighed upon Forrest so heavily that on the morning of the engagement he spoke of the matter in strict confidence to his chief of staff, Major Charles W. Anderson, and to Dr. Ben Wood, of Hopkinsville, Kentucky, then a surgeon connected with his command. He said: "I have a special request to make of you in regard to the proposed attack on Fort Donelson. I have protested against the move, but my protest has been disregarded, and I intend to do my whole duty, and I want my men to do the same. I have spoken to none but you on this subject, and I do not wish that any one should know of the objections I have made. I have this request to make: If I am killed in this fight, you will see that justice is done me by officially stating that I protested against the attack, and that I am not willing to be held responsible for any disaster that may result."[2]

General Wheeler believed, however, that by a simultaneous and

[2] A personal communication from Major Charles W. Anderson, living at Florence, Tennessee, in 1898.

quick rush from two sides the garrison could be overcome with trifling loss, and immediately ordered the advance. The command arrived in sight of the fort about twelve o'clock, noon, on February 3rd, and at once advanced on foot to invest the strong position occupied by a garrison of eight hundred sturdy men of the Eighty-third Illinois Infantry, and a formidable array of light and heavy artillery.

The Eighth Texas, of Wharton's brigade, was sent out on the road to Fort Henry, from which direction the Federals under Colonel Lowe were advancing with reinforcements. After the detachment under Forrest was dismounted and deployed for assault from the east side, and Wharton's fragment of a brigade from the west and southwest, a flag of truce was sent into the fort demanding an immediate and unconditional surrender. The plucky Federal commander replied that he "declined to surrender the forces under his command or the post without an effort to defend them."

The Confederate artillery promptly opened upon the advanced guns of the Union field batteries, and soon compelled these to retire to the immediate vicinity of the fortifications. Forrest was waiting, as he had been directed, until General Wheeler could arrive at Wharton's portion of the line, when, at a fixed moment, a general assault on foot was to be made. Before General Wheeler had reached the point where Wharton was in line, and before the moment set for the general attack, Forrest observed a number of Federal troops (three or four companies) marching at a double-quick in plain view from the fort in the direction of the river. Mistaking this move for the abandonment of the fortifications and an effort to escape, and thinking he would be able to cut off and capture these troops, he immediately ordered his men to mount their horses, and led them in a charge on the Federal detachment.

The Illinois commandant and his soldiers had, however, no idea of abandoning their stronghold. The troops Forrest had observed were several companies of the Eighty-third Illinois, which had been ordered to occupy a deep ravine a little beyond their central position.[3] As Forrest at the head of the few hundred men he had with him rode at the Federal infantry, those most in advance opened upon the charging column and immediately ran back to rejoin their comrades behind the breastworks. In the desperate effort to outrun and capture

[3] *Official Records,* vol. xxiii, part i, p. 36.

them, or go into the works with them and thus shield his men, Forrest and his troopers rode at full speed straight at the trenches.

Unfortunately for him, the distance was so short that the fleet-footed men of Illinois had time to get over the embankment, and with their comrades already there take a hand in the deadly fusillade of small arms poured, right in the faces of the rash horsemen. To this the garrison added a discharge of several of their heavy guns loaded to the muzzle with grape and canister, and the Confederates—horses and men—went down in frightful slaughter. Harding says: "In an instant the siege gun, double-shotted with canister, was turned upon them and discharged, tearing one man and two horses to atoms within ten feet of the muzzle. At the same time I ordered my infantry to fire, and this, with the grape and canister, was too much for them and they gave way."

Forrest's horse was shot and fell within a few paces of the guns. As soon as his troops saw their commander go down, thinking he had been killed, they retreated before the shower of grape and canister which they had unexpectedly met. Forrest disentangled himself from the dead animal, which fortunately had not injured him in falling, and made his way to the rear with scant regard to the order of his going.

General Wheeler says: "Just as I left General Forrest, he, thinking the enemy were leaving the place and being anxious to rush in quickly, remounted his men and charged on horseback. The fire from the enemy was so strong that he was repulsed and obliged to retire."

The discomfited troopers were again formed for assault, this time on foot, and, simultaneously with the advance by Wharton's column, they rushed forward, Forrest again on horseback at the head of his dismounted detachment. The Federal commander says: "The enemy, led on by Forrest himself, moved forward in a solid, motley mass, moving down the river to a point near the jail, and there by the flank up the street towards the southward, then forward in successive lines of battle between our northern line of base and the river, filling the whole open space with mounted men, and the air with yells of triumph."

The Federals were driven from the houses which they had occupied as sharpshooters, and on all sides from the outer intrenchments. They then took cover in the redoubts, from which they again poured a very severe fire into the Confederates. These pressed forward with courage to the breastworks, but were unable to gain a footing within the fort. Forrest's horse was shot down, being the second animal killed under him that day, and the general was badly shaken up in falling. A number of men were killed within a few feet of the breastworks.

The troops now took refuge in the houses near by from which the Federals had been driven. At this moment the garrison commenced running out toward the river, and the Confederates, taking this for a charge upon the held horses that were in that direction, rushed back to protect the horses. General Wheeler was of the opinion that had this position not been abandoned at this crisis the garrison would have surrendered. From the report of Colonel Harding it is evident that this movement of the Federals was a rush on the part of six companies of his regiment to unite with three other companies in the rifle pits, where the reserved ammunition had been kept, and was done with no thought of a surrender.

On the left, Wharton's command easily drove the Federals into their works, capturing a few prisoners and one fine twelve-pounder brass rifled cannon, which was brought from the field. The stubborn resistance made by the garrison had, however, succeeded in holding off their assailants until near nightfall, when, as General Wheeler states, his troops had a secure position not more than ninety yards from the main rifle pits of the garrison. Before making a third assault a conference was held, and it was decided that there was not enough ammunition left in the entire command to justify a further attack. It was also learned at this crisis that reinforcements for the garrison were arriving, and had already fired upon the Confederate outposts. Before retreating a detachment was sent to the river landing near the fort, and there set fire to a boat loaded with supplies, which was soon destroyed. As they retired, other details were made to gather up all the wounded who could be carried away on horseback or in wagons, and to bring off the captured gun and other property, among which was a generous supply of blankets found in the Federal quarters, which were greatly needed, as the weather was intensely cold.

The Confederate troopers, worn out with the exertion of the day and dispirited by defeat, went into bivouac about four miles from Dover and shivered disconsolately through the freezing night. The Union reinforcements, sent over from Fort Henry by Colonel W. W. Lowe, made no effort to follow. The gunboats, five of which came to the rescue of the beleaguered garrison, sent a shower of noisy shells screaming and bursting over the frozen hills, but despite all this the detachment under Colonel Woodward and Major Anderson remained on the field until after dark, and brought away a caisson full of ammunition captured from the garrison.

Here, in a roadside house, by the light of a log fire, Generals Wheeler, Wharton, and Forrest talked over the dismal failure of the day. The former, with singleness of purpose devoted to the cause of the South, his personal courage of the highest order, and his brilliant leadership attested on many more successful occasions than in this disastrous affair at Dover, wrote his report admitting defeat, and without a word of criticism for either of his subordinates. Forrest was, however, in uncontrollable mood, nor was his irritability rendered more easy of concealment by the injury he had received and the great fatigue of the day.

Major Charles W. Anderson says:

It was late when I reached headquarters at Yellow Creek Furnace. Arriving there, I asked for General Forrest. The general, recognizing my voice, came to the door, and as I was too near frozen to dismount, he came out and helped me down and into the house. Without any ceremony he went to the only bed in the room, jerked the covering from two officers who were occupying it, and brusquely ordered them to get out. My boots were pulled off, I was rolled up in blankets and put in the vacated bed. General Wharton was sitting on the side of the fireplace opposite General Wheeler, who was dictating his report to one of his staff. Forrest had resumed his place, lying down on his water-proof coat in front of the fire, his head on a turned-down chair and his feet well on the hearth. General Wharton said: "When the signal was given, my men moved forward, but were met with such a severe fire that, with the exception of the Fourth Georgia and Malone's battalion, they gave way. As we fell back I noticed the garrison from our side of the fort rush across to the other side to take part against General Forrest's attack, and, as his command caught the fire of the entire garrison, he must have suffered severely." Forrest interrupted him, saying in an excited and angry tone, "I have no fault to find with my men. In both charges they did their duty as they have always done." At this moment General Wheeler remarked: "General Forrest, my report does ample justice to yourself and to your men." Forrest replied: "General Wheeler, I advised against this attack, and said all a subordinate officer should have said against it, and nothing you can now say or do will bring back my brave men lying dead or wounded and freezing around that fort tonight. I mean no disrespect to you; you know my feelings of personal friendship for you; you can have my sword if you demand it; but there is one thing I do want you to put in that report to General Bragg—tell him that I will be in my coffin before I will fight again under your command."

Neither the soldier nor the man in "Fighting Joe Wheeler" were ever more in evidence than on this occasion. He both knew and appreciated Forrest, admired his wonderful genius, and loved him devotedly. He proved this in many ways in after-years. Moreover, he knew that when the tempest was raging in this wild and rugged nature he could appeal to it more by gentle word and manner than by the strict rules of military discipline. "Forrest," he said, quietly and with great feeling, "I cannot take your sabre, and I regret exceedingly your determination. As the commanding officer I take all the blame and responsibility for this failure."

After this Wheeler respected in perfect faith Forrest's whim and determination. In Tennessee they served on the opposing flanks of the army, and at Chickamauga Forrest was on the right and Wheeler on the left wing. When Wheeler made his great raid in Rosecrans's rear early in October, 1863, capturing the immense supply train in Sequatchie Valley, and reducing the Union army in Chattanooga to the verge of starvation, he left Forrest in east Tennessee, and in the following month President Davis gave the peerless fighter a separate command, in the district forever famous as "Forrest's Territory."

It was difficult for Forrest to brook command from anyone. He was born a leader of men, not a follower of man. From childhood his existence had depended upon his own exertion, and thus early thrown upon his own resources he had learned to rely entirely upon himself —even in his boyhood he asserted his leadership among his playmates. The rules of discipline which others had learned, and which once learned make the man in war a part of the machine, were to him a sealed book. The methods of these two soldiers were entirely different, and, pursuing them, both won undying fame. Their friendship remained steadfast to the end, and Forrest had no greater admirer than his former chief of cavalry.

In 1897, General Wheeler related to the writer the last interview he had with General Forrest just a few weeks before his death. "I had not seen Forrest for several years, and was struck at the great change his malady (chronic diarrhea) had wrought in his appearance. His face was pale and thin, and it seemed to me his large blue eyes had never looked so clear and penetrating. The stern and at times fierce expression which the hard experiences of his early career and the more exciting times of war had stamped upon his face was gone, and now there was nothing but a gentle look as if at last peace were reigning. I could not help but notice the massive, broad forehead, seemingly so out of proportion to his attenuated frame. No wonder, with such a head, he was an extraordinary man."

The losses at Dover on the part of the Confederates were very heavy for the number of troops engaged. In Wharton's command 17 were killed, 60 wounded, and 8 missing.[4] Forrest, who had not quite 1000 men in the engagement, lost in killed, wounded, and captured 200; and among these Colonel Frank McNairy, of his staff was killed, Colonel D. W. Holman, of Napier's battalion, wounded, and three captains of this command wounded and captured. The Federal commander, Colonel Lowe, on February 4th, reported that 135 Confederate dead had been found, and that they then held 50 prisoners. Major C. W. Anderson says the loss of officers in Starnes's Fourth Tennessee was so great that he was ordered to command a detachment of this regiment, and led it in the last charge. Colonel Harding, in his official report, gives his loss as 13 killed, 51 wounded, and 46 prisoners.

On the morning of February 4th the Confederates resumed their march in the direction of Columbia. Being informed of the approach of a column of Union infantry and cavalry under General Jefferson C. Davis, they were compelled to make a wide detour in the direction of Centerville toward Duck River, and there succeeded in crossing this stream. On the 17th they were once more in camp at Columbia. During the retreat from Dover, Colonel Charles M. Carroll and Major G. V. Rambaut of General Forrest's staff, marching with a small detachment of troops in advance of their column, having mistaken their direction, took the wrong road and, marching unexpectedly into the head of the troops commanded by General Davis, were captured. In the latter part of February, Russell's Fourth Alabama regiment, much to his regret, was detached from Forrest's brigade, and its place was taken by the union of Holman's and Douglas's battalions, which were consolidated to form the Eleventh Tennessee Cavalry. The remnants of Cox's and Napier's battalion were also consolidated and placed under Forrest, forming the Tenth Tennessee Cavalry. Major

[4] *Ibid.,* vol. xxiii, part i, p. 41.

Anderson says: "General Forrest held the Fourth Alabama in high esteem. He always spoke of it as a command he could rely upon to accomplish what it was ordered to do."[5]

The rough handling at Dover and the wear and tear of the hard campaign in bitter cold weather only served to make Forrest the more eager to get even with the enemy. It was on February 17th that he reached Columbia, and the next day he was asking permission to make a descent on Nashville. He notified General Wheeler that there were two thousand mules corralled in the suburbs of Nashville, and as "they are lightly guarded and only one regiment encamped in that direction, a few hundred men might bring them out."[6] He was disappointed in the refusal of his request to undertake this expedition.

On the 18th of February a scouting party of some three hundred Union troopers ventured out from Franklin, but had not proceeded far when they were met by a detachment of Forrest's outpost cavalry under Lieutenant Colonel Woodward, who drove them back.

The necessity of discipline and drill had not appeared at first so important to Forrest as it did now with his widening experience in arms, and, although very busy at the front, he says in one of his dispatches of this period: "I am going to have my forces thoroughly organized before I go into the field again. I have ordered dress-parade twice per week."

Ever on the alert, on February 19th he notified General Wheeler that he should be prepared for a strong movement by the Federals from Franklin. He had positive information that "two regiments of cavalry have reached Franklin, making about two thousand cavalry and four thousand infantry. They are evidently preparing to move out this way, as they are repairing the bridge and putting the telegraph in order. If they should move out this way, I think with General Van Dorn's command and mine to move from here, Colonel Roddey from Chapel Hill, and General Wharton in towards Brentwood, their force can be captured or cut to pieces."

It is noteworthy, as shown by the official dispatches and communications dated prior to the event, in how many instances General Forrest during the war was able to forecast with remarkable exactness the movements of the enemy. In this instance, two weeks elapsed before

[5] Manuscripts of Major Anderson.
[6] *Official Records,* vol. xxviii, part ii, pp. 638 *et seq.*

the advance which he predicted in this dispatch of February 19th was made.

In the early days of March, 1863, Major General Rosecrans became desirous of knowing something more definite of the positions and purposes of the enemy. He ordered various detachments of his troops to proceed on forced reconnaissances from Murfreesboro in the direction of Unionville and Duck River, and from Franklin toward Chapel Hill and Spring Hill. It is with this latter movement that we have to deal, since Forrest's brigade became actively engaged, and, although a subordinate on the field, he, after a very considerable fight, came out of the encounter by all odds the hero of the day.

His vigilance, as we have shown, had led to a thorough preparation to thwart this reconnaissance in force. Near Thompson's Station, on the road along which the Federals were advancing on the 4th of March, Major General Earl Van Dorn, who then commanded on the left wing of Bragg's army, and who had concentrated the cavalry in his department, was stationed. He had five brigades in all, commanded by Brigadier Generals N. B. Forrest, F. C. Armstrong, G. B. Cosby, W. T. Martin, and Colonel (acting Brigadier General) J. W. Whitfield, about 6000 effective troops, and with these Captain S. L. Freeman's six guns of Forrest's command and Captain Houston King's Second Missouri battery of six pieces belonging to Whitfield's brigade.[7] With this force he marched out from Columbia on the morning of the 4th of March and advanced to meet the enemy.

General W. H. Jackson, commanding a division composed of Armstrong's and Whitfield's brigades and King's battery, was given the advance, and proceeded at a considerable distance ahead of the remaining troops. Arriving within four miles of Franklin, they collided with a body of Federal soldiers who were bound for Spring Hill, their object being to find out, if possible, what Bragg's men there were up to.

There were in this Federal column 2837 troops, and, in addition, the Eighteenth Ohio battery of six long-range Rodman rifled cannon. Six hundred of this Union force were of the cavalry; the remainder belonged to the infantry.

When Jackson came in sight of them they were so stretched out along the white macadamized road, with their long train of eighty foraging wagons and their great array of artillery, cavalry, and infantry,

---

[7] *Ibid.*, vol. xxiii, part ii, p. 641.

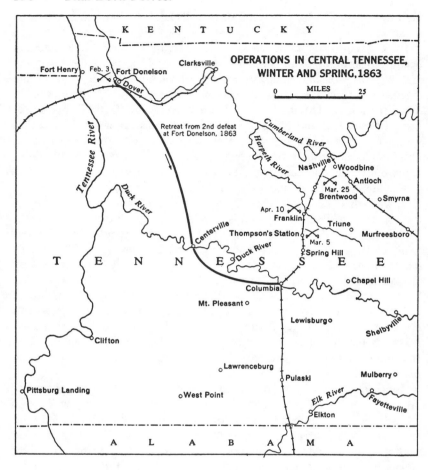

OPERATIONS IN CENTRAL TENNESSEE, WINTER AND SPRING, 1863

that the spectacle impressed the Confederate general with the idea that there were too many in front of him to attack without help. He therefore concluded not to advance upon them, seeing which the Federal commander concluded to advance upon him. At long range the artillery opened on both sides, and for about two hours both commanders seemed to be satisfied with this duel at a distance, which made a great deal of noise but did very little damage.

At last, Colonel John Coburn, of the Thirty-third Indiana Infantry (more known to fame after this event than before), who commanded the Union soldiers, and did it right well and bravely, although he came to grief before he was two days older, advanced his cavalry, and there was precipitated a lively skirmish with small arms. The result was that the Confederates retired in the direction from which they had come, reaching the vicinity of Thompson's Station, on the Alabama and Tennessee Railroad, about nightfall. Here they were joined by the balance of Van Dorn's cavalry, and, almost in sight of each other, the Federal and Confederate columns bivouacked for the night. The casualties of the day were small for either side. The honors of the artillery duel rested rather with the Confederates, for they had succeeded in dismounting one of Coburn's guns, which was sent back to Franklin for repairs.

General Van Dorn says: "During the night my scouts reported the enemy to be a brigade of infantry, two regiments of cavalry, and a body of artillery, and I determined to give them battle."[8] In a military sense this was a very wise conclusion, since Van Dorn, having posted himself as to the number of the enemy with which he had to deal on the morning, had twice as many troops on the ground as his adversary. The information which Colonel Coburn obtained, and upon which he intended to act on the following day, was not, however, so accurate as that possessed by his antagonist. In his official report he says: "On the 5th of March, soon after daylight, two Negro boys, about twelve years of age, came into camp and said that they had come from Van Dorn's army, and that it was out this side of Spring Hill and was coming on to take Franklin."[9]

The Union colonel was not pleased with the reported size of Van Dorn's army. It grew in his mind, for in his official report he stated that there were about 15,000 of them; and between the lines one can clearly read that he did not know whether to fight or run. Spring Hill looked very much farther away than when he started out with the order signed by Brigadier General James A. Garfield, instructing him to proceed to this point. In his perplexity he sent back to Franklin to Brigadier General C. C. Gilbert, informing him that he believed there were more of the enemy confronting him than his superior officer had anticipated, and ended his communication with the very pertinent

[8] *Ibid.,* vol. xxiii, part i, p. 116.
[9] *Ibid.,* p. 86.

inquiry, "What shall we do?" As no answer ever came to this question, early on the morning of the 5th Coburn proceeded to divest himself of all superfluous baggage by sending one-half of his eighty wagons back to Franklin to be cared for by his commanding officer; for now, no matter what might happen, he had to go on, and, although he did it bravely and well, it took five months for his next dispatch to reach General Gilbert, for it was dated at Murfreesboro, August 30, 1863.

Bright and early on the 5th of March, Van Dorn was up and busy, and had his men stretched out in line of battle ready and, although in superior force, waiting for the Union troops to attack him. He had selected an excellent position in the neighborhood of Thompson's Station, had lined up Armstrong's and Whitfield's brigades on either side of the turnpike; and away off to the right of his line, and somewhat to himself (where he always liked to be), was Forrest with his brigade and his six pet guns of Freeman's battery. Our brigadier general was never more anxious for a fight than at this moment, for he and his men were still smarting under the bad whipping they had received at Dover. They had fought hard there and lost heavily in trying to storm a strongly fortified position, and were beaten off; but now they had a chance in the open country, and the men knew from the flushed face and the tone and conduct of their leader that a chance at close quarters would not be missed on this occasion.

Feeling his way along, with as brave a lot of men in blue as any soldier ever commanded, Coburn came on, determined to do his best. However, he advanced slowly and cautiously—so slowly, in fact, that it was not until ten o'clock in the morning that his troops were well engaged with the Confederate cavalry. As the Federal troops advanced, the Thirty-third and Eighty-fifth Indiana, with two guns, formed their right; the Twenty-second Wisconsin and Nineteenth Michigan, with three guns, their left wing. To the left of this line several companies of dismounted cavalry occupied a strong position in a dense thicket of cedars crowning a knoll, and just behind this point the remainder of the cavalry were formed under the command of Colonel Thomas J. Jordan. The One Hundred and Twenty-fourth Ohio was held in reserve with the train.

With these Coburn advanced by a demonstration of his cavalry on his left, and a charge by the two Indiana regiments of his right wing. As this movement began, the artillery of both sides opened with great spirit and with rapid fire. The Federals made lively use of their small arms as they came on in gallant style under orders to charge King's battery, which was in their immediate front.[10] Behind a stone fence, and in excellent position for defending these guns, was Whitfield's brigade, which had been strengthened by Colonel S. G. Earle's Third Arkansas regiment from Armstrong's brigade.

The charge of the Union cavalry under Jordan was of short duration. Forrest, who had the Confederate extreme right, anticipating this effort, ordered Starnes's Fourth Tennessee and Edmondson's regiments to drive their dismounted troopers from the cedar knoll, which they did in quick order. At the same moment he advanced the remainder of his line against Jordan's mounted force, compelling them to take refuge behind the infantry. Seeing his opportunity with the retirement of the Federal cavalry, Forrest hurried Freeman's battery far to the front, and posted it so favorably that it swept not only the advancing Federal infantry in flank, but enfiladed their battery, causing it to limber up and leave its position, and with their cavalry to quit the field. His entire line was now half a mile in front of the main Confederate line of battle.

Colonel Jordan says: "In a moment a battery of the enemy, of four guns, which had heretofore been masked, opened upon our flank, completely covering the ground upon which our infantry and cavalry were placed, and also completely flanking our guns."[11] General Van Dorn says: "While these events were occurring on the Confederate left, General Forrest, on the extreme right, had pushed forward Captain Freeman's battery to a hill in advance of his original position, and completely commanding the enemy's left. The enemy's battery was withdrawn from the cross-fire of this and King's battery, and did not return to the field. The cavalry, with one regiment of infantry, after offering some resistance to General Forrest, precipitately left the field."[12]

At this juncture the charging Federal infantry had reached within two hundred yards of Whitfield's men crouching behind the stone wall. These now arose with a well-directed volley, immediately following which they leaped the fence and charged upon the Union line. With this destructive fire and countercharge from the front, and Forrest's

[10] *Ibid.,* vol. xxiii, part i, p. 88.
[11] *Ibid.,* p. 81.
[12] *Ibid.,* p. 116.

battery playing on their flank and his troopers pushing Jordan's cavalry from the Union left, no wonder the Indianians broke and fled back across the swale and on behind the hill on which they had first been aligned.

Here, although their cavalry and artillery, deeming discretion the better part of valor, had fled the field, the men on foot were rallied. Colonel Coburn says of his troopers, after Forrest had chased them from the field: "I saw them no more, although I sent for them." The Confederates under Whitfield and Earle dashed up the hill, behind which their plucky enemy had halted to dispute their advance, and here they turned upon their pursuers with splendid courage, driving them back down the hill and into the valley to their former position, where the thwarted Southerners held their own.

General Van Dorn again ordered his troops to drive the Federals from the hill they still so stubbornly held. Whitfield and Earle for the second time went at them, and Armstrong's entire brigade joined with them in the charge. The Nineteenth Michigan and Twenty-second Wisconsin rushed to reinforce their comrades, and a fierce combat at close quarters ensued, in which the Southerners again failed to drive them from the coveted position. Armstrong was badly handled in this affray, and left his battle flag in the possession of the Michiganders. In this dilemma, Forrest now charged on the flank and rear, and thus closed all hope of escape. As his troops swept down on the Union flank the Twenty-second Wisconsin broke, and about one-half of this regiment scattered in the woods like frightened partridges, and many of them thus escaped capture; however, only to be taken by Forrest at Brentwood twenty days later. Major General Van Dorn had also considered the possibilities of this movement and had ordered it to be done, but Forrest had accomplished the result independently of his chief, who officially acknowledged that "the final charge by General Forrest decided the fate of the day."

As Coburn retired, his brigade was still in compact order and thorough organization. He says: "Here we met and attacked Forrest's division, which had gained our rear, and had been posted behind fences, trees, and other favorable positions. The brigade was formed with fixed bayonets," etc.

It was a cardinal point of Forrest's military make-up never to stand

and take a charge, but, as he expressed it, to "charge too." Seeing Coburn's maneuver, he says: "I ordered a charge, which was gallantly led by Colonel Biffle and Lieutenant-Colonel Trezevant, commanding Cox's regiment. The enemy opened a heavy fire upon us. Lieutenant-Colonel Trezevant fell mortally wounded, and Captain Montgomery Little, of my escort, was killed. When within twenty feet of their line the enemy threw down their arms and surrendered. The two regiments with my escort numbered about five hundred and sixty men; the balance of effective strength were holding horses. We captured from twelve to fifteen hundred officers and privates."[13] Thus closed this spirited affair, and for Forrest and his men "honors were easy." The defeat at Dover was cancelled.

No sooner had the Union commander thrown in the sponge than Forrest directed a strong detachment to mount their horses and pursue the flying cavalry and artillery and the One Hundred and Twenty-fourth Ohio Infantry, which, being in reserve, had gone to the rear with the wagons. These troops had, however, such a running start that only some seventy-five captures were effected, and chiefly from the regiments which had borne the brunt of the fighting. The Ohio regiment did not lose a man. The Union cavalry lost twenty-seven in all, and their artillery had only one man wounded.

Just before the surrender, Forrest was unhorsed by the killing of his favorite charger, Roderick, a noble animal presented to him by Mr. Cocke of Tennessee. The general led the final assault on foot. Of his command there were on the field about 1700 men—viz., Biffle's regiment, which lost six killed and fifteen wounded; Cox's regiment, one killed and nine wounded; Edmondson's regiment, nine wounded; Starnes's Fourth Tennessee, two killed and twenty-one wounded; McCann's battalion, three wounded and two missing; escort, one (Captain Little) mortally wounded; total, sixty-nine. Lieutenant John Johnson, of Biffle's regiment, was killed while at the front with the colors. Private

---

[13] In addition to Colonels Coburn and Gilbert, Major W. R. Shafter, who in 1898 became the commander in chief in the successful campaign against the Spanish forces at Santiago, was captured in this charge by Forrest. It is stated in the *Official Records,* although the surrender was unconditional, that "the bravery of these Union troops who had been captured was so conspicuous that Forrest permitted the officers to retain their horses and side-arms."—Vol. xxiii, part i, p. 84.

Clay Kendrick caught the flag as it was falling, and held it aloft until his arm was broken with a bullet, when he seized it with his uninjured arm and carried it until Coburn surrendered.

In addition to Forrest's brigade, General Van Dorn had in this action the First and Twenty-eighth Mississippi of Cosby's brigade, about 700 in number, which arrived near the close of the fighting and took only a small part in the affair, their loss being three wounded. The regiments of Colonels T. G. Woodward and J. B. Ballantine, also under Cosby, were in reserve and did not come into action. There were about 1400 of this brigade on the field and available.

The chief loss on the Southern side fell to Whitfield's and Armstrong's brigades in the several attacks and counterattacks gallantly made and withstood by both sides for the possession of "Coburn's Hill." Of the former the Third Texas lost seven killed, twenty-five wounded, and two missing; the Sixth Texas, two killed and thirty-four wounded; Ninth Texas, three killed, nineteen wounded, and one missing; and "Whitfield's Legion," eleven killed, fifty-nine wounded, and seven missing. Total engaged, about 1400—killed, 23; wounded, 137; missing, 10. In Armstrong's brigade the Third Arkansas lost six killed and twenty-eight wounded; the Fourth Mississippi, nine killed and thirty-seven wounded; Saunders's battalion, fourteen wounded; Jenkins's squadron, two killed and twelve wounded. Total engaged, about 900.

The Confederates had in action and in reserve in this engagement, including the two batteries, at a fair estimate, 6000 men. Their antagonists, according to Colonel Coburn's official report, had 2837 men and five guns. His entire cavalry reported as 600, with four regiments of infantry and the cavalry in action, about 2450 in all. They lost in the Thirty-third Indiana, seventeen killed, fourteen mortally wounded, sixty-nine wounded and recovered; Twenty-second Wisconsin, seven killed and nineteen wounded; Nineteenth Michigan, twenty killed, thirteen mortally wounded, seventy-nine wounded and recovered; Eighty-fifth Indiana, thirteen killed, twenty-one wounded and recovered; Ninth Pennsylvania Cavalry, two killed and seven wounded; Second Michigan Cavalry, two killed and eleven wounded. Total killed and mortally wounded, 88; wounded and recovered, 206; total casualties, 292. The One Hundred and Twenty-fourth Ohio, about one-half the Wisconsin Regiment, and all the cavalry escaped, excepting twenty-six troopers killed, wounded, or captured, giving a total in

Federal loss of about 1500 officers and men.

The Union forces placed *hors de combat* 357 Confederates; the fight made by Colonel Coburn and the men of the four regiments who stayed with him was worthy of the admiration of their victors. Had his cavalry held fast, and had the Ohio regiment been added, he might have effected a retreat toward Franklin far enough to have been reached by reinforcements. With the great superiority in numbers, it would seem that better generalship might have succeeded in the capture of the entire Union command. General Van Dorn knew almost exactly the strength of his adversary the night before the engagement, and he had troops in abundance to have interposed in Coburn's rear enough cavalry to have prevented his retreat and insured the capture of all the enemy's wagons, artillery, and practically all of his force. Had Forrest been in command, the tactics of Brice's Crossroads and the terrible pursuit made on that famous field would in all likelihood have been anticipated at Thompson's Station. The general of the army and the powers at Richmond had not yet the discernment to see his great ability. It dawned upon them later, only when stern necessity forced the recognition, but too late for the success of the cause.

General Forrest, in his report of this engagement, says:

By the time the disposition of our force was made, the firing began from the enemy's artillery, and, finding I had no position bearing upon the enemy with my artillery, I ordered Captain S. L. Freeman forward with his battery to a high hill, which placed it advantageously for operating on the enemy's left flank. As this was fully half a mile in advance of my first position, I ordered up all the regiments of my brigade on foot to a line parallel with that hill, and nearly at right angles to the pike. I found two regiments of infantry and a regiment of the Federal cavalry posted behind a stone fence to the left of their artillery. A few shells from my guns drove them from their position to the right of their battery, and, after about twenty rounds, drove it from its position, retreating by the pike towards Franklin.

At this time I was ordered to move forward, and, if possible, get in the rear of the enemy. Ordering up all my troops, we attacked vigorously, and disposed of that portion of the enemy's force moving on the turnpike. The main force of the enemy was posted on the hill in front of Thompson's station and to the left of the pike, and had driven back several times the forces under Generals Armstrong and Whitfield and my two regiments under Colonels Starnes and Edmondson. I now moved Cox's and Biffle's regiments rapidly across the pike in the rear of the enemy, and found they had taken a strong position and were ready to receive us. I immediately ordered the charge, which was led by Biffle and Trezevant, commanding Cox's regiment. The enemy opened a heavy fire upon us, the first volley mortally wounding Lieutenant-Colonel Trezevant and Captain Montgomery Little, who commanded my escort. The men continued to charge to within twenty feet of the Federal line of battle, when the enemy threw down their arms and surrendered.

EIGHT

Brentwood and Franklin

Leaving a strong line of pickets in the neighborhood of Franklin, General Van Dorn, on the evening of the 5th of March, taking the prisoners and captured property, withdrew his force to Spring Hill, and soon thereafter to the neighborhood of Columbia. With the large opposing armies so near each other, the cavalry could not long remain idle. On March 11th, Forrest, now entrusted with a division of two brigades, was ordered to the line of Rutherford Creek, to hold in check a strong force of cavalry backed by a reserve infantry column of 4572 men, reported as advancing upon the Confederate outposts north of Duck River.[1]

This movement was under the immediate direction of Brigadier General Philip H. Sheridan, and for the first and only time these two great soldiers were face to face. Born leaders of their kind, both possessing in a wonderful degree that personal magnetism which attracts men and holds them captive to control, each in his way a genius in the art of war and both loving a fight, it is a wonder that they did not here cross sabers. Forrest not only knew that Sheridan was strong enough to overwhelm him, but he was also under orders to cover a withdrawal of the troops across Duck River, then greatly swollen, and he could not hazard a collision. On the 9th of March, Starnes's Fourth Tennessee, then on picket duty near Thompson's Station, with one of Armstrong's regiments was attacked by a brigade of Sheridan's cavalry under Colonel Robert H. G. Minty, and another brigade under General Green Clay Smith. Skirmishing with his assailants with characteristic stubbornness, Starnes fought his way back to join his chief that night south of Spring Hill.

On the 10th, Sheridan essayed to cross Rutherford Creek at a ford

[1] *Official Records,* vol. xxiii, part i, p. 115.

145

one and a half miles above the Burnt Bridge, on the Spring Hill and Columbia road. Colonel Minty says: "Found the water very deep and rapid, and while making the examination were under fire of a rebel force posted close to the bank. The Fourth Indiana had two men killed and three severely wounded. We camped at Moore's Ford, one mile higher up the creek. March 11th, General Forrest, with five hundred men, advanced to the opposite side. A sharp fire was opened on him. Lieutenant Newell opened on them with his gun, and drove them to the woods. I then crossed the creek, and as I formed on the south bank the enemy dismounted and, with their battle-flag flying, advanced. I sent General Green Clay Smith with a regiment to the left, to get in their rear, and the Fourth Michigan to the right. Perceiving our object, they remounted and retired. At Duck River, Van Dorn's entire force had crossed during the day on a pontoon-bridge and a ferryboat."[2]

Had General Sheridan, with his two brigades, pushed forward with his usual vim, Forrest might not have escaped so easily with his own command; for when he reached Duck River the pontoon bridge had been swept away by the increasing current, and the nearest other point of crossing was twenty-five miles distant. Without halting he rode all night, and happily found this avenue of escape still unoccupied by a hostile force. But Sheridan as well as Forrest was not untrammeled by orders. General G. C. Gilbert had dispatched General James A. Garfield as follows: "General Sheridan will do well to approach with caution Van Dorn's command—it is probably not less than ten thousand men, well trained and well handled."[3] The Union troops returned to Franklin, and on the same day Forrest reported at Columbia. The pontoon bridge was at once replaced, and he, with his division, composed of his own and Armstrong's brigades, recrossed and followed the retiring Federals, reoccupying his old quarters at Spring Hill on March 15th.

General Forrest was now assigned to independent outpost duty in this locality, his picket line extending from Thompson's Station to the vicinity of College Grove on Harpeth River. Beyond the picket posts Forrest kept a swarm of his trusted scouts, who penetrated the enemy's lines around Franklin and Nashville in search of information as to the strength and position of the various outlying detachments. Through these he learned that at and near Brentwood, a station on the Nashville

[2] *Ibid.*, vol. xxiii, part i, p. 131.
[3] *Ibid.*, p. 115.

and Franklin Railroad, about nine miles from the latter place, were stationed two detachments of Union troops from the Twenty-second Wisconsin and the Nineteenth Michigan Infantry, some 800 in all, which were distant from each other about one and a half miles. They were therefore sufficiently isolated to justify the hope of striking them in detail, capturing and bringing them away before succor could arrive. There were 521 men of the Wisconsin regiment in a fortified position near the fork of the Wilson and Franklin pikes, which commanded these approaches and the depot of supplies at the railroad station. The timber in all directions had been felled in order to prevent surprise, and to enable the garrison to cover an advancing enemy. Within a stockade immediately adjacent to the railroad bridge over the Harpeth River, and one and a half miles distant from the camp at Brentwood, were 230 men of the Nineteenth Michigan Infantry.

It will be remembered that in the engagement at Thompson's Station on March 5th this Michigan regiment had greatly distinguished itself, and these troops were the remnant of that command either not on duty on that expedition or escaping from the field. The Wisconsin troops had also been there under Colonel Coburn; and while a portion of the regiment had remained under Colonel Utley, fought well, and were captured, about one-half of this command, when Forrest made his charge by the flank and rear, fell into disorder and, under Lieutenant Colonel E. Bloodgood, had quit the field in time to escape capture. General Forrest asked permission to attack these garrisons, and Van Dorn readily assented. On March 24th, Starnes, in command of the old Forrest Brigade, was directed to proceed in the direction of Brentwood and, leaving Franklin to the left, to cross Harpeth River six miles east of the town.

From this point he was to send a force along the turnpike and railroad between Brentwood and Franklin, cut the telegraph wires, tear up the railroad track, dispatch two regiments to attack the stockade, while the Fourth Tennessee was to be posted so as to prevent escape in the direction of Nashville or Triune. Colonel Starnes was to be on the ground and to attack on daylight of the 25th, with the understanding that Forrest, with Armstrong's brigade and the artillery, would join him by that hour and co-operate with him in the assault.

In obedience to orders, Starnes moved out with Biffle's regiment, his own Fourth Tennessee under Captain W. S. McLemore, and a part of Edmondson's regiment, and at midnight crossed the Harpeth at Davis's Mill. Fifteen men were sent forward to capture the enemy's pickets, which they failed to accomplish. The sentries wounded two of this detachment and alarmed the garrison. One of the sentries rode rapidly into Franklin and notified General Granger of the attack, and this soldier soon had the Union cavalry under Smith marching toward Brentwood. Before three o'clock Starnes had reached the Wilson turnpike near Brentwood, cut the telegraph wires, and destroyed the track near Mallory station. A strong picket force was then stationed on the Franklin turnpike at Holly-Tree Gap. This accomplished, six companies under Captain P. H. McBride were sent forward to take position behind the top of a hill some 350 yards east of the fortified camp at Brentwood. Edmondson's regiment was, as a precaution against surprise, stationed some distance in the rear. Everything was now in readiness for the assault whenever (as was expected) at daylight General Forrest should arrive upon the opposite side of the camp of the enemy.

Daylight came, but Armstrong and the artillery and General Forrest did not appear. Deeming himself too weak to attack so strong a place without cannon, and having waited until half past seven for his commander, Starnes, not doubting that Forrest had been compelled by some unexpected circumstance to abandon the undertaking, proceeded to extricate his command, and withdrew rapidly to the Hillsborough pike. Here he learned to his great chagrin that his chieftain had passed on by another road toward Brentwood at an early hour that morning.

Forrest had met with unlooked-for delay in getting across the Harpeth with his two guns, and when he reached the rendezvous Starnes had left. Nothing daunted, however, he straightway proceeded to business. Two companies of the Tenth Tennessee, under most explicit instructions, were hurried down the Hillsborough pike to guard his rear. There was not to be on this occasion a repetition of the Parker's Crossroads surprise. Two other companies were ordered to the pike in rear of the enemy to prevent their escape, and to warn him of the approach of succor from that direction. The remaining six companies and his escort Forrest led in person to the right of the road running from the Hillsborough pike to Brentwood. To the left of this road he ordered Armstrong to move with his brigade and two of Freeman's guns and at once attack the enemy at Brentwood. Riding with his escort at this moment rapidly to the Franklin turnpike, Forrest captured a courier with a dispatch from Colonel E. Bloodgood, commanding the fortified camp, to his superior at Franklin, asking for help. By this time the Union skirmishers were encountered, and Forrest directed Major Charles W. Anderson, with a white handkerchief on the tip of his saber, to advance and demand the usual immediate and unconditional surrender, with the "Murfreesboro attachment" of no quarter if resistance were made.

Not fully convinced of the vulnerability of his position, Colonel Bloodgood politely invited the Confederate general to come and take him if he could. The Confederate general was pleased to accept the invitation. The six companies of Cox's Tenth Tennessee then present were dismounted and ordered to attack the Federal position in front, while Armstrong was directed to move up with his men on foot and Freeman's artillery and attack from the other side. Meanwhile Colonel Bloodgood was not altogether idle. At a very early hour that morning, when Starnes had rudely awakened him, he had loaded and hitched up his wagon train in the hope of escaping in the direction of Nashville. Several companies of his command were formed as the advance guard of his retreating column. Thinking he might now make a run for it and break through before the cordon was complete, he started for Nashville. As the advance companies moved off, they had not proceeded over four hundred yards before Forrest attacked them with his escort, and they rushed back to the fortified camp. Colonel Bloodgood reports: "The last wagon had not left the camp when those in front were stopped by the enemy. The advanced companies had opened fire." At this juncture Major DeMoss, with the six companies of the Tenth Tennessee, drove in the Union skirmishers and was closing in on the Federal position from the front. The escort had followed the flying train guard to within short range of their stronghold, and with equal eagerness Armstrong came up from the opposite quarter and Freeman ran his guns into battery.

Then Colonel Bloodgood's heart sank within him. He reports: "I had barely time to post the other companies before I discovered that we were completely surrounded by the enemy in overwhelming force; they advanced rapidly, pressing me closely, and soon brought a battery of two pieces of artillery close up to my lines. I had no hope of aid from any quarter. I therefore deemed it best to surrender. The contest, from the opening of our fire to the time when the enemy had succeeded in surrounding me and was about bringing his artillery to bear, was from twenty-five to thirty minutes in duration." The troops surrendered here, which General Gordon Granger intimated were of the "milk-and-water variety," were 521 men and officers of the Twenty-second Wisconsin, with a number of teamsters and a large supply of stores in the depot, and camp equipage, tents, etc.

Fully aware of the fact that his position thus far within the enemy's lines, and between two large bodies of troops stationed at Nashville and Franklin, was one of great danger, Forrest, before hastening to attack the stockade at the Harpeth railroad bridge, ordered his faithful lieutenant, General Armstrong, to hurry the prisoners, arms, wagons, and all portable captured property toward the Hillsborough pike and thence to the rear, and then to destroy the depot, tents, and everything which could not be carried away. He also at this time directed Colonel J. H. Lewis of the Sixth Tennessee Cavalry to dash down the highway toward Nashville, drive in the enemy's pickets at that quarter, and create the impression that an attack was there impending. General Forrest, now with the Fourth Mississippi and Tenth Tennessee, his escort, and Freeman's two guns, scurried away at breakneck speed over the mile and a half between Brentwood and the Harpeth bridge and stockade, and without any preliminary parley surrounded the position, unlimbered one of the guns, and fired a salute which sent the echoes reverberating over the hills and the splinters flying among the astonished Michiganders who composed the garrison.

Turning to Major Anderson of his staff, Forrest said: "Major, take in a flag of truce, and tell them I have them completely surrounded, and if they don't surrender I'll blow hell out of them in five minutes and won't take one of them alive if I have to sacrifice my men in storming their stockade." The staff officer seached in vain for the white handkerchief used at Brentwood. It was the only one in the command, and had been lost. "Strip off your shirt, major!" said the general, fully appreciative of the humor of the situation. Off came the garment (not the whitest of linen, for in those busy days of war the laundry was an unknown quantity), and, tying the shirt to his sword, away rode the messenger of peace. Captain Bassett and the garrison took in the situation and surrendered.

The Federal official records show that 230 officers and men of the Twenty-second Michigan Infantry were surrendered. The other members of this regiment had done very creditable fighting under Colonel Coburn on March 5th.

Colonel James Gordon, commanding the Fourth Mississippi of Armstrong's brigade, says: "General Forrest led the advance in person, followed by one piece of artillery and my squadrons. One gun was fired, and the fort surrendered."[4]

General Forrest reports the capture here of 275 prisoners, eleven wagons, and three ambulances.[5] The railroad bridge and all supplies which could not be brought off were destroyed, and the prisoners and troops hurried away toward Spring Hill via the Hillsborough pike.

So far the expedition was to the Confederate leader, notwithstanding the absence of Starnes's brigade, a gratifying success, and without the loss of a man. Colonel Bloodgood reported the Confederates that captured him as from five to eight thousand men. There were present only Forrest's escort, numbering sixty, the Fourth Mississippi, Tenth and Sixth Tennessee regiments, and two guns—the whole force available for assault not over 1000. In fact, the Sixth Tennessee only arrived in time to see the surrender and "were not engaged" at Brentwood;[6] and had Colonel Bloodgood, with his 750 effective men and teamsters and other camp retainers, made as gallant a struggle as their comrades did at Thompson's Station, they would in all probability have held the Confederates off until help arrived, for Forrest says: "Before the rear of my command reached the Hillsborough pike, they were attacked by a force of Federal cavalry."

It was at this moment that trouble began. Major General Gordon Granger, a vigilant officer, who in this same year of 1863 at Chickamauga won an enviable fame by his "march to Thomas" in the crisis of that battle, and who during that movement was violently assaulted by Forrest, was now almost in contact with this intrepid cavalryman. His headquarters were in Franklin at this date, and when Starnes struck the two Federal outposts, five and seven miles distant, between three and four o'clock on the morning of the 25th, one of these escaped and came tearing like a modern Paul Revere into Franklin at daylight and roused the sleeping major general and the garrison. Granger hastened to the telegraph office to warn Colonel Bloodgood, but, alas, too late!

[4] *Ibid.,* vol. xxiii, part i, p. 190.
[5] *Ibid.,* p. 188.
[6] *Ibid.,* vol. xxiii, part i, p. 191.

Starnes had cut the wires. He says: "Soon after daylight, my pickets on the Columbia, Carter's Creek, and Hillsborough roads were attacked. I had sent the balance of the cavalry to look after the train and guards at Brentwood."[7]

The cavalry sent out to save Brentwood and the bridge consisted of the Second Michigan, Ninth Pennsylvania, and Fourth and Sixth Kentucky (Union) cavalry regiments, under Brigadier General Green Clay Smith; and according to the official report of this affair by the general, he wrought tremendous havoc among the Confederates. The boastful and extravagant tone of this document brings to mind the well-known lines of Praed:

> There was a dragon in Arthur's time,
> When dragons and griffins were quoted prime,
> Of monstrous reputation;
> Up and down and far and wide
> He roamed about in his scaly pride,
> And even at morn and even-tide
> He made such rivers of blood to run,
> As shocked the sight of the burning sun,
> And deluged half the nation.

When Smith reached Brentwood, he says: "The rebels had accomplished their work, burned the bridge, captured the infantry posted there, and were moving westerly with our wagons, guns, and prisoners." The Ninth Pennsylvania, the two Kentucky regiments, and a portion of the Second Michigan were dispatched rapidly after the flying raiders. The balance of the Michiganders were sent, by another route in the same general direction, to close in on the rear of the captured train. Three and a half miles from Brentwood the tail of the procession was struck.

As soon as the prisoners at Brentwood were captured, details from Armstrong's brigade had been called off and the Federals were marched at a rapid pace to the rear. The second detachment taken at Harpeth bridge stockade followed in quick order, the slower-moving wagons came next, and then the work of destruction was completed.

Lewis's Sixth Tennessee went toward Nashville as ordered, drove in the various pickets in sight of the capital, made some captures, marched

[7] *Ibid.,* p. 177.

halfway round that city, and on the 27th, without loss, rejoined its brigade at Spring Hill, bringing a wagon and team taken within three miles of Nashville. The companies of the Tenth Tennessee and Fourth Mississippi (about 400 men left after the detail to guard prisoners had been made) were, under General Armstrong, directed to follow and protect the captured train. The Tenth Tennessee was in the rear, but was destined not long to occupy this position. A dozen stragglers from one of Armstrong's regiments, seeking what they might devour, had lingered too long about the burning storehouse at Brentwood, and were leisurely following in the wake of the rear guard, when they suddenly found themselves run into by the Sixth Kentucky and Second Michigan Cavalry in columns of fours, with drawn sabers and at full speed.

Without firing a shot or making resistance enough to give Major DeMoss warning that the Union troopers were so close upon him in force, this straggling squad stampeded and dashed into the rear company of the Tennessee detachment, throwing them into a panic which spread throughout the command like a prairie fire. In utter and ridiculous confusion these troops, accustomed to different conduct in the presence of an enemy, broke and converted their organization into a helpless mob, each struggling to outrun the other. Some kept to the road, while others took to the woods and byways for escape. The luckless runaways mounted on slow horses were having an unhappy time of it in the rear, and a number were sabered and captured.[8] Colonel Gordon, with only three companies of his Fourth Mississippi, was in front and heard the stampede in time to throw one company into line, and about 200 yards farther back the other two companies were formed. The Union advance was in this way temporarily checked, but the Seventh Pennsylvania, lining up behind the Kentuckians and swinging around Gordon's flank, soon sent him and his Mississippians in wild retreat in the wake of the remnant of the Tenth Tennessee. The Federals had now retaken many of the wagons loaded with the captured property and promptly turned them about toward Franklin.

Forrest, who with his escort and the guns had reached the head of the retiring column, having heard of the disaster at the rear, now hastily retraced his steps and took charge of affairs. With the escort he threw himself in front of the frightened, panic-stricken men and ordered them to halt and fall in line. Seeing that some of these paid no attention

[8] The Tenth Tennessee lost one killed, three wounded, and nineteen captured.

to his command, he seized a double-barrel shotgun from one of his men and emptied both barrels into a squad of the dismayed troopers who refused to halt. This radical measure was immediately effective, and he was soon able to make a very respectable showing with the troops he had rallied.[9]

Fortunately, Starnes, who earlier in the morning had gone in pursuit of a foraging train some two miles distant from his position on the Hillsborough pike, hearing that the captured train had been followed by Smith's brigade, hurried back and came on the scene just as Forrest was rallying the disordered troops of Armstrong's brigade. With Forrest and Starnes at hand, General Green Clay Smith found he had some very serious business before him. His chief, General Granger, says: "At this juncture, and as success seemed certain, Forrest came on with a strong brigade on the left, and General Smith was forced to fall back on Brentwood, burning a portion of the wagons and destroying such arms as he could not bring away.[10]

Colonel J. W. Starnes reports: "I charged them, which caused them to fall back with great precipitation. They were retreating very rapidly when General Forrest ordered us to return."[11] Forrest says: "They succeeded in getting possession of several of the wagons captured at the stockade, and cut out and stampeded the mules. The enemy were repulsed and driven back to Brentwood, but, having no teams, several of the wagons were burned. We brought away three ambulances and harness, nine six-horse wagons and teams and harness, two two-horse wagons, sixty mules and six horses, which were placed in charge of the assistant quartermaster at Columbia. Many of the command who had inferior guns, muskets, shotguns, etc., exchanged them on the field, placing their old guns in the wagons in lieu of them."[12]

The entire Confederate loss in this expedition was one officer and three men killed, three officers and thirteen men wounded, and thirty-nine men captured or missing; total, fifty-nine. The Union loss was four killed, nineteen wounded, and four missing, in Smith's pursuing cavalry; and 750 officers and men captured at Brentwood and Harpeth bridge, all of whom were brought away in safety. Total loss, 758—

[9] Mr. Nat Baxter, Jr., of Nashville, Tennessee, witnessed this incident.
[10] *Official Records*, vol. xxiii, part i, p. 178.
[11] *Ibid.*, p. 184.
[12] *Ibid.*, p. 188.

not including teamsters and other employees. General Smith's report reads like a page from the history of the Knight of Salamanca:

The loss of the enemy was not less, in the judgment of my officers and myself, than from four to five hundred in killed, wounded, and prisoners. My men shot with wonderful and fearful aim. The five-shooters of the Second Michigan, and the rapidity with which the Burnside carbine could be loaded, poured such a constant and deadly volley into their ranks, and felled so many, that but for such overwhelming forces, numbering not less than five thousand, our success would have been unquestioned. Captain Kimmel (of the Seventh Pennsylvania), when falling back, came across some fifteen or twenty loaded guns. He stood, fired, and broke, until all were unloaded at the enemy and broken over a tree. It was a good deed, and he deserves praise.[13]

Brigadier General James A. Garfield, chief of staff to Major General W. S. Rosecrans, complimenting Smith's report with seeming credulity, congratulated him and his command of "six or seven hundred of the Second Michigan, Ninth Pennsylvania, Fourth and Sixth Kentucky, upon the cavalry battle of Little Harpeth with the rebel cavalry under Forrest, Starnes, and Biffle."[14] The facts are that six or seven hundred Union cavalry, excellent and tried soldiers, with the most modern and effective weapons of that period (five-shooting rifles and Burnside breech-loading carbines), attacked vigorously less than five hundred Confederate cavalry guarding a captured train, threw the guard into panic, and ran them for several miles, recapturing a greater portion of the train. Forrest and Starnes then came to the rescue with a superior force, and drove the Federals back almost as rapidly as they had advanced, recaptured or caused the enemy to burn the wagons, and then marched with the prisoners and the remainder of the train to the rear. Not a single Federal prisoner was recaptured.

General Braxton Bragg, on March 31st, officially announced to the army

with pride and gratification two brilliant and successful affairs achieved by the cavalry of Major-General Van Dorn. On the 5th inst. Major-General Van Dorn made a gallant charge upon a large force of the enemy at Thompson's station. He routed them, killed and wounded a large number, and captured 1221 prisoners, including 73 commissioned officers and many

[13] *Ibid.*, p. 181.
[14] *Ibid.*, p. 182.

arms. On the 25th, Brigadier-General Forrest, with the troops of his command, daringly assailed the enemy at Brentwood, who could not withstand the vigor and energy of the attack and surrendered. The result of this successful expedition was the capture of 750 prisoners, and 35 commissioned officers, with all their arms, accoutrements, ammunition, and sixteen wagons and teams. The skilful manner in which these generals achieved such success exhibits clearly the judgment, discipline, and good conduct of the brave troops of their command. Such signal examples of duty deserve the applause and gratitude of their comrades in arms and their country.

The people of the South, and the army, while detracting nothing from the courage and capacity of General Van Dorn, whose death a few weeks later was widely lamented, gave to the genius of Forrest the chief credit for these brilliant results. Of the prisoners taken (about 2000 in all), 1800 surrendered directly to Forrest. Major General W. S. Rosecrans expresses also his appreciation of the Confederate cavalryman at this period. On March 25, 1863, at 9.30 P.M., he wired General in Chief H. W. Halleck: "Rebels appear to me just now engaged in giving me occupation. Regret to learn from Granger that three hundred more of his men were captured to-day at Brentwood, nine miles in his rear, by cavalry. I do not think it prudent to advance from this position until I am better informed."

The affair at Brentwood came very near being the cause of a personal encounter between Generals Van Dorn and Forrest. Both were men of unquestionable courage and of high spirit, not only quick to resent a seeming indignity, but equally quick to make the *amende honorable* when convinced of error. The major general's quartermaster had complained that all of the arms and property captured by Forrest had not been turned over to his department.

Forrest explained that, as was his custom, he had directed the property to be turned over to the quartermaster; but he did not see why, since his men had made the captures, they did not have a right to take the best guns and equipment for themselves, and turn over to the quartermaster those they had discarded. He thought this proper and that his men were entitled to the privilege. Of course, General Van Dorn, who was a West Pointer and a disciplinarian, failed to agree with his subordinate. He was evidently in bad humor on account of the great credit which had been given to Forrest by the Southern papers for the part he had taken in the capture of Coburn's troops at Thompson's

Station. This conversation took place at Van Dorn's headquarters at Spring Hill, and Major J. Minnick Williams of Nashville, and of General Van Dorn's staff, was the only witness present.

Major Williams says that Van Dorn, after questioning Forrest in regard to the property captured at Brentwood, remarked to him: "I am informed that several articles published in the *Chattanooga Rebel,* in which the honors at Thompson's Station and Brentwood were claimed for yourself, were written by one of your staff." Forrest flew into a furious rage at this assertion, and replied in great anger to General Van Dorn: "I know nothing of the articles you refer to, and I demand from you your authority for this assertion. I shall hold him responsible and make him eat his words, or run my sabre through him; and I say to you as well, that I will hold you personally responsible if you do not produce the author." General Van Dorn turned to Major Williams, saying: "Major, do you know the author of those publications?" Major Williams replied: "I do not; and I think, general, that you have done General Forrest an injustice in the suspicion that the articles originated from his headquarters." Van Dorn replied quickly: "I do not assert, nor do I believe, that General Forrest inspired those articles, or had any knowledge of them." Forrest accepted the explanation with quiet dignity and evident satisfaction, saying: "General Van Dorn and I have enough to do fighting the enemies of our country without fighting each other."[15]

The two shook hands and parted, never to meet again. It is a coincidence worthy of remark that within a month from this interview Van Dorn's career was ended, a victim of private vengeance, while Forrest was desperately (at first thought mortally) wounded by a subordinate officer, whose transfer to another command, by order of his superior, he construed as a reflection upon his courage.

From March 25th until April 9th General Forrest and his command were engaged on picket, scouting and outpost duties between Spring Hill and Franklin. Major General Van Dorn, with a view to a reconnaissance in force and a diversion in favor of Bragg's right wing in front of Tullahoma, moved early on the morning of April 10th to attack Franklin, garrisoned by a strong force under Major General Gordon Granger. It would have been better for the Confederate general

[15] The author is indebted to Captain John W. Morton of Nashville for an account of this incident, which he received from Major Williams.

if he had made his assault earlier by twenty-four hours, for Granger received a strong accession to his army just in the nick of time to save him from disaster. General D. S. Stanley, with his brigade of cavalry (1600 effectives), arrived near Franklin at 10 A.M. on the 10th, and later in the day his troops came unexpectedly on the flank of Starnes's brigade and Freeman's battery with very serious results to the Southerners.

That the intention of Van Dorn was to draw troops from Rosecrans's left wing and not to attempt the capture of Franklin (as claimed by Granger in his official report) is evident, not only from the feeble nature of the assault, but from the fact that the Confederate leader had not maintained the secrecy as to his advance which usually characterized such movements by him. In fact, so well was it known that he proposed to assail Granger at this time that General Rosecrans had on the 9th of April hurried Stanley with an excellent cavalry division over from Murfreesboro to be on hand to assist him during Van Dorn's promised attack.[16] General Granger says: "For several days previous I had received information that the attack would be made by General Van Dorn on the 9th."[17]

At 9.30 P.M., after the Confederates had fallen back to their quarters at Spring Hill, Rosecrans dispatched to Halleck: "The attack was repulsed so easily that I am waiting to know whether it was more than a reconnaissance."

In this affair Van Dorn's troops consisted of two cavalry divisions under W. H. Jackson and Forrest respectively, about 3100 in all, with Freeman's battery of six pieces. Forrest, with Armstrong's brigade in front and Starnes's following at an interval of nearly two miles, marched by the Lewisburg pike, while General Van Dorn rode with Jackson's division along the turnpike leading from Columbia to Franklin. These two highways gradually converge to enter this town from the south. On the morning of the attack General Granger states that he had at hand 5194 effective infantry, 2728 cavalry, and eighteen field and two siege guns. There was also a fort crowning a knoll or rise of ground in the town, on the north bank of Harpeth River, with an elevation of forty feet above the surrounding country. There were two twenty-four-pounder siege guns and two three-inch rifled guns in this stronghold. He says: "The fort commands most of the approaches to Franklin

[16] *Official Records*, vol. xxiii, part i, p. 221.
[17] *Ibid.*, p. 222.

north of the Harpeth, and all from the south, save that part of the plateau covered by houses in the southwest part of the town."

With all the evidence now available, even with the memory of the rash and bloody attack on Corinth in mind, it would not be just to accuse General Van Dorn of the supreme folly of trying to capture such a stronghold, protected by a garrison with superior equipment and more than double in numbers the cavalry with which he assailed it. And had not General Granger handled his troops on this occasion so awkwardly, he so far outnumbered the Confederates that he had it in his power to inflict upon them very serious damage.

It was 10.30 A.M. on the 10th when the pickets on the Columbia pike were driven in and the Fortieth Ohio Infantry was attacked by Jackson's advance. About the same time Armstrong's brigade of Forrest's division encountered the Federal infantry stationed in the outskirts of Franklin, where the Lewisburg pike approaches. The attack was made with such lack of vigor that General Granger says he was convinced that the movement on his front was a feint, and that the garrison at Brentwood was again to be the real object of the Confederates. He says: "I received a telegram from General Morgan, at Brentwood, that his pickets were driven in. . . . I sent all of my own cavalry, under Brigadier General G. C. Smith, in great haste to the relief of that post." These troops disappeared down the Brentwood road, on what turned out to be a wild-goose chase, and for that day were lost to Granger and to usefulness. The Union commander adds, in ill-concealed disgust: "Afterwards I learned that General Morgan's pickets had been driven in by three or four Negroes walking along the road, a half-hour after General Green Clay Smith's cavalry had gone, and too late for it to return and take part in the action."

After a very creditable resistance, Jackson had driven the Fortieth Ohio Infantry into Franklin, forcing them into the houses and to the fort for protection and better defense. Armstrong and Forrest were also now making such a show of assault at their end of the line that Granger determined upon a new plan of action. The appearance of two of Freeman's guns, which were in the advance with Armstrong, and some shells they sent flying into the town, emphasized the necessity for the Union general's change of plan. He sent word for all the guns in the fort to open on anything in sight, which they promptly did.

About this time Armstrong's attack suddenly slackened, and for good reason. Something important had transpired about two miles rearward of his position. The Federals had met with the only success achieved for the day, and this came about because General Stanley went contrary to the plan and orders of General Granger. Stanley, with his division of cavalry, had been posted four miles from Franklin, on the Murfreesboro road, with orders to remain on the north side of the Harpeth River and watch the crossing at Hughes's Mill. Having foolishly lost one cavalry division by sending it where it was not needed, Granger now had to send two infantry regiments of Gilbert's division and two guns (he had eighteen in all) to the vicinity of Hughes's Mill to join Stanley, who with the reinforcements was at the proper moment to cross the Harpeth there and throw his troops in Forrest's rear with (as Granger hoped) direful results to the enemy. He said later that if things had gone right he could have taken two or three thousand of Van Dorn's command. But Stanley was in one particular like Forrest—he had not the patience to keep still while anything of interest was transpiring within sight or sound. He convinced himself that the interests of the service required his presence wherever there was a chance for a fight. His gallantry on this same ground on that memorable day in December, 1864, is worthy of record.

Gilbert's infantry had not gone a mile on the second wild-goose hunt of the day when Granger was shocked to learn from Stanley that "he had crossed the river at Hughes's ford, moved to the Lewisburg pike, and had attacked the enemy in flank." The kaleidoscopic changes which had occurred in his command were enough to puzzle even so good a soldier and fighter as General Gordon Granger, but it was too late now to make another change. Stanley had crossed the Rubicon, and nothing was left for Gilbert's infantry but to rush forward as rapidly as possible and to endeavor to reach the ford before he might be driven back. "At the same time I hurried General Baird's division across the pontoon-bridge, but it was too late—he (Stanley) was driven back across the river before the reinforcements could reach it."

As Forrest's division approached Franklin he took two of Freeman's guns in advance with Armstrong's brigade, and it was from these guns that the shells were fired which Granger mentions in his report. Freeman's four remaining pieces, under his personal command, came on with Starnes's brigade, which was more than two miles in the rear of Armstrong. Evidently neither Starnes nor Freeman was deemed necessary to reconnaissance. As they approached Franklin, Biffle's regiment was moving in front, then, at a considerable interval, the four pieces of artillery, followed by the remainder of Starnes's brigade, strung out along the pike upon which they were marching. The cannonade in front gave Starnes notice that the fighting was away off, and this usually vigilant officer did not appreciate the necessity of throwing out flankers at that distance in the rear of the firing. Stanley, intending to strike Armstrong in the rear at Hughes's Mill, had already crossed his division and was moving rapidly toward the Lewisburg pike, along which Starnes in fancied security was then marching in column.

Unexpectedly to General Stanley, as well as to Colonel Starnes, they collided. At the mill, the road leading up to the Lewisburg pike forked. By the route nearest to Franklin it was one mile to the turnpike; by the other it was one mile and a half. On the former road Stanley dispatched one of his brigades, and on the latter another detachment with the Fourth Regular Cavalry in advance. This latter column arrived within one hundred yards of the Lewisburg turnpike before its presence was known to the Confederates. Captain Freeman, seeing them in such close proximity and without adequate protection, instantly threw his four pieces into position; but before he could fire a single shot two companies of these hardy riders swept down upon him, driving off whatever cavalry was near, and capturing him with his guns and about thirty-six members of his battery.

Starnes, who was in advance with Biffle's regiment, which had only a few minutes previous passed toward Franklin, hearing the tumult in his rear, faced his command about and hurried on to the scene of the disaster. As they arrived, the next regiment following Freeman's guns and marching from Spring Hill toward Franklin came up. Colonel Starnes lost no time in retrieving the error made in not guarding his flanks. In person he led a furious assault upon the Union troopers, and drove them in short order from the field, from which they retreated rapidly toward Hughes's Mill and across the Harpeth River. The battery was recaptured and carried safely back to Spring Hill, where the damage done by the Federals while it was in their hands was soon repaired.

Forrest, however, sustained one loss on this occasion which he then deemed irreparable and ever deeply deplored. As the prisoners were being hurried from the field to prevent recapture, it is asserted that Captain Freeman was shot dead by a member of the Fourth Regular

Cavalry because he did not move to the rear as rapidly as he was ordered. As an officer of the artillery he was not in fit condition nor physically able to maintain a rapid pace on foot for the mile and a half which these troopers had to traverse to reach the ford and cross the Harpeth. He soon became so exhausted that he was compelled to slacken his gait, and fell dead from a bullet in his brain.

A survivor of this incident of Freeman's battery, Lieutenant Nat Baxter, has given the writer the following interesting account of this affair:

When we were within a few miles of Franklin, we were surprised by the Fourth Regular Cavalry. Not suspecting the proximity of any Federals nearer than Franklin, where General Forrest was then skirmishing with the enemy, we were utterly unprepared for the sudden collision with this cavalry. Starnes was ahead of us and out of sight on the turnpike, and about a half-mile in our rear another regiment of our cavalry was advancing, and the portion of our battery with us was strung out along the pike. I remember I was riding about the centre of the battery, behind the second gun, with my left leg thrown over the saddle in a careless manner. Captain Freeman was just in front, at the head of the column. On the right of the road, going in the direction of Franklin, was a woodland; between it and the turnpike there was no fence. On the left of the road there was a high new plank fence.

Suddenly I noticed Captain Freeman straighten himself in his saddle, rein his horse up quickly as if much excited, and heard him give a sharp, quick command, which was to throw the guns into action and load them at once. Looking up, I saw a squadron of Federal cavalry charging right at us from this woodland, not more than one hundred yards off, and then at a full gallop. I rushed to the gun, dismounted, turned my horse loose, and took a hand to ram the charge down the piece. I succeeded in loading the gun, which would have been discharged but for a faulty friction-primer which failed to explode. Before we could adjust another primer the cavalry were among us, using their sabres or six-shooters. I endeavored to escape on foot by leaping over the high board fence, but, being unarmed, before I could gain the woods on the opposite side of the field across which I was running I was overtaken and compelled to surrender.

The captured men and officers were immediately sent to the rear on foot. We had not proceeded more than a quarter of a mile from the scene of the disaster before the Federal cavalry that had captured us came running back to where we were moving along in rapid retreat. I did not see Captain Freeman, as he had been taken prisoner a few minutes before I was captured. We were forced to run in front of the Federal troopers at the muzzles of their pistols, they shouting at us constantly that they would shoot us down if we did not make better time. I am convinced from their manner towards myself in this particular that they would have killed me instantly had I slackened my pace.

Another officer of this battery,[18] who was present, has given me the following statement:

I commanded the second section of the battery, but escaped capture by being a short distance in the rear at the time of the attack. Captain Freeman had given me permission to look after my brother, whose horse had fallen with him, and who was reported badly injured. I was just returning and had reached the rear caisson of our battery when the Federals rode among the men in charge of the advanced gun. As Dr. Skelton, assistant surgeon of the battery, and Captain Freeman, both of whom were captured, were being hurried from the field, the Federals ordered them to "double quick" or they would shoot them. Freeman replied that he could not go any faster, as he was thoroughly exhausted with the effort he had already made and was then making. Both he and the surgeon were then shot, a bullet passing through the doctor's hand as he threw it up asking them not to shoot.

After his exchange, Dr. Skelton said that the report that Freeman had offered resistance, or had feigned inability to run faster as ordered, was not true. He was with Freeman when he was killed, and Captain Freeman had told the Federal who shot him that he could not go any faster. He offered no resistance and made no effort to escape.

General Forrest was overwhelmed with grief at the death of his gallant artilleryman. When he arrived on the field and joined in the assault which drove Stanley's troopers across the Harpeth River, Lieutenant Douglas was with him. As he came up to the spot where the body of Captain Freeman was discovered, Forrest, deeply agitated, dismounted and took Freeman's hand in his to see if he were really dead. With tears welling from his eyes, and in a voice trembling with emotion, he said, "Brave man; none braver!"

Some of Forrest's men never forgot or forgave the killing of Captain Freeman, and treasured to the extreme of retaliation a lasting and bitter resentment against this command. In speaking of the bravery of this officer, one who served side by side with him said: "His favorite

[18] Lieutenant E. H. Douglas of Franklin, Tennessee.

pieces were his twelve-pounder howitzers, his preferred ammunition two-thirds canister, and his distance as close as his general would let him go."[19]

The retreat of Stanley ended the fighting. At dark the Confederates retired to Spring Hill and went into camp. General Stanley's division in this affair lost six killed, nineteen wounded, and seventeen prisoners; Armstrong's brigade, one killed, eleven wounded, and two missing; Starnes's, three killed, sixteen wounded, and two missing; Forrest's escort company lost four wounded; Freeman's battery, one killed, one wounded, and twenty-nine prisoners. Total in Forrest's command, seventy. Jackson's division, as reported by Colonel F. G. Mitchell of the Fortieth Ohio, who fought in his front, lost seventeen killed, fourteen wounded, and thirteen prisoners.[20] The Union forces on this part of the field admit a loss of three killed, four wounded, and ten missing.[21] If the Confederate commander or General Jackson ever made an official report of this expedition, it did not find its way into the records. Forrest reported his losses as above given. It is very probable that the death of General Van Dorn soon after this event will explain why his official account does not appear.

[19] *Campaigns of General N. B. Forrest.*
[20] *Official Records,* vol. xxiii, part i, p. 229.
[21] *Ibid.,* p. 240.

The Pursuit and Capture of Streight's Raiders

M AJOR General Braxton Bragg, commanding the Confederate Army of Tennessee in December of 1862, had tried the fortunes of war in the great and bloody battle of Murfreesboro, and, although he was not beaten from the field, the tide of battle did not turn in his favor, and he withdrew his infantry to the line of Tullahoma, two days' march southward from the battlefield. Three months later, in the spring of 1863, it became evident that Major General W. S. Rosecrans was preparing either to fight or to maneuver Bragg south of the Tennessee River. Knowing what a natural stronghold Chattanooga was, he felt sure that the Confederate general would stop there and give him endless trouble unless he could do something which would compel him to continue his retreat beyond that point and into Georgia.

It occurred to his fertile mind that if he could secure the destruction of the two important railroads leading from Chattanooga—one to Atlanta and the other to Knoxville—about the time that he could force Bragg's army southward from Tullahoma, the latter's chance of supplying his troops at Chattanooga, with these highways of commerce destroyed, would appear so slim that he would leave this place behind him and go to Dalton or Atlanta without a stop. General Rosecrans wanted Chattanooga very badly. Two desperate ventures were tried to destroy these invaluable railroads, and both came to grief. The story of Andrews' Raid will ever remain an attractive yet pathetic chapter in American history, and Streight's bold raid and Forrest's relentless pursuit, the story of which "reads like a romance,"[1] will interest the world as long as women "bring forth male children."

Among the subordinates in the Army of the Cumberland who had

[1] General Lord Wolseley.

seriously reflected upon this project, there was a man of great courage and activity, and not lacking in resources. He ventured to submit to General Thomas J. Wood a plan which this officer conveyed to Brigadier General James A. Garfield, who was then chief of staff to Rosecrans, and later President of the United States. Garfield became enthusiastic over Streight's proposition, conveyed it to General Rosecrans, and, after discussion, the following plan of operations was determined upon:

A body of men, of well-attested pluck and endurance, were to be selected, armed, and equipped with a special view to the success of this undertaking. They were to be transported by steamers from Nashville down the Cumberland and Ohio and up the Tennessee to Eastport, Mississippi, near the Alabama interstate line. This would bring the troops, at the beginning of their overland journey, safe from all unnecessary exertion or fatigue until the crucial moment should come.

From twenty to forty miles south of the Tennessee River, and running nearly east and west across the northern portion of the State of Alabama, is a mountainous belt of country sparsely inhabited, and at that time without railroad or telegraphic communications. A good proportion of the inhabitants of this barren tract were Union sympathizers, and many of them had relatives in the Federal army. For the reason that these sympathizers lived along this line, and on account of its remoteness from the telegraph, Colonel Streight had wisely selected this as his route for the movement into Georgia. As there were many rugged hills and mountains to cross, and as the roads were generally in a wretched condition, it was deemed a wise precaution to mount the troops for this expedition on mules, since these hardy animals are surer of foot in difficult going and can stand greater hardships on less forage than horses.

To distract attention from Streight's raid, and at the same time to fight off any pursuing column, a large body of infantry and cavalry was to precede the expedition, attack Tuscumbia on the Tennessee River in north Alabama, drive everything in the shape of a Confederate soldier up the valley toward Decatur, and there hold them engaged until the "flying column" got a running start.

The hero of the hour was Colonel Abel D. Streight, of Indiana. It was he whose plan had been accepted, and he was to have the honor of leadership. On April 7th he received an order to repair to Nashville, and to fit out his command as speedily as possible "for an expedition to the interior of Alabama and Georgia, for the purpose of destroying the railroads in that country."

The command selected by Colonel Streight was his own, the Fifty-first Indiana regiment; the Seventy-third Indiana, Colonel Gilbert Hathaway; the Third Ohio, Colonel Orris A. Lawson; the Eighteenth Illinois, Lieutenant Colonel Andrew F. Rogers; and two companies of Alabama (Union) cavalry under Captain D. D. Smith—about 2000 officers and men.

On April 9th he notified Generals Rosecrans and Garfield: "We can start within three hours from the time of receiving orders."[2] This lively Hoosier was anxious for the foray, and did not propose to lose any time. In his correspondence with the Union headquarters, he desired to know "if it would be violating the rules of war should I see fit to dress any number of men—say two companies—after the promiscuous Southern style?" The reply does not appear in the records, but as his troops went on the march wearing their "blue blouses," there can be no doubt Rosecrans said no to the suggestion. General Rosecrans had not forgotten the unfortunate Andrews raiders, who had dressed themselves after the "promiscuous Southern style," and, being in citizen's clothes when captured, had practically tied the rope around their own necks, and a number of them paid the penalty of their folly with their lives.

On the afternoon of the 10th of April the leader of this expedition received orders from General Garfield to embark at once on steamers and proceed to Palmyra, on the Cumberland River. At this point he was to land his troops and march across the country to Fort Henry, on the Tennessee. Streight reached Palmyra on the 11th, disembarked, and sent the fleet around to the Ohio and up the Tennessee to Fort Henry, where he arrived on the 15th, one day ahead of the boats. He brought with him every mule in all that country upon which he could lay his hands, for he had orders to strip the land of these useful animals as he went. On the 17th the expedition was again afloat convoyed by two gunboats and General Ellet, with a brigade of marines, and reached Eastport, Mississippi, on the 19th of April, where his command was finally disembarked.

Due notice of his coming had been given by General Rosecrans:

[2] *Official Records,* vol. xxiii, part i, p. 225.

"Colonel Streight, with near two thousand picked men, will probably reach Eastport by Thursday. Dodge, with the marine brigade and the gunboats, can occupy or whip the Tuscumbia forces, and let my force go directly to its main object—the destruction of the railroads. This great enterprise, fraught with great consequences, is commended to Dodge's care, enjoining on him to despatch Streight by every means to his destination. Nothing should for a moment arrest his progress."[3]

Colonel Streight had no sooner set foot on land than he hastened to a conference with General Grenville M. Dodge, who with 5500 infantry and cavalry had already arrived at Bear Creek, twelve miles from Eastport. This officer had encountered a small force of Confederate cavalry west of Bear Creek, at Glendale, but these had retired before his advance to the creek; and on April 17th, without much difficulty, he succeeded in crossing this stream, and marched thirteen miles toward Tuscumbia. Colonel P. D. Roddey, with a small brigade of cavalry, attacked one of his columns here with such vigor that he threw it into confusion, captured two pieces of artillery, twenty-two artillerists, and one company of mounted infantry; and although Dodge retook one of the guns, he was so troubled over the results of the day and the non-arrival of Streight's column that be fell back to Bear Creek to await his arrival and to send for more help. He telegraphed to Corinth for Fuller's brigade, 2000 strong, and another battery, all of which reached him in good time, increasing his force, exclusive of Streight's raiders, to 7500 men. At that time he was confronted only by a single brigade of cavalry under Roddey.

At Eastport the woes which an unkind fate had in store for the gallant Hoosier raider and his band began to be in evidence. While he was absent, in conference with General Dodge until midnight, the great cargo of mules had been put ashore, and with clarion tones these noisy animals were celebrating their deliverance from their natural dread of a watery grave. Some irresponsible Westerner, who had nothing to do but to wear a blue uniform, carry a musket, and fight, suggested that since this species of animal did not appear upon the roster of the original ark, they had determined on this occasion to celebrate loud enough to make up for all past slights. The braying of mules was not an unusual sound to Roddey's cavalry, who were hovering about the Federal encampment, with the true instinct of Confederate cavalrymen

---

[3] *Ibid.,* vol. xxiii, part ii, p. 232.

seeking what they might devour. Many of them in this busy time of war were glad enough to get even a mule to ride, and it is said of the men who took General Dodge's cannon only a few days before that they were experts in selecting those which were fast.

During the night, after the fashion of Comanches, they crept into Colonel Streight's corral and, with hoots and yells and the firing of guns and pistols, stampeded this army of mules. This officer says: "Daylight next morning revealed to me the fact that nearly four hundred of our best animals were gone. All of that day and part of the next were spent in scouring the country to recover them, but only about two hundred of the lost number were recovered. The remainder fell into the hands of the enemy. The loss of these animals was a heavy blow to my command, for besides detaining us nearly two days at Eastport, and running down our stock in searching the country to recover them, it caused still further delay at Tuscumbia to supply their places."[4]

Colonel Roddey and his troopers were doing very effective work. They never did better service than this, and when the gallant fight they made under brave Colonel W. A. Johnson at Brice's Crossroads is recalled, no greater compliment could be paid them. The delay thus caused in the execution of this bold conception of the Federal commander and his trusted subordinate was fatal to its success. It gave General Bragg time to hear of it and to select for its defeat the man of all men capable of its accomplishment.

Colonel Streight with his caravan filed out of Eastport on the afternoon of April 21, 1863, and brought up the rear of Dodge's troops, which were continually skirmishing with the enemy as they advanced as far as Tuscumbia. So thoroughly was Roddey doing his work that it took the Union forces (four times his number) until 5 P.M. on the 24th of April to reach Tuscumbia. At this place General Dodge, according to Streight, supplied him with two hundred mules and six wagons to haul his ammunition and rations; but General Dodge officially reports: "I took horses and mules from my teams and mounted infantry and furnished him some six hundred head. I also turned over ten thousand rations hard bread." The troops were now carefully inspected by the surgeon of the command, and all men not fit for the arduous duties to be undertaken were sent to the rear. The colonel says: "This reduced my command to fifteen hundred men."

[4] Colonel Streight's official report.

On the 25th, Colonel Streight received a piece of news which gave him great concern: "General Dodge informed me there was no doubt but Forrest had crossed the Tennessee River and was in the vicinity of Town Creek!" Dodge's information was not altogether correct. Forrest was coming like a whirlwind, by night-and-day marches, and was not far away; but as yet the lion was not in Streight's path, and the way was open. If ever delay was dangerous, the leader of this expedition was now incurring it. Properly employed, the 25th and 26th of April were worth a world to Colonel Abel D. Streight.

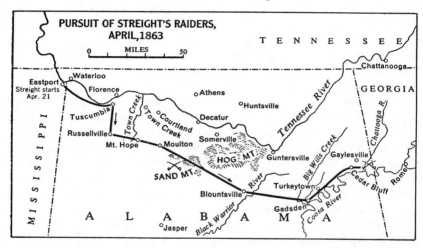

At Spring Hill, on April 23rd, a message had arrived from General Braxton Bragg, directing Forrest to make a forced march with his old brigade to Decatur, Alabama, and, uniting there with the brigade of Colonel Roddey, to take charge of all the Confederate troops and check the Federal advance. On receipt of this order, Colonel Edmondson's Eleventh Tennessee was hurried off with directions to reach Bainbridge on the Tennessee River as soon as possible, cross there, and effect a junction with Roddey. Following with the Fourth, Ninth, and Tenth Tennessee regiments and Morton's battery, Forrest crossed the Tennessee River at Brown's Ferry, near Courtland, Alabama, on the 26th, and was soon in position to dispute the farther advance of General Dodge. Just before crossing this formidable stream he had directed Colonel Dibrell to take his Eighth Tennessee regiment and one gun, march along the northern bank of the river in the direction of Florence, and to use his artillery at every opportunity in order to create as much of a diversion in the Union rear as was possible.

Help had come none too soon for Roddey's brigade, which had struggled manfully with the overwhelming force under the Union leader. General Dodge had pushed out with his legions, and on Monday, April 27th, had driven the Confederates across Town Creek, when he ascertained "that the enemy were in force under Forrest on the opposite bank."

On the 28th, although "the resistance of the enemy was very strong, and their sharp-shooters very annoying," the Union commander succeeded in crossing the creek, the Confederates retiring toward Courtland. Notwithstanding his advantage, Dodge again withdrew to Town Creek that night and there encamped.

It was here, about dark on the evening of the 28th of April, when the fighting had ceased and the Union forces were going into camp on Town Creek, that a well-known citizen of Tuscumbia, Mr. James Moon, after a hurried ride around and through various Federal detachments, reached General Forrest with the startling intelligence that a very considerable body of mounted Union troops, estimated at about two thousand, had passed through Mount Hope in the direction of Moulton, and were probably now at the latter place. In his original plan, General Rosecrans had intended that Dodge should advance no farther than Tuscumbia in aid of Streight; but when at this point he informed the leader of the raiders that Forrest was at Town Creek, Streight insisted that Dodge should attack the latter and drive him at least as far as Courtland, or even to Decatur, and thus hold Forrest off. Streight says, moreover: "It was understood that in the event Forrest took after me in the direction of Moulton, Dodge and his cavalry were to follow Forrest." Swinging loose from all support, and taking advantage of the darkness of night to conceal his departure, Streight's "lightning brigade" marched out of Tuscumbia in the direction of Mount Hope on the 26th of April. Although Mount Hope was the first point aimed for, it must have been that evil forebodings filled the heart of the raider chief as he stumbled and groped his way along the almost impassable roads of northern Alabama. He says: "It was raining very hard, and the mud and darkness of the night made our progress very slow."

Sergeant H. Briedenthal, of Company A, Third Ohio Infantry, in his journal says: "We were aroused from our refreshing slumbers in camp at Tuscumbia at eleven o'clock at night, and prepared our meals and mules. We were in the saddle at 1 A.M., and started on the Russellville road, but made only five miles by daylight, on account of the badness of the roads, and the depth of the streams swollen by the recent rains. We reached Russellville at 10 A.M., a distance of eighteen miles northwest[5] of Tuscumbia. Halted long enough to feed, and at 11 A.M. were in our saddles, and took a westerly[6] direction. At sunset reached Mount Hope, a small village thirty-six miles from Tuscumbia, where we went into camp somewhat fatigued and hungry."[7]

On the night of the 27th, at Mount Hope, Colonel Streight received the cheering news from Dodge that he had Forrest on the run; that he had crossed east of Town Creek, had driven the Confederates away, and that he must now push on. Colonel Streight did push on through mud and slush and rain, and late on the afternoon of the 28th of April woke up the sleepy village of Moulton with the largest procession of Union troopers that secluded spot had yet entertained. Here he fed and rested his weary cavalcade until 1 A.M. (29th), when, saddling up, he moved eastward, with Blountsville as his next objective.

Sergeant Briedenthal says: "After a ride of twelve miles over the most miserable roads, we arrived at dark in Moulton, the capital of Lawrence County, and bivouacked about 9 P.M. At one o'clock on the morning of the 29th we were mounted and off in a westerly (easterly) direction."

As Streight was filing out of Moulton at one o'clock on the morning of the 29th of April, sixteen miles away to the north another body of mounted men was leaving the suburbs of Courtland and heading after them. The plucky raider, relying upon the understanding with Dodge, little dreamed at this midnight hour that the man of all men he most dreaded, at the head of a determined lot of fighters, made veterans under his iron hand and absolutely devoted to his service, had boldly cut loose from in front of Dodge and with rapid stride was bearing down upon him.

When Forrest, at dark on the 28th of April, had received information of the presence of so large a body of mounted troops so far detached from their main column, his quick perception took in the situation at

[5] [Russellville is due south of Tuscumbia.—ED.]
[6] [Mount Hope is really due east of Russellville.—ED.]
[7] *Companion Volume, Rebellion Record,* 1861-64, p. 338.

a glance. Calling his staff at once, he gave explicit directions as to the disposition of the troops whose duty it would be to confront Dodge and hold him where he was or retard any pursuit. He sent a courier to Dibrell to attack at once Dodge's outposts near Florence; to use his artillery freely, and create the impression that a considerable force was threatening the rear of the Union commander. This he did with the hope that it would draw him back to Tuscumbia. In order to prevent any possibility of a return of the raiders to unite with General Dodge's column, or prevent any reinforcements to them from this source, he directed Colonel Roddey to take his Alabama regiment, the Eleventh Tennessee regiment (Edmondson's), and Julian's battalion, to interpose these troops between Dodge and Streight, and then follow on directly after the raiders. Starnes's and Biffle's regiments, two pieces of John W. Morton's battery, and Ferrell's six pieces (heretofore with Roddey) were speedily prepared for the pursuit. Forrest did not leave the details of preparation to any subordinate, however faithful and reliable. He selected the best horses and harness, and double-teamed his artillery and caissons. He even stood by to see the ammunition carefully distributed, with directions to the captains of companies to say to each man that "no matter what else gets wet he must keep his cartridge box dry." He saw to it that the farriers were busy shoeing the horses and tightening the shoes which were loose.

Three days' rations were cooked, and shelled corn issued for two days' forage. To the successful commander, close personal attention to these details was essential, and he knew it. At the bottom of his remarkable and almost unbroken series of brilliant achievements, may not this patient attention to the smallest detail explain in part the wonderful measure of his success?

By one o'clock on the morning of the 29th of April all was ready, and as the cavalcade rode out of the town of Courtland, in the cold drizzling rain which was falling and making the muddy roads still more difficult, there began a race and running fight between two bodies of cavalry which, in the brilliant tactics of the retreat and stubbornness in defense on one side, and the desperate bravery of the attack and relentlessness in pursuit upon the other, has no analogue in military history.

Steadily throughout that night, and well into the daylight of the 29th, the Confederate leader rode without a halt. The mud was deep and the night so dark that even the animals could scarcely find their way. At eight o'clock, an hour for feeding and resting the horses, and then through to Moulton on the forenoon of this day.

In the meantime, Colonel Streight had not been idle. From Moulton he had struck a steady gait and kept it up, and had placed seventeen miles to his credit on the 29th, reaching at dark a defile or gorge which leads to the summit of Sand Mountain and is known as Day's Gap. In addition to this good march over rough and muddy roads on a direct line, his men had swept the country for several miles on each side of the highway, taking all the horses and mules, not only to replace any which might break down, but to prevent them from being used by the enemy, should pursuit be made. He says: "We destroyed during the day a large number of wagons laden with provisions. We were now in the midst of devoted Union people. I could learn nothing of the enemy." And here, at the foot of Sand Mountain, he rested for the night, still unconscious of the fact that the "Wizard of the Saddle" was on his trail.

While the Union troops were sleeping, Forrest's hardy riders were reeling off mile after mile of their heavy task. At Moulton they had stolen another hour of rest, with the saddles off to cool the horses' backs while feeding the hungry animals. Just as the bugle sounded to "saddle up," the sunlight broke through a rift in the western sky, and as their chieftain mounted his horse and gave that ever-famous command, "Move up, men," twelve hundred hats were lifted, and the rebel yell that split the air might well have shaken the sparkling pendants of rain from the tender green leaves of that April afternoon. The moment was auspicious. The wild enthusiasm of his men was to him the harbinger of success. Never was mortal man more in his element than Nathan Bedford Forrest at this hour.

Of him and these men Lord Wolseley says:

They were reckless men, who looked to him as their master, their leader, and over whom he had obtained the most complete control. He possessed that rare tact—unlearnable from books—which enabled him not only effectively to control these fiery, turbulent spirits, but to attach them to him personally "with hooks of steel." In him they recognized not only the daring, able, and successful leader, but also the commanding officer who would not hesitate to punish with severity when he deemed punishment necessary. He thoroughly understood the nature and disposition of those with whom he had to deal, their strong and their weak points, what they could and could not accomplish. He never ventured to hamper their freedom of action

by any sort of stiff, barrack-yard drill, or to embarrass it by any precon-
ceived notions of what a soldier should look like. They were essentially
irregulars by nature, and he never attempted to rob them of that character.
They possessed as an inheritance all the best and most valuable fighting
qualities of the irregulars, accustomed as they were from boyhood to
horses and the use of arms, and brought up with all the devil-may-care,
lawless notions of the frontiersman. But the most volcanic spirit among
them felt he must bow before the superior iron will of the determined man
who led them. There was a something about the dark-gray eye of Forrest
which warned his subordinates he was not to be trifled with and would
stand no nonsense from either friend or foe. He was essentially a practical
man of action, with a dauntless, fiery soul, and a heart that knew no fear.

A little after midnight, Forrest, at the head of the column, had arrived
within four miles of Day's Gap. Here he learned that the Union troops
were encamped at the foot of the mountain, in the mouth of this defile.
Now assured that he had his adversary in striking distance, he halted
the men and told them to feed and rest until near daylight. The roadside
was soon lined with the weary troopers so soundly sleeping that dreams
of neither war nor peace disturbed them. It took several hours for the
column to close up. The trying pace had told on many of the horses,
and it was near daylight when the last of the stragglers caught up. They
in turn were allowed a short respite.

Not all the Confederates, however, were allowed to rest. The general
thought his brother, Captain William Forrest, and his famous "Forty
Scouts" did not need sleep. He ordered him to "keep right on down the
road and get up close to the enemy and see what they are doing." Captain Bill moved on, and in the moonlight succeeded in getting between
an unsuspecting rear vedette of the Federals and their main column, and
capturing them. He then advanced to within sight of the campfires of
Streight's command, and without disturbing their slumbers concluded
to give his own men a rest. It is said that man proposes, but that the
disposition is elsewhere. In any event, the famous scouts were not to
sleep for the short part of the night now at their disposal. One of this
company relates that when they were here, close to the Union camp,
just before daylight, there broke out the most awful noise to which mortal man had ever been called upon to listen. In one mighty effort nearly
two thousand mules, braying in far-reaching and penetrating chorus, set
the echoes in vibration among the Alabama mountains. So loud and
continuous was this unusual noise that Forrest's scouts discarded all

idea of sleep and laughed at the drollery of their serenade.[8]

Over in Streight's camp, the salute to the morning which had so disturbed the Confederate scouts was the breakfast call of the hungry drove. Colonel Streight had determined to be up and away before daylight, and in good time his men were bestirring themselves to feed the animals. At the head of his column, with wagons near the front, and before the day was yet breaking, on April 30th, the Federal commander moved slowly up the narrow, winding, and rocky road by which Sand Mountain is here ascended. In and out as the way runs, it is more than a mile to the summit. From boulders and knobs and trees the gap should be easily held from direct assault, by one against four. It took an hour to make the ascent, and was sunrise when the great undulating plateau was reached.

The caravan almost filled the snakelike highway from top to bottom, and when the advance was on the crest the rear guard of the Union troopers and some loiterers were still lounging about the campfires when suddenly, and from a distance of not over five hundred yards, a cannon boomed on the morning air, and a whizzing shell exploded among the startled stragglers. These and the rear guard did not stand upon the order of their going, but went. In wild disorder the campfires and kettles were abandoned as they chased after the column of raiders climbing up the mountain, with Captain William Forrest and his company in swift pursuit.

Colonel Streight says: "We moved before daylight. I had not proceeded more than two miles at the head of the column before I was informed that the rear-guard had been attacked, and at that moment I heard the boom of artillery."

General Forrest had also moved by daylight, and was in the immediate vicinity of the Union rear before his presence was suspected. Seeing the difficulty of driving Streight from so formidable a position by direct assault, he ordered Biffle's and Starnes's regiments, under McLemore, to hasten by a neighboring pass and take the enemy in flank and rear. The wily Hoosier, however, did not wait for this. His two Alabama companies from this immediate section knew the passes and the country, and in this the Confederates had no advantage. They had told him of the other routes. "I soon learned that the enemy had moved through the gap, and were endeavoring to form a junction in my advance." He

[8] Manuscript of Mr. W. G. Wilkins, in possession of the author.

therefore hurried on across the mountain, his rear guard followed steadily by Captain Bill Forrest's men and the advance of Edmondson's and Roddey's regiments and Julian's battalion. About two miles from the top or western crest of Sand Mountain, Colonel Streight saw he had to make a stand, and standing or running, by night or by day, and without regard to odds, Forrest was determined to fight him whenever he saw him. His order was: "Shoot at everything blue, and keep up the scare."

The country through which Streight was now passing "was of open sand-ridges, very thinly wooded, and afforded fine defensive positions."[9] It was well named Sand Mountain, the topsoil or covering being fine sand or sandstone, in various grades of pulverization. It is the lower or southwestern termination of the great Appalachian range. The elevation is about five hundred feet above the valleys which bound it, and the plateau varies in width from twelve to twenty miles. On top, the land is slightly undulating, with numerous small streams or creeks worn deeply into the surface of the earth, like small canyons or deep ravines, with steep banks, heavily fringed with a thick growth of small trees and dense mountain laurel. Away from these streams there is a fairly rich growth of various species of oak, pine, and hickory trees.

For defensive warfare, as Colonel Streight reports, it is admirably adapted, and here, about two miles from the crest of the mountain, he laid the first ambuscade. His line of battle was formed "along the crest of a ridge circling to the rear. Our right rested on a precipitous ravine, and the left was protected by a marshy run that was easily held against the enemy." Skirmishers extended well beyond either flank to guard against surprise. The mules were to the rear and out of range. In the center of his line and concealed by brush were two twelve-pounder howitzers. He had scarcely got everything in shape, guns loaded, and men all lying down, when his rear guard of the Alabama companies came scurrying down the road, with Bill Forrest leading his men right on their heels.

As soon as Streight's men passed through the gap in the line left open for them, the Federals from either side of the road poured a furious and effective volley into the Confederate scouts. A Minié ball crushed the brave captain's thigh bone, and several of his men were killed or wounded by this deadly fusillade before they could check their horses and run out of range.

[9] Colonel Streight's report.

General Forrest now rode to the front to inspect the Federal position. He had at hand only a portion of Edmondson's and Roddey's regiments, Julian's battalion, his escort company, and the remnants of Captain Forrest's company. In the hard ride since leaving Courtland a number of the horses had not been able to keep up with the advance. Those that came in late to the bivouac, four miles west of Day's Gap, had been left to rest and care for their animals, and were not yet on the ground. There were not one thousand Confederates all told on the top of Sand Mountain at this hour. Dismounting Edmondson's men, Forrest threw them into line, while Roddey and Julian, mounted, were deployed to the right, and to the left his escort and the scouts were placed. The two guns of Morton's battery, having just arrived, were brought up and opened upon the Union line. Edmondson's trained veterans advanced steadily, and when they had reached a point within about a hundred yards of the Federal troops, the two mounted companies on the left rode into the skirmishers on this flank.

At this moment Roddey's and Julian's men recklessly urged their horses well in front of the alignment of Edmondson's men, and by their advanced and exposed position brought on themselves a murderous volley from the greater portion of the Federal line. A number of men and horses were killed or wounded, and, seeing they had been thrown into confusion, the able Federal commander seized the moment to order a charge which, gallantly made, swept the mounted Confederates from the field. As Edmondson was now overlapped and enfiladed, and in danger of having the right files of his regiment captured, he and the escort and Captain Forrest's scouts also fell back, yet steadily and without confusion. Reaching the two guns, they made an effort to take these away, but as several of the horses, having been shot, had become entangled in the gearing, the pieces with their caissons could not be extricated in time and fell into the hands of the advancing Federals.

Whether justly or unjustly, General Forrest never forgave the lieutenant in charge of the artillery for the loss of these guns in this encounter at Day's Gap. In the reorganization of his troops a few weeks later he requested that the artillerist be transferred to another command, and although he preferred no charges against the young officer, the latter, resenting what he interpreted as a reflection upon his courage, in an unfortunate moment attempted to kill his commander.

To those who have been with General Forrest when his troops suffered even a temporary repulse, and know how furious he became, it is not difficult to depict the state of mind he was now in at the loss of his two pet guns. He was praying for Starnes and Biffle to come up; but, alas, they were off on the flank movement and could not be had. He rode in among the men with his saber drawn and accompanied his deft employment of this weapon with a series of remarks well calculated to increase the temperature of the mountain atmosphere. He told every man to get down and hitch his horse to a sapling. There would be no horse-holders in this fight; men were too scarce. Those guns had to be retaken if every man died in the attempt, and if they did not succeed they would never need their horses again. One of Forrest's staff (Captain Henry Pointer), when at last the men were lined up for the charge and the general was riding along to tell every trooper just what he expected of him, rode up to a fellow member of the military family (Major Anderson), drew a modest little bundle of sliced ham and bread from an inside pocket, and, offering half of it to him, remarked: "Major, we had better eat this now, I reckon, for from the way the old man is preparing to get his guns back it might spoil before we get another chance at it."

The order to move up was soon given, and the line of dismounted troopers in desperate mood moved steadily forward. As they neared the strong position from which they had been repulsed, the enemy again opened fire upon them, but without artillery and in feeble, scattering shots. The charge was now ordered, and the men went forward only to see the rear guard of the Union column mount their mules and scamper away in the direction of Blountsville. This was about 11 A.M., on the 30th of April. Streight was satisfied with the first repulse and the capture of the guns, and as soon as the Confederates gave way he had hastily departed, taking the captured pieces with him. He admits in this skirmish a loss of about thirty killed and wounded. Among the mortally wounded was Lieutenant Colonel Sheets, of the Fifty-first Indiana. Forrest claimed about fifty or seventy-five of their killed and wounded were found on the field. The Confederates should naturally have suffered more severely, as they were the assailants and received the fire of the Federals, who were better protected. Of the Confederate officers, Captain William Forrest, brother of the general, was desperately wounded. Fortunately his injury did not prove fatal or permanently unfit him for service.

By the time the Confederate troopers could get back to their horses and resume the pursuit, their vigilant and energetic adversary had a start of nearly an hour. The running fight had opened. The tactics of both leaders were now in evidence. With Colonel Streight it was to move with celerity, until his rear was too hard pressed, and then, whenever a suitable position offered, to ambuscade his adversary, and thus discourage direct assault. Forrest would thus be compelled to attempt to ride around him and head him off.

The raiders were now on the run, and Forrest had no idea of letting them rest until he had worried them into a surrender. His chief anxiety was that Streight might sheer off on some byroad toward the Tennessee River, take the back track, and break for safety by reuniting with Dodge. He did not think Dodge's cavalry was near him, and yet he wanted to make his work sure. With great rapidity he now pressed on after the flying column. Six miles eastward from the battleground of the morning a byroad came in, and along this he saw the Fourth and Ninth Tennessee regiments riding swiftly after their detour around Day's Gap. The distance had, however, been too great to enable them to accomplish the object of this movement. The Federals had passed before they could strike the road. The arrival of these veteran regiments gave great satisfaction to the Confederate leader. He now ordered Colonel Roddey with his regiment and Julian's battalion to retrace their steps and place themselves in observation in front of General Dodge. To preclude the possibility of Streight's escape toward Guntersville, on the Tennessee, Edmondson's regiment, accompanied by Major Charles W. Anderson of the staff, was dispatched toward Somerville and Brooksville in a general direction parallel with the route upon which Streight was moving, and between him and the river.

Under his immediate leadership, in the direct pursuit of Streight, he retained his escort, Captain Forrest's scouts, and the regiments of Biffle and Starnes, and with these moved rapidly on. It was not long before they began to overhaul the swift-marching raiders. The mule tracks in the road grew fresher and fresher at every stride of the pursuers, and soon the moist and dark-colored sand in the deepest hollow of the hoofprints told that they had just been made.

Nine miles from Day's Gap the blue coats of the Federal rear guard came in sight, and the vedettes of the Fourth Tennessee were soon crowding them up on the moving column. For a mile the skirmishing went on, increasing in briskness and gradually demanding more and more attention from the Federal colonel. He says: "Finally the enemy pressed upon our rear so closely that I was compelled to prepare for battle. I selected a strong position on a ridge called Hog Mountain. The whole force soon became engaged about one hour before dark. The enemy strove first to carry our right, then charged the left, but with the help of the two pieces captured in the morning and the two mountain howitzers we were able to repulse them."

This obstinate and plucky encounter did not cease until ten o'clock at night, when Streight retreated. Forrest in person led his men again and again in the assault, with seeming desperation. The Federals stood their ground, and much of the fighting was at close range and at times hand to hand, with no light by which to distinguish friend from foe, except the flash of pistol and carbine and the artillery, which the Federals alone had in the action. Ever in the thickest of the fray, the Confederate commander had one horse killed and two others wounded under him in this bloody encounter; nor did Streight's picked veterans yield until Biffle, with a strong detachment and the daring escort company, had under cover of darkness made a flank movement and borne down upon the mule-holders in the Union rear. Streight then quickly mounted and retreated, leaving his dead and wounded to the Confederates. In the hurry of his retreat he was unable to carry off the two guns he had captured that day, and left them again in the hands of the Southerners. The Union leader says: "The ammunition we had captured with the guns was exhausted, and being very short of horses, I ordered the guns spiked and the carriages destroyed."

The Hoosier colonel had scarcely started again before he had to turn and fight the persistent Tennesseeans who, with the ferocity of blood-hounds, were at his heels. The extreme peril of his situation now began to dawn upon him. He realized that the only safety lay in the integrity of this end of the column. Colonel Hathaway's Seventy-third Indiana regiment was given this important duty, and, as Colonel Streight says: "I remained in the rear in person. We had scarcely got under way when I received information of the enemy's advance." This information came from the cracking carbines of Biffle's picked hundred, who were now Forrest's advance guard. They came on so boldly and became so noisy and insistent that Colonel Streight concluded to give them another check. It was now late in the night; the clouds had disappeared and the moon was shining brightly. The position for the ambuscade was well selected.

On each side of the road along this barren region was a dense thicket of young pines which had sprung up in the track of a hurricane which years ago had mowed a wide swath through the primitive forest of oaks. Here he quickly dismounted Hathaway's men, hurried the mules some distance up the road, and concealed his troops within short gunshot range of the highway by having them lie down in the dark shadows of the saplings.

As the Confederate advance vedette came on at a stiff pace and approached the ambuscade, he was made to suspect the nearness of the enemy by the conduct of his horse, which, with a keener sense of sight and smell than his rider, stopped suddenly in the roadway. Retracing his steps until other troopers of the advance guard came up, he informed the lieutenant in command of the suspected proximity of the Federals. General Forrest was soon notified of the situation, and called for volunteers to draw the enemy's fire. From these, three were selected and told to ride forward, observe closely, and retreat as soon as they recognized the presence of the enemy or received their fire. Moving at a cautious gait, these daring riders became aware of the proximity of Hathaway's men as they were rising from the prone position to deliver their fire. Wheeling quickly about and throwing their bodies well down upon the horses' sides farthest from the enemy, the trained scouts saved themselves from the death trap so skilfully laid. One of these, Private Granville Pillow, of Grove's company, Biffle's regiment, quickly made his way to the rear and guided General Forrest near the position of the ambuscaders.

Forrest ordered one gun of Ferrell's battery, under Lieutenant Jones, to be double-shotted with canister; this was noiselessly shoved by hand along the soft, sandy road until, as indicated by the scout, it was within two hundred yards of the thicket from which the Union troopers had fired. It was a novel experience to the artillerist, but, carefully aiming his piece by the moonlight, he pulled the lanyard, and the charge went crashing through the pines. The Indianians responded with a return salute of small arms. The Confederates brought up a second piece near enough, and several shells were then fired along the road.[10] The raiders, not expecting this turn in affairs, sought their mules and resumed their flight.

[10] *Reminiscences of the Pursuit and Capture of Colonel A. D. Streight,* by Lieutenant Jones of Ferrell's battery.

Colonel Streight says: "We were not again disturbed until we had marched several miles, when they attacked our rear-guard vigorously. I again succeeded in ambuscading them, and we continued our march, and reached Blountsville by ten o'clock in the morning." This last ambuscade was between 2 and 3 A.M. on May 1st, and was practically a repetition of the other. From Day's Gap to Blountsville Colonel Streight had not had a minute's rest or peace, and in making this distance of forty-three miles he had consumed twenty-eight hours.

Forrest now had his antagonist so far from his base at Tuscumbia that he was assured he could not escape in that direction. Should he at Blountsville turn north toward Guntersville, Edmondson and Anderson would head him off until he could close in upon him from behind and destroy him. The only other alternative opened to the raider was to plunge farther into the hopeless distance which lay between him and the arsenals at Rome and the Western and Atlantic Railroad at Dalton. Forrest knew he could wear Streight down before he should reach his goal, and with this in mind, at three o'clock in the morning of May 1st, all hands were ordered to dismount, unsaddle, feed what corn they had brought to their animals, and lie down for a two hours' sleep. This was a short nap, considering the fact that out of the last forty-eight hours they had ridden steadily for forty-four, and for eighteen hours they had fought almost without cessation.

While the Confederates slept, Streight's tired and weary yet determined band was winding down the eastern slope of the Sand Mountain plateau into the valley of corn and plenty. They reached Blountsville at 10 A.M. on May Day, and instead of the usual festivities the citizens of this quiet country town amused themselves in entertaining their first *visitors in blue*. They furnished corn for two thousand hungry animals, and had the pleasure of seeing every horse and mule in all that region gathered up and carried away in speeding the parting guests. Moreover, they witnessed a lively cavalry fight, which was followed by a second entertainment of a second tired and hungry army of horses and men, and all within the short space of three hours. It was the liveliest day in the history of Blountsville, and the pretty Queen of the May was for once neglected.

Colonel Streight did not tarry longer than was necessary to impress all the horses and mules, and corn enough for feed, and to give men and stock a much-needed though very brief respite. The persistent hammering Forrest had given him had taught him the urgent need of a faster pace, and he now determined to rid himself of every possible encumbrance to more rapid flight. A fresh supply of ammunition was distributed to the men, rations issued, and the contents of the wagons transferred to pack mules. The wagons were then bunched and set on fire, but just as the smoke was rising in the air General Forrest, at the head of his escort and a portion of the Fourth Tennessee, charged into the village, driving Captain Smith's rear guard in a whirlwind of dust through and out of the town, to seek shelter in the main column of the flying raiders. Taking possession of the deserted camp, the Confederates soon extinguished the fire in the burning wagons, and secured a rich and much-needed booty.

Colonel Streight says: "After resting about two hours, we resumed our march in the direction of Gadsden. The column had not got fairly under motion before our pickets were driven in, and a short skirmish ensued between Forrest's advance and our rear-guard, under Captain Smith, in the town of Blountsville. The enemy followed closely for several miles, continually skirmishing with the rear-guard, but were badly handled by small parties of our men stopping in the bushes by the side of the road, and firing at them at short range."[11] Despite the great advantages of the Federal leader's position, the Confederates never for a moment relaxed their relentless pursuit, and their general was at the front of it by night and day.

The methods employed by General Forrest to insure discipline and to impress upon the mind of his troopers the importance of obtaining information which was absolutely reliable, and not hearsay, were original and at times extremely severe.

Not far from Blountsville a scout belonging to Captain Bill Forrest's company, who had wandered off a mile or two from the main road to a country blacksmith's shop for the purpose of getting his horse shod, came back to the column at full speed and in great perturbation, anxiously inquiring for General Forrest. Riding up to the commander, he told him in an excited tone that a heavy force of Union cavalry was moving on the road which ran parallel with the one upon which his command was marching, and that they were then not more than four miles off. Forrest said: "Did you see the Yankees?" The man replied: "No; I did not see them myself, but while I was at the blacksmith's shop

[11] *Official Records,* vol. xxiii, part i, p. 290.

a citizen came galloping up on horseback and told me he had seen them."

He had scarcely delivered himself of this piece of information when General Forrest, with both hands, seized the astonished soldier by the throat, dragged him from his horse, and, shoving him against a tree near the roadside, proceeded to bump his head vigorously against the rough bark of the trunk. Having sufficiently punished the unreliable scout, this overbearing leader of men, who, when he found it necessary for the good of his command, constituted himself judge, jury, and executioner, said: "Now, damn you, if you ever come to me again with a pack of lies, you won't get off so easily!" Macbeth, springing upon the messenger with unpleasant and uncertain news, with that fierce denunciation, "The devil damn thee black, thou pale-fac'd loon," was not more ungovernable nor unreasonable than was Forrest in his furious rage.

From Blountsville to the Black Warrior River, a run of about ten miles, the peril of Streight's rear increased to such an extent that he was compelled to turn on his pursuers once more to secure a crossing of this swift and dangerous stream. Under cover of a heavy line of skirmishers he hurried the main portion of the command through the rocky ford, with the loss of only two pack mules (each carrying two boxes of hard bread), which, stumbling over the large, loose stones in the bed of this mountain torrent, went under and were carried away with the current and drowned. On the east bank the two howitzers covered the pell-mell withdrawal of the skirmish line, from which, as the Tennesseeans vigorously charged, several prisoners were taken.

With the exception of two companies, which were ordered to push onward after the Federals and "worry them," Forrest gave his command another respite here for three hours. Some of the Confederates were not so weary of body but that they found time from sleep to strip off and wade in the Warrior, to relieve the dead pack mules of what was "*hard tack*" before it got wet. It did not matter to the hungry troopers if it was wet, for as one freckle-faced, brawny youth remarked, while struggling up the steep bank with the heavy, soaking box on his shoulder: "Boys, it's wet and full of mule hair, but it is a damned sight better than anything the old man's a-givin' us now."

Streight reports that it was about 5 P.M. on the 1st of May when the last of his command crossed the east branch of the Black Warrior. "With the exception of small parties who were continually harassing the rear of the column, we proceeded without further interruption until about nine o'clock the next morning, May 2d, when the rear-guard was fiercely attacked at the crossing of Black Creek near Gadsden."

After the short halt at the Warrior, General Forrest had once more roused his men for their fourth consecutive night march, and, pushing on, overtook his faithful advance guard, which was then skirmishing with the raiders at Big Will's Creek. Sending Biffle's men to the rear for a well-earned rest, and taking their place with his escort, he in person now took charge of the attack, and, gaining rapidly on the Union column, closed in upon the raiders about four miles eastward from where he first struck them, at the ever-famous Black Creek bridge.

Black Creek is a crooked, deep, and sluggish stream with precipitous clay banks and mud bottom. It has its source on the plateau of Lookout Mountain, the southern limit of which range is less than one mile to the north. Only a little farther away, in a series of precipitous falls and whirling cascades, pure and crystal while a mountain stream, leaping from rock to rock it falls from its high estate to mingle with the stained and muddy waters of the lowlands.

Spanning the creek on the main road leading from Blountsville to Gadsden there stood in 1863 a rude, uncovered wooden bridge. There was no other means of crossing the stream (deemed impassable except by bridge or boat) nearer than two miles, where there was a second structure, so rickety and unsafe, however, that it had been abandoned. Colonel Streight, sorely pressed by his pursuers, had built his hopes of escape more upon this obstacle in Forrest's path than any other possible to him before he reached the Chattooga River near Rome, and he bent every energy to cross his command over and destroy this bridge before the Confederates could close in upon him.

This accomplished, and believing the creek could not be forded, he could take it easy for at least half a day and allow his worn-out cavalcade to sleep and to recuperate. By nine o'clock on the morning of May 2nd, despite Forrest's persistent rush at the rear guard for the last four miles, all of his men were over except the rear vedette. His howitzers were in position on the eastern bank, fence rails were piled upon the structure, and it was well in flames. At this moment a cloud of dust came sweeping down the road; in front of it, at full speed, a man on horseback wearing a blue uniform, and in the whirlwind, though not yet distinguishable, a squadron of Confederates. The man in blue, seeing the bridge ablaze and escape now impossible, checked his horse, threw up his hands, and surrendered. The foremost man in the pursuing squadron was General Forrest.

Close by the roadside and some two hundred yards from the westerly approach to the bridge was a plain farmhouse, having only a single story, with two or three rooms on either side of a wide-open passageway, after the fashion of the primitive dwellings of this section of the South. Owning this home, and the small tract of land on which it had been built, there lived a widow and two young unmarried daughters. Their chief means of support had been an only son and brother, and they had sent him to the war in 1861, in one of the first companies that left Gadsden to join the Southern army. He was then away in the Nineteenth Alabama Infantry, and they, with all they had of help given to the cause which they believed was right, were struggling to make the little farm yield enough for their support.

They owned no slaves, nor did at least one-half of the families in the South who gave life and whatever property they possessed to the Southern cause. They fought no war for slavery, but for what they believed to be their right to live like freemen, as they were born, and under whatever form of government the majority decreed. This was the faith of these honest women. The outside world can scarcely appreciate the influence of the women of the Southern states in carrying on the fight when it was once started. Such were their devotion and intensity of purpose that from sixteen to sixty-five years of age no able-bodied male was free from the pressure they exercised in various ways to attach him to the active service. It was this spirit that actuated the widow Sansom and her daughters, and on the 2nd of May, 1863, one of these daughters, Emma Sansom, wrote her name in history.

As Forrest came dashing down the road, close on the fleeing Federals, this girl of sixteen years, recognizing him as a Confederate officer and knowing, as she says, "we were now in the midst of our own men," told him that the bridge was destroyed, and in reply to his questions informed him that there was no other bridge nearer than two miles, but that there was near by, on her mother's farm, an old ford where at times, in very low water, she had noticed the cows wading across the creek, and she believed that he and his men might be able to cross there. No one but her folks knew anything about this "lost ford," and she would guide him to it. So many exaggerated versions of this simple affair have found their way in print that I determined to get from one best able to give it—viz., Emma Sansom, now Mrs. C. B. Johnson, of Calloway, Texas— a true statement of the incident

Emma Sansom was born at Social Circle, Walton County, Georgia, in 1847. In 1852 her father moved from Georgia to the home on Black Creek, Alabama, and there died in 1859. She writes:

When the war came on, there were three children—a brother and sister older than I. In August, 1861, my brother enlisted in the second company that left Gadsden, and joined the Nineteenth Alabama Infantry. My sister and I lived with our mother on the farm. We were at home on the morning of May 2, 1863, when about eight or nine o'clock a company of men wearing blue uniforms and riding mules and horses galloped past the house and went on towards the bridge. Pretty soon a great crowd of them came along, and some of them stopped at the gate and asked us to bring them some water. Sister and I each took a bucket of water, and gave it to them at the gate. One of them asked me where my father was. I told him he was dead. He asked me if I had any brothers. I told him I had *"six."* He asked where they were, and I said they were in the Confederate Army. "Do they think the South will whip?" "They do." "What do you think about it?" "I think God is on our side and we will win." "You do? Well, if you had seen us whip Colonel Roddey the other day and run him across the Tennessee River, you would have thought God was on the side of the best artillery."

By this time some of them began to dismount, and we went into the house. They came in and began to search for fire-arms and men's saddles. They did not find anything but a side-saddle, and one of them cut the skirts off that. Just then some one from the road said, in a loud tone: "You men bring a chunk of fire with you, and get out of that house." The men got the fire in the kitchen and started out, and an officer put a guard around the house, saying: "This guard is for your protection." They all soon hurried down to the bridge, and in a few minutes we saw the smoke rising and knew they were burning the bridge. As our fence extended up to the railing of the bridge, mother said: "Come with me and we will pull our rails away, so they will not be destroyed." As we got to the top of the hill we saw the rails were already piled on the bridge and were on fire, and the Yankees were in line on the other side guarding it.

We turned back towards the house, and had not gone but a few steps before we saw a Yankee coming at full speed, and behind were some more men on horses. I heard them shout, "Halt! and surrender!" The man stopped, threw up his hand, and handed over his gun. The officer to whom the soldier surrendered said: "Ladies, do not be alarmed, I am General Forrest; I and my men will protect you from harm." He inquired: "Where are the Yankees?" Mother said: "They have set the bridge on fire and are standing in line on the other side, and if you go down that hill they will kill the last one of you." By this time our men had come up, and some went out in the field, and both sides commenced shooting. We ran to the house, and I got there ahead of all.

General Forrest dashed up to the gate and said to me: "Can you tell me where I can get across that creek?" I told him there was an unsafe bridge two miles farther down the stream, but that I knew of a trail about two hundred yards above the bridge on our farm, where our cows used to cross in low water, and I believed he could get his men over there, and that if he would have my saddle put on a horse I would show him the way. He said: "There is no time to saddle a horse; get up here behind me." As he said this he rode close to the bank on the side of the road, and I jumped up behind him. Just as we started off mother came up about out of breath and gasped out: "Emma, what do you mean?" General Forrest said: "She is going to show me a ford where I can get my men over in time to catch those Yankees before they get to Rome. Don't be uneasy; I will bring her back safe." We rode out into a field through which ran a branch or small ravine and along which there was a thick undergrowth that protected us for a while from being seen by the Yankees at the bridge or on the other side of the creek. This branch emptied into the creek just above the ford. When we got close to the creek, I said: "General Forrest, I think we had better get off the horse, as we are now where we may be seen." We both got down and crept through the bushes, and when we were right at the ford I happened to be in front. He stepped quickly between me and the Yankees, saying: "I am glad to have you for a pilot, but I am not going to make breastworks of you." The cannon and the other guns were firing fast by this time, as I pointed out to him where to go into the water and out on the other bank, and then we went back towards the house.

He asked me my name, and asked me to give him a lock of my hair. The cannon-balls were screaming over us so loud that we were told to leave and hide in some place out of danger, which we did. Soon all the firing stopped, and I started back home. On the way I met General Forrest again, and he told me that he had written a note for me and left it on the bureau. He asked me again for a lock of my hair, and as we went into the house he said: "One of my bravest men has been killed, and he is laid out in the house. His name is Robert Turner. I want you to see that he is buried in some graveyard near here." He then told me good-bye and got on his horse, and he and his men rode away and left us all alone. My sister and I sat up all night watching over the dead soldier, who had lost his life fighting for our rights, in which we were overpowered but never conquered. General Forrest and his men endeared themselves to us forever.

Emma Sansom's presence of mind and coolness under circumstances which would have paralyzed the faculties of most women enabled Forrest to overcome a very formidable obstacle in his pursuit of Steight, and gained for him at least three hours in time, inestimable in value, since it enabled him to overtake and compel Streight's surrender almost within sight of Rome.

In less than thirty minutes from the time of Forrest's arrival at Black Creek, the artillery was up, and the Federals were driven away from the opposite bank. The "lost ford" was soon cleared and made passable. The cavalry went over, carrying by hand the ammunition from the caissons. The guns and empty caissons, with long ropes tied to the poles, were then rolled by hand to the water's edge, one end of the rope taken to the top of the opposite bank and hitched to double teams of horses. In this original manner the artillery soon made a subaqueous passage to the east bank. The advance guard had already hurried on after the raiders, who, to their great surprise, were hustled out of Gadsden, less than four miles distant from Black Creek bridge, before they could do much damage to the small commissary supplies there.

Another all-night march now became necessary for Colonel Streight, although he says: "The command was in no condition to do so. I only halted at Gadsden sufficiently long to destroy a quantity of arms and stores found there, and proceeded. Many of our animals and men were entirely worn out and unable to keep up, and were captured. It now became evident to me that our only hope was in crossing the river at Rome and destroying the bridge, which would delay Forrest a day or two and allow the command a little time to sleep, without which it would be impossible to proceed."

But alas for all such hope! The relentless hand which had smote him for three successive days and nights, and banished sleep from his worn-out cavalcade, was striking at him yet and had no thought of giving him a respite. Streight, in fact, was not allowed to stop in Gadsden. As he approached the town, he surrounded it, in order to corral all the horses and mules belonging to the citizens. Impressing these, he set fire to several houses containing small quantities of commissaries, and then moved onward with all the speed possible to his mules and men, all now physically exhausted, and the latter mentally dispirited yet ready to fight.

If the state of his men and horses was so deplorable from fatigue and loss of sleep, what must have been the condition of those which were pursuing him? Forrest's men had had no opportunities for obtaining fresh horses or mules when theirs succumbed to the terrible strain to which they were being subjected. The Federals had swept the country clear of livestock as they marched, and in this, as in the tremendous tactical advantage of the ambuscade, they had the Confederate leader at great disadvantage. Many of his men had not tasted food in twenty-four hours, and a number fell from their horses from sheer exhaustion and slept by the roadside as their commands rode almost over their seemingly lifeless bodies. Despite the inspiring example of their leader—who did more work and fighting than any subordinate—and notwithstanding the details, whose duty it was to keep the men awake, rouse up the sleepers, and put them on their horses, Forrest's command had now crumbled away to a mere remnant. From 1 A.M. on April 29th to noon of May 2nd they had marched 119 miles and fought almost without cessation, and still the strongest of them pushed on in desperate emulation of their indomitable leader. Edmondson and Anderson were not up yet —and did not get up until after the surrender. Their duty was to keep Streight from escaping northward, and they were doing this.

Forrest's ever-faithful and efficient escort, now reduced to about forty effectives, some twenty of the remnant of his brother's scouts, and not over five hundred of Starnes's and Biffle's regiments (his entire command) made up the full quota of the troops with which he marched east of Gadsden. In front of him, and fleeing in despair, were more than twice as many brave and picked men of the enemy. From Gadsden on, Streight says, "the enemy followed closely, and kept up a continuous skirmish with the rear of the column, until 4 P.M., at which time we reached Blount's plantation, fifteen miles from Gadsden,[12] where we procured forage for our animals. Here I decided to halt. The command was dismounted, a detail made to feed the horses and mules, while the balance of the command formed in line of battle. Meanwhile the rearguard became severely engaged, and was driven in."

Forrest, continuing his tactics of worrying his antagonist, and knowing the perilous weakness of his own command, advanced his sharpshooters and made all possible show of strength and of assault. This he kept up vigorously until dark. Colonel Streight had set a skillful and

[12] Blount's plantation is twelve miles from Gadsden.

dangerous ambuscade, in which he hoped to entrap his enemy and destroy him, but such cunning was as native to the Confederate leader as to his adversary, and he did not take the bait.

In this affair Streight's right-hand man, brave Colonel Gilbert Hathaway, fell wounded and expired in a few minutes from a carbine bullet fired by a sharpshooter, Private Joseph Martin. The death of Hathaway sealed the doom of the raiders. The Federal commander says: "His loss to me was irreparable. His men almost worshipped him, and when he fell it cast a deep gloom of despondency over his regiment which was hard to overcome. We remained in ambush but a short time when the enemy, who by some means had learned of our whereabouts, commenced a flank movement. I then decided to withdraw as silently as possible."

On through the night struggled this plucky remnant of Rosecrans's picked band of raiders. Bragg's important communications between Chattanooga and Atlanta looked very safe now, but these men were dying gamely. Forrest was at last sure of his quarry, provided he could keep his remnant from destruction by ambush. From Gadsden, by a parallel route, he had dispatched on horseback, to go right through to Rome, a courier who would arrive there in good time to warn the citizens to guard or burn the bridge, and thus stop the raiders short of their spoil. It was too great a danger, with his handful of men, to risk a night fight, with all the advantage on the other side. Therefore, picking out a squadron of his best-mounted troopers to follow on and "devil them all night," he gave his men their first night's rest since leaving Courtland. Forrest's foresight in hurrying a courier to Rome was not the least important of his brilliant moves in this campaign, and was well timed. Colonel John H. Wisdom outdid Paul Revere in this famous ride.

Near Turkeytown, eight miles east of Gadsden, at nightfall of May 2nd, Streight picked out 200 of the best-mounted men of his command, and, placing them under Captain Milton Russell, ordered him to hurry on to Rome and seize and hold the bridge until he could get there with the main column. Captain Russell pushed on, crossed the Chattooga River in a small ferryboat, and on the 3rd approached the city to find the bridge barricaded and defended by a strong company of home guards. He concluded not to attack, and sent word back to his chief of the condition of affairs.

Meanwhile things were going desperately with Streight, without regard to Russell's failure, of which as yet he was in ignorance. With heroic persistence he urged his weary, sleepy, and worn-out cavalcade by starlight, and by the moon when it came out, as far as the Chattooga River, where Captain Russell had crossed. Alas! his subordinate had not left a guard to hold the ferryboat, and some citizens, by this time apprised of the warlike character of the soldiers who had used it, had spirited the boat away to parts undiscoverable.

Many a man would have given up in despair at this moment, but Abel D. Streight was not that sort of man. Several miles distant up this stream there was a bridge, and, Moseslike, he led his people thitherward and verily through a wilderness. He says: "We had to pass over an old coal-chopping for several miles, where the timber had been cut and hauled off for charcoal, leaving innumerable wagon-roads running in every direction. The command was so worn out and exhausted that many were asleep, and in spite of every exertion I, with the aid of such of my officers as were able for duty, could make, the command became scattered and separated in several squads, travelling in different directions, and it was not until near daylight that the last of the command had crossed the river." This bridge was also burned, and still onward Streight plodded with his troopers past Cedar Bluff, twenty-eight miles from Gadsden, at sunup, and then wearily on in the direction of Rome, until at 9 A.M., May 3rd, he stopped at Lawrence to rest and feed. So exhausted were his men that, as soon as they were ordered to halt, they sank down upon the ground and many of them fell asleep at once.

It was with great difficulty that a sufficient number could be kept on their feet long enough to give the mules and horses the measure of provender due them. It was not so, however, with their commander. He had just received a message from Captain Russell that the bridge at Rome was too heavily guarded, and he could not take it. He also had heard that a second column of Confederates was moving parallel with him, and were now nearer to Rome than himself. This was all very depressing news, but at this same moment his quick ear caught a sound he knew too well, and which, more than all else, banished hope as well as sleep. As Sherman called him, "that devil Forrest" was at his heels again, and once more the cracking rifles of his rear guard and their relentless pursuers came ringing through the wood. The Confederate commander had not been long delayed at the Chatooga, where Streight had burned the last bridge. He had discovered that the walking on the bottom of this stream was no worse than at Black Creek, even if still more inconvenient than crossing dry on a bridge.

Ten hours of refreshing sleep and rest had wrought wonders in Forrest's fragment of a command, and by dawn of day, on May 3rd, his less than six hundred were once more in full cry after the raiders. When they reached the burned bridge near Gaylesville, the ammunition was carried over in small boats. The horses swam or forded with the men on their backs, and the cannon and empty caissons were pulled over on the river bottom. So little time was lost by these adepts at war that by 9 A.M. they were up with the Union column, although the latter had trudged along all through the night.

Forrest advanced at once, making the greatest possible display of his small force, yet careful not to make an assault which would demonstrate his numerical weakness. In crescentic line, and at good distance apart, he advanced his skirmishers until he had more than halfway surrounded the Federal position. From the noise these men made, and the orders given as to the disposition and formation of the troops and artillery, one might well have thought a brigade or two was being moved in battle array rather than a corporal's guard of a little over half a thousand men.

In this dire extremity, Colonel Streight gathered his officers about him, and with them tried to arouse his sleeping men. Some of these, when vigorously shaken, raised themselves to a sitting posture, stared drowsily about as if dazed and uncertain as to where they were, then, nodding, closed their eyes, fell over on the earth, and were again asleep. Others made no response whatever to the energetic effort made to awaken them. After strenuous exertion about one-half of the Federal command struggled to their feet, and once more pluckily rallied to their colors. Their commander lined them up for one more desperate effort, and then ordered them to lie down for better protection. They did lie down, their heads to the foe, their loaded guns pointed along the ground in the direction in which Forrest and his men were coming.

Then, instead of shutting one eye in deadly aim along the gleaming barrels of their rifles, both eyes were closed. Gunstock and hammer, barrel and sight and hated foeman faded from their vision in the darkness which overcame them. The brave fellows were asleep in line of battle. The exultant rebel yell, the crack and crackle of pistol and carbine, and the tattoo of horses' feet upon the ground as the rear guard and pickets came rushing into camp no longer aroused them. The man of iron had worn them out. Colonel Streight, in his official report, says: "Nature was exhausted. A large portion of my best troops actually went to sleep while lying in line of battle under a severe skirmish fire."

It was at this propitious moment that General Forrest sent Captain Henry Pointer, of his staff, with a flag of truce to the Union commander, demanding the surrender of himself and command. The wily Confederate, knowing his man, and his own questionable position as well, expressed an earnest desire to avoid "the further effusion of blood," but took especial pains to leave off that terrifying threat of "no quarter, if he had to sacrifice his men in the assault," with which he was wont to bluff his antagonists ever since he used it so successfully in his first attack on Murfreesboro.

Colonel Streight replied that he would meet General Forrest to discuss the question, and in the conference asked what his proposition was. Forrest replied: "Immediate surrender—your men to be treated as prisoners of war; the officers to retain their side-arms and personal property." Colonel Streight requested a few minutes in which to consult his officers. Forrest said: "All right, but you will not require much time. I have a column of fresh troops at hand, now nearer Rome than you are. You cannot cross the river in your front. I have men enough right here to run over you." In all of this there was not one word of truth; but this was war, and in war everything is fair.

Just then one piece of a section of Ferrell's battery, under Lieutenant R. G. Jones, came in sight. This officer says: "I was riding a little in advance of the gun when, suddenly looking up, I saw General Forrest, Captain Pointer, one or two other officers, and several Federal officers sitting down on the north side of the road. A little distance up the road I saw a crowd of Yankees. Captain Pointer motioned for me to halt. He then approached me and said: 'Colonel Streight objects to your coming up so close; drop back a little.' I moved back with the gun, and came to 'action front,' with one wheel in the road and the other at the edge of the wood. Soon Sergeant Jackson came up with the other piece and took position in the other half of the roadway."

Streight returned to his command, called his officers together, and talked over the situation. They voted unanimously to surrender, and their commander, though personally opposed to it, and still ready to fight to the death, yielded to the decision of his subordinates. The men stacked their guns, and were marched away to an open field or clearing, but it was not until the Confederate general got his small command between the Federal troopers and their arms that he felt himself secure.

For seventy-two hours, with no troops in reach excepting the regiments of Biffle and Starnes, his brother's company of scouts, about thirty in number, and his personal escort company, and two pieces of artillery, Forrest had pursued and fought Streight with four regiments and two companies of picked troops and two twelve-pounder howitzers. Moving in front, the Federal commander had cleared up the country of all horses and mules, and in this way kept his men supplied with fresh mounts. He says: "I do not think that at the time of surrender we had a score of the mules drawn at Nashville left." On the other hand, Forrest had had no opportunity of supplying his men with animals. When, from casting a shoe or other injury, or from exhaustion, one of his horses gave out, that was the end of both man and horse as far as this expedition was concerned.

Starting from Courtland, Alabama, at one o'clock on the morning of the 29th of April, he and his command marched sixteen miles to Moulton, thence seventeen miles to Day's Gap. They rode and fought nearly all day of April 30th and through the greater portion of that night, reaching Blountsville, seventy-six miles from the starting point, at ten o'clock on the morning of May 1st, the time consumed being fifty-seven hours, for fifty-two of which his troops were in the saddle. From Blountsville to Gadsden forty-three miles additional were covered, and from Gadsden to Lawrence, where Streight surrendered, thirty-one miles more, making a total distance of one hundred and fifty miles. As the greater part of this march was through a mountainous region and over bad roads, it is not surprising that the thousand troops with which he had started had dwindled down to considerably less than six hundred at the finish. To this small force Colonel Abel D. Streight surrendered all that was left of the two thousand picked troops of the Union army which had left Nashville on April 10th.

Major General Richard J. Oglesby, in his official report, says: "One of Dodge's men, who was with Streight and escaped, says that when taken they were worn out, and Forrest captured them with five hundred men. Streight thought a large force was after him."

On May 10th, Mr. Edwin M. Stanton, Secretary of War, telegraphed General Rosecrans: "The President desires to know whether you have any information on the subject [capture of this force], and whether

Colonel Streight belongs to your command." The answer he received was in the affirmative, and ended with the explanation that the expedition "was deemed feasible and vastly important to us."

General Braxton Bragg reported to the War Department at Richmond: "May 3d, between Gadsden and Rome, after five days and nights of fighting and marching, General Forrest captured Colonel Streight and his whole command, about sixteen hundred, with rifles, horses, etc."

The Congress of the Confederate States of America resolved that "The thanks of Congress are again due to General N. B. Forrest and the officers and men of his command for meritorious service on the field, and especially for the daring, skill, and perseverance exhibited in the pursuit and capture of the largely superior forces of the enemy near Rome, Georgia," etc.

Had the Congress of the Confederate States, or the President, in the light of this brilliant achievement, with the recollection of Fort Donelson, Shiloh, Murfreesboro, Thompson's Station, and Brentwood fresh in mind, appreciated the great military genius they were hampering with such a small force, and had placed him then in command of all the cavalry of the Army of Tennessee, they would have brightened the prospects of an independent Confederacy, and have won the appreciation and confidence of the Southern people.

This relentless pursuit of Colonel Streight's expedition has been considered by capable military critics not only one of Forrest's most brilliant achievements but also one of the most remarkable performances known to warfare.

Had Colonel Streight on the night of May 2nd, instead of wasting the already overtaxed strength of his men and animals, gone into camp as soon as he found out that Forrest was not pursuing him with his entire force, and permitted all or the greater portion of his command to have slept until daylight, and then in their improved condition, and with their superior numbers, had attacked Forrest vigorously, he would in all probability have beaten him. Retracing his steps, he might then safely have reached Dodge in the Valley of the Tennessee near Tuscumbia, and thus saved his command. Among the fatal mistakes made in the conception and execution of this daring expedition, this all-night march, which accomplished such a very short distance, was the greatest. The result was that Forrest and his men and horses were fresh and vigorous in the morning while their enemy was hopelessly worn out. They marched within the first four hours of daylight the same distance that it took the Federals eleven hours to make.

Another error which contributed largely to the failure of Streight was that his command was not suited to the work in hand. It should have been seasoned cavalrymen instead of troops taken from the infantry and mounted without being accustomed to the saddle. It was the universal testimony of the men that they were soon so chafed and sore from being unaccustomed to the saddle that many of them could not retain their seats without great discomfort. It was also an error to suppose that mules were better suited to this work than horses. As shown by the seasoned horses of Forrest's command, they were much better fitted for great and prolonged exertion than mules. These are better draft animals, and can haul heavier loads on less forage than horses, but they cannot get over the ground as well, as shown by the rapidity with which Forrest overhauled the raiders.

Again, General Dodge failed in giving the support to Streight's movement that Streight expected and that the general could have given. On the morning of the day on which Forrest left his front he had a command at Town Creek sufficient to have driven the Confederates across the Tennessee River toward their base at Tullahoma, and had he vigorously attacked the Southern troops left on the east bank of Town Creek, near Courtland, he would have made it impossible for Forrest to have withdrawn as many of his men for the pursuit of Streight as he took with him.

It is safe to say that there entered into Rome, Georgia, on the 3rd of May, 1863, the hungriest triumphal procession in the history of this borough. The victorious troops were royally entertained by the citizens, and men and horses soon forgot the severe ordeal to which they had been subjected. Even the unfortunate prisoners were not neglected. Sergeant Briedenthal, in his diary, from which I have already quoted, says on May 5th: "We have been treated well since our surrender, by Forrest's men, who have used us as a true soldier would treat a prisoner."

The Georgia Romans presented to the Confederate general the finest saddle horse their country afforded. The 6th of May had been set apart as a gala day, with a barbecue and celebration in honor of Forrest and his men; but on the night of the 5th a courier came into Rome from Gadsden with the intelligence that another heavy Federal expedition was advancing from Tuscumbia toward Talladega, Alabama. Instead of the expected feast, the disappointed troopers mounted their horses and followed their leader on a forced march back to Gadsden, where they arrived May 7th, only to learn that, instead of advancing east of Courtland, General Dodge had fallen back to Corinth.

Forrest remained in Gadsden on the night of the 7th, the guest of Colonel R. B. Kyle, still living in that city in 1898. This gentleman says:

As Forrest was returning from the capture of Streight, at Rome, he stayed all night at my house. Forrest's terrific pursuit of Streight, and the capture of his large command with a force only one-third as numerous as the enemy, had, of course, filled the country through which Streight had passed with the idea that Forrest was a tremendous fighter, and gave me the impression that his mind would be occupied only with things concerning the war; but the only thing that seemed to concern him while in my house, for almost a day and all night, was my little two-year-old boy, to whom he took a great fancy, holding him on his lap and carrying him around the place in his arms. The little child showed great fondness for him, and loved to stay with him. The next day, when Forrest rode away in the direction of Guntersville, he took the little fellow two or three miles on the road with him, holding him on the saddle in front of him, and I rode along this distance in order to bring the child home to his mother. He kissed the little fellow tenderly as he bade him good-bye, and, turning to me, said, "My God, Kyle, this is worth living for!"

From Gadsden a detachment was sent back on the line of the recent march to gather up the wounded prisoners and all abandoned supplies. The command was ordered to proceed to Athens, in Limestone County, Alabama, north of the Tennessee River, while Forrest passed through Guntersville and on to Huntsville, where he was given a grand ovation and presented with another superb horse. Arriving at General Bragg's headquarters, he was directed to take command of the cavalry on the left wing of his army, in place of General Earl Van Dorn, who had been killed while Forrest was absent in pursuit of Streight. In obedience to this order, he arrived at Spring Hill on the 16th of May, 1863.

TEN

From Tullahoma to Chattanooga

FOR the last two weeks in May, and until the 25th of June, General Forrest, in command of two brigades (Starnes's and Armstrong's), served on picket and scout duty on the left wing of Bragg's army, in the "neutral ground" between Spring Hill and Columbia on the south and Franklin and Triune on the north. The division under General W. H. Jackson had been sent to the department of Mississippi. Daily encounters between the outpost pickets of the opposing armies and small scouting detachments occurred, but nothing of importance was accomplished beyond maintaining the integrity of the Confederate lines by this vigilance of the cavalry.

It will be remembered that in the engagement on Sand Mountain near Day's Gap, during Streight's raid, two pieces of artillery were captured from the Confederates. General Forrest had never been satisfied with the manner in which these guns were handled on that occasion, and, without pressing any charges against the officer in command, when he returned to Tennessee in May, in the reorganization of the artillery which ensued, this lieutenant was transferred to another battery at Forrest's request. The young officer resented this action as an unjust imputation upon his courage, and in a moment of rashness determined to seek redress even to the extent of making Forrest the victim of his private vengeance. The latter had been called to Columbia on business with the quartermaster's department, and while he was dining at the house of a friend in this city the lieutenant in question called and asked for an interview. He was informed that General Forrest would see him at the quartermaster's office at a certain hour in the afternoon, and at the appointed time the young man arrived.

As there were a number of persons in the room, presuming that he wished to speak privately, General Forrest suggested that they walk out into the hall where they could converse without interruption. The building was so constructed that there was a wide hall running from the front entirely to the rear, with the rooms opening upon this hall-way from either side. While Forrest was yet in the office with the quartermaster, he had in his hand a small penknife, which was closed, and which he was twirling between the thumb and finger of his right hand by striking the end of the knife with the thumb of the opposite hand. As they walked slowly side by side the lieutenant spoke to Forrest in an earnest and excited manner about being left out of the battery in the reorganization, asked why it had been done, and insisted upon being reinstated. General Forrest replied that he did not care to discuss the matter, that his decision was final, and that he need not hope to serve again in his command.

At this moment the lieutenant drew a pistol, and, although Forrest was watchful and exceedingly quick, before he could grasp the weapon which was being drawn and pointed toward him, it was discharged when the muzzle was nearly in contact with his body. The bullet, of large caliber, entered the left hip just above the joint, striking the edge of the bone of the pelvis a little to the outer side of and below the anterior superior spinous process. Being deflected outward, it passed back through the body without coming in contact with the iliac vessels or the intestines. With his left hand (Forrest was left-handed) he grasped the right hand of his assailant, in which the pistol was held, and thus prevented a second shot. Deliberately with the right hand he carried the penknife to his mouth and, holding the handle between his fingers, with his teeth he opened the largest blade and quickly thrust it into the abdomen of his assailant, ripping the peritoneal cavity open and inflicting a mortal wound. At this juncture the lieutenant dropped his pistol and ran to the rear of the building, leaped over a low fence into a side street, and proceeded rapidly a short distance, when he ran into a shop and lay down upon the counter. General Forrest walked out of the front of the building and along the sidewalk to the office of a physician nearby. Removing his trousers sufficiently to permit the wound to be examined, he asked the doctor whether or not, in his opinion, it was a mortal injury. After a brief inspection the surgeon said that he could not tell positively without probing, but from the location and seeming direction of the missile, taking into consideration the warm weather, it was probably a fatal wound.

At this Forrest rearranged his clothes, seized a pistol from a member of his staff who had followed him, and rushed out into the street, saying to those who tried to restrain him, "Get out of my way; he has mortally wounded me, and I intend to kill him before I die." Someone informed the wounded lieutenant that Forrest was coming after him, and he immediately ran out of the building and up the street until he fell from exhaustion. A crowd at once gathered around him, so that Forrest could not get close enough to shoot him. Someone said: "General, you need not trouble yourself to kill him, he is already dying." Forrest said: "All right, if you are sure of this I won't shoot him, but, damn him, he has killed me, and I am determined he shall die too." Being now convinced that the young lieutenant could not live, he directed some of his men to place his assailant on a stretcher, carry him to the hotel, and have him properly cared for. Forrest himself was by this time very weak from loss of blood, and had to be carried to the residence of a friend, where he rapidly recovered from his injury.

Two days later, when the young officer was rapidly sinking from septic peritonitis, which followed a perforation of the intestine, he sent word to General Forrest that, if it were possible, he desired to have him come to see him, as he wished to speak with him before he died. To this request Forrest acceded, and was carried into the lieutenant's room. An eyewitness to the interview informs me that the officer took the general by the hand and held it between both of his, saying, "General, I shall not be here long, and I was not willing to go away without seeing you in person and saying to you how thankful I am that I am the one who is to die and that you are spared to the country. What I did, I did in a moment of rashness, and I want your forgiveness." Forrest leaned over the bed upon which the young man was lying, told him he forgave him freely, and that his own heart was full of regret that the wound he had inflicted was fatal.

My informant says: "Forrest wept like a child. It was the saddest of all the sad incidents of the long and bitter war I witnessed."

Although the authorities at Richmond were yet so blind to the great military ability which Forrest had displayed, those at the head of affairs at Washington were beginning to place a proper estimate upon him. On the 29th of May, Edwin M. Stanton, Mr. Lincoln's famous War Secretary, wired Major General W. S. Rosecrans, at Murfreesboro, that "much apprehension is felt at the North that the enemy would escape from your front and fall on Grant, and we are also anxious on that account to know where Forrest is, for report says he has gone south for that purpose." Stanton knew full well that if Forrest, with a proper command, got after Grant's communications, that general would suffer in consequence, and Rosecrans must keep him busy.

During the first week of June, Forrest was informed that General Granger had transferred his headquarters from Franklin to Triune, a town some fifteen miles eastward from the former place, situated about halfway between Murfreesboro and Franklin. In order to determine the strength of the forces still left in this latter place, he advanced with his two brigades on June 4th. Marching on the Columbia and Franklin pike at the head of Starnes's brigade, he dispatched Armstrong with his troops on the road leading from Lewisburg to Franklin. About three miles distant from Franklin, on both roads, the Federal pickets were encountered and chased into town, a number of captures being made by Colonel Starnes. Forrest, with his accustomed boldness, charged on horseback right into the heart of the borough, shielding his troops as much as possible by keeping the houses between them and the fort.

Here Colonel J. P. Baird, of the Eighty-fifth Indiana Infantry, commanding, had taken refuge with his soldiers, and began a vigorous display of signal flags, calling urgently for help to his chief, General Gordon Granger, who was at Triune. The Confederate commander interpreted this white flag to mean a truce and, ordering his men to cease firing, rode forward with an attendant, displaying a like pacific emblem, cherishing the hope that if he could have an interview with Colonel Baird he might persuade him, by surrendering, to "prevent the further effusion of blood." He had not proceeded sufficiently far on his journey to catch the eye of Colonel Baird when, from a loopholed fence or wall near by, a Union soldier who recognized him shouted out: "General Forrest, you will retire at once. There is no truce; that is a signal flag." Raising his hat in recognition of this generous act, Forrest retraced his steps immediately.

The two guns of Morton's battery that had accompanied him

were now unhitched from the horses and rolled along the principal street by hand, and in this way he advanced with his men on foot, shelling the Union troops in the houses and in the fort. Having possession of the place, with the exception of the fortifications on the bluff and some few loopholed houses immediately under the protection of the garrison, he ordered the jail doors to be battered down, and released a number of political prisoners held in confinement by the enemy. The sutler's stores and commissaries were also promptly emptied by his troopers, and their contents piled into wagons, impressed for this purpose, and hauled away.

While Forrest was having such an easy time in this part of the village, things were not going so smoothly with Armstrong, who had been posted over on the side of Franklin nearest to Triune. In response to Colonel Baird's signals for help, General Granger in great haste had dispatched the First brigade of cavalry, under Colonel A. P. Campbell, to the rescue. This excellent command, composed of the Second Michigan, Fourth and Sixth Kentucky, and Ninth Pennsylvania regiments, reached within one and a half miles of Franklin just before sundown on the 4th of June and dashed into Armstrong's brigade in quick fashion. This officer had advanced Woodward's battalion and five companies of the First Tennessee Cavalry this distance out on the Triune road, and was on the lookout for these very reinforcements. Unfortunately he had not brought up the remainder of his brigade, which was still south of the Harpeth River. With the few he had on hand, Armstrong, with characteristic stubbornness and gallantry, resisted the vigorous attacks of the enemy in his front, in the hope of effecting a safe withdrawal, which he finally accomplished, although the Federal troopers pushed him vigorously to within sight of the river.

Here Colonel Hobson, with his regiment, hearing the brisk firing in his front, advanced hurriedly to reinforce Armstrong, and was successful in covering his retreat across this stream. Forrest, on hearing the heavy sound of musketry in that direction, and noticing that it was drifting southward, gathered from this that Armstrong was being driven back, and, fearing a strong force might be interposed between the detachment under himself and Spring Hill, he immediately withdrew from his point of vantage to the south side of Harpeth River, and soon thereafter joined General Armstrong. Night had now come on, and both brigades retired to a point three miles distant from the river in the direction of Spring Hill, and there encamped for the night. The Federal commander made no attempt to follow the Confederates. He reports fifteen killed and wounded Confederates, and the capture of eighteen men of Armstrong's brigade, among whom were four of the latter's escort. Colonel Baird, who was chief in command of the post, reports, however, only ten prisoners in all, while his own loss "will not exceed ten killed and wounded." Colonel Faulkner, of the Union cavalry, was reported mortally wounded. The Confederates retired the next day to their former position at Spring Hill.

At dark on June 8th, 1863, two men on horseback, clad in the uniform of the Federal army and with equipment belonging to officers in the Union service, arrived in Franklin and called at the headquarters of Colonel J. P. Baird, commanding that post. The two men, whose general appearance and conversation indicated that they were persons of education and presumably of importance, introduced themselves as Inspector General Lawrence Auton, colonel in the United States Army, and Assistant Inspector General Major Dunlap. They presented to Colonel Baird an order from Adjutant General Townsend, assigning them to duty in that quarter; also an order from Major General W. S. Rosecrans, countersigned by Brigadier General James A. Garfield, chief of staff, asking them to inspect his outposts, and enclosing a pass through all lines from General Rosecrans. Colonel Auton told the Federal commander that in coming over from Murfreesboro he had unfortunately wandered off on the wrong road several miles in the direction of Eagleville, had there run into an outpost of rebel pickets. In the effort to escape, his orderly had been wounded and captured, and in his flight he himself had lost his overcoat, and with it his pocket-book with what money he was carrying. He requested Colonel Baird to be good enough to advance him enough money to take him to Nashville, where he would be able to obtain any amount he might need.

While they were conversing upon various subjects with Colonel Baird and his staff, who were entertaining them until some questions could be asked over the telegraph, this officer sent a dispatch to Garfield at Murfreesboro, asking if any such inspectors had received instructions and passes through the lines. Garfield promptly responded that there were no such men of his acquaintance, that no passes had been issued, and added: "The two men are no doubt spies. Call a drumhead court-martial to-night, and if they are found to be spies hang them before morning without fail." Colonel Baird wired back that he had arrested them, and that they had confessed they were Confederate spies. He said: "Their ruse was nearly successful on me. My bile is stirred, and some hanging would do me good."

They were tried and found guilty in short order, but as the trial progressed Colonel Baird's heart softened, and he now wanted to shift the rôle of executioner to someone else. He wired Rosecrans: "If you can direct me to send them to hang somewhere else I would like it." His commander in chief, however, was inexorable, and repeated his order: "If found guilty, hang at once, thus placing it beyond the possibility of Forrest's profiting by the information they have gained." They were hanged early on the morning of the 9th of June, 1863, and Colonel Baird testifies in his report that "they died like soldiers."

It transpired that these unfortunate men were Colonel William Orton Williams and Lieutenant Walter G. Peter, of the Confederate army. They died without making any disclosure of their purposes, nor to this day has it been revealed from whence they came and what object they had in view in this rash enterprise.

General Bragg, on this same day of June 9th, directed Forrest to make a forced reconnaissance of the enemy's position at Triune; and taking his entire division (with the exception of a strong picket line), and also Avery's and Crews' Georgia regiments, he moved out on the morning of June 10th. Approaching Triune on the Chapel Hill pike, the First Tennessee (Union) Cavalry was encountered and driven pell-mell into the town. Following on their heels, Forrest, with his light artillery at hand, came in close range of the Federal encampment, which he at once began to shell, driving everything in his front under cover of the breastworks. Seeing only cavalry in the field, the Federal infantry moved out in force and compelled the Confederates to retire. The number of troops in sight demonstrated to Forrest that the place was occupied by a large force of infantry as well as cavalry, and, as the latter was now menacing both his flank and rear, he retreated rapidly to place the Harpeth River between his command and the enemy.

The First (Union) brigade, under Colonel Campbell, had been hurried, by order of Brigadier General Mitchell, commanding the division,[1] along the right of the pike, while the Second brigade was sent to the left of this highway to gain the Confederate rear. Skirmishing briskly as he retired, Forrest recrossed the Harpeth and continued on his way to Spring Hill without further interruption. General Robert B. Mitchell says: "Being without artillery, and the enemy having obtained such an advance, I did not deem it advisable to follow them farther." The losses were insignificant on either side. General Granger, who was in command, dispatched Rosecrans: "I think it was only a reconnaissance." The Union losses, as officially given, were four killed, eighteen wounded, and six missing. Forrest made no report of his losses which appears in the records. As the casualties were in open fight, and between the cavalry, there should be no material difference in the number of killed and wounded on the two sides.

While the fighting was in progress, Major Jeffrey Forrest, who had been ordered by his brother to take advantage of the retirement of the Union troops and drive off a large herd of beef cattle grazing in a field nearby, accomplished this important duty successfully, and this valuable herd was the chief trophy of the expedition.

General Bragg, being fully informed of the intended advance of the army under Rosecrans, which began on the 22nd of June, 1863, and convinced of the inadvisability of risking a great battle with such a large stream as the Tennessee River immediately in his rear, ordered General Forrest to withdraw his picket lines and retreat via Shelbyville to Tullahoma. In accordance with this order, Forrest, without incident, reached the vicinity of Shelbyville between five and six o'clock on the afternoon of the 27th of June. It was his purpose to unite there with the cavalry under General Wheeler, crossing Duck River on the bridge in that town.

Major General Wheeler, to whom had been assigned the protection of the immense train of wagons which was employed in removing the valuable supplies which had been accumulated at Shelbyville, had been furiously attacked some two miles north of this place about two o'clock of that afternoon. As the wagons were at that time crossing the bridge in Shelbyville, and spread out for many miles along the muddy and almost impassable road leading in the direction of Tullahoma, he felt the urgent necessity of holding the enemy in check until the train could clear the bridge and get a start south of the river. This he

---

[1] *Official Records,* vol. xxiii, part i, p. 375.

had accomplished, although by stress of numbers and by very gallant fighting on the part of the Union troops in this engagement he had at last been driven into Shelbyville near sunset. With slight losses, and after a lively cavalry engagement, he had successfully withdrawn his command, and was on the south bank of Duck River prepared to set fire to the bridge.

At this moment Major Rambaut, of General Forrest's staff, arrived and reported that his commander with two brigades was within sight of Shelbyville and advancing rapidly to secure a crossing. Seeing the danger that threatened Forrest's command, Wheeler, although the Federals in strong force were then in the suburbs of Shelbyville and advancing into the town, hurriedly recrossed to the north side of Duck River in company with General Martin and five hundred men of this officer's division, taking with them two pieces of artillery, which they planted so as to command the approach to the bridge. He had scarcely reached the northerly terminus of the bridge when the Union troopers came charging in columns of fours right down the main street and toward the guns. These had been loaded with canister and were fired at the daring Union cavalry when only a few paces from their muzzles. Generals Wheeler and Martin, with their five hundred men, had lined up as best they could under the pressure of this charge, and held their ground manfully as the Federal cavalry rode through and over them, beat the cannoneers off, and took possession of the two pieces. Having the bridge now in their possession, the Union troopers, thinking they had the forlorn hope of Confederates in their trap, formed their line across the entrance to the bridge and along the bank of Duck River, above and below this outlet.

In the great confusion which had prevailed, a caisson had been overturned, and now thoroughly obstructed the bridge. Realizing the desperate strait in which he was, General Wheeler—as did the brave Poniatowski at Leipzig—saber in hand, shouted to his men that they must cut their way through and swim the river, ordered the charge, and, with General Martin, led in the desperate venture. The Federals, being cut right and left, were forced to yield and let them through. Not stopping for a moment to consider the distance from the crest of the riverbank—which was here precipitous—to the water level, these gallant soldiers followed their invincible leader, and leaped at full speed sheer fifteen feet down into the swift and headstrong current, for the river was then high from recent heavy rains. As they struck the water with such great velocity, horses and riders went out of sight, some of them to rise no more. Those who came up were a considerable distance out in the stream, and had been washed rapidly down with the current when they emerged.

The Federals rushed to the water's edge and fired at the brave men struggling in the river below, who preferred death to captivity. One officer was severely wounded, his arm being broken, but he still held on to his horse's mane, and was carried safely to the shore. Generals Wheeler and Martin escaped uninjured, having clung to their horses, and reached the southern bank. Some forty or fifty were thought to have perished by drowning. The gallant Wheeler never made a braver fight or did a more heroic and generous act than when he here risked all to save Forrest from disaster. That night General Gordon Granger missed the opportunity of a lifetime. Within nine miles of him, stretched along and floundering through the muddy road to Tullahoma, Bragg's enormous train of wagons, for which Wheeler had made his desperate fight and sacrificed his men against overwhelming odds, was creeping at a snail's pace through that dreary night and without adequate protection.

Forrest had turned back when he arrived near Shelbyville and found it and the bridge in possession of the Union forces. As it was four miles to the nearest bridge on which he could cross, he was forced to make a detour of eight miles in order to get back to the rear of the train for its protection. Martin's division was temporarily in disorganization. There was not a handful of effective troops between General Granger and the train, and, with the bridge in his possession, had he been as bold and persistent in pursuit as Forrest, he would have destroyed those wagons before daylight and inflicted a staggering blow to General Bragg. General D. S. Stanley wished to follow on that night, but his chief dissented. Satisfied with the performance of the day, as reported by his subordinate, Colonel R. H. G. Minty, the Federals "bivouacked near the railroad station in Shelbyville."[2]

General Forrest, who had the science and art of running—when it was the thing to do—as well in mind as that of fighting, took to his heels when he learned that Wheeler's men had been driven across Duck River, and sought safety in the crossing of this stream four miles

[2] *Ibid.,* vol. xxiii, part i, p. 558.

east of Shelbyville. General Granger, on June 28th, says: "Forrest passed around our rear last night, moving eastward. Had I known he was so doing, I could have thrown my force between the retreating army and his forces."[3] On the 27th he had dispatched Rosecrans after he entered Shelbyville: "Very few stores are to be found. Their wagon-train cannot possibly be more than nine miles distant, and the roads are very heavy. I hope to be able to destroy it." Wheeler had done his work well in clearing Shelbyville of all supplies and escaping to Tulla-homa with his train. Granger had beaten him in battle with superior forces, but not until he had fought his enemy to a standstill and left him too badly worn out to pursue beyond Shelbyville.

On the next day, June 28th, General Forrest reached the main army at Tullahoma, and was assigned to duty in observation on the Manchester and Tullahoma road. Colonel James W. Starnes, with his brigade, was posted on the route toward Manchester, and Colonel Dibrell, with his regiment, moved toward Hillsboro. On the 30th of June, in front of Tullahoma, Starnes encountered the advance of Rosecrans's army, and with his usual intrepidity assailed it in order to develop its strength. Throwing out a strong skirmish line, and following the precepts of the great soldier under whom he had been trained, he advanced with his skirmishers.

Captain W. A. Hubbard,[4] of Colonel Starnes's Fourth Tennessee regiment, seeing his beloved commander approach his position, where the firing was brisk and at dangerously close range, begged him to retire to the main line. Starnes thanked him for his thoughtful consideration, but, as usual, remained at the front. Within a few minutes a missile from the rifle of a sharpshooter wounded him unto death. Thus fell this worthy physician, brave soldier, and noble man, in the prime of life and on the threshold of a great career. It may be said of him that on every occasion he did his duty. He had no fault, unless it was the constant rash exposure of himself to danger. He believed it was a soldier's duty to fight, and to die when the time should come. When Napier pronounced his ever-to-be-remembered eulogium upon his comrade in arms, he shaped the phrase which may well be applied to Starnes, for "none died with greater glory than he, though many died, and there was much glory!"

[3] *Ibid.,* p. 535.
[4] Personal communication from Captain Hubbard, in possession of the author.

From Hillsboro Colonel Dibrell, hearing that Colonel Wilder with the Seventeenth Indiana mounted infantry and his brigade was marching on Decherd, hastened to the relief of the garrison of one company which was guarding the stockade there. The Federals had only partially destroyed the railroad when Dibrell attacked and drove them off. Wilder says, on the 30th: "A large force was by this time approach-

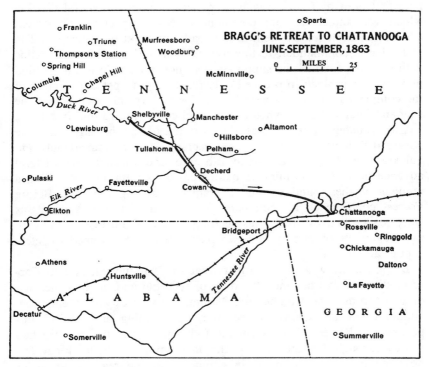

ing, and, having destroyed about three hundred yards of track, we left; believing that I would have but little chance of success in a fight with them, on account of the darkness and our total ignorance of the ground, we retired." Forrest, with his escort in advance, followed by a portion of one of his brigades, started in the direction of Pelham to intercept Wilder. It was raining, and he and his escort of sixty men (their identity concealed by the heavy oilcloth cloaks which housed them in) were well in advance of the command.

Suddenly, and just ahead of them, and also advancing around a short turn in the road, they met a detachment of mounted troops of about equal numbers and similarly clad in noncommittal waterproofs. The two companies were soon side by side in the highway, when Forrest asked what company it was. The captain replied, naming a company in Wilder's mounted infantry. Forrest coolly rejoined that his was Company C in a cavalry regiment, naming a Federal division which was under another commander. Not suspecting the deceit, Wilder's men passed by them in the road, and went on their way. The Confederate commander, feeling assured that they would soon collide with his troops, which he supposed were not more than a mile behind him, had determined to proceed only far enough to get out of sight of the company he had just passed, in order to form his men across the way and intercept them when they should come toward him in retreat.

Unfortunately, not a great distance ahead, as he advanced, he observed Wilder's main column approaching. He then immediately and quickly turned back, and soon ran into and through the Federal advance he had some minutes before passed, capturing and killing a number of these, and causing a stampede among the rest. Before Forrest could reach his command and return to attack Wilder this wary leader had escaped, "just getting ahead of Forrest, who, with nine regiments of cavalry and two pieces of artillery, aimed to intercept us at Pelham."[5]

Bragg's army was now in full retreat to Chattanooga, and to Forrest's division was assigned the duty of securing and holding the pass or gap through the Cumberland Mountains near Cowan, Tennessee. Numerous small skirmishes occurred, but nothing of sufficient importance to be recorded, except the following. After the infantry had passed through Cowan and up the mountain, the Federal cavalry, hovering in their rear, came in contact with the rear guard under Forrest in person. Firing and falling back rapidly, the Confederate troopers went through the village and toward the gap.

As the general, among the last in retreat, was passing a house, he noticed a woman who was berating his soldiers for not turning on the Yankees and "whipping them back." Shaking her fist at Forrest, the stars on whose collar she was too angry to observe or too nearsighted to see, she shrieked out: "You great big cowardly rascal; why don't you

[5] *Official Records,* vol. xxiii, part i, p. 461.

turn and fight like a man, instead of running like a cur? I wish old Forrest was here, he'd make you fight!" The general, unable to control himself, burst into a laugh as he put spurs to his horse and fled the scene. When telling this incident he said that he would rather have faced a battery than that fiery dame. A few days later the army crossed to the south bank of the Tennessee, and in July the cavalry was ordered into various districts in which forage could be obtained, for rest and recuperation.

From Chattanooga, on July 27th, General Forrest ordered Colonel G. G. Dibrell to take his Eighth Tennessee regiment across the Tennessee and proceed to the vicinity of Sparta, Tennessee, to watch a corps of Rosecrans's army, which was then stationed at McMinnville, twenty-six miles from Sparta. Dibrell reached Sparta July 29th and encamped on his own plantation, two miles out from the town. On August 9th, Colonel Robert H. G. Minty endeavored to surprise Colonel Dibrell and his troops. He took the Fourth Regulars, Seventh Pennsylvania, Fourth Michigan, and a battalion of the Third Indiana, numbering, as he states, 774 effectives, and marched all night to pounce upon this single regiment of three hundred men, and managed to put in a very busy day when he found them. Four miles away, Dibrell's pickets at daylight fired into Minty's advance guard, and broke for camp. The Fourth Michigan followed at full tilt, but the Tennesseeans beat them in, and kept up such a racket as they ran that the Confederates in camp were aroused, saddled up, and were ready for the surprise party. A single company was left in front to check their advance, while Dibrell led the other companies behind Wild Cat Creek, where the banks were high and steep, and, by reason of a mill dam, no crossing could be made except over a narrow, rickety bridge, which the Confederates covered with their rifles.

As the Union troopers charged in at full speed, Dibrell, at close range, opened on them with great effect, threw them into confusion, and caused them to retreat precipitately. They re-formed, and on foot made a rush for the bridge, only to meet with a second repulse. They now made a wide detour around Dibrell's position, which caused him to retire to Blue Spring Creek, one mile to the rear. There he took another strong position; but Minty had had enough, and withdrew. Colonel Dibrell reports a loss of four wounded and captured. He found twelve dead Union troopers on the field, and twenty dead horses.

Colonel Minty reports: "Our loss, I regret to say, was heavy."

The presence of Dibrell so far north as Sparta, and of Forrest's cavalry, now in east Tennessee, where a portion of his command were ordered in the vicinity of Kingston, was sufficient to excite the apprehension of Major General George L. Hartsuff, who, on July 21st, from Cincinnati, Ohio, telegraphed General Rosecrans in regard to the looked-for invasion of Kentucky from east Tennessee, as follows: "How much cavalry can Forrest raise? Where is he now? And where will he cross the Cumberland?" Even in faraway Cincinnati the daring raider was deemed a possibility.

Affairs, however, were rapidly shaping themselves which were destined to preclude all notion of invasion of this section of the Union by the Southern troops. Rosecrans, with great boldness, was pushing steadily ahead, and Bragg was on the defensive. The month of August was passed in inactivity on the part of the Southern general, while his enemy was displaying the greatest energy. On the 27th of this month the Federals began the passage of the Tennessee River at Caperton's Ferry, and by the 4th of September the greater portion of Rosecrans's army was on the southern bank.

Threatened by a flank movement, Bragg gave up Chattanooga and retired to Dalton and Lafayette in Georgia, where he rapidly concentrated his troops, calling in with the rest the cavalry under Forrest in east Tennessee. Every movement of Forrest's was closely watched and quickly made the subject of communication to the commander of the Union army. On August 31st, James A. Garfield, chief of staff, was inquiring by telegraph of General Crittenden at Dunlap: "What have you from Forrest?" General Burnside, on the 2nd, telegraphed to Rosecrans: "General Forrest crossed the Tennessee at this place. He was heard to say that he was ordered to Dalton." Rosecrans immediately reported this news to General in Chief Halleck at Washington. The official dispatches of this period are replete with the strongest evidence of the appreciation by the Federal leaders of Forrest's great activity. On the 2nd of September there were "indications that Forrest intended attacking our train." On the 6th, General W. B. Hazen was "anxious about a raid in his rear by Forrest"; and Colonel Minty was notified that "indications pointed to a raid by Forrest to cross the Tennessee River above Harrison." On the 7th, General Wagner sent word to Rosecrans that "Forrest had gone in the direction of Rome," and in this last report there was something of truth. Forrest had been ordered to march in the direction of Alpine and Rome to head off a large force of cavalry under Stanley, upon whom it would seem the mantle of Colonel Abel D. Streight was about to fall.

Rosecrans could not be cured of his longing for a break in Bragg's great feeder, the railroad from Atlanta to Dalton and Chattanooga. If Stanley or Wilder, or some bold cavalryman, could dash in

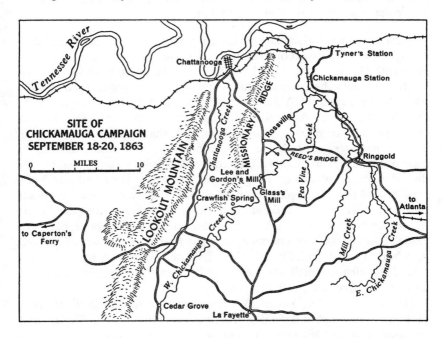

and burn the bridge over the Etowah, or do anything to give Bragg a still greater scare than he had, he might get him still farther into Georgia without a battle. Stanley was ready to try, although he started out with misgivings. Chief of staff and future President Garfield, who was at Trenton, Georgia, with Rosecrans, took a more rosy view of the matter. On the 7th of September he wrote Stanley a very encouraging epistle:

The general commanding thinks it practicable for you to make a successful expedition against the enemy's line of communication. Considering the relative strength of the enemy's cavalry and our own, and the additional fact that Forrest's whole force and nearly all of Wheeler's are in the neighborhood of Chattanooga, and cannot be brought to bear against you, he has the more confidence in your ability to succeed in the expedition. General McCook has been directed to hold the pass to cover your return, and to send two brigades as far as Alpine to aid in securing your route and forming a support. The general commanding directs you to push forward rapidly and with audacity. The severing of the enemy's railroad communication with Atlanta will be most disastrous to him.

With the general of cavalry it was not possible to consider the undertaking as so easy of accomplishment as outlined by the chief of staff. He wrote Garfield that he did not have troops enough—only thirteen small regiments; he wanted Minty and his whole command, and, in addition, that General Wilder should strike at the Chattanooga end of the line and make a diversion. Stanley was correct and Garfield was mistaken. The latter was a better politician than soldier. Forrest was *not* at Chattanooga. He came as near being in both places at once as mortal man ever did. Stanley, backed by McCook's infantry and by the diversion under Wilder on Bragg's right flank near Ringgold and Tunnel Hill, did start. Sweeping down Wills Valley between Sand Mountain on the west and bold Lookout on the east, and then across the latter, he descended into the valley "like the stream from the rock." He reached Alpine and Summerville, near the foot of the mountain, stirred up a hornet's nest, and, like the king of France, went back up the mountain. His thirteen small regiments looked smaller the farther he got away from McCook's infantry.

He found Wheeler, Martin, Wharton, and Forrest all there in front of him. He voted Garfield's information bureau unreliable, and promptly retraced his steps. It was an exceedingly wise move on the part of Stanley. On September 6th, Forrest was at Ringgold, but, having heard of Stanley's movement, by the morning of the 8th he was at Alpine. General Wharton was directed to reinforce him "with three hundred picked men for a reconnaissance" to develop the enemy (Stanley and McCook), and on this date Forrest wrote to Wheeler: "Have arrived at Gowers. If I hear nothing of the enemy to-day, I shall cross the mountain and get in their front. If the enemy do not advance on us *we must move on them.*"

The mystery of Garfield's error in locating Forrest is solved in the official records. On September 7th, Colonel R. K. Byrd, at Kingston in east Tennessee, telegraphed Colonel Minty: "One of Forrest's body-guard came in (deserted) yesterday, and informs me that Forrest is at Philadelphia (in east Tennessee) with three brigades and thirteen pieces of artillery." Forrest's escort were picked men, selected for their devotion to him and their fearlessness, and were always "coming in" to give themselves up, with such "untruthful" reports. It was part of their war trade, and one of the methods employed by Forrest for obtaining information and of deceiving the enemy. Minty rushed to the telegraph and sent this news to Rosecrans and Garfield, and the latter cheered Stanley with such encouraging intelligence as the faraway absence of Forrest.

On September 3rd the division of cavalry under Brigadier General John Pegram had been added to Forrest's command, and when the latter moved to Alpine to aid in forcing Stanley back this division was left to guard the right wing of Bragg's army. As soon as Forrest's reconnaissance demonstrated that the Union cavalryman had given up all idea of striking at the railroad, he hastened back to the neighborhood of Ringgold with the troops he had brought hither. Arriving there on the 10th, Forrest discovered that two divisions of Crittenden's corps had crossed the Chickamauga Creek at Red House bridge, and were practically isolated from the other portions of Rosecrans's army. Seeing at once the possibility of capture or destruction of these troops, he informed General Bragg of the situation, and proposed to throw his troops at once in their rear.

Before any reply or orders could be received from Bragg, Crittenden, who did not seem to appreciate the peril of his situation, continued to advance farther in the direction of Tunnel Hill. Forrest placed his cavalry across his line of march, resisting stubbornly from every point of vantage in the effort to retard his progress until help could arrive. Crittenden's heavy column of infantry gradually forced him back until finally a strong position was found at Tunnel Hill, and here, after a hard struggle, the Union troops gave up and retreated toward Chickamauga.

General Forrest received another wound in this affair, which, however, did not compel him to relinquish the command. It compelled him, nevertheless, to do something which was much against his principles— namely, to take a drink of whisky. Having become faint with pain and loss of blood, he did so at the urgent order of his surgeon. Major Charles W. Anderson, of his staff, says he never knew him to taste liquor unless he was sick or wounded. General Pegram won great and well-deserved credit on this occasion for the desperate fighting done by his division.

Probably no general ever missed so many opportunities to destroy the army of his antagonist as did General Bragg in this month of September, 1863. The escape of Crittenden from his perilous position was the second strategic fiasco that Forrest had witnessed within a fortnight. When Burnside came down out of eastern Kentucky into Tennessee, near Knoxville, he was isolated and hopelessly cut off from all chance of support. The army of Bragg was concentrated, had the inside track or "interior line," and had nothing to do but to move rapidly and overwhelm him before he could either retreat or receive assistance. Forrest was heart and soul in favor of the movement, and did all he could to induce the commander in chief to undertake it. Buckner's corps was at hand, and D. H. Hill was there. There were Confederates enough and available to have annihilated this corps. General Bragg, instead of taking hold vigorously in person and forcing the movement, wrote to Hill: "The crushing of this corps would give us a great victory and redeem Tennessee. By selecting fords, Forrest promises to cross the infantry on horseback." That was the end of it. Burnside was not within five days' march of aid. Crittenden, who could have been surrounded in twenty-four hours with three times his number, could not have received assistance within three days; while McCook's corps, at or near Alpine, was nearly forty miles from Crittenden, and itself isolated and open to destruction.

And yet the Confederate general, able enough to see these grand opportunities, failed to take hold personally and force them to a successful result. On each occasion he seemed content to trust the fate of his army and the cause for which he earnestly fought to subordinates who accomplished nothing. Failure upon failure followed in quick succession. Burnside remained unmolested; Crittenden, McCook, and Thomas in turn escaped. Rosecrans effected his concentration, and then, as a fitting climax to this tragedy of blunders, he forced the army of Bragg to attack him on ground of his own selection.

As Crittenden on the 11th retired with his corps across the Chickamauga and up the west bank of this creek toward Lee and Gordon's

Mill, Wilder's brigade of mounted infantry was employed in protecting his flank nearest to Chattanooga. On the 12th, Pegram, with his Sixth Georgia Cavalry and Rucker's Legion, at Leet's Tanyard came in contact with Colonel Wilder's command, and a desperate encounter followed. The Confederates were overmatched in numbers and in arms (for the enemy had repeating rifles), but held their ground with such determination that the Federal movement was checked. General Pegram reports: "For a time the fight was almost literally hand to hand. My loss was about fifty killed and wounded."

The records show that on this same day another of Forrest's escort deserted and came into the Union camp.[6] He reported that "Forrest had gone toward Lafayette yesterday. Fighting was going on from noon of the 11th until dark, at Lee and Gordon's Mill," etc. Nevertheless, Forrest was at that time at Tunnel Hill, watching Wilder. There was no fighting at Lee and Gordon's Mill, nor was there any intention of accuracy in this statement. The record does not show when the deserter got back to Forrest with the information he was seeking. There was not a general in the Confederacy who had a more thorough and reliable system of scouts than Forrest, and much of his success may be traced to the cunning displayed in this direction.

By September 11th it began to dawn on Rosecrans that the Confederates were at last tired of running, and were about to turn on him for a fight. The chase after Bragg from Tullahoma across the Tennessee had been little more than a summer excursion. He had so little respect for the Southern general that he scattered his troops all over the country, with slight regard to any possible necessity for rapid concentration. The occurrence that opened the eyes of Rosecrans was this: Generals Negley and Baird, who had crossed Lookout Mountain and descended the eastern slope through Steven's Gap into McLemore's Cove, found themselves on this day confronted by a strong force of Confederates, which advanced upon them in such threatening fashion that they rapidly reclimbed Lookout and ran away. The effort to cut them off and capture them was a badly bungled job. Any student of the art of war, desiring to learn how badly a bit of strategy may be spoiled, is referred to the official records of this affair.

On this same 11th of September, Forrest, at Tunnel Hill, had hammered away at Crittenden so vigorously that this officer also discovered

[6] *Ibid.,* vol. xxx, part iii, p. 563.

that "the better part of valor was discretion," and retired toward Chattanooga. The Federal general began at last to display considerable anxiety, and to concentrate his scattered legions. As the hot and dusty days slipped by, his anxiety increased, for he heard that Longstreet was coming, and indeed was near at hand. On the 16th he dispatched to Burnside, who was in the vicinity of Knoxville: "The enemy intend us all the mischief in their power. It is of the utmost importance that you close down this way to cover our left flank. We have not the force to cover our flank against Forrest now. He could cross the river above us before we could discover it. I want all the help we can get promptly."[7]

[7] *Ibid.*, vol. xxx, part iii, p. 691.

ELEVEN

The Battle of Chickamauga

THE battle of Chickamauga opened on Friday, September 18, 1863. In this terrible struggle, one of the bloodiest in history, the Southern cavalry acquitted itself with great credit. It was not beaten on any portion of the field during the three days of the engagement, and fought successfully the retreating army on Monday after the main battle ended, making additional captures of men and wagons. General Joseph Wheeler commanded all the mounted forces on the left wing, and confined his operations exclusively to this portion of the field, leaving Forrest in full sway on the right flank. Practically all the cavalry on the southern side fought at Chickamauga on foot and in line with the infantry. On the left, Wheeler defeated the Union cavalry at Glass's Mill, drove them for nearly two miles to Crawfish Spring, and finally, on Sunday afternoon, September 20th, formed the extreme left of the Confederate infantry line of battle, sweeping the field from Lee and Gordon's Mill back to the rear of Thomas's position, until darkness put an end to the pursuit. On the right it may be said that Forrest struck the first and the last blow—firing the opening and the final shots in this engagement. He acquitted himself with such distinction as to attract the general attention of the Southern people, and once more to win a special vote of thanks from the Congress of the Confederate States.

On the 18th of September, Brigadier General Bushrod R. Johnson, commanding a division composed of his own, McNair's, Gregg's, and Robertson's brigades, was directed to advance from Ringgold to the Chickamauga Creek, cross at Reed's Bridge, and march, prepared for a collision with the enemy, from that point up the creek in the direction of Lee and Gordon's Mill. This force at this moment was the right of the Confederate infantry line, and with it, and on its right flank nearest to Rosecrans's base at Chattanooga, Forrest's cavalry were moving.

In touch with Johnson and to his left, a division of the Confederate reserve corps, under Major General William H. T. Walker, was directed to proceed by a parallel route and cross the creek at Alexander's Bridge, or, if too strongly resisted there, to wade this stream at Byram's Ford, about one mile farther up the creek from the bridge. Next in order was the division of Major General S. B. Buckner, which in like manner had orders to advance and effect a crossing at Thedford's Ford, still farther away, in the direction of Lee and Gordon's Mill. On September 9th, when Forrest had reached Dalton, Georgia, he had dispatched the brigade, under Colonel Hodge, to watch the Cleveland and Dalton road. Colonel Scott's brigade was stationed on the route from Ringgold to Chattanooga. Pegram's division was at Pea Vine Church. Armstrong, with his division, was in front of Cheatham's infantry, along the Lafayette and Chattanooga road; while Forrest, with his escort and about 240 men (a remnant of General John H. Morgan's cavalry which had not been swallowed up in the wild Ohio raid), was stationed at Dalton.

As Johnson approached Reed's Bridge, about noon of Friday, September 18th, Forrest went to the front, having with him his escort and Morgan's remnant—three hundred men in all. Off to the right, as Johnson advanced, Pegram's division was moving, to keep an eye on any Union forces which might be near enough to interfere with the Southern infantry. When General Johnson arrived within one mile of the enemy's position, near Reed's Bridge, over which the Federals had already crossed, he threw his troops into line of battle. He reports: "While forming the line, Brigadier General Forrest joined with his escort, proceeded to the front to develop the position of the enemy, and was soon skirmishing with them."

It must have seemed like old times to Johnson and Forrest to be side by side again as they had stood in loyal and brave support of each other on that bitter cold Saturday in February, 1862, when they shattered Grant's right wing at Fort Donelson. Had everyone on that field done their work as well as Forrest and Johnson, and brave, loyal, and unjustly treated Gideon J. Pillow, it might not have been necessary to shed the river of blood which the Chickamauga, within the next three days, was to carry away on its tinted current and pour into the beautiful Tennessee. There, as now, Forrest had opened the ball.

From Pea Vine Creek, where the skirmishing commenced, the Federals were driven back by Johnson and Forrest, but not without creditable resistance. At Reed's Bridge they made a final and more stubborn stand, as the Confederates crowded them with artillery, and then charged with infantry and cavalry, driving them away so precipitately that they did not take time to burn the bridge. The entire force now moved across the Chickamauga, and, being joined by Pegram's division, marched up the creek toward Alexander's Bridge.

About 4 P.M., Major General John B. Hood arrived and took command of all the troops on this part of the field. The infantry slept in line of battle that night about eight hundred yards from the Vineyard House, and near the little log schoolhouse, on the highway from Lee and Gordon's Mill to Chattanooga. Forrest scouted and picketed the country a mile to the right of this position, and went into bivouac with the main body of his troops in the rear of Hood's line, near Alexander's Bridge. The Federal forces encountered here were a brigade of cavalry under Colonel Minty. Very early on the 19th General Forrest was ordered to move with his command to the Confederate right, in the direction of Reed's Bridge and Chattanooga, and to develop the enemy.

Advancing promptly with Pegram's division near the bridge, he was soon engaged with the Union troops in such strength that help was needed. Forrest sent a courier to the infantry with the message that he had raised a hornet's nest, and could not hold on long unless reinforcements were sent to him. It was evident to him now that the Federal commander had outwitted General Bragg. While the latter was marching his troops from the neighborhood of Reed's Bridge up the Chickamauga all that same night Rosecrans was sliding his long line of battle in the opposite direction to get nearer to Chattanooga, so that in case of disaster his antagonist could not get in between him and that place of refuge. Wise Rosecrans; for here now, a mile at least to the right of this flank of the Southern infantry, was a large force and a long line of Union troops. D. H. Hill, who passed up that way, says: "I found that while our troops had been moving up the Chickamauga, the Yankees had been moving down, and thus outflanked us."[1]

As no reinforcements came, General Forrest sent Major Anderson of his staff to General Polk, asking him to give him Armstrong's division. Polk, needing half of this cavalry for his portion of the line, an-

[1] *Official Records,* vol. xxx, part ii, p. 140.

swered with the other half, sending General Dibrell's brigade, which double-quicked and, with the faithfulness and celerity of this gallant soldier, was in short order dismounted and in the thickest of the fray. As no satisfactory answer had come to Forrest's repeated messages for the infantry line to be moved in his direction, he now instructed Pegram to hold what he had, "no matter what might happen," until he could go for help and return with it.

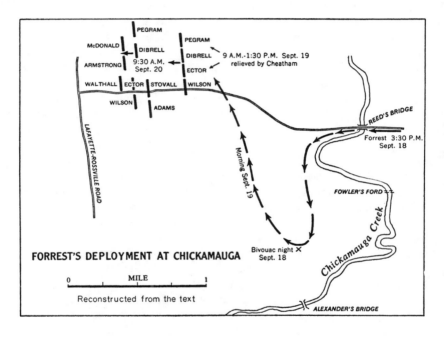

FORREST'S DEPLOYMENT AT CHICKAMAUGA

0   MILE   1

Reconstructed from the text

Pegram promised to do it, and did it well, though at terrific cost. From behind trees and logs, and every possible point of vantage, these cavalrymen on foot fought with the stubbornness and precision of infantry. They held on like grim death, and grim death held on to many of them. One-fourth of their number went down then and there, although Forrest hurried back and brought the foot soldiers with him. Pegram says: "It became apparent that we were fighting overpowering numbers. General Forrest having sent several messengers for the infantry to come up, finally went for them himself, ordering me to hold the position until their arrival. In obeying this order our loss was about one-fourth of the command."

The brigades of Colonel Claudius C. Wilson and General Edward C. Walthall, coming up at Forrest's request, took their place in line immediately on his left and moved forward. They were not going to yield the palm to Forrest and Pegram's horsemen. These veterans of other bloody fields moved forward rapidly and with directness to close range before they delivered their well-aimed volleys into the Union line, which yielded under the pressure, and was pursued by all. Forrest was elated over the conduct of Wilson's men. "They advanced in gallant style, driving the enemy back and capturing a battery of artillery, my dismounted cavalry advancing with them." He was in command of all the troops now at this end of the line, and pushed forward, and with Wilson drove back the second Federal line of battle, following this until a third line, behind well-constructed defenses, was developed. Colonel Wilson was now ordered by General Forrest not to attempt to carry this position until more troops could be brought up. At this moment the brigade of General Matthew D. Ector appeared on the field, having orders to report to Forrest, who placed it on the right of Wilson, the dismounted cavalry being pushed still farther over on Ector's right flank. Meanwhile the Union lines had been reinforced, and now felt themselves strong enough to take their turn as the aggressors.

Before Forrest could get Ector's men in place and ready for a general assault, a heavy column of Federals had advanced well beyond Wilson's left flank, overlapping him and opening a severe enfilading fire, which forced this brave officer to retire his brigade, in doing which Forrest's entire line was carried back. The horses in the captured battery had been killed, and though the Confederates tried to roll them off by hand, they could not succeed, and these guns again fell into the hands of their former owners. Morton's and Huggins's batteries had done excellent work, and, as was Forrest's practice, their pieces were shoved to the front almost up to shotgun range. As they retired, the thick woods and, in places, the dense undergrowth made it no easy matter to bring away their artillery, as the plucky Federals were coming on in steady lines and with fixed bayonets. The general held his troops steadily at work as they gave back. There was no break to the rear, but from tree to tree and from behind every point of shelter these trained woodsmen, making plucky resistance, loaded and fired their guns with deadly effect.

The horses of one of Captain Huggins's pieces, in charge of Lieutenant Edwin H. Douglas, were all killed or wounded. Douglas told Forrest that he would have to leave the gun unless he could get help to pull it out. Alive to the urgency of the situation, and quick in expedient, the general called to four of his escort who were mounted and nearby, and, quickly throwing the collars and hames over the troopers' saddled horses, the traces were attached, and away rode the cavalrymen, dragging the precious gun to safety.

The men fell back in good order, the Federals not following beyond their original position. Just at this minute, Major General W. H. T. Walker came up and took command of his infantry. The fighting here had lasted from early in the morning to 1.30 P.M. Cheatham's division came on the field to relieve them, and with Cleburne succeeded after a terrific struggle in driving the Federals from their entire line, and slept on their arms that night, masters of the bloody field. General Walker paid a high and well-earned compliment to the fighting qualities of the men under Forrest in this hot and sanguinary morning's work. "The unequal contest of four brigades against such overwhelming odds is unparalleled in this revolution, and the troops deserve immortal honor for the part borne in the action."

In the hottest of the fight, General Forrest's horse, presented to him by the citizens of Rome in token of their appreciation of his capture of Streight, was mortally wounded. As the troops were retiring, here also occurred an incident which will throw light upon two of this man's characteristics. Major Anderson was with the general in the rear of the line, up and down which he was galloping, encouraging his men to stand to their work, and ready to threaten, or do more than threaten, any who dared to give back too rapidly. At one moment of this trying time, a private soldier, having parted company with his courage, cut loose from his place in front and broke at top speed for the rear. He unfortunately ran very near to the general and his aide. Forrest whipped out his six-shooter, ordered the man to halt, and was in the act of making an example of him when Major Anderson exclaimed, "Oh, general, think"; the general did think and, lowering his pistol, let the unhappy mortal go in peace.

In relating this incident the faithful aide-de-camp remarked: "I knew him and his moods so well that I had learned just how to take him. I am confident that, in the excitement of the moment, knowing the supreme disregard he felt for life—even his own, when the fate of battle hung in the balance—had I said, 'General Forrest, don't do that!' he would have killed the·man without a doubt, and I might have gotten a turn too."

Ex-Congressman and later United States District Judge C. B. Kilgore related to the writer the following, which occurred on this portion of the field:

On Friday night, September 18, 1863, Ector's brigade, of which I was adjutant, crossed Chickamauga Creek, and on Saturday morning, the 19th, formed on the extreme Confederate right, supporting General Forrest's cavalry, which was very heavily engaged. The fighting soon became fierce for us, and we were barely able to hold our ground. General Ector became uneasy in regard to the protection of his right flank, and asked me to go to General Forrest and urge him to be very vigilant in his protection of it. I galloped up to where one of his batteries was engaged, as I had been told he was there. He had on a linen duster, with a sword and pistol on the outside of the duster, and was exposed to very heavy fire of infantry and now and then a shot from the enemy's batteries.

I said: "General Forrest, General Ector directed me to say to you that he is uneasy in regard to his right flank." He replied: "Tell General Ector that he need not bother about his right flank, I'll take care of it." I reported to my commander, and about an hour later news reached us that Wilson's brigade had been hard hit and driven back, and General Ector sent me again to Forrest to tell him that he was now uneasy about his left flank. I found him near the same spot, right in the thickest part of the fight, the battery blazing away and every man fighting like mad. I told him what General Ector had directed me to say, and this time he got furious. He turned around on me and shouted, loud enough to be heard above the terrible din that was in the air: "Tell General Ector that, by God, I am here, and will take care of his left flank as well as his right." It is hardly necessary to add that we were not outflanked on either side.

Saturday night General Frank C. Armstrong arrived with his second brigade, and took command of his division, which, with Pegram's, was thrown out to the extreme right, guarding that flank, contiguous to the Reed's Bridge road. During the night of Saturday the 20th, a general readjustment of the opposing lines of battle was made. The struggle of the 19th, severe and bloody as it was, had never become general. The firing had at no time swept continuous down the lines. The advantage was decidedly with the Confederates, who held all the ground upon which the contest had opened, and more. Rosecrans's anxiety about his left wing and the path to the rear and Chattanooga had greatly increased. By an all-night march Thomas's corps, heavily reinforced, was placed at his left, and all through this night and during the early morning the axes were ringing along the five or six miles of battlefront, trees were crashing to the ground, and the busy picks were playing a tattoo on the earth as the Union beavers toiled to strengthen their position. They had been beaten on Saturday, and they knew the morrow would require all that art and skill and courage could do to hold the Southerners back.

At daybreak on Sunday morning General Forrest and his cavalry found themselves in line with the division of Major General John C. Breckinridge, which, a little after daylight, reached Cleburne's right, and now became the extreme right of the Confederate infantry. Still to the right of these, in line of battle at dawn of day, were Forrest's troopers. General Bragg had given explicit directions as to the hour of battle. In his official report he says: "Lieutenant-General Polk was ordered to assail the enemy on our extreme right at daydawn on the 20th." Daylight came; the troops were there, but the attack was not made. Polk's order to Hill was not delivered. The courier could not find General Hill in time. Breckinridge says: "Soon after sunrise I received a note from Lieutenant-General Polk, directing me to advance. Cleburne received the same order at this time."[2] Breckinridge adds: "Lieutenant-General Hill having arrived, the notes were placed in his hands. By his order the movement was delayed for the troops to get their rations, and on other accounts." The whole army was waiting for the sound of cannon and musketry from Polk and Breckinridge and Hill. It did not come until 9.30, and these three hours of priceless daylight were gone forever.

Breckinridge, advancing at 9.30, soon came in contact with the Federals, and was fully engaged by ten o'clock. As his troops moved forward, Forrest also moved, a continuation of the infantry line. Armstrong's division, with the exception of the First Tennessee regiment arfd McDonald's battalion, was dismounted and sent in well on the right. Pegram's division, having already suffered extremely, was at this time held in reserve, while the two mounted detachments were kept out

[2] *Ibid.,* vol. xxx, part ii, p. 198.

on the flank. Breckinridge had met with determined resistance. The enemy was strongly intrenched, and it seemed almost impossible to dislodge them. Time and again his gallant troops assailed the works, only to be driven back with terrific slaughter. In those two desperate hours men perished by hundreds. The Kentuckians gave up their lives in reckless fashion, and, without a peer among these gallant spirits, General Ben Hardin Helm passed in the twinkling of an eye from the storm of battle "To where beyond this presence there is peace."

Armstrong and Forrest moved over to the right and, reaching a little beyond the Union intrenchments, found open going, and pushed well beyond the alignment of the infantry. It was glorious work for the cavalry. General D. H. Hill, just from the mighty battle scenes of the army of northern Virginia, riding with his staff to this quarter and seeing these men sweeping in steady line around the Union left, asked Major Charles W. Anderson, "What infantry is that?" "That is Forrest's cavalry," he replied. General Hill looked at him with an expression of surprise, if not of incredulity, and said, "Can I see General Forrest?" "Yes; he is there with his men. I will take you to him." As they approached, Forrest rode back to meet them. His artillery had just been advanced to the open field in front of Cloud's Spring, and Huggins, Morton, and gallant Captain Gracey (whose guns had been borrowed for this urgent occasion) were hurrying into this advanced position.

As Forrest approached, General Hill, raising his hat in salutation, said: "General Forrest, I wish to congratulate you and those brave men moving across that field like veteran infantry upon their magnificent behavior. In Virginia I made myself extremely unpopular with the cavalry because I said that so far I had not seen a dead man with spurs on. No one can speak disparagingly of such troops as yours." Forrest, concealing whatever of pride or elation he felt at this high compliment to himself and his troops, simply said: "Thank you, General," waved his hand, wheeled his horse, and galloped away to his favorite position by Morton's battery.

Well may General Breckinridge report that "this was one of the bloodiest encounters of the day." The threatening position of Forrest's men, reinforced by Adams's and Stovall's brigades of Breckinridge's division, gave General Thomas so much concern that he called loudly for help, and Rosecrans materially and fatally weakened his line farther toward the (Union) right. At this moment Granger's corps came on the scene at double-quick from the direction of Rossville. Forrest's vigilant scouts had wind of their coming, and informed their leader of Granger's advance. The cavalryman sent quickly to Breckinridge for more artillery, and this was why Gracey with his Napoleons was charging out with Morton and Huggins. As Gordon Granger came in sight with the reserve corps of the Army of the Tennessee, Forrest's three batteries opened on the head of his column with such vigor and precision that his rapid march toward Thomas was arrested, and he was compelled to throw himself into line of battle and fight his way through. Forrest now held the Lafayette road, the Federal camps and hospitals, and a number of prisoners. For more than an hour Granger's march was here retarded.

Then Thomas sent help over to him, and, thus reinforced, charging down the road from the direction of Chattanooga, Granger compelled this portion of the Confederate line to retire, though for not more than two hundred yards. Here Forrest held on stubbornly, forcing Granger to make a considerable detour to reach his destination. He says: "As Granger approached, by shelling his command and manoeuvring my troops he was detained nearly two hours and prevented from joining the main force until late in the evening, and then at a double-quick, under a heavy fire from Freeman's battery and a section of Napoleon guns borrowed from General Breckinridge."

After Granger had effected a junction with Thomas, Forrest again advanced to the Lafayette road. Another bold charge by the plucky defenders of this portion of the Union line drove his troops and the infantry again back, until now, as the sun was about to set on one of the bloodiest fields in history, Breckinridge's line was only six hundred yards in advance of the position where it had opened its fire at ten o'clock in the forenoon. These brave fighters had not made much headway in ground wrested from their equally gallant antagonists; but they had so hammered Thomas that Rosecrans was compelled to strip other portions of his line, giving Longstreet an opening on the Confederate left, an advantage which this brilliant fighter did not fail to take. It so happened that the weak point in the Union line was in front of one of the bravest and most skilful division commanders in Bragg's army, and it was thus that Stewart threw forward his sturdy Tennesseeans and cut their line in twain.

Longstreet followed this up by hurrying the troops under Preston,

Buckner, Hindman, and Johnson immediately to the support of Stewart, and these, rushing forward at this propitious moment with irresistible force, knocked the right wing and center of Rosecrans's line of battle to pieces. On this part of the field the Federals melted away, a disorganized and beaten mass, and within a few minutes were in wild flight in the direction of Chattanooga. Carried away with this flying mob were the commander in chief of the army, two corps commanders, and with them the Assistant Secretary of War, all in the ruck, and never halting until they reached Chattanooga, ten miles from the battlefield. Night alone saved this army from annihilation.

While all this was transpiring on the Federal right and center, Cleburne and Breckinridge, whose troops had rested for an hour and replenished their ammunition, once more advanced for a desperate effort to break through on the Union left where Thomas was. This time nothing could withstand the impetuosity of their assault. Thomas's center gave way to Cleburne's onslaught, and his left yielded to Breckinridge and Forrest. So quickly was this work done that several hundred of the Union troops could not get away, and threw down their arms and surrendered. The whole Federal army now on the field withdrew inside of Thomas's horseshoe defenses on Snodgrass Hill; beaten but still under the leadership of this indomitable soldier, presenting still a fighting front. The Confederates had followed after them until now night had settled down, and the tired and hungry Southerners sank upon the ground for rest and sleep. Not so with the Federals, who were retreating for the greater part of the night in the direction of Chattanooga. Forrest says of this final assault that he employed "fourteen pieces of artillery, terminating on the right flank the battle of Chickamauga. My command was kept on the field during the night of the 20th, and men and horses suffered greatly for want of water. The men were without rations, and the horses had only received a partial feed once during the two days' engagement."

It may be said without contradiction that on no field of the war did cavalry ever do such persistent and efficient fighting as was done by Forrest's command at Chickamauga. In the Southern army he became more popular than ever, and with the people at large he had already become one of the most romantic figures of the war.

General Daniel H. Hill, who was immediately with Forrest on the 19th and 20th, says, in mentioning the advance of Granger: "That ever-watchful officer, General Forrest, reported to me soon after that a heavy Yankee column was coming from the direction of Chattanooga. His active scouts soon brought in some prisoners. His artillery opened upon it, and a portion of it went to the left of the corps, and, advancing upon Cleburne, was met with a storm of shot and shell and driven back in confusion. General Forrest agreed to move forward and seize the Chattanooga road. The left wing was driving the Yankees everywhere. Forrest was thundering on the right." He closes by saying: "No eulogy of mine could add to the reputation of General Forrest and his soldiers, who, though not under my command, most heartily co-operated and rendered the most valuable service. I would ask no better fortune, if again placed on a flank, than to have such a vigilant, gallant, and accomplished officer guarding its approaches."

Speaking of this attack, the author of the *Life of General George H. Thomas* says (p. 395):

Forrest's men had passed beyond Van Derveer's left, and formed for assault on his front, and also directly on his flank. But the vigilant skirmishers and prisoners taken by them made known the movement. The left was thrown back in time, and the line presented an obtuse angle opening towards the enemy. Into this, and heavily against the left of it, Forrest hurled his columns, four deep. On came these men in gray in magnificent lines, which showed clearly through the open forest, bending their faces before the sleet of the storm, and firing hotly as they advanced. As they came within the range of the oblique fire from Van Derveer's right they halted within forty yards of his left, and for a few moments poured in a destructive fire. A wheel of Smith's regular battery, and of a section of Church's guns, which had reported, brought them where they poured a nearly enfilading fire of canister down those long lines, standing bravely there and fighting almost under the mouths of the guns.

General Bragg, on December 28th, wrote his report of this battle, and the meed of praise measured out to Forrest and his men occupied only a line and a half: "Brigadier-General Forrest's report will show equally gallant and valuable services by his command on our right." Had the commanding general's report been made within a week of this battle, it is safe to say that General Forrest would have received a much more commendatory paragraph. In the meantime, as will appear later, an event had transpired which had greatly embittered General Bragg, and made an irreparable breach between these two soldiers, which the President of the Confederacy, then on the ground, tried in vain to repair.

The battle of Chickamauga is seriously claimed by writers of history as a Union victory; but the human mind, as allotted by the Creator to certain of His creatures, is capable of receiving any impression it chooses, and holding it as a fixed conviction. Other minds may gather a different and more rational conclusion of this great struggle, and from sources not then or ever in sympathy with the Southern side. In *McClure's Magazine* for February, 1898, Mr. Charles A. Dana, who in an official capacity was representing the President of the United States and the Secretary of War on this battlefield with General Rosecrans, thus describes some of the incidents of "September 20th at Chickamauga":

At daybreak we at headquarters were all up and on our horses ready to go with the commanding general to inspect our lines. We rode past McCook, Crittenden, and Thomas to the extreme left, Rosecrans giving as he went the orders he thought necessary to strengthen the several positions. The general intention of these orders was to close up on the left, where it was evident the attack would begin. We then rode back to the extreme right, Rosecrans stopping at each point to see if his orders had been obeyed. In several cases they had not been, and he made them more peremptory. When we found that McCook's line had been elongated, so that it was a mere thread, Rosecrans was very angry, and sent for the general, rebuking him severely; although, as a matter of fact, General McCook's position had been taken under the written orders of the commander-in-chief given the night before. About half past eight or nine o'clock the battle began again on the left, where Thomas was. At that time Rosecrans, with whom I always remained, was on the right, directing the movement of the troops there.

I had not slept much for two nights, and, as it was warm, I dismounted about noon, and, giving my horse to my orderly, lay down on the grass and went to sleep. I was wakened by the most infernal noise I ever heard. Never in any battle I had witnessed was there such a discharge of cannon and musketry. I sat up on the grass, and the first thing I saw was General Rosecrans crossing himself; he was a very pious Catholic. "Hello," I said to myself; "if the general is crossing himself, we are in a desperate situation." I was on my horse in a moment. I had no sooner collected my thoughts and looked around towards the front, where all this din came from, than I saw our lines break and melt away like leaves before the wind. Then the headquarters around me disappeared. The gray-backs came through with a rush, and soon the musket-balls and cannon-shot began to reach the place where we stood. The whole right of the army had apparently been routed. My orderly stuck to me like a veteran, and we drew back for greater safety into the woods a little way.

There I came upon General Horace Porter (Captain Porter it was then) and Captain Drouillard—an aide-de-camp infantry officer attached to General Rosecrans's staff—halting fugitives. They would halt a few of them, get them into some sort of line, and make a beginning of order among them, and then there would come a few rounds of cannon-shot through the tree-tops over their heads, and the men would break and run. I saw Porter and Drouillard plant themselves in front of a body of these stampeding men and command them to halt. One man charged with his bayonet, menacing Porter, but Porter held his ground, and the man gave in. That was the only case of real mutiny that I ever saw in the army, and it was under such circumstances that the man was excusable. The cause of all this disaster was the charge of the Confederates through a hiatus in our line, caused by the withdrawal of Wood's division, under a misapprehension of orders, before its place could be filled.

I attempted to make my way from this point in the woods to Sheridan's division, but when I reached the position where I knew it had been placed a little time before I found it had been swept from the field. Not far away, however, I stumbled on a body of organized troops. This was a brigade of mounted riflemen, under Colonel John T. Wilder, of Indiana. "Mr. Dana," asked Colonel Wilder, "what is the situation?" "I do not know," I said, "except that this part of the army has been routed. There is still heavy fighting on the left front, and our troops seem to be holding their ground there yet." "Will you give me any orders?" he asked. "I have no authority to give orders," I replied; "but if I were in your situation, I should go to the left, where Thomas is." Then I turned my horse, and, making my way over Missionary Ridge, struck the Chattanooga valley and rode to Chattanooga, twelve or fifteen miles away. Everything on the route was in the greatest disorder. The whole road was filled with flying soldiers, and here and there were piled up pieces of artillery, caissons, and baggage-wagons.

When I reached Chattanooga, a little before four o'clock, I found Rosecrans there. In the helter-skelter to the rear, he had escaped by the Rossville road. He was expecting every moment that the enemy would arrive before the town, and was doing all he could to prepare to resist his entrance. Soon after I arrived, the two corps commanders, McCook and Crittenden, both came into Chattanooga. The first thing I did on reaching the town was to telegraph Mr. Stanton. I had not sent him any telegrams in the morning, for I had been in the field with Rosecrans, and part of the time at some distance from the Widow Glenn's, where the operators were at work.

The boys [telegraph operators] kept at their work there until the Confederates drove them out of the house. When they had to run, they went, instruments and tools in hand, and as soon as out of reach of the enemy set up shop on a stump. It was not long before they were driven out of this. They next attempted to establish an office on the Rossville road, but before they had succeeded in making connections a battle was raging around them, and they had to retreat to Granger's headquarters at Rossville. Having been swept bodily off the battle-field, and having made my way into Chattanooga through a panic-stricken rabble, the first telegram I sent to Mr. Stanton was naturally colored by what I had seen and experienced. I remember that I began the dispatch by saying: "My report to-day is of deplorable importance. Chickamauga is as fatal a name in our history as Bull Run."

Mr. Dana subsequently modified his first telegram; yet he felt, as most normal men do, that winning generals do not celebrate victories by running twelve miles away from the field of battle and leaving their artillery and thousands of muskets and prisoners in the enemy's hands.

On Monday morning, September 21st, General Forrest, with a strong advance guard from Armstrong's brigade, and accompanied by this latter general, moved forward on the Lafayette road toward Chattanooga. When nearing Rossville they came upon a rear guard of Federal cavalry, seeing which Forrest remarked, "Armstrong, let's give them a dare." He immediately ordered a charge, and the two generals, at the head of some four hundred Confederate cavalry, at full speed rode down upon the Union troopers, who fired a volley and fled in the direction of Chattanooga. Forrest's horse was fatally wounded by this volley, a Minié ball passing through his neck and severing one of the large arteries. The blood spurted from the divided vessel, seeing which Forrest leaned forward from the saddle, inserted the index finger of his hand into the wound, and thus, stanching the hemorrhage, the animal was still able to carry his rider onward with the troops pursuing the Federals. As soon as the field was cleared, Forrest, removing his finger from the wound, dismounted when his noble charger sank to the earth and was soon lifeless.[3]

General Armstrong says that just as the pursuit ceased he and Forrest found themselves on the point of a knoll or spur of Missionary Ridge, and that, looking up in a clump of oak trees, they saw three or

[3] The author is indebted to General Frank C. Armstrong for a description of this unusual scene.

four Federals perched in the timber upon little wooden platforms, where they had evidently been placed with field glasses for purposes of observation. So rapid had been Forrest's advance that these men of the signal corps had no time to descend from their perches and escape. He called to them to climb down, which they immediately did. Taking a pair of glasses from one of the prisoners, he then climbed the tree, from the top of which he had a full sweep of the Chattanooga valley, of the town, Lookout Mountain, the Tennessee River, and Walden's Ridge to the far north.

From his perch in the treetop he dictated to Major Charles W. Anderson the celebrated dispatch, an engraving of which is here presented, for which I am indebted to Dr. William M. Polk, of New York, who found it among his distinguished father's effects after his death. It was

On the Road
Sept 21st 1863

GENL

We are in a mile of Rossville—Have been on the Point of Missionary Ridge can see Chattanooga and every thing around   The Enemey's Trains are leaving going around the point of Lookout Mountain—

The Prisoners captured report two pontoons thrown across for the purpose of retreating   I think they are evacuating as hard as they can go—

They are cutting timber down to obstruct our Passage

I think We ought to push forward as rapidly as possible—

Respectfully yr

N B FORREST
Brig Gen

Lt Gen L Polk
Please forward to Gen Bragg

written upon a pale-blue sheet of paper, evidently torn out of a pocket memorandum book. By pulling taut on the stirrup and holding it up high, the flat leather shield of this part of the saddle served as a table to support the paper as the dispatch was written out. The switching of the horse's tail and the movement of his feet and legs, as he stamped to disengage the flies which were fretting him, will account for the staggering chirography.[4]

In 1896 the writer sent a copy of this dispatch to General James Longstreet, and in reply he received a letter which contains the follow-

---

[4] Manuscripts of Major Anderson, in possession of the author.

On the Road
Sept 21st 1863

Genl

We are in a mild ~~threatening~~ of Rossville - Have been on the Point of Missionary Ridge Can see Chattanooga and every thing around. The Enemy's trains are leaving going around the point of Lookout Mountain - The Prisoners captured report two pontoons thrown across for the purpose of retreating I think they are evacuating as hard as they can go - They are Cutting timber down to obstruct Poor Passage I think we ought to press forward as rapidly as possible -

Respectfully &c

[signed] Lt Genl Polk [signed] NB Forrest
Brig Genl

Please forward Genl Bragg

ing: "It was that despatch which fixed the fate of the Confederacy. General Bragg had decided to march around Rosecrans, leaving him in Chattanooga, when the despatch was received which caused Bragg to think that the place would be abandoned on the night of the 22d, when he decided to turn back and march through Chattanooga." General Longstreet had advocated this immediate movement across the Tennessee, throwing his army, flushed with victory and full of confidence, between Burnside and Rosecrans, and cooping the latter up in Chattanooga, where he would soon have been starved into surrender or forced to retreat over Walden's Ridge and the Cumberland Mountains, with all the loss of morale and prestige this would have induced. The army of Rosecrans at this crisis was not in good fighting trim. The corps of Thomas alone was solid and fully effective.

Dissensions, not to the point of mutiny, but serious enough to impair their effectiveness, had crept into the corps of McCook and Crittenden. The subordinate officers in these corps had complained to Rosecrans about their fleeing from the field of battle, and threatened to resign unless they were removed. Rosecrans did not exhibit a disposition to proceed with severity against Crittenden and McCook for quitting Thomas and the field, for he was in the same boat. Taking it all in all, it was not a happy family. As it turned out, the rations got so low that the men were put on half-allowance. Mr. Dana says, "We were on the verge of starvation." Never was an army more at the mercy of another than was the army of the Tennessee had there been a big-brained, bold, and vigorous leader for the army of the South confronting it.

When Forrest had heard the axes ringing again down in the gap at Rossville, he dismounted Dibrell's old regiment, now commanded by Captain McGinnis, and made a strong reconnaissance, only to discover that Thomas was fortifying himself here to hold back too vigorous pursuit. Though he brought up his guns and shelled them for several hours, he could not move them. That night he camped on the ridge while the Federals stole away under cover of darkness and safely reached the protection of the heavy earthworks around Chattanooga. From the moment that Rosecrans reached this place, about four o'clock on Sunday, after his rapid journey from the field, he expected Bragg to come right on after him. With an energy born of despair, he immediately put every man and beast to work upon the defenses. If Bragg could be kept away for twenty-four hours, he might yet be safe. Mr. Dana says:

"Rosecrans gave orders for all our troops to prepare for the attack; no attack was made that day, however, nor the next, and by the morning of the 24th the herculean labors of the army had so fortified the place that it was certain it could only be taken by a regular siege or a turning movement."

On the 22nd the cavalry under Forrest moved into the suburbs of Chattanooga. During that night his troops were kept in line of battle, his left, under Dibrell, resting on the base of Lookout Mountain, his right on the Tennessee River. On Monday the 23rd, he had occupied the point or peak of Lookout Mountain, where his troops were relieved by the infantry. The cavalry were then ordered to Byrd's Mill to rest and forage, shoe the horses, and cook rations. By September 25th the forces of Burnside were reported as being at Harrison, and General Forrest was directed to proceed thither. Marching at once, he had proceeded as far as Chickamauga station when a courier overtook him with orders to hasten via Cleveland to Charleston, drive off any of the enemy in that vicinity, and, if necessary, to cross the Hiawassee River. On the morning of the 26th, at Charleston, he discovered the Union troops on the opposite side of the river, opened on them with his artillery, under cover of which he crossed his command, and drove the enemy away. Pressing this detachment to Philadelphia, his advance under Dibrell came upon the Union cavalry under Colonel Wolford, and, after a very brilliant fight on the part of Colonel Dibrell and his men, the Federals were badly beaten and driven in full flight from the field. One hundred and twenty prisoners were captured and sent to Dalton. The important part taken by Forrest and his troops during and immediately following the battle of Chickamauga may be more fully appreciated by extracts from his official report, which was dated at Dalton, Georgia, October 22nd, 1863. After detailing his advance from Dalton to Ringgold, on Thursday, the 17th, and the action which occurred between his command at Pea Vine Creek, where he came into contact with Minty's brigade of the Union cavalry on the 18th, he states:

On the morning of the 18th I was ordered to move with my command down the road towards Reed's Bridge and develop the enemy, which was promptly done, and their advance was soon engaged at the steam saw-mill at that point. Finding the enemy too strong for General Pegram's force, I despatched a staff officer to Lieutenant General Polk, asking for Armstrong's division. He could only spare Colonel Dibrell's brigade, which arrived shortly after we engaged the enemy; was speedily dismounted and formed, and, with General Pegram's division, were able to hold position until infantry re-enforcements arrived, the first brigade of which, under Colonel Wilson, formed on the left, advanced in gallant style, driving the enemy back and capturing a battery of artillery, my dismounted cavalry advancing with them. The superior force of the enemy compelled us to give back until re-enforced by General Ector's brigade, when the enemy was again driven back. From statements of prisoners captured, the enemy's force engaged was four brigades of infantry and one of cavalry; but when driven back the second time, with the loss of another battery, their full strength was developed, and being met and overpowered by vastly superior numbers, we were forced to fall back to our first position. A cavalry charge was made to protect the infantry as they retired, which they did in good order, but with loss. We captured many prisoners, but were unable, for want of horses, to bring off the guns captured from the enemy.

Until the arrival of Major-General Walker (being the senior officer present) I assumed temporary command of the infantry, and I must say that the fighting and the gallant charges of the two brigades just referred to excited my admiration. They broke the enemy's lines, and could not be halted or withdrawn until nearly surrounded. We fell back, fighting and contesting the ground, to our original position near the mill on the Reed's Bridge road. General Cheatham's division coming up and engaging the enemy, drove them for some distance, but was in turn compelled to fall back. Seeing General Maney's brigade hard pressed and retiring before the enemy, I hastened to his relief with Freeman's battery of six pieces, dismounting Colonel Dibrell's brigade to support it.

The conduct of Major John Rawle, chief of artillery, and the officers and men of this battery on this occasion deserves special mention. . . . They were gallantly protected by Colonel Dibrell in retiring, who fell back with the line of infantry. General Armstrong, having been relieved by General Polk, arrived with his brigade, and took command of his division, forming it, and, with Pegram's division, holding the road to Reed's Bridge, which had been repaired during the day.

On Sunday morning, the 20th, I received orders to move up and keep in line with General Breckinridge's division, which I did, dismounting all of General Armstrong's division, except the First Tennessee Regiment and McDonald's battalion, holding General Pegram's division in reserve on my right. The two commands of General Armstrong's division which were mounted took possession of the La Fayette road, capturing the enemy's hospitals and quite a number of prisoners. They were compelled to·fall back, as the enemy's reserves, under General Granger, advanced on that road. Colonel Dibrell fought on foot with the infantry during the day. As General Granger approached, by shelling his command and manoeuvring my troops, he was detained nearly two hours, and prevented from joining the main force until late in the evening, and then at double-quick, under a heavy fire from Freeman's battery and a section of Napoleon's guns borrowed from General Breckinridge.

After Granger's column had vacated the road in front of me, I moved my dismounted men rapidly forward and took possession of the road from the Federal hospital to the woods on the left, through which Infantry was advancing and fighting. My artillery was ordered forward, but before it could reach the road and be placed in position, a charge was made by the enemy, the infantry line retreating in confusion and leaving me without support, but held the line long enough to get my artillery back to the position from which we had shelled Granger's column, and opened upon the advancing column with fourteen pieces of artillery, driving them back, and terminating on the right flank the battle of Chickamauga. This fire was at short range, in open ground and was to the enemy very destructive, killing two colonels and many other officers and privates.

It is with pride and pleasure that I mention the gallant conduct of the officers and men of my command. General Armstrong's division fought almost entirely on foot, always up and frequently in advance of the infantry.

My command was kept on the field during the night of the 20th, and men and horses suffered greatly for want of water. The men were without rations, and the horses had only received a partial feed once during the two days' engagement.

It was while in pursuit of the retreating enemy, on September 30th, that Forrest received from General Bragg the following order:

MISSIONARY RIDGE, *September 28, 1863*
Brigadier-General Forrest, near Athens:
GENERAL—The general commanding desires that you will without delay turn over the troops of your command, previously ordered, to Major-General Wheeler.[5]

Upon the receipt of this message he flew into a violent rage, at the height of which he dictated a letter to Major Anderson, who says: "The general dictated a letter which I wrote to Bragg, resenting the manner in which he had been treated, and charging the commander of the army in plain, straight language with duplicity and lying, and informing him

[5] *Official Records,* vol. xxx, part iv, p. 710.

that he would call at his headquarters in a few days to say to him in person just what he had written. He concluded by saying he desired to shirk no responsibility incurred by the contents of his letter. When Forrest read the letter over and signed it, it was sealed and handed to the courier, and, as he rode away, the general remarked to me, 'Bragg never got such a letter as that before from a brigadier.' "

He kept the promise he had made in his wrathy letter, and called upon the commander in chief at his headquarters on Missionary Ridge to give that distinguished general a "piece of his mind." The only witness of this remarkable scene, Dr. J. B. Cowan, of Tullahoma, Tennessee, is still living (in 1898) and in the active practice of his profession. The high standing of this gentleman renders his statement absolutely reliable.

Dr. Cowan, Forrest's chief surgeon, had been left in charge of the hospital near Alexander's Bridge, on the battlefield. Having finished his work there, he notified the general that he was ready to report in the field when needed, and in reply received a dispatch directing him to be ready to join Forrest at Ringgold the next day. They proceeded by train to Chickamauga Creek bridge, and rode thence to the headquarters of General Bragg on Missionary Ridge. Dr. Cowan says:

I observed as we rode along that the general was silent, which was unusual with him when we were alone. Knowing him so well, I was convinced that something that displeased him greatly had transpired. He wore an expression which I had seen before on some occasions when a storm was brewing. I had known nothing of the letter he had written General Bragg, and was in utter ignorance not only of what was passing in Forrest's mind at this time, but of the object of his visit to the general-in-chief. As we passed the guard in front of General Bragg's tent, I observed that General Forrest did not acknowledge the salute of the sentry, which was so contrary to his custom that I could not but notice it. When we entered the tent where General Bragg was alone, this officer rose from his seat, spoke to Forrest, and, advancing, offered him his hand.

Refusing to take the proffered hand, and standing stiff and erect before Bragg, Forrest said: "I am not here to pass civilities or compliments with you, but on other business. You commenced your cowardly and contemptible persecution of me soon after the battle of Shiloh, and you have kept it up ever since. You did it because I reported to Richmond facts, while you reported damned lies. You robbed me of my command in Kentucky, and gave it to one of your favorites—men that I armed and equipped from the enemies of our country. In a spirit of revenge and spite, because I would not fawn upon you as others did, you drove me into west Tennessee in the winter of 1862, with a second brigade I had organized, with improper arms and without sufficient ammunition, although I had made repeated applications for the same. You did it to ruin me and my career. When in spite of all this I returned with my command, well equipped by captures, you began again your work of spite and persecution, and have kept it up; and now this second brigade, organized and equipped without thanks to you or the government, a brigade which has won a reputation for successful fighting second to none in the army, taking advantage of your position as the commanding general in order to further humiliate me, you have taken these brave men from me.

I have stood your meanness as long as I intend to. You have played the part of a damned scoundrel, and are a coward, and if you were any part of a man I would slap your jaws and force you to resent it. You may as well not issue any more orders to me, for I will not obey them, and I will hold you personally responsible for any further indignities you endeavor to inflict upon me. You have threatened to arrest me for not obeying your orders promptly. I dare you to do it, and I say to you that if you ever again try to interfere with me or cross my path it will be at the peril of your life.

Dr. Cowan says this whole transaction was so unexpected and startling that he was almost dumfounded. When Forrest refused to take the proffered hand, Bragg had stepped back to one corner of his headquarters tent, where there was a little field desk or table, and seated himself in a camp chair. He seemed at a loss to know what to do or say in the presence of this violent outburst of rage in one who was so desperately resenting what he considered a systematic and revengeful persecution of himself. He realized that in his stormful mood Forrest acknowledged no accountability to law, civil or military, human or divine, as he stood there towering above him, launching at him this fierce denunciation, and emphasizing each expression of contempt with a quick motion of the left index finger, which he thrust almost into Bragg's face. The general did not utter a word or move a muscle of his face during this shower of invective from his brigadier. The scene did not last longer than a few minutes, and when Forrest had finished he turned his back sharply upon Bragg and stalked out of the tent toward the horses. As they rode away Dr. Cowan remarked, "Well, you are in for it now!" Forrest replied instantly, "He'll never say a word about it; he'll be the last man to mention it; and, mark my word, he'll take no action in the matter. I will ask to be relieved and transferred to a different field, and he will not oppose it."

Forrest was correct. If General Bragg ever took any official notice of the incident it did not find its way into the records.

Forrest did not offer to resign his commission, because he did not want General Bragg to think he was trying to escape any consequences of his violent denunciation of the man—no matter how high in authority—who had grievously and unjustly wronged him, and who he was convinced was incapable of commanding an army. Bragg could have court-martialed his insurbordinate brigadier, but did not do it. He never replied to the letter, nor did Forrest ever hear from him concerning the intemperate interview.

General Bragg was a brave man, intensely loyal to the cause for which he was fighting, but he was none the less a strict and severe disciplinarian. It is probable that he felt that no personal grievance would justify him in causing such tremendous loss to the Confederacy as would occur should he force the fighting in the case of Forrest.

Between the two, friendly relations were never re-established, although President Davis, who was at last beginning to realize the great ability of Forrest, used his personal influence to bring about a reconciliation.

Even after Bragg was moved to Richmond as military adviser, etc., to the President, the records show his animosity to his former brigadier, and also the continued friendship and admiration of Mr. Davis for Forrest. The latter made known to him his grievance and his determination to serve no longer in Bragg's department. Mr. Davis invited him to a personal interview in Montgomery, and Forrest straightway went there. En route, Colonel R. B. Kyle, of Gadsden, Alabama, traveled with him. He says: "Forrest told me he would not serve longer under Bragg; that he was not competent to command any army; that the army had whipped the Federals badly at Chickamauga, and that he, with his command, had followed them almost to the suburbs of Chattanooga; that they were demoralized and could have been captured, and that he rode back himself, after sending couriers and getting no replies, and found General Bragg asleep. He urged that they move on in pursuit of the enemy at once, as their capture was certain. Bragg asked how he could move an army without supplies, as his men had exhausted them. Forrest's reply was: 'General Bragg, we can get all the supplies our army needs in Chattanooga.' Bragg made no reply, and Forrest rode away disgusted.'"[6]

The conference with the President was satisfactory in every way to Forrest. The President assured him of the full appreciation by the Southern people and by himself of the important services he had rendered, and of his desire to conform to Forrest's wishes for an independent command in Mississippi and west Tennessee. He reverted to the communication he had received some few weeks before, and suggested some slight modifications in the plan as laid out by Forrest. The document referred to is worthy of careful scrutiny.

It was written while Forrest was stationed at Kingston in east Tennessee, on August 9th, 1863,[7] and addressed—through General Bragg's headquarters—to General S. Cooper, adjutant general, at Richmond, Virginia. Ten days later[8] a copy of this letter was sent to President Davis direct. To the President he wrote:

Having understood that it was likely it would not be forwarded by the general commanding the department, and believing the matter of sufficient importance to merit the consideration of your Excellency, I have taken the liberty of sending a copy direct. While I believe the general commanding is unwilling for me to leave his department, still I hope to be permitted to go where (as I believe) I can serve my country best, especially so as an experienced and competent officer, Brigadier-General Armstrong, would be left in command of my division.

The letter is as follows:

GENERAL—Prompted by the repeated solicitations of numerous friends and acquaintances resident in west Tennessee and northern Mississippi, also by desire to serve my country to the best of my ability, and wherever those services can be rendered most available and effective, I respectfully lay before you a proposition which, if approved, will seriously, if not entirely, obstruct the navigation of the Mississippi River, *and in sixty days procure a large force now inside the enemy's lines, which without this, or a similar move, cannot be obtained.*[9]

The proposition is this: Give me the command of the forces from Vicksburg to Cairo, or, in other words, all the forces I may collect to-

[6] Personal narrative.
[7] *Official Records,* vol. xxiii, part ii, p. 955.
[8] *Ibid.,* vol. xxx, part iv, p. 507.
[9] Italics added.

gether and organize between those points—say in northern Mississippi, west Tennessee, and those that may join me from Arkansas, Mississippi, and southern Kentucky. I desire to take with me only about four hundred men from my present command—viz., my escort, sixty; McDonald's battalion, one hundred and fifty; the Second Kentucky Cavalry, two hundred and fifty—selected entirely on account of their knowledge of the country in which I propose to operate. In all, say, men and outfit, four hundred men, with long-range guns (Enfield), four three-inch Dahlgren or Parrott guns, with eight number-one horses to each gun and caisson, two wagons for the battery, one pack-mule to every ten men, and two hundred rounds of ammunition for small arms and artillery.

I would like to have Captain (W. W.) Carnes, now at Chattanooga, in some portion of General Bragg's army, to command the battery, and, in case he was detached for the expedition, that he be allowed to select his cannoneers, etc. I have resided on the Mississippi for over twenty years, was for many years engaged in buying and selling Negroes, and know the country perfectly well between Memphis and Vicksburg, and also am well acquainted with all the prominent planters in that region, as well as above Memphis. I also have officers in my command and on my staff who have rafted timber out of the bottoms, and know every foot of the ground between Commerce and Vicksburg. With the force proposed, and my knowledge of the river-bottoms, as well as the knowledge my men have of the country from Vicksburg up, I am confident we could so move and harass and destroy boats on the river that only boats heavily protected by gunboats would be able to make the passage.

I ask also authority to organize all troops that can be obtained, and that I be promised long-range guns for them as soon as organizations are reported. There are many half-organized regiments, battalions, and companies in northern Mississippi and west Tennessee, but they are without arms and have no way of getting out, and it only requires a little time and a nucleus around which they can form, to organize and put them in the field. I believe that in sixty days I can raise from five to ten thousand men between Vicksburg and Cairo, well mounted and ready for service as soon as provided with guns and ammunition.

In making this proposition, I desire to state that I do so entirely for the good of the service. I believe that I can accomplish all that I propose to do. I have never asked for position, have taken position and performed the duties assigned me, and have never yet suffered my command to be surprised or defeated. I should leave this department with many regrets, as I am well pleased with the officers in my command and with the division serving under me. I shall especially regret parting with my old brigade. It was organized by me, and a record of its past services and present condition will compare favorably with any cavalry command in the service, and nothing but a desire to destroy the enemy's transports and property, and increase the strength of our army, could for a moment induce me voluntarily to part with them. There are thousands of men where I propose to go that I am satisfied will join me, and that rapidly (otherwise they will remain where they are), until all the country bordering on the Mississippi from Cairo down is taken and permanently occupied by our forces.

I am, general, very respectfully, your obedient servant,

N. B. FORREST, Brigadier-General

This document had, undoubtedly, in whole or in part reached Richmond at an earlier date. Mr. James A. Seddon, Secretary of War, August 19th, says, in a letter to General Joseph E. Johnston: "It is not of less importance that the use of the Mississippi River for trade should, if possible, be debarred to the enemy. If this could be done effectually, it would deprive the North of most of the fruits of their late successes in Mississippi, and satisfy the Northwest of the impossibility of ever enjoying the Mississippi as an avenue of trade without peace and amity with the Confederate States. I should think, in the present low state of the water, *field artillery, with cavalry, might find ready access to the bank of the river for hundreds of miles, and render the passage of trading-boats entirely impracticable.*"[10]

Mr. Davis hesitated, and lost the untold benefits which might have accrued had this genius in war been turned, *loose and untrammeled,* to employ his never-failing resources in this important work. The Mississippi was the only route left open to the Federal army in Mississippi and Louisiana. After the west Tennessee raid, General Grant had abandoned the railroads as unsafe and unreliable, and henceforth he said he would rely upon the Mississippi River. Forrest would have made this so unsafe that it too must have ceased to be successfully utilized. The President endorsed upon this letter, which was officially submitted to him: "The services of Brigadier-General Forrest would no doubt be valuable in that portion of the country to which he refers, and in the character of the service described. The propriety of detaching him, with a portion of his brigade, could be better decided after a report from his commanding general."

But the commanding general did not want to lose Forrest at that time. They were on good terms then. His endorsement reads: "I know

[10] Italics not in original.

no officer to whom I would sooner assign the duty preferred, than which none is more important, but it would deprive this army of one of its greatest elements of strength to remove General Forrest." Here was a dawn of the appreciation of the "unlettered general" at his worth. Bragg had his way this time with the President. Mr. Davis, on August 28th, wrote: "The endorsement of General Bragg indicated the propriety of a postponement. Subsequent events have served to render the proposition more objectionable. Whenever a change of circumstances will permit, the measure may be adopted." The chief subsequent event was the great battle of Chickamauga.

As a result of the conference with Mr. Davis, Forrest, although he objected to the restrictions placed upon him, accepted the service offered him in the West, and early in November of that year bade farewell to the brigade which had served so faithfully under him, and then left for the new field of duty. The parting with his old command was mutually sad and full of lasting regrets, especially with that splendid brigade composed of Starnes's Fourth, Biffle's Fifth, Dibrell's Eighth, Edmondson's Eleventh, and Cox's Tenth Tennessee regiments, and Freeman's famous battery.

TWELVE

In the New Field of Duty

GENERAL BRAGG did not withdraw his objections to the transfer of Forrest to the West until October 13, 1863. On this date he wrote to President Davis that he had withheld his approval because he deemed "the service of that distinguished officer necessary with this army. As that request can now be granted without injury to the public interests in this quarter, I respectfully ask that the transfer be made."

On the 29th of this same month Mr. Davis wrote to General Forrest, directing him "to proceed to his new field of duty." From Atlanta, Georgia, on November 7, 1863, Forrest wrote to General S. Cooper, at Richmond: "Major McDonald's battalion, my escort company, and the battery will comprise my entire command, which is wholly inadequate to the undertaking; yet I will use all the energy I possess to accomplish the object I have proposed." He enclosed the following list of the command:

Field and staff	8
Escort company	65
McDonald's battalion	139
Captain J. W. Morton's battery	67

Total effectives	279[1]

In assigning Forrest to his new command in west Tennessee, General Joseph E. Johnston wrote: "He will, on arriving there, proceed to raise and organize as many troops for the Confederate service as he finds practicable. Colonel Richardson will report to General Forrest, of whose command his troops will form a part."

[1] *Official Records,* vol xxxi, part iii, p. 646.

The fact that Forrest was to take charge of affairs in west Tennessee had already reached the ears of General Hurlbut, the Federal commander of this district, whose headquarters were at Memphis. On November 3rd he wrote to General Grant: "It is currently believed that Forrest has been assigned to this department. If so, there will be more dash in their attacks."

Although it was not until the 16th of November that Forrest reached Okolona, in Mississippi, General McPherson had two days before telegraphed General Sherman that Forrest was organizing a force to operate on the river south of Memphis, and that he had as much as six pieces of artillery. Two days later, General Hurlbut, at Memphis, was informed that Forrest was coming, and would surely attack Collierville before the 18th; and this officer assures his superior, General Sherman, that he would try "to be ready for him, though he may break through and pass north." These and other dispatches of like note found in the official records of this period are indications of the importance attached by the Union authorities to his advent in the West.

From Atlanta to Rome, and thence westward, along the route over which a few months before he had pursued and captured Streight's raiders, Forrest marched with his handful of men—a brigadier general with an army of 279 men. After more than two years of hard service, successful in results beyond any commander of mounted troops, he had been deprived of two different brigades which he had organized and made effective; and now, at the head of this small cavalcade, with four pieces of artillery, he was on the way to a new sphere of action, in which he was to build up again a new army. If the ingratitude of his government or the persecution of Bragg caused any bitter reflections in his mind, he was careful to refrain from expressing them. His loyalty to the cause of the Confederacy was not diminished, and he permitted no doubt of ultimate success to find a lodging place within him.

Arriving at Okolona, Forrest was disappointed in the small number of troops that Colonel R. V. Richardson had present for duty to turn over to him. Forrest informed General Johnston, on the 21st of November: "I think two hundred and fifty will cover all the troops Colonel Richardson has. He desires to command a brigade, but as I shall have only about a thousand men with which to cross the Memphis and Charleston railroad, I shall take direct and immediate command of all the troops myself."

It will give the reader an idea of the difficulties which beset General Forrest from the outset in his military experience in northern Mississippi and west Tennessee to state the fact that when he asked Colonel Richardson where the men he was reported to have were, the latter replied that he had brought out of west Tennessee with him about eight hundred troops; that as they had come away from home during the warm season, they had provided themselves only with light summer clothing, and, with the first approach of cold weather, without asking permission, they had gone home to get heavier apparel for winter use. The inventory of arms and equipment showed that there were only 271 guns and 151 pistols in the entire command of Colonel Richardson, and 247 horses that were fit for duty.[2] The men who had returned to their homes within the enemy's lines had carried with them 517 serviceable Enfield and Austrian rifles. Although Forrest had been promised another regiment, when it finally marched into Okolona to report to him it numbered 150 men, and about a fourth of these did not have any arms. Four hundred new troops in all to add to the forlorn hope of 271, which followed his banner into Mississippi, did not at this time make a very formidable showing, but, formidable or not, he had determined to attempt to break through the strong cordon of Federal troops along the Memphis and Charleston Railroad, march into west Tennessee, establish his headquarters in the neighborhood of Jackson, far within the enemy's lines, and recruit his army by first calling for volunteers, and, if this were not successful, by conscription.

In this important enterprise Forrest had enlisted the energy and loyalty of Tyree H. Bell, a man of great influence in this section of Tennessee, and a leader of dauntless courage and ability. His selection of such a lieutenant demonstrated again the fine judgment of men which General Forrest possessed. They had become acquainted while serving in Bragg's army, and when General Forrest was promised an independent command in west Tennessee he requested Bell, who was the senior colonel in Preston Smith's brigade, to go with him, promising him a commission as brigadier general if he would raise a command sufficient to justify the promotion. Colonel Bell, with a small detachment, had been sent in advance into the counties west of the Tennessee River "to spy out the land," and had spread throughout all that quarter the information that Forrest was coming to occupy that section and hold it for the Confed-

[2] *Ibid.,* vol. xxxi, part iii, p. 731.

eracy. General Forrest and Colonel Bell had also secured the assistance of several able and devoted officers, who were an invaluable aid in organizing the new command. Among these were Colonels A. N. Wilson, John F. Newsom, R. M. Russell, and Lieutenant Colonel D. M. Wisdom, all of whom had already seen service and were favorably known to the people of this region.

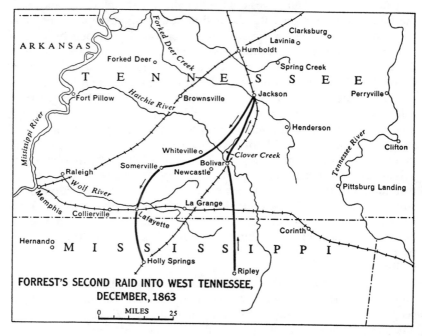

FORREST'S SECOND RAID INTO WEST TENNESSEE, DECEMBER, 1863

Such was the enthusiasm aroused by their labors and the presence of General Forrest that when he invaded the country, in December of 1863, three regiments were recruited, and, although without arms and equipment, marched out under these officers. Colonel C. R. Barteau's Second Tennessee regiment was later on joined with the regiments of Wilson, Newsom, and Russell, forming a brigade of which Brigadier General Bell was placed in command.

On December 1st, Forrest headed his small battalion northward toward the Memphis and Charleston Railroad. Such was the difficulty in securing horses that at the last moment he found he had only enough to pull two of his small pieces of artillery. In order to make a diversion in his favor, Generals Lee and Chalmers had with two detachments of troops moved up in the direction of Memphis, feigned an attack upon this position, which caused a concentration of Federal troops who were scattered along the railroad at various points, and thus enabled Forrest to break through between the depleted outposts. Moving swiftly, with nothing to impede his progress excepting the two pieces of artillery and five light wagons loaded with ammunition, on the 4th of December he passed the railroad safely without molestation. General S. D. Lee dispatched to General Joseph E. Johnston that Forrest had "marched into west Tennessee with four hundred and fifty men and two guns, having been compelled to leave the balance of his artillery for lack of horses to pull them."

General Sherman, who always kept an eye open for the Confederate cavalryman, was at once informed of Forrest's movement, and in reply telegraphed to Hurlbut that he did not attach a great deal of importance to the movement. He said: "I have made the junction at which I was aiming, and am rather indifferent to Forrest's reported expedition. He may cavort about the country as much as he pleases." Sherman's indifference was, however, not to be of long duration. Once more on his old stamping ground, far within the Union lines, the bold raider was soon "cavorting" in such lively fashion that both Grant and Sherman were compelled to concentrate an overwhelming force against him in order to drive him back to Mississippi; not, however, until he had raised a small army within the limits of the "enemy's country," with which he was to accomplish wonders and cause infinite trouble to those great leaders of the Union hosts in 1864.

The Confederates were successful in avoiding any conflict with the Federals until they neared the Hatchie River at Bolivar, in Tennessee. At this point they collided with a body of cavalry belonging to General B. H. Grierson's command, and a lively skirmish ensued. In a dispatch informing his superior that Forrest had crossed the Hatchie at Bolivar, this officer says: "Colonel Hatch was wounded through the lung. Our loss, four or five killed and about twenty wounded. The Sixth Illinois lost thirty or forty horses killed."

As might have been expected, the advent of Forrest created considerable excitement in the various military posts scattered along the Tennessee, Ohio, and Mississippi rivers. On December 7th, General A. J.

Smith, who was at Columbus, Kentucky, received a dispatch that Forrest had passed into west Tennessee for the purpose of organizing all the guerrillas and local companies into his command, and was concentrating them in the neighborhood of Jackson and Trenton. He expressed to his subordinate a "desire to make thorough work of these trespassers." General J. G. Stevenson, another of these post commanders, on the 11th of December informed General Hurlbut at Memphis that Forrest was conscripting every man in west Tennessee capable of bearing arms, and taking all Negroes fit for soldiers.

On the 6th of December, Forrest advised General Johnston that he had "arrived safely at Jackson, and was highly pleased with the prospect; that a healthy spirit manifested itself among the people; that he had already gathered together about five thousand men, and thought it likely, if unmolested until the 1st of January, he should be able to put about eight thousand effective troops into the field."

The citizens of this section of the Union must have been impressed with the fact that a state of war really existed. The Federal authorities had already established recruiting bureaus, and had been doing all in their power to induce the male citizens, black and white, eligible to military service to enlist in the Union army; and now Forrest and his lieutenants were calling for volunteers, and conscripting all those who would not answer to the call. The few troops he had brought with him, and others that had immediately on his arrival rallied to his standard, were scattered throughout the country under trusted subordinates, and recruiting stations were established in every county of west Tennessee and Kentucky. As the Federals were occupying most of the important towns, this work had to be done with great care and secrecy, and was attended with considerable risk. Rendezvous were established in unfrequented spots, often in the dense canebrakes and in the ravines and thickets of the river bottoms, to which only the initiated could find their way. In these lonely places, as fast as the new levies were secured they were enlisted. Those who volunteered, and were therefore trustworthy, were placed as guards over those who had been forcibly conscripted.

Such was his success in attracting recruits that it soon excited the apprehension of General Grant, who, with his devoted subordinate, Sherman, immediately ordered a combination of movements to destroy Forrest or drive him out of this section. The wily leader was not, however, to be taken by surprise or outwitted by any combination.

Without being a student of the science of war, he knew intuitively that success depended first of all upon being thoroughly informed in regard to the movements and intentions of the enemy. The most daring and trustworthy men enlisted in his service were detailed in the performance of scouting duty.

The movements that Grant and Sherman had ordered were not under way before Forrest informed Johnston that they were preparing expeditions against him from the direction of Columbus, Kentucky, and Fort Pillow on the Mississippi. For these he cared little, but he expressed an anxiety in regard to a movement which he had anticipated from Memphis and the South. He requested his department commander that General S. D. Lee be directed to occupy the attention of the Federals along the line of the Memphis and Charleston Railroad, and hold them there. "If this were done," he says, "I will be able to take care of any force that can come at me from the North." He adds:

I am exceedingly anxious to get the arms promised me by the President, and earnestly ask that General Lee, with all the cavalry that can be spared, be brought up to west Tennessee at this juncture, bringing with him the arms and ammunition needed for the new troops. If this were done, we could effectually destroy the Memphis and Charleston railroad, and drive out from here between four and six thousand head of good beef cattle for the use of the army. If I hear that he is coming to help me, I will build a pontoon-bridge across the Hatchie, and will have the cattle gathered up by the time he can reach me. I am in great need of money, and have had to advance to my quartermaster and commissary $20,000 of my private funds to subsist the command thus far.[3]

So impressed was Forrest with the advantages that would accrue to the Confederate arms by holding possession of the fertile country west of the Tennessee River that he dispatched Major M. C. Galloway to Richmond to lay the facts before the President. He says: "The destruction of the Memphis and Charleston railroad, and the block-ading of the Tennessee River, which is easy of accomplishment, gives us west Tennessee. With the means asked for, I am satisfied we can hold the country, and secure for the army a vast amount of provisions and supplies not to be obtained in like quantity at so little cost anywhere else."

He made a special request that General Gideon J. Pillow be sent to

[3] *Ibid.*, vol. xxxi, part iii, p. 789.

serve with him there, and also General Frank C. Armstrong. "With such assistance and experience I am confident that I shall have in a short time eight thousand effective men in the field, besides some thousand belonging to various infantry commands, all of whom will be sent back at the earliest possible moment."

Forrest never for a moment neglected to show his appreciation and friendship for General Pillow. He could not forget the courageous fight this brave and loyal soldier had made side by side with him at Fort Donelson, and the determination he had displayed never to surrender, but to fight it out to the last; and he believed, as did the vast majority of the rank and file of the Confederate army, that General Pillow had unjustly suffered at the hands of the government at Richmond for the failure to extricate the army which unnecessarily surrendered at Donelson. But the request for General Pillow was without avail, nor was General Armstrong sent to the aid of Forrest. On December 13th, Mr. Davis informed General Johnston that "Brigadier-General Forrest is promoted to the rank of major-general, and will, I hope, supply your wants in northern Mississippi and west Tennessee, so as to enable you to draw Major-General Lee to the southern portion of your department."

At this time Forrest was led to believe that an expedition from the direction of middle Tennessee was on its way to unite with the other movements which had been organized against him. General William Sooy Smith, with whom the Confederate leader was soon to have an interesting experience, had appeared on the horizon from this quarter. On the 28th of December he marched out of Nashville toward Columbia and thence westward to swoop down upon Forrest, who, as he stated in his report at that time, was at Jackson, Tennessee.

Being now convinced that the Federals were in earnest to close in upon him from all directions, the Confederate commander deemed it a wise precaution to send some of his unarmed troops southward for safety. Colonel R. M. Russell, who had recruited one of the new regiments, accompanied by a small detachment of men who had arms, left Jackson on the morning of December 13th and, traveling at night by forced marches along unfrequented ways, succeeded in eluding observation and pursuit, and reached Mississippi without molestation. Forrest had calculated, as he had informed General Johnston, that the enemy would reach him about the 25th, and asked his commander to send what troops could be spared from Generals Chalmers's and Ferguson's commands without delay to a point within reach of him, to aid him in taking the cattle and other supplies out, and to assist in meeting any expedition of the enemy against him.

He suggested that these officers bring their troops to cross the Hatchie at·Estenaula, where he would have forage prepared for them and boats ready for crossing. "If this be done, I am able to protect myself against any move from Union City. Should they, however, send two expeditions against me, one from Fort Pillow, I am afraid I will have more than I can manage with the raw and unarmed troops that I have, especially so should they move on me from below at the same time. I have reliable information that they are pressing every horse in Memphis to mount their infantry, and that all the enemy's force at La Grange has been sent down to Memphis, and thence up the river in boats."

Although he had diligently scoured the country for arms, Forrest was still far from being prepared to meet any considerable body of the enemy's troops with his new command; and when on the point of moving southward, under pressure of the columns that were advancing upon him, he sent another courier to General Polk, saying that unless the assistance he had asked for was sent to him, he would have to abandon the cattle and much of the supplies he had collected.

The Confederate leader's flight out of west Tennessee, with his raw levies, was none too soon. That able leader, General A. J. Smith, from the direction of Columbus, and General Grierson, from the direction of Memphis, were moving upon him. Minzer's brigade had been ordered from Corinth to march to Purdy to hem him in on that side, while all the Federal cavalry that had been at La Grange were advanced to Bolivar, directly in his route to the south. The same day General William Sooy Smith was reported, with about 2500 veteran cavalry, coming from the east towards Jackson in Tennessee.

When it was known that Forrest was to command the cavalry in the new department, Generals Grant and Sherman had put their heads together to find a cavalry leader of ability sufficient to cope with so formidable an adversary. General Grant's selection fell upon General William Sooy Smith, and on the 11th of November he was made chief of cavalry for the military division of Mississippi. General Sherman did not altogether approve the selection. The blunt soldier wrote to his superior on December 19th: "I deem General William Sooy Smith too mistrustful of himself for a leader against Forrest. Mower is a better man for the duty." Subsequent events showed the superior judgment of Sherman in weighing men in the balance.

Well might General Hurlbut congratulate himself that the fox was in the toils: "Forrest must fight or run. I think we shall cure him of his ambition to command west Tennessee." And last of all, to make assurance sure, General Grant ordered Brigadier General Crook to move with his command from Huntsville, Alabama, with a view to operate against Forrest in west Tennessee.

On the 22nd of December, Chalmers appeared in the neighborhood of Memphis, along the southern border of Tennessee, and this movement General Hurlbut properly construed into a diversion to enable Forrest to make his escape. He dispatched Grierson immediately: "Close watch must be kept that Forrest does not slip by you on some of the roads."

The vigilant Grierson had already concentrated the larger portion of his command at La Grange, from which point he could move readily toward Bolivar and throw himself directly in the route he presumed Forrest would take from Jackson toward Holly Springs, in Mississippi. At daylight on the morning of the 23rd of December he took the further precaution to send Colonel Prince with the Seventh Illinois, five hundred effectives, northward to the Hatchie River, at Bolivar, with orders to follow this stream from that point toward the Mississippi River, and destroy all the ferryboats and any bridges that might have been overlooked.[4] Prince arrived at Bolivar at six o'clock in the afternoon of the 23rd, and sent details up and down the Hatchie to carry out the orders of his superior.

He learned on his arrival there that Forrest's men had taken the ferryboat from Bolivar, and that it was concealed in Clover Creek, a tributary of this stream; but upon arriving there, in the hope of destroying this boat, it had been removed to Estenaula. Forrest had taken the precaution to secure this ferryboat, knowing full well that the Federals would do everything possible to prevent the passage of his command over that stream, thus forcing him to a long detour around the headwaters of the Hatchie and Wolf rivers above Bolivar and toward Corinth, where he would fall an easy prey to the troops which

[4] *Ibid.,* vol. xxxi, part i, p. 607.

had been stationed along that line for his destruction. The boat had been scuttled, and was watched by a detachment of his trusted scouts, and it was impossible for the Federals to find it. Judging, however, from what he had heard, that Forrest would attempt a crossing somewhere in the neighborhood of Estenaula, Colonel Prince moved directly to that point along the south bank of the Hatchie. He arrived just in time to meet with a very serious rebuff at the hands of the Confederates, who had stolen a march upon him and were already on the south bank of the river at this point.

When Forrest started on his march southward he had divided his command into three separate detachments; the most important, consisting of the larger portion of his recruits, more than half of whom were unarmed, he placed under the command of his trusted lieutenant, Colonel Tyree H. Bell, and started them in advance with the two pieces of artillery, some forty or fifty wagons loaded with very needful supplies, and a drove of several hundred beef cattle. Bell pushed on toward Estenaula with as much rapidity as the terrible condition of the roads would permit, but with the wagon and cattle his progress was necessarily slow.

As soon as he was well under way, a second detachment, under Lieutenant Colonel D. M. Wisdom, comprising about five hundred armed men, was ordered toward Mifflin and Jack's Creek, in a southeasterly direction from Jackson, to dispute the advance of another column of the enemy who were coming from that quarter. A third detachment, under General Richardson, had been sent by a different route a day ahead of Bell's march, with directions to reach the Hatchie at or near Estenaula, throw an advance guard of picked men across this stream, and secure a landing upon the southern side.

The first collision, which occurred as the Confederates were moving south, was at daylight on the 24th of December; and while the fighting did not amount to a general engagement of all the troops of either side upon the ground, it was at one time quite animated. Colonel Wisdom handled his command with ability, and so maneuvered as to give out the impression that there was with him a much larger number of troops than he really had, and in this way held the enemy in check until the main column, under Bell and Forrest, had made good headway in their march to the river.

Once during the day his position was seriously threatened by a movement upon his flank and rear, made with considerable boldness by the Federal commander. He immediately ordered eighty picked men, under Lieutenants H. A. Tyler and John O. Morris, who were directed to check this advance of the Federal flankers. Tyler, the senior lieutenant, was placed in command of this detachment of Kentuckians. This sturdy fighter, who made a brilliant reputation under the inspiring leadership of Forrest, no sooner had his men in line than he gave the order to draw their six-shooters and charge. He and Morris, at the head of their respective squadrons, rode with reckless daring right into the Federal line. The firing was exceedingly severe for a few minutes, and at such close quarters that the clothing of some of the killed and wounded was ignited by the burning powder.

Lieutenant Morris, while grappling with a Union trooper, their horses dashing at full speed along the highway, was mortally wounded. He and his antagonist, thrusting the muzzles of their pistols against each other, fired almost simultaneously, and both fell to the ground mortally hurt. It was brief but bloody work, and, as the Federals gave way, the column under Forrest was not molested by further pursuit from this direction.

Wisdom, at nightfall, withdrew his troops, and by a forced march joined the main command at daylight on the following morning. The rear guard, under Forrest, following after Bell, had also had a sharp collision with a Union column coming up from Corinth, not far from Jackson. With his plucky escort the general had succeeded in repulsing this detachment of the enemy, and had moved swiftly in the wake of Bell to Estenaula. General Richardson, with commendable celerity, had successfully carried out his part of the program. Arriving ahead of Bell at the Hatchie, and raising the sunken boat, he had ferried over that portion of his command that had arms, and secured a foothold on the south side of the stream.

Here also, on the evening of the 24th, Forrest came up with his escort and crossed over to the southern bank. He had no sooner made this junction with Richardson than he was informed that sharp firing had just begun about five miles away, in the direction of Bolivar. Colonel Prince's Seventh Illinois regiment, on the lookout for ferryboats, had arrived, as he says in his report, within four and a half miles of Estenaula, when he came upon the Confederate pickets, and immediately attacked the advance guard of the troops under Richardson. Driving these back to the Slough Bridge, one and a half miles from the Hatchie at Estenaula, his advance was here successfully resisted. "At this point we were unable to drive them farther. We were, however, able to hold our ground without difficulty, and did so until 8 P.M."

Later in the night this officer reports that he was again attacked, and it was necessary to retire farther. He marched all night, reaching Somerville about daylight.

The rout of Prince's regiment was the work of that reckless body of fighters which formed General Forrest's personal escort. They were under the command of Lieutenant Nathan Boone, and numbered at this time sixty men. An officer present on this occasion writes:

When we reached the Hatchie at Estenaula, at dark on the 24th, General Richardson's command, which had crossed before we arrived, had already been engaged with a column of the enemy and had been driven back. The river was very much swollen by recent rains, and we had to ferry over in a small boat. Reaching the southern side, General Forrest directed General Richardson to get together as many men as were available and follow him. He ordered an advance-guard of ten men from the escort, commanded by Sergeant George L. Cowan; instructing them to move down the Memphis road and to keep a sharp lookout for the enemy. We moved off briskly, followed closely by Forrest and the remainder of the escort, with Richardson's men bringing up the rear. About two miles distant from the river we came upon the first Union picket, and as our order was to ride right on and into them until we came upon something that was formidable, we put spurs to our horses and rode as fast as the flying picket could.

We went pell-mell into the reserve, about forty strong, but were so close upon them and going at such great speed that we could not check up in time to avoid a collision even had we so desired. Taken by surprise, and evidently thinking we were more numerous than we really were, they also broke and ran towards their main camp. We soon saw, just in our front, their camp-fires scattered on both sides of the road, and slowed up for a minute or two, until General Forrest arrived with the balance of the escort under command of Lieutenant Nathan Boone. He at once directed the entire escort, under Boone, to go forward and reconnoitre the camp while he brought up Richardson's brigade.

As we moved forward to the edge of a corn-field towards the enemy's camp, Lieutenant Boone, with the reckless daring which was so characteristic of him, determined to take matters into his own hands, and, forming us into as long a line as we could be stretched into, there being about ten paces between each member of the escort, he told us he was going to charge into that camp, no matter what it cost; that he wanted each one of the lieutenants and sergeants to give orders as if commanding a company, and in as loud a voice as possible, and when all were ready he would give the order to charge. In the mean time we could see by their camp-fires that they were in considerable disorder, trying to mount their horses and forming in line. At this moment Boone gave the order, "Forward, brigade; charge!" and we swept across the corn-field, making a tremendous racket. It was a clear, frosty night, and as our horses' feet trampled the corn-stalks down they made noise enough, with the yells we were giving, to represent at least a regiment. The Federals evidently believed that we were upon them in force, for they broke and ran in great disorder. We dashed through the camp, and though many of us would have liked to have stopped and helped ourselves from the pots of meat that were on the fire, we kept on after the enemy. It must have been at least two miles beyond the camp before the pursuit was stopped.

All through the bitter cold night Colonel Bell and his faithful soldiers, with tireless energy, were ferrying the wagons and their precious loads, and the two guns of Morton's artillery, across the swollen stream. With the exception of one teamster who was drowned, with the two horses attached to his wagon, by an upsetting of the boat in one of the trips, by daylight of the 25th everything was safe on the southern bank. Forrest was now with his entire command across the first real obstacle in his march back to Mississippi, but this Christmas week—as was the one of the preceding year in this same section of Tennessee—was to be full of danger and perplexity.

On all sides he was confronted by a host of Federal troops, well mounted, well armed, and in the main bravely and well officered. A strong detachment was placed at Bolivar, while others were posted southward from this point as far as Grand Junction, closing in the line of escape between the headwaters of the Hatchie and Wolf rivers. They had him now penned in between these two streams, and as the bridges had already been destroyed, and as Wolf River, which, rising near Bolivar, flows due west into the Mississippi at Memphis, was at this season of the year very deep and could in no place be forded, the Federal commander congratulated himself that at last he had the famous raider in the toils. Moreover, large bodies of infantry were stationed along the line of the Memphis and Charleston Railroad from

Captain Frank B. Gurley, Russell's Fourth Alabama Cavalry

Captain William M. Forrest, aide-de-camp

Lieutenant Nat Baxter, Jr., Freeman's battery

Major J. P. Strange, assistant adjutant general

M. C. Galloway, aide-de-camp

Captain Nathan Boone, commanding Forrest's escort

Colonel E. W. Rucker, commanding a brigade of Forrest's escort

Brigadier General Tyree H. Bell, commanding "Bell's Brigade" of Forrest's cavalry

Captain John C. Jackson, Forrest's escort (From a photograph taken after the war)

(top right) Brigadier General H. B. Lyon, commanding the "Kentucky Brigade" of Forrest's cavalry

(center right) Captain John W. Morton, chief of artillery, Forrest's cavalry

(bottom right) Brigadier General A. Buford, commanding a division of Forrest's cavalry

Colonel Robert McCulloch, Second Missouri Cavalry, commanding brigade

Colonel Jeffrey E. Forrest, commanding brigade

Captain H. A. Tyler, Co. A, Twelfth Kentucky Cavalry

Colonel W. L. Duckworth, Seventh Tennessee Cavalry

Men of Forrest's Command

Major C. S. Severson, chief quartermaster, Forrest's cavalry

Lieutenant William Richardson

Captain Reuben R. Ross

Colonel A. A. Russell, Russell's Fourth Alabama Cavalry, commanding brigade (From a photograph taken after the war)

Major G. V. Rambaut, chief of subsistence, Forrest's cavalry

Colonel James W. Starnes, Fourth Tennessee Cavalry, commanding brigade

Brigadier General George G. Dibrell (From a photograph taken after the war)

Dr. J. B. Cowan, chief surgeon, Forrest's cavalry

Men of Forrest's Command

Colonel W. A. Johnson, commanding brigade of Forrest's cavalry

Colonel D. C. Kelley (Forrest's old regiment), commanding brigade, Forrest's cavalry

Brigadier General W. H. Jackson, commanding division of Forrest's cavalry

Brigadier General James R. Chalmers

Men of Forrest's Command

Lieutenant George L. Cowan, Forrest's escort

Brigadier General Frank C. Armstrong

Lieutenant John Eaton, Forrest's escort

Major Charles W. Anderson, assistant adjutant and inspector general, Forrest's cavalry

Collierville as far east as Corinth, while at Grand Junction and at Collierville heavy detachments of troops were kept night and day upon capacious trains, the engines of which, with steam up, were ready at a moment's notice to transport these soldiers to any required point.

Although the torch had been applied to every bridge in the entire length of Wolf River, Forrest, before quitting Jackson, received a bit of information which was invaluable to him in the present emergency. Colonel Thomas H. Logwood, a devoted friend, and a man of great personal courage, had ventured into the section of Tennessee immediately north of Memphis on recruiting duty for his regiment, and while thus engaged he heard that General Forrest was near Jackson. He had discovered that near Lafayette station, on the Memphis and Charleston Railroad, there was a bridge over Wolf River which had been only partially destroyed, the fire having consumed but a single span. As the detachment sent to burn it had not waited to see it entirely consumed, the fire had been extinguished before the string timbers were materially weakened. He sent a trusted messenger to General Forrest with this information, telling him that it could be quickly repaired and used for conveying his troops across should he desire to escape by that route. To Colonel Bell was entrusted the important and dangerous duty of selecting three hundred of his best men and going in advance of the train and remainder of his troops, driving away any detachment of Federals which might be near at hand, effecting a lodgment on the southern bank, and placing the bridge in condition for the rapid crossing of the troops and train when these should arrive.

It will be remembered that on Christmas night Colonel Prince's Illinois cavalry had been driven from the neighborhood of Estenaula in the direction of Somerville, and on the following day General Forrest at an early hour took up his line of march on their trail. General Richardson's command had preceded him by another route, and between four and five o'clock in the afternoon, about four miles from Newcastle, in the vicinity of Somerville, had come in collision with the Federal cavalry. As General Forrest approached with his escort and a detachment of McDonald's battalion, he immediately took command, and, throwing the unarmed as well as the armed men of Richardson's detachment in line of battle, in order to present a more formidable appearance, they moved forward upon the enemy, who, however, did not give way until after a serious struggle, in which several Confederates were killed or wounded. Among the latter was Lieutenant Boone, and this brave officer lost a younger brother, first sergeant of the escort, who was killed here. The result of this affair may be inferred froin the official report of Colonel Prince, who says: "The enemy having gained our rear, we were compelled to retire, and, owing to the broken character of the ground, in considerable disorder. The loss the enemy sustained in killed and wounded must have exceeded our entire loss, which will not exceed forty killed, wounded, and missing."

General Forrest reports that here he killed and wounded eight or ten, and captured thirty-five prisoners. The detachment under Colonel Prince did not further molest him on the retreat.

At daybreak on the morning of the 27th, the advance, under the energetic leadership of Colonel Bell, had reached the burned bridge at Lafayette, and, advancing under cover of a dense wood, had succeeded in crossing on the unburned string timbers, and had surprised and driven off the small body of Federals that had just taken a position a short distance from the southern end of the bridge. It was only the work of an hour or two to relay the flooring of the bridge, and by the time the Confederate column came up it passed without delay over Wolf River and continued without interruption on the road toward Holly Springs, in Mississippi. The crossing at Lafayette was entirely unexpected by General Hurlbut, who had not dreamed that the Confederate leader would have the audacity to venture with his unarmed mob and his wagons and drove of cattle to the door of his headquarters and within sound of the large garrison at Memphis. It was, indeed, a bold stroke, and one of the cleverest pieces of strategy that Forrest practiced during the war. Had he marched out through the open country by Bolivar or Purdy or Corinth, he would have been overwhelmed, for in this direction he was expected; but Forrest, as a rule, did what was least expected.

Still further to throw Hurlbut off the scent, he had ordered Colonel Faulkner to proceed to Memphis and to attack the pickets within the suburbs of that city and, if hard pressed, to escape by way of Hernando. The Federal general was nonplused by the audacity of this movement, and only too late learned that Forrest's main column and train, having seized the bridge at Lafayette, had repaired it and crossed, and was already south of the Memphis and Charleston Railroad. Before reaching this highway of commerce, his advance guard had already placed obstructions upon the track two miles on either side of the point at which he proposed to cross it, and in this way the approach of the trains loaded with troops was prevented. In the darkness of the night they were compelled to remain without attacking, and by daylight the Confederates were miles away. Forrest, in his report, says the last fight took place at Collierville, about eight o'clock at night, at which point he drove the enemy into their fortifications and passed on to the south.

General Hurlbut, on the 28th of December, wired Sherman: "Forrest, after having been driven from the neighborhood of Jackson, has eluded Grierson, and crossed the railroad last night."

Colonel W. H. Morgan, who did not pass entirely without censure for his failure to intercept the Confederates on the 29th, wired to his commander the doleful doxology, "Forrest is certainly far away." On this same day the Confederate chieftain reached Holly Springs and reported to his superior, General S. D. Lee, that he had arrived there safely with the greater portion of his troops, regretting very much that he had to leave Tennessee so early. He reported to the Adjutant General at Richmond that he had come out of west Tennessee with about three thousand troops, fragments of sixteen different commands, with companies varying from fifteen to thirty-five men each. "I can see no way of making these troops effective, except by an order from the War Department annulling all authority previously given to raise troops, accompanied with the order to consolidate into full companies and regiments all the troops that can be gotten together in west Tennessee and north Mississippi. By adopting this method, I can get six full regiments of cavalry of about four thousand men. The balance would have to be conscripted. I think with this cavalry organized I can conscript ten thousand men and place them in the service."

On the 24th of January the Secretary of War acceded to his request, and he was directed to organize these troops, following the plan he had submitted. It began to look as if Forrest was about to receive some recognition at Richmond. Elsewhere the escape from the network which had been woven around him received considerable comment. A correspondent of a Northern paper, writing from Memphis, January 12, 1864, says: "Forrest, with less than four thousand men, has moved right through the Sixteenth Army Corps, has passed within nine miles of Memphis, carried off a hundred wagons, two hundred beef cattle, three thousand conscripts, and innumerable stores; torn up railroad-tracks, destroyed telegraph-wires, burned and sacked towns, ran over pickets with a single derringer pistol, and all in the face of ten thousand men."[5]

[5] *Campaigns of General N. B. Forrest.*

THIRTEEN

Meridian Expedition

Having captured Vicksburg, and thus completed the possession of the Mississippi River, General Grant had no sooner cut the Confederacy in twain than he determined to attempt a further subdivision of the eastern half of the southern country by a movement of the army under Sherman from Mississippi and west Tennessee into Alabama for the capture of Selma and Mobile.

In the early days of January, 1864, he and Sherman, the Damon and Pythias of the Union hosts, had put their heads together in formulating a plan for the accomplishment of this end. The official records point clearly to the intention of the campaign which was instituted in February of this year. After it was all over, and had, as a result of the genius of Forrest, failed in its ultimate purpose, General Sherman, in his official reports, published then, and in his *Memoirs,* written several years after the war, endeavored to convey to the mind of the reader that the object of his enterprise was fully attained in the destruction of the railroads at and near Meridian.

While it is true that General Sherman was given a wide discretion to act as his judgment might suggest after he started out upon his campaign, there can be no doubt in the mind of the close student of the records that it was the joint intention of Grant and himself not only to reach Meridian, but to go farther if possible, destroy the foundries and arsenals which were supplying the Confederate armies from Selma, and, still farther, to secure the seaport of Mobile, the value of which, as estimated by the Federal authorities, was ultimately shown in the desperate battle fought by Farragut for its capture.

As early as January 6, 1864, General Sherman, in a letter to Grant, says: "General W. S. Smith is supposed to be crossing the Tennessee to-day. I will aim to reinforce him with cavalry, and with infantry occupy the attention of the enemy, so as to enable him to reach Meridian, and, if possible, Selma."[1] Six days later he reverts to the same theme in a communication addressed to General Halleck at Washington: "I think by the 24th I can make up a force of twenty thousand men to strike Meridian, and, it may be, Selma."

On the 15th of January General Grant also addressed to Halleck, in Washington, a dispatch as follows: "I shall direct Sherman to move out to Meridian with his force—the cavalry going from Corinth—and destroy the roads east and south so effectually that the enemy will not attempt to rebuild them during the rebellion; he will then return, *unless the opportunity of getting into Mobile with the force appears perfectly plain.*"[2]

General S. A. Hurlbut also admits in the records: "I am ordered by Major-General Sherman to draw in my entire line of cavalry and all my available force, and proceed on the expedition south, towards, and probably to, Selma."

General Grant, in a letter to General Thomas, dated on the 19th of January, directing him to co-operate with Sherman in this enterprise by a movement from Chattanooga upon the army of Johnston at Dalton, says that Sherman is to proceed to Meridian and, if possible, as far east as Selma, "or, if he finds Mobile so far unguarded as to make his force sufficient for the enterprise, he will go there."[3]

The plan finally adopted was that General Sherman should concentrate at Vicksburg, during the month of January, 1864, an army of 20,000 effective troops, and march thence at a given time eastward through Jackson, direct to Meridian, which point is near the Alabama state line and only a short distance west of Selma. To co-operate with this movement from Vicksburg, and to unite with it at Meridian, a large cavalry force was to proceed from Memphis in a direction a little east of south, traversing the State of Mississippi, destroying the Mobile and Ohio Railroad from Corinth down to Meridian, at the same time spreading devastation in all that rich section of the South by burning the granaries, ginhouses, and all the cotton that could be found. They were to spread through the country as they passed a proclamation inviting the Negroes to leave their masters and homes, and bring with

---

[1] *Official Records,* vol. xxxii, part ii, p. 36.

[2] *Ibid.,* p. 100. (Italics not in original.)

[3] *Life of General Leonidas Polk,* vol. ii, p. 298 (Longmans, Green & Co., 1894).

them what livestock they could, and follow in the wake of the invading army. Uniting ultimately at Meridian, the combined army of invasion was to proceed at its leisure for the capture of Selma, the destruction of the arsenals and foundries there, and thence march to Mobile, which seaport they would open to the navies of the United States. General Sherman reports: "I ordered all the effective cavalry at once to be assembled and got ready for the field; there were ready for duty at Memphis 9231 cavalry, with 7638 serviceable horses. This force, with the 2500 brought with General Smith, gave us over ten thousand effective cavalrymen and horses."[4]

On or before the 1st of February, with an active force of seven thousand cavalry, lightly equipped and furnished with the most thoroughly effective weapons which the wealth of the United States could purchase, General William Sooy Smith, selected by General Grant for his special fitness to command such an important expedition, was directed to leave Memphis, march to Meridian direct, going by way of Pontotoc, Okolona, Columbus Junction, and Macon; the distance being about 250 miles, it was computed that he would reach there about the 10th of February. General Sherman moved out of Vicksburg, with his army of twenty thousand troops, on the 3rd of February, his command divided into two columns, which moved eastward along parallel routes.

It is somewhat singular, since the co-operation of Smith was deemed by Sherman so essential to the success of this campaign, that he did not inform himself as to the certainty of Smith's departure in time to effect the junction agreed upon. Telegraphic communication was open between Vicksburg and Memphis; General Smith was still in this portion of the world when Sherman sallied forth on the 3rd of February, and could easily have told his superior that he was not ready to start, and at the same time have informed him of the date when he would put his troops in motion. It would have been better for the full success of his project had Sherman waited four or five days until Smith could get ready, or, not wishing to tarry longer in Vicksburg, to have ordered him to go ahead without waiting for Waring's brigade (which was the reason of his long delay). Without this small brigade, the cavalry, properly handled, would still have been strong enough to have fought its way to Sherman, at Meridian, on time.

[4] *Official Records,* vol. xxxii, part i, p. 174.

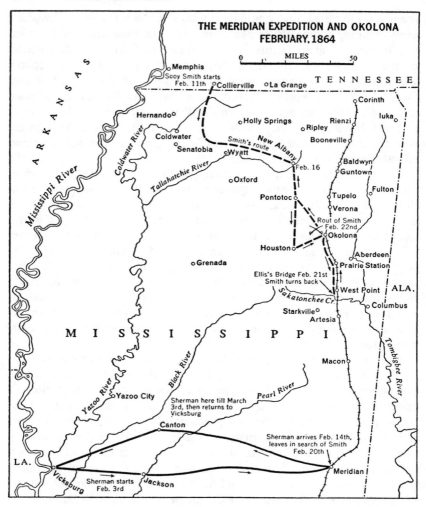

THE MERIDIAN EXPEDITION AND OKOLONA
FEBRUARY, 1864

Nevertheless, on the 3rd of February, General Sherman started with his force and, meeting with a resistance so slight as scarcely to cut him short of a single full day's march, went through to Meridian, arriving there at 3.30 P.M. on the 14th of February. Halting here, his command was busy with the destruction of the railroads and other public property in this section of country until the 20th of the month. Then, "hearing nothing whatever of General Smith, I ordered McPherson to move back slowly on the main road, while I moved towards the north to feel for General Smith." On the 23rd Sherman was at Hillsborough, in Scott County, Mississippi, and thence he moved westward to Canton, where his army remained until the 3rd of March, still hoping against hope that Smith might come to him. Then, finally despairing, his troops were ordered to return to Vicksburg.

General Smith did not start with his portion of the expedition until the 11th day of February. About the 1st of this month he had concentrated his command at Collierville, a station on the Memphis and Charleston Railroad, near the northern boundary line of Mississippi, some twenty-five miles eastward of Memphis. Instead of pushing on, as he was expected to do by his superior, with the troops he had in hand, with a hesitation which characterized him at times he wasted day after day awaiting the arrival of a single small brigade commanded by Colonel George E. Waring, Jr., which had been ordered to join him from Columbus, Kentucky.

Waring was making every effort to reach Collierville, but the fates were against him. The rivers and creeks which traverse west Tennessee were swollen; the cold winter weather had caused the ice to form, not strong enough to bear up under horse or man, but sufficiently thick and heavy to interfere with swimming or crossing in the small ferryboats which are common to this section. Even when the weather moderated, the muddy bottoms of the Obion and the Hatchie had rendered his progress so slow that it was noon of February 8th when the head of his column of worn-out men and horses reached Collierville.

Even after the arrival of Waring, with a strange fatality General Smith still lingered nearly three days more, waiting for Colonel Waring to have his horses shod and to give his troops time to recuperate from the severe ordeal through which they had passed. He says: "At last, by great effort, the whole command was prepared for the movement, and put in motion on the 11th day of February." Upon this day he marched out of Collierville at the head of seven thousand picked cavalry, armed with Colt's repeating rifles, modern carbines, and army revolvers—in all probability the most formidable cavalry command which had ever been organized in the Western armies.

There went with it twenty pieces of artillery, and, as a part of the initial movement, a brigade of infantry, under an efficient commander,

Colonel William L. McMillen. General Smith knew that Forrest would be in his path, and believed at this time that he had his forces scattered along the south bank of the Tallahatchie River awaiting his advance. In order to effect the crossing of this stream without serious opposition, he had called in the aid of this brigade of infantry. McMillen had preceded Smith's advance, having reached Hernando, due south of Memphis, on the 7th. On the 9th he had taken Senatobia, and on the 13th, having skirmished almost incessantly with Forrest's vedettes, he reached the Tallahatchie at Wyatt, advancing as far as this point for the purpose of making a diversion in favor of General Smith.

In the meantime, in order to produce the impression that he would cross the Tallahatchie at that point, while holding McMillen's infantry engaged with the Confederates across the river at Wyatt, Smith had also marched from Collierville in that direction. Turning suddenly to the east, he then moved with his entire cavalry column by way of New Albany, in Union County, Mississippi, where, on the 16th and 17th, his troops crossed without molestation to the south bank of this stream. Smith had already written to General Sherman that he thought Forrest would show fight between the Coldwater and the Tallahatchie, and he had promised his superior that he would pitch into him wherever he found him.

For two weeks following his escape from west Tennessee with his new levies, Forrest, who on the 4th day of December, 1863, had been promoted to the rank of major general, had busied himself in organizing and perfecting the discipline of his troops. He found this no easy task. It required all the energy, tact, and good sense which he possessed to consolidate into companies and regiments the various fragments of commands and organizations these recruits represented. Naturally the men desired to keep over them the officers they had elected, and, as far as this could be made consistent with the good of the service, Forrest permitted it, but in many instances his better judgment told him that this was impracticable. Then, by persuasion or force, they were merged into other companies under new officers, or scattered in squads of half a dozen or more among the older companies which had already seen service under some of his trusted subordinates.

As a result of these labors four skeleton brigades were formed. The first was placed under Brigadier General R. V. Richardson, numbering about fifteen hundred rank and file; the second, about twelve hundred effectives, was placed under Colonel Robert McCulloch; the third, two thousand strong, under General Tyree H. Bell; and the fourth, one thousand rank and file, under Colonel Jeffrey E. Forrest, brother of the general. McCulloch's and Forrest's brigades constituted a single division, over which General James R. Chalmers was placed.

Such was the influence exercised by this remarkable man over the restless class with which he was now dealing that only a very small number deserted his standard.[5] To nip this evil in the bud Forrest had placed a cordon of his most reliable troops across the roads leading northward. Taking advantage of the darkness of night, about twenty malcontents slipped away and started full tilt for their native country. They were arrested, brought back in a body, paraded through the camp as deserters; a court-martial was summoned, and they were tried and condemned to be shot. Whether Forrest, in order to exert a healthy influence upon the balance of his troops, had determined to make an example of these men, or whether he merely intended to frighten them for this offence, was known only to himself. In any event, they were condemned to be shot, placed in wagons, each one seated upon a coffin, and in solemn fashion were driven to the place of execution. Before their open graves the sentence of the court was read, and they were given a few minutes for prayer. There was not one of them who was not now convinced that his hour had come. Just as the prayer was ended and the soldiers were about to take their place to fire the fatal volley, Forrest rode to the spot and announced to the offenders that if they would promise to serve as faithful soldiers of the Confederacy, he would pardon them for this offence; but that if any further desertions or disobedience of orders occurred in his command, he would not again show such leniency.

Preparation on the part of the enemy for the cavalry expedition from Memphis was now well known to the Confederate commander. On the 6th of February, five days before Smith started, Forrest informed Chalmers of the impending movement from Collierville, and directed him to send twenty reliable men well to his front to watch the enemy. On the 8th he informed General Gholson, commanding the state militia, that McMillen's column was moving on the Hernando

[5] A majority of these recruits were men who had either served for one year in the Confederate army, and, having refused to enlist for the war, had sought refuge from conscription within the Union lines, or, for reasons satisfactory to themselves, were absent without leave.

road, and he adds in one of his dispatches of this date: "They will move in two columns, one by Panola to Grenada, the other by New Albany and Pontotoc, towards Okolona." With remarkable prevision he had judged the routes the enemy would take. On the 16th he informed General Polk that the destination of the expedition was a junction with Sherman; that they were about ten thousand strong, with some thirty pieces of artillery, and had crossed the river at New Albany.

As Smith advanced, Forrest, who had withdrawn south of the Tallahatchie, posted small detachments of his troops to watch the crossings of this stream, while with Bell's brigade he retired in the direction of Grenada. The remainder of his troops were ordered through Houston in the direction of West Point and Columbus. Forrest pushed rapidly across the country from Grenada to Starkville, where he arrived on the 18th of February. Jeffrey Forrest, with his brigade, was now directed to proceed in a northerly direction in the route along which Smith was marching, and to oppose his advance sufficiently to develop his strength and purposes. While Forrest was convinced that Okolona would be an important point in Smith's raid, he was uncertain whether the Union general would turn eastward across the Tombigbee River to reach Columbus, or would attempt the passage of the Sakatonchee near West Point, and march by way of Artesia toward Meridian. He therefore took the precaution to post Bell's brigade along the Tombigbee to arrest any movement in that direction.

The march of the invaders thus far had been uneventful. No obstacles had been encountered save at the crossing of the Tippah, a narrow stream with treacherous bottom, which, being swollen, delayed General Smith nearly two days until a bridge could be constructed. Occasionally the rifles of the advance guard and some Confederate outposts or stray scouts cracked away at each other in noisy fashion, but the Southerners were not yet ready, and took good care to scurry away to longer range. When within ten miles of Houston, in Chickasaw County, the Federal advance guard came upon a squadron of General Gholson's state militia, which with their shotguns and squirrel rifles delivered a volley, and then, as General Smith says in his report, "retired precipitately." These, he further says, he brushed away, and continued to advance until he encountered the enemy in stronger force, guarding the crossing of a swamp which could only be passed by a corduroy road which was narrow and about a mile in length. Some sharp fighting occurred here, which was finally overcome and the crossing made. Three miles north of Houston the roads again entered the slashes, too miry for flanking, and the causeway dangerously narrow for a direct advance.

As Gholson's partisans were gathered in force at the southerly end, the Union commander concluded not to attempt the passage, and turned back for several miles, until he struck a road which led eastward towards Okolona and thither he marched. From Okolona he passed almost due southward and here entered the prairie country, the rich corn-producing section of Mississippi, which was baptized during the Civil War "The Land of Egypt." One object of his expedition was the devastation of this granary, and corncribs, ginhouses, cotton, homes, and everything which could support or protect life went up in smoke or settled in ashes in the wake of the diligent detachments which shot out from the main column for miles on either side of the line of march.

At Prairie station, about fifteen miles north of West Point, General Smith concentrated his entire command, and on the 20th of February moved toward that place. The Union column had proceeded only five miles when the advance guard was vigorously assailed, and came back in some confusion on the leading regiment. He had encountered something more than Gholson's militia. It turned out to be Colonel Jeffrey Forrest's brigade, which had been sent in this direction, and was found here in line of battle and in plain view across the prairie. There were not many of them, but they were not to be run over without a fight, for the younger brother had not only the courage but a good share of the ability which the general possessed. The Federal commander formed to attack, and threw out his flankers to gain the Confederate rear. A short, sharp fight occurred, and when about to be overlapped on the flanks Colonel Forrest retreated in the direction of West Point, through which place, after offering resistance at every available position along the way, he passed, at three o'clock on the afternoon of the 20th, the Federal army immediately occupying the town.

From West Point, Jeffrey Forrest continued his retreat some three miles southward to the Sakatonchee Creek at Ellis's Bridge. Major D. E. Coon, who commanded the Second Iowa Cavalry, which formed the advance guard in the march from Prairie station to West Point, and which command was armed with Colt's repeating rifles and "navy sixes," says that five miles beyond Prairie station to the south they came in contact with the Confederates, and skirmished with them for five miles.[6] He then ran into a column of about 250, which gave way before a charge made by a portion of his regiment. The Confederates still skirmished with them for some three miles farther, when another stand was made, compelling Major Coon to dismount his men, in order to drive the Southern troopers from the field. He says:

"This was not done, however, without the loss of Lieutenant Dwyer, killed, and four men wounded. On reaching West Point it was ascertained that the three Forrests—the general, the colonel, and the captain —had just left and passed west, crossing the Sakatonchee, some three miles distant." This officer reports that, up to the time of reaching West Point, the largest force encountered at any time was 250 or 300 men. "Having had the advance during the entire day of the 20th, I had good opportunities for gathering information of the location and numbers of Forrest's command, and at no time placed the force at the Sakatonchee Bridge above two thousand men, and this force without artillery."[7]

Arriving at West Point on the 20th of February, General William Sooy Smith found himself in great perplexity, and it is not improbable that the fact that he was now at last face to face with the redoubtable Forrest had something to do with his state of mind. The man whom he had, as he expressed himself, been anxiously looking for and ready to "pitch into wherever he found him" was at last directly across his path. Although he had accomplished considerably more than half of the distance from Memphis to Meridian, and General Sherman was still within reach of him, he hesitated and was lost. Three or four days of energetic marching would have brought him to Sherman's camp, between Meridian and Canton.

In this hope Sherman's army lingered in the neighborhood until the 6th of March. Smith says he made a careful reconnaissance of the Sakatonchee swamp and the crossings of the various streams in that neighborhood, and they were all found strongly held by the enemy. Exaggerated statements of the strength of Forrest's command had been brought to him, and for this the Confederate leader was of course responsible. It was an invariable part of Forrest's strategy in every campaign to impress upon his enemy the idea that he had a force very

[6] *Official Records,* vol. xxxii, part i, p. 298.
[7] *Ibid.,* vol. xxxii, part i, p. 298.

much larger than he actually commanded.

General Smith says: "It was reported that Lee was about to reinforce Forrest with a portion or the whole of his command"; and to add to his discomfiture and increase his responsibilities, about three thousand Negroes, whom he had induced to desert their owners, had taken refuge with his troops, mounted on as many horses and mules brought in with them. These formed a serious impediment to his progress. "The ground was so obstructed as to make it absolutely necessary that we should fight dismounted, and for this kind of fighting the enemy, armed with Enfield and Austrian rifles, was better prepared than our force, armed mainly with carbines."[8] Strangest of all his excuses, after carefully selecting this command, he says: "There was but one of my brigades that I could rely upon with full confidence."

General Forrest had been directed by his superiors, Generals Polk and S. D. Lee, to retire in front of Smith's advance, in order to draw him as far as possible from his base at Memphis, and then to turn upon him and endeavor to destroy him. To retire in front of the enemy was one of the most difficult things for Forrest to do, but on this occasion he was making a tremendous effort to accomplish it. He says in his report that he offered some opposition to Smith's advance at the crossing of the Sakatonchee, for the reason that he wanted to protect this one bridge and hold it intact, so that he could cross his command rapidly in the pursuit when he should ultimately drive him toward Memphis.

The Union commander, however, had no intention of attempting to cross this Rubicon. In the crucial moment his heart failed him. On the morning of the 21st Major Coon, of the Second Iowa Cavalry, was directed to take his command and make a demonstration against the Confederates stationed in front of Ellis's Bridge, while the remainder of the Federal column would begin the retreat from West Point by way of Okolona.

On the night of the 20th General Forrest had stationed his troops along the southern bank of the Sakatonchee, at Ellis's Bridge. The brigade of Jeffrey Forrest was left on the northern side of this stream, about a half-mile from the bridge. During the night this careful officer busied himself in throwing up temporary breastworks of rails and logs for the protection of his men and to strengthen his position for the

[8] Official reports.

fight which he anticipated would take place on the ensuing morning. At a late hour in the night General Forrest was informed that a column of Federal cavalry had crossed the Sakatonchee at a point some four miles distant from Ellis's Bridge and were destroying houses and barns and property in that direction. He at once ordered his escort and a picked body of men to mount their horses, and, placing himself at their head, he came suddenly upon the raiders, and, getting between them and the bridge over which they had crossed, captured the entire party, consisting of about thirty troopers of the Fourth United States Regulars. He then returned to Ellis's Bridge, where early on Sunday morning, the 21st of February, he was informed by Colonel Jeffrey Forrest that the Federals were advancing upon his position from the direction of West Point.

Colonel Forrest was ordered to hold his ground stubbornly, and to retire across Ellis's Bridge only when forced to do so by overwhelming numbers. Major D. E. Coon, commanding the Federal troops, dismounted four rifle companies of his regiment, threw them out as skirmishers, brought forward two twelve-pounder howitzers, and these were soon briskly engaged with Jeffrey Forrest's force. For an hour and a half the firing continued briskly, but the younger Forrest held his position, and about ten o'clock in the morning the Federals ceased firing and disappeared toward West Point. Major Coon said in his report that Forrest had no artillery in front of him, and that he was convinced that the Union troops were at least four to one of the Confederates.

While the skirmish was in progress an incident occurred which is worthy of narration, since it gives something of an insight into one phase of Forrest's character, and serves to illustrate one of the various methods he pursued in controlling the men in his command. While the firing on the northern bank of the Sakatonchee was at its fiercest, General Chalmers, seated upon his horse, had taken a position on the south bank of the creek, near the short bridge over that stream. He had but recently been attached to Forrest's command, and had never before been with him under fire. He says:

I had considerable curiosity to observe General Forrest, but up to nine o'clock that morning he had not appeared upon the scene. Suddenly, out of a cloud of dust, accompanied by an orderly, he came dashing up the road towards the bridge. As he approached me and reined up his horse

I noticed that his face was greatly flushed, and that he seemed very much more excited than I thought was necessary under the circumstances. In rather a harsh, quick tone he asked me what the condition of affairs was at the front. As I had not been on the firing-line, and did not know anything definite excepting that the firing indicated quite a severe skirmish, I replied that Colonel Forrest had reported nothing to me beyond the fact that there was some skirmishing going on at the front, and added that I thought it was not a very severe affair. Forrest said quickly, and with evident impatience: "Is that all you know? Then I'll go there and find out for myself."

It was about four hundred yards from the bridge to where Jeffrey Forrest was in line, and a portion of the Federal advance had now reached a position where their shots were falling pretty thick in the road, and where they could readily fire at any one crossing on the bridge. Even as we were conversing the bullets were falling about us, and I thought, even there, we were unnecessarily exposed; but as General Forrest and his orderly dashed across the bridge (it seemed to me then in a spirit of bravado), I follcwed him, more out of curiosity to observe him than for any definite purpose. As we galloped over the bridge and up the road the enemy's skirmishers singled us out and commenced firing directly at us.

We had proceeded not more than a hundred yards in the direction of the skirmishers when I noticed, coming at full tilt towards us from that direction a Confederate soldier, who, dismounted and hatless, had thrown away his gun and everything else that could impede his rapid flight to the near. He was badly demoralized and evidently panic-stricken. As he approached General Forrest, the latter checked up his horse, dismounted quickly, threw the bridle-reins to the orderly who accompanied him, and, rushing at the demoralized soldier, seized him by the collar, threw him down, dragged him to the side of the road, and, picking up a piece of brush that was convenient, proceeded to give him one of the worst thrashings I have ever seen a human being get. The terror and surprise of the frightened Confederate at this unexpected turn in affairs, at a point where he thought he had reached safety, were as great as to me they were laughable. He offered no resistance, and was wise in this discretion, for the general was one of the most powerful men I ever saw, and could easily have whipped him in a free-for-all encounter.

At last he turned him loose, faced him again in the direction of his comrades, and thundered at him: "Now, ——— damn you, go back to the front and fight: you might as well be killed there as here, for if you ever run away again you will not get off so easy." It is unnecessary to say that the poor fellow marched back and took his place in line, a wiser if not a braver man. The news of this incident spread rapidly through the command and even through the Southern army, and, almost as soon, it appeared in one of the Northern periodicals of this time, which came out in illustrated form, and was entitled, "Forrest breaking in a conscript."

Colonel Waring, in his entertaining book, writing of this campaign, says: "Forrest was in our front with about our own number of cavalry, but without artillery, of which we had twenty good pieces. The open country was good fighting ground, and gave to our better drilled and more completely organized force a decided advantage, even without our great odds in artillery. Could we effect a junction with Sherman, we should enable him to divide the Confederacy from Vicksburg to Atlanta. No sooner had we turned tail than Forrest saw his time had come, and he pressed us sorely all day and until nightfall."[9]

The moment that Colonel Forrest reported that the Federals were retiring from his front the general became convinced that they had commenced a systematic retreat, and that the fight made here was simply for the purpose of gaining time. He at once ordered Captain H. A. Tyler, who had won his spurs in the spirited dash at Jack's Creek, to take his own company and one other company of Faulkner's Twelfth Kentucky, numbering in all one hundred and fifty men, and to push on in the direction taken by the retreating enemy. At the same time, the purpose of the enemy being now fully developed, he ordered the rapid concentration of his scattered troops, for the purpose of closing in upon General Smith. Dispatches were sent to General Richardson, who was some twelve miles westward, to move at once to the bridge across Line Creek, and to push on in the direction of Okolona. The state troops, under Gholson, were to move in the same direction, bearing a little westward, toward Houston. Jeffrey Forrest and Chalmers were to follow in the wake of Captain Tyler, while General Forrest, with his escort, would press forward to keep up with the Kentucky captain. Bell's brigade, which, owing to the illness of this officer, was temporarily under Colonel C. R. Barteau, and which had been thrown to the east to guard the crossings of the Tombigbee, was ordered to move with all possible celerity and endeavor to intercept the retreating column of General Smith at Okolona.

[9] *Whip and Spur,* by George E. Waring, Jr., formerly colonel of the Fourth Missouri Cavalry, U. S. V.

While these dispositions were being made, Captain Tyler was vigorously pursuing the retiring Federals. He says:

General Forrest in person gave me my orders to push forward and ascertain quickly what direction the enemy had taken. I followed at a stiff pace, but did not come up with them until I reached West Point. Their rear-guard was passing through this town, when I charged them with my two companies, driving them without serious resistance through the village, capturing and killing several. At this time the escort had not come up, nor were there any other Confederate troopers in sight, excepting my detachment. At West Point I learned that the entire Federal force had gone northward on the road to Okolona, and were evidently in rapid retreat. I reported this by courier to General Forrest at once. Slight skirmishing continued along the road, but no decided opposition was encountered till a point about six miles north of West Point had been reached. Here I became convinced that we had come up with a considerable body of the main column. There were in sight, as near as I could estimate, about fifteen hundred mounted troops and several pieces of artillery, in well-selected position. The country was open in their immediate front, while just behind them was some heavy timber, which offered good protection, and also prevented me from determining the exact number of their troops.[10]

The courage and vigor which characterized the pursuit of Captain Tyler may be inferred from the report of Major Coon, who commanded the rear of Smith's column at this juncture: "After having passed through West Point," he says, "the firing began in the rear, and increased for an hour, when I was called upon by Captain Graves, who was in command of the rear-guard, for assistance, as the enemy's forces were pressing him and threatened his flanks. One battalion of rifles was dismounted and placed behind the fence and brought into line. The enemy, thinking the road clear, came up with great boldness. At this time two or three shells and three or four rounds of the rifles checked their movement, and my men retired in good order. From the demonstration of the enemy, I deemed it necessary to dismount another battalion of rifles."

Meeting with such formidable opposition, Captain Tyler wisely halted his column, threw it in line on one side of the road, out of reach of the enemy's artillery, and awaited the arrival of Forrest with his escort, who came up in a few minutes at a gallop. The general immedi-

[10] Manuscript in possession of the author.

ately took command of the squadron and the escort, and advanced in the direction of the Federals.

Their battery soon opened upon him with such precision as to convince him of the rashness of attempting to move through the open field upon a superior force admirably posted. Telling Captain Tyler that McCulloch's and Forrest's brigades were immediately in the rear and would soon be up, he directed him to remain where he was while he would take his escort and pass to the flank and rear of the enemy in order to reconnoiter their position. He also ordered Tyler, in case the enemy began to give way, to charge them and to press the pursuit as vigorously as he had already done.

Forrest, moving to the flank and rear, was observed by the enemy, who immediately limbered up their artillery and retreated in great haste. Tyler followed, moving directly down the lane, and once more closed in upon the retreating rear guard. General Forrest was considerably disappointed that his main column had not come up at this point.

From the Union reports it is evident that they had considerable difficulty in getting away fast enough to save themselves. Major Coon says: "I got my led horses and howitzers out of the timber in time to save them; but my men on foot had become so completely exhausted that I felt at one time that half of them must be captured."

Forrest's report reads: "I soon came on their rear-guard; charged with my escort and Faulkner's command, and drove it before me."

A mile or two farther up, in the direction of Okolona, the Federals had determined upon another effort to check the pursuit, which at this early hour was presaging disaster to the flying column. They had selected a place naturally strong, and in addition had thrown up protecting breastworks of rails, and had taken advantage of a large ginhouse and other outbuildings of a plantation which was situated on either side of the road from West Point to Okolona. Tyler, who was still in advance, rushed dangerously close to the Federal line, which opened upon him a scathing volley and emptied several saddles of his troop. This officer immediately withdrew his command, which was at this moment joined by General Forrest with his escort. McCulloch's brigade was now ordered to the front. Dismounting, he advanced with about a thousand troopers, who, under the intrepid Missourian, soon drove the Federals from their position. They no sooner turned to run than Forrest dashed at their rear, leading in person his escort and Tyler's Kentuckians. Within about one-half mile the best mounted of the Confederates had closed in with the laggards of the Union rear, precipitating one of the severest combats at close quarters which took place on this day.

Seeing the desperate predicament in which their comrades were, some of the Federals not immediately in the rear turned boldly on their pursuers. Here General Forrest, whose skillful horsemanship, dexterity with the saber, and great muscular strength stood him well in hand in these frequent combats at close quarters, killed a Federal trooper, who, relying upon his pistol, had fired at and missed his adversary. This brief yet bloody affair seemed to convince the Union forces that another stand for that day was injudicious. They continued their retreat, and the Confederates pursued them until nightfall, when General Forrest ordered his men to take a much-needed rest.

General Smith had wisely determined to put as great a distance as possible between his rear guard and the Confederates. He urged his weary troopers on until near midnight, when he halted and encamped three miles south of Okolona. Forrest had no thought of allowing his enemy much time for rest and recuperation. By four o'clock on the morning of the 22nd he had dispatched Jeffrey Forrest's brigade by a road which gradually converged toward the route along which the enemy had retreated, and united with this about one mile south of Okolona. Placing himself at the head of his escort before the day had yet dawned, the Confederate general moved rapidly to the front, followed in close order by the ever-faithful McCulloch and his gallant brigade. He soon encountered Smith's outpost pickets, which he charged at sight, chasing these and the rear guard into and through the town of Okolona.

Just beyond the limits of this village a considerable body of Federal troops were now discovered drawn up in line of battle in the open prairie, and apparently ready to attack. Across the prairie, and distant about a mile, Forrest was rejoiced to see another line of battle, which he recognized as Bell's brigade under the intrepid Barteau, who, true to his promise to unite with his commander at Okolona at an early hour on the 22nd, had arrived at that point an hour before Forrest and the escort came up. He found himself with a single brigade in the immediate presence of a force of the enemy sufficiently large to overwhelm him, had General Grierson taken proper advantage of the absence of Forrest with Chalmers's division. Fully realizing the peril of his position, Barteau assumed a bold front, threw his troopers into line, advanced his skirmishers, and maneuvered his force in such a fashion that an assault upon him was deferred while a careful reconnaissance was being made upon either flank of the Confederate force. The time thus gained in all probability saved him from disaster, as Forrest came up before Grierson had determined to attack.

Forrest had no sooner caught sight of Barteau's line than, leaving half of his escort as skirmishers, whom he directed to engage the attention of the enemy, with the other half he galloped across the plain and joined Barteau. The yells of the Tennesseeans as they recognized their idolized chieftain, in whose courage and skill everyone had implicit faith, told Forrest how thoroughly he might depend upon the devotion of his followers. He congratulated Barteau on the disposition he had made of his troops as he rode along the lines, stretched to the utmost to make the largest possible display of force, and encouraged the men with a few timely words. He told them that all the day preceding he had whipped the enemy in engagement after engagement, and chased them until night compelled him to stop; that they were already cowed and beaten, and if his men would follow him into their ranks with the courage they had shown in their work in west Tennessee, the Federals would not stand the pressure. With rare tact he added for their greater encouragement that Chalmers's division and Richardson's brigade were close at hand and would join in the attack.

Both lines of battle were in plain view of each other across the open prairie, and the Confederates so far on the ground were greatly overmatched. Forrest looked with longing eyes in the direction of West Point, but as yet McCulloch's and Jeffrey Forrest's brigades were not in sight. With all in readiness, noticing a point in Grierson's line where the Federal troopers were apparently in confusion, rising in his stirrups, he yelled at the top of his voice, "Charge!" and away he went, the foremost horseman of the line.

Colonel Barteau, who was frequently in battle with Forrest, says: "One of his many peculiarities was that in battle he never seemed to touch his saddle, but 'stood up' in his stirrups, an attitude which gave him the appearance of being a foot taller than he really was. As he was over six feet in stature and of large proportions, and of necessity rode a large horse, it was not difficult to recognize his imposing presence at any ordinary distance along the line."

As the Confederates came on the Union troopers gave them a single volley and retreated to find shelter behind a second line of General Smith's cavalry. Unwilling to jeopardize further the small force at this moment under him by a further attack on the strong lines which his advance had developed, Forrest called a halt to his men, threw forward his skirmishers, and, taking advantage of a "stake-and-rider" fence, dismounted about two-thirds of his command, and for a short time engaged the enemy on foot.

The Fourth United States Regulars, who were considered. by all odds the best fighters with Smith's expedition, ventured at one moment to make a rush upon the skirmish line that Forrest had advanced. They compelled these to retire within supporting distance of the dismounted Confederates along the line of fence, who, opening upon the Union cavalry, drove them back in disorder.

Having observed the head of McCulloch's column, which was followed by his brother's brigade, now coming into Okolona and on to the field from the south, Forrest sent word for them to press forward in his rear, and, mounting all the troops of Barteau's command, the Confederate general took immediate advantage of the disorder into which the Fourth Regulars had been thrown, and gave his well-known order to "Move up!" Taking the lead with the escort and the Second Tennessee, he charged and broke the Federals, and pressed them with such vigor that they fled the field in great confusion.

No sooner had the Fourth Regulars given way than the Seventh Indiana rallied to its support, but this in turn suffered defeat. Then the Third brigade of Smith's expedition, under Colonel Lafayette McCrillis, was lined up for their assistance, but Forrest's onslaught was irresistible, and the defeat of the enemy was now complete.

Colonel George E. Waring, who commanded the First brigade on this occasion, says: "On the 22nd the first brigade was ordered to form in line and prepare for a fight. It formed in the open country, with the enemy in sight about a mile away across the prairie. As we passed to the left of Okolona, one regiment, the Seventh Indiana, was ordered to fall out and support the Fourth Regulars. The Third brigade had the rear of the column, the Regulars and the Seventh Indiana were engaged, and this brigade was ordered to the attack. It soon broke in disgraceful flight and confusion, abandoning five guns of its battery without firing a shot."[11]

Colonel McCrillis reports that he was directed by General Grierson to form his brigade in line, while he (Grierson) would place himself at the head of the Fourth cavalry and the Seventh Indiana, and engage the enemy in front. He says:

At this time the column in front moved suddenly and rapidly as the firing commenced in the rear, and the column of the enemy on our right charged down on the Third Illinois. I was sent forward to reinforce this regiment, to halt the column and reinforce the rear. The Third Tennessee was ordered into an open field on our left to protect the Second Tennessee and Fourth Regulars, who were hard-pressed and outflanked by a superior force. These regiments were forced upon the rear of the column by the enemy, and the Third Tennessee was ordered back. They were driven in, and charged on in rear and flank, and all three of the regiments —the Fourth Regulars, and the Second and Third Tennessee—became entirely disorganized. I then passed to the head of the disorganized regiments, and found General Grierson and a part of his staff trying to check the column, but with their aid and part of my own staff I found it only partially practicable.

The confusion into which this division of General Grierson's cavalry was thrown was complete, and the relentless pursuit and vigorous pressure which Forrest brought to bear upon them soon developed their flight into a hopeless stampede. Officers as well as men stood not "upon the order of their going," but went as best they could. Along the road and through the woods or fields on either hand, paying slight heed to commands from any source, the crowds of panic-stricken soldiers rushed and crowded until the way was choked with the surging mass of men and animals. Five pieces of artillery, retarding their disordered flight, were forced from the road into a field, and fell a prey to the fierce-smiting Forresters.

Lieutenant I. W. Curtis, of the First Illinois Light Artillery, says:

We had not proceeded very far from Okolona when we were unexpectedly surprised by the presence of flying cavalry on both sides of us. They were in perfect confusion; some hallooing "Go ahead, or we will be killed!" while some few showed a willingness to fight. After several unsuccessful attempts to form my battery, I gave it up, and

[11] *Battles and Leaders of the Civil War*, vol. iv, p. 417.

marched as best I could until I received an order for me to try to save the artillery by marching through the field to the right. I proceeded to comply with orders. After crossing some two or three almost impassable ditches, and my horses being nearly exhausted, I came to another ditch some six feet deep. I managed to get one gun over safe by the men dismounting and taking it over by hand, and one other which, by the time we got it over, was broken so that we had to leave it. I ordered them to cut the horses loose, to cut the gearing, and to go ahead with the led horses.[12]

From the point where the first dispersion of General Smith's rear guard took place, within sight of the village of Okolona, no resistance save an occasional rifle shot from the fleeing rear guard was made, until a point westward about five miles was reached.

Colonel Waring, who with his brigade was in advance at this time, says that when five miles west of Okolona he received a message from the rear informing him of the disaster that had happened to McCrillis's brigade and the other troops which had been sent to reinforce him. He was ordered to form a line in the first available position and fortify it; get together what artillery could be had, and to allow the stampeding cavalry to pass through its lines and hold the enemy in check, if possible, until they could be in a measure reorganized at some safe distance in his rear.

The Federal commander and his subordinates realized that the situation was desperate. As the disorganized cavalry came in sight of Waring's position and passed through, they gave evidence of such complete demoralization that this officer became seriously alarmed as to the safety of his own command. He says:

"I formed my brigade in line, with skirmishers far out on each flank, and remained until the Third brigade had passed through, portions of it in such confusion as to endanger the morale of my own command."

He then abandoned the line he had formed, under orders from his superior, and fell back to a stronger position, about a mile distant. At this point another stand was made. The Second New Jersey, the Second Illinois, Seventh Indiana, and Fourth Missouri bore the brunt of the fight, until they in turn were overwhelmed by Forrest's irresistible onslaught. Meanwhile General Smith seemed at last to be aroused to a full appreciation of his desperate condition. About two miles in the

[12] *Official Records,* vol. xxxii, part i, p. 301.

rear of the line which Waring had first taken to check the flight of Grierson's troops, Smith had selected a position of great natural strength on a farm called Ivey's Hill, near Tallaboncla. Northward from Okolona the road to Pontotoc, along which this relentless pursuit was being pressed, passes from the open prairie into a wooded and hilly country; and at the point chosen by General Smith, for the purpose of checking the advance of the enemy, and giving him time to reorganize his broken column, the highway ran directly along the backbone or summit of a narrow ridge.

On Ivey's Hill, just where the houses, ginhouse, and stables of a large plantation were erected, the road coming from the direction of Okolona turned almost at a right angle in its course toward Pontotoc. Taking advantage of this deflection and the houses, which offered great protection to his command, and hastily throwing the rails from the fence into temporary breastworks and massing his artillery, General Smith had at last with skill so disposed his forces as to command the long, narrow road which approached his formidable position.

As General Forrest came in sight, two separate lines of the Federals were now in plain view. He ordered the two brigades which were immediately with him, Jeffrey Forrest's and McCulloch's, to form in columns of four to one side of the highway, taking advantage of the protection which the wooded land afforded. They could thus advance without being exposed to the artillery, from which they would necessarily suffer had they moved forward in the open lane.

Bell's brigade, having borne the brunt of the fighting in the earlier part of the day, had been replaced by the two commands just named, and was now bringing up the rear at a slow pace. It was only the work of a few minutes for these rough riders and hard fighters to be in readiness for the advance. They did not number twelve hundred in both brigades. Eighteen hours of hard riding had broken down a large number of the horses, and, although the men whose animals gave out struggled along on foot as ordered, they could not keep in sight of their mounted comrades. The bugle sounded, and away the two columns sped parallel with each other. Coming near the enemy, they changed their formation from columns of four into line, and then swept forward. Within about three hundred yards of the advance line of the Union troops a thundering volley rolled from the artillery and the small arms on the hill in front, and a number of the Southerners went down.

At the first volley Colonel Jeffrey Forrest, with the reckless daring which he had shown in many other encounters, and which was characteristic of the five brothers who won distinction under the flag of the Confederacy, while leading this charge at the head of his brigade, met the glorious death of a soldier. He was instantly killed by a Minié ball which passed through his neck, cutting the carotid artery and dividing the spinal cord. Colonel McCulloch, who occupied the same position at the head of his brigade, was also, by the same volley, painfully wounded.

Staggered by this terrific fire, the death of the younger Forrest, and the wounding of McCulloch, the troops wavered and then halted. This was the moment when General Smith might have won success, but, seemingly content with checking the Confederate advance, the Federals made no effort to advance from behind their works.

Colonel W. L. Duckworth, of the Seventh Tennessee, who at once assumed command of Jeffrey Forrest's brigade, with the aid of Lieutenant Colonel D. M. Wisdom and Colonel Russell, steadied the command, dismounted their men, and prepared to defend to the last the position they had gained. At the same time, Colonel Robert McCulloch, refusing to quit the field, also dismounted his troops and sent the horses to the rear, to a place of safety. While the fighting still continued, the "lion-hearted McCulloch" had the surgeon dress his wound, and never left the head of his command until late in the night, when all signs of the enemy had disappeared.

The death of Jeffrey Forrest overwhelmed the general with grief. His love for this youngest brother surpassed the ordinary affection which exists in this relationship. He was the pride as well as the best beloved of his brothers. Jeffrey had been given every opportunity to reach a high place in the social and professional world, and was ambitious to make his mark high enough to satisfy his brother's pride. When the war came on, laying aside every civil aspiration, he entered the service, and, though only twenty-four years old, had risen by merit to the command of a brigade.

When General Forrest saw his brother fall from his horse he rushed to the spot, dismounted, and, kneeling, held the lifeless form in his arms, and called him several times by name, in a voice choking with anguish. Realizing then that he was dead, he kissed him on the forehead, laid him gently down again upon the earth, called his aide-de-camp, Major Strange, and with tears in his eyes asked his faithful adjutant to take charge of his brother's remains.

In the immediate presence of this affecting scene the Confederate troops had ceased firing; to the right and left, however, along the lines, the rifles of the dismounted men were cracking away at the Federals on the hill. Several minutes must have elapsed while the small group of officers and men gathered around their grief-stricken commander. To those present it seemed as if for once, in the agony of a great personal loss, this strong leader of men had lost sight of the greater obligation which he owed to the safety of his devoted followers. But it was only for a few minutes at the most, and so deep was the sympathy of these men with their leader that they would have submitted to any exposure and taken any risk out of respect for his deep affliction.

Meanwhile a portion of Bell's brigade had come in sight. Mounting his horse, and looking rearward to assure himself of this fact, General Forrest rode a few paces to the front and, despite the heavy firing which had not for a moment ceased, surveyed quickly yet carefully the position of the enemy on the hill. He then directed a portion of the Forrest brigade under Duckworth to mount and ride to the left and on the flank and rear of the Federals. This detachment had scarcely started to make this movement when the entire command present was ordered to mount and prepare to advance; then, waving his saber in the air, Forrest ordered his bugler to sound the charge and shouted to his men to follow him. With his ever-faithful escort at his heels, he dashed at full speed in the direction of the Union position, and to some of his officers who witnessed it, it seemed an act so rash as to savor of madness. Major Strange was at the time fearful that his commander had been made desperate by the death of his brother and, wild with despair at such misfortune, was rushing headlong in the hope of a like fate to himself.

The Federal line gave way before the desperate onslaught which Forrest was making. The movement of the Confederate troops toward the flank and rear had evidently frightened General Smith, who ordered his troops to retire, which they did with great rapidity. Forrest followed as swiftly as was his wont, and soon was dangerously far in advance of any strong support. The escort was with him, some sixty in number, and close behind, not more than a like number of the best-mounted men of the troops, who were endeavoring to keep pace with him. The Union retreat, impeded by a piece of artillery which had met with an accident and was abandoned, with two or three wagons and caissons of ammunition, was just at this moment retarded, and, as the Confederates were close at hand and following at full tilt, the Federal commander had thrown some five hundred of his rear guard into line across the road. Into these Forrest dashed, and here one of the most sanguinary hand-to-hand engagements of the war occurred. Dr. J. B. Cowan writes:

I had just reached the spot where Jeffrey Forrest was lying dead, when Major Strange said to me as I rode up, "Doctor, hurry after the general; I am afraid he will be killed!" Putting spurs to my horse, I rode rapidly to the front, and in about a mile, as I rounded a short turn in the road, I came upon a scene which made my blood run cold. There in the road was General Forrest with his escort, and a few of the advance-guard of the Forrest brigade, in a hand-to-hand fight to the death, with Federals enough, it seemed to me, to have pulled them from their horses. Horrified at the situation, I turned back down the road to see if help was at hand, and, as good-fortune would have it, the head of McCulloch's brigade was coming in full sweep towards me.[13]

The position occupied by the Federals at this time was a strong one, and the number of Federals engaged with the general and his escort seemed so large, and the undertaking to drive them off so great, that for a moment McCulloch's men hesitated. They did not usually stop at anything which looked like a fight, but to them it seemed certain death to rush into the trap in which Forrest and his escort had seemingly fallen, and an effort to rescue them seemed hopeless. It was here that the heroic McCulloch proved his devotion to his leader. The dressing of his wounded hand had become saturated with blood, and, seeing the momentary hesitation on the part of his troops, he held his bloody hand high above his head and shouted at the top of his voice, "My God, men, will you see them kill your general? I will go to his rescue if not a man follows me!" With this he dashed toward the enemy, followed by his troopers to a man, and was soon in the thickest of the fray.

[13] Manuscript in possession of the author.

This short encounter did not consume much more time than it requires to describe it, for the Federals turned in flight, and were sorely pursued by the Missourians. It is said on excellent authority that in this single encounter General Forrest placed three of the enemy *hors de combat.*

Inside of a mile from the scene of this last encounter the rear guard had taken up another position. As General Forrest approached, Dr. Cowan was riding by his side. The Federals opened upon them, and the bullets were falling in alarming proximity, when the doctor said: "General, I think you should get out of the road; it is not right unnecessarily to expose yourself." Forrest replied: "Doctor, if you are alarmed, you may get out of the way; I am as safe here as there." The doctor continues:

> At this moment a piece of artillery which had not been observed opened upon us, and the general's horse fell dead. I dismounted at once and offered him my own, but he said, "No, I will take Long's" (calling to a member of his escort by this name), "and he can go to the rear."
>
> Just here, where this horse was killed, there was a little log cabin, and we noticed a woman and some children huddled in behind the house in a corner of the chimney. Touched by the terror of the mother for herself and her children, Forrest said, "Dr. Cowan, please put that poor woman and her children in that hole" (pointing to a pit in one corner of the yard from which the earth had been taken for making the mortar in the construction of the rude chimney), and added, "In there they will be perfectly safe!"

In a few minutes the whole command had moved forward again, and another short, sharp fight occurred, in which the general's second horse was also shot down, after which he had the famous old charger King Philip brought up, and he rode him to the close of the day. King Philip also received a slight wound in the neck on this sanguinary day, but was not fatally hurt.

In this last charge the gallant Lieutenant Colonel James A. Barksdale of the Fifth Mississippi fell mortally wounded, just as the Federal line gave way.

From this time the Federals offered no further resistance at any point. Discouraged and beaten, they hurried on their weary journey toward Memphis, bending every energy to escape capture. In the language of one of the brigade commanders, Colonel Waring, "The retreat to Memphis was a weary, disheartening, and almost panic-stricken flight, in the greatest disorder and confusion, and through a most difficult country. The First Brigade reached its camping-ground five days after the engagement, with the loss of all its heart and spirit, and nearly fifteen hundred fine cavalry horses. The expedition filled every man connected with it with burning shame, and it gave Forrest the most glorious achievement of his career."

Colonel Joseph Kargé of the Second New Jersey Cavalry bears testimony to the dilapidated condition of the Federal command as it journeyed toward Memphis: "The regiment lost by death on the march and in camp the majority of its horses, and of the remaining one hundred and sixty-one only fifty-five can be called serviceable."

Lieutenant Curtis, whose battery, with the exception of a single piece, was captured in the stampede, reports: "I then proceeded to gather up my company with my single gun. I lost thirty horses during the march."

The commander of the expedition reports that from West Point he retired, "fighting for over sixty miles, night and day"; and of the closing fight on the 22nd, he says: "The Second Tennessee Cavalry, the last regiment that I had thrown into the line to cover the passage of our column, broke from line, stampeded, and galloped over our rear-guard, drove a battery of little pop-guns into a ditch, where they were so badly smashed we could not get them out, so we unhitched the horses, destroyed the ammunition, and spiked the guns. This spread confusion everywhere, which the rebels took advantage of, pitched into us, and gave us pretty rough handling, inflicting a loss upon us of about three or four hundred men—killed, wounded, and missing. Our total loss, killed and wounded, will reach about four hundred, and of stragglers they must have picked up about two or three hundred, possibly more, but this is immaterial."

In his official report, General Forrest says of the last resistance offered on this day:

They made a last final effort to check pursuit; from their preparations, numbers, and advantageous position no doubt indulging the hope of success. They had formed in three lines, crossing a large field on the left of the road, but which a turn in the road placed directly in our front. Their lines were at intervals of a hundred paces, and the rear and second lines longer than the first. As the advance of my column moved up, they opened on it with artillery. My ammunition was nearly exhausted, and I knew that if we faltered they in turn would become the attacking party, and disaster might follow. Many of my men were broken down and exhausted with climbing the hills on foot and fighting almost constantly for the last nine miles. I determined, therefore, to rely upon the bravery and courage of the few men I had, and advance to the attack. As we moved up, the whole force charged down at a gallop, and I am proud to say that my men did not disappoint me. Standing firm, they repulsed one of the grandest cavalry charges I had ever witnessed. The Second and Seventh Tennessee drove back the advancing line, whose head wheeled into retreat, pouring a destructive fire on each successive line of the enemy, who soon fled the field in dismay and confusion, losing an entire battery of artillery, and leaving the field strewn with dead and wounded men and horses.

Half of my command were out of ammunition, men and horses were exhausted and worn out with two days' hard riding and fighting, and as night was at hand farther pursuit was impossible. General Gholson arrived during the night with his command, which was small but comparatively fresh. I ordered them to follow the next morning, and to press forward and cross the Tallahatchie.

Considering the disparity in numbers and equipment, I regard the defeat of this force, consisting as it did of the best cavalry of the Federal army, a victory of which all who were engaged in it may justly feel proud. Its moral effect upon the raw, undisciplined, and undrilled troops in this command is of a value incalculable. It has inspired them with courage and given them confidence in themselves and their commanders. Although many of them were but recently organized, they fought with a courage and daring worthy of veterans. They captured six pieces of artillery, three stands of colors, and 162 prisoners. My force in the fight did not exceed 2,500 men, while that of the enemy, twenty-seven regiments, cavalry and mounted infantry, numbered 7000 strong.

I regret the loss of some gallant officers. The death of my brother, Colonel Jeffrey E. Forrest, is deeply felt by his brigade as well as by myself, and it is but just to say that for sobriety, ability, prudence, and bravery he had no superior of his age.

General Forrest pays grateful tribute to the memory of Lieutenant Colonel Barksdale, who fell, mortally wounded, soon after Jeffrey Forrest was killed, and also to the heroism of Colonel Robert McCulloch, who, although wounded, continued in command. The charge led by McCulloch, and the desperate encounter south of Pontotoc, will never be forgotten by those who witnessed and survived it, and ought not to be forgotten as long as courage and heroism are appreciated by the human race. Captain H. A. Tyler, who joined in the charge, said of it: "McCulloch, with his bandaged hand, all blood-stained and raised high above his head, recalled the plume of Henry of Navarre, and we rode after it as faithfully as did the followers of the peerless prince."

Colonels Russell, Duckworth, and Barteau, and Lieutenant Thomas S. Tate, who commanded the escort in the terrible melee, were especially mentioned, as was Captain Jackson and other officers of this command. It is to Lieutenant Tate that we are indebted for a description of the exciting combat in which his life was saved by the quick eye of Forrest, who, although sorely beset, saw the danger in which his devoted subordinate was in and, rushing to his rescue, slew the Federal trooper with a stroke of his saber.

The corrected reports of the losses in the two commands, in the engagements of the 20th, 21st, and 22nd, showed 27 killed, 97 wounded, and 20 missing in the Confederate army. General Smith lost 54 killed, 179 wounded, and 155 missing. Total, 388.

General Gholson, with the state militia, kept up the chase as far north as the Tallahatchie, which was crossed on the 23rd at New Albany, and from thence the Federals pursued their way unmolested to Memphis.

Gathering up his wounded, who were taken back to the hospital at Okolona, and leaving details to bury those who had fallen in the various encounters, General Forrest returned and established his headquarters at Starkville, where, on the 26th, he was joined by his entire command, which in the latter part of February went into camp at Columbus, Mississippi.

For the failure to join him at Meridian, as agreed upon in the plan of campaign, General Sherman never forgave his unfortunate subordinate. In his *Memoirs* he says:

General Smith was ordered to move from Memphis straight for Meridian, Mississippi, and to start from there the 1st of February. I explained to him personally the nature of Forrest as a man, and his peculiar force; told him that in his route he was sure to encounter him; that he always attacked with vehemence, for which he must be prepared, and that were he repelled at a first attack, he must in turn assume a most determined offensive, overwhelm him, and utterly destroy his whole force. He knew that Forrest could not have more than four thousand cavalry, and my own movements would give employment to every other man in the rebel army not immediately present with him, so that General Smith might safely act on this hypothesis. I wanted to destroy General Forrest, who was constantly threatening Memphis and the river above, as well as our route to supplies in middle Tennessee. In this we failed utterly, because General Smith, when he did start, allowed General Forrest to head him off and to defeat him with an inferior force near West Point, below Okolona.

Of course I did not, and could not, approve of his conduct. I had set so much store on his part of the project that I was disappointed, and so reported officially to General Grant. General Smith never regained my confidence as a soldier, though I still regard him as a most accomplished gentleman and a skillful engineer. Since the close of the war he has appealed to me to relieve him of that censure, but I could not do it, because it would falsify history.

The disappointment of Sherman was scarcely less keen than that of his superior, the general in chief of the army. Grant, in his *Memoirs,* vol. ii, p. 108, in speaking of the Meridian expedition, says: "Forrest had about four thousand cavalry with him, composed of fairly well-disciplined men, who, under so able a leader, were very effective. Smith's command was nearly double that of Forrest, but not equal man to man, for the lack of a successful experience such as Forrest's men had had. The fact is, troops who have fought a few battles and won, and followed up their victories, improve upon what they were before to an extent that can hardly be counted by percentage. The difference in result is often decisive victory instead of inglorious defeat. This same difference, too, is often due to the way troops are officered; and for the particular kind of warfare which Forrest had carried on neither army could present a more effective officer than he."

As these *Memoirs* were written years after the war was over, when General Grant had access to all the records which bore upon this enterprise, it is a matter of astonishment that he could submit such an entirely mistaken view of the condition of Forrest's command, no matter how anxious he might have been to excuse his friend, General Smith, whom he had appointed to this position against the judgment and silent protest of the far-sighted Sherman. It is true that Forrest did have with him about four thousand cavalry, but his command was at no time concentrated and available for an attack upon General Smith. Many of his troops in this pursuit had never been under fire before, and not five hundred of them had ever fought a battle under their present leader. About three thousand of these men he had brought out of west Tennessee only six weeks before the expedition of Smith was encountered at West Point. They had had scant time for drilling, and in no sense should be considered as "thoroughly well-disciplined men."

As compared to their opponents, they were badly equipped, and it is a matter which redounds to the credit and proves the wonderful ability of General Forrest, that with a command which at no time in action exceeded three thousand newly organized and insufficiently armed troops, he confronted, defeated, and pursued for more than fifty miles seven thousand of the best cavalry in the Union army, backed by twenty pieces of artillery, and equipped with Colt's repeating rifles and pistols and modern carbines, the most effective weapons then known to warfare.

General Grant was more nearly correct when he speaks of Forrest as "so able a leader." He proved it not only here, but on many occasions before he encountered this expedition. It is evident to the military critic that all the advantage was with the Federal commander. He had every reason to become acquainted with the small available force of his antagonist. When he turned back at West Point to retreat to Memphis, and was here assailed by Forrest, it was in the open wide prairie country. As Colonel Waring says: "Below Okolona we entered the beautiful prairie region of east Mississippi, and a finer country for cavalry is nowhere to be found."

Forrest drew his men up in line of battle in plain view of the extended lines of his adversary. Why Generals Smith and Grierson did not overwhelm him then and there may well be considered a matter of surprise to the student of this brief campaign. Smith had him in full view, and in the open country, and had on the field more than twice as many troops as the Confederate general. Forrest maneuvered his forces with his usual audacity, and evidently impressed General Smith with the idea that he had at command and in reserve an overwhelming force.

In speaking of this affair, Forrest said: "General Grierson left a weak place in his line, and I carried my men right through it." Once started on the run, he never ceased his relentless pursuit for two entire days and a portion of two nights, fighting at almost every bend in the road, as General Smith reports, for nearly sixty miles; and when finally night fell upon his exhausted troops in sight of Pontotoc, on the 22nd of February, the Federal column was in such panic and confusion it is probable that nothing but nightfall saved the entire command from destruction.

Not only was the open country between West Point and Okolona entirely favorable to General Smith's superior force, but in retreat the advantage is always in favor of the pursued. From every available position ambuscades may be laid, narrow roadways obstructed and commanded by artillery, where a few troops properly posted can hold at bay a largely superior force, inflicting heavy loss or compelling the assailants to make wide detours to dislodge them, at great expense of time and energy.

After Okolona is passed, the road for mile after mile runs along the back of a narrow ridge, and such is the nature of the country and the peculiar location of this highway that it is admirably adapted for successful defense from pursuit.

On March 3rd General Polk issued a special order congratulating Major General Forrest upon the brilliant and successful campaign just closed. "It marks an era in this war, full of honor to our arms, and calculated to teach a useful lesson to our enemies. The lieutenant-general commanding tenders thanks, and the thanks of his countrymen, to Generals Lee and Forrest and the gallant spirits who follow them." On the 11th of the same month, from Columbus, Forrest issued an address in which he says:

The major-general commanding desires to return his thanks and acknowledgments to the officers and men of his command for the recent gallant and meritorious conduct in defeating and routing the largest, most carefully selected, and best-equipped cavalry and mounted-infantry command ever sent into the field by the enemy. It affords him pleasure and pride to say that by your unflinching bravery and endurance a force three times your own was defeated and driven from the country. Thus by your valor and courage you have given safety and security to the homes of the defenceless, whose grateful acknowledgments are showered upon you, and whose prayers daily and nightly ascend unto heaven for you future prosperity and success. Deploring the loss of some of our bravest officers and men, he desires that you cherish their memory, emulate their example, and achieve your independence or perish in the attempt.

FOURTEEN

Storming Fort Pillow

F ORREST'S defeat of William Sooy Smith attracted more attention at Richmond than any of his previous achievements, and the eyes of the authorities were at last opened to the suggestions which some months earlier he had made. The assignment of General T. H. Bell and other influential citizens of west Tennessee to duty with him had attracted to his standard a very considerable number of recruits from this section, who, under his magnetic and inspiring leadership, had developed into a body of fighters equal in effectiveness to any in the Southern army.

It will be remembered that General Forrest, when first ordered to duty in the West, had requested that a battalion of Kentuckians under Colonel Woodward should be permitted to accompany him as part of his command. He argued that as these men were natives of the western portion of their state, they would be useful not only on account of their intimate acquaintance with the country he was about to invade but also as a nucleus around which might be gathered additional recruits from this quarter. The government at Richmond now concluded that what Forrest and Bell had accomplished in west Tennessee might be done in Kentucky.

About the 1st of March, 1864, Brigadier General Abe Buford, a member of one of the most influential families of this commonwealth and an officer who had already demonstrated both courage and ability in the service, was ordered to report to Forrest in Mississippi, and to take with him the fragments of three Kentucky infantry regiments which had formerly served in Bragg's army. Having become decimated in the numerous battles and hardships through which they had passed, they had applied for service as mounted infantry. As it was impossible for the Confederate government to furnish them with horses, they were transferred on foot to General Forrest's department, and to him the government turned for their equipment. General Sherman had paid the Confederate leader a high compliment on his ability to equip his men when he said that it was foolishness for him to leave any horses in the country through which he passed, since Forrest would be sure to steal them if he did not!

The Kentuckians joined Forrest near Columbus, Mississippi, where he had concentrated the various detachments of his cavalry and had completed the organization of four small brigades.[h]

During the two weeks immediately following the defeat of the Meridian expedition, with the exception of Richardson's brigade, Forrest's troops were comparatively inactive. General R. V. Richardson's brigade had been ordered by General Lee to proceed rapidly to Yazoo City, upon the river of that name, there to unite with a brigade of cavalry under General L. S. Ross for the purpose of repelling an expedition which was reported to be moving upon Grenada from that direction. Richardson and Ross arrived in front of Yazoo City at eight o'clock on the morning of March 5th, and at once attacked the enemy, who took refuge in the houses of that town, and in a fort which had been there constructed. The Confederates were defeated with consider-.able loss, Richardson's brigade leaving on the field thirty-seven killed and wounded. They then withdrew from the scene of the encounter without being pursued, and remained in sight of the enemy until they in turn evacuated the place on the following day.

The men and animals having now thoroughly recuperated from the exhaustion following their recent arduous campaign, with improved equipment and replenished ammunition, and with no immediate prospect of an incursion into his territory, General Forrest, impatient to be at the enemy, determined once more to try his fortune in west Tennessee.

On the 18th of March General Hurlbut, at Memphis, dispatched: "It is reported that Forrest, with about seven thousand men, was at Tupelo last night, bound for west Tennessee. I think he means Columbus and Paducah."

Forrest had, with his entire force, marched northward on the 15th. Buford's division, comprising Thompson's and Bell's brigades, with the Seventh Tennessee and McDonald's battalion, took the advance, the unmounted Kentuckians trudging along on foot, happy at the thought of having their faces turned once more to their homes, whither they were now going to replenish their wardrobes and to secure horses to carry them henceforth with the Wizard of the Saddle.

By March 20th the mounted troops had reached Jackson, Tennessee, and from here Colonel Crews was sent with his battalion in the direction of Memphis, to keep a sharp lookout for the advance of any Federal force from that direction; while Colonel Wilson, with his regiment, was left to garrison Jackson and to prepare for the reception of Buford's dismounted men, who would arrive in two or three days. On the 22nd of March General Forrest, with his escort, the Seventh Tennessee and Twelfth Kentucky regiments, proceeded to Trenton to take possession of this borough and establish there a bureau for recruits. On the 23rd Colonel Duckworth was given command of a detachment consisting of his own regiment, the Seventh Tennessee, and of Faulkner's regiment, to which McDonald's battalion, marching toward Memphis, was ordered to report and move with them for the capture of Union City.

Early on the morning of the 24th Colonel Duckworth arrived in front of this place and at once proceeded to invest it, closing in upon the garrison on all sides. Some lively skirmishing ensued, in which several of the Confederates were wounded, and as a result of which the Federals were driven within a strong redoubt constructed near the railroad station. As Duckworth was without artillery, and the garrison, numbering five hundred men, was too strong to justify an assault on his part, he determined to effect by strategy what he could not accomplish by force.

He was encouraged to take this course in good part from his acquaintance with the character of the Federal officer in command of the garrison. This person was Colonel Hawkins, of the Second West Tennessee Cavalry, who on a former occasion, during Forrest's first raid into west Tennessee in 1862, had been surprised and so easily taken in then that he was not now held by Forrest's men to be a dangerous or hard-fighting antagonist. Colonel Duckworth, a man whose experience as a physician as well as a minister of a large congregation had not been without value in turning him out a diplomatist, knowing the weight that Forrest's name would have, sent with a flag of truce a demand for surrender written in Forrest's blood-curdling style and with his name attached. It stated that as he had invested the place

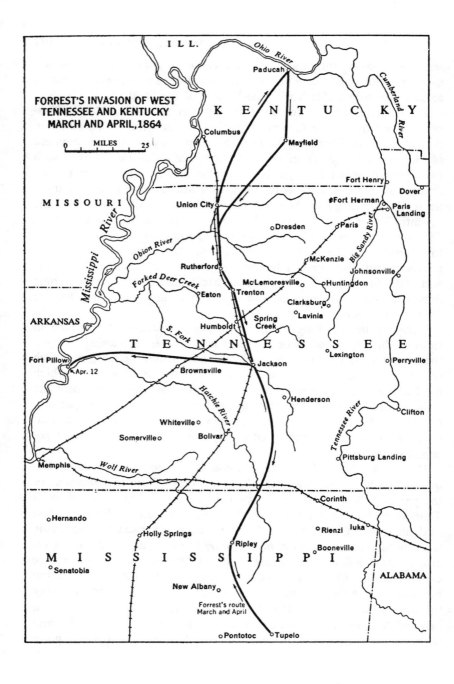

FORREST'S INVASION OF WEST
TENNESSEE AND KENTUCKY
MARCH AND APRIL, 1864

MILES
0   25

I L L.

Ohio River

Paducah

K E N T U C K Y

Cumberland River

Columbus

Mayfield

MISSOURI

Mississippi River

Fort Henry

Dover

Union City

Fort Herman

Paris Landing

Dresden

Paris

Big Sandy River

Obion River

McKenzie

Rutherford

Johnsonville

Forked Deer Creek

McLemoresville

Huntingdon

Eaton

Trenton

Clarksburg

Lavinia

ARKANSAS

S. Fork

Humboldt

Spring Creek

T E N N E S S E E

Fort Pillow
Apr. 12

Jackson

Lexington

Perryville

Brownsville

Henderson

Tennessee River

Hatchie River

Clifton

Whiteville

Somerville

Bolivar

Wolf River

Pittsburg Landing

Memphis

Corinth

Hernando

Rienzi

Iuka

Holly Springs

Ripley

Booneville

M I S S I S S I P P I

ALABAMA

Senatobia

New Albany

Forrest's route
March and April

Pontotoc

Tupelo

with a view to its capture, and was prepared by reason of the superior force he had on the ground to take the place by storm, in order to prevent the loss of life which would necessarily follow a bloody assault he now gave him the opportunity to surrender, promising him that he and his men would be treated as prisoners of war. Otherwise he would not be responsible for the fate of the garrison.

The Federal commander, who was aware that reinforcements were coming toward him at that time, pleaded for time to consider the proposition. On the 23rd of March he had wired General Mason Brayman that Forrest was approaching and at that time was about sixty miles away. General Brayman had immediately assembled a force of some two thousand men and started for Union City. He says: "I became satisfied that Union City was the point of attack." He had already notified Colonel Hawkins that he was coming, and expected him to hold out until rescued. The Federal commander, in reply to Duckworth's summons to surrender, declined unless he could have a personal interview with General Forrest.

As Forrest was not present, this would have checked an ordinary man; but Colonel Duckworth was not an ordinary man, and his cunning was equal to the occasion. Turning shortly on his heel, he remarked to Hawkins that he didn't care whether he surrendered or not; that General Forrest was not in the habit of holding interviews with officers not of his own rank, and that if he didn't make up his mind to surrender within five minutes he would charge the place and not spare a single member of his command.

This threat, with the alternative of kind treatment, which Hawkins knew he would get, because he had surrendered to this command once before, induced him to capitulate. Greatly to the chagrin of General Brayman, who was at that time only six miles away, with reinforcements sufficient to have picked Duckworth's command up and marched away with it, the garrison laid down its arms. He says:

At 11 A.M. on the morning of the 25th I was within six miles of Union City, and there learned with pain and surprise that Colonel Hawkins had surrendered at eleven o'clock, and had with his force been removed and his fortifications destroyed. The force of the enemy does not appear to be more than a quarter of the number represented, and without artillery. The number of men surrendered is probably five hundred; all were armed and equipped—about three hundred mounted; a few mules and wagons and a considerable amount of public property were lost and destroyed. Colonel Hawkins and his command had been recently paid for over a year's service, and the aggregate of individual loss on the part of the officers and soldiers will reach some $60,000.[1]

Selecting a detachment to convoy the prisoners southward, and sending McDonald's battalion on toward Memphis, as directed by General Forrest, Colonel Duckworth removed the supplies which were needed and portable, set fire to all which could not be taken away, and straightway marched to rejoin the main command in the neighborhood of Jackson. While he had been moving on Union City, General Forrest, from Trenton, with a portion of Buford's division from near Jackson, had pressed farther northward for the purpose of attacking the garrison stationed at Paducah.

On the 26th of March Captain H. A. Tyler, with his company and two other detachments of Confederates, was sent in advance of General Buford's troops to dash into Paducah along several separate roads, in order to drive the enemy to their gunboats and into the fort. This fort at Paducah was a strong earthwork, situated in the western portion of the town, near the bank of the Tennessee River. It was surrounded by a deep ditch, in front of which fallen timber had been formed into an abattis. It was garrisoned by 665 men, commanded by a brave and resolute officer—Colonel S. G. Hicks, of the Fortieth Illinois Infantry. These advanced companies were followed by other detachments of Forrest's command, and, crowding up as close to the fort as was advisable, under the protection of the houses they opened a brisk fire upon the Federals in the fort, as well as those on board the gunboats at the landing.

After about one hour of this firing General Forrest sent a flag of truce to Colonel Hicks with a demand for the surrender of the garrison. It was couched in language almost identical with that used by Forrest on all former occasions, stating that he had a force amply sufficient to storm the works, but in order to avoid the unnecessary effusion of blood he demanded the surrender of the troops, with all public property. "If you surrender you shall be treated as prisoners of war, but if I have to storm your works you may expect no quarter."[2] The plucky Federal colonel, however, did not intend to give up without a fight.

---

[1] *Official Records,* vol. xxxii, part i, p. 503.
[2] *Ibid.,* p. 547.

Forrest had no intention of making a needless sacrifice of his troops in an assault. His object was to hold the Federals there and on board of their gunboats until he could remove all the supplies and horses which could be obtained in Paducah. The casualties in his command at this time had been insignificant, amounting to not more than five or six men wounded. Unfortunately one of his brigade officers, Colonel A. P. Thompson, without authority from Forrest, having at the head of his command reached a point where the street along which he had marched opened out upon the space in which the fort was situated, concluded to attempt to capture the garrison by a sudden assault.

Captain H. A. Tyler, who was present, says:

> With my company I had reached a point where the fort or stockade into which the Federals had retreated was in plain view across the open space. My men had been firing at the Federals running to get into the stockade, and at those already firing back at us from the embankment, but we had not suffered any material loss, by reason of the protection afforded by the houses. About this time Colonel A. P. Thompson, moving at the head of his brigade, came up the street to where I was, and in answer to my inquiry as to what was next to be done, replied: "I am going to take that fort." Supposing that the charge had been ordered by General Forrest, and being too far away from my own regiment to join it in time, I asked permission to accompany him in this assault, and rode away by his side. Just as we reached the open space he gave the command to charge, and we dashed forward in a wild rush in the direction of the fort. The enemy opened upon us with a most terrific volley. Colonel Thompson was slain and a number of the troops killed or wounded by this discharge. The rest of us sought safety in a rapid retreat, taking shelter in and behind the houses, from which we resumed our fire.[3]

In his official report of this affair General Forrest says: "I drove the enemy to their gunboats and fort, and held the town for ten hours; captured many stores and horses; burned sixty bales of cotton, one steamer, and a dry-dock, bringing out fifty prisoners. My loss, as far as known, is twenty-five killed and wounded, among them Colonel A. P. Thompson."[4]

Returning from Paducah with his captured horses and prisoners, a portion of Buford's division was sent in the direction of Mayfield, in southwestern Kentucky, and there his troops were temporarily dis-

[3] Manuscripts of Captain H. A. Tyler, in possession of the author.
[4] *Official Records,* vol. xxxii, part i, p. 607.

banded and permitted to visit their homes, to replenish their clothing and improve their mounts, under promise to report at Trenton on the 3rd of April. To the lasting honor of these men be it said that not one took advantage of this opportunity to desert the cause in which he had enlisted.

The report of General Forrest, made from Jackson, Tennessee, on April 4th, is worthy of reproduction in its entirety, for the reason that it not only shows how busily engaged he and his troops were in harassing the Federals and in gathering up recruits, but it gives some idea of the energy displayed in securing much-needed supplies for the Confederate army. It shows, moreover, the clear conception in his mind of the plans and coming movements of the enemy.

HEADQUARTERS FORREST'S CAVALRY DEPARTMENT
Jackson, Tennessee, *April* 4, 1864

I desire respectfully and briefly to state that Lieutenant-Colonel Crews, commanding battalion, met the enemy yesterday morning, and after a sharp little engagement repulsed and drove them back to Raleigh. The enemy's force was two regiments of cavalry of Grierson's command. The fight occurred fifteen miles east of Raleigh, on Somerville road. Colonel Crews lost: one man severely and one slightly wounded. The enemy had six killed and fifteen or twenty wounded and three prisoners.

In all engagements so far in west Tennessee my loss in the aggregate is fifteen killed and forty-two wounded. Among the killed, Colonel Thompson, commanding Kentucky brigade, whose death was reported to you by telegraph. Lieutenant-Colonel Lannum, of Faulkner's regiment, reported mortally wounded, is, I am glad to say, rapidly recovering.

The loss of the enemy thus far is as follows: 79 killed, 102 wounded, and 612 captured.

I have, as far as prudent, allowed my troops an opportunity of going home. Am now concentrating and preparing for any move the enemy may make, or for offensive operations, provided they do not move on me. I feel confident of my ability to whip any cavalry they can send against me, and can, if necessary, avoid their infantry. If permitted to remain in west Tennessee, or, rather, if it is not the purpose of the lieutenant-general commanding to order me elsewhere until driven out by the enemy, would be glad to have my artillery with me, and will send for it, as I could operate effectively with my rifle battery on the rivers. With the small guns I have here it would be folly to attempt the destruction or capture of boats. I am yet in hopes the lieutenant-general commanding will repair and operate the railroad to Corinth, as suggested in a former letter. I, of course, cannot tell what demands are being made on him for troops, but am clearly of opinion that with a brigade of infantry at Corinth, as a force upon which I could fall back if too hard pressed, that I can hold west Tennessee against three times my numbers, and could send rapidly out from here all conscripts and deserters for service in infantry. At present it is impracticable, as I am without the transportation necessary to supply them with rations to Okolona, through a country already depleted and whose inhabitants are suffering for food. I find corn scarcer than I had thought, but have plenty of meal, flour, and bacon for troops. If supplied with the right kind of money or cotton, can furnish my command with all small-arm ammunition required, and I think with small arms also.

General Chalmers is here, and will be kept in readiness for any move that may be made from Memphis. General Buford's division is above this, and concentrating at Eaton, ten miles west of Trenton. As I came up here I employed a man to get up lead. He writes me that he has from eight to ten thousand pounds, which I shall send out as soon as possible, and will continue to get up all that can be had. *There is a Federal force of five or six hundred at Fort Pillow, which I shall attend to in a day or two, as they have horses and supplies which we need.* There are about six thousand troops now at Memphis—all else gone up the river. *It is clear that they are concentrating all their available force before Richmond and at Chattanooga.*[5] They have attempted to send their cavalry across the country to Pulaski, Tennessee. Have driven them back, and hope yet to be able to make them take water. I have ordered everything belonging to my command at Columbus moved up to Aberdeen, and Morton's battery up to Tupelo to report to General Gholson, and shall bring it on here unless ordered to the contrary, as the little guns I have are of no use to me. You will please send any orders or despatches for me through General Gholson, at Tupelo. I am, very respectfully, your obedient servant,

N. B. FORREST, Major-General Commanding.

While operating in the neighborhood of Paducah, General Forrest, as shown in the above report to General Polk, had ordered General Chalmers to follow him into west Tennessee, and bring with him all the scattered remnants of his command, which had been on duty in various parts of northern Mississippi. Moving north, one of these detachments, under Colonel J. J. Neely, arriving at Bolivar on the 29th, had come in contact with a battalion of west Tennessee Union troops commanded by a bitter partisan, Colonel Fielding Hurst. Neely made short work in the encounter which resulted, killing and wounding quite

---

[5] Italics not in original.

a number, capturing some prisoners, their wagon train, and a supply of ammunition which the Southern troopers much needed at this time. Chalmers had come up by way of La Grange, and here he furnished a strong guard for the six hundred prisoners which Forrest had captured and sent south.

In the first week of April, General Buford, whose troops, having been furloughed, had reported promptly at Trenton, was ordered by General Forrest to proceed again in the direction of Columbus and Paducah, not only to obtain additional horses and supplies for his cavalry but also to make a diversion in favor of a movement that General Forrest was now contemplating for the capture of Fort Pillow and its garrison, and the horses which, in his report, he says he "very much needed."[6] Buford arrived in the neighborhood of Columbus on the 12th of April, the same day upon which Fort Pillow fell. Here he detached his trusted subordinate, Captain H. A. Tyler, with a picked detachment of about 150 men, to make a demonstration on Columbus.

General Buford, having learned from one of his scouts that since the former attack on Paducah a number of horses and mules belonging to the Union government had been collected there for distribution, determined to make a rapid descent upon the place for the purpose of securing these animals, and started at once for that point, where he arrived unexpectedly on the morning of the 14th. Advancing on the place with a great show of force, he drove the Federals once more to their gunboats, which were lying at the dock, and into the fort, and held them there long enough to obtain the horses which had been the object of his expedition, coming off successfully with about 150 excellent animals. As a part of his movement, as soon as he had driven the pickets in he sent a flag of truce to the Federal commander, with a note, to which the name of General Forrest was signed, demanding the surrender of the garrison and fort, and threatening to give no quarter if he were compelled to carry the place by assault.

Meanwhile Captain Tyler was carrying out the same game of bluff upon the commandant of the post at Columbus. Arriving in sight of the place, Captain Tyler states that he marched his men across an open space on a hill in full view of the garrison, repeating the circuit several times and changing the position of the horses in order to

---

[6] *Official Records,* vol. xxxii, part i, p. 609.

create the impression that he had a large number of men with him.[7] He then sent in a flag of truce demanding the surrender, to which he signed General Buford's name. It was practically a copy of the note sent by General Buford at Paducah under Forrest's name, and of other notes demanding surrender that Forrest had himself dictated.

HEADQUARTERS CONFEDERATE FORCES
Before Columbus, Kentucky, *April* 13, 1864

The Commanding Officer United States Forces, Columbus, Kentucky:

Fully capable of taking Columbus and its garrison by force, I desire to avoid the shedding of blood, and therefore demand the unconditional surrender of the forces under your command. Should you surrender, the negroes now in arms will be returned to their masters. Should I, however, be compelled to take the place, no quarter will be shown to the negro troops whatever; the white troops will be treated as prisoners of war.

I am, sir, yours,
A. BUFORD, Brigadier-General.[8]

Although there were only 150 men engaged in this diversion, it is worthy of comment to note how much importance was attached to it by the commander of the post at that time, who on April 13th says: "The only information we could obtain was that they had a division under Buford, principally of mounted infantry." There is also published his reply to Tyler's demand for the surrender, in which he says that "surrender is out of the question."

About forty miles in a direct line northward, or up the Mississippi River from Memphis, a bar of sand and mud stretches from the western or Arkansas bank across this mighty stream well over to the opposite or Tennessee shore. In the lowest stage of water much of this obstruction to navigation is for several months of each year many feet above the surface of the river, and spreads out, a flat, monotonous plain, as dry and verdureless as a patch of the Libyan Desert. Acting as a dam, it has turned the current or channel of the Mississippi close in to the eastern shore, so that for the greater portion of the year all manner of craft which ply the Father of Waters are forced to steer within a stone's throw of the Tennessee side.

Just opposite to the "point" of this bar, emptying into the Mississippi

---

[7] Diary of Captain Tyler, in the author's possession.
[8] *Official Records*, vol. xxxii, part i, p. 553.

from the east, and almost perpendicular to its course, is a small stream known as Cold Creek. In the angle of junction of this creek with the river, and stretching back along the south shore of the estuary and along the river as well, there is a high clay bluff which slants rather sharply (yet not precipitately) from the crumbling edge above, some seventy-five to one hundred feet, to the waterline below. Fort Pillow was constructed upon this angular bluff.

Early in the war, when General Gideon J. Pillow was in command of the Tennessee troops, he recognized the strength and importance of this position in commanding the traffic of the Mississippi, and commenced the fortifications which, when completed, were named in his honor. Three separate lines of works were constructed. The most exterior, which at the greatest convexity was about six hundred yards from the river, extended from the bank of Cold Creek above to the bluff of the river below—a distance of nearly two miles along the trench, which was slightly curved outward, or to the east. There was the usual ditch in front, with the earth thrown up on the inner edge of the excavation. About halfway between this trench and the river, and immediately in front of the fort, a second defense, covering about two acres of ground, was constructed along the crest of a commanding hill. The third and strongest of all was a small fort built just at the angle of junction of the river bluff with that of Cold Creek, extending in irregular semicircular outline from bluff to bluff.

From one end of this horseshoe to the other, as measured along the edge of the bank, the distance was about seventy yards. Walking along the parapet, from end to end, the distance was about 120 yards. The earth wall or parapet was six feet high, six feet thick, and flat on top. Exterior to this was a ditch twelve feet wide and eight feet deep. Along the inner face of the parapet a bench was constructed, upon which the garrison could stand and fire over the wall, with nothing exposed below the head and shoulders. From this they could step down to the ground to load their guns, and be entirely concealed.

At six places there were protected openings or embrasures, through each of which a cannon commanded the approaches from as many directions. Along the face or slope of the bluff, above and below, and about seventy-five yards distant from each end of the embankment, rifle pits had been constructed for defending the approaches from either direction near the water's edge, and to shelter sharpshooters while firing at boats upon the river. Looking eastward and along the bank of Cold Creek from the edge of the ditch for a distance of about 150 feet, the surface of the earth descends gradually and then sharply

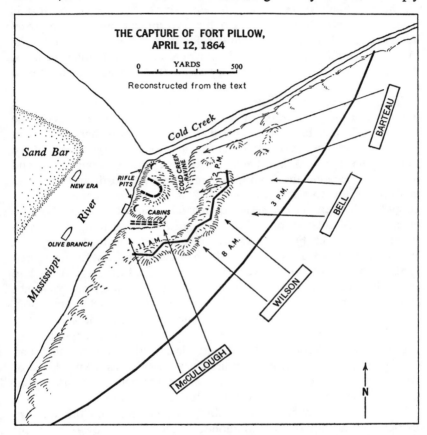

THE CAPTURE OF FORT PILLOW,
APRIL 12, 1864

YARDS

0   500

Reconstructed from the text

down into a crescent-shaped ravine which encircles the fort for nearly one-half of its extent. This hollow opens into Cold Creek bluff, near the mouth of this stream, and is known as the Cold Creek ravine.

On the south side of Fort Pillow there is another depression, well marked, yet not so precipitate as that just described. The deepest portion of this ravine is about 450 feet from the parapet, and the ground surface descends gradually to the bottom of the ravine. At the time of the battle, along the deeper portions of this depression there were two rows of log cabins or shanties, extending from the mouth of the ravine on the riverbank almost to a point opposite the center of the fort in front. These structures were used for government and private storehouses, and for bunks for the white soldiers of the garrison. Within the fort proper, and rather near the bank, were erected a number of tents, with plank floors covered with dry straw, for the use of the Negro troops.

In the rear of the fort the face of the river bluff was covered with trees and bushes, a portion of which had been cut down, leaving the stumps, logs, and brush half buried in the mud, with here and there a tree still standing. Just below the fort and near the log houses in the south ravine the bank had been cleared to enable steamboats to land with safety. Beyond the Cold Creek ravine to the north and east, and in front of the fort for two-thirds of its extent, the contour of the ground is broken into a series of irregular hillocks or knolls, with intervening depressions or gullies. Many of these elevations are as high as that upon which Fort Pillow was erected, and vary in distance from one to four hundred yards from the parapet. For fully four hundred yards from the fort, and in every direction, most of the larger trees had been felled and the undergrowth cut away, so that an enemy could not approach without exposure. As this work was done in 1861 and 1862, the stumps and logs were still on the ground, and a considerable undergrowth had been reproduced in the two years which had elapsed.

I have thus carefully and at length described this stronghold and the topography of the ground immediately about it, as a knowledge of these features is essential to a proper comprehension of the great tragedy which happened here on the 12th of April, 1864.

Major General Stephen A. Hurlbut, who commanded this military district, with headquarters at Memphis, deemed Fort Pillow of sufficient importance, even when no enemy was in west Tennessee, to keep it well garrisoned, and also to use it as a recruiting post and place of refuge for fugitive slaves, and other citizens of the regions roundabout, who might desire the protection of the United States. He testified in 1864 that "the steamboat channel at Fort Pillow runs right under the bluff, and brings every boat within musket-shot of the shore. A couple of guns mounted up above would stop most effectively the navigation of the river," etc.[9]

At the time of the fight, according to the official report of Lieutenant Colonel T. H. Harris, Assistant Adjutant General, dated April 26th, the garrison at Fort Pillow consisted of the First Battalion, Sixth United States Heavy Artillery (colored), 8 commissioned officers and 213 men; one section Company D, Second United States Light Artillery (colored), 1 commissioned officer and 40 men; First Battalion, Thirteenth Tennessee Cavalry, Major W. F. Bradford, 10 commissioned officers and 285 enlisted men. Total white troops, 295; total colored troops, 262; grand total, 557. Six fieldpieces, two six-pounders, two twelve-pounder howitzers, and two ten-pounder Parrotts. In addition to the enlisted troops there were in the fort about twenty white men (noncombatants), some of whom took an active part in the defense of the position. On March 28th, Major L. F. Booth, by order of General S. A. Hurlbut, had been placed in command of this position. Next in rank was Major W. F. Bradford, a native Tennesseean, with whom the post commander was advised to "confer freely." Major Bradford was recommended as "a good officer, though not of much experience."

The order to Booth says: "There are two points of land fortified at Fort Pillow. You will occupy both, either with your own troops alone, or holding one with yours and giving the other in charge to Major Bradford. The positions are commanding, and can be held by a small force against almost any odds."[10] Hurlbut adds: "I think Forrest's check at Paducah will not dispose him to try the river again. Nevertheless, act promptly in putting the works into perfect order and the post into its strongest defence." On April 3rd Booth wrote his general: "Everything is quiet within a radius of thirty or forty miles around, and I do not think any apprehensions need be felt or fears entertained in reference to this place being attacked or even threatened; I think it perfectly safe."[11] (This was, ironically, just the day before Forrest wrote Polk of his intention shortly to "attend to" the garrison at Fort Pillow.)

Thus, in fancied security on the part of the Union commander and

---

[9] *Rebellion Record*, vol. viii.
[10] *Official Records*, vol. xxxii, part i, p. 556.
[11] *Ibid.*, p. 557.

a determination on the part of the Confederate to appropriate the much-needed horses and supplies of the garrison, stood affairs as the 12th of April approached. On the 10th of this month, while General Buford was absent in Kentucky, Major General Forrest, with his command at and near Jackson, Tennessee, placed Brigadier General James R. Chalmers in charge of the movement against Fort Pillow, and this officer made the following disposition of his troops. The First brigade, Colonel J. J. Neely commanding, marched rapidly from Whiteville toward Memphis with orders to spread the report, so that it would get to Hurlbut's ears in Memphis that Forrest's whole command was coming that way to attack him. At the same time, Colonel John McGuirk, with the Third Mississippi State Cavalry and the First Mississippi Partisans, was ordered to advance on that city from the south and to let it be known that General S. D. Lee was also advancing with all his troops to join in the attack.

Neely moved swiftly to Wolf River, almost in sight of Memphis, and made a great show of building pontoon bridges and other structures for throwing a large force across this stream, while McGuirk drove in the pickets from the southern side and made his presence felt in the suburbs of Memphis. The strategy of Chalmers was not without the desired effect upon General Hurlbut. On April 15th he reported: "I have ordered up the four regiments of the third division of the Seventeenth Corps, now in Vicksburg, as soon as practicable, that I may have some movable troops."[12]

While these detachments of the Confederates were maneuvering around Memphis, a fragment of one division, made up respectively of portions of McCulloch's and Bell's brigades, under General Chalmers, moved on the 11th from Sharon's ferry, on Forked Deer Creek, toward Brownsville, and thence on toward Fort Pillow by a rapid all-night march of forty miles without stopping. The Confederates were fortunate in securing as a guide Mr. W. J. Shaw, a citizen of this vicinity, who had recently been arrested by Major Bradford and confined within the limits of the fort.[13] Having escaped on the 11th, he was entirely familiar with the topography of the enclosure, as well as the number of troops defending the works.

[12] *Ibid.,* vol. xxxii, part i, p. 551.
[13] Personal narrative by Captain W. J. Shaw, of Forked Deer, Tennessee, in possession of the author. Captain Shaw enlisted in Forrest's command after this fight.

Approaching just at break of day, Colonel McCulloch with his brigade was given the advance, and this excellent soldier dispatched the Second Missouri Cavalry under Lieutenant Colonel R. A. McCulloch, with directions to drive in the pickets and feel their way to the vicinity of the Federal camp. All the Confederates advanced to the charge the moment the rifles were cracking at the picket line, and so sudden was the attack that the Federals abandoned the entire outer line of defenses without serious resistance. Forrest, who with his escort and some of Wisdom's regiment was following in the rear, had directed Chalmers to invest the stronghold in order to prevent the garrison from running away, and then await his arrival. McCulloch's brigade advanced rapidly down the Fulton road to Gaines's farm, then north to the fort on a road running parallel with the Mississippi River, bringing his troops in sight of the redoubt from the side upon which the stores and barracks were situated. Wilson's regiment of Bell's brigade moved on the direct road from Brownsville to Fort Pillow, while Barteau's and Russell's regiments marched west along the bank of Cold Creek and came into position from the north side.

While these movements were being made the skirmishers of the garrison, consisting of Companies D and E of the Thirteenth Tennessee (Union) Cavalry, and the advance line of the Confederates were briskly engaged, the artillery of the fort, firing furiously over the heads of the Union skirmishers. Adjutant Mack J. Leaming of this regiment reports that these companies, about 8 A.M., were compelled to retire to the fort after considerable fighting, in which Lieutenant Barr of Company D was killed. "The firing continued without cessation, principally from behind logs, stumps, and under cover of thick underbrush, and from high knolls. *We suffered pretty severely in the loss of commissioned officers by the unerring aim of the rebel sharp shooters,*[14] and among this loss I have to record our post commander, Major L. F. Booth, who was killed almost instantly by a musket-ball through the breast."[15]

Colonel Robert McCulloch, coming in range of the fort, now advanced cautiously, his men taking advantage of logs, stumps, and knolls, and slipping along the gullies and ravines with the dexterity of frontiersmen. In this way, shielded from the artillery of the fort, which

[14] Italics not in original.
[15] *Official Records,* vol. xxxii, part i, p. 559.

was firing with rapidity, while the gunboat *New Era,* well out in the river and directed by signals from the garrison,[16] was throwing shells from its battery on all parts of the Confederate line, they reached a position within three hundred yards of the fort. On the side nearest to Cold Creek, Bell had in like cautious yet steady manner, but not without brisk skirmishing, advanced his lines to a point about 250 yards from the parapet. Colonel Wilson, directly in front, together with the right of McCulloch's line, had, at an earlier hour, in a brilliant dash driven the Federals out of the middle redoubt, which they now occupied, and were thoroughly protected behind the east face of the breastworks, and only three hundred yards away from the fort yet to be assaulted. Having, as instructed by his superior, invested the stronghold so thoroughly that escape was impossible, General Chalmers made no further effort to advance, but kept up a continuous fire from his sharpshooters at any of the garrison who exposed themselves.

This was the general position of the troops when, at 11 A.M., General Forrest with his escort and a detachment of Colonel Wisdom's regiment arrived and assumed command. Colonel Robert McCulloch says: "About eleven o'clock General N. B. Forrest arrived, and, after a survey of the ground and the lines we had established, asked me what I thought of capturing the barracks and houses which were near the fort and between it and my position. I replied that if I could get possession of the houses I could silence the enemy's artillery. He then said, 'Go ahead and take them.' I made the charge in short order, and very soon had my men in and behind the houses, from which the artillery on that side was silenced by sharp-shooters."[17]

Adjutant Leaming of the Thirteenth Tennessee (Union) Cavalry in his report, already cited, says:

At about 11 A.M. the rebels made a second determined assault on our works, and were again successfully repulsed with severe loss. They succeeded, however, in getting possession of two rows of barracks running parallel to the south side of the fort and distant about one hundred and fifty yards. The barracks had previously been ordered to be destroyed, but after severe loss on our part in the attempt to execute the order our men were compelled to retire without accomplishing the desired end, *save only to the row nearest to the fort.* From these barracks the enemy kept up a

---

[16] *Ibid.,* p. 620.
[17] Private manuscript in possession of the author.

murderous fire on our men despite all our efforts to dislodge him. *Owing to the close proximity of these buildings to the fort, and to the fact that they were on considerably lower ground, our artillery could not be sufficiently depressed to destroy them or even render them untenable for the enemy.*[18]

Especial attention is called to this official report of the adjutant of this regiment. It is a positive admission, and shows beyond all shadow of doubt that McCulloch's brigade was in position in this ravine, where it was shielded from the fire from the fort long before the flag of truce was sent in.

It was characteristic of Forrest that, no matter how much confidence he had in his officers, he never entrusted to anyone the task of making him acquainted with the strength of a point to be assailed, the topography of the ground to be traversed, or the various obstacles to be overcome. He was after success first, and with the smallest possible loss of men. Hard fighter as he was, and even reckless of all when occasion demanded, he took infinite pains to shield his faithful soldiers when he could.

His first act on reaching the field at Fort Pillow was to increase largely the corps of sharpshooters on every commanding position, and these were instructed to shoot at anything which showed itself from the fort. They were directed to crawl up behind logs and stumps and get as close as possible. He then made a close and careful study of the ground from one end of the crescent to the other. The rifles from the fort soon began to single him out, and almost before the reconnaissance had begun his horse received a shot which wounded it mortally and rendered the unfortunate animal so frantic from pain or fright that it reared and fell over upon the general, who was badly bruised by the accident.[19] He, however, was soon mounted on another horse, and continued the survey of the enemy's position. Major Charles W. Anderson (then captain and acting adjutant general on the staff), who was riding with the general at this time, begged him to dismount and make the inspection on foot, but Forrest made no other reply than that he was "just as apt to be hit one way as another," and that he could see better where he was. Before the day was over two other horses that he was riding were shot, one being killed, the other slightly wounded. More than an hour was consumed in this reconnaissance, and nearly

[18] Italics not in original.
[19] Narrative of Captain Shaw, the guide, and of Major Anderson.

two hours elapsed before the ammunition wagon, which could not keep up with the rapid movements of the column, arrived on the scene and the cartridge boxes were refilled.

It was now one o'clock, and Forrest ordered the advance of the troops under Colonels Bell and Wilson to a line fully as near the fort as that which McCulloch on the south had earlier in the day secured. While making the reconnaissance, General Forrest had at once perceived the great advantage which was offered by the ravine that circumvented the parapet on the north or Cold Creek side, as far as the position of Colonel Wilson in front, and realized that, if he could get his men once in that sharp depression, they would be so far beneath the fort that the artillery could not be sufficiently depressed to strike them, and they would then be as safe there as were McCulloch's troops on the other side. To make a rush for this point for two or three hundred yards would expose him to great loss, for although there were numerous depressions intervening, there were just as many hilltops which could be swept by the artillery and small arms from the east and north faces of the parapet.

By moving cautiously along the face of the bluff of Cold Creek, Colonel C. R. Barteau, who was on the extreme right, after considerable time succeeded in placing his Second Tennessee regiment, not without some loss, however, in this ravine, where they were not more than seventy-five yards from the fort. Colonel (afterward General) T. H. Bell, one of Forrest's bravest and most capable officers, had to exercise greater precaution and consume more time in moving the balance of his line to this advanced position. It was finally accomplished under the protection of the heavy body of sharpshooters, which, as Bell's troops would rush over the exposed places, would open in lively fashion at any men of the garrison who would show their heads and shoulders in the endeavor to fire upon the advancing line. Meanwhile the gunboat *New Era,* scarcely without cessation, shelled the Confederates as they were skirmishing and maneuvering for the positions now obtained, and it was not without serious loss that the Confederates were able to advance practically into the teeth of their adversaries.

Feeling assured now that he could take the fort by a quick rush, and hoping that he could convince the commander of the fort of this fact and save any further loss of life, Forrest, who had ridden to a knoll some four hundred yards distant, directed General Chalmers to display a flag of truce and to ask for a parley. This was between 3 and 3.30 P.M., and firing immediately ceased. Captain Walter A. Goodman, of Chalmers's staff, was selected to convey the following message, which was written by, and is copied from the original now in possession of, Major Charles W. Anderson:

HEADQUARTERS FORREST'S CAVALRY
Before Fort Pillow, *April* 12, 1864
Major Booth, Commanding United States Forces, Fort Pillow:
MAJOR—The conduct of the officers and men garrisoning Fort Pillow has been such as to entitle them to being treated as prisoners of war. I demand the unconditional surrender of this garrison, promising you that you shall be treated as prisoners of war. My men have received a fresh supply of ammunition, and from their present position can easily assault and capture the fort. Should my demand be refused, I cannot be responsible for the fate of your command. Respectfully,

N. B. FORREST
Major-General Commanding

The Federal commander, as soon as the truce was indicated by the Confederates, had answered by his flag and by signaling the gunboat, which, with the garrison, immediately ceased all hostilities. Captain Goodman, accompanied by Captain Thomas Henderson, commanding scouts, and Lieutenant Frank Rodgers, now advanced toward the fort with their white flag, approaching from the rear of McCulloch's advanced position, along the riverbank from the south.

As the bearers of the flag of truce were approaching the fort along the riverbank, they observed the smoke of a steamer which was approaching from above, and a messenger was immediately dispatched to inform General Forrest of the fact that a boat loaded with Federal troops was coming down the river toward the landing at Fort Pillow, presumably to reinforce the garrison. General Forrest rode as rapidly as he could from his position, which was four hundred yards distant and required a considerable detour on account of the conformation of the ground and of the fallen timber, to reach the riverbank. The steamer was now in sight, and blue with troops coming down the stream toward the beleaguered garrison and the gunboat. If she had been signaled that a truce was prevailing, she did not respect the signal by stopping or putting about or sheering over to the Arkansas shore, but came steadily on.

General Forrest, believing that these were reinforcements for the garrison, in order to prevent their landing and notwithstanding that a truce was in force, ordered Captain Anderson of his staff to call off two hundred men from McCulloch's brigade and take a position immediately under the bluff, below the fort, where the steamboat landing could be commanded, and to fire into the steamer should such effort be made. A similar detail was ordered from Colonel C. R. Barteau's regiment of Bell's brigade, to take a corresponding position along the bluff near the mouth of Cold Creek, to aid Anderson in preventing the landing of the reinforcements. The movements of these two detachments were made in full view of the garrison, the troops under Anderson marching rapidly through the open space just behind the barracks from the fort. The force from Barteau's Second Tennessee rushed out of their position in the ravine to the Cold Creek bluff, and there concealed themselves.

As has been stated, the flag of truce was flying when the disposition of these two detachments of two hundred men each was made. The officers of Fort Pillow knew for what reason it was made and, as their reports show, made no formal protest against it at the time. They could see this loaded steamer coming as readily as did the Confederates; she was in full view; the gunboat, also under truce, was bound by the obligations incurred in accepting a cessation of hostilities, and should have signaled the steamer that the truce was prevailing, that she must put about and not approach. That was the plain duty of Captain Marshall and Major Bradford. Forrest did not intend to be robbed or cheated out of his prey while it was nearly in his grasp. Moreover, there now appeared in sight two other steamboats coming up the river from the direction of Memphis, and the Confederate general had every reason to hasten matters to a conclusion. The Union commander had equally strong reason to secure delay in the hope of succor.

Fortunately for the reputation of Forrest, which was bitterly and unscrupulously assailed after this affair, the proof of all that is here said is indisputably established by the Federal reports as well as by those of the other side. Adjutant Leaming was plainly in error in the deductions made from the movements of Anderson's and Barteau's detachments. He says: "During the cessation of firing on both sides in consequence of the flag of truce offered by the enemy, and while the attention of both officers and men were naturally attracted to the south end of the fort, where the communications were being received and answered, Forrest had resorted to means the most foul and infamous ever adopted in the most barbarous ages of the world for the accomplishment of his design. Here he took occasion to move his troops partially under cover of a ravine and thick underbrush into the very position he had been fighting to obtain throughout the entire engagement up to 3.30 P.M."

It is upon this statement that the charge of a violation of the flag of truce by Forrest rests. General Forrest denied it most positively at the time, and General Chalmers, General Bell, Colonel McCulloch, Major Anderson, and many others now living say that the charge is unequivocally false, and make affidavit to the same. The report of the Committee of the United States Congress admits that these two ravines were held by the Confederates before the truce. What Adjutant Leaming mistook for the occupation of this position was the movement of Barteau's detachment out of the position they had already obtained. Colonel Barteau, now living, testifies that he had this position prior to the truce, and that he had these men moved out of it during the truce to prevent the landing of the boats with reinforcements.

It so happened that a distinguished Union officer, Brigadier General George F. Shepley, who had just resigned the position of Military Governor of Louisiana, was on one of these boats approaching Fort Pillow at this very hour. His report to the Committee on the Conduct of the War contains full proof of all that is here stated.[20] From his evidence it is clear that as their boats, loaded with artillery and infantry, were approaching and were not signaled by the fort or gunboat *not to approach,* it was no violation of the truce by General Forrest to take such steps as were necessary to prevent a landing by these or any other boats which might attempt it, to relieve the garrison. As it was, the movement diminished the assaulting column by four hundred men, for these men took no part whatever in the assault on the fort, and only fired on the Federals when they endeavored to escape. It will be remembered that Adjutant Leaming admits that McCulloch's brigade was in close proximity to the redoubt, and so placed that the guns of the fort could not be trained on them before

[20] *Official Records,* vol. xxxii, part i, p. 572.

the truce was declared. This malicious and foolish charge is thus shown to be false. It should never have gained credence, even in times of war and bitterness, when men's minds were inclined to accept as truth anything injurious to an enemy.

While these things were transpiring on the river and beneath the bluff just above and below the fort, the note of Forrest was under consideration by the commander of the post. Adjutant Leaming was directed to make the following reply, which he placed in a sealed envelope and delivered to Captain Goodman:

General Forrest, Commanding C. S. Forces:

SIR—I respectfully ask one hour for consultation with my officers and the officers of the gunboat. In the meantime no preparations to be made on either side.   Very respectfully,

L. F. BOOTH, Major Commanding

Major Booth had been dead since about nine o'clock, and this subterfuge was intended to conceal the fact from the Confederate leader. This note was at once taken to General Forrest. Meanwhile it is the general testimony of the survivors among the Confederates that the troops of the garrison, especially the colored soldiers who now had mounted the parapet in considerable numbers, shouted to McCulloch's men, many of whom had come out from behind the barracks and houses which concealed and protected them, daring them to try to take the fort, and hurling epithets at them couched in most obscene and abusive terms and accompanied by gestures and actions not to be described. If their officers made any effort to put a stop to this unusual exhibition, it was without effect. In about fifteen minutes Captain Goodman returned with this reply from Forrest:

Major L. F. Booth, Commanding U. S. Forces, Fort Pillow:

SIR—I have the honor to acknowledge the receipt of your note, asking one hour to consider my demand for your surrender. Your request cannot be granted. I will allow you twenty minutes from the receipt of this note for consideration; if at the expiration of that time the fort is not surrendered, I shall assault it. I do not demand the surrender of the gunboat.

Very respectfully,   N. B. FORREST, Major-General[21]

Adjutant Leaming says: "After a short consultation with the officers of the garrison, it was unanimously voted not to surrender." He

[21] All these notes are copied from the originals.

then, as directed, wrote and delivered to General Forrest in person the following:

GENERAL—I will not surrender.
Very respectfully, your obedient servant,
L. F. BOOTH, Major Commanding

Forrest, in his official report, says: "While these negotiations were pending the steamers below were rapidly approaching the fort. The foremost was the *Olive Branch,* whose position and movements indicated her intention to land."[22] He believed, and was justified in the conclusion, that the request for delay by the Union commander was a subterfuge to gain time, so that the boats might land before the hour asked for should expire.

In the light of the published official records there is also clearly seen the explanation of the unanimous vote of the officers of the garrison not to surrender. It came out in the investigation which followed that Captain Marshall, who commanded the gunboat *New Era,* testified as follows: "We (Major Bradford and Captain Marshall) had agreed on a signal that if they (Bradford's troops) had to leave the fort they would drop down under the bank, and I was to give the rebels canister."[23] In this admission will be found the prime reason of the tragedy which here ensued.

The second reason was the condition of intoxication which prevailed with a large part of the garrison. Major Booth, from all accounts an excellent and brave commander, was dead. Major Bradford, evidently, as stated by Major General S. A. Hurlbut, "without experience," had succeeded to the command, and had made the fatal error of giving his men free access to the liquor with which the commissary of the fort was supplied. The sworn testimony of a large number of honorable and trustworthy men establishes this fact beyond contradiction. Forrest so stated this fact, and Generals Chalmers and Bell, Colonels Mc-Culloch, Wisdom, and Barteau, and many more surviving Confederates swear that vessels containing whiskey were distributed along the inside of the works, with cups and dippers convenient for use. To those familiar with the two classes, black and white, which composed the bulk of the private soldiers in the garrison at Fort Pillow, and their

[22] *Official Records,* vol. xxxii, part i, p. 614.
[23] *Rebellion Record,* vol. viii, p. 55.

fondness for intoxicating drinks, especially so with the Negroes just free from slavery, it will readily be accepted that they did not fail to take advantage of the opportunities here offered to drink to excess. Their conduct during the truce and the insane resistance beneath the bluff bear out the allegation that many were intoxicated.

Major Bradford and his subordinates were foolish enough to believe either that a ditch twelve feet wide and eight feet deep, with a wall of earth six feet high, would be impassable to the Confederates or that, should they not be able to repel the assault, they could rush beneath the bluff and near the water's edge, while Captain Marshall would rake the crest of the bluff with canister and thus, with the aid of the troops, keep off the assailants until succor could arrive. To this end preparations were made. *The gunboat was ready, and Bradford had six cases of ammunition carried down below the bluff in anticipation of this; the tops were removed, and the cartridges were ready for distribution when needed.* The garrison evidently was instructed as to this movement, for they carried their guns with them when they left the fort, and fought to the last, as will be shown by their official report. There is sworn testimony that some 275 guns of the Federal troops were picked up below the crest of the bluff, where they were carried by the retreating garrison. Lieutenant Van Horn, who took part in the fight, testifies that they never surrendered and fought with desperation to the last.

As soon as the flags of truce were withdrawn both sides prepared quickly for the final grapple. The soldiers of the garrison loaded their muskets and filled their six pieces with grapeshot. A number of noncombatants, refugees, sutlers, etc., were given muskets and took their places in line. All along the inner aspect of the embankment they crouched beneath the parapet, their guns resting on the crest, and all ready for the onslaught. The gunboat *New Era* was in the place and ready, but alas! it was a broken reed upon which this weak and foolish commander was leaning. Forrest had long since solved the problem of silencing such craft at canister range. He instructed Anderson and Barteau to watch the boat, and when her ports were opened to have their sharpshooters cut down the gunners. "Shoot everything blue betwixt wind and water until their flag comes down," were his exact words.

His orders to the troops were explicit: they were told that they must storm the fort; every gun and pistol was to be loaded; not a shot was to be fired by the assaulting line until they were inside the works and hand to hand; they must make it quick work. The men were informed that the sharpshooters would keep the heads of the Federals behind the parapet until they could cross the ditch and climb the embankment. He would be where he could watch the entire field, and would note which command would be first over the walls; when Gaus's bugle sounded the charge, they were to go.

General Forrest then rode slowly to the hillock, some four hundred yards from the fort, which he had formerly occupied, and waited a few minutes longer. They were anxious and exciting moments for those daredevil spirits he was proud to command. It was now nearly four o'clock. Intently scanning the fort and the ground about it, without turning his head, Forrest said: "Blow the charge, Gaus." The faithful German raised the battered bugle (it had two bulletholes through it) to his mouth, and away through the air rang out the thrilling sound. Only the first few notes, however, were audible. Other and harsher sounds broke on the ear and swallowed up the bugle's blast.

From the space around the entire front of the crescentic earthworks twelve hundred Confederates sprang from the ground, rent the air with their war cry, the rebel yell, and with bodies bent low to the earth to escape the shower of bullets which greeted them from the parapet, they rushed like the wind and jumped into the wide and deep ditch. It was too wide to jump across. Few men with gun in hand and cartridgebox buckled on could leap twelve feet and land upon the slanting bank of earth where ditch and embankment met; and as for scaling ladders, Forrest's men would sooner have thought of using Jacob's ladder than of preparing such apparatus to cross a ditch. They jumped straight to the bottom. It was April weather, and the bottom was mud and water. They did not mind that on such an occasion. From where they stood it was fourteen feet of climbing to the parapet. Where were the hand grenades? the shells with short fuses? Bradford might have exterminated these reckless horsemen who stormed forts and captured gunboats and manned them and had the effrontery to fight a naval battle. There was neither reason nor an ordinary knowledge of war behind the earthworks. When the wild yell of the assailants brought the garrison to their feet, they raised their heads above the works and fired a deafening volley of musketry, and simultaneously the gunners pulled the lanyards of their six pieces.

It made an awful din—the wild, defiant yell of the assailants, mingled with the crackle and roar of musketry and the thundering cannon. The shower of grapeshot swept the hilltops in the distance, but sped over the heads of the Confederates. The guns could not be sufficiently depressed to harm the charging line. The volley from the small arms was more effective; a number of the assaulting line went down, and more would have fallen but for the foresight of their commander, who from his distant position was a spectator intensely interested in the event which was transpiring. As the blue caps of the garrison rose above the horseshoe line of the parapet to deliver their volley, a shower of missiles whizzed by and into them, while bits of pulverized earth flew in their faces as the bullets from the unerring aim of 250 sharpshooters sped through the air and plowed miniature furrows along the floorlike top of the embankment or went home in mortal spite at some unhappy victim. Moreover, in order to render their arms effective, so close were the cavalrymen to the works that they must of necessity expose at least one-fourth of their bodies in order to bring the muzzles of their guns in proper range.

Meanwhile, at the bottom of the ditch the human scaling ladders were not idle. These hardy riders were playing the most serious game of leapfrog they had ever undertaken. Broad backs bent over, and on them as stepping blocks their comrades clambered to the narrow ledge of solid earth above, where embankment and ditch almost joined. From this landing they reached down and lent a hand to pull the others up. They soon thickly lined the facing of the wall of earth, and as yet had not fired a single shot. The sharpshooters now had of necessity ceased their work for fear of hitting their own men, whose heads were nearly level with the parapet. The fire of the garrison, too, had suddenly stopped. It was an ominous silence. Their guns were loaded, and they were waiting for the heads of their enemies to show along the crest. Only the artillery blazed away, shooting at the air and the hills around, hitting no one but making a terrific noise. There was no wild, disordered rush of Forrest's men, no helter-skelter advance, which would have been fatal. They moved together and under orders. Bell, the two McCullochs, Barteau, Alexander Chalmers, Wilson, Russell, and Wisdom were there with their soldiers.

What they were doing and did consumed only a few minutes, yet it

took time and order to accomplish with the minimum loss of life
what they were doing. It was a bold and daring feat, without a parallel
in the history of cavalry. It was another stroke of that rare combination
of caution and audacity which Forrest practiced at all times, and
almost always with success. To rush through a blaze of musketry
and cannon and gain that ditch, jump into it and clamber out, halt
for a minute on the base of the embankment, and in one solid line from
all sides spring over the parapet ablaze with the flash of powder from
the very muzzles of the muskets of the garrison, still reserving their
fire, then to leap in among them and grapple hand to hand in mortal
combat, took these daredevil horsemen less time to do than it takes
to tell of it. But there they were, and every man knew it was a fight to
the death. The garrison had resolved to die—*not to surrender.* The
Confederates were there to take that fort or die in the attempt. No
marvel the loss of life was terrible.

With a fierce shout, with guns and pistols cocked and ready, with
finger on the trigger, they sprang on to the parapet. A circle of fire
flashed in their faces, and the ground shook with the terrific explosion
which greeted them the instant their heads began to show, and backward into the ditch reeled and fell a number of the assailants. This
did not stop the rest; the front rank, six hundred strong, leaped down
among the garrison, shoved their guns and six-shooters against their
blue blouses, and lead and powder and wadding tore them to instant
death. White and black of the Union forces, with guns in hand, some
turning and firing as they were swept back, now, as ordered, sought
safety beneath the bluff. *They had no thought of surrender then, and in
defiance of Forrest they left their flag floating from the staff.* They had
been promised aid from the gunboat, and safety from pursuit when
once below the crest of the riverbank. No man surrendered or tried
to surrender above the bluff.

The Confederates lining the embankment, and those on the ground
within the fort—twelve hundred in all—from pistol and musket poured
into them a deliberate and converging fire as they retired, and with
fearful execution. There were some tents erected within the fort
nearest the river, and these blocked the way to rapid egress. As the
retreating mass crowded the narrow paths between the tents, they
were pelted by the shower of lead which slaughtered them by scores.
They fell in piles three or four deep, heaps of bleeding, mangled

bodies. It was a frightful holocaust; fully 250 of the 557 soldiers who were defending Fort Pillow lay dead or wounded within that small enclosure. Reloading as they advanced, the victors followed as far as the crest of the bluff, beneath which the remnant of the Union forces had disappeared.

When Major Bradford and the survivors of the garrison reached the bank they leaped over and ran toward the water's edge and down the bluff to where the ammunition was stored. They did this to get out of the way of harm and to make room for Captain Marshall to carry out his promise of "giving the rebels canister" from the gunboat just off the shore. Alas! not a porthole was opened, not a cannon flashed or roared from across the smooth surface of the Mississippi. The flash and roar came from another and an unexpected quarter. As Bradford and his men leaped over the bluff and rushed southward along its face, they had not gone fifty yards when Captain Anderson, who with his detachment of two hundred men was stationed one hundred yards below the fort, gave the command to fire, and sent a furious and fatal volley into their midst. Staggered and bewildered at this unexpected turn of affairs, the decimated garrison, now panic-stricken, turned upon their tracks and rushed wildly along the face of the bluff up the river, thinking that way was open for escape. As they reached the upper limit of the fort, the detachment from Barteau's regiment stationed opposite the mouth of Cold Creek ravine opened upon the fugitives another volley which stopped their flight in this direction, and turned them like frightened sheep once more back in the direction they had first taken when they sought safety beneath the bank.

Many of the survivors now realized that escape or rescue was hopeless and threw down their guns; some, wild with fright or frenzied by liquor or the wounds they had received, rushed into the river and were drowned or shot to death as they attempted to swim away. Many of the white men, more intelligent than their colored comrades, threw themselves behind the logs, stumps, brush heaps, or into the gullies which they encountered in their flight, and thus saved themselves from the frightful mortality which befell the terror-stricken Negroes, some few of whom, either insanely intoxicated or convinced from the slaughter that had transpired that no quarter would be shown them, and determined to sell their lives as dearly as possible, still offered resistance and continued to fire at the Confederates. There were not many who were guilty of this insanity, but there were enough to justify their assailants to close in upon them from the bluff above and from either side of the riverbank and continue to shoot them down. Others broke through the investing lines and, refusing to halt, were pursued and killed. A number who had thrown their guns away, holding up their hands, ran up toward the Confederates on the crest of the bluff and were spared, while others who did this were shot down. But for the insane conduct of their drunken and desperate comrades, a great many of those who perished would have escaped.

This frightful scene of carnage was fortunately of short duration. General Forrest, from his position four hundred yards distant from the fort, as soon as he saw his men gain the parapet and leap in among the garrison, rode at once to the scene and ordered all firing to cease. As he entered the fort a soldier of Barteau's Second Tennessee regiment, Private John Doak Carr of Hartsville, Tennessee, cut the halyards of the Union flag and, as it fell to the ground, he picked it up and carried it to the general. When Forrest ordered the firing to be stopped, Generals Chalmers and Bell, and Colonels McCulloch, Barteau, Wisdom, and Captain Anderson, who were immediately with their troops, enforced the order. Among the mass of sworn testimony examined by the author, it is shown that with but one exception, the perpetrator of which was arrested by General Chalmers on the spot and placed under guard, not a gun was fired or a prisoner injured after the flag of the garrison fell.

The gunboat *New Era,* with steam up, was still lying at anchor, or under a "slow wheel," to steady her in the current. She had not opened a port or fired a cannon. Only a few musket shots came from her sides. One of the Parrott guns of the fort was now rolled to the bluff and opened upon her, at which she steamed up stream and was soon out of range, though still hovering in sight.

As soon as the firing ceased, Forrest ordered Colonel McCulloch to take charge of the enemy's camp, prisoners, and captured property. McCulloch says: *"I ordered the survivors to gather up their wounded and bury their dead."*[24] The wounded were placed in the tents at the rear of the fort and in the barracks and other buildings to the south of the stronghold. In this work some of the Confederate officers took part. The dead were buried entirely by details from the Union

[24] Report of Colonel Robert McCulloch.

survivors, and if, as charged, some of the wounded were buried alive, they were thus interred by their own comrades. Meanwhile Forrest directed Captain Anderson to take one of the prisoners, Captain John T. Young (Twenty-fourth Missouri Infantry), provost marshal of the fort, with a white flag, and have him proceed along the shore and signal the *New Era* to send off a boat and convey to Captain Marshall the following note, copied from the original:

Captain Marshall, Commanding Gunboat No. 7, United States Navy:

SIR—My aide-de-camp, Captain Charles W. Anderson, is fully authorized to negotiate with you for the delivery of the wounded of the garrison at this place on board your vessel.

I am, very respectfully yours, etc.,
N. B. FORREST, Major-General

Captain Young went up the bank waving his flag, but Captain Marshall, if he saw it, paid no attention to it other than to move off up the river and disappear around a bend. In his sworn statement to the committee he said: "I was fearful that they might hail in a steamboat from below, capture her, put on four or five hundred men, and come after me."[25]

Captain Anderson and a detail of Confederates were now busy gathering up the arms and all captured property, and placing it in wagons to be hauled away. Fully one-half of the muskets and carbines of the garrison were picked up by Anderson below the crest of the bluff, and six cases of cartridges with the tops removed, ready for distribution, were found behind the trunks of trees below and between the rear of the fort and the water's edge.[26]

At five o'clock General Forrest and a portion of the troops moved away. Bell, with his brigade, followed with all the unwounded prisoners and those whose injuries were not serious enough to prevent them from marching. Forrest, on account of his injuries, was unable to proceed more than five miles on that afternoon. Bell marched ten miles from the battlefield and encamped for the night. McCulloch, with Chalmers, followed at dark, leaving the fort entirely abandoned by the Confederates. The Federal wounded were left in charge of their surgeon. The rear guard of the Confederates encamped for the night two miles from the river.

[25] *Rebellion Record,* vol. viii, p. 55.
[26] Sworn statement.

After dark that evening not a soldier of Forrest's command was nearer Fort Pillow than two miles, where General Chalmers went into camp. If the excesses charged by some of the survivors were committed after that time and before six o'clock of the following morning (April 13th), they were done by guerrillas, robbers, and murderers, with which this section of the country, as is well known, was then infested, and who, following in the wake of either army like hyenas, preyed without mercy upon the weak and defenseless.

At daylight on the 13th, General Forrest, before proceeding on his way to Jackson, directed Captain Anderson of his staff to return to the battlefield and endeavor to secure the landing of some passing steamer to take the Federal wounded on board. Captain Anderson's report,[27] written on April 17th, states that, accompanied by three men of the escort, he rode toward the battlefield, and when about two miles from the fort he came upon General Chalmers's camp, and requested permission to take Captain Young, a Federal prisoner, with him. At this moment a gunboat was shelling the woods about the fort. On nearing the bluff Captain Anderson raised the white flag, and the boat ceased firing. A small boat came off to inquire what was wanted. Captain Anderson informed the officer in command of the boat—the *Silver Cloud*—that General Forrest desired to place the Union wounded, "white or black," upon his boat.

Acting Master William Ferguson, U.S.N., accepted the truce and at once landed at the fort. This was at 8 A.M. It was then agreed between these officers that the flag of truce should remain in force until 5 P.M. General Chalmers, who had also now returned to the river, approved of this agreement. No armed Confederates were to come within the outer line of works, which was about one-half mile from the bluff. The task of burying the dead and carrying the wounded on board was completed by four o'clock, when the boats left and Captain Anderson lowered the flag of truce. He then set fire to all remaining tents and houses, and rode away with the few soldiers who had remained at the outer works.

Captain Ferguson says that at 6 A.M. his boat arrived off the fort, and he began to shell some rebel pickets who were seen hovering near the fort. About 8 A.M. the flag of truce was seen, and he made the agreement with Captain Anderson as just given. He also hailed the

[27] *Official Records*, vol. xxxii, part i, p. 598.

steamer *Platte Valley,* and had her land to assist him. Upon these boats the wounded men were placed, a detail of Confederates assisting in this work, as acknowledged by Captain Ferguson, and at 4 P.M. the boats proceeded up the river.[28]

The casualties among the Confederates were fourteen officers and men killed, and eighty-six wounded. Lieutenant Colonel Wiley M. Reid, Captains J. C. Wilson and W. R. Sullivan, Lieutenants N. B. Burton, Ryan, Hubbard, and Love were among the slain. Considering the stubborn character of the resistance offered by the garrison and the strength of the position, the loss of the Southern troops was small. This is in great part accounted for by the woeful incompetency of the officer who at 9 A.M. succeeded to the command of the Union forces after the death of Major Booth, and by the intoxication of very many of his troops, a condition which, while it made them reckless and indifferent to danger or death, also rendered them inefficient for an intelligent defence of the fort.

In Forrest's superior skill in the management of the attack will, however, be found the chief reason for the small loss his men suffered. His genius in aggressive warfare was probably never more brilliantly exhibited than in this small affair. The accurate and persistent work of his sharpshooters either kept the heads of the garrison below the parapet or, when they rose to fire, made the discharge of their pieces premature and their aim too uncertain to be effective. Once inside the works, the Confederates had all the advantage, and their loss after the first volley from the Federals was exceedingly small. The loss with the garrison was very heavy. Of the 557 enlisted troops there were 226 who were marched away with Bell's command to Mississippi.

There were about fifty whose wounds were so slight as not to interfere with their marching south. Captain W. Ferguson, commanding the United States steamer *Silver Cloud,* reports that he received on board of his boat on the 13th, at Fort Pillow, about one hundred men, and that about seventy of these were wounded. Thirty-four of this group of seventy were whites; the remainder were Negroes. Captain A. M. Pennock, United States Navy, testified that two days after the battle, April 14th, ten additional wounded soldiers were picked up by Captain Fitch.[29] This would make the killed of the garrison, 221;

---

[28] *Ibid.,* p. 571.
[29] *Rebellion Record,* vol. viii, p. 38.

wounded, 130; unwounded, 206; ratio of killed to troops engaged, 39 per cent; killed and wounded, 63 per cent.[j]

On the 15th of April, three days after the capture of Fort Pillow, General Forrest sent a brief and imperfect report to his immediate commander, Lieutenant General Polk. In this dispatch he states that he

arrived at Fort Pillow on the morning of the 12th, with about fifteen hundred men of McCulloch's and Bell's brigades, and after a sharp contest captured the garrison and all of its stores. A demand was made for a surrender, which was refused. The victory was complete, and the loss of the enemy will never be known, from the fact that large numbers ran into the river and were shot and drowned. The force was composed of about five hundred negroes and two hundred white soldiers [Tennessee Tories]. The river was dyed with the blood of the slaughtered for two hundred yards. There was in the fort a large number of citizens who had fled there to escape the conscript law. Most of these ran into the river and were drowned. The approximate loss was upward of five hundred killed, but few of the officers escaping. It is hoped that these facts will demonstrate to the Northern people that negro soldiers cannot cope with the Southerners. We still hold the fort. My loss was about twenty killed and about sixty wounded.[30]

Upon the same day he wrote to President Davis, giving a report of his campaign in west Tennessee, including the capture of Fort Pillow. This report differs in no essential particular from that made to General Polk. April 26th, Forrest, having the reports of his subordinates at hand, forwarded his full report of this engagement. He says:

My command consisted of McCulloch's brigade of Chalmers's division, and Bell's brigade of Buford's division, both placed for the expedition under the command of Brigadier-General James R. Chalmers, who by a forced march drove in the enemy's pickets and gained possession of the outer works, and by the time I reached the field, at 10 A.M., had forced the enemy to their main fortification. The fort was garrisoned by seven hun-

[30] In this report General Forrest was in error both as to the loss of the Federals, which was much less than he stated, and also as to his own casualties, which were in excess of his figures. It will be remembered that he left the scene of the battle immediately after it was over and before any definite knowledge could have been obtained. The expression that "the river was stained with the blood of the slaughtered" was used by General Grant in his *Memoirs* to injure the reputation of Forrest, and unjustly, since the facts were accessible to him at the time his *Memoirs* were written.

dred troops, with six pieces of field artillery. A deep ravine surrounds the fort, and from the fort to the ravine the ground descends rapidly. I ordered General Chalmers to advance his lines and gain position on the slope, where our men would be perfectly protected from the heavy fire of artillery and musketry. The enemy could not depress their pieces so as to rake the slopes, nor could they fire on them by small arms except by mounting the breastworks, and exposing themselves to the fire of our sharp-shooters, who, under cover of stumps and logs, forced them to keep down inside the works. After several hours' hard fighting the desired position was gained, not, however, without considerable loss. Our main line was now within an average distance of one hundred yards from the fort, and extended from Cold Creek on the right to the bluff or bank of the Mississippi on the left.

During the entire morning the gunboat kept up a continuous fire in all directions, but without effect; and being confident of my ability to take the fort by assault, and desiring to prevent further loss of life, I sent under flag of truce a demand for an unconditional surrender of the garrison. [This dispatch and others mentioned below appear on pages 319, 322, and 323.]

The gunboat had ceased firing, and the smoke of three other boats ascending the river was in view, the foremost boat apparently crowded with troops; and believing the request for an hour was to gain time for reinforcements to arrive, and that the desire to consult the officers of the gunboat was a pretext by which they desired improperly to communicate with her, I at once sent a reply by Captain Goodman, who bore the flag, directing him to remain until he received a reply, or until the expiration of the time proposed.

My dispositions had all been made and my force was in a position that would enable me to take the fort with less loss than to have withdrawn under fire, and it seemed to me so perfectly apparent to the garrison that such was the case that I deemed their capture without further bloodshed a certainty. After some little delay, seeing the message delivered to Captain Goodman, I rode up myself to where the notes were received and delivered. The answer was handed me, written in pencil on a slip of paper without envelope, and was, as well as I remember, in these words: "Negotiations will not attain the desired object." As the officers who were in charge of the Federal flag of truce had expressed a doubt as to my presence, and had pronounced the demand a trick, I handed them back the note, saying: "I am General Forrest; go back and say to Major Booth that I demand an answer in plain, unmistakable English. Will he fight or surrender?" Returning to my original position, before the expiration of twenty minutes I received a reply. [See dispatches.]

While these negotiations were pending, the steamers from below were rapidly approaching the fort; the foremost was the *Olive Branch*, whose position and movements indicated her intention to land. A few shots fired into her caused her to leave the shore and make for the opposite side. One other boat passed up on the far side of the river; the third one turned back.

The time having expired, I directed Brigadier-General Chalmers to prepare for the assault. Bell's brigade occupied the right, with his extreme right resting on Cold Creek. McCulloch's brigade occupied the left, extending from the centre to the river. Three companies of his left regiment were placed in an old rifle-pit on the left and almost in the rear of the fort. On the right a portion of Barteau's regiment was also under the bluff, and in rear of the fort. Fearing the gunboats and transports might attempt a landing, I directed my aide-de-camp, Captain Charles W. Anderson, to assume command of the three companies on the left and rear of the fort, and hold the position against anything that might come by land or water, and to take no part in the assault on the fort. Everything being ready, the bugle sounded for the charge, which was made with a yell, and the works were carried without a perceptible halt in any part of the line. As our troops mounted and poured into the fortification, the enemy retreated into the river, arms in hand and firing back, colors flying, no doubt expecting the gunboat to shell my men away from the bluff and protect them until they could be taken off or reinforced.

As they descended the bank an enfilading and deadly fire was poured into them by the troops under Captain Anderson on the left and Bell's detachment on the right. Until this fire was opened upon them, at a distance varying from thirty to one hundred yards, they were evidently ignorant of any force having gained their rear. The regiment which had stormed and carried the fort also poured a destructive fire in the rear of the retiring and now panic-stricken and almost decimated garrison. Fortunately for those of the enemy who survived this short but desperate struggle, some of our men cut the halyard, and the United States flag which floated from a tall mast in the centre of the fort came down. The force stationed in the rear of the fort could see the flag, but were too far under the bluff to see the fort, and when the flag descended they ceased firing; but for this, so near were they to the enemy, that few, if any, would have survived unhurt another volley. As it was, many rushed into the river and were drowned, and the actual loss of life will perhaps never be known, as there were quite a number of refugee citizens in the fort, many of whom were drowned, and several killed in the retreat from the fort. In less than twenty minutes from the time the bugle sounded the charge, firing had ceased and the work was done.

One of the Parrott guns was turned on the gunboat; she steamed off without replying. She had, as I afterwards understood, expended all her ammunition, and was therefore powerless for affording the Federal garrison the aid and protection they doubtless expected of her when they retreated towards the river. Details were made, consisting of the captured Federals and negroes, in charge of their officers, to collect together and bury the dead, which continued until dark. I also directed Captain Anderson to procure a skiff, and take with him Captain Young, a captured Federal officer, and deliver to Captain Marshall, of the gunboat, a message. [See dispatches.] All the boats and skiffs having been taken off by citizens escaping from the fort during the engagement, the message could not be delivered, although every effort was made to induce Captain Marshall to send his boat ashore by raising a white flag. She finally moved off, and disappeared round the bend above the fort. General Chalmers withdrew his force from the fort before dark, and encamped a few miles east of it.

On the morning of the 13th I again despatched Captain Anderson to Fort Pillow for the purpose of placing, if possible, the Federal wounded on board a transport, and of reporting to me on his return the condition of affairs at the river. We captured six pieces of artillery and about three hundred and fifty stand of small arms; the balance of the small arms had been thrown into the river. All the small arms were picked up where the enemy fell, or threw them down in the fort; the balance scattered from the top of the hill to the water's edge.

It should be borne in mind that this official report was written before General Forrest could have known of the action of the congressional committee.

On April 24th, General Polk, in a dispatch to Major General Forrest, says: "Your brilliant campaign in west Tennessee has given me great satisfaction and entitles you to the thanks of your countrymen. Appropriate orders in writing will be transmitted you immediately."[31] On May 23, 1864, it was resolved by the Congress of the Confederate States of America "that the thanks of Congress are eminently due and are hereby cordially tendered to Major-General N. B. Forrest and the officers and men of his command, for their late brilliant and successful campaign in Mississippi, west Tennessee, and Kentucky, a campaign which has conferred upon its authors fame as enduring as the record of the struggle which they have so brilliantly illustrated."

For many reasons the capture of Fort Pillow attracted wide at-

[31] *Official Records,* vol. xxxii, part i, p. 619.

tention. It was considered a remarkable achievement for a small force of cavalry, one-half of whom were recruits of four months' service, and badly armed, to storm a stronghold deemed impregnable, the garrison of which was thoroughly well equipped with the most modern and effective small arms, with six pieces of artillery, and these aided by a gunboat with an additional heavy battery. No wonder, after the capture of such a stronghold, that Major General Hurlbut should declare in his testimony before the congressional committee: "Forrest is desperate. He will carry his men farther than anybody I know of."[32]

Moreover, this was the first occasion on which the Negro troops came prominently to notice in conflict with their late masters. About one-half of the Union troops were runaway slaves, and were considered as private property by the Confederates, who did not recognize Mr. Lincoln's proclamation as giving their slaves legitimate freedom.

There can be little doubt, however, that it was the heavy loss of life—the unusually large proportion of killed and wounded to the number of soldiers engaged—which led to the report of the committee of Congress, and caused this engagement to pass into history as the "Fort Pillow Massacre."

To the rational mind, capable of carefully weighing the evidence on both sides, and arriving at a conclusion unbiased by prejudice, it must be clear that there was no massacre as charged. Had a wholesale and merciless slaughter been intended by General Forrest and his subordinates, it could and would have been carried out, as there was nothing to prevent it. The fact that so many escaped death is of itself a proof that a massacre was not premeditated or permitted. It is true that more of the garrison were shot after the Southern troops were in possession of the breastworks than was necessary for the full success of the assault, but under the conditions which prevailed during the attack, it is clearly shown that an unusually large loss in killed and wounded was inevitable, even had no excesses been indulged in by the captors.

From a careful study of the subject, I am convinced that a few desperate or insanely intoxicated soldiers of the garrison resisted to the very last, and even after escape was hopeless continued to fire at the Confederates. On the other hand, notwithstanding this extreme

[32] *Rebellion Record,* vol. viii, p. 42.

provocation, there were a number of men, both white and black, shot down who were trying to surrender and should have been spared. About an hour before the assault was made a detachment of Forrest's command posted at the extreme left of his line broke into the quartermaster's stores which had been captured at this time, and before they could be compelled to quit the building had had access to a supply of whisky which they discovered there. The moment Forrest learned that his men were pillaging the captured stores he rode there rapidly and put a stop to it in person.

The incidents, however, which did occur were greatly exaggerated and cleverly distorted in the reports. In extracting the testimony, the committee, for political purposes, and as part of an important war measure, gave a bloody coloring to the whole. Everything considered, it may well be a matter of surprise that the slaughter was not greater. Human life was held exceedingly cheap in 1864, and especially in west Tennessee; the scenes of bloodshed which stained this section of the South may well suggest the reddest days of the French Revolution.

It is difficult for those who did not live through this unhappy period, and in this immediate section, to appreciate the bitterness of feeling which then prevailed. Three years of civil war had passed, not without a deplorable effect upon the morals of the rank and file of either army. War does not bring out the noblest traits in the majority of those who from choice or necessity follow its bloodstained paths. Too often the better qualities hide away, and those that are harsh and cruel prevail. Some of Forrest's men treasured a deep resentment against some of the officers and soldiers of this garrison. They had been neighbors in times of peace, and had taken opposite sides when the war came on. These men had suffered violence to person and property, and their wives and children, in the enforced absence of their natural protectors, had suffered various indignities at the hands of the "Tennessee Tories," as the loyal Tennesseans were called by their neighbors who sided with the South. When they met in single combat, or in scouting parties, or in battle, as far as these individuals were concerned, it was too often a duel to the death. Between the parties to these neighborhood feuds the laws of war did not prevail. Here in this melee, in the fire and excitement of the assault, they found opportunity and made excuse for bloody vengeance. No official surrender; the flag still flying; some of the Federals, no matter how few, still firing back, and they shot them down regardless of the cry for quarter.

Some of those high in authority on the Union side may, in a measure, be justly held accountable for the deep hatred which existed among' these men. General William Sooy Smith, the chief of cavalry of the military division of the Mississippi, no later than January 17, 1864, had, in writing to General Grant, said: "We have given Colonel Hurst a roving commission with his regiment (the Sixth Tennessee Union Cavalry), and directed him to 'grub up' west Tennessee. I think he will reduce that district to order."[33]

That Colonel Fielding Hurst proceeded thoroughly to "grub up" west Tennessee is evident from the fact that, as stated in the records, he and his command were assessed by the Federal authorities at Memphis, and forced to repay a very considerable sum of money extorted from citizens.[34] A trusted officer (killed in the assault), sent by General Forrest to investigate the conduct of Hurst's command, reports:

> About February 15th, 1864, Lieutenant Joseph Stewart and Privates John Wilson and Samuel Osborn, members of Newsom's regiment (Forrest's cavalry), while on duty under orders from their commanding officers, were captured by Hurst's command, and three days thereafter their bodies were found, they having been shot to death. About the 5th of February, 1864, Private Martin, of Wilson's regiment (Forrest's cavalry), was captured by this same command and was shot to death, and the rights of sepulchre forbidden while the command remained, some four days. Lieutenant Willis Dobbs, of Newsom's regiment, while under orders of his superiors, was arrested at the residence of his father, in Henderson County, Tennessee, about March 9, 1864, and put to death by torture. Private Silas Hodges saw the body of Lieutenant Dobbs very soon after his murder, and states that it was horribly mutilated. Private Alexander Vale, of Newsom's regiment (Forrest cavalry), was arrested and shot to death in Madison County, Tennessee, about March 8, 1864.[35]

In view of these reported facts, General Forrest on March 22, 1864, authorized Colonel Reed, in the event that Colonel Fielding Hurst was not surrendered to him to answer for these deeds of murder, to

[33] *Official Records,* vol. xxxii, part ii, p. 124.
[34] *Ibid.,* p. 118.
[35] *Ibid.,* part iii, p. 118.

declare the aforesaid Fielding Hurst and the officers and men of his command outlaws, and not entitled to be treated as prisoners of war when falling into the hands of the forces of the Confederate States.[36]

Forrest brought this matter forcibly to the attention of Major General C. C. Washburn, who succeeded General Hurlbut, upon whom this demand was made, denouncing "one Colonel Fielding Hurst, and others of his regiment, who deliberately took out and killed seven Confederate soldiers, one of whom they left to die after cutting off his tongue, punching out his eyes, splitting his mouth on each side to his ears, and inflicting other mutilations."[37]

Lieutenant Colonel James P. Brownlow, son of the Union Governor of Tennessee, commanding the First Tennessee (Union) Cavalry, had on December 1, 1863, established the precedent of "no quarter." In the official report of a skirmish in which he and his regiment had been successful, he says, significantly: "I would take no prisoners."[38]

These are horrible recitals, but they give some idea of the disregard for life in those days of bloodshed and distress, and it would seem that their perpetrators were not without encouragement. General W. T. Sherman in this same year wrote to one of his subordinates: "Cannot you send over about Fairmouth and Adairsville, burn ten or twelve houses of known Secessionists, kill a few at random, and let them know it will be repeated every time a train is fired on from Resaca to Kingston."[39]

In this same year this distinguished soldier made use of his prisoners of war for the purpose of exploding torpedoes which had been planted by the enemy. One of his officers had been wounded by the explosion of a torpedo planted in the road in the Georgia campaign. He says: "I immediately ordered a lot of rebel prisoners from the provost-guard armed with picks and spades, and made them march in close ranks to explode their own torpedoes, or discover them and dig them up. They begged hard, but I reiterated the order, and could hardly help laughing at their stepping so gingerly along the road, where it was supposed some of the torpedoes might explode at each step, but they found no others until near Fort McAllister."[40]

[36] *Ibid.,* p. 119.
[37] *Ibid.,* vol. xxxii, part i, p. 592.
[38] *Ibid.,* vol. xxxi, part i, p. 591.
[39] *Ibid.,* vol. xxxix, part iii, p. 494.
[40] *Memoirs of Sherman.*

There is an adage that in war as in love all means of accomplishing the end desired are permissible. In the crisis of a great civil war, when each side was bending every energy for success, the leaders of the opposing forces justified a resort to measures of diplomacy in order to weaken their antagonists which a strict construction of right and truth would not have allowed. The proclamation of emancipation may be mentioned as such a measure—the unlawful and unjust sweeping away of private property. The refusal of the United States Government to exchange prisoners, thus condemning to a lingering death those of its own and its enemy's soldiers, was a war measure. In this same category should be placed the report of the congressional committee upon the capture of Fort Pillow, and the story of a massacre which was deftly woven out of the exaggerated testimony of two or three of the officers and some of the Negroes and whites who were of the garrison, much of which testimony was so self-contradicting as to prove its falsity, and all of which was *ex parte* and inadequate in establishing the trumped-up charges of a violation of the rules governing civilized warfare.

Forrest had become a man of great importance in the mighty struggle the South was making. The opportunity which now presented itself to injure his reputation and blacken his character and that of his men was not to be lost.

To further excite the indignation of the Northern people and of the civilized world by the wide publication of a horrible story of massacre which could not be refuted before it had done irreparable damage to the cause of the South, and further to impress upon the minds of the Negroes who were then flocking to the ranks of the Union army that in future battles they could not expect quarter, and must therefore fight with desperation to the last, was a stroke of policy the advantage of which the shrewd politicians at Washington did not intend to lose.[k]

FIFTEEN

Expedition Under General S. D. Sturgis, and the Battle at Brice's Crossroads

IN THE spring and summer of 1864 two great masters in strategy were playing a memorable game of war among the pine-clad hills of Georgia. Sherman, fiercely aggressive, with an army larger and better equipped, was slowly yet surely pushing Johnston back upon Atlanta. The latter, with matchless skill, was contesting every foot of ground and inflicting heavy loss upon his antagonist; but despite these losses it was clear to the Union commander that he had this army of the Confederacy at his mercy if he could keep his troops well supplied from the north and west until the corn with which the Southern fields were teeming was sufficiently ripened to supply subsistence to his men and animals.

It would seem from his official dispatches that his chief source of anxiety was that "that devil Forrest" would get into Tennessee and break the railroads in his rear. From the time immediately after the Meridian expedition, when Sherman was ordered to Nashville and thence to Chattanooga to take command of the Army of the Tennessee, the burden of his correspondence was that Forrest must be killed or crippled. He even went so far as to offer a major general's commission to one of his brigadiers if he would kill Forrest. "It must be done, if it costs ten thousand lives and breaks the Treasury."[1] In case the wily fox could not be killed or crippled he must be kept busy where he was.

When in March the Confederate cavalryman broke through the Union cordon and settled himself down in west Tennessee, as if he had come there to stay, Sherman directed the Federal commander at Memphis to leave Forrest where he was, saying that he could do less harm by "cavorting over the country" there than elsewhere. It was only after General Grant had become convinced that Forrest was making a too profitable use of this territory that he urged Sherman to send enough

[1] *Official Records*, vol. xxxix, part ii, pp. 121, 142.

troops there to drive him back into Mississippi. This, as has been shown in a preceding chapter, they succeeded in doing, and now that they had him south of the Tennessee border it became the prime object of Sherman and Grant to keep him so engaged that he would not get into Tennessee again.

The first essential to success was to find a commander equal to the emergency. General William Sooy Smith had been tried and found wanting, and Major General Stephen A. Hurlbut, who had been at the head of this department with headquarters at Memphis, had also fallen into disfavor by reason of his failure to defeat the redoubtable Confederate; General C. C. Washburn had been appointed in his stead. The choice fell upon General Samuel D. Sturgis, who as brigadier general commanding the cavalry corps in the Department of the Ohio had, in this same year of 1864, achieved such success in his operations in east Tennessee as to receive the special congratulations of the commanding general "upon your handsome success."[2]

He had taken part in the movement which drove Forrest from Tennessee in April and the early part of May of this same year, and had then been ordered by General Washburn to pursue him into Mississippi and punish him. Although on this occasion he did not succeed in catching "the scoundrel," he does not seem to have incurred the displeasure of his commander for this shortcoming. He kept on in the hopeless chase as far as Ripley, Mississippi, and then gave it up. In his official dispatch to General Washburn, dated May 7th, he says: "Upon reaching Ripley I found that the rear of Forrest's command had passed through that place nearly two days before. It was here that I had hoped, almost against hope, to intercept him, but as he was abundantly supplied with forage he was able to travel day and night, and thus elude our most strenuous exertions. It was with the greatest reluctance that I resolved to abandon the chase. Although we could not catch the scoundrel we are at least rid of him, and that is something."[3]

From Memphis, on May 13th, he wrote Sherman in the same vein of disappointment, but promised greater things when another occasion should offer:

My little campaign is over, and I regret to say Forrest is still at large. He did not go to west Tennessee for the purpose of fighting, unless it might

[2] *Ibid.,* vol. xxxii, part i, p. 138.
[3] *Ibid.,* vol. xxxii, part i, p. 697.

so happen that he could light upon some little party or defenceless place; and being well mounted, and having, of course, every facility of gaining information of our movements, it is idle to follow him except with an equal force of cavalry, which we have not in that part of the country. I say "except with an equal force of cavalry," but even then he has so many advantages, and is so disposed to run, that I feel that all that could be done in any case would be to drive him out, unless, indeed, he might be trapped, as might have been the case if a force had been sent to co-operate with mine at Purdy. I regret very much that I could not have the pleasure of bringing you his hair, but he is too great a plunderer to fight anything like an equal force, and we have to be satisfied with driving him from the State. He may turn on your communications—I rather think he will, but I see no way to prevent it from this point with this force.[4]

General Sturgis's prognostications were in part correct. Forrest was about to turn on Sherman's communications, and although he (Sturgis) saw no way of preventing it, the great soldier who was controlling the destinies of the Army of the Tennessee did see a way to keep him off. General Washburn was urged to send at once a formidable expedition in the direction of Tupelo, or wherever Forrest was; and for this purpose there marched out of Memphis and Lafayette on the 1st of June, 1864, 4800 infantry, 3300 cavalry, and about 400 artillerists with 22 pieces, and a supply train of 250 wagons and ambulances.[5]

In his official report General Washburn says: "The number of troops deemed necessary by General Sherman was six thousand, but I sent eight thousand. Everything was in complete order, and the force consisted of some of our best troops. I saw to it personally that they lacked nothing to insure a successful campaign."

Not only were these troops selected for their special fitness for fighting, but they were armed with Colt's repeating rifles and breech-loading carbines, the most formidable and effective weapons known to warfare at that date. The cavalry was divided into two brigades; the first, 1500 strong, accompanied by a battery of six pieces of artillery, was commanded by Colonel George E. Waring, Jr.; on record as an excellent soldier and good fighter, having led in person in the fight with Forrest at Okolona one of the most brilliant cavalry charges made during the war, and although, as Colonel Waring modestly says, "the charge was without effect, except as a diversion," and although, when repulsed, his

[4] *Ibid.,* p. 698.
[5] *Ibid.,* vol. xxxix, part i, pp. 89-90. Sturgis's report.

men were driven with considerable precipitation back to their starting point, General Forrest reported it as "the grandest cavalry charge I ever witnessed." The second brigade, of 1800 men and four guns, was commanded by Colonel E. F. Winslow, and this officer had shown such ability as to win the commendation of General Sherman for his conduct when in command of the cavalry in the expedition from Vicksburg to Meridian in February, 1864. These two brigades formed a division, under the command of Brigadier General B. H. Grierson, one of the best cavalry commanders at that date in the Federal army.

The infantry was divided into three brigades: the first, commanded by Colonel A. Wilkins, 2000 strong, with six pieces of artillery; the second, under Colonel G. B. Hoge, 1600 strong, with four guns; the third, 1200 colored troops, with two pieces of artillery, under Colonel Edward Bouton. These three brigades were formed into a division and placed temporarily under the direction of an excellent soldier, Colonel W. L. McMillen. The entire expedition was under Brigadier General Samuel D. Sturgis. Colonel Waring says: "We were a force of about nine thousand infantry, cavalry, and artillery, sent out by Sherman as a tub to the Forrest whale, a diversion to keep this commander from joining Hood in northern Georgia, though I doubt if even General Sherman in his moments of wildest enthusiasm anticipated just the issue that followed. We were well supplied for a campaign of any length, and, judging from the mess-tables we were invited to, others of the command were no less well provided."[6]

General Sturgis's orders were to strike the Mobile and Ohio Railroad at or near Corinth, Mississippi, to capture any force that might be there, proceeding south, destroying the railroad to Tupelo and Okolona, and as far as possible towards Macon and Columbus; thence back to Memphis by way of Grenada, and incidentally to disperse and destroy Forrest's cavalry. These orders also embraced the destruction of everything in that rich section, which was then called the "granary of the South," which would support life.

On the third day out, having learned that the Confederates had evacuated Corinth and gone south, Sturgis changed his direction, intending to strike the Mobile and Ohio Railroad below this point, and to intercept the Confederates, who had advanced in the direction of Corinth two days before, and were now, as he was informed, retreating toward Okolona.

[6] *Whip and Spur.*

On the 4th of June, Grierson, who was in the lead with the cavalry, dispatched Colonel Joseph Kargé, with four hundred troops, to march to Rienzi on the Mobile and Ohio Railroad, some ten miles south of Corinth. When this expedition reached Rienzi, the Confederates had already passed south. Colonel Kargé destroyed the depot buildings, but before the railroad could be materially damaged, Forrest's troopers turned on him and drove him away precipitately. General Sturgis, bearing farther southward with his command, struggled slowly on through the mud and rain over bad roads, traversing a section of country at that time stripped of supplies and almost deserted by its inhabitants; and although the distance was but seventy-five miles from his starting-point, it was not until the 7th of June that he reached the town of Ripley in Tippah County. On this day (June 7th) Winslow's brigade, which had been ordered by General Grierson to advance on the New Albany road, came into collision with two regiments of Confederates under Colonel Edward W. Rucker, who had been sent "to feel the enemy," with orders to retire when he met them, without bringing on an engagement. Holding Winslow at arm's length, Rucker reported to Forrest at Booneville on the night of June 9th.[7]

On this same night General Sturgis had concentrated his entire command and went into camp at Stubbs's farm, on the road leading from Ripley's by Brice's Crossroads in a southeasterly direction to Guntown, a station on the Mobile and Ohio Railroad, six miles beyond Brice's place. Here, as he reports, he sent back to Memphis "four hundred worn-out, sick, and disabled members of his command," about one hundred of whom belonged to the cavalry, leaving ready for duty and to take part in the battle of the next day 3200 cavalry, 4500 infantry, 400 artillerists (8100 men) with 22 pieces.

On the 1st of June, as Sturgis had marched out of Memphis, General Forrest, under orders from General S. D. Lee, had left Tupelo, Mississippi, with 2000 men, and started on a raid into middle Tennessee, directed against the Nashville and Chattanooga Railroad in Sherman's rear. Several days earlier (on the 26th of May) the Confederate general, who did not seem to pay much respect to the presence of Sturgis at the

---

[7] Colonel Rucker, on May 24th, had been placed in command of a fragment of a brigade composed of the Seventh Tennessee, Colonel W. L. Duckworth; Eighth Mississippi, Colonel W. L. Duff; and Lieutenant Colonel A. H. Chalmers's Mississippi battalion, with Captain J. C. Thrall's battery attached. Under his resolute leadership they won great fame as desperate fighters.

head of the cavalry about Memphis, had sent a request to General Lee, asking whether an expedition against that city would meet with his approbation, and no doubt he astonished his superior by saying "a few hours' work would enable me to fight successfully all the so-called gunboats they have. This would be a means of preventing reinforcements to the trans-Mississippi Department, and from thence, if necessary, we would move into middle Tennessee. If, however, it is deemed better to move into middle Tennessee, I can do so from here (Tupelo) better than from Corinth, as it would be nearer, and the enemy would have but little opportunity to know of it until we reach Tuscumbia."

The proposed movement on Memphis and west Tennessee was not, however, approved, for General Lee had determined to send Forrest to middle Tennessee to break up the railroads leading from Nashville to the south. On the 29th of May, from Tupelo, General Forrest telegraphed General Lee that "the time has arrived, and if I can be supported and allowed two thousand picked men from Buford's division and a battery of artillery, I will attempt to cut the enemy's communications in middle Tennessee."

With this in view, Forrest on the 3rd of June had proceeded as far as Russellville, in Franklin County, north Alabama, where he was overtaken by a dispatch from Lee, stating that an expedition had left Memphis, as he believed, for the invasion of Mississippi, and directing him to retrace his steps as rapidly as possible. This Forrest did, as is shown from the fact that he arrived in advance of his command in Tupelo by the 6th of June. Here he learned of the general direction of Sturgis's march, and of the detachment which had started toward Rienzi. Ordering Rucker to proceed to that village, and directing him to reconnoiter from thence in the direction of New Albany while Bell followed Rucker as far as Rienzi and halted, General Forrest, with his escort and the artillery, advanced to Booneville, on the Mobile and Ohio Railroad, where he was joined by Colonel Rucker at sundown on the 9th of June. At this time, while Sturgis had concentrated his entire command at Stubbs's, nine miles from Brice's Crossroads, where the battle was to be fought on the morrow, Forrest's command was distributed as follows:

Bell's brigade, of Buford's division, numbering, as shown in the official report of this officer for that day, 2787 men, was at Rienzi, twenty-five miles from Brice's; Rucker's brigade, 700 strong, was with

Forrest[8] at Booneville, eighteen miles from where the battle was fought; while Johnson's and Lyon's brigades, 500 and 800 respectively, were at Baldwyn, a little village six miles from Brice's Crossroads, these villages being on the road leading from Rienzi through Booneville and Baldwyn in a southwesterly direction toward Pontotoc. This road upon which Forrest would move, and that along which Sturgis was to march, running southeasterly to Fulton, crossed each other nearly at a right angle at Brice's farm, better known as Brice's Crossroads. The artillery, under Captain John W. Morton, consisting of his own and Rice's battery, was also at Booneville at this time, where General Lee had just arrived in order to confer with General Forrest.

It was Lee's opinion that the cavalry should retire in the direction of Okolona, permitting Sturgis to advance as far as possible away from his base of supplies and place of refuge in Memphis before giving him battle. He therefore directed General Forrest to march on the following morning from Booneville in the direction of Brice's Crossroads, and thence toward Prairie Mound and Okolona. Orders to this effect were immediately issued by Forrest, and three days' rations prepared. Two batteries of artillery, Thrall's and Ferrell's, and all supplies not needed there, were placed on the train and sent southward by rail on the night of the 9th with General Lee. It became a matter of discussion, after the campaign was over, whether General Forrest fully concurred in the opinion of his superior as to the propriety of retreating in advance of Sturgis, and of permitting him to further devastate the prairie country. The statement of Colonel Rucker is sufficient evidence upon this question. He says: "Late that night Forrest called a council of his officers, more to discuss the reports that he had received than for any other purpose."[9]

General Buford, Colonel Rucker, and Captain Morton, commanding the artillery, were present. General Bell was absent, being at Rienzi, seven miles farther north, while Lyon was at Baldwyn, twelve miles away to the south. General Forrest stated that he had information which was reliable, that the enemy was then encamped at Stubbs's farm on the Ripley and Guntown road, and that while he would prefer to get

---

[8] In addition to the troops here mentioned, General Forrest had his escort company of about eighty-five under Captain Jackson, and a company of Georgians under Captain Gartrell, about fifty strong, on headquarters duty, reinforcing his escort.

[9] The author is indebted to Colonel E. W. Rucker for these details.

them into the open country, as desired by General Lee, where he could "get a good look at them," he added that an emergency might arise which would necessitate a conflict before the prairie country could be reached and before a concentration with Generals Lee and Chalmers in the vicinty of Okolona could be effected.

It was evident then to the mind of Forrest, from the situation of the two forces, that a conflict was almost inevitable, and it is a fact that he had foreseen this collision at the point where it did take place, two days before it occurred.

Colonel D. C. Kelley, now living at Columbia, Tennessee, states that he was the bearer of a dispatch from General Forrest to Colonel W. A. Johnson of Roddey's division, who at that time was on the way from north Alabama to effect a junction with Forrest near Rienzi or Corinth. On June 8th, two days before the battle, Forrest requested him to hasten as quickly as possible to meet Colonel Johnson and tell him to press forward with all possible speed in the direction of Baldwyn and Brice's Crossroads, that from the direction the enemy were moving, and from their present position and his own, he expected to be obliged to fight them there about the 10th of June.[10]

General S. D. Lee, in a personal communication in 1897, informs the writer that Forrest had not been ordered to avoid a conflict with Sturgis under any and all circumstances. While he believed that Sturgis could ultimately be defeated, and that the defeat, taking place farther down in Mississippi, would prove more disastrous to the Federal expedition, he left General Forrest with full discretion to act in any emergency as his judgment might dictate.

On the night of the 9th of June, after the meeting just detailed, General Forrest sent a courier to Bell to have rations issued to his men and everything in readiness to move promptly before daylight in the morning, and to push forward as rapidly as possible in the direction of Brice's Crossroads. Similar instructions were conveyed to Colonels Rucker, Lyon, and Johnson, and to Captain Morton of the artillery. Lyon's brigade was ordered in the advance; Rucker, and then Johnson, who with a portion of his brigade had just arrived, jaded and worn out by a forced march from Alabama, were next in order, while Bell brought up the rear. The artillery, twelve pieces in all, was at Booneville, and had eighteen miles of muddy road to cover; but, rain or shine, Forrest

[10] Manuscript of Rev. D. C. Kelley, in possession of the author.

well knew that Morton would be where he could put his hand on him when most needed.

A heavy rain had fallen on the 8th of June, and on the afternoon and evening of the 9th it came down in torrents, and did not cease until after midnight; but about daybreak the clouds broke away and vanished, and when the sun came up it ushered in one of those hot, humid, and depressing days characteristic of this season of the year in this section of the Southern country.

By the time it was light enough to see the roadway, the Confederate troops were in motion. Between seven and eight o'clock in the morning, while riding at the head of his column, Colonel Rucker says that General Forrest rode by his side. He told Rucker that he intended to attack the Federals at Brice's. "I know they greatly outnumber the troops I have at hand, but the road along which they will march is narrow and muddy; they will make slow progress. The country is densely wooded and the undergrowth so heavy that when we strike them they will not know how few men we have. Their cavalry will move out ahead of the infantry, and should reach the crossroads three hours in advance. We can whip their cavalry in that time. As soon as the fight opens they will send back to have the infantry hurried up. It is going to be as hot as hell, and coming on a run for five or six miles over such roads, their infantry will be so tired out we will ride right over them. I want everything to move up as fast as possible. I will go ahead with Lyon[11] and the escort and open the fight."

[11] Colonel, afterward Brigadier-General, Hylan B. Lyon was one of Forrest's most devoted followers, a stubborn fighter, exhibiting at times a recklessness akin to desperation.

An incident which occurred at a small village known as Red Hill, in Marshall County, Alabama, will serve to show the spirit and determination of this officer.

Having been sent on detached duty in this section, Lyon, who had been promoted to a brigadier generalship, with two members of his staff was staying for the night at the residence of a Mr. Noble. A little before daylight they were awakened by a knock at the door and a sound of persons conversing without. Thinking he recognized one of the voices as that of Captain Terry, one of his subordinates, General Lyon went to the door and said: "Is that you, Terry? What do you want?" A voice replied: "Yes, I want to see you, general." With this Lyon opened the door, and to his surprise a Federal officer followed by several soldiers, with pistols cocked and presented, rushed in upon him, the officer saying: "I am an officer of the Fifteenth Pennsylvania Cavalry, and you are my prisoner." Colonel Lyon made no resistance, but asked to be permitted to dress himself. The officer consented, and with his men followed him to the

While Forrest had everything on the move by four o'clock on the morning of the 10th, the Federals were still in camp. Their commander was not in the happiest frame of mind. He was weighed down by the responsibility of his position and experienced, as he states in his official report, "a sad foreboding of the consequences."[12] He was practically in ignorance of the position and number of the enemy. The white citizens in the country through which he had traveled would give him no information, and the Negroes who flocked to him told such conflicting stories that he placed little reliance on their reports. He had, however, learned enough to know that Forrest was somewhere in his front or flank and not very far away, and that he could not proceed much farther southward without finding him in his path.

At 5.30 the Union cavalry under Grierson mounted their horses

---

door of the sleeping room from which he had been aroused. It was pitch dark, and the Union officer, standing at or in the door of the room, insisted that a light should be made. General Lyon responded, as he was drawing on his trousers and boots, that the fire was entirely out, and that he had no possible means of making a light.

Just at this moment a considerable uproar was heard in the yard and surrounding the house, and in the road just in front of it. A number of voices cried out: "Yonder comes the cavalry!" Taking advantage of this commotion and, of course, unobserved by the Federal officer, who, notwithstanding the darkness, by the sound of his voice was readily located as standing in the door, General Lyon, with his trousers and boots on but in his shirtsleeves, reached quickly under the pillow of his bed and drew out his two army pistols which had been placed there, as was his custom, on retiring. With one in each hand he stepped toward the door and fired both at once, killing the officer, as it happened, instantly; then, continuing to fire, he jumped over the dead body into the hallway and ran toward the rear of the house. The other Federals hesitated to fire at him for fear of shooting each other, and in this way the general made his escape across the back porch of the residence and out into the darkness.

One of his fellow officers, hearing the firing, had jumped out through the window of an adjoining room. General Lyon, in order to stampede the Federal troops which were around the house as he gained the yard, shouted: "Surround them, men, and capture all of them!" The sudden firing, the death of the officer, and the clatter of horses in rapid movement, which was heard only a short distance down the road, as well as the command of General Lyon to surround and capture the enemy, impressed the Federals that they had fallen into a trap and caused them to retreat precipitately. Taking advantage of the situation, Lyon and his companion escaped.

The record in the War Department at Washington bears this note: "Sergeant Arthur P. Lyon, Company A, Fifteenth Pennsylvania Cavalry, killed on the morning of January 15th by the rebel General Lyon, after he had taken him prisoner."

[12] *Official Records,* vol. xxxix, part i, p. 91.

and moved out in the direction of Brice's. With fateful leisure the infantry cooked their breakfast, and did not march until seven o'clock. The advance guard of Waring's brigade of Grierson's division encountered the Confederate outposts at the Tishomingo Creek bridge, drove these away, reached Brice's Crossroads at 9.45, and pursued the flying Confederates, who, turning to the left at Brice's, ran in the direction of Baldwyn. Along this road Waring proceeded for a mile until he came to the edge of a field through which the road runs, and here he encountered the advance of Lyon's brigade, which had just arrived upon the opposite side of this clearing about four hundred yards distant.

Two companies of Faulkner's Kentuckians, under Captain H. A. Tyler, formed Lyon's advance, and by a dashing charge had not only developed Waring's brigade, but a battery of artillery, which, being in position, opened upon Tyler's troopers and drove them rapidly back upon the main column.

By ten o'clock, when Lyon had thrown out his skirmishers, Forrest in person had come up with his escort, took command of Lyon's troops, which numbered eight hundred riflemen, and opened the famous battle of Brice's Crossroads, which took place in Lee County, Mississippi, on the 10th of June, 1864. It has passed into history as one of the most signal victories of the Civil War, considering the forces engaged. On this field General Forrest displayed not only that bulldog tenacity of purpose which characterized his aggressive method of warfare, but his remarkable ability as a strategist and those original methods of fighting which then won success and have since attracted the closest attention of students of military science.

The contending forces were: on the Union side, 3200 cavalry and 4500 infantry, with 22 pieces of artillery, commanded by General Samuel D. Sturgis; on the Confederate side, 4713 mounted troops, with 12 pieces of artillery, under General N. B. Forrest.[13]

At Brice's the main highway, leading from Memphis to Ripley, and on in a direction slightly east of south to Fulton in Mississippi, intersects almost at a right angle another important road leading from Corinth through Rienzi, Booneville, Baldwyn, and in a southwesterly direction to Pontotoc.

With the exception of two or three cleared patches of land, not exceed-

---

[13] The artillery companies are not included in this enumeration. These would bring the Union strength to about 8000, and the Confederate to about 4875.

ing six acres in extent, immediately around Brice's house, the country, which is only slightly undulating, for a mile in every direction was at the time of the battle not only heavily timbered, but there was an undergrowth of blackjack and scrub oak so dense that in places the troops could with difficulty force their way through, and, being then in full leaf, it was possible to approach within a few yards without being seen. About one mile northeast of Brice's, the Corinth road, with a worm fence on either hand for about a quarter of a mile, passed through a field, to the outskirts of which on all sides the dense undergrowth extended. This field was enclosed by a heavy rail fence reinforced on top with poles and brushwood. About the same distance on the highway leading from Brice's toward Ripley and Memphis the roadbed descended some twenty feet into the Tishomingo Creek bottom, along which stream there was a large cornfield, at that time in cultivation, and here this sluggish stream was spanned by a small wooden bridge.

Grierson, satisfied that the Confederates were in considerable strength, dismounted Waring's brigade (1450 strong), which he posted behind the fence in the edge of the dense timber, about equally divided on the north and south side of the road along which Forrest was advancing. Two rifle guns and two howitzers were thrown into position on a slight elevation just behind his line, and 100 picked men armed with revolving rifles were sent forward and concealed in the fence corners of the lane about a hundred yards in advance of his main line.

To the right of Waring was dismounted Grierson's other brigade under Winslow (numbering 1750), and the extreme right of this portion of the Union line was slightly "refused," or drawn back, in the direction of Brice's house. It will be seen that at this critical moment (for General Forrest) General Grierson had on the field 3200 cavalry, with four pieces of artillery in position and six others in reserve, confronted four hundred yards away by 800 mounted troops of Lyon's brigade, with the escort company of 85 men, and Gartrell's company, 50 strong, and with no Confederate artillery within eight miles.

Forrest was naturally an offensive fighter. He rarely stood to receive an attack. If his troops were mounted and the enemy moved first upon him, he always advanced to meet their charge. In a memorable interview with a Federal officer he said he would "give more for fifteen minutes of bulge on the enemy than for a week of tactics." He believed that one man in motion was worth two standing to receive an attack.

When he realized how strong the enemy in his immediate front was, his chief anxiety was that they might charge in force and run over his small command. Rucker was still two miles in the rear and Johnson was yet behind him. He immediately had Lyon's troops dismounted and thrown into line, and their position behind the fence strengthened by

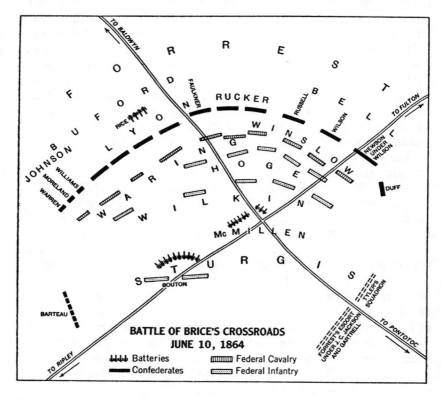

BATTLE OF BRICE'S CROSSROADS
JUNE 10, 1864

Batteries   Federal Cavalry
Confederates   Federal Infantry

brush and logs. To prevent Grierson from attacking, it was important to make a show of force, and with characteristic effrontery, having alternate panels of the worm fence thrown down, he ordered Lyon to make a demonstration by advancing from the edge of the woods into the open field. Lyon threw out a double line of skirmishers and marched boldly toward the enemy's position.

That Forrest's advance was "pure bluff" should have been clear to

Grierson, for Lyon's right just reached the Baldwyn road, while his left extended only a little beyond the junction of Waring's and Winslow's brigades. He was thus widely overlapped on either flank. Major E. Hunn Hanson of Waring's brigade says of this movement: "The Confederate line advancing was shorter than our own, their left ending in front of the left and centre of Winslow's brigade."[14]

With artillery and small arms the Union line opened upon the Confederates, who kept up their feigned attack for about an hour, when they withdrew without confusion to the edge of the woods from which they had started, and there resumed their position behind the layouts.

It was at this moment that Colonel E. W. Rucker, with his brigade of 700 mounted men, came on the scene. When within two miles of Lyon's position, hearing the cannonade, he put spurs to his horse and went rapidly forward with his hardy riders to the relief of his chieftain. Forrest at once dismounted the Seventh Tennessee regiment and Chalmers's Eighteenth Mississippi battalion of Rucker's command, placing them in line to the left of Lyon's troops, opposing the center of Winslow's brigade. The Eighth Mississippi, under Duff, was kept mounted, and thrown well over to the left toward the Guntown road to protect that flank of the Confederates from being turned. All told, the Confederates now had on the field 1635 men, with Grierson's division, 3200 strong, in line of battle opposing them.

Forrest again ordered his lines forward, with the same purpose for which the original attack was made, and after some sharp firing, although not at close range, the Confederates again retired. Chalmers's battalion, mistaking the object of the movement, had advanced too far to the front and received an enfilading fire from the right of Winslow's line, which threw them into confusion, but they rallied on the main Confederate line. As the troops came back a second time, Colonel W. A. Johnson arrived with 500 Alabamians, being that portion of his brigade whose horses had not given out in the forced march they had just made from northern Alabama. These troops Forrest directed to dismount, take position on Lyon's right, and move forward to engage the attention of the left of the Union line. After some desultory fighting, lasting not longer than five minutes, Johnson also retired.[15]

It was now about eleven o'clock, and although Bell's brigade, which

[14] *Battles and Leaders of the Civil War,* vol. iv, p. 420.
[15] *Ibid.,* vol. iv, p. 420.

numbered more than the Confederate troops at the front, and the artillery under Morton were not within supporting distance, Forrest determined to close in with Grierson in deadly earnest. He rode hurriedly along his entire line with words of encouragement to his troops, telling them that he expected every man to move forward when the signal was given. It was not to be a feint, but desperate work, and at close quarters. At the sound of the bugle the dismounted troopers sprang from the edge of the timber, leaped through the fence, and with a wild yell rushed into the open space toward the Union line. Such was their eagerness that the commands seemed to vie with each other as to which should first reach their antagonists. The men of Waring and Winslow seemed imbued with the same desperate purpose, for they stood their ground manfully, their repeating rifles crackling away in deafening roar, first at a distance, and then, as the lines came clashing together, into the very faces of the Confederates.

It fell to the gallant Rucker to make the first impression upon the Union position. At the head of the Seventh Tennessee and Chalmers's battalion, he swept onward with such impetuosity that he carried his part of the line fully one hundred yards in advance of Lyon and Johnson. Concentrating his fire on this part of the Confederate line, Waring had hoped to check or break it here, and when, under the fearful ordeal, it wavered for a moment, he sprang forward with two of his regiments to drive it from the field. To make assurance doubly sure, this vigilant officer brought up the Second New Jersey and the Seventh Indiana to fill the gap made by his countercharge and to reinforce his line. It was a brave and desperate venture, and worthy of the brave Waring. But Rucker's men were not to be denied. As the Union troops rushed forward, he shouted to his Southerners to draw their six-shooters and close with them hand to hand, and in one of the most fiercely contested short encounters of the war the Federals were finally forced to retire. The desperate character of this attack, and the obstinate resistance with which it was met, may be appreciated from an account by a participant, in J. P. Young's *History of the Seventh Tennessee Cavalry:*

The Federals occupied a wood on the far side of the field behind a rail-fence, greatly strengthened with logs and brush piled up against it. It was very hot and sultry when the command was given, and as we approached the fence seemed ablaze with crackling breech-loaders. The fire was so terrific that the regiment staggered for a moment, and some of the men fell flat upon the earth for protection. They again pushed forward, reached the fence, and began to pull the brush away in order to close with the Federals. So close was this struggle that guns once fired were not reloaded, but used as clubs, and pistols were brought into play, while the two lines struggled with the ferocity of wild beasts. Never did men fight more gallantly for their position than did the determined men of the North for this black-jack thicket on that hot June day. Sergeant John D. Huhn, of Company B, being a few feet in advance, came face to face with a Federal, presented his gun, and ordered the Union soldier to throw his weapon down. Several Federal soldiers rushed to the rescue of their comrade. With clubbed guns they broke Sergeant Huhn's arm and struck him over the head until he fell senseless. Privates Lauderdale and Maclin, of the Seventh Tennessee, ran to his aid, shot two of his stout-hearted assailants, and drove the others away with clubbed guns.

Of these attacks Colonel George E. Waring, Jr., says: "They were exceedingly fierce. The first assault was repulsed. The second one, after a hand-to-hand fight, was successful, and forced back my right, although the whole Second New Jersey and the Seventh Indiana were brought into action. After falling back a short distance I succeeded in forming a second line, which was held until the infantry came up to relieve my command, the men being much fatigued and out of ammunition."[16]

Forrest had only 2080 men on the field at that moment, and as every regiment but one was fighting dismounted, deducting the troops left with the horses, he had actually engaged in this fierce and successful attack not more than 1700 troops. He had strengthened his center, and, while the enemy's flanks were strongly assailed, he had broken through the Union line at this point. Just as this was accomplished, Johnson and Lyon, with equal courage, had closed in with the left of the Federal forces, while Duff's Mississippi regiment, mounted, on the extreme Confederate left, was vigorously engaged in holding the attention of the extreme right of Grierson's line. As Waring's center gave way, the gallant W. A. Johnson and his Alabamians advanced so rapidly and eagerly that he had gained a point fully halfway between his original position and the road leading from Ripley to Brice's, along which the infantry coming to reinforce Grierson was now advancing.

Still pushing onward, Rucker, leading this brilliant assault mounted, was too fair a target to escape. Several bullets passed through his cloth-

[16] *Official Records,* vol. xxxix, part i, p. 132.

ing; his horse, five times wounded, fell at last from a mortal shot. His rider received a bullet in the abdomen, which, though painful, was fortunately not fatal; nor did he yield his position at the head of his troops until the field was won.

The Union cavalry was now beaten at all points of the line, and by 12:30 Forrest had carried out the first part of his program—namely, that he would have their cavalry whipped by the time the infantry could get up.

At ten o'clock in the morning, when Forrest came on the field, he dispatched Major Charles W. Anderson, of his staff, toward Booneville with the order, "Tell Bell to move up fast and fetch all he's got," and for Morton to bring the artillery on at a gallop. Nor had he forgotten the famous movement upon the flank and rear of his opponent which he always employed, and which in all probability was one of the chief factors in his wonderful success. He directed General A. Buford (his division commander) to take Colonel C. R. Barteau's Second Tennessee regiment of Bell's brigade, when it should have arrived within five miles of the battlefield, and to proceed across the country through the woods and byways until he struck the road over which Sturgis would pass from Stubbs's to the crossroads. Barteau says: "My instructions were to take my regiment, numbering then 250 men, across the country by out-of-the-way routes, to slip in upon the Federal flank and rear, and to attack them in co-operation with Forrest's force in front."[17]

How well Barteau did his work and what commotion he caused in the Union lines will appear in the course of the narrative.

When the Confederates were first encountered, General Grierson had sent a courier to Sturgis, who was then some six miles back, for reinforcements, and this request was repeated with greater urgency when Rucker and Johnson came on the field and joined hands with Lyon in their desperate onslaught. It was, however, not until twelve o'clock that the Union commander in person came upon the scene, and more than an hour later when the head of the infantry column began to appear. These had been urged forward as fast as the condition of the road and the extreme heat would permit.

Colonel Hoge, who led the advance brigade of infantry, says: "It was impossible to keep up the rapid gait. I received a peremptory order to move forward rapidly, as the enemy was gaining ground, and the only

[17] Diary of Colonel C. R. Barteau, in possession of the author.

thing that would save us was the infantry. Three-quarters of a mile from the field I received an order from Colonel McMillen in person to move forward at double quick, which was done."[18] Coming upon the scene, Hoge's brigade, the One Hundred and Thirteenth, One Hundred and Eighth, Ninety-fifth, and Eighty-first Illinois Infantry, with Battery B of the Second Illinois Artillery (four guns), were immediately thrown into line, their battery being placed at Brice's house.

These reinforcements had not all formed in line before the first brigade, under Colonel A. Wilkins, also arrived. The Ninety-fifth Ohio, One Hundred and Fourteenth Illinois, Ninety-third Indiana, and Seventy-second Ohio Infantry were thrown into line at points most needed, while Mueller's section of the Sixth Indiana battery, reinforced by Chapman's full battery, were posted on an eminence in the rear of Brice's house. Battery E of the First Illinois Light Artillery and the Nineteenth Minnesota Artillery were held in reserve at the cross roads. Thirty-six hundred Union infantry, who as yet had not fired a shot, with three batteries of artillery additional, had come upon the scene, reinforcing Grierson's division, which Forrest had already beaten, and this entire force was confronted by the two thousand Confederates which General Forrest had at hand. Behind this bulwark of infantry the Federal troopers, exhausted and beaten, mounted their horses and took refuge, some even quitting the field, as the official records show, "without orders." Still back of these, and then in sight, was another infantry brigade of colored troops, with artillery under Colonel Bouton, held in reserve.

In crescentic line, and this in some portion of double formation, the Federal army now extended from well north of the Baldwyn road across to, and some two hundred yards beyond or west of, the road from Ripley to Guntown. At this propitious moment for the success of Forrest's battle, just as the Federal infantry were swinging into line, Morton came up with the artillery, and at his heels were Generals Buford and Tyree H. Bell, with the latter's full brigade of fresh troops, which within the last six months had been recruited within the Union lines in west Tennessee. The artillery consisted of Morton's and Rice's battery, which had traveled eighteen miles since daylight over roads so muddy that for much of the distance it was with great difficulty the horses could drag the pieces along. For the last six miles it required the most vigorous urging with whip and spur to push them forward in a trot.

[18] *Official Records*, vol. xxxix, part i, p. 119.

To the right of the road from Baldwyn, as Morton advanced in rear of Lyon's position, his batteries were brought into action, and opened with telling effect. General Sturgis says of this particular period of the engagement: "Finding that our troops were being hard pressed, I ordered one section to open on the enemy's reserve. Their artillery soon replied, and with telling accuracy, every shell bursting over and in the immediate vicinity of our guns."[19]

With fatal precision, scarcely excelled by the sharpshooter with his Whitworth, globe-sighted rifle, Captain John W. Morton, the famous young artillerist who had celebrated his twenty-first birthday on the bloody field of Chickamauga, with clear eye and steady heart was sending his shells with deadly purpose right to the spot.

Placing Buford in command of the right wing, where Johnson and Lyon were operating, Forrest, with Bell's troops, moved to the Confederate left and dismounted to the left of Rucker, extending his now strengthened line westward of the road leading from Brice's to Guntown.

Still farther to the Confederate left, mounted and guarding that wing, and ready to swoop around and upon the Union flank and rear, were two companies of Kentuckians, upon which, under their dashing leader, Captain H. A. Tyler, Forrest knew he could rely for most desperate work when the occasion offered. The other mounted companies, his famous escort, under Captain Jackson, and Gartrell's Georgians, on headquarters duty with Forrest, were kept immediately with the general.

The two opposing armies now faced each other for the supreme effort. About 8000 Federal soldiers, with twenty-two pieces of artillery, confronted Forrest, who, with an audacity born of supreme confidence in his men as well as in himself, moved forward to attack them. As most of the Confederates fought dismounted, deducting those left with the horses in the rear, the Confederate commander could not have carried into action in this desperate encounter over 3300 troops, with twelve pieces of artillery—a proportion of less than one to two.

For some thirty minutes the sounds of war had ceased. A rifle here and there from some sharpshooter or venturesome skirmisher spoke out in vicious challenge, but the wild fusillade and the crackle and roar of hundreds and thousands of guns no longer swept to and fro along the

[19] *Ibid.*, p. 92.

double rainbow of men in deadly earnest for the undoing of each other. It was the calm before the storm—the ominous silence which precedes the cloudburst and the angry onslaught of the winds. The atmosphere was heavy with humidity, the day depressing and intensely hot. Not a cloud was in the sky to shield friend or foe from the burning rays of the sun. Nothing but the thick foliage intervened, and this was motionless, for not a breath of air was stirring. Forrest, in apt phraseology, more forcible than elegant, had measured the heat when he said to Rucker that morning, in his forecast of the fight and of the day, "It is going to be as hot as hell." The troops, and animals as well, in both contending armies had suffered extremely, and a goodly number had fallen from exhaustion and sunstroke.

On the Union side, Grierson's cavalry had been fighting steadily from ten until two, and fighting is terribly exhausting work. They had been roughly handled to boot, and had a right to be wearied and worried. On the Confederate side, Johnson's, Rucker's, and Lyon's men, who had "knocked out" Waring's and Winslow's brigades, were equally fatigued. Bell's famous brigade, which had just arrived, had traveled twenty-five miles to reach the battlefield, and for the last fourth of the journey their horses had been urged to the full limit of their endurance and speed. The Union infantry had also suffered much—in fact, more than any of the troops upon the field. They had marched nine miles since seven o'clock, and under the urgent appeals of Grierson and Sturgis the last three miles had been made at a trot, and the final mile at a double-quick.

Forrest was fully alive to the conditions which, in spite of his numerical weakness, favored him. He had no thought of giving his enemy an opportunity to "catch their wind." He had informed Buford that everything was ready on the left, and that he must push his end of the line (the right) and engage as much as possible the attention of the enemy in that direction. He added that they were massing in front of him, and that their left would not offer as much resistance as he and Bell would encounter. Johnson, on the extreme right of the Confederate line, was urged to crowd in as closely as possible on the road leading from Ripley to Brice's.

The two Federal brigades of infantry under Hoge and Wilkins had scarcely effected their alignment when over to their left the rifles of Johnson and Rucker told them the fight had reopened, and at this moment everything in the Confederate line of battle moved to the front. There was now no open country except a few acres immediately about Brice's house. Through the thick and almost impenetrable undergrowth, just where Hoge had formed his sturdy Westerners in double array, both ranks lying prone upon the ground for concealment as well as protection, there came with guns trailing and bodies bent as close to the earth as possible the rustling sound of a moving body of men among the foliage as with difficulty they pushed their way forward. These were the Tennesseeans, as stanch and brave a set of men as ever served in war, under Tyree H. Bell, the Blücher of this hard-fought field. When within only a few paces of the Federal line, which as yet they could not see, the rifles of Hoge's infantry burst forth, a withering flash and murderous roar into the very faces of the Confederates. Under this fierce and sudden fire, which inflicted serious loss, a part of Bell's men gave way. Taking quick advantage of the momentary confusion he had caused, Hoge, with great gallantry, believing that the entire line of the enemy would yield if a general advance was made, ordered his whole force forward, directing his attack principally on the right of Bell and the left of Rucker's position.

Forrest, knowing the heavy fighting would be just at this point, had remained with the troops, and, seeing the disaster which now threatened him, dismounted from his horse, called to his two escort companies to dismount and hitch their horses to the bushes, and with these daring fighters gathered about him he rushed into the thickest of the fray, pistol in hand, to take his place in the front rank with his men. With equal dash and courage, Bell did the same; and with such examples and under such leadership the Tennesseeans quickly rallied, and, being reinforced by Lieutenant Colonel D. M. Wisdom, who with 280 men of Newsom's regiment had been held in reserve behind this portion of the line, they checked the retreat and advanced again upon the enemy.

Arrested in front of Bell, the Federal infantry pushed on in gallant style against the thinner line of Rucker; but this sturdy fighter had no notion of yielding the position he had won after such a fierce struggle. He knew from the way the rifles were crackling on his left that Forrest was hard at work there and was holding his own. As the Federal infantry came on with bayonets fixed, Rucker shouted, "Kneel on the ground, men, draw your six-shooters, and don't run!" Against this plucky wall the onrushing Federals struck hard, but rebounded. They could not break through it, and in fierce and bloody hand-to-hand combat the bayonet was no match for the repeating pistol, and the Union troops gave way as the whole Confederate line rushed forward with irresistible force.

As the center of Hoge's line crumbled away in this terrific onslaught, Johnson, with Lyon's prompt aid, had pushed back the extreme left of McMillen's line until it was now doubled back upon the Ripley road. At this important juncture Forrest received a message from the ever-watchful Buford which was invaluable to him. From the open position occupied by this officer on the extreme right, he had observed a sudden movement of the Union cavalry from near Brice's house to the rear, and could now distinguish musketry off to his right in the direction of Tishomingo Creek. Barteau was there with the Second Tennessee. He had arrived just in the nick of time and had struck the rear and flank of Sturgis's column. The brilliant strategy of Forrest was now to prove its value in deciding the fate of the Union army. Of this moment Colonel Barteau says: "I succeeded in reaching the Federal rear just as the fighting seemed heaviest in front. I at once deployed my men in a long line, had my bugler ride up and down sounding the charge at different points, and kept up as big a show as I could and a vigorous fire upon the Federals until their complete rout was evident. I was in the flank and rear of their position when Waring's and Winslow's brigades came back."[20]

This brilliant movement, executed with vigor and precision, had, at this crisis of the battle, not only thrown the reserve brigade of infantry and the train guard into commotion, but had withdrawn from Forrest's immediate front practically all of Grierson's cavalry that could offer him effectual resistance.

Forrest's perception told him that the crisis of the day had come, and that now the battle must be won or lost. It was past four o'clock. For more than two hours these desperate men of either army had been in murderous strife at close range since Bell and Morton had arrived. With savage fierceness, against heavy odds, Forrest's men had fought, and it seemed that the extreme of human endurance had been reached.

Riding along the rear of the line, encouraging his troops by telling them that the enemy were giving way, that their rear was attacked by Barteau, and that only one supreme effort was necessary to sweep them

[20] Manuscripts in possession of the author.

from the field, he hastened to the position of Morton with the artillery, upon whom at this moment he greatly depended. As he rode up to Morton, whose guns were then in action, the position being one at close range to the enemy and of great exposure, the artillerist ventured to say to his general that it was too dangerous a place for him, and suggested that he should go to the rear a short distance, where it was safer. He noticed that Forrest was much exhausted, and was surprised that he yielded to the advice of his subordinate. Riding back some thirty or forty yards, he called Morton to him as he laid himself upon the ground at the root of a big tree.

Here he said to the artillerist that he believed he had the enemy beaten, and that while they were still holding on with considerable stubbornness near the crossroads, he felt convinced that one more vigorous charge along the whole line, in which the artillery should take an active part, would be successful. He said that he would order this charge within ten minutes, and directed him to take four guns, double-shotted with canister, and, as soon as the bugler sounded the charge, to hitch the horses to them, gallop forward as close as possible to the enemy, and open upon them at close range. The signal for Morton was the heavy firing on the right. Forrest then rode farther over to the right to give Buford his final instructions. General Buford said that when Forrest told him what part Morton was to play he suggested that it would be dangerous to send the guns forward without any support; but Forrest replied, "Buford, all the Yankees in front of us cannot get to Morton's guns."

After the battle and pursuit were over, and two days later when the artillerist was returning with his pets, Forrest rode up to him, laid his hand on his shoulder, and said, "Well, John, I think your guns won the battle for us." Flushing with pride at this great praise from the man he idolized, Morton said, "General, I am glad you think so much of our work, but you scared me pretty badly when you pushed me up so close to their infantry and left me without protection. I was afraid they might take my guns." To this Forrest replied as he rode away, "Well, artillery is made to be captured, and I wanted to see them take yours."

Hurrying back to Bell, he ordered Tyler, with his two companies of Kentuckians, Captain Jackson of the escort, and Captain Johnson, with Gartrell's Georgians, that when the firing became general along the line they must charge around the Federal right flank and into their rear, rush in, and engage at pistol range any Federal troops between their right and the Tishomingo Creek bridge.

Forrest's famous tactics were now to be demonstrated—namely, the fierce onslaught from the front, with a charge upon both flanks and in the enemy's rear by a few well-chosen and desperate horsemen. As Gaus's bugle sounded the charge, Buford and Lyon and Johnson went forward with the right of the Confederate line; in face of a tremendous discharge of small arms and artillery, and amid the wild yells of the successful Confederates, the Federal line gave way stubbornly for a little space, and then yielded in disorder. Morton, with his horses hitched to the guns, swept forward along the country road, so narrow that only four pieces could be employed, with such boldness that in all probability the Federal commander at this point felt he was heavily supported, and when within short range of the center and right of the Union line he made his double-shotted canister tell on their ranks with frightful effect. Rucker's final charge on the center and Bell's quick rush to the left carried away the last vestige of organization on the part of the Federals, and their line was at last irreparably broken.

Colonel McMillen, commanding the infantry, says:

> As the enemy on our right were being driven back by the Ninth Minnesota and Ninety-third Indiana, I directed Captain Fitch to put one section of his artillery into position on the Guntown road and sweep it with grape and canister. Soon after the left and left-centre gave back in considerable confusion, the rebels (Johnson and Lyon) following them in force up to the road over which we had advanced, and from which they were kept by the Seventy-second Ohio and Mueller's battery. I endeavored to rally the different regiments and get them to advance to their original position, but failed. I sent word to General Sturgis I was hard pressed, and unless relieved I would be obliged to abandon my position. I was informed that he had nothing to send me. I therefore determined to retire and form another line a short distance in the rear, to keep the enemy from the cross-roads until the artillery could be moved.

As the Federals retired, Lieutenants Haller and Mayson, under orders from Morton, pushed their guns still farther by hand along the narrow roadway to the front, and firing as they advanced. Coincident with this, Buford, Lyon, and Rucker closed in from all directions upon the Union forces, now in confusion, crowding them to the crossroads at

Brice's house, where three pieces of artillery were captured and turned upon the fleeing enemy.

General Sturgis, referring to this period of the engagement, says: "I now endeavored to get hold of the colored brigade which formed the guard of the wagon-train. While traversing the short distance to where the head of that brigade should be found, the main line began to give way at various points. Order soon gave way to confusion, and confusion to panic. . . . The army drifted toward the rear and was beyond control. The road became crowded and jammed with troops, wagons and artillery sank into the deep mud and became inextricable. No power could check the panic-stricken mass as it swept toward the rear."

The panic of the troops was not without effect upon the Union commander. Colonel D. C. Thomas testifies that General Sturgis at this period in the fight proposed to save himself by taking the Nineteenth Pennsylvania Cavalry as an escort, to turn off into some byway and make his escape.[21]

About one-quarter of a mile north of the crossroads, where the Fourth Iowa Cavalry of Winslow's brigade had dismounted, sent their horses across Tishomingo Creek, and were making a final and desperate stand, Colonel McMillen endeavored to stem the current of disaster by throwing the Fifty-fifth Colored Infantry across the line of retreat. The Fifty-ninth Colored Infantry and Lamberg's section of artillery were placed somewhat in rear of them, and for the same purpose; but the onsweeping tide of the Confederates was running high and could not be withstood. General Buford had pushed Johnson's Alabamians so far forward on the extreme Confederate right that they struck the flank of Bouton's Africans from the direction of Tishomingo Creek; and at the same moment, upon the extreme left of the Confederate line, the troopers of Forrest's escort, under Jackson and Gartrell, with Tyler's two Kentucky companies mounted, swept around the right of the Federal line and rode squarely into the colored infantry with their six-shooters just as Johnson's troops came in range and opened upon them from the other side. To add to their discomfiture, Morton and Rice, pushing their guns by hand, were crowding along the main road from Brice's to the bridge, and now, within gunshot range, rattled away with their charges double-shotted with canister.

Nothing could surpass the desperate earnestness of these heroic men

[21] *Official Records,* vol. xxxix, part i, p. 171.

who stood to their work throughout this hot and depressing day. Suffering so intensely with thirst, they drank the blackened, powder-stained water from the sponge buckets, which was being used to cleanse and cool the guns, rather than send one needed man away. Even some of the wounded refused to go to the rear.[22]

McMillen's forlorn hope was demolished so quickly that he scarcely checked the onward rush of Forrest's men.

Rearward of this position, across the sluggish Tishomingo Creek, there was a narrow wooden bridge, which had become hopelessly blocked by the overturning of a wagon and the impaction behind this of several other vehicles. Onto this bridge, clambering over the wreckage of wagons and the fallen horses struggling to free themselves, mad with fright, the fugitives rushed pell-mell, the soldiers pushing each other off into the stream on either side in their wild efforts to escape. Others, seeing the hopelessness of attempting to cross by the bridge, threw themselves into the creek and waded or swam across, while many were drowned or shot as they were floundering in the water.

The Union loss was fearful. Reaching the creek, the Confederates cleared the bridge by pushing the wagons and the dead or wounded animals into the stream.

Meanwhile a detachment of Forrest's escort under Lieutenant George L. Cowan had effected a crossing about a quarter of a mile below the bridge and, sweeping around upon the flank of the enemy, charged boldly in among the panic-stricken crowd of fugitives, and cut off and captured a large number of prisoners and some wagons. So far was Cowan within the Federal lines that he came in range of Morton's relentless guns, and it was only when the battle flag of the escort was waved that he was recognized and the firing in that direction ceased.

The sun was now just above the western horizon, but Forrest had no idea of calling off the chase. The men who had been detailed as horse-holders, and were therefore comparatively fresh, were hurried to the front, and under the personal leadership of Forrest and Buford went forward upon the heels of the beaten army. Two miles from the battlefield McMillen succeeded in rallying a portion of the first and second brigades under the command of the brave Colonel A. Wilkins,

---

[22] James Moran, a mere lad, who was badly wounded, when told by Captain Morton to go to the hospital, replied: "Captain, I don't want to go; I can stand it until we run 'em away."

who later fell on the bloody field of Harrisburg. This line, however, could not stand longer than to permit Bouton to pass through with his Africans, for Morton came upon the scene with two of his pieces, and after a single round the Federals vanished. From this point on resistance practically ceased.

Of the result of the fighting until after twelve o'clock Colonel Waring says:

It was seen at half-past twelve that our ammunition was reduced to five rounds per man; and when our battery had fired its last shot the infantry began to arrive, and then they came a regiment at a time, or only so fast as the Forrest mill could grind them up in detail. Little by little the enemy pressed upon us, gaining rod after rod of our position, until finally our last arriving troops, a splendid colored regiment, reached the field of battle at double quick, breathless and beaten by their own speed, barely in time to check the assault until we could cross the creek and move toward the rear. The retreat was but fairly begun when we came upon our train of two hundred wagons piled pell-mell in a small field and blocked in beyond the possibility of removal. The train was our tub to the whale; and while Forrest's men were sacking our treasures we had time to form for the retreat, more or less orderly according as we had come early or late upon the field.[23]

Major E. H. Hanson reports:

All through the night the beaten army kept on their way, reaching Ripley, twenty-two miles from the battle-field, on the morning of June 11th. During the retreat the enemy captured fourteen pieces of artillery, our entire train of two hundred and fifty wagons loaded with ammunition and ten days' rations. At Ripley an attempt was made to reorganize our troops into companies and regiments, but the enemy appeared on two sides before this could be accomplished, and we were only able to check them until the retreat could be resumed. It continued in this way to Collierville, Tennessee. The bitter humiliation of this disaster rankles after a quarter of a century. The enemy may have numbered three thousand five hundred or four thousand, but it must be reluctantly confessed that not more than this number is believed to have been in action. If there was, during the war, another engagement like this, it is unknown to the writer; and in its immediate results there was no success, among the many won by Forrest, comparable to that of Guntown.[24]

[23] *Whip and Spur.*
[24] *Battles and Leaders of the Civil War,* vol. iv.

An amusing incident of the flight of Sturgis's command is given by Colonel George E. Waring, Jr., who says:

Grierson ordered me to prevent the pushing ahead of the stragglers of the other brigades, who were to be recognized, he reminded me, by their wearing hats (mine wore caps). The order was peremptory, and was to be enforced at the cost of cutting the offenders down. We were all sleeping more or less of the time, but constantly some hatted straggler was detected pushing toward the front, and ordered back. Close to my right, and pushing slowly to the front, came a gray horse with a hatted rider, an India-rubber poncho covering his uniform. I ordered him back, and the adjutant, eager for the enforcement of the order, remonstrated at the man's disobedience. I ordered him again, but without result. The adjutant ejaculated, "Damn him, cut him down!" I drew my sabre, and laid its flat, in one long stinging welt, across that black poncho. "——! Who are you hitting?" Then we both remembered that Grierson, too, wore a hat, and I tender him here my public acknowledgment of his good-nature and generous silence.[25]

Forrest's men, who had done the fighting on foot, were allowed to rest until one o'clock, while the horse-holders kept hammering away at the fleeing enemy, to give them no respite. At 3 A.M. Buford in force came upon their rear in the Hatchie bottoms, and here the balance of the wagon train and fourteen pieces of artillery additional fell into the hands of the gallant Kentuckian. Four miles from Ripley, Grierson had rallied a forlorn hope, but, with the escort and the Seventh Tennessee alone, Forrest, leading the charge in person, attacked them and after a feeble resistance scattered them "like chaff before the winds."

All through the day and until nightfall on the 11th the pursuit was continued, and only closed when, near Salem, in sight of the home of his youth, Forrest, completely exhausted, was seized with a fainting spell, fell from his horse, and remained unconscious for nearly an hour, to the great alarm of his devoted followers.

The battle at Brice's Crossroads demonstrated the truth of the adage that "the battle is not to the strong." The Federals were not defeated for lack of courage, as the fighting qualities of these men, when properly handled, was in a succeeding engagement fully proven.

From ten until four, beneath the fierce heat of a Southern sun, the men of Alabama, Mississippi, Kentucky, and Tennessee had struggled

[25] *Whip and Spur.*

in desperate and often hand-to-hand conflict with the sturdy soldiers of Indiana, Illinois, Minnesota, Iowa, and New Jersey; and while there can be no doubt that great credit was due to the splendid fighting qualities of the men under Forrest, and to his officers, as determined and courageous as himself, nothing on that day, and against such odds, could have saved his army from defeat and destruction but the marvelous genius of the "unlettered soldier."

He had fought on the field a body of veteran troops which greatly outnumbered him and were, withal, advantageously posted, as he had been the assailant from the beginning. To reach the battlefield the Federals had only nine miles to march; the greater portion of Forrest's command had covered twenty-five miles, and his artillery had made eighteen miles before they came into action. The vigorous and tireless pursuit was as wonderful as the victory on the field. It seems almost incredible that men could have endured what this little army of Forrest's endured on those two days of June.

The artillery of Morton and Rice had started from Booneville at 5 A.M. on the 10th, and marched eighteen miles, and then for five hours had been engaged without intermission in desperate conflict; had followed the enemy from the field until well into the night, and, after seven hours of rest, pushed onward, keeping up with, and at times even in front of, the advance guard of Forrest's cavalry; had reached Salem on the night of the 11th, making sixty-one miles in thirty-eight hours, besides fighting for five hours of that time, a record possibly without a parallel in artillery fighting. So energetic had been Morton's pursuit that fifteen horses fell dead in harness from exhaustion.

Bell's brigade, at 4 A.M. on the 10th, had left Rienzi, marched twenty-five miles to the battlefield, fought from 2 P.M. until 5 P.M., pursued the enemy from the field until 7, and at 8 P.M. on the night of the 11th camped at Davis's Mill, twelve miles north of Salem, having made eighty miles in forty hours.

No wonder the army of Sturgis had melted away in a wild stampede, until it was everyone for himself. Few escaped, excepting those who had horses, or who cut them loose from the wagons and the artillery. The infantry suffered most heavily in killed and captured, while the colored troops, believing that no quarter would be shown them, scattered in all directions, taking to the woods and bottoms for safety. On the morning of the 11th, at Ripley, General Sturgis writes:

"Nothing was left but to keep in motion." On the 12th he was at Collierville, after a run of forty-eight hours with scarcely a halt, and on the 13th, at 9 A.M., a fragment of his fleeing command was at White's station. It had taken his army nine days to march from this point to Brice's Crossroads. The return trip was made in sixty-four hours.

General Washburn says: "The expedition left the railroad terminus on June 1st, and reached Brice's Crossroads on June 10th. The force that escaped returned to this point in one day and two nights."

The Confederates lost heavily in killed and wounded. The report of the chief surgeon, Dr. J. B. Cowan, gives 493 killed and wounded. In Rucker's brigade the loss was 23 per cent, and in Lyon's command over 20 per cent were killed and wounded.

General Sturgis, in his official report, made on the 24th of June, gave his loss of killed, wounded, and missing, as 2240. The detailed reports of his brigade and regimental commanders show his loss to have been 2612.

General Forrest captured 250 wagons and ambulances, 18 pieces of artillery, 5000 stands of small arms and 500,000 rounds of small-arm ammunition, and all the enemy's baggage and supplies.

That the Federals threw away everything which would impede their flight is evident from the reports of the subordinate officers. Colonel George B. Hoge gives the original strength of his brigade at 1674, of which 748 were killed, wounded, and missing.[26] Of the remaining 926 who escaped, *only* 267 *had not thrown away their guns!*

In his official report General Sturgis says: "I need hardly add that it was with feelings of the most profound pain and regret that I found myself called upon to record a defeat and the loss and suffering incident to a reverse. Yet there is some consolation in knowing that the army fought nobly while it did fight, and only yielded to overwhelming numbers. The strength of the enemy is estimated by the most intelligent officers as fifteen to twenty thousand men."[27] He adds: "A very intelligent sergeant who was captured says the enemy had actually engaged 12,000 men, and had two divisions of infantry in reserve."

The overthrow of Sturgis caused scarcely less anxiety at the headquarters of Generals Grant and Sherman, and at Washington, than

[26] *Official Records,* vol. xxxix, part i, p. 120.
[27] *Ibid.,* p. 95.

was felt by General Washburn at Memphis. Grant says, in his *Memoirs:* "Farther west, also, the troubles were threatening. Some time before, Forrest had met Sturgis, in command of some cavalry in Mississippi, and handled him very roughly, gaining a great victory over him. This left Forrest free to go almost where he pleased, and to cut the roads in rear of Sherman, who was then advancing. Sherman was abundantly able to look after the army that he had immediately with him, and all of his military division, so long as he could communicate with it, but it was my place to see that he had the means with which to hold his rear. Two divisions, under A. J. Smith, had been sent to Louisiana some months before. Sherman ordered these back, with directions to attack Forrest."[28]

General Sherman, who on the 23rd of May had addressed the governors of Missouri, Indiana, Iowa, and Wisconsin, calling for militia to be sent to Memphis to co-operate with him in preventing Forrest and Lee from swinging over against his communications,[29] was now more than ever upset. The anxiety which he felt is shown in a dispatch to General Thomas, dated June 9th, which says: "I cannot hear of Forrest, though I believe the expedition which left Memphis June 1st, composed of three thousand cavalry and five thousand infantry, will give him good employment." Again, on the 13th, to Halleck, he insists that "there are troops enough in Tennessee to watch Forrest, should he make his appearance there, as Johnston doubtless calculates."

Stanton, Secretary of War, on June 14th telegraphed General Sherman that he had just received the report of the battle between Sturgis and Forrest, "in which our forces were defeated with great loss. Washburn estimates our loss at not less than three thousand. Forrest is in pursuit."[30]

Sherman replied that he had just received the same news of the defeat of Sturgis, "whose chief object was to hold Forrest there to keep him off our road. Of course it is to be deplored, but we must prepare for all contingencies. I have ordered A. J. Smith not to go to Mobile, but to go to Memphis and to defeat Forrest at all cost. Forrest has only his cavalry; I cannot understand how he could defeat Sturgis

[28] *Memoirs of U. S. Grant,* vol. ii, p. 306.
[29] *Official Records,* vol. xxxviii, part iv.
[30] *Ibid.,* p. 474.

with eight thousand men." On the 15th he adds to Stanton: "I will have the matter of Sturgis critically examined, and if he should be at fault he shall have no mercy at my hands. I cannot but believe he had troops enough. I know I would have been willing to attempt the same task with that force; but Forrest is the devil, and I think he has got some of our troops under cower. I have two officers at Memphis who will fight all the time—A. J. Smith and Mower. The latter is a young brigadier of fine promise, and I commend him to your notice. I will order them to make up a force and go out to follow Forrest to the death, if it costs ten thousand lives and breaks the Treasury. There never will be peace in Tennessee until Forrest is dead!" And with an evident air of satisfaction this bloody-minded warrior closes this dispatch by saying: "We killed Bishop Polk yesterday and have made good progress to-day."[31]

The disturbance of the various plans of campaign which were then in operation as the result of this victory of Forrest's is further shown from General McPherson's dispatch to General Dodge on the 15th of June, saying that on account of the defeat of Sturgis by Forrest, Colonel Howe would remain at Decatur with his brigade until further orders.

Sherman, on the 16th of June, dispatched Stanton that he would send as large a force as he could get on Forrest's trail and harass him and the counties through which he passed. "We must destroy him if possible." On the 20th of this month he telegraphed to Rousseau, at Nashville, that he had determined to wait to see what Forrest would do, adding: "I propose to keep him occupied from Memphis. He whipped Sturgis fair and square, and now I have got against him A. J. Smith and Mower, and will let them try their hands."

At the close of this campaign, on the 28th of June, General Forrest issued an address to his soldiers, recapitulating their achievements in the defeat of William Sooy Smith, the successful expedition into west Tennessee, with the capture of Union City and Fort Pillow, and the overthrow of Sturgis's command at Tishomingo Creek.[1] While these were triumphs of which any general might well feel a great and just pride, between the lines of this eloquent address one can recognize the cleverness of the diplomatist. Lauding to the skies their past performances, this skillful leader of men no doubt

[31] *Ibid.*, p. 480.

intended to stimulate his soldiers to further effort under his command. It has a touch of the old-fashioned Fourth-of-July oratory which was in vogue in the Southern states in the period preceding the Civil War. General Forrest was remarkable for his ready command of language.

This address, as well as all of his reports and addresses, was dictated by him to Major Charles W. Anderson, or some other member of his staff. Major Anderson states that often after the first draft of a report or address was made it would be read over to the general, who, although a man of limited education, would not only quickly detect a grammatical error, but would criticize and correct a phrase improperly constructed. His usual remark was, "That hasn't got the right pitch."

SIXTEEN

The Tupelo Expedition, July, 1864

O<small>N</small> JUNE 16th Sherman tele-
graphed Edwin M. Stanton, Secretary of War: "I have made necessary
orders, through General McPherson, to inquire well into the Sturgis
matter; also to send as large a force again as he can get on Forrest's
trail, and harass him and the country through which he passes. We
must destroy him if possible."

The undoing of Sturgis had for the second time thwarted Sherman's designs against Mobile. In a dispatch of this date to McPherson
he says: "We will not attempt the Mobile trip now, but I wish to
organize as large a force as possible at Memphis, with General A. J.
Smith or Mower in command, to pursue Forrest on foot, devastating
the land over which he has passed, or may pass, and to make the
people of Tennessee and Mississippi feel that although a bold, daring,
and successful leader, he will bring ruin and misery on any country
where he may pass or tarry. If we do not punish Forrest and the people
now, the whole effect of our vast conquest will be lost."[1]

The people and not Forrest were punished by this terrible policy of
General Sherman. True to his instructions, General Smith laid waste
this beautiful country, burning towns, private residences, as well as
granaries, ginhouses, and plantations. The city of Oxford and the
country around might well have stood for the picture of the abomina-
tion of desolation.

The expedition under Smith was only one of a series of movements
which were intended to hold Forrest away from Sherman. On June
28th General Canby telegraphed Major General H. W. Slocum at
Vicksburg that "Smith's expedition would move from Memphis early
in July, that a large cavalry force would leave the Mississippi River
near Baton Rouge, to operate against the Mobile and Ohio railroad,

[1] *Official Records*, vol. xxxix, part ii, p. 123.

while another invasion in the direction of Mobile will start about the 6th of July."

This same officer reports to the General of the Army of the Tennessee: "I had previously written to General Washburn that he should employ A. J. Smith's troops, and any other that he could reach, to pursue and if possible destroy all of Forrest's command. I have placed under his control all the militia of the Northwestern States that were ordered to report to me, and several regiments of old troops from Missouri. This will give Smith an effective force of 12,000 or 15,000 men, and leave a reserve of 5000 for other operations. I will start the expedition against Mobile four days later. A cavalry expedition will start at the same time from Vicksburg for the purpose of distracting the attention of the enemy from Smith's operations."[2]

Sherman, on the 30th of June, instructed Major General Rousseau, in middle Tennessee, as follows: "The movement that I want you to study and be prepared for is contingent on the fact that General A. J. Smith defeats Forrest, and holds him well in check; and after I succeed in making Johnston pass the Chattahoochee with his army, I want you to take twenty-five hundred good cavalry, with pack-mules, ammunition, etc., and two light Rodman guns, and start from Decatur to Blountsville, cross the Coosa at Ten Islands, thence rapidly to the railroad between Tuskegee and Opelika, tearing up the road and twisting the irons, threaten Columbus, Georgia, and then join me between Marietta and Atlanta."[3]

General Sherman lost no opportunity to impress upon General Mower, whom he considered one of his ablest men and best fighters, that his rapid promotion depended upon his destruction of Forrest's command and the death of its leader. From near Kennesaw, Georgia, he sent, on June 24th, the following message:

To Abraham Lincoln, President of the United States:
SIR—I have ordered General A. J. Smith and General Mower from Memphis to pursue and kill Forrest, promising the latter, in case of success, my influence to promote him to a major-general. He is one of the gamest men in our service. Should accident befall me, I ask you to favor Mower, if he succeeds in disposing of Forrest.

WILLIAM T. SHERMAN, Major-General.[4]

[2] *Ibid.,* p. 149.
[3] *Official Records,* vol. xxxviii, part ii, p. 910.
[4] *Ibid.,* vol. xxxix, part ii, p. 142.

While the great soldier of the Union cause was moving heaven and earth to keep the man he most dreaded from breaking in upon his rear, several of the most farsighted men of the Confederacy were in vain pleading with the government at Richmond to give up Mississippi, if necessary, for the time being, and place General Forrest in command of all the cavalry in the Department of the Army of Tennessee, to conduct the operations for the destruction of the railroads supplying Sherman's army. Unfortunately these suggestions did not proceed from sources calculated to influence President Davis, for among the chief movers in this matter were two men toward whom he entertained a bitter personal animosity.

The one was General Joseph E. Johnston, Sherman's most formidable antagonist in the brilliant strategic game which these two great soldiers were then playing in the remarkable campaign from Dalton to Atlanta. Johnston states that on June 13 and July 16, 1864, he suggested to the President of the Confederacy directly, and on four other occasions through General Bragg to Mr. Davis, that "an adequate force under the most competent officer in America for such service, General N. B. Forrest, be sent to operate against Sherman's communications." He says: "I did so in the confidence that this cavalry would serve the Confederacy far better by insuring the defeat of a great invasion than by repelling a mere raid."[5]

The other, a personage of scarcely less importance, one of the ablest of the war governors of the South, Joseph E. Brown of Georgia, in a formal document addressed to Mr. Davis, requested that General Forrest be placed in command of all the cavalry, with a special view of operating with the army of General Johnston. His request having been refused, in a telegram to the President of the Southern Confederacy, dated June 5, 1864, he says:

> I regret that you cannot grant my request. I am satisfied that Sherman's escape with his army would be impossible if ten thousand good cavalry under Forrest were thrown in his rear this side of Chattanooga, and his supplies cut off. The whole country expects this, although points of less importance should be for a time overrun in the destruction of Sherman's supplies. Destroy these, and Atlanta is not only safe, but the destruction of the army under Sherman opens Kentucky and Tennessee to us. Your information as to the relative strength of the armies in northern Georgia

[5] *Battles and Leaders of the Civil War*, vol. iv, p. 276.

cannot be from reliable sources. If your mistake should result in the loss of Atlanta, and the capture of other strong points by the enemy in this State, the blow may be fatal to our cause, and remote posterity may have reason to mourn over the error.

Mr. Davis did not delay his reply to this "impertinent" suggestion of a civilian, for on the date of its reception he answered by wire in a manner which displayed his feelings toward the Governor of Georgia and his indignation at and contempt for the criticism that this state officer had ventured to make upon his conduct of the war:

Your telegram received. Your dicta cannot control the distribution of troops in different parts of the Confederate States. Most men in your position would not assume to decide on the value of the services to be rendered by troops in distant positions. I would be glad to know the source of your information as to what the whole country will expect and posterity will judge.

General Howell Cobb, of Georgia, in July, 1864, also joined in this suggestion to Mr. Davis, in a letter addressed to Mr. James A. Seddon, Secretary of War: "Allow me to express to you an opinion that the defence of Atlanta, Georgia, and the certain defeat and destruction of Sherman's army are involved in some movement to be made by Forrest, if possible, on Sherman's line of communication. Unless it is done, I see no end to the slow process of Sherman's advance through Georgia. If his communications were cut for ten days, his army would be destroyed. To effect such a result, could we not afford to uncover for a short time the country protected by Forrest?"

General Joseph Wheeler, who at that time was in command of all the cavalry operating with Johnston's army, gave once more a demonstration of his nobility of character and unselfish devotion to the Southern cause by endorsing General Johnston's recommendation. It was he, in fact, who made the suggestion to General Johnston that General Forrest be placed in command of the cavalry, offering his co-operation in any capacity Johnston might desire.[6]

Meanwhile the subject of these dispatches, unconscious of the importance which in the high places was being attached to his movements, found himself with plenty to do where he was. In A. J. Smith, he was at last confronted by the ablest soldier who so far had been pitted

[6] Personal communication to the author from General Joseph Wheeler in 1897.

against him, a man who evidently had made a careful study of his adversary, and, while fully appreciating his great ability, had with unusual discernment discovered his weakest point. Smith was ably seconded by Brigadier General Joseph A. Mower. Together these two presented a combination well calculated to give Forrest such a fight as he had never before experienced. There was to be no repetition of the Sooy Smith or the Sturgis disasters. These men marched forth determined not to be surprised, and to fight, and succeeded admirably in their effort. They did not accomplish all that they had intended, or all that was expected of them by the general who, from the battlefields of northern Georgia, was watching with intense interest the progress of their expedition. They wounded instead of killing their game.

There is a ring of evident satisfaction in Sherman's dispatch of the 2nd of July to Thomas, when he says, "I see Forrest is at Tupelo"; for he turns to Rousseau on the same date and advises him by telegraph: "Now is the time for the raid on Opelika. Forrest is in Mississippi, and Roddey has also gone there." To Grant, on the 12th of July, Sherman says: "I have now fulfilled the first part of the grand plan. Our lines are up to the Chattahoochee. Morgan failed in his Kentucky raid, and we have kept Forrest employed in Mississippi. The defeat of Sturgis was unfortunate; still, he kept Forrest away from us, and now A. J. Smith is out with a force amply sufficient to whip him."

This force, which marched from La Grange, near Memphis, on the 5th day of July, 1864, "amply sufficient to whip him," consisted of 3200 cavalry (under General Grierson), 11,000 infantry, 24 pieces of artillery, and 500 artillerists. Major General Andrew J. Smith, commanding the right wing of the Sixteenth Army Corps, was in chief command. The infantry comprised the first division of the Sixteenth Army Corps, Brigadier General Joseph A. Mower commanding; third division of the Sixteenth Army Corps, Colonel D. Moore commanding; first brigade of the United States Colored Troops, Colonel E. Bouton commanding.

The destination of Smith's expedition was the prairie country in the region of Okolona and West Point, in Mississippi. Its chief object was Forrest. It passed through Ripley on the 8th of July, meeting with no resistance beyond slight skirmishing with the vedettes and outpost detachments which Forrest kept always well in front of his main force as a part of his thorough system of observation. Marching from Ripley southward, toward New Albany and Pontotoc, crossing the Tallahatchie on the 9th of July at New Albany, General Smith moved without incident, camping, on the night of the 10th, five miles north of Pontotoc. After crossing the Tallahatchie, the wary commander of the Union expedition moved with the greatest possible caution. His main column was preceded by a line of battle fully a mile in length, while the cavalry was kept in heavy columns as flankers and in front. The rear was pro-

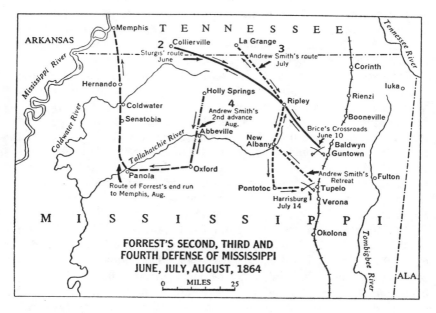

FORREST'S SECOND, THIRD AND
FOURTH DEFENSE OF MISSISSIPPI
JUNE, JULY, AUGUST, 1864

0   MILES   25

tected with a double guard of infantry, and the wagons were kept closed up between the infantry in front and rear.

On the morning of the 11th of July, as General Smith approached the town of Pontotoc, he met with the first serious resistance to his advance. Chalmers and Buford, now fairly well concentrated, were in his front. So formidable did this array seem to the cautious Union general that he did not advance more than two miles from Pontotoc in the direction of Okolona on this day. General Chalmers says: "I placed Barteau's regiment on the Tupelo road, and Rucker's brigade on the Cotton-Gin road, with orders to watch the Tupelo road and reinforce

Barteau if necessary. Lyon's and Mabry's brigades, under General Buford, were placed on the Okolona stage road, and McCulloch's brigade was stationed on the Harrisburg road. All these dispositions were communicated to Major-General Forrest."[7]

Brigadier General Buford, on the 10th, had been ordered by Forrest to send one hundred picked men to the rear of the enemy, to cut off his communications, and to make as much of a diversion as possible between him and his base of supplies. He says: "I immediately detached one hundred picked men under Captain H. A. Tyler, Company A, Twelfth Kentucky regiment. On Monday morning, the 11th, the enemy made his appearance. This force was admirably equipped, commanded by an officer of experience and skill, and moved with great caution, always prepared."

On Tuesday, the 12th of July, General Stephen D. Lee, commander in chief of this department, arrived on the field with Forrest, and to these officers General Buford reported the cautious advance of the formidable army under General Smith. On the morning of the 12th the Union commander moved forward, in the hope of being able to force his way to Okolona. He says:

> The enemy were discovered to be in force about nine miles from Pontotoc, on the opposite side of a low, swampy bottom, through which ran two creeks. This bottom was about a mile and a half in width, densely timbered, which the enemy has rendered almost impassable by felling trees across the road. I did not deem it prudent to attack from the front, and on the morning of the 13th I moved towards Tupelo, making nearly a right angle at Pontotoc, following the cavalry with the infantry and train, and leaving the colored brigade and the Seventh Kansas to bring up the rear. I then ordered in my skirmish-line on the Okolona road, and commenced to march towards Tupelo, a distance of about eighteen miles. While this march was in progress, there was almost continuous skirmishing from the front and rear of the column.

General Smith reports:

> Almost immediately upon leaving Pontotoc, skirmishing commenced in the rear; but as my object was to secure Tupelo, and thus gain possession of the railroad and have the opportunity to choose my own ground for the battle, I directed the column to keep well closed up, and to move steadily forward without halting, unless absolutely necessary. When we were within

[7] *Official Records,* vol. xxxix, part i, p. 325.

about six miles of Tupelo the enemy made a charge with four brigades of cavalry upon the train. A sharp fight occurred, lasting about half an hour. The enemy were repulsed. Our loss was twenty-seven mules killed, seven wagons broken by the carelessness of the teamsters and burned by my order.[8]

Lieutenant General Lee arrived on the field on the 12th and took command of all the forces. General Forrest says: "With Mabry's brigade, my escort, and Jeffrey Forrest's old regiment, I was ordered to attack and press upon the rear of the enemy. At the same time General Lee moved with Chalmers's and Buford's division on the right, with a view to attacking him in motion at every vulnerable point." As Forrest advanced, he found the enemy about a mile from Pontotoc, on the Okolona road and, after a short, brisk skirmish, drove him into Pontotoc, and then out eastward on the Tupelo road.

Taking advantage of every favorable position in his line of march, General Smith, with the rear guard, resisted the advance of the Confederates, and about ten miles east of Pontotoc he made a formidable stand and held Forrest in check until the latter brought up a battery of artillery, which compelled the Federal rear guard to abandon their position and fall rapidly upon their main column. It was evident from the rapid movement of General Smith's column at this time that he had no idea of stopping to fight short of Tupelo. Forrest says:

I had now driven the enemy ten miles, and, as his flanks had not been attacked, I was fearful he was being driven too rapidly. I therefore halted my command and waited the attack upon his flanks. In about an hour our guns opened upon him three miles ahead. I resumed the march and hurriedly pressed forward, and on reaching the ground I found that General Chalmers had dashed into the road, surprised the enemy, and had taken possession of his wagon-train. He, however, threw back a large force upon Chalmers, and forced him to retire, although not until he had killed and wounded many men and horses, which forced the enemy to abandon and burn several wagons, caissons, and ambulances. About this time heavy firing was heard still farther up in the direction of Tupelo, which admonished me that General Buford was also attacking the enemy's flank. As night approached, the enemy became more obstinate in his resistance, but I attacked his rear with renewed energy until nine o'clock, when I reached a point two miles from Harrisburg, where I was joined by my entire com-

[8] General Smith's report.

mand, which halted for the night. Being anxious to learn the exact position of the enemy, I moved Mabry's brigade forward, and opened with four pieces of artillery. At a late hour in the night, accompanied by one of my staff officers, I approached Harrisburg, and discovered the enemy strongly posted and prepared to give battle the next day.

The firing which Forrest had heard was from a vigorous dash made by General Chalmers upon the flank of Smith's column while in motion, about eight miles west of Tupelo. For a moment General Mower had relaxed the vigilance which had characterized his movements since crossing the Tallahatchie. It was observed by General Lee, who ordered Chalmers to attack the exposed position with Rucker's brigade. With Duff's Mississippians in advance, Rucker took temporary possession of one section of the train, killing a number of mules, which forced the Federals to abandon and burn several wagons, one caisson, and two ambulances; "but his infantry rallied, and by superior numbers forced us to retire."[9] The Confederates paid dearly for this bold attack.

General Smith reports: "Immediately after this attack I learned from General Grierson that he had possession of the town of Tupelo. I immediately passed the train to the front through the first division, and parked it about two miles west of Tupelo, at the same time forming line of battle, with the third division on the left of the road, making Pontotoc the objective point."

The position selected by General Smith was one admirably adapted for successful defense. His line of battle, running nearly north and south, extended along the crest of a low ridge, which formed the center of a large clearing or open field. From the summit of this elevation, looking nearly due west toward Pontotoc, the direction from which the Confederates would advance upon him, the surface of the ground gradually descended to the level of a small valley or swale, beyond which the country was an undulating woodland with scant undergrowth and fairly heavy timber. From the Federal line, which was a little more than a mile and a half in length, the distance to the edge of the timberland in front varied with the meanderings of the shallow ravine which marked the limit of the clearing. Just opposite their center it was about three hundred yards from the timber to the crest of the ridge, while the woods here were so open that the Confederates were

[9] Chalmers's report.

in plain view for the last five hundred yards of their approach. In other portions of the line the assailing troops were of necessity exposed to an artillery and small-arm fire for a distance varying from four hundred to one thousand yards.

During the night the Federal commander had taken the precaution to strengthen his position by constructing light breastworks of rails and other materials. The most commanding points had been chosen for the artillery, and by break of day the entire twenty-four guns were posted and ready for battle. The cavalry were deployed, one brigade on either wing of the Union line, and were for most of the time mounted. However, as the engagement progressed, detachments from this arm of the service were dismounted and hurried on foot to reinforce the infantry.

Between sundown and dark of the 13th, after the Confederates had encamped for the night, the scouts having reported that the Federals were bivouacking in line of battle about a mile in front, General Forrest determined to make a careful reconnaissance of their position. Greatly fatigued by the heavy work and intense heat of the day, he and General Lee had dismounted from their horses, and were conversing at some distance from their respective staffs. Lee was seated upon the ground, leaning against the trunk of a tree, while Forrest, in his shirtsleeves, having pulled off his coat and spread it on the ground, was lying down at full length.

Suddenly he started up, put on his coat, mounted his horse, and called to Lieutenant Samuel Donelson of his staff to mount and come with him. Riding through the woods, they made a wide detour, and in about an hour, or an hour and a half, it being by this time very dark, they came up well in the rear of the Federal army, and soon found themselves among the wagons where the Union teamsters were busily engaged feeding their animals. About a half-hour after they had started Forrest remarked to Donelson, "I have left my pistols." The lieutenant replied that he had one, and offered it to the general, who, however, declined, saying, "It doesn't matter much anyway. I don't think we will have any use for them." As it was so dark, the color of their uniforms could not be seen, and no notice was taken of the two horsemen as they deliberately passed along the rear of the Union encampment. Having satisfied himself as to the position of the enemy, Forrest then turned in the direction of his own camp.

They had proceeded about two hundred yards when they were suddenly halted by two Federal soldiers who were on picket. Riding directly up to these men, Forrest, in a tone of affected indignation, said, "What do you mean by halting your commanding officer?" and without other remark passed the sentries, who did not discover the ruse which had been practiced upon them until it was too late. Realizing the mistake they had made, they again challenged the horsemen, who by this time were some seventy or eighty yards away, and on account of the darkness could not now be seen. Anticipating that they would be fired at, Forrest and Donelson crouched down quickly upon their horses, put the spurs to them, and broke into a full run along the narrow roadway through the woods. The pickets fired, but the shots which came whizzing in that direction did no damage.[10]

Of this incident, Forrest in his report says: "At a late hour in the night, accompanied by one of my staff officers, I approached Harrisburg, and discovered the enemy strongly posted and prepared to give battle the next day."

By daylight on the morning of the 14th the Confederates, who had encamped for the night about two miles distant from Harrisburg on the Pontotoc road, were in motion in the direction of Tupelo. Almost immediately upon their advance they became engaged with the skirmishers of the wary Union commander, but these were gradually driven back until they retired within their fortified line.

As Generals Lee and Forrest came in sight of the formidable array upon the heights in their front, they were fully impressed with the strength of the position and the difficulties they must encounter in the effort to carry it by assault. It became a matter of serious discussion between them as to whether under the circumstances it would not be wiser to postpone the attack until General Smith should resume his line of march, when they might force him to battle under conditions less disadvantageous to the Confederates.

General Lee stated to Forrest that it was a matter of great importance that the force under General Smith should be dealt with vigorously and at once, so that he might be able to give much-needed attention to other portions of his department, which were then being heavily pressed.[11] A large force was at that moment threatening Mobile,

[10] Manuscript of Lieutenant Donelson, in possession of the author.
[11] Manuscript of Lieutenant General S. D. Lee, in possession of the author.

and from the direction of Vicksburg an expedition was advancing into his territory, while from northern Alabama a third invasion (under Rousseau) was about to descend upon him. He admitted that it would be safer to wait until the Federals in their immediate front were on the march, and then strike them, but that it was impossible to say how long the Union commander would remain in his present position, and that the circumstances he had just detailed would not admit of delay. He stated, in conclusion, that they would have to fight then and there, or he would be compelled to withdraw a portion of the troops which were now on the ground and ready for battle, in order to meet the other dangers which were imminent.

In view of these facts, General Forrest concurred in the attack, stating that all that could be done was to go forward and fight the enemy. This statement of General Lee is in accord with that made to Colonel C. R. Barteau by General Buford, who was present at this conference.[12] At the close of this interview General Lee offered to Forrest the command of all the forces on the field, agreeing to render him every assistance in his power. "I said to General Forrest that a large proportion of the troops now on the ground belonged to his immediate command, had served under him in his recent successful campaigns, and had just won the splendid victory at Brice's Crossroads, having beaten some of the troops that they would have to encounter to-day, and that, knowing Forrest better than myself, they would have more implicit confidence in his leadership. General Forrest, however, positively declined to take the command, saying that I was his senior, and that I should take the responsibility. I replied, 'Then let it be a fight to the bitter end.' "[13] It should be borne in mind that General Forrest was at that time ill in health and had requested Lee a fortnight earlier to relieve him from command.

From Tupelo, on June 28th, he wrote: "I am suffering with boils. If the enemy should move out, I desire you to take command of the forces. Our force is insufficient to meet this command. Can't you procure some assistance?"

General Lee then gave Forrest his choice of what part of the line he would care to direct personally during the battle. Forrest selected the extreme right, or Roddey's division, while General Lee,

[12] Manuscript of Colonel C. R. Barteau, in possession of the author.
[13] Manuscript of General Lee, in possession of the author.

placing Buford on the left, took his position near the center of the Confederate line, where he could observe the entire field. As had been shown, the Union forces in line of battle were not quite 15,000, with twenty-four pieces of ordnance. The Confederates numbered 9460 effectives, with twenty pieces of artillery. The composition of this force was as follows: Chalmers's division, composed of McCulloch's and Rucker's brigades, 2300; Buford's division, Bell's, Lyon's, and (temporarily) Mabry's brigades, 3200; Roddey's division, composed of Patterson's and Johnson's brigades, 1500; Beltzhoover's battalion of infantry, and the dismounted troopers of Gholson's and Neely's brigades, 2100; 360 artillerists with twenty guns. Deducting the horse-holders from the 7000 cavalry—as these were dismounted to fight—and including the 2100 infantry which were in line of battle, the Confederate force available in the attack did not amount to more than 7500 troops.

It was nearly seven o'clock by the time all of the Southern troops had arrived and taken their places in the line of battle, which was formed under the protection of the timber, nearly a mile distant from the Federal position. Mabry's brigade formed their extreme left; touching this and to the right was Bell's brigade, both of these commanders being to the left, or north, of the Pontotoc road as one approaches Tupelo from the direction of Pontotoc. Crossland's brigade of Kentuckians came next in order, while still to the right of this, and somewhat refused or drawn back, was Roddey's division. Hudson's battery was detailed to move with Roddey, while with Mabry and Bell the batteries of Morton and Rice were in line.

Thrall's guns were held in reserve with Chalmers near the center of the Confederate alignment, where two brigades (McCulloch's and Rucker's), formed as a reserve, were deployed some four hundred yards in rear of Crossland. Rucker's men were to the left and in the rear of Bell, while McCulloch stood ready to support Colonel Crossland when needed. Still to the rear, a quarter of a mile, the 2100 dismounted cavalry and the battalion of infantry formed a second reserve of the Confederate line under General H. B. Lyon.

As the Confederates moved forward under protection of the timber in which they had been deployed, General Lee wisely concluded to use every means possible to draw the enemy out of their intrenchments and induce them to assume the offensive. With this end in view, upon reaching the limit of the timber, just on the edge of the opening, the troops were halted, and a brisk fire at long range opened upon the Federals. In this preliminary firing the artillery on both sides took an active part. Fully an hour was spent in this futile effort to draw the Federal commander from his stronghold, with no other effect than to attract his attention in the direction of the Confederate right, where Roddey, across the clearing and well back in the timber nearly a mile away, was deploying his division. Evidently taking the movement of the troops in this quarter as a threat upon the weakest portion of his line, the left, Smith immediately hurried reinforcements to that quarter. He says: "On the morning of the 14th the battle opened by the enemy attempting to secure a commanding position on our left. Advancing the third brigade of the third division into line with the remainder of the division, and throwing out a brigade of colored troops on the left of the third, but facing nearly to its flank, we easily drove the enemy from the hill, and retained possession of it during the entire battle."[14]

By this time it was eight o'clock. The sky was cloudless, and the heat of the mid-July sun was already intense. For thirty days so little rain had fallen in this section that the earth was parched, the blades on the cornstalks were twisted, the leaves were withering, the highways were filled with dust, and the wet-weather streams and branches were now as dry as the roadbeds. It was with difficulty that enough water could be obtained to fill the canteens of the troops of the two small armies which stood facing each other in battle array.

As the Confederates stood ready to advance they were facing directly east, so that the morning sun fell in their faces, giving their antagonists a great advantage of firing with their backs to the light. Just before giving the order for the troops to move to the attack, General Lee directed Forrest to repair to his portion of the field and at the proper moment swing Roddey's division against the Union left. Comparing their watches, the two generals agreed upon the time when the attack should be made. Forrest rode away at full speed in the direction of Roddey, who was then nearly a mile to the right. General Lee says: "At the expiration of the time agreed upon between us when comparing our watches, I ordered the left wing in."[15]

There was now precipitated a battle tragedy for a parallel to which

---

[14] *Official Records,* vol. xxxix, part i, p. 251.
[15] Manuscript of General Lee, in possession of the author.

the historian will in vain search the records. Without co-ordination or concert of action between the different portions of the assailing line, and without proper control even of the separate commands, one brigade after another, in isolated rashness, precipitated itself against this exceedingly strong position; and as wave after wave of the ocean is scattered in spray against the unyielding cliffs, these waves "of living valor rolling on the foe" were dashed to pieces.

When General Buford, whose troops composed the center and left of the Confederate line, received the order to advance, and had proceeded in company with General Lee as far as the edge of the open space across which in full sweep of the enemy's artillery and small arms his troops must pass before closing in upon them, he recognized the desperate character of the work and the heavy loss of life it would involve. He says: "I modestly expressed the opinion that the attack should not be a direct one; that the majority of the forces should be thrown on the Verona and Tupelo road and a vigorous assault made on his left flank; that a direct charge was what the enemy most desired and for which he was strongly posted, both by nature and art."[16]

Buford's advice, however, came too late; the order of battle had been given, Forrest had ridden away to the attack on the right, and evidently, in the opinion of the commanding general, it could not be changed. In moving forward, the Kentucky brigade under Colonel Edward Crossland obliqued to the right in order to be in touch with Roddey's portion of the line; while the brigade of Mabry, which had been temporarily attached to General Buford's division, obliqued to the left. In the interval between Mabry and Crossland, Bell, with his brigade, was directed to advance. Meanwhile the Federal and Confederate batteries were heavily engaged, Walton and Thrall taking the chief part at long-range practice on the Southern side.

It so happened that the Kentucky brigade debouched into the open space considerably in advance of Bell and Mabry, and these gallant spirits, believing themselves invincible when Forrest was on the field, eager to close in upon the enemy in hand-to-hand combat, could not be restrained, and, despite the orders and entreaties of their officers, in suicidal rashness rushed at full run upon the center of the Federal position. General Lee, whose plan of battle, after having determined

---

[16] *Official Records*, vol. xxxix, part i, p. 330.

to attempt this desperate assault, was excellent, had ordered the entire left wing to attack at the same time and coincident with Forrest's attack on the right. Colonel Crossland says:

> Though ordered to move surely and steadily, it was impossible to restrain the ardor of my men. Believing that they were strongly supported both on the right and left, raising a shout, they charged forward on the enemy's line, which was keeping up a constant, destructive fire. Arriving within two hundred yards of the enemy, exposed during the whole time in an open field and under a most terrific fire of artillery and small arms from a force greatly superior to their own and strongly intrenched, the enemy suddenly opened an enfilading fire from both flanks.

For fully five hundred yards across this open field, without a fence or gully or any protection whatever, swept by two full batteries discharging grape and canister, these fearless troopers, not seven hundred in number, reserving their fire, braved this storm and pressed up to within one hundred yards of the Federal breastworks. Then from their place of safety, with guns at rest, fully four thousand rifles of the Union infantry, from front and on both flanks, opened upon this forlorn hope a murderous volley. They fell by scores, and for a moment the thin line staggered as if about to yield.

Realizing now that to retreat would be more dangerous than to go on, Crossland and Faulkner, in desperate mood, still mounted, rode out in front shouting, "Forward, men; forward!" The men quickly rallied and again pressed on toward the enemy. Within a few yards of their breastworks Faulkner's horse was killed, and he, twice wounded, went down and was left on the field. The color-bearer was killed, but the flag of the Twelfth Kentucky, perforated by eighteen bullets, was saved from capture. Some half a score of the Confederates reached the works, jumped in among the Federals, and were killed or taken prisoners. At this crisis the Federals to the right of the assaulting line rushed forward from their position on the flank and poured an enfilading fire on the unfortunate Kentuckians. Flesh and blood could not stand before such a withering storm of lead, and at last those who had thus far escaped broke for shelter to the woods in which a few minutes before they had been deployed.

Seeing the desperate situation of Crossland's brigade, Buford hurried forward Mabry and Bell to strike the right of the Union position in order to divert a portion of the fire which was being concentrated upon the Kentuckians. Mabry's advance, as has been shown, was obliquely to the left, and in making the movement through the woods he reached the open space a hundred yards in front of Bell's Tennesseeans, who had not yet cleared the timber. In the emergency which existed, Mabry did not await an alignment with Bell, but charged forward with great bravery, only to meet a fate scarcely less tragic than that which had almost annihilated the brigade of Crossland. He says: "As soon as my command advanced within range of the enemy's artillery, he opened on me a furious cannonade. My line advanced steadily. When within about three hundred yards of the works a terrific fire of small arms was opened on me. I immediately ordered a charge, but the heat was so intense and the distance so great that some men and officers fell exhausted and fainting along my line, while the fire from the enemy's line of works, by both artillery and small arms, was so heavy and well-directed that many were killed and wounded, leaving my line almost like a line of skirmishers." As bravely as men ever fought in this world, these fearless soldiers continued to advance. Arriving within sixty yards of the enemy's works, Colonel Mabry says: "Seeing that my line was too much weakened to drive the enemy, I halted and directed the men to protect themselves by lying down in a hollow behind a low fence which covered a part of my front."

The Federal troops from behind their protection had made short work of the Mississippians, who had lost fully one-third of their command before Bell's brigade rushed into the breach between them and the Kentuckians. Bell and his famous brigade were never laggards on any field, and here they did their duty nobly and well; but so close was the range and so concentrated the fire from the greatly superior numbers in their front that even such valor as they were wont to display was of no avail. After a desperate yet vain struggle, in which many of their bravest and best officers and men fell, they relinquished their effort, but not until the surviving remnant of Mabry's Mississippians had been withdrawn under their protection, and Colonels R. M. Russell, C. R. Barteau, A. N. Wilson, J. F. Newsom, Lieutenant Colonel D. M. Wisdom, and Major W. T. Parham—in fact, the commander of every regiment—were shot down, and in Barteau's Second Tennessee only one commissioned officer escaped. General Bell says: "My brigade marched out just in rear of Mabry's, which, after fighting some time in front of the enemy's fortifications, retired, leaving my brigade to take its place."

In the desperate fighting which was going on the Confederate artillery was taking its full share, and was handled with the boldness and precision which characterized these splendid artillerists which Forrest had trained. As the troops were forming in the woodland, two of these batteries (Walton's and Thrall's), with guns of somewhat longer range, had been responding to the fire from the Union pieces which lined the heights in their front. As the troops marched onward into the open field and began the descent of the slope which lay between them and the enemy, these daring cannoneers unlimbered their guns and at close range pushed them forward with the line of battle. Rice's battery went in with Crossland's brigade, and to its support, somewhat in the rear, Thrall now advanced his guns.

On the left, the old Morton battery, commanded then by Lieutenant Sale, took its place in the rear of Mabry's and Bell's brigades, and, marching boldly, unlimbered its pieces within four hundred yards of the intrenched position of the Union forces. The fine practice of Morton and his batteries was soon in evidence. A Federal officer, Captain W. S. Burns, who took part in this engagement, says: "Forrest's artillery was very active; one battery in particular was handled with great accuracy, throwing its shot and shell into the Twenty-first Missouri, Fifty-eighth Illinois, and Eighty-ninth Indiana until the Illinois and Indiana batteries engaged their attention."[17]

So terrific was the fire concentrated upon this battery on account of the execution it was doing that five of the seven gunners and six of the eight horses of one piece were disabled, and the sergeant (Brown) in command, though three times wounded, refused to quit his gun, and when the Confederates retired from the field it was rolled off by hand. Another piece, the wheel of which was shattered, was also dragged away and saved.

Although the Kentuckians under Crossland had wavered for a moment under the murderous fire which had been directed at them, as soon as they saw the advance of Mabry, and Bell's troops coming out of the woods a little farther back on their immediate left, they rallied. As their commander reports: "They seemed imbued with fresh vigor, and again charged forward, intent upon taking the enemy's

[17] *Battles and Leaders of the Civil War,* vol. iv, p. 422.

works and driving him before them; but the fire was too galling. The ranks were decimated—literally mowed down. Some of my best officers were either killed or wounded. The brigade was compelled to fall back; not, however, until it had reached the enemy's line."[18]

The rash advance of Crossland's brigade, which can only be accounted for by the lack of that rigid discipline which holds men in strict obedience to command, whether in advance or retreat, was the first great misfortune of the day, and probably contributed most to the severe repulse and terrific losses which the Confederates received on this bloody field. The second and scarcely less serious misfortune was the failure on the part of Generals Forrest and Lee to estimate accurately the time which should have been allowed for Forrest to reach the right wing where Roddey's division was. This portion of the Confederate line of battle was, on account of the greater distance from the edge of the timber to the Federal position, some four or five hundred yards refused or drawn back; and although General Forrest rode with the greatest speed and carried his line forward to the attack as rapidly as possible, he had not approached near enough to engage the Federals in his front before Crossland's men in their mad rush had been destroyed.

General Forrest says in his official report: "General Lee gave the order to advance, and directed me to swing the right around upon the enemy's left. I immediately repaired to General Roddey's right with all possible speed, which was nearly a mile distant, and, after giving him the necessary orders, I dashed across the field for the purpose of securing a position in which to place his troops. On reaching the front I found the Kentucky brigade (Crossland's) had been rashly precipitated forward, and were retiring under the murderous fire concentrated upon them."[19]

Forrest, who at this time was on the left of Roddey's division and nearest to Crossland, seeing the Kentuckians in confusion and being beaten back, rushed in among them, seized their colors, and rallied the men at the edge of the timber to which they were retiring as he rode up to them. Having failed to close in with the enemy in time to attack in concert with Crossland, he wisely desisted from repeating an isolated assault with his division. He says: "The terrific fire poured

[18] *Official Records,* vol. xxxix, part i. Crossland's report.
[19] *Ibid.*

upon the gallant Kentucky brigade showed the enemy was supported by overwhelming numbers in an impregnable position, and, wishing to save my troops from the unprofitable slaughter which I knew would follow any attempt to charge his works, I did not push forward with Roddey's command when it arrived, knowing it would receive the same concentrated fire which had repulsed the Kentucky brigade."

General P. D. Roddey states: "I was ordered by General Forrest to swing the troops under my command around on the enemy's left, covering the railroad south of his position, and to advance to the attack. The movement was executed in so far that the troops were in line facing the enemy's left, and had sufficiently advanced to drive his skirmishers back on his main force, when General Forrest ordered an immediate retreat to the horses, saying that Buford was badly cut up."[20]

While all this was transpiring in the center and to the left, where the remnants of Mabry's brigade were being withdrawn to the timber, the first line of reserves under Chalmers was ordered to their support. Rucker's brigade was directed to move forward to the position of Mabry and Bell, and advanced gallantly to their work. Marching through the Mississippians, Rucker's men took their place at the front, and swept across the field and up the slope in the direction of the Federals, and these now turned their death-dealing fusillade upon this stubborn fighter, who at the head of his veterans was twice wounded and carried from the field. So heavy was the fire upon this portion of the Confederate line at this time that, after severe loss, they in turn were compelled to retire to the edge of the timber. Captain Burns, speaking of the persistent gallantry of these men, says:

> For an hour and a half the struggle continued, until the enemy were driven from the front of Moore, leaving the ground covered with their dead and dying. Instead of retiring to the woods (where their horses were held in reserve, for Forrest's army was always "mounted infantry") they moved in what at first appeared a confused mass to their left, crossed to the north of the Pontotoc road, turned, and in good line of battle swept down upon Mower, whose men (under orders) reserved their fire until the enemy were quite near, when they opened upon them with musketry and canister shot. Human beings could not stand such a storm, and the attacking line fell back, only to return to a somewhat exposed part of Mower's line.

[20] Letter from General Roddey to General Lee. Copy in possession of the author.

Coincident with Rucker's advance, McCulloch's brigade was thrown forward to relieve Crossland, but fortunately was not permitted to advance farther in this hopeless enterprise, Generals Lee and Forrest ordering the attack to be stopped.

The able commander on the Union side did not fail to take advantage of the lack of co-ordination which characterized the advance of the Confederates. Referring to the isolated attack of the Kentucky brigade, in his official report General Smith says: "The enemy advanced in line upon the right or third division near the Pontotoc road. They drove in our skirmishers, and were allowed to come within about one hundred yards of the main line, when our forces rose and delivered one volley at short range, and charged with their bayonets, driving the enemy with a heavy loss from the field, and killing even more while running than in the first volley."[21]

In referring to the attack by Mabry and Bell on the left, he says:

Passing towards our right, they rallied at the edge of the timber, and were reinforced and strengthened by their whole available force, and once more returned to the attack, which was this time made on the first division, Brigadier-General Mower commanding. The enemy started from the edge of the timber and advanced in three lines. At first their lines could be distinguished separately, but, as they advanced, lost all semblance of lines, and the attack resembled a mob of huge magnitude. There was no skirmish line, main line, or reserve; but it seemed to be a foot-race as to who should reach us first. They were allowed to approach, yelling and howling like Comanches, to within canister range, when the batteries opened upon them. Their charge was evidently made with the intention of capturing our batteries, and was gallantly made, but without order, organization, or skill. They would come forward, fall back, forward again, and fall back with a like result. Their determination may be seen from the fact that their dead were found within thirty yards of our batteries. After two hours of fighting in this manner General Mower advanced his line about a quarter of a mile, driving the enemy before him from the field. This ended the fighting of the day.

The Confederates having absolutely failed to make any impression upon the Union line, General Forrest now ordered four pieces of artillery to be advanced on the Verona road in the direction of Tupelo, and moved Roddey's division there, making a demonstration upon the

[21] *Official Records,* vol. xxxix, part i, p. 252.

left of Smith's position, but no further assault was made by the Confederates. They were withdrawn to the woods, where Forrest quickly threw up breastworks, behind which his troops remained in line of battle for the remainder of the day. General Forrest says:

> About one o'clock Lieutenant-General Lee ordered me to fall back to the residence of Mrs. Sample, and form a new line fronting a large open field. The position selected was a strong one. I ordered the immediate construction of temporary fortifications, and in a short time the men along my entire line were protected. . . . The approach of the enemy was anxiously awaited, but he still remained behind his fortifications. At night he commenced burning the houses in Harrisburg.[22] General Chalmers advanced with one of his batteries and McCulloch's brigade, and did good execution by throwing shells among the enemy, who could be plainly seen by the light of the burning houses. At the approach of darkness I ordered Rucker's brigade to report to me mounted, and with it I moved to the right, cautiously approaching the enemy's left, with a view of determining his position and strength. By meandering through the woods I approached very near his camp before he discovered my presence. I ordered my men to open fire upon him, and the first line fell back to the main body. Then they opened upon me one of the heaviest fires I have heard during the war. Returning to camp, I ordered General Buford to move to the right with his division and occupy the road between the enemy and Verona, and oppose any advance in that direction.

Forrest, from his fortified position, was destined to disappointment in the hope of an advance upon him by General Smith, who had not only determined not to attack the Confederates, but to retreat to Memphis as rapidly as possible. The Union commander says:

> My troops were so exhausted with the heat, fatigue, and short rations that it was not possible to press them farther. Sixty prisoners were captured unwounded. During the afternoon the enemy attempted to attack our rear from the east side of Tupelo, and were repulsed. At sundown, as they were making no demonstration whatever, I directed the main bodies of my command to fall back about six hundred yards towards the wagons. At 11 P.M. the enemy attempted a night attack, drove in the skirmishers, but were promptly met and repulsed. On the morning of the 15th . . . it became

[22] The devastation by fire of this portion of the country by General A. J. Smith was complete, and was in line with General Sherman's war policy as expressed in his correspondence—namely, to let the people know that wherever Forrest and his men were found the land would be laid waste with fire and sword.

a matter of necessity to return. I am sorry to say that for lack of transportation, and the character of their wounds, I was obliged to leave about forty of the worst wounded of my command at Tupelo. I sent out one brigade of cavalry on the Pontotoc road to bring off a gun of the enemy which had been disabled the day before, which they did after some slight skirmishing. Being now nearly noon, and no demonstration from the enemy, I directed Colonel Moore, commanding the third division, to withdraw his line and take the advance and proceed on the Ellistown road, moving very slowly, the train to follow with sick and wounded, General Mower and the remainder of the cavalry covering the withdrawal. On reaching Old Town Creek we encamped for the night. The first division was ordered to pass the third and take position in advance, so that it might be in readiness to take the advance in the morning. It had scarcely advanced when a small force of the enemy, numbering perhaps a thousand men, took position on a hill, and commenced shelling the camp. General Mower turned back two of his regiments, and, with the brigade of the third division, drove them back about a mile, with heavy loss. We encamped at Ellistown on the 16th, near New Albany on the 17th, at Tippah on the 18th, reached Salem on the 19th, on the 20th moved to Davis's Mills, and on the 21st were at La Grange, having been gone seventeen days.

The position that Forrest had already taken on the morning of the 15th on the Verona road with Roddey's division was reinforced by General Buford, who, advancing, forced in the Federal skirmishers and drove their main line back for about a mile. The heat was so oppressive that in this advance eighty of Buford's men were left unconscious on the field from sunstroke. At two o'clock the enemy were in full retreat, and Bell's brigade was placed in front with Rice's battery and ordered to press them vigorously. He came up with their rear guard at Old Town Creek, four miles from Tupelo, where he vigorously attacked, and where Mower as vigorously in turn attacked Bell and Crossland. It was here that Colonel L. J. Sherrill of the Seventh Kentucky was killed, and Colonel Crossland, commanding the brigade, was seriously wounded. Mower, who was in command of the Federal rear guard here, handled his troops with his usual skill and courage, and the Confederates were repulsed. McCulloch came up to the relief of Bell and Crossland, and succeeded in holding his ground, but in so doing was most desperately wounded.

General Forrest says: "The enemy continued his retreat, and was pursued for two days by Rucker and Roddey. My force during this engagement did not exceed five thousand men. The enemy fought behind fortifications, and in positions of his own selection. Three of my brigade commanders—Rucker, McCulloch, and Crossland—were severely wounded, and all the colonels were either killed or wounded; 210 were killed, 1116 wounded."[m]

When McCulloch fell, and while Forrest was riding with Rice's battery to an advanced position in order to open upon Mower, he received a painful wound through his right foot which incapacitated him for the time being from active service. The command then devolved upon General Chalmers, who held his position until the enemy retired.

Shortly after Forrest was wounded the rumor spread among the troops that he had been killed, causing the greatest consternation among the soldiers. When this was reported to Forrest, who had been taken some distance to the rear, where the hemorrhage was arrested and his wound dressed, he mounted his horse at once and, without even taking time to put on his coat, rode in his shirtsleeves at a gallop along the line of troopers, cheering them not only by his presence, but with encouraging words, assuring them that it was only a slight flesh wound and he was still able and ready to lead them. Dr. C. W. Robertson, of Somerville, Tennessee, who was then a private soldier under Forrest, says: "The effect produced upon the men by the appearance of General Forrest is indescribable. They seemed wild with joy at seeing their great leader was still with them."

In the battle at Harrisburg, as between the contending armies, honors were easy. While the bloody repulse of the Confederate assault on the morning of the 14th of July was a victory for the Union commander, the ultimate result of the engagement cannot in fairness be so considered.[23] The retreat of the Federal army from the field, the close and vigorous pursuit of the troops under General Lee, a portion of which harassed the rear of the retiring column for four days after the battle, demonstrated that Generals Smith and Mower, in being so

---

[23] The losses on the Confederate side in the engagements of the 13th, 14th, and 15th of July were: Chalmers's division, 57 killed and 255 wounded; total, 312. Buford's division, including Mabry's brigade, 153 killed and 798 wounded; total, 951. Morgan's squadron of 80, 5 killed and 19 wounded; total, 24. Total loss in killed and wounded, 1287. Total missing, 50—48 in Buford's brigade and 2 in Morgan's detachment.

remote from succor and their base of supplies, did not feel that sense of security which usually belongs to the victor in battle.

The battle of Gettyburg is justly pronounced a great Union victory, notwithstanding the fact that General Robert E. Lee, after the bloody repulse of Longstreet's corps, retired to his original position on the field and for twenty-four hours offered battle, which was refused by his antagonists. Had General Meade on the day after the close of the struggle withdrawn his forces in the direction of Baltimore or Philadelphia, leaving General Lee in possession of the field, history would have recorded the Confederates as victorious there.

In like manner, when at noon on the day after this smaller battle near Tupelo, General Smith retreated from the field, it was an acknowledgment of his inability to hold his position and an abandonment of the object of his expedition, and therefore a Confederate victory. He had been sent out to destroy Forrest's command, and if possible to kill the Confederate leader, and incidentally to tear up the Mobile and Ohio Railroad and invade the prairie country. With the exception of about four miles of track torn up at Tupelo, not a single object of the expedition was accomplished. In support of this is the fact that Sherman was dissatisfied with his early return and the manner of his coming, with the beaten Confederates at his heels, and directed Washburn to send him back at once to keep Forrest busy.

It has been stated that General A. J. Smith's chief claim for recognition as a general of ability was his defeat of Forrest at Tupelo. Even if the result at Harrisburg had been a victory for the Federal commander, it could not in fairness be considered a defeat of Forrest. While it is true that fully three-fourths of the troops on the field, and all of those who took part in the encounter, belonged to Forrest's command, he positively refused to take charge of the battle and, as General Lee states, left him to assume the responsibility of the engagement.

Forrest did not even command the troops that went into action, nor did the portion of the line of which he was in command fire a single volley. Had the Union troops been driven from the field, General Lee would have been entitled to the credit of this achievement.

It is worthy of comment that in this brief and desperate encounter of the 7500 Confederate troops in line of battle and ready to engage, fully 4000 did not fire a shot. The reserve under Lyon, 2100 strong, were never in gunshot range. Roddey's division under Forrest, 1500 strong, drove in the skirmishers in their immediate front, but advanced no nearer than within about four hundred yards of the Union left. McCulloch's brigade, 1400 strong, advanced from the first line of reserves, but did not approach near enough to the Federals to engage their attention. If such an impression could have been made upon the Union position by this small proportion of the assaulting line, it is exceedingly probable that had all the Confederates on the field moved forward in proper alignment, with the supporting columns close up, as General Lee intended, and had all fought with the desperate valor exhibited by those engaged, General Smith's army would have been beaten and destroyed.

In his official report the Federal commander states as his reason for retreating to Memphis that "much of his bread was spoiled when drawn from the commissary depot, and that there was on hand but one day's rations left." If this be accepted as a fact, his army must have lived for four days upon a single day's rations, because it took him that length of time to reach his commissary at La Grange. He says in his report: "We reached Salem on the 19th, where we found supplies awaiting our arrival."

It must be borne in mind that the country around Tupelo at that time abounded with growing corn, and the wheat and rye had been already garnered. General Smith was within one day's march of the prairie region of Mississippi, which was then one vast field of ripening grain and bountifully afforded all the necessaries for the support of an army. He could have sustained his troops there for months, and if, as he claimed, he defeated the Confederates so signally here, he had nothing to do but to march after the beaten forces, drive them into and beyond the prairie country they were fighting to defend, and permanently establish himself in this rich land.

It may be proper to inquire why did not this careful and competent commander—for such he proved himself to be—assure himself before starting on a march so far from his base of supplies, and to meet such a formidable adversary as he knew Forrest to be, that his supplies were sufficient for the campaign? He also says: "Our ammunition was issued, and we had remaining only about one hundred rounds per gun; it therefore became a matter of necessity to return." One hundred rounds of artillery ammunition to each of twenty-four guns would seem to have been sufficient for all practical purposes had General Smith felt himself safe to try again the gage of battle.

Between the lines it is not difficult for the careful student to read the real cause of General Smith's retreat. He had never seen men fight with such desperate (if misdirected) valor. After this exhibition he did not dare to advance upon his antagonist, in compact line and behind defenses, nor could he safely remain where he was.

SEVENTEEN

General A. J. Smith's Second Invasion of Mississippi

THE wound received by General Forrest at Old Town Creek on the 15th of July, 1864, was the most painful of the many injuries from which he suffered during his career of hard fighting. The ball penetrated the right foot near the base of the great toe, and ranged through the most sensitive portion of the sole. Dr. J. B. Cowan, his chief surgeon, who was with him constantly throughout the war, while testifying that as a rule his patient exhibited great fortitude under these trying ordeals, says that in this instance his strong will gave way to the intense pain which this wound caused.

Moreover, for some time past, symptoms pointing to a general impairment of his health were evident. The tremendous strain through which mind and body had passed for the three years since he entered active service was telling even on his strong physique, but the will of iron was as yet unbroken. Before General A. J. Smith's first expedition left Memphis, General Forrest had requested a leave of absence, stating that he was afflicted with a number of boils which almost prevented him from moving about; but as soon as his territory was invaded these ills of the flesh were forgotten. Now, as the Federals were in retreat toward Memphis, his surgeon advised him to give up active duty, take the rest he so much needed, and have his wound properly cared for; but this advice was also unheeded.

As the injury to his foot prevented him from riding on horseback, he secured a light buggy, had it arranged with a rest or frame projecting over the dashboard to maintain his leg and foot in an elevated position, and in this way was able to continue in the personal direction of affairs. It was a novel sight, this major general of cavalry in the field seated in a dilapidated wartime buggy, guiding a spiritless nag among the trees and along the highways of Mississippi, carefully dodging stumps and roots and stones, or anything which might jolt the crippled foot! The day after he was wounded he was occupied in visiting the houses near the battlefield and in Tupelo where the wounded soldiers were collected. Incidentally he drove over the battlefield, superintending the gathering up of all abandoned property. Meanwhile his mind was busy, not only with the present disposition and reorganization of his troops, and the restoration of confidence, which had necessarily been impaired by the bloody repulse at Harrisburg, but also with plans for future movements upon the enemy.

On July 17th he submitted to General S. D. Lee the following suggestions:

In the event the enemy does not threaten any immediate movement against us, I respectfully suggest that Roddey's command remain or be encamped at Tupelo, Mabry's at or near Camargo, and Buford's and Chalmers's divisions and Neely's brigade be sent in the neighborhood of Pikeville, on Chuckatouchee Creek, to be fitted up, rested, and reorganized. With this disposition of the command, at least one hundred captured negroes, now putting up forage, can be placed at work on the railroad, and in a short time have it opened and running to Corinth. Mabry's brigade can be supplied with forage in the neighborhood of Camargo, and there is plenty of forage (tax in kind) on the Chuckatouchee for the other commands, and the men can also eat vegetables, which they very much need. I could establish my office and headquarters at this place (Okolona), remaining nominally in command, and have to a great extent the direction of affairs in reorganizing and fitting the troops for active service in the field, and in gathering up the absentees. With the horses now being recruited in pasture, and those of dead and permanently disabled officers and men, I think the battalion of dismounted men can be remounted and sent to their respective regiments. I am also of the opinion that it would be a good plan to send home one officer from every company to get absentees, and to bring horses to those who have them at home but have not been granted the privilege of going after them, limiting the absence of the officers to fifteen days.

Forrest's mind was as busy with the future as with the present. The rebuilding of the railroad from Tupelo to Corinth, although accredited by General Taylor to Fleming, the military superintendent of railroads, was clearly the work of this farsighted commander, who intended to use it—as he did a few weeks later—in transporting his troops in order to throw himself rapidly and unexpectedly on Sherman's communications in north Alabama and Tennessee.

It was about this period, on August 7th, 1864, that General Forrest was greatly disturbed by a communication received from Richmond which foreshadowed an interference with the appointment of officers made by him in the various regiments and companies he had brought out of west Tennessee. Hoping to forestall the measure, he appealed personally to the President in the following comprehensive document:

His Excellency Jefferson Davis, President C. S. A.:

Sir—I have the honor to state that I am just in receipt of a letter from the Adjutant and Inspector-General's Office, under date of 19th ultimo, accompanied by a memorandum of instructions as to the irregularities and illegalities occurring in the organization of the various regiments of my command, which instructions require the election of field-officers for several of the regiments as organized by me at Oxford, Mississippi, in February last. It is due to myself to state that, in organizing the west Tennessee regiments referred to, it was my understanding that elections for field-officers could not be held, and that, being made up as they were from the odds and ends of some twelve or fifteen reputed commands and of unattached companies and squads raised inside the enemy's lines, the field-officers were to be appointed by the War Department; hence, in nominating the field-officers for these commands, I was governed by the claims of the parties instrumental in raising the troops, also by their ability and merit as officers. Your Excellency is aware of the condition of affairs as I found them in west Tennessee and north Mississippi, and the circumstances of my entering this department, and the limited means placed at my command for the accomplishment of my mission here. With great labor, and under many difficulties and disadvantages, I succeeded in bringing order out of confusion, and organized and placed in the service a majority of the troops now constituting my command. The enemy in heavy force is in my front, and any attempt, by elections, to fill the field positions of the west Tennessee regiments I am satisfied will disorganize my command and be injurious to the service. They are all contented, and everything is moving along harmoniously, and an election will surely result in the loss of the best field-officers I have, who by strict discipline have kept the men together. Many of them have distinguished themselves by gallantry in the recent engagements of Tishomingo Creek and Harrisburg, and quite a number are now absent, wounded. I have no desire to see the rights of any one disregarded. I believe the appointing of field-officers, upon proper recommendations, the legal method of supplying field-officers of regiments composed of parts of so many different unattached commands, and now that it has been done and has proved satisfactory to all parties, I do hope the appointments will be made as per roster forwarded to the department. I should not trouble your Excellency with this matter but for the fact that the good of the service and the efficiency of my command, and justice to the officers who have served so faithfully, require that I should lay this matter before you. I shall, as soon as practicable, forward a detailed statement of facts and recommendations relative to all parties referred to by the department in its instructions, and do hope that no changes will be made in the new commands raised under your authority. At this particular time it would be disastrous to change the field-officers of the west Tennessee regiments, and it is my firm conviction that to do so at any time will be highly injurious. I distinctly disavow any assumption of any power or authority to make these appointments, but selected the very best men in the commands for the positions, and in doing so believed I was acting properly and legally, and that the officers nominated and placed in command would be appointed to the positions to which they were assigned. Having done all, as I conceived, for the best, and having organized a fine command, which since its organization has performed more and better duty than perhaps any other new cavalry command ever did in the same length of time, I do hope that nothing will now be done to destroy its effectiveness or weaken my influence and control over it. I regarded the commands as detached, raised under various authorities, at different times and by different parties, and that field-officers could only be made by appointment from the War Department.

I have the honor to be, very respectfully, your obedient servant,

N. B. FORREST, Major-General

The position taken by Forrest was thoroughly sustained by the report of the inspector general, which was forwarded to Richmond, and for the time being his recommendations were respected. Later, and possibly at the insistence of General Bragg, who was at this date in Richmond as military adviser of President Davis, and who lost no opportunity to throttle Forrest, the authorities there disregarded General Forrest's wishes, and as a result of the changes which were thus effected, and which Forrest conscientiously carried out to the best of his ability, a large number of his troops quit the service and were therefore lost to the Confederacy.

On the 20th of July, General S. D. Lee was transferred from this department to the army under General J. B. Hood at Atlanta, and, pending the arrival of General Richard Taylor, General Dabney H.

Maury was placed temporarily in charge of the department in which Forrest was operating.

The small battalion of infantry which was present at Harrisburg had been returned to Mobile. Roddey's division in the last week of July was dispatched to northern Alabama for the protection of that section, which was then threatened with a raiding expedition from Nashville. The other dismounted troops and the cavalry were scattered throughout the prairie region of Mississippi, where sustenance could be obtained. A remnant of Mabry's brigade had been ordered southward toward Canton to repel a raid moving eastward from the Mississippi River.

Although General A. J. Smith had reported his "defeat of Forrest at Tupelo," and the Northern press was filling columns with the great exploit, it was early in evidence that Generals Sherman and Grant were not satisfied with the result of his campaign. With characteristic discernment the commander of the Army of the Tennessee realized that his subordinate had "scotched the snake, not killed it," and that Forrest, albeit in a buggy, was still on the rampage.

On July 19th General Grant, from City Point, Virginia, telegraphed Sherman: "Smith ought to be instructed to keep a close watch on Forrest and not permit him to gather strength and move into middle Tennessee."

Taking his cue from this, Sherman on the next day dispatched to Washburn at Memphis: "Order Smith to keep after Forrest all the time. I think a few more days will bring matters to a crisis. Johnston is relieved and Hood succeeds to the command"; and to General Halleck he says: "A. J. Smith has orders to hang on to Forrest, and prevent his coming to Tennessee."

When Smith received these urgent orders from headquarters it dawned upon him that his victory was not properly appreciated by Sherman, and he said as much to Washburn, who on the 23rd, from Memphis, wired the commander of the Army of the Tennessee: "General Smith thinks you have a wrong impression in regard to his fight. He has returned for lack of supplies. I have ordered him to move again against Forrest. He will move as soon as he can get ready, unless you think that he had better go to Mobile."

Acting upon the urgent instructions of Sherman, Generals Washburn and Smith brought all their energies in play to collect a force large enough to return at once to the invasion of Forrest's territory.

At one moment while thus engaged their hearts were gladdened with a rumor that the Confederate commander was no more. Washburn gave it so much credence that on August 2nd he wired Sherman: "I have a report that Forrest died some days ago of lockjaw." Such news was too good to be kept, and Sherman repeated to Grant: "Washburn thinks that Forrest is dead of a wound he received in his battle with General Smith." To Washburn he next turned with the query: "Is Forrest surely dead? If so, tell General Mower I am pledged to him for his promotion, and if 'Old Abe' don't make good my promise, then General Mower can have my place."[1]

Forrest, however, was not yet out of the way, and, although Mower had not killed him, "Old Abe" made good his promise, for on the 12th of August Sherman wired Stanton: "Please convey to the President my thanks for the commission for General Mower, whose task was to kill Forrest. He only crippled him; he is a young and game officer."

The experience General Smith had acquired in his first expedition was not without value in his second essay. This time he did not intend to be drawn so far away from his base of supply, and instead of marching directly overland to assail Forrest on his old stamping ground near Tupelo and in the prairie country, the Federal general's first move was to rebuild the railroad from Memphis to Holly Springs in Mississippi, from which point he did not intend to advance any considerable distance, being content to hold Forrest engaged from that quarter until he had further extended his line of road.

Early in August, Generals Washburn, Smith, Mower, and Grierson had concentrated a heavy force, consisting, according to General Sherman's dispatch of August 11th, "of 10,000 infantry and 4000 cavalry, with 3000 colored troops from Memphis, and in addition three Minnesota regiments sent from St. Louis." Moving his cavalry overland and his infantry by rail, General Smith by the 9th of August had reached the Tallahatchie River between Holly Springs and Oxford.

Fully informed of Smith's movements by General Chalmers, who was in immediate command of the troops north of Oxford, Forrest made his dispositions accordingly and, jointly with his trusted lieutenant, sent the following communication to the general commanding the department at Meridian:

[1] *Official Records,* vol. xxxix, part ii, p. 233.

Our scouts report that the enemy is making preparations to move from Memphis, Vicksburg, and north Alabama at the same time, and if successful to concentrate at Selma. There are now 14,000 infantry and cavalry assembled at La Grange, and they are reported repairing the Mississippi Central railroad. Three regiments of infantry and two of cavalry are reported moving from Decatur to Moulton. The communication with Little Rock by White River is open, and the troops of Smith reported as going up White River have returned to Memphis. Some troops, number unknown, have been sent down the river towards Vicksburg. If the enemy moves in three columns, as expected, it will be impossible for us to meet him; and, after consultation, Major-General Forrest and I have concluded to recommend a consolidation of the troops in this department to meet one column. The northern column will be the largest; if we can defeat it the others may be easily overtaken and crushed. We have accumulated supplies at Grenada and Oxford, so that the cavalry from Jackson can be well subsisted, should you think it advisable to move them there. We can subsist our force better upon this line than any other, and it is more valuable to the Confederacy, therefore more important to be defended. The column from Vicksburg could do but little damage before reaching Demopolis, and if we should defeat him here, could by means of the railroad intercept him at Meridian on that line. The force moving from Decatur is, as yet, reported small, and ought to be checked by the reserves and other troops in Alabama. We beg leave, therefore, to suggest for the consideration of the major-general commanding the department that the forces from below be concentrated with this command on the northern line; but should he disapprove, we still recommend a concentration of our whole force to meet one of the columns. We are preparing fortifications here which, if manned by the whole force we had here before, may enable us to defeat the enemy. Our effective force is 5357, but we are very much crippled in officers. Both of my brigade commanders are wounded, also a brigade commander of General Buford's division, and most of the field-officers of the command were either killed or wounded in the late engagement.

I am, Colonel, very respectfully, your obedient servant,

JAMES R. CHALMERS, Brigadier-General

This letter is given here because it explains the situation of affairs in the department at this juncture, and demonstrates the wonderful accuracy of Forrest's knowledge (obtained through his system of scouts) of the movements and strength of the enemy. Moreover, since the reinforcements were not available, and the Confederate leader found himself hard pressed by the overwhelming numbers of Generals

Washburn, Smith, Grierson, and Hatch, it emphasizes the brilliant strategy which he executed within the next few weeks, encompassing the defeat of these threatening invasions.

When General Maury had been placed temporarily in command of the department in which Forrest was operating, he had suggested to his subordinate that the chief object in view was the defense of the rich farming region of central Mississippi, but with excellent judgment gave him the widest discretion. He wrote: "The prairie country appears to me to be the first object of your care. I know how disproportionate the forces at present under your command are to those which we understand the enemy has, but it will be difficult for him to advance far into the country while you are before him. I would not, if I could, undertake to prescribe to you any plan of operations. I wish you to understand that I intrust to you the conduct of affairs, and desire only to be able to aid you effectively with the means of executing your own views."

Upon receipt of information that the Federal expedition had started south from Memphis, Forrest immediately took to the field in his buggy, ordered ten days' rations prepared for the troops, one hundred rounds of ammunition for small arms and two hundred for the artillery issued, and started at once in the direction of Oxford, in Lafayette County, which point was about thirty miles south of the terminus of General Smith's railway line at Holly Springs. General Chalmers had been ordered to destroy any remaining trestles or bridges on the railroad leading south from Holly Springs, and to fall back to the Tallahatchie, cross to the south side of this stream, and offer as much resistance as possible.

In obedience to these orders, Chalmers, fighting persistently as he retreated, was beaten back to Oxford by the 10th of August, where he was joined by General Forrest, with Bell's and Neely's brigades and Morton's artillery. Chalmers's division, which now comprised McCulloch's, Neely's, and Mabry's brigades, was reinforced by Bell's brigade, and was placed in position at Hurricane Creek, a small stream which crossed the road from Oxford to Holly Springs about eight miles north of the former place. Here the Confederates made such stubborn resistance that for three days there was almost continuous firing.

By nightfall of the 13th General Smith had succeeded in throwing a heavy force around the flank and threatened the rear of the Confederate general, who immediately withdrew his entire force to Oxford. On the 14th of this month he reported to General Maury that the enemy in his front consisted of 18,000 infantry and 7000 cavalry, under Generals Washburn, Smith, and Grierson, and that they had forced him back to Oxford. It is clear from the correspondence of General Forrest, which is given in the official records, that he had long since become convinced of his inability, by reason of the small force at his command, to cope successfully with the superior numbers under Smith and Mower, and had conceived a movement which, as daring as it was brilliant, wrought confusion upon the Federal generals, causing them to abandon the invasion of Mississippi and retreat to their stronghold at Memphis.

In a dispatch dated August 8th to Chalmers, General Forrest had inquired as to the facilities for crossing the river at Panola, wanting to know definitely how many boats could be obtained there. He had now sufficiently recovered from his wound to enable him once more to take the saddle, although, as he said, he "had only one foot in the stirrups."

On the 18th of August, selecting two thousand of the best-mounted men of his command, and with four pieces of artillery, leaving Chalmers in command in the immediate front of the enemy, with orders to make the greatest possible demonstration of force by attacking him vigorously at various points, Forrest, under cover of darkness on the night of the 18th, left Oxford, taking a direction nearly due west, and by daylight, despite the bad condition of the road and the swollen streams, had cleared the right wing and was miles away to the rear of Smith without a suspicion on the part of his adversary that he had left his front.

By seven o'clock on the morning of the 20th Forrest had reached Senatobia, in Tate County, from which point he sent a courier back to Chalmers stating that he had bridged and was crossing the Hickahala, and expected to have to go to Quinn's Mills to get over the Coldwater. He directed him to "hold the enemy hard and press them up so as to engage their whole attention." This Chalmers was doing so well that he received the highest commendations from his commander.

The success of the enterprise which Forrest had on hand depended upon the celerity of his movements. North of Senatobia, by reason of the heavy rains which had fallen during the last forty-eight hours, and which are common to this part of the country in the early weeks of August, the streams ordinarily fordable were now "bank full," and it became necessary to construct temporary bridges for the rapid passage of the troops and artillery. The first obstacle of this nature was encountered at a creek known as the Hickahala, a few miles north of Senatobia. There were no bridges in all this country, and the only way of crossing the stream was to ferry the men, their accouterments, the ammunition and the artillery across in a very small boat, the only one obtainable, and then compel the horses to swim. This would require at least twelve hours, and such delay would in all probability be fatal.

The genius of Forrest in surmounting obstacles stood him well in hand in this emergency. His quick brain, ever fertile in resources, had planned the crossing long before he reached the stream. He had sent in advance a detachment of his best-mounted troops with instructions to pick out some suitable place for a crossing, to fell four trees, two on either bank, leaving the stumps convenient for the support of cables, and to have cut, twisted together, and in place by the time he should have arrived a cable made of the heavy grape and muscadine vines which grow in great profusion and of unusual size and length in the fertile alluvial bottoms of the Mississippi country. These novel cables were all ready when he reached the stream. Twisted around and lashed to the stumps on either side, by their weight they curved down until they were only two or three feet above the water at the middle of the stream. Just under the middle the ferryboat was anchored, and on either side of this a series of cypress logs were floated in and fixed at certain distances to add support where, by reason of the heavy weight of the flooring and of the troops passing over, it would sag in the middle. As the command approached within three or four miles of the Hickahala every ginhouse and cabin was stripped of its flooring, and as each trooper rode up he brought on his shoulder his burden of planks.

Within an hour's time of the arrival of the head of the column at this stream, the planks had been laid and the entire command had crossed over, the troops dismounting and crossing over in single file, each leading his horse.

Colonel J. U. Green, who commanded one of Forrest's regiments, informs the writer that in crossing on one of these grapevine pontoons the cables stretched or yielded until the center was well submerged before the last of the troops passed over. Seven miles farther north it became necessary to build a similar structure over the Coldwater, a stream twice as wide as the Hickahala, and here three hours were consumed in crossing. Notwithstanding all these hindrances, at dark on the 20th Forrest with his command had arrived at Hernando, only twenty-five miles distant from Memphis. On account of the wretched condition of the roads some of the artillery horses had given out, and, as these could not be replaced, two of the four guns had been left at Panola. It required ten horses to drag each piece and keep up with the cavalry. At Hernando, where Forrest had lived for several years in his younger days, and where he had many friends, he stopped for a few hours to feed and rest, and then pushed on in the direction of Memphis, where, at three o'clock Sunday morning, August 21st, he arrived with 1500 of the original 2000 troops which had started with him. Fully five hundred horses had given way under the great strain to which they had been subjected, and as their riders could not secure fresh mounts they were allowed to drop out and make their way back to Chalmers.

For the assault on Memphis, General Forrest had matured his plans with great care. His scouts had given him definite information as to the location of three general officers of the United States army who were then stationed in the city, and it was his purpose to capture these and whatever troops they might have immediately about them. The strong fort, which was then heavily garrisoned, he had no thought of assailing.

The headquarters of Major General C. C. Washburn were on Union Street, and the house in which he was sleeping was to be surrounded as the most important feature of the attack. Major General Stephen A. Hurlbut made his headquarters at the Gayoso House, while General R. P. Buckland was in another quarter of the city.

The troops were now, about an hour before daylight, gathered closely around the general and his officers, and the commander of each detachment as well as the men received specific instructions as to what he was expected to do. The greatest silence was enjoined upon all; not a word was to be spoken, not a shout, not a gun to be fired under any circumstances.

Each detail was to move under its leader directly to the spot indicated, without stopping for a moment even to fire at any detached bodies of Federals who might be encountered en route. To his brother,

Captain William H. Forrest, and his reckless forty scouts was given the advance, with orders to capture the pickets without firing, and as soon as this was done he was to ride at full speed, without halting, until he reached the Gayoso House, and then to place guards at all the outlets of that hostelry to prevent the escape of General Hurlbut or any other Federals quartered there.

Colonel Neely was placed in command of a second detachment, with orders to attack and engage the attention of a regiment of Illinois infantry which was encamped in the suburbs of Memphis and near the road over which the Confederates would be compelled to travel.

To the gallant Colonel Logwood was given another force, which was to follow immediately behind Captain Bill Forrest. Arriving at the corner of Main and Shelby streets, he was to station a portion of his troops there as a reserve, and send a second detachment to the wharf to capture any transports which might be there.

Lieutenant Colonel Jesse Forrest, with his picked detachment, was to move straight to the house of General Washburn on Union Street, and effect the capture of the commander of the department.

General Forrest, with Colonel T. H. Bell and detachments of New-som's, Russell's, and Barteau's regiments, and the two pieces of artillery under Lieutenant Sale, remained in the suburbs in order to cover the withdrawal of the columns which were to make the dash into and out of the city.

Everything being in readiness, the troops moved quietly forward just as the first streak of dawn shot up from the eastern sky. Approaching a small bridge which spans Cane Creek in the suburbs of Memphis, Captain Forrest, with ten men well in advance, was challenged by the Union sentry. To the question "Who goes there?" he replied, "a detachment of the Twelfth Missouri Cavalry, with rebel prisoners." He was told to "dismount and come forward alone on foot." As the doughty captain knew he could not be recognized until he had arrived almost in touching distance of the unsuspecting sentinel, he replied, "All right!" but, instead of dismounting, he rode up, having previously directed his men to follow close at his heels. As soon as the dim outline of the Federal cavalryman was discernible, Forrest, sticking spurs to his horse, the animal sprang forward, when, with his heavy army pistol, he knocked the trooper senseless to the ground. As the man fell, Captain Forrest dashed forward and surprised the reserve pickets, which were some thirty or forty yards farther up the road.

Unfortunately, one of these was quick enough to discharge his gun, and this aroused the second reserves, which were farther in the rear. Knowing now that the alarm would spread rapidly and that no time was to be lost, General Forrest ordered the troops to go in, and the whole Confederate force moved forward at a swift run. The excitement of the moment, and the eagerness of the men, who were now engaged in work which they enjoyed most keenly, were too much for their better judgment and lax discipline, and, forgetting the injunction of silence which their commander had placed upon them, they began yelling and shouting like so many wild and ungovernable Indians. What wonders these men accomplished under Forrest! but what greater wonders they might have achieved had he been able to have thoroughly disciplined them!

As Captain Forrest swept forward in the direction of the Gayoso House he came suddenly upon a Federal battery of six pieces, which was posted in an open space right at the side of the street on which he was passing. Several of his men dashed in among the surprised and demoralized artillerists, who, deserting their pieces, took to their heels and sought shelter among the houses in the immediate neighborhood. They were followed no farther than this, and unfortunately the precaution was not taken to spike these guns, or in some way to render them useless. Arriving at the Gayoso House, Captain Bill, scorning the preliminary courtesy of dismounting to enter the hotel, rode directly from the sidewalk into the office of the hotel, and there gave further instructions to his men, who barred all egress and streamed through the corridors in search of their prey.

Major General Stephen A. Hurlbut no doubt thanked his stars for many a day thereafter for the good fortune which befell him in sleeping elsewhere that night than in his own room in the hotel. When Colonel Aleck Chalmers battered in the door of his room, he was not at home. Colonel Chalmers for many years after the war told the amusing story of how, as he rushed into one of these rooms in the Gayoso House, he was met by a beautiful damsel with disheveled locks and becoming dishabille, who threw her arms about his neck, imploring his protection, which he claimed he was only too glad to give if she would not take up her arms until regularly exchanged as a prisoner of war.

When Lieutenant Colonel Jesse Forrest, whose duty it was to attempt the capture of Major General Washburn at his headquarters on Union Street, arrived there, he found that that distinguished officer had already been warned of the impending danger and, without taking time to arrange his wardrobe, had in his "cutty sark" made his escape to Fort Pickering. Lieutenant Colonel Forrest, however, succeeded in capturing one or two members of the general's staff before they could follow their leader.

General Cadwallader C. Washburn was in all probability the most astonished Federal soldier in Memphis on the morning of August 21, 1864, when just at dawn of day a trooper, sent in great haste by the vigilant Colonel Starr of the Sixth Illinois Cavalry, galloped to his house, rapidly dismounted, rushed to the door, and in Macduff's heroic style banged upon it with the handle of his saber. Aroused thus unceremoniously, to the inquiry of "What is wanted?" the trooper might with propriety have responded "Your honor," but he did not. In an excited tone he told the general that Forrest's cavalry were in possession of the town, were rapidly approaching and within sight of his house, coming at full tilt for his capture. The commander in chief of this department did not for a moment stand upon the order of his going, but made his exit through the back door, crossed the garden to an alley which was convenient, and then after a run of half a mile he was safe in the fort.

Lieutenant Colonel W. H. Thurston of the United States army, who was then stationed in Memphis, was bold enough to say in his official report of this affair, that "the general ran away for a safe place in the fort, which was fully a half-mile from his home, when he was but three squares away from the provost marshal's office; and all this without giving any orders or commands as to what should be done by the troops." If Lieutenant Colonel Jesse Forrest did not bring away the general, he did bring away his uniform and personal effects, which he delivered as a trophy to his elder brother, and these, with his personal compliments, General Forrest returned by flag of truce to Washburn. With becoming courtesy, which showed his appreciation of the delicate attention paid him, some two or three weeks later General Washburn sent by courier to his friend the enemy a handsome suit of Confederate gray which had been made by Forrest's old tailor in Memphis, and for which the Confederate general was very grateful.

The detachment which had been sent to surround the house of General Buckland also came too late to capture that officer. The yells of the Confederates as they rode through the suburbs, and the crack of rifles here and there, had attracted the attention of the sentry guarding his residence, who immediately awakened the general and called his attention to the uproar, whereupon he also sought safety in a change of residence.

The detachment led by Colonel Neely came in contact with a regiment of Federal infantry which, aroused by the picket fire in the direction of Cane Creek Bridge, had sprung to their arms and were in battle array when the Confederates came in sight. As soon as they began firing at Neely's command, General Forrest, who was nearby with Bell's brigade, seeing the condition of affairs in that direction, moved forward promptly upon the flank of the infantry, and in this movement, coming upon a detachment of Union cavalry who were encamped there, charged in among them, capturing a number of their horses and some prisoners, and putting the rest to flight. As Forrest moved forward, Neely also advanced upon the infantry and drove them from their camp. These, uniting with the cavalry that had been driven from their horses, now took refuge in a large brick building or seminary, and opened fire upon the Confederates with considerable annoyance.

Failing in the capture of the distinguished officers for whom they had been sent, Colonel Logwood and the two Forrests, after breaking open a number of livery stables and taking what horses could be obtained, united their forces within the city and started to retrace their steps to rejoin the main column under General Forrest. They were soon confronted by the battery of six pieces which had been captured earlier, but had not been spiked, and which was now manned and ready to be turned upon them. Without hesitation the Confederates rode at the guns and drove the gunners away; but as the garrison in Memphis were now thoroughly aroused and were running in large detachments to plant themselves across the streets in their front and thus hem them in, they could not take the pieces away with them, but rushed onward in their retreat.

General Forrest, greatly chagrined in not having effected the capture of either of the three generals known to be in Memphis that morning, withdrew his entire command in the direction of Hernando.

As they were marching out of town a detachment of the Sixth Illinois Cavalry, under Colonel Starr, made a vigorous assault upon the Confederate rear guard, which was commanded by General Forrest in person. Having his escort at hand, Forrest met the Federal cavalry with a countercharge, and a sharp hand-to-hand encounter ensued, in which, in a personal combat with General Forrest, Colonel Starr, the Federal commander, was seriously wounded and placed *hors de combat.*

After this affair no further pressure was made upon the rear of the retreating command, and from Cane Creek Bridge the Confederate commander sent Major Anderson with a flag of truce and a dispatch to General Washburn proposing to exchange prisoners; also informing him that a number of officers and men had been captured and hurried away before they could be properly clad, and requesting him to send their clothing. Forrest said he would wait at Nonoonnah Creek for a reply. At this place, General Washburn's note was received, stating that, as he had no authority, he declined the exchange of prisoners, but that he sent therewith the clothing for his men.

In the afternoon of the 21st of August, General Forrest, with his prisoners, reached Hernando, and from there by courier reported as follows: "I attacked Memphis at four o'clock this morning, driving the enemy to his fortifications. We killed and captured four hundred, taking their entire camp, with about three hundred horses and mules. Washburn and staff escaped in the darkness of the early morning, Washburn leaving his clothes behind."

Here he also paroled the prisoners captured at Memphis, directing them to return thither, and then proceeded to Panola, which place he reached on the 22nd of August. From this point he dispatched a courier to Chalmers, urging him: "If the enemy is falling back, pursue them hard. Send Buford to capture their foraging-parties. Keep close to their camp. Order Captain Henderson to scout well to their right to ascertain if there is any movement this way." He closed this communication by saying he would rest with his troops two or three days at Grenada if possible.

On the 23rd of August, General Maury reported that Forrest's movement in the rear of General Smith had caused him to pause in his advance into Mississippi, and on the following day he was gratified to receive from Maury a dispatch in which he said: "You have again saved Mississippi. Come and help Mobile. Fort Morgan, after a long and fierce struggle, was captured by the enemy yesterday. The attack on the city will be made at once, I expect. Will the retreat of the enemy from north Mississippi enable you to come with any of your force? We are very weak."

Sherman on the 24th of August telegraphed to Washburn: "If you get a chance send word to Forrest that I admire his dash but not his judgment. The oftener he runs his head against Memphis the better. This case illustrates the importance of converting those armories into regular citadels with loop-holes and flanks. See to it." The result showed that the Confederate general had attained fully the object of his strategy, for as soon as Washburn's telegram reached Smith at Oxford he immediately withdrew his troops across the Tallahatchie in the direction of Holly Springs, and on the 29th of August Forrest telegraphed to Maury: "Enemy left Holly Springs at two o'clock yesterday, marching rapidly in the direction of Memphis and La Grange. They say they are ordered to reinforce Sherman."

Although the Federal generals escaped capture and the Confederates were in rapid retreat, the greatest consternation prevailed in Memphis and in the mind of the commander in chief there, General Washburn, who immediately took steps to inform General Smith at Oxford of the condition of affairs at headquarters, and to insist upon the capture of Forrest's raiders and the protection of Memphis. So widespread was the feeling of panic in the city that two days after Forrest had left, and in fact when he was well beyond the Tallahatchie, a general stampede was caused by the rumor that he was returning in force.

Colonel Thurston, inspector general at this station, in his report says: "On the 23rd of August the whole town was stampeded at about ten o'clock in the morning by a report that Forrest had returned in force and was again in town. It was the most disgraceful affair I have ever seen, and proves that there is demoralization and want of confidence by the people in our army, and by our army in some of its officers. On this day there were no Confederate troops nearer than Forrest's rear, which was probably not less than twenty-five or thirty miles distant, and the alarm was caused by some of the troops firing off their guns, which had been loaded since Sunday."

On the 24th of August Washburn reported to Canby:

At daylight on Sunday morning, the 21st inst., Forrest attacked Memphis. The force was led by Forrest in person, and left Smith at Oxford, Mississippi, on the evening of the 18th, and marched day and night, the distance being about one hundred miles. One-third of his force dashed right over the pickets and through two regiments without stopping to fight, dividing into three parties, one coming to our house (headquarters), another to Gayoso House, where Major-General Hurlbut was supposed to be staying, and the third to the headquarters of Brigadier-General Buckland, commanding district of Memphis. Hurlbut was out of the house that night and escaped without molestation, while General Buckland and myself were barely able to do so. They were driven out of the city, taking about twenty-five private horses and the horses belonging to one section of the battery. We had about thirty killed and eighty wounded. Smith was instructed to send 1500 cavalry at once to Panola, and hold the crossing, and come around on Forrest's rear. I hope that they will be intercepted and captured. Smith has between four and five thousand cavalry with him, and in the exhausted condition that Forrest's men and horses are in, it would seem that if our cavalry does its duty they should not get away.

General R. P. Buckland reports that he was awakened by loud raps upon his front door, the sentinel exclaiming, "General, they are after you!" He inquired who were after him, and the answer came, "The rebels." He says: "I dressed myself as speedily as possible and ran to the barracks, where I found the soldiers had been alarmed and were collecting in the street. Colonel Starr, of the Sixth Illinois Cavalry, informed me that General Washburn's headquarters were in possession of the enemy, and that the general was undoubtedly captured. He organized all the available troops, and marched out towards the Hernando road. Forrest's plan was well laid. The morning was exceedingly foggy, and the state of the atmosphere such that the report of small arms, and even artillery, was heard but a short distance. They passed through the Seventh Wisconsin battery, killing one officer and several men, but without disturbing the guns or ammunition."

As soon as Forrest was well on his way toward Hernando, Washburn hastened to inform General Smith of the attack that had been made on him, and to advise him as to the direction of Forrest's retreat, urging him to take the necessary steps for the discomfiture or capture of his command. His wily enemy, however, was not to be so easily entrapped. He had taken the precaution, several hours before he reached Memphis and charged into the heart of the city, to have the wires leading eastward cut, thus delaying any communication with the Union forces at Oxford.

General Washburn says:

As soon as possible on the morning of the attack I endeavored to get a despatch through to La Grange, to be expressed from there to Major-General Smith, but it was found that during the night the wires had been cut between Collierville and Germantown. They were, however, repaired, so that by 12 M. the following despatch was sent to General Smith: "We were attacked at three o'clock this morning by a force said to be led by Forrest in person. The fight is still going on. They left Oxford two days ago, and crossed the Tallahatchie at Panola. You will at once order all your cavalry to move to intercept them. You will move one-half across at Panola, and the rest at Abbeville. They must be cut off and caught. Move rapidly and spare not horse-flesh. Their horses must be much jaded, and they can be caught."

This dispatch was ordered to be sent from La Grange with an escort of one hundred men. It started at one o'clock on that day, but before it left General Washburn sent two other dispatches in the following order:

Major-General A. J. Smith:
The enemy has retired on the Hernando road. He has five hundred prisoners, but failed to take the battery. I am at a loss to know whether he means to cross at Panola or go *via* Holly Springs. With a force to dispute the Panola crossing, and another force crossing at Abbeville and moving towards him until they strike his trail, and then following him until overtaken, he may be captured. His men and horses will be so much worn down that they will be an easy prey. . . .

You had better send fifteen hundred cavalry to hold the crossing at and above Panola, and send the rest of your cavalry across at Abbeville. If vigorously pressed they can be caught.

General Washburn asserts that these dispatches were received by General A. J. Smith at Oxford between ten and eleven o'clock on the morning of the 22nd. Moreover, that as soon as it became absolutely certain that Forrest would cross at Panola on his way out, he notified General Smith by telegram, which he received early on Tuesday morning, that Forrest had left Hernando that morning, the 22nd, intending to cross the Tallahatchie at Panola, and that his horses were jaded, and that he would probably cross during the night. In case Smith did not intercept him at Panola he should catch him between Yocona and Tallahatchie.

General Washburn further states that Smith, instead of moving to Panola, as all of his dispatches ordered him to do, sent the following dispatch to him:

From ABBEVILLE, Mississippi, *August 24th*

Major-General C. C. Washburn:

On arriving at Oxford yesterday morning, Brigadier-General Hatch was detailed to proceed to Panola and destroy the railroad from that point south along the line. Then we heard of Forrest's raid to Memphis, but could not believe it. I soon received your despatches of the 21st, and was induced to believe from your last telegram and information received at Oxford that Forrest would retreat through Holly Springs. I at once ordered the second division of cavalry to this point, with instructions to Hatch to return to Abbeville and join the second division, and proceed at once towards New Albany and intercept Forrest. I arrived with the infantry command about 10 A.M. to-day, and find the river booming and our bridge broken down. Recent rains in this region have made the roads almost impassable. I hope to communicate by telegraph by 12 M.

Washburn in his criticism of Smith's conduct says: "There were but two lines of possible retreat for the enemy, one *via* Holly Springs and the other by way of Panola. The Tallahatchie was very high and impassable, except upon the bridge at Panola. Had my orders been obeyed, Forrest would have found himself penned up between the Coldwater and the Tallahatchie, and escape would have been impossible. That Forrest should have left our immediate front at Oxford and made this move on Memphis without being discovered is somewhat strange. Forrest made a forced march in advancing and retreating."

EIGHTEEN

Forrest's Raid into Northern Alabama and Central Tennessee, from September 16 to October 6, 1864

THE President of the Southern Confederacy had at last appreciated the necessity of turning Forrest loose upon the railroads and other sources of supply of the Army of the Tennessee. His conversion, however, was too late for the good of the cause which he above all men had at heart, and in which he demonstrated, in the long years of disaster which fell to his lot, a heroism and a loyalty unsurpassed among men. Sherman, in his grand strategy, had now reached a point so far away from his base that, like Macbeth, who said,

> I am in blood
> Stepp'd in so far, that, should
> I wade no more,
> Returning were as tedious as go o'er,

he found it just as easy to go on as to stand still or turn back. Earlier in this campaign, when the line of the Chattahoochee had been reached, before the ripening corn in middle and eastern Georgia offered him the means of sustenance for his troops in a march to the sea, the thorough destruction of the Nashville and Chattanooga and the Alabama and Tennessee railroads, with a closure of the Tennessee and Cumberland rivers, all of which could have been done by a proper employment of the genius of Forrest, would have insured the defeat of Sherman's plans and in all probability the destruction of his army. But Johnston, the man who had so stubbornly and skillfully retarded the advance to Atlanta, had been removed, and Hood (for whom Sherman had little respect as a military leader) was in his stead. Moreover, all the broad fields of Georgia were teeming with ripening corn, and the able commander of the Army of the Tennessee now knew that he could march through Georgia and find enough to support his army on the route.

There is a dispatch in the official records, dated October 1, 1864, from Sherman to Howard, in which he plainly indicates his intention of cutting loose from Atlanta and leaving Tennessee and northern Georgia and Hood's army behind him. This strategic move he later carried into execution, with results that demonstrated his consummate generalship. "I have not yet heard from Lieutenant-General Grant as to my proposed campaign, but it is well for you to bear in mind that if Hood swings over to the Alabama road and then tries to get into Tennessee, I may throw back to Chattanooga all of Major-General Thomas's men as far down as Kingston, and draw forward all else; send back all cars and locomotives; destroy Atlanta, and make for Savannah or Charleston *via* Milledgeville and Millen."

General Richard Taylor, a brother-in-law of President Davis, had at this date become the commander in chief of the Department of the Southern states, in which General Forrest was engaged in his military operations. Forrest had written to President Davis a personal letter, asking permission to move into Tennessee with a strong force of cavalry, in order to cut the railroads, interfere with Sherman's supplies, and at the same time divert as many men as possible from the army that was pressing Hood so severely in Georgia.

Upon the 6th of September the President telegraphed General Taylor in regard to Forrest's dispatch: "General Forrest telegraphed me, on the 5th instant, that, if permitted to select from his present command four thousand men and six pieces of artillery, he thought he could, in middle and west Tennessee, disturb the enemy's communications and recruit his command. If circumstances permit it, I think it would be well to employ him in operations on the enemy's lines of communication, as well as to interfere with the transportation of supplies and reinforcements to General Sherman's army. Of this you must inform yourself and freely exercise your judgment." General Taylor was fully informed of the importance of this movement and immediately proceeded to exercise his excellent judgment.

Forrest's strategic move on Memphis, which produced such consternation in the mind of General Washburn and brought the army under Smith back to Memphis in short order, had liberated northern Mississippi from Federal occupation. The Confederate leader had stationed the various detachments of his command in northern Mississippi at points not only convenient to forage and supplies, but where they would also be in readiness to meet any further incursion into his territory. Making his headquarters at Grenada, he stationed Chalmers's division at West Point, on the Mobile and Ohio Railroad, ready to move to the assistance of General Maury in Mobile, who had already indicated the probability that he would need assistance. The remnant of Mabry's brigade had been dispatched toward the western portion of the State of Mississippi to act in concert with General Wirt Adams in the Yazoo country. Brigadier General H. B. Lyon, since the infantry over which he had been temporarily placed in command had been returned to Mobile, now rejoined Buford's division, while Colonels McCulloch and Rucker, both of whom had been wounded in the engagements at Harrisburg and Old Town Creek, emulating the example of their commander, although not fully recovered, had again reported for duty in the field.

On the 4th of September, in answer to an urgent call from General Maury, Forrest had started in the direction of Mobile, to take charge of Chalmers's division, which was also en route for that destination. On reaching Meridian he was met by General Richard Taylor, to whom he had been directed to report when he should arrive there, and here for the first time these two soldiers came face to face. It is interesting to note what Taylor's first impressions of Forrest were, as given in his entertaining book, *Destruction and Reconstruction:*

An hour later a train from the north, bringing Forrest in advance of his troops, reached Meridian and was stopped, and the general, whom I had never seen, came to report. He was a tall, stalwart man, with grayish hair, a mild countenance, and slow and homely of speech. In few words he was informed that I considered Mobile safe for the present, and that all our energies must be directed to the relief of Hood's army, then west of Atlanta. The only way to accomplish this was to worry Sherman's communications north of the Tennessee River, and he must move his cavalry in that direction at the earliest moment.

To my surprise, Forrest suggested many difficulties, and asked many questions: how he was to get over the Tennessee; how he was to get back if pressed by the enemy; how he was to be supplied; what should be his line of retreat in certain contingencies; what he was to do with prisoners if any were taken, etc. I began to think he had no stomach for the work; but at last, having isolated the chances of success from causes of failure, with the care of a chemist experimenting in a laboratory, he rose, and asked for Fleming, the superintendent of the railway, who was on the train by which he had come. Fleming appeared—a little man on crutches, but with the energy of a giant—and at once stated what he could do in the way of moving supplies on his line, which had been repaired up to the Tennessee boundary. Forrest's whole manner now changed. In a dozen sharp sentences he told his wants, said he would leave a staff-officer to bring up his supplies, asked for an engine to take him back north twenty miles to meet his troops, informed me he would march with the dawn, and hoped to give an account of himself in Tennessee.

Moving with great rapidity, he crossed the Tennessee River, captured stockades with their garrisons, burned bridges, destroyed railways, reached the Cumberland River below Nashville, drove away gunboats, captured and destroyed several transports with immense stores, and spread alarm over a wide region. The enemy concentrated on him from all directions, but he eluded or defeated their several columns, recrossed the Tennessee, and brought off fifteen hundred prisoners and much spoil. Like Clive, nature made him a great soldier, but he was without the former's advantages.

General Forrest proceeded with his usual energy to prepare for this expedition. Buford's division was ordered to Verona, while the military superintendent of the Mobile and Ohio Railroad was urged to repair that highway as far as Corinth at once for the transportation of Forrest's forces as far as possible on their route toward northern Alabama and middle Tennessee. Chalmers was ordered to take General Forrest's place at Grenada, in command of all the troops not to accompany him on the expedition. A courier was sent to General Roddey in northern Alabama, with instructions to repair the Memphis and Charleston Railroad, and place it in running order from Corinth as far as Cherokee station, near the interstate line of Alabama and Mississippi. Bell's, Lyon's, and Rucker's brigades, with the artillery, were concentrated with Buford at Verona. Everything being in readiness, on September 16th Forrest moved from Verona with 3542 effectives, and on the 18th arrived at Cherokee station, Alabama, which was then the eastern terminus of the Memphis and Charleston Railroad, and here the following order was issued:

1. This entire command will be in readiness to move on the morning of the 16th instant, with four days' cooked rations. They will leave all baggage except one blanket and one change of clothing. All ordnance stores will be shipped by railroad, and the ordnance trains of the command will assist in

transporting forage, forage and ordnance trains moving together. Three days' rations of corn for the command will be carried in the ordnance and forage trains.

2. The command will be supplied with one hundred rounds of ammunition to the man, forty of which will be taken in the cartridge-boxes, the balance to be shipped by railroad.

3. Adjutants will not be allowed to take any more papers than will be necessary for active field-service. No desks will be taken, or other boxes or baggage allowed to be carried.

4. All extra wagons, disabled horses, and baggage will be sent back to Sakatonchee Creek, near West Point. One officer from each brigade and one man to every ten horses will be sent back with the extra wagons, baggage, and unserviceable horses.

5. All dismounted men will be ordered to report to Lieutenant-Colonel Barnett, for the purpose of being organized into a battalion.

6. Lieutenant-Colonel Barnett will organize all dismounted men into a battalion, and be in readiness to move on the morning of the 16th instant with rations and ammunition as above.

7. A full and complete field report of arms, ammunition, horses, and their condition will be sent to these headquarters by the morning of the 15th instant."

After a careful inspection of his command, preparatory to crossing to the north side of the Tennessee River, the men were provided with ammunition and rations, and at daylight on the morning of the 21st of September marched out from Cherokee with their faces toward the north. The artillery, ordnance, and wagon trains were placed in charge of Major Charles W. Anderson, with instructions to be ferried across the Tennessee River at Newport, where boats had already been provided for that purpose. Proceeding with the troops, General Forrest moved to Ross's Ford, at Colbert's Shoals, and with but little difficulty forded the river, which is here about one mile in width. The artillery and wagon trains were safely and rapidly ferried over, and joined the main body of the command five miles west of Florence, where they went into camp. Such was the celerity of movement of the various columns of this expedition that between daylight and dark of the 21st this command had crossed so formidable a barrier as the Tennessee River, and in addition had marched twenty-five miles!

At daylight on the 22nd of September the troops were in the saddle and moving rapidly toward Athens, the county seat of Limestone

County, north Alabama, where was stationed a strong Federal garrison. At Shoal Creek, six miles east of Florence, General Forrest was joined by 900 men from Roddey's division, under Colonel William A. John-

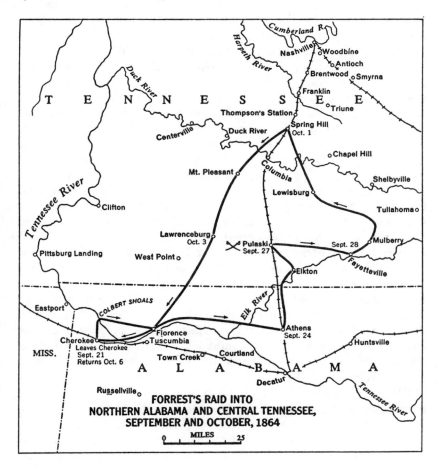

FORREST'S RAID INTO
NORTHERN ALABAMA AND CENTRAL TENNESSEE,
SEPTEMBER AND OCTOBER, 1864

son, who had previously been ordered to cross at Bainbridge and report to him at that point. It will be remembered that this gallant soldier had commanded the right of Forrest's line, and contributed so much to the defeat of Sturgis at Brice's Crossroads. Forrest's entire force now amounted to 4500 effectives, 400 of whom were as yet dismounted and were following on foot, with the expectation of securing horses by capture from the enemy.

The command, having halted only a sufficient time to supply Colonel Johnson's troops with ammunition, continued their march toward Athens. At ten o'clock on the night of the 22nd, the Twentieth Tennessee Cavalry, under Lieutenant Colonel Jesse A. Forrest, and the Fourteenth Tennessee, under Lieutenant Colonel White, of Kelley's brigade, were sent forward under cover of darkness to McDonald's station, a point between Decatur and Athens on the Nashville and Decatur Railroad (called the Alabama and Tennessee Railroad in 1864), to destroy the railroad track and cut the telegraph wires, and to capture a corral of government horses and mules located there.

On the morning of the 23rd the main column moved forward, and arrived near Athens late in the afternoon of the same day. About a mile from town the pickets of the enemy were developed and driven into the village and thence into the fort, from which the garrison opened upon the Confederates with two pieces of artillery. When the outposts were first fired upon, hearing the whistle of a locomotive coming from the direction of Nashville toward Athens, General Forrest ordered Colonel C. R. Barteau, with the Second Tennessee, aided by Major Charles W. Anderson, who was placed in charge of the escort, to move rapidly to the north side of the town and obstruct the railroad, so that the train, having passed, could not escape capture. They were instructed also to cut the wires in that direction. In the prompt and successful execution of this order these two efficient officers were fortunate enough to capture about one hundred horses which were being run out of Athens in the hope of preventing their falling into the hands of the Confederates.

General Tyree H. Bell at the same time was directed to move his brigade to the right and occupy the eastern portion of the suburbs. Meeting with some resistance, Bell, with his well-known intrepidity, forced his way through and bivouacked for the night in the position designated by his commander. Colonel D. C. Kelley, with his brigade, was ordered to move around and occupy the southeastern portion of the town, his left resting near the railroad and his right in touch with Bell.

General Buford, with Lyon's brigade, was stationed on the west, his left on the Florence and Athens road. Colonel Jesse A. Forrest and

Lieutenant Colonel White, who had successfully performed the duty assigned to them on the previous night and were marching from the direction of Decatur toward Athens, halted and deployed between the Brown's Ferry road and the railroad. Colonel W. A. Johnson, with his brigade, was ordered to occupy the street leading from the courthouse toward Florence.

So sudden and unexpected was the appearance of General Forrest, and so rapid was the disposition of his troops, that before escape was possible the Federals found themselves hopelessly corralled in the fort and blockhouses. Taking advantage of the darkness, the Confederate artillery was brought up and placed in position where it could bear upon the fort with the greatest efficacy. Hudson's battery, commanded by Lieutenant E. S. Walton, was placed northeast of the fort; one section of Morton's old battery, commanded by Lieutenant J. M. Mayson, on the west side; another section of this battery, commanded by Lieutenant J. W. Brown, on the north—all the artillery was under the command of Forrest's chief of artillery, Captain John W. Morton.

At seven o'clock on the morning of the 24th of September a general advance was ordered upon the fort, and at the same time the artillery opened upon it. Bell's brigade moved promptly on the east and advanced across the railroad in full view of the fort, while Generals Buford and Lyon, with the latter's brigade, were moving forward at the same moment on the west. Colonel Kelley was ordered to remain in his position, to throw out flankers, and to hold in check the reinforcements reported to be advancing at that time from the direction of Decatur. It was at this moment, while making this great display of force, yet without risk to his men, with the artillery pouring in a concentrated fire upon the garrison, that General Forrest brought into exercise that shrewdness which in a high degree he possessed, and which, as practiced by him, contributed so largely to his success. Appreciating the fact that it would cost heavily to storm and capture the fort, which was well-nigh impregnable, he ordered his troops and the artillery to cease firing.

His chief of staff, Major J. P. Strange, was then sent under a flag of truce to the commander of the garrison with the following communication:

HEADQUARTERS FORREST'S CAVALRY
In the Field, *September* 24, 1864

Officer Commanding U. S. Forces, Athens, Alabama:

I demand an immediate and unconditional surrender of the entire force and all government stores and property at this post. I have a sufficient force to storm and take your works, and if I am forced to do so the responsibility of the consequences must rest with you. Should you, however, accept the terms, all white soldiers shall be treated as prisoners of war and the negroes returned to their masters. A reply is requested immediately.

Respectfully,

N. B. FORREST, Major-General C. S. Army

Forrest's descent upon Athens had been so swift and his movements made with such secrecy that his presence was not suspected until his troops were already in sight and had cut the railway and telegraph south of this important position. Colonel Wallace Campbell of the One Hundred and Tenth United States Colored Infantry, commanding, reports that on the 23rd of September, about three o'clock in the afternoon, he was informed by an employee, who had been at work on the railroad about four miles south of Athens, that two or three hundred Confederates were tearing up the track at that point. He immediately detailed one hundred men to report at the station, ready to board the evening train then due from Nashville.

At four o'clock this detachment was placed on the cars, and had proceeded only four miles in the direction of Decatur when it ran into the pickets of Colonel Jesse Forrest's command, who, it will be remembered, had been sent ahead of the main column to destroy the track and telegraph wires south of Athens. After the train had passed through Colonel Forrest's line of pickets, the Confederates, knowing it would be stopped lower down where the rails had been removed, hastily obstructed the track in its rear. Seeing the trap into which they had fallen, the Federals abandoned the train, made a desperate effort to return to Athens, and after a brisk skirmish broke through Jesse Forrest's picket line and retreated in that direction, taking refuge at first in a blockhouse in the suburbs of the town. Here they engaged the forces under Colonel Forrest for an hour and fifteen minutes, losing three men killed and four wounded, when Colonel Campbell fled from the blockhouse and escaped into the fort in Athens.

Just as the Federal colonel reached his stronghold he learned that the Confederates had already captured the commissary buildings which were near the railway station and some distance removed from the stockade. He learned at the same time that General Forrest, with a force estimated at from ten to twelve thousand troops, with nine pieces of artillery, had completely invested the town. The Confederate leader was playing his old game of magnifying the strength of his command. Colonel Campbell immediately ordered all the Union forces to take refuge in the fort after attempting to destroy what government property he could reach.

To the demand of surrender which Forrest now sent him, he replied: "I have the honor to decline your demand of this date." Upon receipt of this message from the Federal colonel Forrest sent a reply requesting an interview with Colonel Campbell outside the fort, at any place he might designate. This interview was granted, and the Federal commander was invited to inspect the troops of General Forrest's command and judge for himself as to his ability with the force at hand to storm the stockade. Forrest assured Colonel Campbell that he was actuated by the highest principles of humanity in endeavoring to prevent a scene of slaughter which he would be unable to control should the place be carried by storm. At the same time he impressed his antagonist with the idea that he was determined to capture the garrison, no matter at what sacrifice. He says in his report that "Colonel Campbell, accompanied by another officer, went along our lines, and, seeing the number and enthusiasm of the men, he surrendered the fort with its entire garrison."

Colonel Campbell says:

I sent Lieutenant-Colonel J. A. Dewey and acting assistant Adjutant-General William T. Lewis to receive the Confederate flag of truce. They met Major Strange, General Forrest's chief of staff, and Colonel Galloway, and held conversation with them. They said from the conversation held with General Forrest they knew he was determined to take the fort, and if he were compelled to storm it no lives would be spared. I refused to comply with the last demand as with the first, when General Forrest sent in a request for a personal interview, reading as follows:

COLONEL—I desire an interview with you outside of the fort, at any place you may designate, provided it meets with your views. My only object is to stop the effusion of blood that must follow the storming of the place.

N. B. FORREST, Major-General

Accompanied by Lieutenant-Colonel J. A. Dewey, I immediately met General Forrest. He told me that he was determined to take the place, that his force was sufficiently large, and have it he would; and if he was compelled to storm the works, it would result in the massacre of the entire garrison. He told mè what his force was, and said myself and one officer could have the privilege of reviewing his force. I returned to the fort, when, after consultation with the commanders of various detachments in the fort, it was decided that if, after reviewing the force, I found he had eight or ten thousand troops, it would be worse than murder to attempt to hold the works. I then took Captain B. M. Callender and rode round his entire line, thereby satisfying myself and the captain accompanying me that there were at least ten thousand men and nine pieces of artillery. It was now 11 A.M. I had been "dilly-dallying" with General Forrest since 8 A.M., expecting reinforcements would be sent from Decatur. Believing they could not reach me, I ordered the surrender of the fort.

The legerdemain by which Forrest made 4500 troops, the sum total of his command, count up to 10,000 in the eyes of his adversary was the result of the sharp practice to which he was wont to resort. He had so arranged his troops that he displayed a portion of them dismounted and passed them off as infantry, and then, when the Federal colonel had passed to another detachment in the line of Confederates which was stretched around the town, the dismounted troops were made to get on their horses and present themselves in another position as cavalry. The artillery was also moved about to produce a similar impression. In the capture of Streight, near Rome, Georgia, in 1863, Forrest had practiced this device successfully, and on several other occasions since that day.

The expected reinforcements to which Colonel Campbell refers were nearer at hand than he dreamed of at that time, and it was a stroke of good-fortune that Forrest, by his diplomacy, had driven him to the wall when he did and secured the capitulation of the garrison before the firing could be heard from the small arms of the troops which were then not a mile distant and bravely fighting their way to his relief. Forrest was well informed while negotiations were pending that reinforcements were near at hand and were endeavoring to cut their way through to the beleaguered fort. A detachment of the Eighteenth Michigan and One Hundred and Second Ohio Infantry, under Lieutenant Colonel Elliott, had been hurried forward from Decatur by train, but had been intercepted by the Confederates under

Colonels Kelley and Jesse Forrest and Lieutenant Colonel Logwood. The Union troops had taken a strong position behind a lot of cordwood piled along the railroad, which afforded excellent protection.

The Fifteenth Tennessee, under Logwood, with two companies of Forrest's regiment, pluckily charged on the flank of the Federals, and drove them from their breastworks, killing several and capturing eight prisoners. Beaten from this point of vantage, the Union infantry, quitting the railroad, made a detour through the woods in the hope of avoiding a further collision and of reaching Athens; but by a rapid movement Jesse Forrest, with the remaining eight companies of his regiment, placed himself across their path. A desperate encounter at close quarters ensued, in which Colonel Forrest was severely wounded through the thigh and a number of Confederates were placed *hors de combat.* While this struggle was at its height, Confederate reinforcements arrived and, attacking the Federals in flank and rear, compelled the entire force to throw down their arms and surrender unconditionally.

In the negotiations for the surrender of the garrison it was stipulated that the commissioned officers should be permitted to go to Meridian or some other point in Mississippi and, as soon as Major General Forrest could communicate with Major General Washburn, be released on their paroles of honor not to act in opposition to the forces of the Confederate States until they were duly exchanged. The officers were also permitted to retain all personal property, including horses, saddles, sidearms, and clothing. It was agreed that the enlisted men of Colonel Campbell's command should be kindly and. humanely treated and turned over to the Confederate government as prisoners of war, to be disposed of as the War Department of the Confederate States should direct.

There now remained to be captured only two small blockhouses with their garrisons, and one of these surrendered as soon as a demand was made; the other refused, and the artillery immediately opened upon it. The second shot penetrated the walls, killing two and wounding another of the defenders, whereupon a white flag was raised, and these troops also capitulated. Two locomotives, two trains of cars, a large quantity of government stores and ammunition, two pieces of artillery (twelve-pounder howitzers), about one thousand stand of small arms, thirty-eight wagons, two ambulances, and three hundred horses were the booty of the Confederates in this brilliant affair. The prisoners and captured property, under a suitable escort, were at once started for the south side of the Tennessee River under the command of Colonel Nixon.

Immediately after the surrender of the Federal troops, General Forrest moved northward with his command, and four miles from the scene of his first encounter another blockhouse was situated, defended by a garrison of thirty men, who surrendered without resistance. The railroad bridge, for the defense of which this blockhouse was built, was destroyed, and the command encamped, on the night of the 24th of September, eight miles north of Athens.

The work of the day was briefly reported to General Taylor by courier: "My force captured this place (Athens) this morning, with thirteen hundred officers and men, fifty wagons and ambulances, five hundred horses, two trains of cars loaded with quartermaster's and commissary stores, with a large quantity of small arms and two pieces of artillery. My troops in fine spirits. My loss, five killed and twenty-five wounded."

With all this important business pressing upon him, General Forrest was not unmindful of the interests of his old department in northern Mississippi. He wrote General Taylor that he had received information which led him to believe that another move from Memphis toward the prairie country was under consideration, and that in order to keep them as far away from Corinth as possible he had directed Chalmers to destroy all the trestles and bridges along the line of the Memphis and Charleston Railroad from La Grange to a point as near Memphis as he could reach.

Early on the morning of the 25th the command moved upon the heavy stockade at Sulphur Springs trestle, where the pickets were driven in and the place soon invested. There were here two blockhouses and a formidable fort situated upon an eminence, all strongly garrisoned and thoroughly well protected by the art of the engineer, as this was considered one of the most important bridges on the Alabama and Tennessee Railroad. At a considerable distance from the fort, yet within reach of his long-range guns, Forrest noticed an elevation which would enable him to command the most important of the Federal defenses, and here he placed the two heavy Parrott guns of Hudson's battery, commanded by Lieutenant E. S. Walton; another section of Ferrell's battery and the two sections of Morton's old battery—all in command of Captain John W. Morton—were placed on different sides of the

Federal stockade. These dispositions were quickly made, and the guns opened without the prelude of a demand for surrender.

Under cover of the artillery, General Buford moved forward with alacrity, while Colonel Kelley's brigade was led by this gallant officer in a rush across an exposed clearing to a position where his men could use their rifles with great effect. In this advance several of Kelley's troopers were killed and wounded, and the colonel's horse fell dead beneath him. Having his troops in position, so accurate was the fire of Colonel Kelley's men that the enemy scarcely dared to raise their heads above their works. At the same time the artillery from four different points poured in such a concentrated and destructive stream of shell that the garrison was thrown into a state of great consternation and suffered tremendous loss. In a very short while no resistance whatever was offered by the Union forces within the fort, observing which, Forrest says:

I deemed this an appropriate occasion to demand a surrender, and sent a flag of truce for that purpose. After a short parley with Colonel J. B. Minnis, the commanding officer, the fort surrendered. The enemy suffered severely in this assault. The colonel (Lathrop) commanding was killed early in the fight. Almost every house was perforated with shell, and the dead lay thick along the works of the fort. The fruits of this victory consist, besides the prisoners, of seven hundred stands of small arms, two pieces of artillery, three ambulances, sixteen wagons, three hundred cavalry horses and equipments, medical, quartermaster's, and commissary stores. The trestlework at this place was seventy-two feet high and three hundred feet long, and defended by two large block-houses, all of which were consumed by fire. The prisoners were turned over to Colonel Logwood, who started with them to the Tennessee River.

The number of prisoners captured here is incorrectly stated in the official reports. Captain H. T. Hanks of Company C, Fifteenth Tennessee, Colonel Logwood's regiment, was placed in command of these prisoners immediately after their capture and personally made a careful roster of the prisoners, a copy of which he retained and which was reported to General Forrest's adjutant, showing 973 captured Federals.[1]

While the fight at Sulphur Branch trestle was in progress, Colonel George Spalding, of the Twelfth Tennessee Union Cavalry, was march-

[1] Diary of Captain H. T. Hanks of Ripley, Tennessee, in possession of the author.

ing to the reinforcement of the beleaguered Federals, but concluded after approaching within sound of the fire to retrace his steps to a safer quarter. He reports: "In accordance with orders from General Stark-weather I moved about 3 A.M. on the 25th for Elk River bridge. I was ordered to assume command of all the forces between Sulphur Branch and Elk River. I arrived at Elk River about 8 A.M. on the 25th, and as soon as the horses of the command were fed I moved to the support of Sulphur Branch, the troops at that place being very hard pressed. I had eight hundred men, and arrived near the trestle at 11 A.M. on the 25th and found the enemy in strong force. I engaged them immediately with my small but gallant force, and after fighting about twenty minutes I learned that the fort near the trestle had surrendered. I therefore deemed it prudent to withdraw to Elk River."

It was to have been expected that Forrest's sudden appearance in northern Alabama and middle Tennessee would excite considerable concern at the headquarters of the commanders of the armies of the Potomac and of the Tennessee. Major General Rousseau, on the 25th of September, had informed his immediate superior (Thomas) that Forrest was tearing up the track and burning blockhouses as he went, and playing the mischief generally:

Despatches just received indicate that this afternoon the forces at Sulphur Branch trestle, consisting principally of dismounted men from the Ninth and Tenth Indiana Cavalry, eight hundred strong, with two pieces of artillery, and in a fort, surrendered to Forrest, who appears to be tearing up the track and capturing blockhouses and forts as he goes. Rebel forces were reported advancing on Elk River bridge. General Croxton left Franklin with brigade of cavalry at daylight this morning. I have sent by train to Pulaski thirteen hundred cavalry and a battery, and will follow in an hour with all the other force that can be spared from here. Troops sent to reinforce the Nashville and Chattanooga road should report to General Milroy at Tullahoma, as he has full instructions where to place the men.

It is also evident that Forrest's invasion had seriously interfered with the grand strategy of Grant and Sherman, as shown from the following dispatches of that day on record. On the 26th of September, from City Point, Grant telegraphed Sherman: "It will be better to drive Forrest from middle Tennessee as a first step, and do anything else that you may feel your force sufficient for"; and Sherman answered: "I have your dispatch of to-day. Have already sent one division (General Newton's to Chattanooga, and another (Corse's) to Rome. *Our armies are much reduced, and if I send back more I will not be able to threaten Georgia much.*[2] There are men enough to the rear to whip Forrest, but they are necessarily scattered to defend the road. Can't you expedite the sending to Nashville of the recruits that are in Indiana and Ohio? They could occupy the forts. Forrest is now lieutenant-general and commands all the enemy's cavalry."

From these dispatches some idea may be formed of the effect such a movement by Forrest, as suggested by Generals Johnston and Cobb and Governor Brown of Georgia, would have had upon Sherman's advance to Atlanta earlier in the campaign.

The morning of September 29th found Forrest pushing still farther north with his raiders. With the horses captured at Athens and Sulphur Branch trestle he was now able not only to mount the detachment of his men which had accompanied the expedition on foot but also to supply those whose horses had given out. General Buford, with a portion of the command, was ordered to follow along the line of the railroad as far as Elk River, and in so doing he came upon a blockhouse which had been evacuated by the enemy. This he destroyed, together with the extensive bridge across Elk River, and the long trestle which approached it from one side.

With the main column, General Forrest marched to Elkton, and thence to a government corral at Brown's plantation, near Pulaski, where he captured some two thousand Negroes and a large amount of commissary stores and medical supplies. For the first time in many months the Confederate troopers enjoyed the luxury of as much sugar and "sure enough" coffee as they wanted. Forrest says in his report: "Here I issued to my entire command several days' rations, distributing among the troops as much sugar and coffee as they needed. The negroes were all ragged and dirty, and many seemed in absolute want. I ordered them to remove their clothing and bedclothes from the miserable hovels in which they lived, and then burned up this den of wretchedness. Nearly two hundred houses were thus consumed."

Colonel Spalding, who had withdrawn from in front of Sulphur Branch trestle while Forrest was hammering away at the garrison with his artillery, had retreated to the Elk River stockade and placed his men in the blockhouses and fort there, but later, as Buford approached,

[2] Italics added.

had concluded to abandon this position and move still farther toward Pulaski. He says:

> At 3 A.M. on the 26th, reinforcements not having arrived, and the enemy having driven in my pickets, left and front, I deemed it necessary to move my cavalry out of such a position as soon as possible. Before morning I sent for the officers commanding the colored troops at Elk River bridge, and ordered them to hold the block-houses at all hazards; and also exhibited the despatches in regard to reinforcements. I told them I would be obliged to withdraw my cavalry or Forrest would have me surrounded before day-light. They promised to hold the block-houses until they were knocked to pieces. I then moved off gently in the direction of Pulaski, until daybreak, when I halted to learn the location of the country. To my great surprise I found that the negro soldiers and their officers whom I had left to hold the bridge had abandoned the stockade, and had been in advance of my cavalry all the morning, having evacuated the stockades without firing a shot. I arrested all of my colored soldiers, and sent them under guard to Richland Creek bridge, that being the nearest block-house. At Richland Creek I found that the officer in charge of the block-houses had ordered the colored soldiers to pack their knapsacks, preparatory to a move to Pulaski. I immediately sent directions to the captain in command to make a stubborn resistance, and also stated that I would support him, and shoot every officer and soldier that I found deserting his post.

Neither the colonel's orders nor threats availed, for after a short resistance the garrison of fifty men surrendered, after which the Confederates crossed the creek and encamped for the night ten miles from Pulaski. From this point Forrest reported to General Taylor: "I succeeded yesterday in capturing three block-houses and the fort at Elk River, with about fifty prisoners, without the loss of a man, and have entirely destroyed the railroad from Decatur to Pulaski, and five large railroad bridges, which will require sixty days to replace."

On the 27th Buford's division, moving along the railroad toward Pulaski, was thrown forward, while Kelley and Johnson's brigades were ordered to proceed by a parallel route in the same direction. Six miles from Pulaski the advance guard of Forrest's command collided with a heavy force of the Federals and was driven back. General Buford hurried forward with his division and, notwithstanding the strong position occupied by the enemy, attacked vigorously. Resisting every inch of ground with great stubbornness, the Federals gradually retired to within three miles of the town, where they made a still more desperate and determined stand. Colonel Kelley now occupied the extreme Confederate left, Johnson the center, and General Buford the right, and the engagement soon became general. The Union commander, with great boldness, extended his right and advanced it for the purpose of enfilading Forrest's troops upon the left of the Confederate line; but General Forrest, making his accustomed excellent use of the artillery, defeated this effort, breaking their line at this point, upon which he immediately ordered a charge, and the Federals gave way precipitately. In this spirited affair Colonel Johnson received a severe wound through the knee joint, from which he suffered greatly to the time of his death, some twenty years after the war.

Retreating in haste, the Union troops were closely pursued into Pulaski and behind their breastworks. It was one o'clock in the afternoon when this was accomplished. Placing himself at the head of his escort, General Forrest moved to the right and rear of the Federal position in order to make a careful reconnaissance, in which he satisfied himself that the Union forces were too numerous and too well posted to justify an assault. Remaining in their front until nightfall, and maneuvering his troops as if bent upon a further attack, the Confederate leader then ordered campfires to be built for the purpose of deceiving the Federal general. Leaving pickets so placed as to notify him of any advance on the part of the Union forces, General Forrest, under cover of darkness, withdrew and eight miles from Pulaski bivouacked for the night. Just before retreating, Colonel Wheeler, with a detachment of about three hundred men, was ordered to proceed north of the town and destroy the railroad and telegraph line between Pulaski and Columbia, which duty he faithfully and successfully performed, burning at the same time a large supply of wood intended for the use of the locomotives.

From here Forrest reported to General Taylor, on the 27th: "I have driven the enemy, after fighting all day, into his fortifications at this place, and find General Rousseau with a heavy force well fortified. I will move to the Nashville and Chattanooga railroad. My loss to-day about one hundred; enemy's much heavier, having contested ground for several miles. Enemy concentrating heavily against me."

On the 28th Forrest had reached Fayetteville, and from this place ordered Captain Boone, with twenty picked men of the escort, to proceed as rapidly as possible to the Nashville and Chattanooga Railroad, at some point north of Tullahoma, and there to cut the telegraph wires and tear up the rails. At the same time, Captain Kelleher was detailed with thirty men of the Twelfth Kentucky to strike this same railroad south of Tullahoma, and also to remove some of the rails and destroy the telegraph wires.

On September 29th General Forrest moved toward Tullahoma with the main column, but, on arriving at Mulberry, his scouts informed him that the enemy were in heavy force and strongly posted in the town and along the railroad, and that heavy columns of reinforcements were coming by train from Chattanooga and Nashville.

The information of Forrest's scouts was correct. A large army of Federals, under Generals Thomas, Rousseau, Schofield, Steedman, Croxton, Webster, Granger, Washburn, and A. J. Smith, was gathering in upon him. Fully 30,000 men were for the time being diverted from the grand purpose of the Georgia campaign, and this whole force, General Thomas says, "should press Forrest to the death, keeping your troops well in hand and holding them to the work. I do not think that we shall ever have a better chance than this."

Sherman had wired General Webster at Nashville: "Rousseau should collect all the force he can, and move straight for Pulaski and Florence. Call forward from Kentucky any troops that can be spared there, and hold all that come from the rear, until Forrest is disposed of. Caution Rousseau to unite this movable force and let it not be picked up in detail. Ask Rosecrans for me if he cannot spare A. J. Smith, and explain to him that he may be needed. I wanted him for this very contingency, which I foresaw. Use my name and concentrate at Nashville all the men you can. Recall Generals Steedman and Schofield if you know where they are. The policy should be, small but well-commanded bodies in the block-houses, and a movable force to act straight against Forrest, who must scatter for forage."

General Thomas's report says: "As Forrest changed the scene of his operations from the Decatur railroad over to the one leading to Chattanooga, General Rousseau moved rapidly by rail around through Nashville to Tullahoma, and prepared for his reception. On the same day, 5000 men under General J. B. Steedman crossed north of the Tennessee River from the direction of Chattanooga. Newton's division was ordered from Atlanta on the 26th of September, and Morgan's corps started on the 29th of September to reinforce the troops operating against Forrest." In this report General Thomas speaks of Forrest and his command as "an enthusiastic cavalry command led by one of the boldest and most successful commanders of the rebel army."

On the 28th Sherman had dispatched Grant: "I send back to Stevenson and Decherd, General Thomas to look to Tennessee, and have ordered a brigade of the Army of the Tennessee up to Eastport, and the cavalry across to that place from Memphis, to operate against the flank of any force going into Tennessee by way of the fords near Florence. Forrest has got into middle Tennessee, and will, I feel certain, get on my main road to-night or to-morrow."

Again on this day he telegraphed to General Webster at Nashville: "General Grant telegraphs me that he has ordered many troops to Nashville. I want you to recall General Burbridge and concentrate all the troops possible to push Forrest. I send General Thomas up to Stevenson to work from this direction. I can hold Atlanta and my communications back to Chattanooga."

This was followed by a second dispatch, which says: "I will send up the road to-night another division, and want you to call forward from the rear all you can get, to operate in Forrest's rear."

To Granger the wily Sherman, who gave his personal attention to the smallest details of his campaign, telegraphed that he should drive any squads of Forrest's men across the Elk and threaten the fords at Lamb's and Elkton, and act in concert with Rousseau. "Keep your surplus men so as to move quick and to strike Forrest's line of retreat or communication."

On the 29th of September Sherman telegraphed to Halleck: "I take it for granted that Forrest will cut our road, but I think we can prevent his making a serious lodgment. His cavalry will travel one hundred miles in less time than ours will ten. I have sent two divisions up to Chattanooga and one to Rome, and Thomas started to-day to clear out Tennessee, but our road should be watched from the rear, and I am glad General Grant has ordered reserves for me to Nashville. I can whip his infantry, but *his cavalry is to be feared.*"

To Major General Thomas, on the 29th of September, he says: "If Forrest is about the tunnel and Decherd you must look out for him coming down by the University and Battle Creek to Stevenson and Bridgeport. General Granger should open communication with Rousseau at Pulaski, even if he has to risk a fight, for Forrest will only leave a detachment at Elkton or Prospect."

To General Elliott, chief of cavalry, Department of the Cumberland, on the same date he telegraphed: "Our cavalry must do more, for it is strange Forrest and Wheeler should circle around us thus. We should at least make ten miles to his hundred."

To Granger a second warning: "A strong division has gone up the road, and will act against Forrest. Don't scatter too much or try to hold too many points. We will have some heavy reinforcements from the North."

To General Ammen, commanding district of east Tennessee, he dispatched: "Recall General Burbridge with his forces, to come to Nashville."

On the 29th, Stanton, Secretary of War, telegraphed the governor of Michigan: "There is urgent need that every enlisted man be hurried forward to Nashville, to guard General Sherman's communications, without an hour's delay."[8]

Stanton had been stirred up by the telegram received this day by Thomas from Rousseau: "Forrest struck the road, and destroyed it thoroughly from Athens to within a few miles of Pulaski. He will not leave until he has thoroughly destroyed the railroad, unless killed or captured. His force is an effective one, and amounts to six or seven thousand men, with artillery."

On the 30th of September Sherman telegraphs Thomas to "push right at Forrest with as heavy a force as you can get and as soon as possible. If you can turn him towards Lamb's ferry, Granger should hold him in check until the infantry can get up. We will never have a better chance at him than now. I will watch Hood here."

To General Cox, at Decatur, Sherman says: "I know that desperate efforts will be made to render our roads useless. Forrest is in middle Tennessee, but I think will have his hands full, for I have sent up two divisions of Thomas's, and Thomas went up himself yesterday."

Rousseau summed up the situation to Sherman as follows:

Forrest struck the road at Athens, and destroyed it to within a few miles of Pulaski, where I had repulsed him on the 27th instant. He is here to stay, unless driven back and routed by a superior cavalry force. Infantry can cause him to change camp, but cannot drive him out of the State.

[3] *Official Records,* vol. xxxix, part ii, p. 531.

Forrest's movements are much more cautious than formerly. He has attacked no place held by white men, but every post held by colored troops has been taken, and his destruction of railroad was most thorough. I have here about three thousand cavalry, not enough to fight him without support. This is much more than a raid; I regard it as a formidable invasion, the object of which is to destroy our lines, and he will surely do it unless met by a large cavalry force, and killed, captured, or routed. The cavalry, supported by infantry, can fight and defeat him, but he must be caught. He will not give battle unless he chooses to do so.

With all this concentration against him, it was wisdom on the part of Forrest to call a halt. At Athens, Sulphur Branch trestle, and Pulaski, and the other small engagements, he had expended nearly all of his artillery ammunition, and his force had been considerably depleted by the large details sent back to guard prisoners and take care of the captured property sent south. He therefore abandoned for the present any idea of destroying extensively the Nashville and Chattanooga Railroad. General Buford, with a portion of his division and Kelley's and Johnson's brigades, was ordered to proceed in the direction of Huntsville and along the line of the Memphis and Charleston Railroad from Huntsville to Decatur, tearing up the track and destroying the trestles and bridges.

With the remainder of his troops, consisting of Lyon's and Bell's brigades, the Seventh Tennessee, and Forrest's old regiment, General Forrest in person, moving to the right of Shelbyville, and by an obscure, circuitous route to Lewisburg, reached the latter place at twelve o'clock on the 30th of September and encamped that night on the north side of Duck River. On the 1st of October he reached Spring Hill, captured at that place some government horses and wagons, and from thence proceeded in the direction of Columbia. At Spring Hill the telegraph wires were tapped and important information secured in regard to the movements of various bodies of troops sent to intercept the Confederates. Forrest also took occasion to send to the Federal commander of this department (General Rousseau) a series of dispatches tending to mislead him in regard to his own line of march. These dispatches were signed by the Federal commander in the field, and stated that Forrest was still destroying the railroad from Nashville to Decatur.

Twelve miles from Columbia he captured four blockhouses and

their garrisons of 120 men. The blockhouses, a large government saw-mill, and three railroad bridges were burned. A fifth blockhouse was encountered, but the plucky commander declined to surrender; and as General Forrest had no artillery with him at this time, all the ordnance having been dispatched south with Buford and Kelley, it became necessary to call for volunteers to attempt the destruction of the bridge which was so resolutely guarded by this small but formidable garrison. Bundles of dry wood saturated with turpentine were prepared, and with these the daring men who undertook the destruction of this trestle, protected by sharpshooters favorably posted by Forrest, crawled along the edge of the stream under shelter of the bluff bank nearest to the Federals and, placing their kindling wood and combustible material upon the woodwork of the bridge, quickly ignited it and made their escape, fortunately without loss. The firing was still continued in order to prevent a sortie on the part of the garrison to extinguish the conflagration until the bridge was destroyed.

On the morning of the 2nd General Forrest continued his march upon Columbia, and when within six miles of the town a detachment under Colonel Wheeler was sent in advance to drive in the enemy's pickets, while Bell's brigade proceeded to invest the town on the northern side, with Lyon on the west. Having convinced himself by a careful reconnaissance that the place was heavily garrisoned, and being without artillery, he made no further attempt to take it by assault, but withdrew his troops and encamped for the night at Mount Pleasant. On the 3rd of October, moving now with all possible celerity in the direction of the Tennessee River to escape the Federal columns that were concentrating in that direction to prevent his escape, he camped on the night of the 3rd at Lawrenceburg.

The march southward was continued all day on the 4th, and on the 5th he reached Florence, where he found the river, which had been forded two weeks before by the troops, so swollen by recent rains that it could no longer be crossed on horseback. General Buford, who, it will be remembered, had been detached in front of Pulaski and ordered to make a feint upon Huntsville and Athens and proceed thence rapidly to Colbert Ferry on the Tennessee River, had arrived at Florence thirty-six hours ahead of Forrest, and had already ferried the artillery wagons and a large portion of his own command safely to the south bank of this stream. There were only three ordinary ferryboats which could be obtained, and these were kept going night and day transporting the men, ammunition, guns, and saddles, and the weaker horses, which from their run-down condition would be less able to swim the river should this become necessary on the near approach of the pursuing Federals.

On the 6th, hearing that the Federals in force had already arrived in Athens, and in two columns were advancing toward his place of crossing on the Tennessee River, General Forrest sent a detachment of troops under Colonel Windes of Roddey's division to Shoal Creek, to contest the advance of the enemy there, with orders to hold him back as long as possible and, when beaten, to retreat in a direction down the river in the hope of decoying the Union forces in that direction. The troops under Colonel Windes were reinforced a few hours later by two regiments of Bell's brigade, and, upon their arrival at Shoal Creek, Windes was directed to lead his detachment on the flank and rear of the approaching column of the enemy in order to make a diversion in that direction. These troops so thoroughly performed the work which was entrusted to them that it was not until the 8th of October that they were driven back and the head of the Federal column entered the town of Florence.

As there were still more than a thousand of Forrest's men on the northern bank of the river (in addition to the detachment of Bell's brigade and Colonel Windes' troops), the situation, with an overwhelming force of the pursuing Federals almost in sight, was indeed precarious; but Forrest's brain had proved itself equal to more desperate emergencies than this. A few miles down the Tennessee River from the point where he had been crossing, there was situated in this stream a long island, covered with an almost impenetrable growth of cane and, in addition, heavy oak and hickory timber. The slough, or portion of the river between the mainland and the northern shore of the island, was not more than two hundred feet in width. At the upper end of the island sand and driftwood had accumulated, and, while along the entire northern shore the bluff was so steep that men and horses could only with great difficulty ascend it, at this point the water was shallow and the bank sloped gradually to the edge of the cane and timber.

The troops were moved rapidly to a point on the riverbank somewhat above the upper end of the island; the ferryboats were dropped down with the current; the saddles and accouterments were stripped from the animals, piled into the boats in great haste, and ferried over to the southern shore of the island, where the boats could not be seen from the north bank of the Tennessee. The horses were then led close to the edge of the steep bluff and pushed into the water, tumbling down fifteen or twenty feet into the stream. One or two of these, with halters attached, were then caught and the strap held by a trooper in a skiff, which was rowed to the upper point of the island. The other horses, as fast as they were thrown into the stream, followed the pilots which were being towed across, and within an hour's time, with the loss of six horses, the men and animals had landed on the island, had made their way into the depths of the canebrakes, and were safely hidden along the southern shore. Unobserved by the enemy who a few hours later were lining the northern bank, the ferriage was continued to the southern bank of the Tennessee River for two days and nights, when all the troops were safely over.

Throughout these busy days and nights Forrest was one of the most indefatigable of workers. Nothing seemed to tire him, and he had little patience with any man who showed a disposition to shirk. After having reached the island in safety, although it was quite cold, the men were not allowed to build fires for fear the smoke might attract the attention of the enemy and lead to their discovery. Several detachments on picket duty had been left along the northern bank of the island, to give timely notice in case an attempt should be made by the Federals to cross the slough. As the last boatloads were about ready to put out, these detachments were called in; but in order to be sure that no men were left, Forrest in person made a tour of the outposts. Coming upon four troopers who had been overlooked, and who were thus saved from capture by his precaution, the general, stalking in among them, said: "I thought I would catch some of you damned fools loafing back here in the cane as if nothing was going on; if you don't want to get left all winter on this island you had better come along with me; the last boat is going over right away."

A survivor of this incident[4] states:

When we reached the boat we were all made to take our turn at the oars and poles, and do our share of the work in ferrying across the river. The general, evidently worried and tired out, was on the rampage, and

[4] Dr. Z. T. Bundy, of Texas. Manuscripts in possession of the author.

was showing considerable disregard of the third commandment. There happened to be standing in the bow of the boat a lieutenant who took no part whatever in the labor of propelling the craft, noticing which, Forrest said to him: "Why don't you take hold of an oar or pole and help get this boat across?" The lieutenant responded that he was an officer, and did not think he was called upon to do that kind of work as long as there were private soldiers sufficient to perform that duty. As the general was tugging away with a pole when this reply was made, he flew into a rage, and, holding the pole in one hand, with the other he gave the unfortunate lieutenant a slap on the side of the face which sent him sprawling over the gunwale and into the river. He was rescued by catching hold of the pole held out to him and was safely landed in the boat, when the irate general said to him: "Now, damn you, get hold of the oars and go to work! If I knock you out of the boat again I'll let you drown." Forrest's rough-and-ready discipline was effectual; the young officer made an excellent hand for the balance of the trip.

The troops which had been left on the north side of the river to retard the advance of the Federals who were closing in upon Forrest, as soon as they were informed that the general had safely reached the island, retreated down the Tennessee River, and on the 13th of October safely crossed, with a loss of two men killed and four missing. Colonel Wilson, of Bell's brigade, received special commendation for the successful manner in which he conducted this movement. Forrest says: "He is entitled to the commendation of his government and its lasting gratitude for the faithful manner in which he performed this important and hazardous trust. Surrounded by fifteen thousand of the enemy for three days, he hung upon his flanks, assaulted him on every favorable occasion, retiring to the hills when pushed, and subsisting upon supplies captured from the enemy. He made no effort to escape from his perilous situation until every Confederate soldier was across the river, when he ferried over his own regiment and joined his command."

On the 6th of October General Forrest was again at Cherokee station, in Alabama, which place he had left on the 21st of September. Having been informed of the approach of a flotilla up the river with reinforcements for General Rousseau, which it had been intended should arrive in time to prevent the passage of the Tennessee by Forrest, he dispatched about five hundred men under Colonel D. C. Kelley, with a section of artillery from Hudson's battery, under the command of Lieutenant Walton, to take position at or near Eastport in order to prevent any advance from that direction. Colonel Kelley, by a skillful disposition of his troops and by masking his batteries, succeeded in concealing the presence of his command from the enemy, who on the 10th came in sight, steaming up the river with two gunboats and three transports.

The Federal troops in this expedition (commanded by Colonel George B. Hoge) consisted of the One Hundred and Thirteenth and One Hundred and Twentieth Illinois and the Sixty-first Colored Infantry, and Company G of the Second Missouri Light Artillery. They formed part of the expedition of three thousand troops under General C. C. Washburn which had sailed on the 1st of October from Cairo to Florence, Alabama. Hoge was ordered on the 8th of October to proceed up the Tennessee River to Eastport, move rapidly out to Iuka, break the railroad and destroy the bridges, and then to hold Eastport until he could hear from General Washburn. In his report Colonel George B. Hoge says:

On nearing Eastport the gunboat *Key West* went above the landing, and seemed to be satisfied that there was no enemy near, and I immediately landed the troops. Lieutenants Lytle and Boals, as soon as they could land their horses, started out to reconnoitre, and about five hundred yards off the landing came upon the pickets of the enemy. A masked battery (I think it was a battery of at least six rifled guns), and shortly after a battery of three rifled guns at Chickasaw, opened on us. I immediately went on shore and had a line of battle formed. The enemy had got a perfect range of the transports, every shot doing more or less execution. One of the gunboats (*Undine*) had become disabled and was dropping down the river, and the *Key West* followed her. I ordered the troops to be placed on board.

I then went on board the transport *City of Pekin,* when a shell from the enemy struck a caisson of the battery on board the *Kenton,* exploding it and setting fire to the boat. Immediately after this a caisson exploded on the *Aurora,* setting fire to her, and also bursting her steam-pipe. A scene of confusion then began. The boats, in spite of all I could do, backed out, parting their lines, leaving about two-thirds of the command on the shore. The troops that were left on the bank were commanded to keep in good order and proceed down under the river-bluff, and they would all be taken on board. A number were thus rescued. I am sorry to have to report the loss of the four guns of the battery.

After this disastrous termination to the expedition, Colonel Hoge concluded to return to Johnsonville, where he arrived that day. He reports 18 killed, 31 wounded, 25 missing: total 74. This brilliant affair entitled Colonel D. C. Kelley to the unstinted praise which his commander bestowed upon him.

General Forrest, in his official report, says:

During the expedition I captured 86 commissioned officers, 67 government employes, 1274 non-commissioned officers and privates, 933 negroes, besides killing and wounding in the various engagements about 1000 more, making an aggregate of 3360, being an average of one to each man I had in the engagements. In addition to these I captured about eight hundred horses, seven pieces of artillery,[5] two thousand stands of small arms, several hundred saddles, fifty wagons and ambulances, with a large amount of medical, commissary, and quartermaster's stores, all of which have been distributed to the different commands. The greatest damage done to the enemy was in the complete destruction of the railroad from Decatur to Spring Hill, with the exception of the Duck River bridge. It will require months to repair the injury done to the road, and may possibly be the means of forcing the evacuation of Pulaski and Columbia, and thus relieve the people from further oppression.

Forrest lost, in the expedition, 47 killed, 293 wounded, making a total of 340 killed and wounded.

The amount of damage done to the various stockades and fortified places along the route may be gathered from the following report of Brigadier General D. C. McCallum, General Director of Railroads of the United States, dated the 13th of October, 1864:

Forrest burned one engine and twelve cars at Decatur Junction; three cars between Huntsville and Stevenson; all the bridges and trestles between Pulaski and Athens, a distance of thirty miles. This embraced Elk River bridge, and the most formidable trestle on the Decatur and Stevenson line, eleven hundred feet long and about ninety feet high; and also partially destroyed two miles and a half of track. Between Spring Hill and Columbia three bridges and two to three miles of track were destroyed. The Chattanooga line was uninjured, except the tearing up of one or two rails by small guerilla parties. It will take until the 20th of the present month to

[5] He captured eight pieces of artillery: two at Athens, two at Sulphur Branch trestle, and four at Eastport.

restore the communication between Chattanooga and Atlanta. Many engines have been thrown from the track by the removal of the rails, but no very serious accidents have occurred.

Lieutenant Albert Kramer, Sixty-eighth New York Infantry, Assistant Inspector of Blockhouses, reports:

On Saturday, at 1 P.M., came General Forrest and staff with flag of truce to block-house No. 5, in command of Lieutenant E. Nixon, and demanded the surrender of the block-house and garrison, which demand Lieutenant Nixon complied with without firing a shot. Lieutenant Nixon ordered block-houses No. 3, No. 4, and No. 5 to surrender. On demand of the surrender of block-house No. 6, bridge No. 5, refusal was made. Lieutenant Long fought the enemy from 2 P.M. until 12 midnight; killed ten rebels, and wounded several, but they succeeded in destroying his bridge. Lieutenant Long reports the surrender of block-houses No. 3, No. 4, and No. 5; also bridges No. 3 and No. 4. Block-house No. 6 and bridge No. 5 refused to surrender, and the rebels, under cover of the railroad bank, succeeded in firing the bridge with turpentine. One end was burned, and the whole fell in. Block-houses No. 3, No. 4, and No. 5 are burned to the ground; also bridges No. 3 and No. 4. At Carter's Creek station the water-tank and saw-mill were destroyed, and the railroad rendered useless from there to Spring Hill. The rebels had no artillery, and the three block-houses were double cased up to the top log of the loop-holes. The garrisons of the three block-houses, water-tank, and saw-mill were taken prisoners, except one man who escaped. Block-house No. 3 was garrisoned with thirty-two men; block-house No. 4 with twenty-two men; block-house No. 5 with thirty-one men; and thirty men garrisoned the water-tank and saw-mill; altogether, one hundred and fifteen men captured.

From Cherokee station General Forrest moved his troops to Corinth, where he arrived on the 12th of October. From Cherokee, on October 8th, the following letter had been written to General Taylor:

CHEROKEE, *October* 8, 1864

Lieutenant-General R. Taylor, Commanding, etc.:

GENERAL—I have been constantly in the field since 1861, and have spent half the entire time in the saddle. I have never asked for a furlough for over ten days in which to rest and recruit, and except when wounded and unable to leave my bed have had no respite from duty. My strength is failing, and it is absolutely necessary that I should have some rest. I left a large estate in Mississippi, and have never given my private affairs a day's attention at any one time since the war began. Will make the trip to west

Tennessee, and hope as soon thereafter as you can do so you will relieve me from duty for twenty or thirty days to rest and recruit. I have received letters from Colonel McCulloch at Mobile. He and his command are much dissatisfied, and I respectfully ask that my two divisions be placed, as they originally were, under the command of Brigadier-Generals Chalmers and Buford, and that Mabry's brigade be substituted for McCulloch's, which change would in my opinion be satisfactory to all parties. I have captured since I came into this department over thirty pieces of artillery, fitting up my command with four batteries (in all sixteen guns).[6] They are now scattered, and I desire, if possible, to get all my command together, and with General Chalmers as senior officer feel that it would be safe to leave the command for a short time, which, in my present state of health, is absolutely necessary, and which you will confer a favor on me by granting as early as consistent with the good of the service.

I am, General, very respectfully, your obedient servant,

N. B. FORREST, Major-General

Sherman had at least begun to despair of keeping intact his communications from Atlanta to Nashville. On the 9th of October he had telegraphed Grant: "It will be a physical impossibility to protect the roads, now that Hood, Forrest, and Wheeler, and the whole batch of devils are turned loose without home or habitation."

The invasion of north Alabama and middle Tennessee had forced his hand, and now to Grant he said: "I propose we break up the railroad from Chattanooga and strike out with wagons for Savannah."

[6] The records show that Forrest, from the time he assumed command in Mississippi, had captured thirty-nine pieces of artillery, including those taken from General W. Sooy Smith.

NINETEEN

The Johnsonville Expedition

THE raid from which Forrest was just returning had seriously interfered with the transportation of supplies toward Sherman's army in Georgia, and had emphasized the determination already arrived at in the mind of that officer to establish another route by which his army could be reached. He had, in fact, already made Johnsonville, on the Tennessee River, an important base for his commissariat, and Forrest, fully informed of this, had reported it to his superior, General Taylor.

His request for a leave of absence could not be entertained for the present, and he had scarcely dismounted from the saddle after reaching Cherokee when he received orders from Lieutenant General Taylor to start at the earliest practicable moment into west Tennessee, in order to interrupt the navigation of the Tennessee River and to destroy at Johnsonville the immense stores which the Federal government were gathering at that important center of distribution. It was while this correspondence was being carried on that General Taylor took occasion to refer in terms of high appreciation to Forrest's recent achievements: "Could anything add new lustre to your already justly earned reputation, I feel assured the complete success of your last expedition would do all that the most ambitious could desire. Permit me, General, to thank you and your noble followers, and to express the hope that all your future expeditions may prove as advantageous to our cause and as hurtful to that of the enemy as your last."

The much-needed rest was promised upon his return from this proposed expedition, but events over which neither he nor General Taylor could exercise control were then transpiring which were to carry him beyond Johnsonville into middle Tennessee again, and into a campaign so disastrous that it practically wiped out of existence one of the bravest armies of the South and sealed the doom of the Confederacy.

Forrest now applied himself with great energy to the transfer of his troops from Cherokee station to Corinth, in Mississippi, and to the repair of the Mobile and Ohio Railroad from that point northward to Bethel or Henderson station for the transportation of his troops and artillery. Chalmers, who had been left in the neighborhood of Memphis, was directed, if the condition of affairs there would permit, to move with his division and unite with Forrest at Jackson in west Tennessee about the 16th of October. He informed Chalmers that he would be at Corinth by the 12th, and would proceed immediately to Paris, and thence to Jackson at the date above given.

The movement of the Confederate army through northern Alabama to Decatur and Florence, and thence across the Tennessee River toward Franklin and Nashville, was now in full swing. Realizing that Hood's invasion of middle Tennessee would necessitate such a concentration of the Union forces about Nashville as would weaken the garrisons in Memphis and other stations in the section where Forrest was operating, he earnestly requested to be permitted to remain with his command in the west. He argued that this section would now be practically at his mercy, and he could still further strip it of supplies for the use of the army. Should Hood succeed in his essay he could then cross the Tennessee River and unite with him in the forward movement to Kentucky. To Chalmers he writes: "I think the expedition to west Tennessee will enable me to get out a considerable amount of stock and accomplish very important results, which can hereafter be explained."

On the 12th of October he informs General Taylor: "I will move into west Tennessee in a few days, and you may rely on my doing all I can towards accomplishing your desires and in facilitating your suggestions."[1] He was of the opinion that the cars would be running to Bethel for the transportation of his troops and supplies within two weeks.

I am satisfied the amount of supplies reported as being in west Tennessee has been greatly exaggerated. I can subsist my command there and will be able to gather up some wheat and hogs, but not in amounts as large as has been suggested. Our currency cannot be used in that region, and the people, instead of collecting their surplus supply of hogs, will scatter them in the woods to prevent them falling into our hands. To hunt up and press

[1] *Official Records,* vol. xxxix, part iii, p. 815.

the needed supplies will require much time, and will take all of my command to accomplish much. If you can furnish salt, or anything the people could use at home, they would interest themselves in hunting up and furnishing the government with every article of supply that they could possibly spare.

It is my present design to take possession of Fort Heiman, on the Tennessee River, below Johnsonville, and thus prevent all communication with Johnsonville by transports. It is highly important that this line be interrupted, if not entirely destroyed, as I learned during my recent operations in middle Tennessee that it was by this route that the enemy received most of his supplies at Atlanta. I shall exercise diligence in gathering up the large number of deserters and absentees in Tennessee. As fast as these are gathered up I would suggest that they be sent to you and placed at once in the infantry service. The facilities of these men for running away is much greater in the cavalry service, and they should be placed in positions remote from their country. *The great, predominating, absorbing desire is to cut Sherman's line of communication.* I did something towards accomplishing this result in my recent expedition, and am anxious to renew the effort, but nothing can be done without a pontoon across the Tennessee River.

I suggest that the railroad be repaired from Cherokee to Tuscumbia and Florence, and that a bridge be thrown across the river there. This can be accomplished without much difficulty, as the columns or piles of the old bridge will furnish ample supports for ropes. I presume it is the only place on the river that a bridge can be built. The road for several miles has been destroyed, but the iron necessary for repairs can be procured on the west end of the road between this place and Grand Junction. If this bridge was built, I could strike the Tennessee and Alabama road or the Nashville or Chattanooga at pleasure, and return when hard pressed in safety. My men and horses are greatly jaded by the labors of the recent raid. Both need more rest than I am able to give them at present. It will require a month to recuperate and place my command in proper condition. In the recent engagement I lost in killed and wounded about 400 men. I still have on the other side of the river about 500 men unable to cross.[2] These losses, with those ordered back to Georgia by General Hood, have greatly reduced my command. General Chalmers's brigade of 500 men will probably swell my command to 3400 troops.

During my recent trip I killed, wounded, and captured 3000 of the enemy, and destroyed the Tennessee and Alabama railroad from Decatur

---

[2] These troops subsequently escaped in small squads to the south bank of the Tennessee.

to Spring Hill. It cannot be repaired in sixty days, and the engineer captured by me gives it as his opinion that the road cannot be placed in good running order during the winter. I captured on the road upward of 1000 negroes. I understand only about 800 have reached you. This matter should be investigated, and I shall endeavor to learn where the blame should rest and punish the delinquent. I find a few smiths were retained here to shoe up my command, all of which will be reported to you and accounted for.

A sense of duty to my government constrains me to call attention to the large number of stragglers in General ——'s command. I do so in no spirit of unkindness towards that gallant and meritorious officer, who will certainly remedy the evil when his attention shall have been called to it. On my recent trip I found his men at every stopping-place, some of them with passes, from every grade of subordinate officer, and many with no passes at all. At Burnsville I found many stragglers, and on my approach they fled as if the enemy had made his appearance in their midst. Such a state of affairs is disreputable, and humiliating to my feelings. It is a burlesque upon military discipline. All applications for leave of absence for a longer period than ten days I shall refer to you for your action, and, unless something of this sort is required of General ——, his command will still be found scattered over the country, with furloughs and passes from all grades of officers. It is no spirit of dictation, but a desire to promote the good of the service, that prompts me to make these suggestions. I have commenced repairing the telegraph-line from Grand Junction to this place (Corinth), and from here to Jackson. Both lines will be in operation in a few days.

On this same day (October 12th) a more urgent order was telegraphed to Chalmers, which read: "Fetch[3] your wagons and the two batteries with you. I will supply you with the artillery ammunition at Jackson." This urgent dispatch to General Chalmers was with a view of pouncing upon General Edward Hatch, who was then reported to be making for the crossing of the Tennessee River into west Tennessee, and Forrest was anxious to meet him there with his entire force.

All necessary preparations having been made, on the 16th of October Colonel Bell, with his brigade, was directed to advance from Corinth and to take post at Lavinia, in west Tennessee. Two days later General Buford, with the Kentucky Brigade, took up his line of march for Lexington, a point eastward of Jackson and between this

[3] "Fetch" was one of his favorite verbs, and he would never permit his aides to substitute for it the more modern and accepted word "bring."

town and the Tennessee River. With his escort and Rucker's brigade (which on account of the wounds of Colonel Rucker was still under the command of Colonel D. C. Kelley), General Forrest in person left Corinth on the 19th of October, and on the 21st established his headquarters once more at Jackson. From there he took occasion to report to General Taylor the unserviceable condition of his command, stating that a large number of the horses had died as a result of the great exposure and fatigue to which they had been subjected in the recent hard campaigns, that many of his men were sick and worn out, and that he had been compelled to permit a large number to go to their homes in west Tennessee and Kentucky to procure horses and clothing. "Mabry's brigade now numbers only three hundred and fifty men, and my total effective force for the expedition in hand is three thousand troops." Forrest himself was also "sick and worn out" in body, but the indomitable will was still on duty.

At Jackson the ever-faithful Chalmers reported with 250 men of McCulloch's brigade and the 300 of Mabry's, which, with Rucker's old brigade, now constituted his division. Buford, having advanced from Lexington toward the Tennessee River, and thrown his scouts across that stream, reported to Forrest that there were no indications of the enemy in the neighborhood of Clifton, and upon receipt of this information he was directed to move northward to Huntington and thence by way of Paris to the mouth of the Big Sandy River.

On the 29th of October Chalmers was also sent forward to co-operate with Buford, who with excellent judgment had established himself at Fort Heiman and Paris Landing on the Tennessee. The judicious disposition of the troops and batteries was highly complimented by Forrest, who arrived in person on the morning of the 29th. On this date also, Colonel Edward W. Rucker, having sufficiently recovered from the wounds received at Harrisburg, rejoined the command and took charge of the remnant of his old brigade. Bell, with his Tennesseeans and one section of the old Morton battery, was now stationed near Paris Landing, the guns commanding a stretch of the river for about a mile up and down the stream. About five miles below, at Fort Heiman, General Buford, with his division and the two twenty-pounder Parrotts, thoroughly guarded the river at that point.

The Confederates had not long to wait for their game. Forrest, as usual, had moved with such celerity and covered his approach so suc-

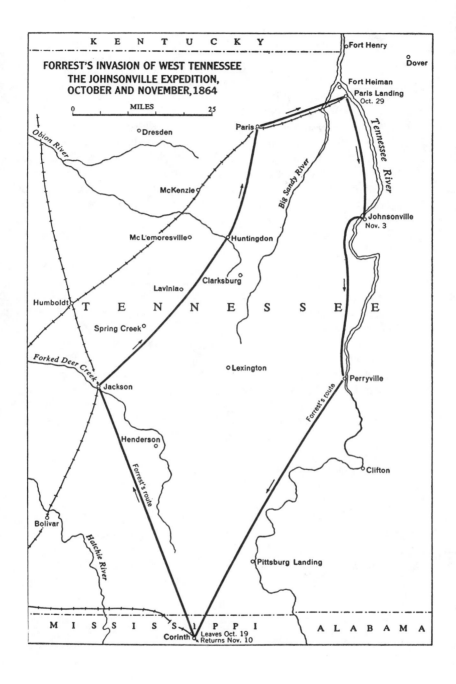

KENTUCKY

Fort Henry
Dover

FORREST'S INVASION OF WEST TENNESSEE
THE JOHNSONVILLE EXPEDITION,
OCTOBER AND NOVEMBER, 1864

MILES
0   25

Fort Heiman
Paris Landing
Oct. 29

Obion River

Dresden

Paris

Tennessee River

McKenzie

Big Sandy River

McL'emoresville

Huntingdon

Johnsonville
Nov. 3

Clarksburg

Laviniao

Humboldt

T E N N E S S E E

Spring Creek

Forked Deer Creek

Lexington

Perryville

Jackson

Forrest's route

Henderson

Clifton

Forrest's route

Bolivar

Hatchie River

Pittsburg Landing

M I S S I S S I P P I

ALABAMA

Corinth   Leaves Oct. 19
            Returns Nov. 10

cessfully that the Federals were in utter ignorance of his presence on the Tennessee.

Early on the morning of the 29th of October the Federal transport *Mazeppa,* a rich prize, heavily laden with freight, and with two barges in tow, en route to Johnsonville, was seen rounding a bend in the river from below. She was permitted to pass the lower battery, which, being masked, her officers did not discover. When well in the stretch between the two lower batteries they opened upon her, and so accurate was the aim of these veteran gunners that every shot passed through her. At the third fire she was so badly crippled that the pilot headed her for the opposite shore, where she was abandoned by the crew, who, with the exception of the commanding officer and two men, fled to the woods in wild dismay.

As the Confederates did not even have a canoe or skiff, volunteers were called for to swim the river and take possession of the boat. Several offered their services, but to Captain Frank P. Gracey more than all others is due the credit on this occasion. With him, Captain John Horn, Lieutenant E. B. Ross of the Third Kentucky, and others volunteered. A crude raft was constructed of logs and driftwood, but at the first essay it went to pieces, whereupon Captain Frank P. Gracey, who had won especial notice for his conduct as an artillerist at Chickamauga, not waiting for his comrades, and using a portion of the raft to sustain in part his weight, made his way alone across the river and boldly took possession of the boat. The boat's yawl was launched and by means of a line the steamer was warped to the side where the Confederates were.[4]

Forrest's men now found themselves bountifully supplied with blankets, shoes, clothing, and all the necessaries and not a few of the luxuries of life. It was the richest capture in many a day, and immediate steps were taken to have the cargo removed some distance from the riverbank, where it could be carefully guarded until carried away for the use of the command. While this was being done three gunboats made their appearance from below, and began vigorously to shell the men who were engaged in unloading the *Mazeppa.* The Confederate batteries, however, forced them to retire, and, after the boat was

[4] I am indebted for this correction to General H. B. Lyon, living in 1906 at Eddyville, Kentucky, who was an eyewitness to Captain Gracey's feat, and to Lieutenant E. B. Ross and Captain John Horn, who were also witnesses.

emptied of her contents, fearing the gunboats might return in force, General Buford ordered her to be set on fire.

On the following morning, October 30th, the steamer *Anna* came down the river from the direction of Johnsonville, and successfully ran the gantlet of all the Confederate batteries. She was struck a number of times, but unfortunately the gunners, usually so accurate, did not hit a vital spot. Her success tempted a repetition of the feat by the transport *Venus,* which was towing two barges and was convoyed by the gunboat *Undine,* which latter craft, it will be remembered, had already had an unhappy experience with Colonel D. C. Kelley at Eastport soon after the Confederates had recrossed the Tennessee from the expedition into north Alabama and middle Tennessee. These boats, coming in range of the guns in front of Colonel Tyree H. Bell's command, were by instructions permitted to pass into the trap, and when well below his guns Bell opened upon them and struck them repeatedly, but without material damage. They soon ran in range of the lower batteries in front of Lyon's and Buford's positions, and these, having a better chance, opened with such telling precision that the Federal steamers put about and tried to escape again up the river toward Johnsonville. In this attempt they were, however, thwarted by the Confederate batteries which they at first succeeded in passing, and were now caught halfway between the two batteries, though beyond accurate range of either.

At this moment Colonel E. W. Rucker asked that he be given two pieces of artillery, with which he would undertake to reach the riverbank at a point close enough to the boats to enable him to sink or capture them. Before he could get into position and open fire, however, another steamer, the *J. W. Cheeseman,* approached the upper battery (Rice's) and, under directions, was also allowed to pass into the trap unmolested; but as soon as she came opposite Hudson's guns, both Hudson and Rice opened upon her and in short order completely disabled her. At the same time the troops concealed in the undergrowth and cane along the bank poured a heavy fire of small arms into her, compelling her to surrender. By this time Rucker, who had met with great difficulty in getting through the tangle and undergrowth with the two ten-pounder Parrotts of Hudson's battery, accompanied by the Fifteenth Tennessee regiment and the Twenty-sixth Tennessee battalion, had attacked the *Undine* "with such vigor and success that, after a severe artillery duel between his battery and the gunboat, the latter was disabled and driven to the opposite bank, where all of its officers and crew, who were able to do so, abandoned it and escaped."

General Chalmers in his official report continues: "At the same time Lieutenant-Colonel Kelley, commanding the Twenty-sixth Battalion Tennessee Cavalry, attacked the transport *Venus,* which was defended by a small detachment of Union infantry, so sharply that she surrendered to him, and the gallant colonel, going on board of her with two companies of his battalion, crossed the river, took possession of the gunboat, and brought both safely to the landing."

While this fight was going on, another gunboat, the *No. 29,* appeared from above, and, anchoring about one and a half miles from Rice's battery, opened upon the Confederates. Rice returned the fire, but found the distance too great to be effective. General Chalmers then ordered him to move nearer with the guns, accompanied by the general's escort and a company of vedettes attached to the Seventh Alabama Cavalry. As soon as Captain Rice approached sufficiently near to open upon the newcomer, she steamed up the river out of range. It was now found upon inspection of the captures that the *J. W. Cheeseman* was so badly damaged that she could not in any way be useful to the Confederates, and Forrest ordered her, after all the property on board had been removed to the shore, to be set on fire. The transport *Venus* and the gunboat *Undine* were only slightly injured and were soon put in repair.

The *Undine* was one of the largest boats of her class on the Tennessee, carrying eight twenty-four-pounder brass howitzers, and when captured had all of her armament and equipment on board. An attempt had been made to spike two of the guns and to disable another by jamming a shell in the muzzle, but these obstacles were soon removed. The Confederate loss in this day's work was one man in Rucker's command severely wounded. The enemy lost five killed and six wounded on the *Venus;* three killed and four wounded on the *Undine;* one wounded on the *Cheeseman;* and forty-three prisoners captured, among whom were one officer and ten men of the Union infantry; the others belonged to the crews of the different boats.

Forrest now conceived the novel idea of manning the captured boats and using them in co-operation with his land force in the proposed attack on Johnsonville and the Federal flotilla there. Colonel W. A.

Dawson was ordered to take charge of the fleet, and with a volunteer crew of "horse marines" raised the commodore's flag on the *Venus,* and Captain Gracey was placed in command of the *Undine,* on which the two twenty-pounder Parrotts were placed. It will be remembered that this officer served on the right wing of the Confederate army with Forrest at Chickamauga, taking an active and brilliant part in the effort to prevent Gordon Granger from uniting with Thomas near the close of this battle on September 20th, 1863.

"Commodore" Dawson was directed to proceed up the river toward Johnsonville, but not to venture beyond the support of the batteries, which with the troops would march along the road parallel with the bank of the river. As Dawson went on board his vessel he said to Forrest: "General, I will go with these boats wherever you order, but I tell you candidly I know very little about managing gunboats. You must promise me that if I lose the fleet you won't give me a cursing when I wade ashore and come back on foot." Forrest said: "No, Colonel, you will do the best you can; that is all I want. I promise not to haul you over the coals if you come home wet; but I want you and Gracey, if you see you are going to be caught, to run your boats into the bank, let your men save themselves as best they can, and then set the steamers on fire." A trial trip was now made with the fleet, and although the boats behaved awkwardly enough to frighten a riverman, since these landlubbers were able to maintain steam enough to overcome the force of the current and to keep the boats from running into the woods it was deemed a sufficient experience to justify an engagement with the enemy.

On November 1st the "horse marines" steamed slowly and cautiously up the river, keeping in close touch with the troops and artillery that were plodding along the bank in the direction of Johnsonville. Forrest's sailors were for the present, at least, enjoying their novel situation, and, as occasion would offer, spoke words of affected sympathy to their unfortunate comrades who had to ride horses and drive artillery. Their sarcasm even went so far as to offer to carry their guns and forage sacks if the cavalrymen would only wade out in the stream and hand them on board. The men on shore, however, were equal to the emergency and, while appreciating the kindness of their webfooted comrades, declined assistance, on the ground that the sailors would soon be drowned by the Yankee gunboats, and their guns and forage sacks were too valuable to be risked in such hands.

For two days the history of the fleet was uneventful, but on the 2nd of November, having gained courage with experience, they ventured too far in advance of their land supports and collided with the Union flotilla with dire results. At three o'clock on this date, Lieutenant Commander King, U.S.N., with gunboats *No. 32* and *No. 29,* started from Johnsonville, and five miles below that point, rounding a bend in the river, came suddenly in range of the *Undine,* which was well in advance of the *Venus,* and immediately engaged her. The trained navy of the Federal Lieutenant Commander made short work of Forrest's sailors. Seeing that the *Undine* was about to be captured, Gracey ran her nose into the bank, and he and his men jumped ashore after the vessel had been set on fire. The *Venus,* a witness to the disaster to her sister ship, turned about and sought safety in flight, reaching the Confederate batteries on the riverbank.

Lieutenant Commander King later picked up the *Undine,* which had not been destroyed by the fire, and which had on board when captured the two twenty-pounder Parrotts, with 200 rounds of ammunition (a great loss to General Forrest), also 100 boxes of shoes, two bales of blankets, and 576 boxes of hard bread and other freight which had been taken from the *Mazeppa* and placed on this boat for convenience of transportation. The Federals ultimately took the guns and ammunition from the *Undine* and used them against the Confederates during the bombardment of Johnsonville. The other property was destroyed with the boat, by Forrest's command, in the general conflagration a few days later at Johnsonville.

On November 3rd the *Venus* again proceeded up the river, this time more cautiously, and as the Federal boats came in sight she made a show of fight, in an effort to decoy them into an ambuscade of the Confederate batteries below. The *Key West,* the advance gunboat of the Federals, ran into the Confederate battery two miles below Johnsonville, and received nineteen shots before she was able to escape, but finally got away. The remainder of the Union flotilla, however, closed in upon the *Venus* in such desperate fashion that the brave Colonel Dawson was compelled to abandon her, but not until she was set on fire and destroyed. The Federal boats pressed Dawson so closely that he could not land on the western shore, upon which the Confederate cavalry was. He, however, succeeded in escaping to the opposite side, where he and his men concealed themselves in the canebrakes until dark and then on logs and rafts crossed the river to rejoin their command.

While the *Key West* was engaged with the upper batteries, five additional gunboats came up the river from the direction of Paducah and engaged the Confederate batteries near the foot of Reynolds Island, but were repulsed and failed to unite with the upper fleet.

The extent of the damage which Forrest had so far inflicted upon the Union vessels in the Tennessee may be gathered from the report of Brigadier General James L. Donaldson, who says: "The new boat, *Mazeppa*, with seven hundred tons of freight from Cincinnati, was captured Friday. The *Naugatuck* and *Alice* were captured at Widow Reynold's Bar on Saturday. Gunboat *No. 55* and transports *Venus* and *Cheeseman* were captured yesterday without being disabled. Gunboat *No. 55* and the two transports are now in the hands of the rebels on the river. The steamer *Dave Hughes,* with barges loaded with government stores, was burned yesterday afternoon fifteen miles from Clarksville."[5]

Late in the afternoon of the 3rd Forrest reached the bank of the Tennessee River opposite Johnsonville and, accompanied by his chief of artillery, Captain John W. Morton, made a careful reconnaissance, with the view of selecting the most favorable positions for the batteries. The river landing at Johnsonville was lined with transports and gunboats and barges. Upon the bank were large warehouses filled with valuable supplies, while several acres of the shore were covered with every description of army stores.

Waiting until night came on, all the guns were silently placed in position and the batteries so masked that their presence was not suspected until they were ready to open fire. Thrall's guns, which had arrived on the day before in company with Mabry's fragment of brigade, were placed in position above Johnsonville, while the old Morton battery and Hudson's pieces were placed nearly opposite and just below the town. Forrest ordered the attack to begin at three o'clock in the afternoon. His movements had been so carefully made that the enemy were loath to believe he could be on the opposite side of the river. About two o'clock a gunboat, evidently bent upon a reconnaissance, steamed toward the western shore, but put back in great haste as one of the Confederate guns sent a shell through its side.

---

[5] *Official Records,* vol. xxxix, part i, p. 863.

The cannonading was commenced by a section of Morton's battery commanded by Lieutenant Brown, and the other batteries chimed in promptly. From the forts on the opposite side of the river and the fleet of gunboats the enemy returned the fire with spirit. Captain Morton and the commanders of the various batteries soon obtained the range, and, by cutting the time fuses with precision, spots of smoke and flame soon began to break out here and there among the boats which lined the riverbank and in the warehouses and piles of goods along the wharf. The conflagration spread rapidly, and by nightfall the wharf for nearly a mile up and down the river presented a solid sheet of flame. The Union reports assert that some of the boats along the wharf were fired by order of the Federal commander for fear that they would be captured by the Confederates.

General Forrest, who was as great a believer in artillery as Napoleon, was in the habit of spending many of his spare moments in camp or on the march with the artillery companies. While Freeman lived, and when Morton commanded a separate battery, they always made it a point to have something tempting for the general to eat, and when they bivouacked for the night or for the midday feed for men and horses, whether he messed with them or not, they always had a place ready for him, and he never missed an opportunity of showing his appreciation of these excellent fighters for the effective work they were doing under his directions.

The battery of Captain J. C. Thrall exceptionally distinguished itself by the steadiness and accuracy of its fire at Johnsonville. The troops had nicknamed this company, which was made up chiefly from Jackson County, in the White River country of Arkansas, "The Arkansas Rats." Riding along with them as they were leaving Johnsonville, Forrest complimented them very highly upon their conduct. He said: "Boys, after this fight we will have to find a better name for you than 'The Arkansas Rats.' I am going to baptize you now 'The Arkansas Braves.' " A waggish sergeant of one of the guns, finding this a good opportunity to close in with his general, said: "General, talkin' may be very good, but something to eat would sound a heap better; we have been living on wind for two days." Forrest smiled appreciatively and, turning to one of his staff, said: "Go back to my headquarters wagon, where you will find four boxes of hard-tack and three hams; have them brought right up here and issued to Captain Thrall's men."[6]

Lieutenant Colonel William Sinclair, Assistant Inspector General of the United States Army, in his official report, says: "The total money value of the property destroyed and captured during the operations of the rebels on the Tennessee River, including steamboats and barges, is about $2,200,000."[7] Colonel Thompson estimated the rebel forces operating under Forrest, Chalmers, Buford, Bell, and Lyon at 13,000 men, with twenty-six guns, twenty of them twenty-pounder Parrotts. He says:

The rebel cavalry under Forrest appeared October 28th before Fort Heiman, and captured the steamboat *Mazeppa* and a barge with a valuable cargo of quartermaster's and subsistence stores. The *Undine*, the *Venus*, and the *Cheeseman* fell into the enemy's hands on the evening of the 30th of October. At this time the military and naval forces off Johnsonville, on November 4th, were as follows: Forty-third Wisconsin Volunteers, seven hundred men; detachments of the Twelfth, Thirteenth, and One Hundredth United States Colored Infantry (numbers not given); and quartermaster's employés numbering eight hundred men; six ten-pounder Parrott guns, four twelve-pounder Napoleon guns, and two twenty-pounder Parrott guns (captured on the *Venus*), and the gunboats *Key West, Elphin,* and *Tawah*. In the fight which ensued the gunboats were abandoned and burned, and all the transports were destroyed by fire, the fire extending to the large pile of stores on the levee, and from that to the warehouse, which was destroyed.

No marvel that Sherman on November 6th reported to Grant: "That devil Forrest was down about Johnsonville, making havoc among the gunboats and transports."

Forrest says:

Having completed the work designed for the expedition, I moved my command six miles during the night by the light of the enemy's burning property. The roads were almost impassable, and the march to Corinth was slow and toilsome, but we reached there on November 10th, after an absence of over two weeks, during which time I captured and destroyed four gunboats, fourteen transports, twenty barges, twenty-six pieces of artillery, and $6,700,000 worth of property, and captured one hundred and fifty prisoners. General Buford, after supplying his own command, turned over to my chief quartermaster about nine thousand pairs of shoes and

[6] Manuscripts of Mr. John Sherrer of Thrall's battery.
[7] *Official Records,* vol. xxxix, part i, p. 860.

one thousand blankets. My loss during the entire trip was two killed and nine wounded.

In his official report of this remarkable expedition, General Forrest pays high tribute to Brigadier Generals Chalmers, Buford, and Lyon, and to Colonels Bell, Rucker, Crossland, and Mabry, for the skill, coolness, and undaunted courage which they exhibited. He pays an especial tribute to Captain John W. Morton, his chief of artillery, and the brave troops under his command: "My thanks are especially due for their efficiency and gallantry on this expedition. They fired with a rapidity and accuracy which extorted the commendation of even the enemy."

The Union commanders in this immediate section, as well as the generals of departments elsewhere, were considerably stirred up by this unlooked-for incursion of the Confederates and the destruction which they had accomplished of the gunboats, transports, and an enormous quantity of supplies. Forrest had thrown the Federal officers off the scent by a feint upon Memphis. Just before starting for Jackson and Johnsonville he had directed Chalmers to leave troops enough under an efficient officer in the neighborhood of Memphis to worry the commander there and to give out the impression that he was moving to attack that place. The official records show that he was expected there on the 16th of October, for it was telegraphed from Memphis that Forrest intended to attack at an early date, and General M. L. Smith reports: "The houses along the Gayoso bayou are loop-holed for sharpshooters, and our inner line of defense constructed of cotton and hay. Forrest himself was at Grenada on Friday night, and consulted with General Dick Taylor."

Halleck also wired Thomas that Forrest was threatening Memphis and Paducah. He says: "If by the help of Burbridge and Washburn I could drive him south, it would relieve that part of the country from all danger."

Thomas, who in one of his dispatches dubbed Forrest "a tricky fellow," agreed fully with the general in chief that it would relieve that part of the country from all danger if Forrest were out of it, but did not consider it an easy task. In reply to Halleck he says: "The best way to get rid of Forrest would be for Sherman to let me have one of my corps, with which, and the cavalry now in Tennessee, I could soon move Forrest south, after which I could return to the main army."

The general in chief at Washington on October 21st advised Thomas to lay the matter seriously before Sherman, saying: "So long as Forrest holds Corinth he threatens several very important points. Please consult General Sherman as to the best means of getting rid of him." Two days later President Lincoln wired Thomas that he had received information, "having great appearance of authenticity, that there is to be a rebel raid into western Kentucky, sent from Corinth, Mississippi, on the 4th day of November." The President of the United States was about two weeks behind the starting of the raid, for it was on the 4th of November that Johnsonville and the fleet were destroyed and the object of the expedition accomplished.

Sherman meanwhile had received so many different irreconcilable dispatches as to Forrest's whereabouts in various parts of the country that, with evident humor, he wired Grant on November 1st: "Forrest seems to be scattered from Eastport to Jackson, Paris, and the lower Tennessee; General Thomas reports a capture by him of a gunboat and five transports."

That he was also located elsewhere is evident from the following dispatch, which was received by General Hooker in Cincinnati, at sunset on November 7th, 1864:

Forrest has been in disguise alternately in Chicago, Michigan City, and Canada for two months; has 14,000 men, mostly from draft. On the 7th of November, at midnight, he will seize telegraph and rail at Chicago, release prisoners there, arm them, sack the city, shoot down all Federal soldiers, and urge concert of action with Southern sympathizers.

W. FITHIAN, Captain and Provost Marshal

The effective work the Confederate leader was accomplishing with the small number of troops in his command had produced the impression that his force had been greatly augmented.

General James H. Wilson, in a dispatch to General Grant, says: "Sherman estimates that Forrest has 26,000 men mounted and menacing his communications."

Evidently under a similar impression, on the 4th of November, while Forrest was busily engaged in destroying Johnsonville and the supplies there, Thomas telegraphed to Halleck at Washington: "I have determined to send the Twenty-third Corps to Johnsonville, and have telegraphed Colonel Thompson, who has a force of 4000 men, not to abandon Johnsonville."

To the commander at Columbus, Kentucky, Sherman telegraphed: "If the enemy approaches Columbus, the guns of large caliber must be defended to the death, and the town should be burned by you rather than Forrest should get a pound of provision or forage."

While these various telegrams were flying over the wires, describing the doings or warning commanders as to the supposed whereabouts of the redoubtable Confederate, he and his victorious troopers, laden with booty, were floundering through the mud, trying to get out of west Tennessee over roads which were in such wretched condition that it required eight yoke of oxen to pull a single piece of artillery.

General Forrest had received a dispatch from General Beauregard directing him as soon as he had accomplished the object of his expedition to move with his entire command to middle Tennessee and co-operate with General Hood in the advance of the main body of the Confederate army toward Franklin and Nashville; and in obedience to these orders, while Johnsonville was still in flames, he turned in the direction of Perryville, where he encamped on the night of the 6th of November.

It had been Forrest's intention to throw his command across the Tennessee River at Perryville, and with this end in view he had hastened on in person with his escort and a few picked men, arriving there some twelve hours ahead of the main body of his troops. A search for ferryboats, yawls, and skiffs was immediately instituted up and down the river, but so thorough had been the work of destruction of these small craft by the Federal gunboats, which had been constantly patrolling the stream, that no boats could be found. The two yawls which had been taken from one of the captured gunboats and hauled on wagons to this point were the only means at his disposal. Not easily baffled, he undertook to build rafts upon which, with the yawls, the men and artillery might be carried over, while the horses could be made to swim.

The Tennessee River, as a result of the frequent and heavy rains, was now rising rapidly, the current had become very swift, and there was such a quantity of heavy driftwood in the stream that it was found impossible to use the rafts with safety to the men; nor was it safe for the horses, who were much weakened by the hard campaigning they had undergone, to try to make their way by swimming across a river so full of the trunks of trees and other floating material. By dint of hard work with the two yawls, by nightfall of the 7th of November, some four hundred men of Rucker's brigade had been transferred to the eastern bank.

The folly of any further effort in this direction was now apparent to Forrest, who, directing General Rucker to move on in the direction of Florence, Alabama, with the troops already across, on the next day, with the remaining portion of his command and the artillery, took up his line of march south in the direction of Corinth, parallel with the west bank of the Tennessee. The roads were in such wretched condition and the horses so greatly weakened that it became necessary to impress oxen from the citizens living along the line of march, in order to pull the artillery through the mud. The horse teams were doubled, as many as sixteen horses being attached to a single cannon, while from four to eight yoke of oxen were necessary to drag a single piece along. Each relay of steers would be carried fifteen or twenty miles from the point of impressment, and then turned over to their owners, who were permitted to drive them back to their homes. Others were now impressed, and in this way, finally, on the 15th, the command reached Iuka and, on the 16th, Cherokee station, at which point they were transferred to the cars and proceeded without further interruption to Florence, where on the 18th of November they effected the junction with Hood's army.

Such was the scarcity of nails and shoes for his horses on this march that he was compelled to take the tires from the farm wagons along the route and have these made into horseshoes to supply the needs of his command.

At Corinth, on November 12th, in view of his orders to report to General Hood, Forrest wrote the following letter, which breathes so much the spirit of personal and official friendship for General Richard Taylor, his immediate superior, and of that unselfish, undying devotion to the Confederate cause which characterized his whole conduct during the Civil War:

HEADQUARTERS FORREST'S CAVALRY
Corinth, *November* 12th.

Lieutenant-General R. Taylor:

GENERAL—In a few days I will forward you a report of my recent operations on the Tennessee River, together with a report of my expedition to Memphis. These two documents will, I presume, for the present terminate my official connection with you—an event which I deeply deplore. Our intercourse has not been of long duration, but to me it has been most pleasant and agreeable, certainly of such a character as to render our separation a source of regret; but duty calls me elsewhere. I got to share in the toils and, I trust, in the victories of other fields; but in leaving you I shall carry with me a sincere friendship, made so by your kindness and official courtesy. I congratulate you, on leaving, that so much of the territory under your jurisdiction has been rescued from the grasp of the invader. Twelve months ago I entered your department and found the people groaning under the most cruel and merciless oppression. They were despondent, and traitors exultant. I leave the department in security and the people hopeful. I know not how long we are to labor for that independence for which we have thus far struggled in vain, but this I do know, that I will never weary in defending our cause, which must ultimately succeed. Faith is the duty of the hour. We will succeed. We have only to "work and wait." Be assured, my dear general, that wherever I may go, I shall deeply sympathize in all that concerns your interest and always exult in your success.

With great respect, I am, General, your friend and obedient servant,

N. B. FORREST, Major-General

TWENTY

The Nashville Campaign, November 19 to December 27, 1864

ARRIVING at Florence, General Forrest was placed in command of all the cavalry with the Army of Tennessee. In addition to the troops which had been serving with him in west Tennessee, this gave him a division under General W. H. Jackson and a fragment of Dibrell's brigade. Some of these had served with distinction under Forrest in the famous brigade organized shortly after the retreat from Kentucky in 1862, with which he had made the successful foray into west Tennessee in December of that year. Forrest, with the entire cavalry force of Hood's army, numbering 5000 effectives, immediately moved out from Florence in advance of the infantry and encamped at Shoal Creek. From this point Buford and Jackson were ordered to advance northward over the military road.

On the following day, the 19th of November, at Butler's Creek a foraging detachment of the Kentuckians came in collision with a brigade of Union cavalry under Colonel Datus Coon of Hatch's division, which pounced down upon the Confederates so vigorously that the latter gave way, abandoning to the Union troopers one or two wagons from General Buford's headquarters train. By a rapid and successful movement on the part of General Frank C. Armstrong of Jackson's division, who was near enough to hear the fighting and with characteristic alacrity marched toward it, the Federals were caught between Armstrong's brigade and Buford's men, who had rallied promptly after the first flurry of surprise, and so roughly handled was the Federal brigade that it sought safety in flight, leaving several prisoners in the hands of the victors. In this affair the brave Colonel Edward Crossland, who had scarcely recovered from the painful injuries received at the battle of Harrisburg in July, was again severely wounded.

Despite the weather, which was exceedingly inclement, on the 21st

471

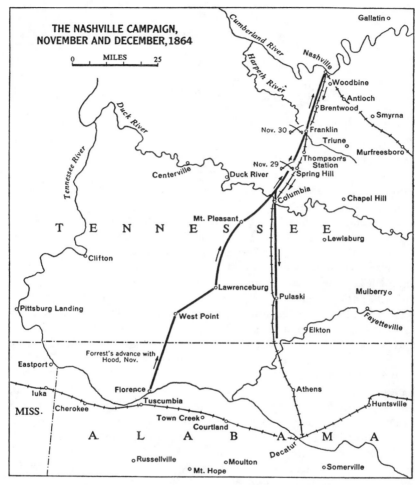

THE NASHVILLE CAMPAIGN,
NOVEMBER AND DECEMBER, 1864

of November Forrest, with the remaining division under Chalmers,
set out on the march toward Nashville. His force consisted of the three
divisions under his able lieutenants, Chalmers, Buford, and Jackson.
Chalmers's division, with Forrest, took the road by way of West Point
and Kelley's Forge to Henryville, which latter place they reached on
the 23rd. Meanwhile, on the 22nd, Buford and Jackson arrived at
Lawrenceburg, where they had again encountered a portion of Wilson's

cavalry, which, however, offered but slight resistance, and retreated toward Pulaski.

That Forrest was carrying everything before him is gracefully recorded by Colonel Henry Stone, United States Army, an officer on the staff of General George H. Thomas, who says: "The Confederate army began its northward march from Florence on the 19th of November, in weather of great severity. It rained and snowed and hailed and froze. Forrest had come up with about six thousand cavalry, and led the advance with indomitable energy. Hatch and Cox made such resistance as they could, but on the 22d the head of Hood's column was at Lawrenceburg, sixteen miles west of Pulaski."[1]

On the 23rd of November, at Henryville, Chalmers's division came in contact with another column of the Union cavalry and drove them after slight resistance through and beyond this town for a distance of several miles. Finally, at Fouché Springs, the Federals were found drawn up in line of battle in considerable force. Taking command of that portion of Chalmers's division which was immediately on the field, General Forrest directed Rucker to go forward with his brigade and to skirmish lightly with the enemy, and to hold them where they were until he could gain their flank and rear. Colonel D. C. Kelley, with his battalion, was sent around the left flank of the Federals, while Forrest, placing himself at the head of the escort, about eighty in number, made a rapid detour to the right of the Union line, in order to gain their rear in this direction.

Moving with celerity, Forrest soon found himself far to the rear of the Federal line, which was then skirmishing with Rucker. The Union commander evidently did not believe that the Confederates were in force in his front, nor that he would be seriously attacked at so late an hour. In any event, Forrest, while it was yet light, found himself in sight of a considerable body of the enemy's cavalry who had dismounted, unsaddled their horses, and were building fires preparatory to going into camp for the night. His presence so far in their rear was entirely unsuspected, and, notwithstanding that his force was numerically much inferior to the Federals, seeing that they were thoroughly unprepared to make any resistance, at the head of the escort he rode at full speed into their encampment, firing right and left with pistols

---

[1] *Battles and Leaders of the Civil War*, vol. iv.

at short range, throwing the enemy into such confusion that they broke and scattered in all directions.

Forrest says in his official report: "Taking with me my escort I moved rapidly to the rear. Lieutenant-Colonel Kelley being prevented from joining me as I had expected, I made the charge upon the enemy with my escort alone, producing a perfect stampede, capturing about fifty prisoners, twenty horses, and one ambulance."[2]

It was so near dark by the time this charge was made that the Federals had no means of knowing how few their assailants were, but as they yielded so readily they probably believed, from the vigor and boldness of the assault, that the Confederates were in strong force. At the same time Rucker, hearing the firing from Forrest's attack, now, as agreed upon, charged from the front and drove them from the field in great confusion. The Federals, fleeing before Rucker, bore down upon Forrest and his escort in such a throng that he was compelled to turn off into a byroad for fear of being run into by a detachment too large for him to cope with.

Notwithstanding this precaution, while riding at the head of the escort, side by side with Major Strange, his adjutant general, they suddenly came upon a squadron of Federals led by an officer, who ordered the Confederates to halt. Paying no attention to the command, Forrest continued boldly to approach, and it was only when they were practically in touch that in the darkness it was discovered that they were Federals. The Union officer quickly levelled his pistol at Forrest, the muzzle of which was almost in touch with the general's body, and was just in the act of firing when Major Strange, by a quick movement of the hand, knocked the weapon of the plucky Federal upward so that as it exploded it missed its aim. By this time the escort, with pistols in hand, had closed up on the Federal detachment, who, seeing that they were outnumbered, immediately surrendered.[3]

Early on the following morning Rucker continued his march to Mount Pleasant, where he captured 35,000 rounds of small-arms ammunition, together with the guard left in charge. From this point the stubborn enemy was pursued to the suburbs of Columbia, where, in a desperate hand-to-hand fight with a small but determined detachment of Union cavalry, the brave Colonel W. A. Dawson, who may be re-

[2] *Official Records,* vol. xlv, part i, p. 752.
[3] Manuscripts of Lieutenant G. L. Cowan of Forrest's escort.

membered as having been placed in charge of the gunboats which Forrest had captured on the Tennessee River near Johnsonville a few weeks earlier, and had acquitted himself most gallantly, was killed in a hand-to-hand encounter with the Union color guard. Chalmers says: "In this pursuit Lieutenant-Colonel Dawson, of the Fifteenth Tennessee, was killed while leading his regiment in the charge. He had emptied his revolver and was endeavoring to wrest one of the enemy's flags from its bearer when he was killed."[4]

Brigadier Generals Buford and Jackson, from Lawrenceburg, had steadily driven the Federals toward Pulaski, and at Campbellsville engaged Edward Hatch's division, which after a short but vigorous resistance was driven from the field.

Arriving in front of Columbia on the 24th, General Forrest invested this place and held his position here until the morning of the 27th, when, on the approach of Hood's infantry, the Federals evacuated the town, and on the 28th the main portion of the Confederate cavalry crossed Duck River—Chalmers's division at Carr's Mill, Jackson's at Holland's Ford, while General Forrest crossed at Owen's with the remainder of the troops. The boldness and rapidity of Forrest in leading Hood's invasion had given General Thomas at Nashville good reason for concern as to the safety of his troops south of Duck River.

A Federal writer says: "The situation at Pulaski was anything but cheering. Thomas directed Schofield to fall back with two divisions to Columbia on the 22d. On the 23d the other two divisions under Stanley were to follow. It was not a moment too soon. On the morning of the 24th General Cox, who had pushed on to within nine miles of Columbia, was aroused by sounds of conflict away to the west. Taking a cross-road leading south of Columbia, he reached the Mount Pleasant pike just in time to interpose his infantry between Forrest's cavalry and a hapless brigade under command of Colonel Capron, which was being handled most unceremoniously. In another hour Forrest would have been in possession of the crossings of Duck River, and the only line of communication with Nashville would have been in the hands of the enemy."[5]

Major Henry C. Connelly, of the Fourteenth Illinois Cavalry, on

---

[4] *Official Records,* vol. xlv, part i, p. 763.
[5] Colonel Stone of General Thomas's staff, *Battles and Leaders of the Civil War,* vol. iv.

August 8, 1887, wrote to the editors of the *Century Magazine,* describing this attack of Forrest:

> Capron's brigade was on the extreme right of our army, and from the 19th of November until the 24th, the day Columbia was reached, we fought Forrest's cavalry. I was with the rear-guard on the occasion referred to: it fell back and found the brigade in good position in line of battle. I rode to Colonel Capron and expressed the opinion that he could not hold his position a moment against the troops pressing us in the rear and on the flanks, which we could easily see advancing rapidly to attack us. Capron replied that he had been ordered to make a decided stand if it sacrificed every man in his brigade; that we must hold the advancing forces in check to enable the infantry to arrive and get in position. I replied: "We are destroyed and captured if we remain here." While passing through a long lane south of Columbia, Forrest's forces charged the brigade in rear and on both flanks with intrepid courage. Our command was confined to a narrow lane, with men and horses in the highest state of excitement. We were armed with Springfield rifles, which after the first volley were about as serviceable to cavalry as a good club. The men could not reload while mounted, in the excitement of horses as well as soldiers. The only thing that could be done was to get out as promptly as possible and before Forrest's forces should close in and capture the command. The brigade was composed of the Fourteenth and Sixteenth Illinois and Eighth Michigan Cavalry.

The Confederate leader was pushing northward with such vigor that Colonel Stone further says: "In spite of every opposition, Forrest succeeded in placing one of his divisions on the north side of Duck River before noon of the 28th and forced back the Union cavalry on the roads leading towards Spring Hill and Franklin."

By the night of the 28th, Forrest, with Chalmers's division, had advanced boldly eight miles beyond Columbia on the Spring Hill and Carr's Mill road. It was here that he was much disappointed by receiving a dispatch from Buford, at eleven o'clock that night, informing him that the enemy had made such stubborn resistance to his crossing that he would be unable to join him before the morning of the 29th. Meanwhile Jackson was directed to move along the Lewisburg pike toward Franklin until he developed the enemy. It was not long before Armstrong of Jackson's division sent word back that he had struck them in force and awaited instructions. He was ordered not to press too vigorously, as Forrest, if he could hold them still where they were, would endeavor to gain their flank and rear with Chalmers's division.

Forrest then moved rapidly toward Spring Hill with his entire command. Two miles from this place the Union pickets were encountered, and soon heavy skirmishing began, and Buford, with Chalmers's division, advanced upon the position of the enemy. The Federals, however, were very strongly posted and stood their ground so manfully that the Confederates were compelled to fall back. A strong barricade had been erected by the Union troopers here, who had also been reinforced by Coon's brigade of Hatch's division. Forrest now dismounted his entire command and, making his usual flank movement, succeeded in dislodging the enemy.

General James H. Wilson, commanding the Union cavalry, speaking of this, says: "Heavy skirmishing ensued, the enemy pressing forward with the greatest celerity, endeavoring to push around and strike our column in flank."[6]

The Confederates were now ordered to press the enemy with all possible vigor. A courier was sent to General Buford to dispatch a mounted regiment at once, and this, the Twenty-first Tennessee, under Colonel Wilson, coming in sight, Forrest ordered a charge, which was gallantly made; Wilson at the head of his splendid regiment, riding across the open field, received three wounds, but refused to leave his command. The fight by this time had become general and brisk, as Forrest had received word from General Hood to hold the position at all hazards, as the advance of his infantry column was only two miles distant and rapidly approaching. Bell's brigade having arrived, it was deployed immediately and ordered to the attack. Following this came Chalmers's division, which moved upon the enemy from the Confederate left. As the troops advanced, Bell reported to his commander that he had only four rounds of ammunition to the man, but despite this he was ordered to charge the enemy.

Forrest says: "This order was executed with a promptness and energy and gallantry which I have never seen excelled. The enemy was driven from his rifle-pits, and fled towards Spring Hill."[7] General Jackson was now ordered to move rapidly with his division towards Thompson's Station, and to throw himself across the line

[6] *Official Records*, vol. xlv, part i, p. 550.
[7] *Ibid.*, vol. xlv, part i, p. 753.

of retreat of the Union army. He struck the road at 11 P.M., just as the front of the enemy's column was passing, and attacked at once. He held possession of the pike, and fought the enemy until near daylight, when, receiving no support, he was compelled to retire.

Colonel Stone (already quoted) says:

As Stanley was approaching Spring Hill, just before noon, he met a cavalry soldier who seemed to be badly scared, and reported that Buford's division of Forrest's cavalry was approaching from the east. The troops were at once double-quicked into the town, and the leading brigade, deploying as it advanced, drove off the enemy. The possession of Spring Hill would not only shut out the Union army from the roads to Nashville, but would effectually bar the way in every direction. Stanley's arrival was not a moment too soon for the safety of the army. The three brigades had hardly reached their position when they were attacked by the Confederates. At the same time a dash was made by a detachment of the Confederate cavalry on the Spring Hill station, northwest of the town. It seemed as if the little band, attacked from all points, was threatened with destruction. The third assault on the Federals was more successful, and they were driven back to the edge of the village. Except this one small division, deployed in a long, thin line to cover the wagons, there were no Union troops within striking distance. The cavalry were at Mount Carmel, five miles east, and fully occupied in keeping Forrest away from Franklin and the Harpeth River crossings. The nearest aid was Kimball's division, seven miles south, at Rutherford's Creek. The other three divisions which made up Schofield's force—Woods's, Cox's, and Ruger's—were still at Duck River. A single Confederate brigade planted squarely across the pike either south or north of Spring Hill would have effectually prevented Schofield's retreat, and daylight would have found his whole force cut off from every avenue of escape by more than twice its numbers, to assault whom would have been madness and to avoid whom would have been impossible.

It was upon this momentous occasion, when General Jackson was making his gallant fight to retain possession of the pike and cut off the Federals, that Hood, with Cheatham's corps, was in such close striking distance to the line of retreat; and had these troops been thrown boldly and vigorously upon the enemy, the overthrow of the Union army would without any doubt have been accomplished, and the success of Hood's campaign in Tennessee and Kentucky would have been assured. As already shown, the Confederates on the ground greatly outnumbered the Federals, and the troops of Cheatham and

Cleburne were among the best fighters in the Southern army. It was concerning this failure to take advantage of one of the most brilliant opportunities ever offered a commanding officer that such a bitter controversy subsequently arose between Generals Hood and Cheatham.

Speaking of this incident, Major General David S. Stanley says: "Many of our men were overtaxed and broken down, and fell into the hands of the enemy. On two occasions they were very near obtaining the advantage sought. The greatest escape for us was at Spring Hill, where, with a whole corps in line of battle, the left of the line within six hundred yards of the road, they allowed all our army, excepting Wagner's division, to pass them with impunity in the night."[8]

So close to the turnpike along which the Federals marched during the night were the Confederates posted that the conversation of the troops moving on the highway was distinctly overheard by the Confederate pickets.[9]

Lieutenant General Hood, in his official report, says:

When I had gotten well on his flank the enemy discovered my intention, and began to retreat on the pike towards Spring Hill. The cavalry became engaged near that place about mid-day, but his trains were so strongly guarded that they were unable to break through them. About 4 P.M. (29th) our infantry forces, Major-General Cheatham in the advance, commenced to come in contact with the enemy, about two miles from Spring Hill, through which place the Columbia and Franklin pike runs. The enemy was at this time moving rapidly along the pike, with some of his troops formed on the flank of his column to protect it. Major-General Cheatham was ordered to attack the enemy at once vigorously, and get possession of this pike, and although these orders were frequently and earnestly repeated, he made but a feeble and partial attack, failing to reach the point indicated. Had my instructions been carried out there is no doubt that we should have possessed ourselves of this road. Stewart's corps and Johnson's division were arriving upon the field to support the attack. Though the golden opportunity had passed with daylight, I did not at dark abandon the hope of dealing the enemy a heavy blow.*

On the morning of the 30th the entire cavalry was ordered to press the enemy on the Franklin pike. This was vigorously done, the Federals retiring to Winstead's Hill, where they again offered resistance and from

[8] *Ibid.,* vol. xlv, part i, p. 117.
[9] Personal communication from Captain P. H. Coleman, First Florida Infantry, in charge of Confederate pickets on this occasion.

their point of vantage held Forrest at arm's length until the infantry arrived, when the Union troops abandoned their position and took refuge behind the fortifications in Franklin.

General Forrest, as was his invariable practice, immediately proceeded to make a thorough personal reconnaissance of the position occupied by the enemy.

Chalmers, in his address before the Southern Historical Society in August, 1879, says: "Without knowing it, he was following Napier's precept of the art of war, always in front making personal observations. This practice brought him into many personal conflicts and exposed him to constant danger. It led to imitation by his general officers, and near Franklin I witnessed Forrest with two division and three brigade commanders all on the skirmish-line."

When General Hood arrived upon the field, which was about one o'clock in the afternoon, Forrest reported to him that the position of the Federals was exceedingly formidable, and that in his opinion it could not be taken by direct assault, except after great and unnecessary loss of life. General Hood replied: "I do not think the Federals will stand strong pressure from the front; the show of force they are making is a feint in order to hold me back from a more vigorous pursuit." Still maintaining his position, Forrest remarked: "General Hood, if you will give me one strong division of infantry with my cavalry, I will agree to flank the Federals from their works within two hours' time."

Hood's reply to this was a direction to General Forrest to take charge of the cavalry for the battle which had been ordered.[10] These orders were for Forrest to post cavalry on both flanks and, if the assault proved successful, to complete the ruin of the enemy by capturing those who attempted to escape in the direction of Nashville.[11]

By three o'clock on the afternoon of November 30th two corps of Hood's infantry were up and were taking position, while the third corps, under General S. D. Lee, was held in reserve. Cheatham's corps formed the Confederate left, and Stewart's the right. Under instructions, Forrest placed Jackson's and Buford's divisions immediately on the right of Stewart's line of battle, while Chalmers's division, with the fragment of a brigade under Biffle, was placed on the extreme

[10] Letter from Rev. D. C. Kelley to author.
[11] *Advance and Retreat,* by Lieutenant General J. B. Hood.

left of Cheatham's corps along the Carter's Creek pike. Buford's men were at first deployed in immediate contact with Stewart's right wing, and on the south side of the Harpeth River; somewhat eastward of Franklin along the Lewisburg pike, and between this highway and the river, Jackson's command were thrown boldly across to the north bank of the Harpeth, where they were immediately confronted by Wilson's cavalry in superior force.

As the Confederate infantry moved upon the Union breastworks the cavalry on either flank joined in the advance. Upon the extreme left of the Confederate line Chalmers became heavily engaged with an infantry force posted behind a formidable stone wall, strengthened by hastily constructed breastworks of earth, from which he was unable to dislodge them. Advancing as close as possible to their line, he ordered his men to protect themselves in every way possible and to maintain a constant fire in order to hold the enemy employed there. On the Confederate right wing, Forrest, who was in immediate command, with Buford and Jackson, had already encountered Wilson's cavalry and some infantry which were posted in an advanced position on Schofield's left. Buford, pushing forward with his accustomed pluck and determination, had soon driven the Federal cavalry and infantry which were confronting him to the northern bank of the Harpeth, which his dismounted troops immediately waded and effected a junction with Jackson and Forrest, who were already across.

The fighting now became extremely severe on this part of the line. General James H. Wilson, who was in command of the Union cavalry, says that, simultaneously with the assault of Hood's infantry, Buford's and Jackson's divisions, under Forrest, advanced to the attack and drove back Croxton's brigade from the Lewisburg turnpike north of the Harpeth River, when he immediately dispatched Hatch's, Johnson's, and Harrison's troops to cover and watch the fords and protect the left and rear of Schofield's army.

Realizing the importance of holding this position, as soon as the rebel cavalry had made their appearance on the north side of the river, which properly formed the real line of defence for the Union army, I ordered Hatch and Croxton to attack the enemy with vigor and drive him into the river if possible, while Harrison, with Capron's old brigade, would look well to the left and rear. The occasion was a grave one. My subordinate commanders dismounted every man that could be spared, and went in with a rush that was irresistible. Towards the middle of the afternoon the fighting became exceedingly sharp. The enemy's troopers fought with their accustomed gallantry, but the Union cavalrymen, outnumbering their antagonists for the first time, and skilfully directed, swept everything before them. Upon this occasion Hood made a fatal mistake, for it will be observed that he had detached Forrest, with two divisions of his corps, on a side operation, which left him only Chalmers's division to co-operate with the main attack of his infantry. Had his whole cavalry force advanced against me, it is possible that it would have succeeded in driving us back.

The battle between the two forces of cavalry raged with great fury until nightfall, and Wilson was unable, notwithstanding his superior force upon this part of the battlefield, to drive the Confederates south of the river until dark, when Forrest, having been informed of the failure on the part of Hood to dislodge the Federal infantry from its position in Franklin, withdrew his troops to the south side of the Harpeth.

From about four o'clock until dark the battle of Franklin raged with unsurpassed fury. It has passed into history as one of the bloodiest battles of the Civil War as far as the Confederates were concerned. Never in the history of any war did troops, both officers and men, fight with more desperate valor than upon this field of slaughter. The generals vied with the enlisted men in the recklessness with which they offered up their lives in the heroic yet vain struggle for victory. Here fell the immortal Cleburne, and here John Adams, intent on victory, found undying glory, his horse falling lifeless across the enemy's breastworks and he, sword in hand, dying in their midst.

Though the Confederates did not succeed in carrying all points of the Federal breastworks, they effected an entrance at one or two points, and maintained their position until late in the night, when the enemy left the field and retreated toward Nashville.

General Hood's report might well have been written in blood: "We captured about one thousand prisoners and several stands of colors. Our loss in killed, wounded, and prisoners was forty-five hundred. Among the killed were Major-General P. R. Cleburne, Brigadier-Generals Gist, John Adams, Strahl, and Granbury. Major-General Brown, Brigadier-Generals Carter, Manigault, Quarles, Cockrell, and Scott were wounded, and Brigadier-General Gordon captured."

The Union army marched northward, "Forrest, with his cavalry, pursuing the enemy vigorously.["12] Chalmers moved across to the Hillsboro pike, and along that to a point opposite Brentwood, where he crossed over to the Franklin pike. Arriving within four miles of Nashville, he encamped for the night.

Moving with Buford and Jackson, General Forrest at daylight on the 1st also crossed the Harpeth River and, advancing up the Wilson pike, struck the enemy in strong force at Wilson's Crossroads. Morton was directed to open upon them with one of his batteries. Forrest ordered General Buford to charge, which order he executed with great gallantry, dislodging the enemy and capturing several prisoners. Without further resistance a portion of Forrest's command continued its march toward Nashville.

On the 2nd of December the troops under Chalmers were thrown out along the Hillsboro and Hardin pikes, while Forrest directed Buford to take his division to Mill Creek and form in line of battle across the Murfreesboro highway. Jackson's division was ordered to take position so as to cover the Nashville and Mill Creek pike. When the infantry arrived, late in the afternoon, General Forrest proceeded to operate upon the various blockhouses and detached garrisons in the immediate neighborhood of Nashville, and to interfere with navigation on the Cumberland River below that point. Lieutenant Colonel D. C. Kelley, with a detachment of three hundred men and two pieces of artillery, reached this stream at a point about twelve miles from Nashville, where this gallant and efficient officer, arriving unexpectedly, captured two transports laden with horses and other property belonging to the United States government. The horses he hastened to unload; but before he had succeeded in getting all of the cargo on shore, the enemy's gunboats, coming down from Nashville, recaptured the transports and a portion of the freight.

Kelley brought off 56 prisoners and 197 horses and mules. On this same day (December 3rd), Forrest, with Buford's division, had succeeded in capturing Stockade No. 2, with eighty prisoners, besides killing and wounding several more by the opening shots from Morton's battery. While this attack was in progress a train of cars loaded with troops came in sight at a considerable distance down the road, and before the engineer could reverse his engine and escape

[12] *Official Records,* vol. xlv., part i, p. 659.

it was crippled by Forrest's skillful artillerists. The Union troops, meanwhile, before the Confederates could arrive, had stampeded from the train, and, scattering in the woods, almost the entire command escaped capture.

On the 4th of December Buford's division captured Blockhouse No. 1 on Mill Creek, and No. 3, with thirty-two prisoners. After this, under orders from Hood, Forrest, with Buford's and Jackson's divisions, proceeded toward Murfreesboro, where he was engaged in picketing along the line of the Nashville and Chattanooga Railroad and as far north as the Cumberland River.

General W. H. Jackson, on December 5th, captured near Lavergne a redoubt with the garrison of eighty men, two pieces of artillery, a number of wagons, and a considerable supply of government stores. Another detachment of the cavalry succeeded in capturing a blockhouse near Smyrna station, adding thirty-five prisoners to the list of those already taken on this day. It was here, on the evening of the 5th, that Major General Bate arrived with his infantry division, having been ordered to report to General Forrest, and to operate under his directions upon the enemy's forces in and about Murfreesboro.

Forrest, in his official report, says: "Four miles from Lavergne I formed a junction with Major-General Bate, who had been ordered to report to me with his division for the purpose of operating against Murfreesboro. I ordered General Jackson to send a brigade across to the Wilkinson pike, and, moving on both pikes, the enemy was driven into his works. After ordering General Buford to picket from the Nashville and Murfreesboro to the Lebanon pikes on the left, and Jackson to picket on the right to the Salem pike, I encamped for the night."[13]

At this time the other division of Forrest's cavalry, under Chalmers, was still operating northward on the line of the Cumberland. On the 6th of December, an infantry force having been sent to relieve Colonel Rucker, who with his small brigade was operating on the Hillsboro pike, Chalmers moved to the Charlotte pike to assist in the blockade of the Cumberland.

On the morning of the 7th a monitor appeared in front of the Confederate guns and attempted to force the passage of the river,

[13] *Ibid.*, vol. xlv, part i, p. 755.

but was badly damaged and driven back, and on several subsequent occasions several gunboats repeated the attempt without success. Here Chalmers remained, effectually closing the Cumberland to all transports until the 12th of December.

The boldness and activity of Forrest's command excited the apprehension of General Grant, who, as commander in chief of the armies of the United States, was showing considerable irritation at the delay of Thomas in attacking Hood in front of Nashville, and was justly fearful that if Forrest should throw his troops across the Cumberland River it might cause Thomas to retreat in the direction of Louisville. On December 2nd, in a dispatch to Stanton, he says: "It looks as if Forrest would flank around Thomas until Thomas is equal to him in cavalry." On the 5th he telegraphed Thomas direct: "Is there not danger of Forrest moving down the Cumberland to where he can cross it? It seems to me while you should be getting up your cavalry as rapidly as possible to look after Forrest, Hood should be attacked where he is." Thomas immediately replied: "I have no doubt Forrest will attempt to cross the river, but I am in hopes the gunboats will be able to prevent him."

On the 10th of this month General McLean dispatched: "There is a rumor that Forrest has crossed the Cumberland. Keep scouts out as far as possible in the direction of Nashville. Should a force approach, destroy the pontoons and fall back."

While Thomas had established his headquarters with the reserves at Nashville, in addition to throwing Schofield's column forward as far south as Columbia on Duck River (which army we have followed on their retreat to Franklin and from this battleground to Nashville), he had posted General Lovell H. Rousseau in Murfreesboro, with about 7000 infantry, cavalry, and artillery, and had strongly fortified this position. As soon as the Confederates reached the vicinity of Nashville, General Hood had skillfully maneuvered so as to cut off the troops under Rousseau from communication with those in Nashville under Thomas and Schofield.

On December 6th General Forrest determined upon a forced reconnaissance of the enemy's works at Murfreesboro, and advanced in line of battle, his force consisting of Jackson's and Buford's divisions of his own command, Bate's division of infantry, and the two brigades additional under Sears and Palmer. Driving the Federal pickets and skirmishers in, the Confederates advanced, and, after some two hours of light skirmishing, the Union troops retired within their intrenchments, ceased firing, and showed no further disposition to give battle. Forrest ordered the Confederates to remain in line while he, with a single regiment, made a careful inspection of the fortress, which convinced him that the Federal position was too strong to justify a direct assault. He therefore determined to attempt nothing more than to hold the Federal forces here engaged, and to prevent their union with Thomas in Nashville until he could receive further instructions from General Hood.

The Union commander, General Lovell H. Rousseau, had, however, determined upon the offensive, and on the morning of the 7th Forrest, who was stationed with Palmer's brigade of infantry, observed the Federals moving out in strong force on the Salem pike, with infantry, cavalry, and artillery. He immediately withdrew his command something over a mile to the Wilkinson pike, and formed there a new line in a more favorable position. His chief object in this retrograde movement was to entice the Union troops sufficiently far from their base in Murfreesboro to permit him to throw Jackson's and Buford's divisions between them and their stronghold, and capture them, when he, with the infantry, upon which he felt that he could implicitly rely, should have beaten them in front. These he directed to throw up such temporary protection as they could, and this was hastily done, a very satisfactory line of breastworks being constructed from rails, logs, and stones; and here, in strong position and in fancied security, he calmly awaited the approach of the attacking force.

This force, as given in the official records, consisted of two brigades of infantry and 1326 cavalry, all under the immediate command of Major General R. H. Milroy. His troops moved out on the Salem pike about ten o'clock in the morning, with the Fifth Tennessee (Union) Cavalry in advance. Advancing to within one-half mile of the Wilkinson pike, after a spirited artillery duel lasting about thirty minutes, the Federal commander fell back into a thick wood, until he was out of sight of the Confederate line of battle. He had evidently found this too strong in his front to justify a direct assault.

Taking advantage of the covering afforded by the thick wood, General Milroy moved by the right flank in a northeasterly direction,

Picking off the Federals at Fort Pillow

McCulloch's men taking the first line of fortifications

Lieutenant Leaming delivering the reply, "I will not surrender."

The Confederates storming Fort Pillow

The hand-to-hand struggle between the troops of Rucker and Waring at Brice's Crossroads

Charge of the artillery under Captain Morton at Brice's Crossroads

Retreat of the Federals across Tishomingo Creek after Brice's Crossroads

The Confederate cavalry charging through the streets of Memphis—
Escape of General Washburn

until his line of battle was astride the Wilkinson pike, and here in double alignment his troops were formed. To meet this movement of the enemy, Forrest was compelled to make a change of front by withdrawing a portion of his line and placing it directly across the pike in the path of the advancing Federals. Riding hastily along the line, he addressed the infantry with encouraging words, telling them that they were fully as strong as the attacking party, and that in addition he had his cavalry ready to gain their rear and cut them to pieces and capture the entire command the moment they were repulsed.

Captain P. H. Coleman, of the First Florida Infantry, says: "General Forrest rode to where my company was in position and said by way of encouragement to us: 'Men, all I ask of you is to hold the enemy back for fifteen minutes, which will give me sufficient time to gain their rear with my cavalry, and I will capture the last one of them.' "[14]

Advancing with great gallantry, the Federals, only halting to deliver their volleys, came on in short range of the Confederate infantry, when, to the great surprise and dismay of Generals Forrest and Bate, these soldiers, who had stood their ground and fought with wonderful valor on other fields, broke in disorder and fled in wild panic. Forrest reports: "The enemy moved boldly forward, driving in my pickets, when the infantry, with the exception of Smith's brigade, from some cause which I cannot explain, made a shameful retreat, losing two pieces of our artillery. I seized the colors of the retreating troops and endeavored to rally them, but they could not be moved by any entreaty or appeal to their patriotism. Major-General Bate did the same thing, but was equally as unsuccessful as myself. I hurriedly sent Major Strange, of my staff, to Brigadier-Generals Armstrong and Ross, of Jackson's division, with orders to say to them that everything depended on their cavalry. They proved themselves equal to the emergency by charging on the enemy, thereby checking his further advance."

General Hood says: "I had sent Major-General Forrest, with the greatest part of his cavalry and Bate's division of infantry, to Murfreesboro, to ascertain if it was possible to take the place. After a careful examination and reconnaissance in force, in which I am sorry to say the infantry behaved badly, it was determined that nothing could be

[14] Manuscripts of Captain P. H. Coleman, in possession of the author.

accomplished by assault. Bate's division was then withdrawn, leaving Forrest with Jackson's and Buford's divisions of cavalry in observation. Mercer's and Palmer's brigades of infantry were sent to replace Bate's division."[15]

Forrest was wild with fury at the behavior of the infantry, and took it upon himself to resent personally their shameful conduct. While they were running from the field he dashed in among them, commanding and entreating them to rally and again face the enemy. Mr. W. A. Calloway of Atlanta, Georgia, who was an artillerist in Young's battery on this important part of the field at that time, says: "I was an eye-witness to an interesting incident of this fight at Murfreesboro. During the stampede or retreat, which almost amounted to a panic, Forrest rode in among the infantry, ordering the men to rally, and doing all in his power to stop the retreat. He rode up and down the lines, shouting, 'Rally, men—for God's sake, rally!' The panic-stricken soldiers, however, paid no heed to the general. Rushing towards a color-bearer who was running for dear life, he ordered him to halt. Failing to have his command obeyed, he drew his pistol and shot the retreating soldier down. Dismounting, Forrest took the colors, remounted his horse, and, riding in front of the soldiers, waved the colors at them and finally succeeded in rallying them to their duty."[16]

The resistance offered by the cavalry under Armstrong and Ross succeeded in checking the Federals, who immediately retired within their fortifications. The rapid withdrawal into Murfreesboro was in part due to a bold movement of Buford, who, having been ordered by Forrest to operate upon the left of his line, had taken advantage of the opportunity which offered to attack Murfreesboro from his portion of the field, and had succeeded in penetrating well into the heart of the city. This created such consternation in the mind of the Federal commander, General Rousseau, that he directed Milroy to retreat at once within the fortifications. Milroy says that while thus engaged with the Confederates he received a dispatch from the general, admonishing him of the advance of a large rebel infantry force from the north, directing him to return to the fortress.

On December 11th Buford was directed to picket the Cumberland

[15] *Official Records,* vol. xlv, part i, p. 654.

[16] Personal communication in possession of the author. I have received a corroboration of this statement of Mr. Calloway from another eyewitness.

River in the direction of the Hermitage. On the 12th the infantry were engaged in destroying the railroad from Lavergne to Murfreesboro. On the 13th General Jackson, who had been previously ordered to operate south of Murfreesboro, again distinguished himself by the capture of a train of seventeen cars and the Sixty-first Illinois Regiment of infantry. The train was loaded with supplies, and was destroyed. The prisoners, about two hundred in number, were sent to the rear.

On the morning of the 14th General Forrest moved with Olmstead's and Palmer's brigades of infantry northward across Stone River and east of Murfreesboro, with the view of capturing the enemy's forage train. While on this expedition he received a dispatch from Hood that a general engagement was in progress in front of Nashville, and directing him to hold himself in readiness to move to his assistance at any moment. On the morning of the 16th Forrest retired with his entire command to the Wilkinson Crossroads, six miles from Murfreesboro, and here at nightfall he received the first notice of the great disaster which had befallen the Confederate forces. This courier also brought urgent orders, from the commander in chief at Nashville, for Forrest to fall back toward Duck River and concentrate the cavalry to protect the rear of the beaten army.

While the operations in and about Murfreesboro were in progress, Chalmers's division was still engaged in immediate duty with the infantry in front of Nashville.

On the 12th of December Biffle's brigade had been ordered by General Hood to take position on the extreme Confederate right, leaving Chalmers in charge of the left of the Confederate line, with no other troops than the small brigade of Rucker. Informing General Hood of the extreme weakness of his force, and its inability to cover the ground allotted to it, on the 14th the general in command reinforced this portion of his alignment with Ector's brigade of infantry.

When the battle of Nashville was precipitated on the morning of the 15th of December, 1864, Wilson's corps on the extreme Federal right, advancing in largely superior force and with great gallantry, struck Ector's brigade of infantry so heavily that this officer was compelled to withdraw his command to the main infantry line, and with such precipition that he was unable to convey to Chalmers, who was still farther to his left, any notice of his retreat. The Hardon pike being thus left wide open, General Wilson took prompt advantage of the opportunity presented and threw forward a strong body of his mounted troopers. Ector's infantry had retired eastward to place itself in closer relation to Hood's left wing, and there was at this time in front of the Federal cavalry a single regiment, the Seventh Alabama, which, though fighting bravely, was unable to offer effectual resistance to the Union Troopers.

Advancing some two miles along this highway, General Wilson succeeded in capturing Chalmers's headquarters wagon and ordnance train before this officer had received any intelligence whatever of the disaster which had befallen Ector. The position of Chalmers so far in the rear of the Federal line, with the Cumberland River hemming him in on the west, was now precarious in the extreme. Wilson was fully informed that Forrest, with the two divisions of Jackson and Buford, was absent, at or near Murfreesboro, and not in supporting distance. "The fortunate absence of Forrest, with a large part of his cavalry, relieved the operations of the Federal cavalry from the great peril it would have otherwise incurred."[17]

There can be little doubt that had General Wilson made full use of the strong and thoroughly equipped force at his command, he might have destroyed Chalmers on this occasion. His reports show that during the battle at Nashville his effective force was "12,500 men, having 9000 horses, 2000 of which were scarcely fit for service." He says: "At 10 A.M. on the 15th of December, the sixth division, under Brigadier-General R. W. Johnson, moved on the Charlotte pike, clearing it as far as Davidson's house, driving a battery and a part of Chalmers's division of cavalry from their position on Richland Creek. Croxton's brigade formed on the left of the sixth, between the Hardin and Charlotte pikes, advanced, and turned the enemy's position in front of Johnson's division. The fifth division, Brigadier-General Edward Hatch, formed on the Hardin pike, its right acting with Croxton, advanced simultaneously, and encountered a strong force of the enemy's cavalry well intrenched on both sides of Richland creek. After a sharp fight the enemy was driven from his works and pushed rapidly beyond Hardin's house, near which place part of

[17] Official report of General Wilson.

Hatch's command captured the headquarters train of General Chalmers."

While Croxton's brigade was moving between the Hardin and Charlotte pikes, Hatch's division had full command of the Hardin pike. At the same time, Chalmers, who was with Rucker and his brigade, had also been vigorously assailed on the Charlotte turnpike by R. W. Johnson's division, but held his ground with great bravery until the enemy, as before stated, had swept Ector from the field, pushed the Seventh Alabama rapidly back, and was nearly two miles in his rear, having captured his ordnance and headquarters trains. He skillfully extricated himself, and late in the afternoon effected a junction with the left wing of Hood's army, which as yet held the battlefield, with the exception of that portion on the extreme left from which he and Ector had been driven.

On the following morning (the 16th) the cavalry under Chalmers was again ferociously attacked by a heavy column under Wilson, who was now moving heaven and earth to turn this flank and gain the rear of the Confederate infantry. Realizing how disastrous this movement, if successful, would prove to the army of Hood, he concentrated all his available forces and moved rapidly to the Granny White turnpike, there securing a strong defensive position. He had made the movement none too soon, for shortly after arriving there he received a courier from Hood informing him of his defeat and instructing him to hold the Granny White turnpike at all hazards. The message had been repeated, for one copy was in the hands of Wilson, who says: "It was during this stage of the battle that a most important dispatch from Hood to Chalmers was captured and brought to me, and forwarded by me at once to Thomas. In substance the dispatch was: 'For God's sake, drive the Yankee cavalry from our left and rear, or all is lost.' "

In obedience to this urgent order from the commanding general, Chalmers, Rucker, and Kelley hastened to strengthen their position further by obstructing the road with trees and constructing a barricade of rails and brush. Here, just at dark on the 16th, the Federal cavalry, flushed with the overwhelming success of the day, and still reckoning that Forrest had not yet reached Hood's rear, bore down upon the Confederates with courage and confidence. Rucker, who bore the brunt of this fierce onslaught, held his men to their work, and there occurred all along the Confederate line one of the most desperate and gallant hand-to-hand conflicts which have been recorded in the history of any war.

The weather was intensely cold and the rain, which had been falling, had turned into sleet, which covered the surface of the earth with a coating of ice and made it extremely difficult for the horses to retain their footing as they reared and plunged in this desperate melee. Moreover, the fingers of many of the troopers were so benumbed with the cold that it was difficult for them to cock their pistols or hold their weapons in hand. As Colonels Rucker and Spalding were slashing and thrusting at each other in the darkness, other troopers and officers of the two sides were engaged in like fierce combat, neither side willing to yield.

A Federal writer says:

On the 16th of December, down the Granny White turnpike at dark, Hatch's division pushed onward, followed by Hammond and Croxton. After going two or three miles the advance squadron came upon part of Chalmers's division of Forrest's cavalry formed across the road behind a fence-rail layout. It was too dark to discern anything except the flash of the rebel fire-arms. Colonel George Spalding, commanding the leading regiment, ordered it to follow him in a headlong charge. A running fight took place, charge and countercharge following in quick succession, in which the shouts of the combatants, the clang of sabres, and the rattle of pistols and rifles made the night one never to be forgotten. During this demoniac scene, Colonel Spalding encountered the Confederate general Rucker, and a conflict as between two knights of old took place. They were men of great personal strength and skill, and yet it was so dark that both were at a disadvantage. Grappling at each other blindly, each wrested the sabre from his antagonist's hand and renewed the fight with the other's weapon. They were both well mounted and both good horsemen, and the issue was doubtful till a stray shot broke Rucker's sword-arm, when he was compelled to surrender. Rucker's sword was Spalding's trophy, gallantly won. It remained in his possession at Monroe, Michigan, for a quarter of a century, when it was returned to its owner, now a successful business man at Birmingham, Alabama.[18]

It is possible that the desperate fight made here by Chalmers, Rucker, and Kelley led General Wilson to believe that there was a much larger force in his front than he anticipated, and that Forrest

[18] *Life of General George H. Thomas,* by Donn Piatt and Henry V. Boynton.

had probably reached the scene and was there to confront him. Rucker, who was the heroic figure in this unique encounter, and who possessed not only the stubborn fighting qualities of his superior but in a certain measure that cunning which served Forrest so admirably in many of his desperate situations, had informed the Federal general that he was acting immediately with and under Forrest, who was in front, and this information may have determined the cessation of pursuit on the part of General Wilson. General Rucker's courage and tact on this occasion contributed so largely to the salvation of the remnant of Hood's army from capture before they reached the south side of Duck River that the following authentic statement is worthy of record here.

It was about four o'clock on the afternoon of the 16th of December that Rucker had been ordered to retire with his command, select a strong position on the Granny White pike, and to hold the enemy in check at all hazards. He was told that Hood's army was completely routed and in wild retreat, and that if Wilson's advance was not detained then and there all was lost. He was also informed that General Forrest was expected every moment from Murfreesboro with his cavalry. In order to encourage his men as much as possible, Rucker put out the report that Forrest was near at hand and would soon take command of all the troops.

When he reached the position which had been designated, it was beginning to grow dark. The ground was covered with snow, which had fallen during the afternoon, and at this hour there was a drizzling rain, which congealed as it came in contact with the snow and made it as slippery as glass. Directing one of his regiments to construct breastworks of rails and brush and logs across and on either side of the pike, Rucker rode a short distance to the left to place the Seventh Alabama Cavalry in such position that he could enfilade the Federals when they should charge upon the breastworks. As Rucker was returning, after having posted this regiment, he rode into and among a body of mounted troops which he had mistaken for his own men.

As it was now very dark, the uniforms could not be recognized, but from the orders which were being given to the troops he soon became convinced that they were Union soldiers. Rucker, who had his saber already in hand, rode up close to an officer who was giving the various orders and asked him who he was. The officer replied that he was

Colonel Spalding of Wilson's cavalry, upon which Rucker struck him a blow over the head and shoulders with his saber. Colonel Spalding quickly returned the compliment, but fortunately for Rucker he was so near his adversary that as he brought his saber down at full swing the basket, or guard, of the handle only came in contact with the top of the Confederate officer's head. Rucker again struck at his adversary, but at this moment his horse reared up on his hind feet, the stroke fell short, and in the effort to recover his seat his saber fell from his hand. Nothing daunted, he spurred his charger so as to bring him again close to Colonel Spalding, whose saber he now seized and wrenched from his hand.

The Federal troopers now came to the rescue of their leader, and Rucker, appreciating the hopelessness of the contest, struck spurs to his horse, a large, powerful animal, snow-white in color, and endeavored to escape. Colonel Spalding yelled out to his men, as Rucker drew away, to shoot the man on the white horse. This was a signal for a volley to be fired at Rucker, one of the shots taking effect near the elbow of his left, or bridle, arm. As the bone was shattered by the missile, the member, of course, became powerless, when the animal, released from the restraint of his rider, leaped wildly forward and threw Rucker violently to the ground, where he was made a prisoner.

He was immediately taken some fifty or one hundred yards to the rear, where he was interviewed by General Hatch, to whom he remarked: "Forrest has just arrived with all the cavalry, and will give you hell to-night. Mark what I tell you." He was closely questioned as to the coming of Forrest, and repeated the statement in such a manner that in all probability he convinced the Federal commander that Forrest was on the field. About this time, Randolph, who was in command of one of Rucker's regiments, opened a side volley upon the Federals, which threw them into confusion, and they retreated several hundred yards. It was at this point that Rucker says he was greatly gratified to hear someone say, "General Wilson has ordered everything in camp."

It is an agreeable task to write of the chivalric conduct of Generals Wilson and Hatch and Colonel Spalding toward this wounded and brave Confederate. He says: "During the night General Hatch came to me and said that he wanted to make me more comfortable, and offered me his bed. I thanked him very much, and he made a courteous reply. I was taken to a room in which there were two beds. One of these I occupied, and later in the night General Wilson came into the room, and was told that the other bed was for him. He did not retire, however, but sat up in that bed, crosslegged like a tailor, all night, writing orders and receiving despatches. I do not think that either General Wilson or I slept a wink. I certainly didn't. General Hatch laid down on the floor by my side, and (God bless him) got up frequently during the night and gave me water, and the next morning, when we left for Nashville, he provided me with a small flask of good whiskey."[19]

In later years General Hood expressed his full appreciation of Rucker's clever stategy on that night, and told him that it did much to save his army from complete destruction.

From an article on the "Cavalry Corps in the Nashville Campaign," which forms a chapter in the *Life of General George H. Thomas,*[20] the following is quoted:

The victory was as complete as it could be made in a short December day. The pursuit was begun at once, but it must not be forgotten that the entire cavalry force on the field had been dismounted and engaged in the attack against the rear of Hood's intrenchments. There was absolutely no reserve, and the horses of the entire force were from a half to three-quarters of a mile in the rear, and, with all the officers could do, aided by the cheerful alacrity of the men, over half an hour was consumed in getting to the horses and mounting for the pursuit. There was no warning of the rebel intention to break, except that contained in Hood's despairing cry to Chalmers; they fought on doggedly and steadily, every man in his place, till the infantry advance began, and then, seeing that further resistance would be in vain, they broke all at once and hastened to the rear as rapidly as possible. The break occurred at about four o'clock. The pursuit by the first mounted troops began at about half past four. The clouds hung low and were dense and black. It had already begun to rain, and this hastened the on-coming of night. By five o'clock it was dark, and by six a cavalryman could scarcely see his horse's ears, but there was no hesitation or delay. Following the Granny White turnpike, the gallant horsemen pushed onward into the darkness, picking up prisoners and ruthlessly charging every semblance of a rear-guard. Hammond and Croxton followed close upon their heels, and no one in the entire cavalry force thought of halting or going into camp, although the day had been a hard and toilsome one with but little cessation from marching and fighting. The pursuit had not been

[19] Based on manuscript of Colonel E. W. Rucker, in possession of the author.
[20] It is stated in this volume that General Wilson had rendered full assistance "in connection with this portion of the work."

carried on for more than two or three miles before the advanced squadrons found a part of Chalmers's division of Forrest's cavalry formed across the road behind a fence-rail lay-out.

It was here that the signal resistance of Chalmers and Rucker took place, practically ending the Federal pursuit for that day.

Referring to this fight, General Wilson says: "The gallant Confederates were driven in turn from every fresh position taken up by them, and the running fight was kept up until near midnight. Chalmers, however, had done the work cut out for him gallantly and well. He was overborne and driven back, it is true, but the delay which he forced upon the Federal cavalry by the stand he had made was sufficient to enable the fleeing Confederate infantry to sweep by the danger-point that night, to improvise a rear-guard, and to make good their retreat the next day."

In the desperate straits in which he found himself toward the close of that disastrous day of December, 1864, General Hood turned to his famous lieutenant for help, and Forrest never showed himself a greater soldier or a more successful fighter than in this trying emergency. When on the afternoon of the 15th of December he had received by courier a message stating that the battle in front of Nashville had been begun, his sound military judgment told him that the contest between the greatly superior army of Thomas and the troops under General Hood would end in the overthrow of the latter.

He knew full well that the battle of Franklin had broken the spirit of this army. Up to that date, inspired with fresh hope of success by the invasion of Tennessee, pushing the enemy in front of them as they did from the Tennessee River to Franklin, they had rushed upon the foe here in the full confidence of victory; and when the survivors of this gallant army saw that their commanders and their comrades had been slaughtered in such fearful numbers, and that, after all, the enemy had escaped and had taken post behind their breastworks in Nashville and were now stronger than ever, they had lost heart and hope, and were practically beaten before a gun was fired in the battle of the 15th and 16th of December.

With this in mind, as soon as he heard that the battle was in progress, although the Confederates were still holding their position, Forrest hastened Buford's division in the direction of Nashville and Franklin, where it would be ready to unite with Chalmers and offer what resistance it could in the protection of the army when it should retreat. It will be seen that this division arrived just in the nick of time to unite with Chalmers at Franklin on the early morning of the 17th of December.

Forrest had already started southward, in the direction of the Tennessee River, his prisoners (some four hundred in number), the wagon trains, the sick and wounded, and several hundred infantry who were unfit for active duty by reason of being barefooted, and with these a considerable drove of beef cattle and hogs which had been gathered up for the use of the army. Thus encumbered, his march along the almost impassable road was unavoidably slow, and had he not started in advance he would not have been able in safety to reach Duck River and unite with General Hood there as he did on the 18th of December.

When the courier arrived with the information that Hood's lines were broken, from Triune he hastened Armstrong's brigade westward in the direction of Spring Hill, and threw the remainder of Jackson's division on that route to unite with the rear guard then, under Chalmers and Lee, struggling against the onslaughts of Wilson's corps. The single brigade of Ross accompanied his train across Duck River, near Columbia, on the 18th, and early on this morning Forrest in person reported to General Hood and was immediately assigned to the command of the rear guard of the Army of Tennessee.

General Grant, in front of Petersburg, had now no longer any anxiety in regard to General Hood, but as to the commander of the Southern cavalry his mind was not so much at ease. He wired Thomas: "The armies operating against Richmond have fired two hundred guns in honor of your great victory. In all your operations we hear nothing of Forrest. Great precautions should be taken to prevent him crossing the Cumberland or Tennessee below Eastport."

General Thomas had heard on the 17th that Forrest had been killed, but awaited the confirmation of this news, which was almost too good to be true, before answering the dispatch of his chief. On December 17th Schofield had informed him that "citizens on the road in rear of where we fought yesterday report that the universal testimony of rebels, officers and men, is that Forrest was certainly killed at Murfreesboro, where they admit their cavalry was badly whipped."

General Wilson had been urged to inform his commander as to what had become of the redoubtable Confederate cavalryman, and on the 17th he telegraphed as follows: "Cannot hear definitely, though it is reported he withdrew from Murfreesboro yesterday." On the 18th the official records contain the following: "General Rousseau reports Forrest killed, and fifteen hundred of his men captured at Murfreesboro."[21] While the wires were burdened with these messages, Forrest, by night and day, was marching to throw himself between the beaten infantry and their victorious pursuers.

At daylight on the morning of the 17th the troops of both armies were astir. The Federal cavalry, however, had had the longer rest, since they encamped for the night about eleven o'clock and did not mount their horses until between four and five on the following morning. The Confederate horsemen, under Chalmers, had had little respite from the desperate work in which all day of the 16th they had been engaged. When the Union troopers desisted from further pursuit the Confederate general had left a thin line of skirmishers to offer what resistance they were able, should any advance be made, and these had built fires in order to impress the Federals with the idea that the entire cavalry had gone into camp in their front. With the remainder of his command, which had by this time become considerably scattered and not a little disorganized, Chalmers hastened, despite the darkness of the night, toward Franklin, where he arrived early in the morning and, in the absence of Forrest, was placed in command of all the cavalry at that point, to act with General Stephen D. Lee in protecting the rear of the army. It was at this opportune moment that General Buford arrived with his division and reported to Chalmers.

General Stephen D. Lee, who had handled his corps with such marked ability and success in the two days' battle in the front of Nashville, still held his immediate command together in excellent fighting shape, and selecting two brigades—Pettus's Alabama and Stovall's Georgia troops—he, with the cavalry of Chalmers and Buford, organized these into a temporary rear guard and awaited the onslaught of the Union cavalry.

Major General Wilson was early in the saddle and pressed forward vigorously with the brigades of Hammond, Croxton, and Knipe. Near Brentwood his advance struck the outposts of the Confederate cavalry and drove these without great difficulty as far as four miles north of Franklin. Pursuing with a boldness amounting to rashness, the Union troopers here ran into a stronger detachment of Forrest's cavalry and

[21] *Official Records,* vol. xlv, part ii, p. 252.

the two brigades of infantry under Stephen D. Lee, and suffered a temporary check. General Lee reports:

Their boldness was soon checked by many of them being killed and captured by Pettus's Alabama and Stovall's Georgia brigades and Bledsoe's battery under General Clayton. I was soon compelled to withdraw rapidly towards Franklin, as the enemy was throwing a force in my rear from both the right and left of the pike. This force was checked by Brigadier-General Gibson with his brigade and a regiment of Buford's cavalry under Colonel Shacklett. The resistance which the enemy had met with early in the morning, and which materially checked his movement, enabled us to reach Franklin with but little difficulty. About 4 P.M. the enemy, having crossed a considerable force over the Harpeth, commenced a bold and vigorous attack, charging with his cavalry and pushing forward his lines in our front. A more persistent effort was never made to rout the rear-guard of a retiring column. This desperate attack was kept up till long after dark, but gallantly did the rear-guard, consisting of Pettus's Alabama and Cummings's Georgia brigades—the latter commanded by Colonel Watkins, of Stevenson's division—repulse every attack. Brigadier-General Chalmers with his division of cavalry recovered our flanks. The cavalry of the enemy succeeded in getting in Stevenson's rear and attacked Major-General Clayton's division about dark, but were handsomely repulsed, Gibson's and Stovall's brigades being principally engaged. Some four or five guidons were captured from the enemy during the evening.[22]

Of this incident General Wilson says: "The rebels, finding Johnson on their flank, fell back to a strong position on the Columbia pike two miles south of Franklin."

During the desperate fighting of the rear guard under General Lee on the 17th of December, this gallant officer covered himself with glory, not only in the reckless exposure to every danger which the fighting at close quarters made necessary, but in the ability with which he handled the brave troops under his immediate command. Toward the close of the day he was seriously wounded, but declined to relinquish his command until the safety of the troops was assured, when near nightfall he was succeeded by Major General C. L. Stevenson. Chalmers and Buford, realizing the critical situation of the army, fought with bulldog tenacity and great courage.

So bold was the pursuit on the part of the Federal cavalry that for mile after mile in the running fight of the day officers and men alike of

[22] *Ibid.*, vol. xlv, part i, p. 689.

the contending forces were mingled in hand-to-hand assault. They slashed or thrust at each other with their sabers, or drew their six-shooters. The hands or fingers of many of these men were so benumbed with cold that they were compelled to use both hands to cock their pistols. The two cavalry generals moved in the thickest of the fray, and emptied all the chambers of their "navies" in hand-to-hand combat more than once during the arduous work of this bloody day. Language is inadequate to depict the suffering of the soldiers of both armies. For several days during and after the battle it sleeted and rained and froze alternately; the roads were deep in mud and covered with thin ice, which broke under foot and added to the difficulty of marching; the weather was intensely cold, the troops were wet and hungry, and the horses and men were jaded and worn out. With unsurpassed heroism these brave soldiers of both armies stood uncomplainingly to their desperate work. Their leaders were men of indomitable will. There was not to be a Fort Donelson surrender because the weather was cold or the enemy in superior force.

Wilson says:

Late in the evening of the 17th, apparently exhausted with rapid marching, the enemy took up a strong position in the open fields about a mile north of the West Harpeth River. It was then so dark from fog and the approaching night that Hatch's men had become somewhat intermingled with the sullen and taciturn Confederate stragglers, and began to doubt that the ranks which were now looming up in front were really those of the enemy's rear-guard. The momentary hesitation caused by this doubt gave Forrest an opportunity to strengthen his line and to post his single remaining battery in position so as to sweep the turnpike. Hatch on the left and Knipe on the right were at once ordered to charge the enemy's flank. The Confederate battery opened with canister at short-range, but hardly had Forrest emptied his guns before the storm broke upon him as well as upon the entire rebel line. This fight was most desperate, and extended well into the night. Every musket-flash and every defiant shout was a guide to the gallant and unrelenting pursuers. It was a desperate hand-to-hand fight, mounted men against footmen, sabre and pistol against stout hearts and clubbed muskets, with the pall of darkness still over all; the enemy was again scattered, the guns captured, spreading confusion and terror throughout the retreating mass of now completely disorganized Confederates.

Early on the 18th of December the Confederates continued their retreat toward Columbia, but beyond one or two slight skirmishes between the advance of Wilson's corps and the extreme rear guard of the Confederate cavalry, in which the casualties were insignificant, no fighting occurred. The relaxed vigor in the pursuing enemy was a godsend to the beaten Confederates. Rutherford Creek, which was now level with the top of the banks from the heavy rainfall, was the first formidable obstacle in the path of the retreating army. While the cavalry of Forrest was holding Wilson's men at bay, Cheatham, arriving near this stream, halted his corps a few miles south of Spring Hill and threw up intrenchments in order to protect the passage of the wagon train. This safely over, he crossed to the southern bank, and was immediately followed by the entire cavalry, who succeeded in destroying the bridge over which they crossed before it was captured.

It was not until the 19th that the head of General Wilson's column reached the northern bank of Rutherford Creek. In his report, reciting the difficulties which confronted him in the pursuit of Forrest, he says: "At early dawn on the 19th, the cavalry corps, although entirely out of rations, resumed the pursuit, Hatch and Knipe, pressing close upon the enemy's rear-guard, which had again been formed and was now commanded by Forrest in person, while Croxton and Johnson endeavored to reach around it and strike the retreating Confederates at Spring Hill. The haversacks and forage-bags were emptied, and there was no alternative but to wait for the supply-trains which had been ordered forward, and which arrived late in the night."

These difficulties, not only for the pursuers but for the pursued, were not lessened by a terrific winter rainstorm which set in late on the afternoon of the 19th.

It had been the intention of General Hood, in case of failure at Nashville, to fall back no farther than the line of Duck River and there maintain himself throughout the winter. So overwhelming, however, was the defeat, and so greatly disorganized was his army, that when he arrived at Columbia, he says, "I became convinced that the condition of the army made it necessary to recross the Tennessee without delay." What General Hood implied by the "condition of the army" may be judged from the losses he had sustained, as given in the official reports of General George H. Thomas: "We captured 13,189 prisoners, including seven general officers and nearly one thousand other officers of all grades, and seventy-two pieces of serviceable artillery. During the same period over two thousand deserters were received, to whom the oath was administered."[23]

Forrest fully concurred in the conclusion of the commanding officer to reach the Tennessee River with the greatest expedition, giving as his opinion that if this was not done the entire army would be captured. He proposed to General Hood to undertake the protection of his rear and to hold the enemy in check long enough for the escape of the army across the Tennessee, if in addition to his cavalry, which now numbered 3000 effectives, he would place under his command 4000 serviceable infantry, and requested that Major General E. C. Walthall be placed at the head of the infantry to act under his orders during the retreat. These suggestions of Forrest were accepted.

This ever-famous rear guard, in addition to Forrest's cavalry, was composed of fragments of the following commands: the brigades of General W. S. Featherston, Colonel J. B. Palmer, Colonel C. W. Heiskell (who had succeeded General Strahl, who was killed at Franklin), Colonel C. H. Olmstead (who had succeeded General Smith), Colonel H. R. Field (who had succeeded General Maney), General D. H. Reynolds, General D. Coleman (who had succeeded Ector), General J. B. Johnson (who had succeeded General Quarles). These remnants were consolidated by placing Palmer's and Smith's brigades under Colonel Palmer, Field's and Heiskell's under Colonel Field, Reynolds's and Coleman's under General Reynolds, Featherston's and Johnson's under General Featherston.

In General Thomas's report, he says: "Forrest and his cavalry, and such other detachments as had been sent off from his main army, joined Hood at Columbia. He had formed a powerful rear-guard, numbering about four thousand infantry and all his available cavalry. With the exception of this rear guard, his army had become a disheartened and disorganized rabble of half-armed and barefooted men, who sought every opportunity to fall out by the wayside and desert their cause, to put an end to their sufferings. *The rear-guard, however, was undaunted and firm, and did its work bravely to the last.*"[24]

Of the infantry which volunteered its services to cover the Confederate retreat fully three hundred were without shoes, and their feet were so badly cut by the ice and the rough marching that they could

[23] *Ibid.*, vol. xlv, part i, p. 46.
[24] Italics not in the original.

scarcely hobble along. They wrapped pieces of blankets around their raw and swollen feet, tied them on with thongs, and still trudged on, staining the snow and slush as they went, until Forrest ordered some of the wagons to be emptied of their contents in order to give transportation to these unconquerable men. When it became necessary to fight off the Union advance guard they left the wagons, took their place in line, and did effective service. When the uncomplaining sacrifices which these heroic spirits made is fully known, the historian and the poet will transmit to posterity in lasting form the thrilling story of the immortal rear guard of Hood's army under Forrest and Walthall.

The successful passage of Rutherford Creek gave the Confederates forty-eight hours of valuable time, and enabled Forrest to effect the passage of Duck River and to destroy all the bridges which might be available to the enemy before Wilson could reach its banks.

It is clear that the plans of Thomas and Wilson fell short of perfection at this important juncture. Having calculated upon the defeat of Hood in front of Nashville, these generals had wisely delayed their attack until they had completed the organization of this magnificent cavalry corps, so that they might fall upon him in retreat, convert his rout into panic, and destroy him before he could reach the Tennessee River. They had also constructed as a part of this pursuit a train of pontoons, and were abundantly supplied with wagons, supplies, and light artillery. Notwithstanding this, they were so slow in moving to the front that the train with rations did not arrive at Rutherford Creek until the 20th of December, more than three days after the close of the battle in front of Nashville, and it was not until the 21st that the Federal cavalry succeeded in crossing so small a stream as Rutherford Creek. This delay gave Forrest the opportunity of which he took immediate advantage, and saved the remnant of Hood's beaten forces.

No sooner had Forrest been placed in charge of affairs at Columbia, on the 18th, than he began to impress oxen and to have the wagons and artillery double-teamed in order to pull one-half of the train and guns more rapidly over the quagmire roads leading toward the Tennessee. By this method he knew he could surely save at least one-half his train.

An official Union dispatch of this period says: "They report that the Confederate artillery horses have all given out, and the guns are being hauled by oxen. Forrest's cavalry is in fair condition, but it does not amount to more than fifteen hundred mounted, while their dismounted troops are thirty-five hundred."

Forrest had made a clean sweep of the Duck River bridges. For many miles above and below Columbia not even a piece of string timber remained. To the Federal horsemen, strong enough to have run over and swallowed up the Confederate mounted troops facing them, was left the alternative of swimming this stream, a madly sweeping torrent at this season, or of awaiting the arrival of their pontoons. Wilson was too wise a commander and knew his antagonist too well to attempt to swim, with Forrest's riflemen behind logs and trees on the other side. Chafing at the enforced delay, he sent messenger after messenger to have the bridge train hurried on.

To his chagrin he learned that the pontoons had taken the wrong road. He says: "Duck River proved impassable for the national cavalry until the single pontoon-train of the army could be brought forward, and this, owing to the condition of the roads and a mistake which had started it in the wrong direction, involved a further delay of twenty-four hours." These various delays gave Forrest time to return with the teams from the first trip to the Tennessee and save the remaining half of the wagons and artillery.

It was not until the morning of December 24th that the Union general crossed to the south side of Duck River with his corps and resumed the pursuit. Forrest, meanwhile, had fallen back and taken up a strong position at Richland Creek, south of Columbia, and was prepared to meet him. Six pieces of artillery were placed in well-selected positions on the main pike, and these were supported by Buford's and Chalmers's divisions and Ross's brigade of Jackson's division. General Wilson, after a careful reconnaissance, was so well convinced of the inadvisability of attempting to cross this creek at the place where Forrest had posted his guns and troops that he took immediate steps to throw his men across above and below the Confederate position. He says:

On the morning of the 24th the pursuit was resumed. Hood's reorganized rear-guard, under the redoubtable Forrest, was soon encountered by the cavalry advance-guard, and he was a leader not to be attacked by a handful of men however bold. The few remaining teams and the rabble of the army had been hurried on towards the Tennessee, marching to Pulaski by turnpike and thence to Bainbridge by the dirt roads of the country. The rear-guard had thus a clear road, and when hard pressed could fall back rapidly.

The open country to the right and left of the turnpike was much broken, heavily wooded, and almost impassable, while the turnpike itself, threading the valleys, depressions, and gorges, offered many advantageous positions for defence; hence, with a few men, the pursuing force could be made to develop a front almost anywhere, and its progress was at times comparatively slow.

General Wilson finally succeeded in crossing Richland Creek well upon the flanks of the Confederate position, as a result of which Forrest was forced back in the direction of Pulaski. In the fighting here, which was at times a hand-to-hand affair, Brigadier General Buford was badly wounded and was compelled to relinquish command of his division, which was for the time being consolidated with that of Chalmers.

On Christmas morning, after destroying the ammunition and stores which could not be moved, Forrest, leaving a light rear guard under Jackson, moved rapidly seven miles south of Pulaski, and near King's, or Anthony's, Hill again awaited the advance of the enemy. The approach to this hill was through a narrow valley, shut in on either side by ridges of considerable height. Morton's artillery was placed on the crest of the ridge and masked in position to sweep the valley along which the enemy must approach. Armstrong's and Ross's brigades were dismounted and thrown into line with Featherston's and Palmer's infantry in easy support, and to one side of the artillery. From the opposite side of this crescentic formation Jackson's division, mounted, was lined up with Reynolds's and Field's infantry. Breastworks of logs and stone and brush were hastily constructed and a line of skirmishers thrown well out in front. In order to prevent any possibility of a flank movement on the part of Wilson to gain the Confederate rear, Chalmers had been placed upon the right flank in observation.

A half-mile in front of this position, toward Pulaski, a small force of Confederates, mounted, was left at the mouth of the gorge, with directions to fire and to retreat rapidly in order to entice the Union horsemen into the ambush. As soon as the Federals came in sight they charged the rear guard; but, advancing into the narrow path between the hills, their cautious commander felt assured that Forrest would not fail to take advantage of his strong natural position. Suspecting the trap which had been laid for him, he called off a pursuit on horseback and ordered one of his regiments to dismount, and these he carefully pushed forward with a single piece of artillery. The Confederates remained concealed until the enemy were within close range, when, upon a given signal, Morton opened with his battery, which was double-shotted with canister, and at the same time the Confederates in ambush on either side delivered a volley of musketry. The Federals broke in great disorder, and the Confederates, leaving their breastworks, charged upon them, General W. H. Jackson's mounted detachment leading and capturing a number of prisoners, one piece of artillery, and several hundred horses of the dismounted troopers.

General Wilson at this juncture sent the following message to General Wood, commander of Fourth Army Corps: "We are four miles from Pulaski, on the Lamb's Ferry road, and have met a slight check. If you bring up your infantry we may get some prisoners, and I think I shall be able to drive Forrest off. Your infantry can materially assist me."[25] And further: "Just before sundown on Christmas eve, Forrest, in a fit of desperation, made a stand on a heavily wooded ridge at the head of a ravine, and by a rapid and savage counterthrust drove back Harrison's brigade, captured one gun, which he succeeded in carrying away as the sole trophy of that desperate campaign."[26]

Notwithstanding General Wilson's statement that this was the last flicker of aggressive temper shown by any of Hood's beaten and demoralized army, on the following day, the 26th, a very decided stand was made by the rear guard under Forrest, about which there was no suggestion of demoralization or defeat. The Union general, advancing, drove in easily the pickets of Ross's brigade, but struck something heavier at a small stream called Sugar Creek. Here Forrest had encamped for the night, and had again strengthened his position by a layout of rails and logs. In the early morning a dense fog prevailed, and this effectually concealed not only his troops but the breastworks. As the Federals came on they could not know of the presence of the Confederates until they were within very close musket range. Then a volley was opened upon them, and again they were thrown into confusion and retreated in disorder.

Two mounted regiments of Ross's brigade and two of the infantry regiments were ordered to charge at this opportune moment, which was done, throwing the enemy into a complete rout. The Confederates fol-

---

[25] *Official Records,* vol. xlv, part ii, p. 348.
[26] *Battles and Leaders of the Civil War,* vol. iv, p. 471.

lowed for nearly two miles. Coming upon them in stronger force, Forrest then withdrew his troops back to Sugar Creek, and remained in line of battle for two hours. As the enemy did not put in an appearance, he then retreated toward the Tennessee River. Forrest says in his report: "The enemy made no further attack between Sugar Creek and Tennessee River, which stream I crossed on the evening of the 27th of December."

General Wilson says:

From that time till the Tennessee River was reached Forrest made a frequent show of resistance, each of which ended with nothing more serious than an insignificant skirmish. The weather had become worse and worse; it was cold and freezing during the nights, and followed by days of rain, snow, and thaw. The country, which was poor and thinly settled at best, had been absolutely stripped of forage and provisions by the march of contending armies. The men of both forces suffered dreadfully, but the poor cavalry horses fared still worse than their riders. Scarcely a withered corn-blade could be found for them, and thousands, exhausted by overwork, famished with hunger, or crippled so that death was a mercy, with hoofs dropping off from frost and mud, fell by the roadside never to rise again. By the time the corps found rest on the Tennessee River, it could muster scarcely seven thousand horses fit for service. The failure of the light-draft gunboats on the Tennessee to reach and destroy the pontoon-bridge which Hood had kept in position insured his safe retreat. The cavalry advance-guard, under the active and enterprising Spalding, reached the north bank of the river just as the bridge had been swung to the south side and the last of the rebels were disappearing in the distance."[27]

It was said of Forrest through this trying ordeal, by Captain Walter A. Goodman of Chalmers's staff: "At no time in his whole career was the fortitude of General Forrest in adversity, and his power of infusing his own cheerfulness into those under his command, more strikingly exhibited than at this crisis."[28]

Colonel D. C. Kelley says: "The part which he took in the Hood retreat from Nashville, in directing almost every movement of the army, suggesting the roads that should be taken, the manner in which the artillery and baggage-trains were to be moved, sending messengers every few hours to General Hood, giving the minutest practical details,

[27] *Battles and Leaders of the Civil War.*
[28] *Campaigns of Lieutenant-General N. B. Forrest.*

showed him fully capable of handling an army of any size. All this while he was actively engaged in covering the retreat, inflicting upon the enemy blow after blow, until his latest capture of men and artillery induced them to cease their pursuit. When he had reached Iuka, Mississippi, I heard General Hood heartily thank Forrest for the suggestions he had sent him in reference to the movements of the army, saying to him that without his aid he should never have brought his army across the Tennessee River."

Diplomatist as well as soldier, Forrest knew that his troops could not fail to be influenced by the gloom and despondency that had settled down upon the remnant of Hood's infantry which had survived this campaign of disasters. He was, moreover, a born orator, possessed a wonderful command of language, and was eloquent and impressive in delivery. On reaching the south side of the Tennessee, he addressed his men as follows:

SOLDIERS—The old campaign is ended, and your commanding general deems this an appropriate occasion to speak of the steadiness, self-denial, and patriotism with which you have borne the hardships of the past year. The marches and labors you have performed during that period will find no parallel in the history of this war.

On the 24th day of December, 1863, there were three thousand of you, unorganized and undisciplined, at Jackson, Tennessee, only four hundred of whom were armed. You were surrounded by fifteen thousand of the enemy, who were congratulating themselves on your certain capture. You started out with your artillery, wagon-trains, and a large number of cattle, which you succeeded in bringing through, since which time you have fought and won the following battles—battles which will enshrine your names in the hearts of your countrymen and live in history an imperishable monument to your prowess: Jack's Creek, Estenaula, Somerville, Okolona, Union City, Paducah, Fort Pillow, Bolivar, Tishomingo Creek, Harrisburg, Hurricane Creek, Memphis, Athens, Sulphur Springs, Pulaski, Carter's Creek, Columbia, and Johnsonville—fields upon which you have won fadeless immortality. In the recent campaign in middle Tennessee you sustained the reputation so nobly won. For twenty-six days, from the time you left Florence, on the 21st of November, to the 26th of December, you were constantly engaged with the enemy, and endured the hunger, cold, and labor incident to that arduous campaign without murmur. To sum up, in brief, your triumphs during the past year, you have fought fifty battles, killed and captured sixteen thousand of the enemy, captured two thousand horses and mules, sixty-seven pieces of artillery, four gunboats, fourteen transports, twenty barges, three hundred wagons, fifty ambulances, ten thousand stands of small arms, forty block-houses, destroyed thirty-six railroad bridges, two hundred miles of railroad, six engines, one hundred cars, and $15,000,000 worth of property.

In the accomplishment of this great work you were occasionally sustained by other troops, who joined you in the fight, but your regular number never exceeded five thousand, two thousand of whom have been killed or wounded, while in prisoners you have lost about two hundred.

If your course has been marked by the graves of patriotic heroes who have fallen by your side, it has, at the same time, been more plainly marked by the blood of the invader. While you sympathize with the friends of the fallen, your sorrows should be appeased by the knowledge that they fell as brave men battling for all that makes life worth living for.

Soldiers, you now rest for a short time from your labors. During the respite prepare for future action. Your commanding general is ready to lead you again to the defence of the common cause, and he appeals to you, by a remembrance of the glories of your past career, your desolated homes, and, above all, by the memory of your dead comrades, to yield a ready obedience to discipline, and to buckle on your armor anew for the fight. Bring with you the soldier's safest armor—a determination to fight while the enemy pollutes your soil; to fight as long as he denies your rights; to fight until independence shall have been achieved; to fight for home, children, liberty, and all you hold dear. Show to the world the superhuman and sublime spirit with which a people may be inspired when fighting for the inestimable boon of liberty. Be not allured by the siren song of peace, for there can be no peace save upon your separate, independent nationality. Be patient, obedient, and earnest, and the day is not far distant when you can return to your homes and live in the full fruition of freemen around the family altar.

TWENTY-ONE

Closing Campaign of 1865, January 1 to May 9

THE opposing cavalry forces of the Federal and Confederate armies, under Wilson and Forrest, were at last separated from each other, and were mutually content to have the broad Tennessee River between them. Forrest's command, if anything, was even more jaded and worn out than Wilson's. It had passed through the severe and trying experiences of the Johnsonville expedition, and without a day of rest had been hurried forward to join Hood at Florence. Then, from the 19th of November to the 27th of December, in a season of great inclemency, it had marched and fought every day, and at times for several nights in succession. Many of the horses had died on the march and in battle, and a goodly number of those which survived were in such a deplorable condition that they had to be abandoned without any hope of procuring new animals in their place.

The advantages of the situation were greatly in Wilson's favor. For several weeks before Hood crossed the Tennessee Wilson had had possession of all the country between this river and the Cumberland at Nashville, and while the rigorous general impressment of animals was not begun until Hood was in front of Nashville, it goes without saying that Wilson's veteran troopers did not leave any serviceable animals in that region, but appropriated them for the large cavalry command which he had skillfully organized. He did not leave a horse or a mule in all this land. All the streetcar, omnibus, and private horses and mules in Nashville which were fit for service had been taken. So exacting was the impressment of this officer that Andrew Johnson, Vice-President of the United States, had to give up his carriage team. Not a circus within this territory but what had been compelled to disband for the reason that General Wilson had appropriated its livestock. Sherman had for years been praying for a cavalry commander who could, as he termed it, "beat Forrest stealing horses." His prayer had at last been answered.

A fair idea of the terrible hardships of this Nashville campaign may be gathered from the fact that even Wilson's command, freshly mounted and thoroughly provided for with all the vast resources of the Federal government, had in thirty days marched and fought itself almost to a standstill. General Wilson says that his troops were "nearly on foot when his advance-guard reached the Tennessee River, to see the last of the Confederates disappearing in the distance beyond the southern shore."

Looking backward now, it would seem that the war for the establishment of the Southern Confederacy should have ceased with the battle at Nashville. The demoralization of Hood's army, with the conditions prevailing at Petersburg, and Sherman's unresisted march to Savannah and northward, leave slight justification for the sacrifices which the Southern soldiers were called upon to make after this date. Forrest himself was fully impressed with the hopelessness of the struggle, but as a soldier he was in honor bound to fight to the bitter end unless the authorities should direct otherwise.

Major Powhatan Ellis, writing of him at this period, says: "I had at this time a conversation with General Forrest which impressed me very deeply. The turn which events soon took showed how thoroughly he grasped the situation and saw the inevitable end. He began the conversation by asking me what I intended to do when the war was over. I replied, 'I do not exactly understand what you mean.' He said: 'To my mind it is evident that the end is not far off; it will only be a question of time as to when General Lee's lines at Petersburg will be broken, for Grant is wearing him out; with unlimited resources of men and money, he must ultimately force Lee to leave Virginia or surrender. Lee's army will never leave Virginia; they will not follow him out when the time comes, and that will end the war.' "[1]

After the Tennessee had been crossed on the 27th of December, Forrest, with the approval of General Hood, moved his command to the neighborhood of Corinth, at which point he was better able to secure forage for his horses and food for his men. Roddey's brigade alone was left to look after the crossings of the Tennessee between Decatur and Waterloo, and to protect that section from incursions by the

---

[1] Manuscript notes in possession of the author.

Federal cavalry. With the exception of Ross's brigade, which was composed of Texans, all of the remaining troops under Forrest were from Kentucky, Tennessee, Mississippi, and northern Alabama. Retaining the Texans to do scout, picket, and guard duty, the other brigades were given furlough for twenty days, in which time they were to return to their various homes, procure new clothing, and, if possible, horses, and gather up stragglers from the Confederate army. They were also to capture any outlying detachments of Federal troops, fire into the transports on the various streams, and in every way to annoy the enemy as much as possible.

General T. H. Bell and other officers accompanied their commands on furlough, and under their direction numerous minor expeditions and raids throughout the occupied territory were made, capturing supplies and horses and greatly disturbing the navigation on the Cumberland, Tennessee, and Mississippi rivers. Acting Rear Admiral Lee, in January of 1865, wrote to General Thomas: "I respectfully suggest that, if consistent with your plans and views, Forrest and his gang be entirely cleaned out of western Kentucky and Tennessee."

General Sherman, in a dispatch to Thomas at this time, says: "I suppose Forrest is again scattered to get horses and men and to divert attention. I would like to have Forrest hunted down and killed, but doubt if we can do that yet."

Meanwhile Ross's Texans were busily engaged on picket duty along the boundary line between northern Mississippi and west Tennessee. To such an extent were desertions from Hood's infantry prevailing that this general directed Forrest on the 14th of January to "keep picked bodies of cavalry near at hand, that they may be ready to pursue and capture any men that may desert from the army. If the first party of deserters can be caught and promptly punished, it will perhaps deter others from doing the same."

While Forrest was at Corinth, Roddey's brigade, which had been left in the Tennessee Valley, in northern Alabama, had signally failed in the duty to which it was assigned. By a movement of great boldness, Colonel Palmer of Wilson's command had crossed the Tennessee River with a picked detachment, surprised and beaten Roddey's cavalry, and captured and destroyed Hood's pontoon and wagon train. This disaster called forth a communication from General Beauregard to General Cooper at Richmond, dated January 22, 1865: "General Hood reports the loss of his pontoon-train, eight-three boats, one hundred and fifty wagons, and four hundred mules, due to inability of General Roddey to bring his troops from their homes. I wish to substitute another brigade in its place, and put all the cavalry of this department under one commanding officer, Forrest."

This recommendation was promptly approved by the Confederate authorities, and on the 24th of January, in the following model circular, Forrest assumed command of the department. No more comprehensive papers were drafted by any commander than the official communications dictated by this man, who said he never "saw a pen but what he thought of a snake."

HEADQUARTERS CAVALRY DEPARTMENT OF ALABAMA, ⎱
MISSISSIPPI, AND EAST LOUISIANA   ⎰
VERONA, Mississippi, *January* 28, 1865

In obedience to orders from department headquarters I hereby assume command of the District of Mississippi, east Louisiana, and west Tennessee. In doing so it is due both to myself and the troops thus placed under my command, to see that every effort will be made to render them thoroughly effective. To do this, strict obedience to all orders must be rigidly enforced by subordinate commanders, and prompt punishment inflicted for all violations of law and of orders. The rights and property of citizens must be respected and protected, and the illegal organizations of cavalry, prowling through the country, must be placed regularly and properly in the service or driven from the country. They are in many instances nothing more or less than roving bands of deserters, absentees, stragglers, horse-thieves, and robbers, who consume the substance and appropriate the property of citizens without remuneration, and whose acts of lawlessness and crime demand a remedy, which I shall not hesitate to apply, even to extermination. The maxim "that kindness to bad men is cruelty to the good" is peculiarly applicable to soldiers; for all agree, without obedience and strict discipline troops cannot be made effective, and kindness to a bad soldier does great injustice to those who are faithful and true; and it is but justice to those who discharge their duties with promptness and fidelity that others who are disobedient, turbulent, and mutinous, or who desert or straggle from their commands, should be promptly and effectively dealt with, as the law directs. I sincerely hope, therefore, while in the discharge of the arduous duties devolving upon me, and in all the efforts necessary to render the troops of this command available and effective to suppress lawlessness and defend the country, I shall have the hearty co-operation of all subordinate commanders and the unqualified support of every brave and faithful soldier.

N. B. FORREST

One of Forrest's first acts after being made commander in chief of the cavalry in this district was to reorganize his troops, placing all the Mississippians in Chalmers's division, the Alabamians and Kentuckians in a single brigade under Buford, the Tennessee troops under Brigadier General T. H. Bell, while Ross's Texans were placed under Brigadier General W. H. Jackson. Colonel Robert McCulloch, with his famous regiment, the Second Missouri, was made an independent command and moved directly with General Forrest.

During the months of January and February, 1865, nothing of importance occurred in Forrest's territory. With untiring zeal and energy he applied himself to refitting his command and to improving their discipline and effectiveness. On the 28th of February he received his commission as lieutenant general. On the following day, March 1st, he transferred his headquarters to West Point, Mississippi, near the Alabama line.

One of the most difficult problems with which he was confronted was the correction of certain grave abuses which had been encouraged by the issuance of orders from Richmond granting authority to various persons to raise troops within the territory occupied by the Union forces. Forrest was convinced that in many instances these commissions were being used simply to evade actual service in the army, and his views as to the manner in which these agents should be dealt with are given in the following letter:

HEADQUARTERS FORREST'S CAVALRY CORPS
WEST POINT, Mississippi, <i>March</i> 18, 1865</div>

Hon. John C. Breckinridge, Secretary of War, Richmond, Virginia:

GENERAL—I take the liberty of addressing you relative to the state of affairs in the district of southern Kentucky, and to bring to your notice and knowledge existing evils which can alone be corrected by yourself as the chief of the War Department. It is due to myself to state that I disclaim all desire or intention to dictate. So far from it, I hesitate even now to make known the facts or to suggest the remedies to be applied. No other motive than the good of the service prompts me to address you. A military district was formed in southern Kentucky, including a small portion of west Tennessee, and Brigadier-General A. R. Johnson assigned to the command of it. The object of creating this district was doubtless for the purpose of raising and organizing troops for our army. Its permanent occupation by any force raised within its limits was not expected or calculated upon. If it was, the sequel shows that both in raising troops or holding the territory the experiment is a complete failure. General Johnson, who was often reported to have from twelve to eighteen hundred men, was finally wounded and captured, and his men scattered to the four winds. Brigadier-General Lyon then succeeded him, and was driven across the Tennessee River into north Alabama, with only a handful of men. Nothing has been added to our army, for while the men flock to and remain with General Johnson or General Lyon as long as they can stay in Kentucky, as soon as the enemy presses and they turn southward the men scatter, and my opinion is that they can never be brought out or organized until we send our troops there in sufficient numbers to bring them out by force. So far from gaining any strength for the army, the Kentucky brigade now in my command has only about three hundred men in camp (Third, Seventh, and Eighth Kentucky regiments). They have deserted and attached themselves to the roving bands of guerillas, jayhawkers, and plunderers who are the natural offspring of authorities given to parties to raise troops within the enemy's lines. The authorities given to would-be colonels, and by them delegated to would-be captains and lieutenants, have created squads of men who are dodging from pillar to post, preying upon the people, robbing them of their horses and other property, to the manifest injury of the country and our cause.

The same state of affairs exists in west Tennessee and along the Mississippi River. The country is filled with deserters and stragglers, who run away and attach themselves to the commands of those who have the authorities referred to. They never organize, report to nobody, are responsible to no one, and exist by plunder and robbery. There may, perhaps, be a few exceptions, but, as a general thing, men who besiege the department for such authorities are officers without position or command, who by flattering representations, recommendations, and influential friends avoid the ranks by obtaining authority to raise troops within the enemy's lines. I venture the assertion that, where one succeeds and organizes a command, ninety-nine fail, and that they take twenty men out of the army to one placed in it. I therefore unhesitatingly recommend that all parties holding such authorities, or acting under orders from those who do hold them, be ordered to report with what men they have to the nearest department commander within a limited period, for consolidation and organization, and those failing so to report to have their authorities revoked and themselves subjected to conscription whenever caught. Do not understand me as reflecting on General Johnson or General Lyon. They did all they could, no doubt, to carry out the objects of the department in their district. They have failed, and the fact to my mind is demonstrated most clearly that the conscripts and deserters in west Tennessee and Kentucky will never come out until brought out by force. If all authorities to raise troops in the enemy's lines are revoked and the mustering officers ordered out, troops can be occasionally sent in under good and reliable officers to arrest and bring out deserters and break up the bands of lawless men who not only rob the citizens themselves, but whose presence in the country gives a pretext to Federal authority for oppressing the people.

I am, General, very respectfully, your obedient servant,

N. B. FORREST, Lieutenant-General[7]

During January and February Forrest's scouts had reported a concentration near Waterloo and Gravelly Springs on the Tennessee of a large cavalry command under General James H. Wilson. Other expeditions for the invasion of his territory were being organized in Memphis and in the neighborhood of Vicksburg and Baton Rouge on the Mississippi River. In addition a heavy concentration of Federal infantry was being made in the vicinity of Mobile, under General Canby, while still another army of invasion was forming in Pensacola. Fully 75,000 Union soldiers were by March 1st ready, as soon as the conditions of the weather and the streams were favorable, to march into his department. It was, however, the command of Wilson, on the Tennessee River, which gave him the greatest concern. He clearly foresaw that their object was the invasion of Alabama, and in all probability of the destruction of the large Confederate arsenals at Selma. It was for this reason, so convinced was he of the intention on the part of the Federal commander, that he moved his headquarters to West Point, near the Alabama line, and concentrated his troops in that region.

He also took the precaution, early in March, in order to prevent any possible error on the part of his subordinates in moving rapidly to the relief of Selma or Tuscaloosa when ordered, to have the roads leading thither newly signboarded. A general notice recites that "One road will have a sign-board 'Tuscaloosa'; the other a sign-board 'Pleasant Ridge, Clinton, Eutaw.' The road to Tuscaloosa, then, will have the mark X on the trees. The road to Finch's ferry will have the trees marked $\overline{X}$." He also directed at this early date that a pontoon bridge be placed over the Warrior River at Finch's ferry, and supplies accumulated so that five days' rations would always be on hand ready to be cooked as soon as the troops should receive orders to march.

Forrest's formidable adversary, General James H. Wilson, was no less busy than himself in increasing the efficiency of his cavalry command during the early months of 1865. With remarkable zeal he had completed by the middle of March the organization of the most magnificent body of mounted troops ever gathered under one commander on the western hemisphere. He had called to his assistance young men of experience who had already won reputation for courage, ability, and energy. An English military critic, Colonel Chesney, says of Wilson's staff that it was the best cavalry staff ever organized, and in every way worthy of imitation.[2]

By the first week of March, 27,000 cavalrymen, 17,000 of whom were mounted, were gathered in the camps between Gravelly Springs and Waterloo on the Tennessee River.[3]

Generals Thomas and Wilson had determined upon the invasion of Alabama with this large force for the purpose of destroying the valuable arsenals and government stores of the Confederacy at Selma. This accomplished, circumstances were to decide the further movements of the expedition. General Grant had advised Thomas, with some 5000 men, to make simply a demonstration on Tuscaloosa and Selma, but to this both Thomas and Wilson objected so strenuously that the order from headquarters was rescinded. They argued wisely that so small a force, so remote from its base of supplies, would place itself practically at the mercy of Forrest.

In the *Life of General George H. Thomas* there occurs the following:

It was known that the hitherto invincible Forrest had been put in command of all the cavalry in Alabama, Mississippi, and eastern Louisiana, and he, after the retreat from middle Tennessee, had taken post at Corinth, where he devoted himself to the concentration, discipline, and reorganization of his command. Forrest was an active and resourceful commander, who did not fail to patrol all the country of northern Alabama, Mississippi, and Tennessee beyond the lines of Federal occupation. He not only gathered in all absentees that he could find, but mercilessly conscripted all the able-bodied men that were fit for service, while his picked and trusty scouts, familiar with the country, were sent into the Federal lines to gather

---

[2] *Life of General George H. Thomas,* by Donn Piatt.

[3] Knipe's division of 5000 mounted men was sent by steamer to Canby, and Hatch's division (dismounted), about 7500 in number, was left in camp, making 14,500 ready for duty with Wilson.

all the information they could in reference to the strength and future movements of the Federal forces.

On the 22nd of March, General Wilson, with the first, second, and fourth divisions (14,000 effectives), consisting of 12,500 mounted and 1500 dismounted men—the latter being used to act as train escort until they could secure horses—started southward from Waterloo on the Tennessee River, their immediate destination being Selma. These troops were armed with the Spencer magazine repeating rifle, the most formidable weapon known to warfare at that time.

General Boynton says: "They were all veterans, in excellent discipline and condition, and full of enterprise and zeal. The division and brigade commanders were mostly young men, but they had been in the war from the beginning, had had plenty of experience, and knew both how to inspire and command the confidence necessary to success." He further says: "It may be doubted if a better cavalry command had ever been organized in any country in so short a time. Each trooper carried five days' light rations, one pair of extra horseshoes, and one hundred rounds of ammunition. Five days' rations of hard bread and ten of sugar and salt were taken on pack-animals. A light wagon-train carried forty-five days' rations of coffee, twenty of sugar, fifteen of salt, and eighty rounds of ammunition. The supply-train consisted of two hundred and fifty wagons, which were sent back to the Tennessee as fast as the contents of each was consumed. There was, besides, a canvas pontoon-train of thirty boats, hauled by six-mule teams."

Starting on diverging roads, the command moved southward in three columns, with directions to rendezvous at Jasper, the county seat of Walker County, Alabama, where they arrived without opposition, and proceeded thence to Elyton, in Jefferson County, arriving there on the 29th and 30th of March.

At Jasper, on the 27th, Wilson learned of the advance of a portion of Forrest's command, under Chalmers, which was reported to be coming toward Tuscaloosa by way of Bridgeville. Knowing so well with whom he had to deal in this crisis, he displayed a promptness and boldness which proves him to have been an able and resolute commander. He knew that he must move with lightninglike rapidity in order to beat his adversary. He therefore determined to strip himself for the race to Selma. He ordered his division commanders to replenish the haversacks, pack everything they must take with them on mules, leave the

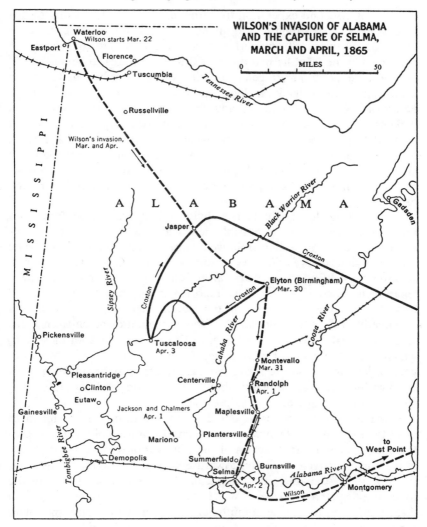

WILSON'S INVASION OF ALABAMA
AND THE CAPTURE OF SELMA,
MARCH AND APRIL, 1865

wagons, haul nothing but the artillery, and march with the greatest possible rapidity by way of Elyton to Montevallo.

Forrest had kept himself fully informed as to Wilson's movements. His position, however, was one of great perplexity, by reason of the advance of a second expedition from the direction of Pensacola toward Montgomery, compelling him to divide his command, which even when concentrated was still numerically much inferior to the army of Wilson.[q] On the 23rd he had directed Buford to hurry to Selma and to complete the pontoon bridge at that city. From there he was to detach a portion of his brigade to look out for the Federal invasion from Pensacola. Chalmers had already been thrown forward as far as Pickensville, in Alabama, and on the 25th, two days before Wilson reached Jasper, one of Forrest's brigades (Armstrong's) and Hudson's battery were ordered to move via Finch's ferry, where a pontoon had already been laid, toward Selma. They were ordered to take 80 rounds of small-arm and 250 rounds of artillery ammunition to the piece.

Starke's brigade of Chalmers's division was ordered to follow on the next day as rapidly as possible, and with the same amount of ammunition. Adams's brigade followed Starke's, and on the same date Jackson's division was directed to follow without delay. This order to Jackson says: "Report your arrival at Selma by telegraph to the lieutenant-general commanding. Also report by return courier the time you leave Pickensville. It is important that you move at once." Jackson was to move by way of Tuscaloosa, as is shown from a dispatch from Lieutenant General Taylor, at Meridian, to Forrest, on the 26th of March, which says: "In view of movements from Russellville and Moulton, your order for Jackson to move *via* Tuscaloosa is right. Jackson, with his own and Lyon's command, should meet, whip, and get rid of that column of the enemy as soon as possible."

Leaving as many troops as could be spared from the command to meet the expedition which was threatening from Memphis, and to protect the country in the direction of the Mississippi River toward Vicksburg, Forrest moved in person toward Selma, reaching the bridge over the Sipsey, in Alabama, on March 29th, from which point he sent the following dispatch to General W. H. Jackson: "The lieutenant-general directs that you leave one commissioned officer with twenty men here for the purpose of guarding the three crossings—this bridge, and Carter's and Colter's ferries, one above and one below. They will remain here until day after to-morrow morning, when they will bury the two men who have been shot here at the bridge to-day, then follow on and report to their commands at Marion, Alabama, or wherever they may be. Should the officer left behind catch other deserters, he will take them to the bridge and execute them."

When it became known that General Forrest was ordered by General Taylor to lead his troops to Selma, a number of men, fearing this movement would ultimately carry them into Johnston's army in North Caroline, left the command without permission and made for their homes within the enemy's lines. The commander was greatly exasperated at these desertions, and left guards at the various crossings of this stream, with stringent orders to arrest any soldiers moving through the country on detached duty without proper written authority.

At Sipsey bridge two men were brought in as deserters. They acknowledged that they had been in the service, and were then on their way to their homes in Kentucky. A drumhead court-martial was called and they were put on trial. They had no furloughs or passes or official papers showing to what command they belonged or why they were quitting the army. One of the prisoners claimed that he was over age, while the other asserted that he was too young to be liable to military duty. They were condemned and executed. The bodies were exposed by the side of the road in plain view of where the troops should pass, and upon a tree was nailed a placard in large letters:

SHOT FOR DESERTION

The execution of these men was extremely unfortunate. Their statements turned out to be true in every particular, but they were not credited by the court-martial which pronounced sentence. Forrest was entirely justified, not only by military law, but by the desperate dilemma in which he found himself placed, in having the sentence of the court executed. Moreover, he had been directed by General Hood, just before this officer was relieved from command, to make an example of the first deserters he should catch.

By the afternoon of March 30th General Wilson had concentrated his entire command in and near the village of Elyton, where the city of Birmingham now stands. He had quit his wagon train between the two forks of the Warrior River, in a wild and rugged region, where he felt it could be successfully defended by the dismounted veterans left there for that purpose. He was now in light weight and evidently full of confidence that even Forrest could not stand up before him. Nothing but overconfidence would have justified the detachment from his main column of Croxton, who with 1800 effective troops was sent on an extremely hazardous enterprise.

It was an error which might have annihilated Croxton and placed his own column in extreme jeopardy had proper advantage been taken of it. While he was a soldier of first-class ability, and his men were tried veterans, Jackson so outnumbered him that it would seem that nothing but great good luck and fast horses rescued Croxton from the critical position in which the orders of his commander had placed him. General Wilson was not aware that Forrest's command, advancing from the direction of West Point toward Tuscaloosa, was so near him at that time. Croxton's orders were to proceed to Tuscaloosa, capture that place, and destroy the bridge there, the factories, and other public property. This accomplished, he was to rejoin the main corps in the vicinity of Selma, traveling by the Centerville road. He was only cautioned to look out for Lyon, who with a small brigade was expected to be at Tuscaloosa on the 29th, marching toward Montevallo.

In explanation of this division of his force in the presence of the enemy, Wilson says: "In addition to covering our front and inflicting a heavy blow upon the enemy, I hoped by this detachment to develop any movement on his part intended to intercept my main column."

So near were the Confederates in force to Wilson that Croxton had not marched a day until he was practically surrounded by the Confederate cavalry, and, as far as General Wilson's expedition was concerned, this brigade disappeared from view at four o'clock on the afternoon of the 30th of March and was not again seen until it rejoined him at Macon, Georgia, in the latter part of May.

Moving as ordered, Croxton camped, on the night of the 30th, eight miles from Elyton. On the 31st of March, pushing onward in the direction of Tuscaloosa, at four o'clock in the afternoon he came into the road along which the rear of one of Forrest's columns (Jackson's division) had just passed in the direction of Plantersville. Here was a dilemma, or, as he termed it, "a state of case," which the orders to the wandering brigadier did not contemplate. In his perplexity Croxton took the bull by the horns and turned aside from the direct route to Tuscaloosa. He says that he determined to follow Forrest during the night, hoping to be near enough to co-operate with the main column in the fight which he felt sure would come off on the following day. At the same time he attempted to notify Wilson and McCook of his change of direction. That night Croxton again changed his mind and concluded to go on to Tuscaloosa, as he had been ordered. Posting two companies of the Sixth Kentucky as a rear vedette, he retraced his steps and pushed rapidly westward.

He had proceeded only a few miles when one of these rear companies, under Captain Parrish, was fiercely attacked, early on the morning of April 1st, and surrounded. Parrish was wounded and his command captured. Had Croxton at this moment known what an advantageous position he occupied he might have performed one of the most brilliant exploits of the war. By mere good luck he had come in between the rear of Jackson's division and his artillery and wagon train, which were struggling along some four miles distant, in the vain endeavor to keep in sight of the swift-moving horsemen. Jackson was for the time entirely ignorant of Croxton's presence, and had the Union commander moved rapidly westward he could have captured and destroyed every gun and wagon of this Confederate division. Instead of doing this he trailed along after the Confederate rear guard until Jackson had discovered his presence and turned upon him. Even then the road was wide open for Croxton to move to Tuscaloosa, but he did not take advantage of it. When Jackson retraced his steps to strike him, instead of marching rapidly on a direct route to this city he turned squarely to the west, and ran away with such celerity that he soon had Jackson many miles behind him. The Federal brigadier reached Johnson's Ferry on the Black Warrior River, some fifteen miles northward from Tuscaloosa, where on the 2nd of April he succeeded in getting across.

The ever-vigilant Jackson had meanwhile sent a courier to the commander of the small garrison of militia at Tuscaloosa to be on his guard and not let Croxton outwit him, and had then turned eastward toward Plantersville, in order to be ready to throw himself upon the flank and rear of Wilson, according to the strategy of Forrest, who had thus laid his plans for the destruction of Wilson's corps.

The presence of Croxton's small force in Jackson's rear was probably the salvation of Wilson, for it delayed Jackson's eastward march for several hours, enabling General Wilson to hurry McCook and La-Grange to destroy the Centerville bridge. Had Jackson pushed on regardless of Croxton, he could have secured this crossing, and with his superior force should have whipped McCook and then pounced upon the rear and flank of Long and Upton, as Forrest had planned. In all probability this would have held Wilson in check sufficiently to have allowed Chalmers time to reach Plantersville when Armstrong did. The fortunate capture of the dispatches of Major Anderson in all probability prevented a cavalry fight between Forrest and Wilson the like of which had not been seen on the American continent.

Moving with boldness and celerity early on the morning of April 3rd, Croxton, coming from a direction entirely unsuspected by the small garrison of home guards or militia which had been left in Tuscaloosa, reached the suburbs on the west side of the river, seized the bridge, captured the city without opposition, and promptly destroyed all government property there, together with the state university. He was now so completely isolated from Wilson that nothing was left to him but to wander as far out of harm's way as possible, until he could hear something definite from his commander. On April 6th he unexpectedly collided with the command of General Wirt Adams, was worsted in the encounter, but escaped with the loss of two officers, thirty-two men, and two ambulances.

Continuing on in his wanderings, on April 19th he arrived at Jasper, from which point he had started twenty days earlier. A waggish trooper suggested that General Croxton had been allotted one of the horses Wilson had impressed from a circus—it could not get out of the habit of moving in a circle. Here at Jasper for the first time he received information that Wilson's corps had captured Selma, and had gone to Montgomery and was marching east. He straightway headed for Georgia, and on the 20th of May rejoined his commander at Macon.

At the time that Croxton was detached, on the afternoon of the 30th of March, near Elyton, Upton's division had advanced rapidly, driving in the Confederate pickets to Montevallo, arriving there about dark on the 30th. He was followed by the division of General Long and La-Grange's brigade of McCook's division. General Wilson reached Montevallo at one o'clock on March 31st. On this afternoon a sharp engagement took place between the Federals and a small force of Confederates—three hundred Kentuckians of Crossland's brigade, Roddey's division, and a detachment of militia under General Dan Adams. The Confederates were forced back to a creek some five miles south of

Montevallo, where they again made a stand, and after a sharp, short fight at close quarters they were finally driven from their position by the enemy in superior force.

Upton's division encamped for the night fourteen miles southward from Montevallo, and at daylight of April 1st, himself in the lead, the entire cavalry corps of General Wilson, with the exception of Croxton's brigade, moved forward to Randolph. This done, General Upton, with his division, was directed to take the road leading somewhat to the east by way of Maplesville, and thence by the old Selma road south, while Long was instructed to push forward on the new road. General Wilson was playing in great good luck at this crisis of his campaign. To Croxton's bold dash at Tuscaloosa and his fortunate escape, and McCook's safe return from his isolated position at the Centerville bridge a few days later, there was added at Randolph, on the morning of April 1st, another stroke of fortune.

On this morning a detachment of Upton's division captured a Confederate courier with dispatches which led to the complete undoing of Forrest. As Lee's dispatch in the Maryland campaign, found in the roadway by McClellan, told of the Confederate general's movements and intentions, so these communications placed in the hands of Wilson the fullest information of the exact position of Forrest's various detachments at that hour. McClellan failed to take advantage of his great find, but with Wilson it was otherwise.

The Confederate commander had not failed to appreciate the necessity of a rapid concentration of his command, in order to throw his troops in full force between the Union column and Selma. He had taken every precaution which was necessary, and his plan of attack upon Wilson at this time was one of his most brilliant conceptions. It failed only because of the capture of these dispatches. At 2 P.M. on the 31st of March, while on the Montevallo road, nine miles from Centerville, he sent Lieutenant Glass of the First Mississippi Cavalry to General Jackson, directing this officer to repair straightway to the plantation of Mr. James A. Hill, "where General Jackson will find orders for his movement. Should Brigadier-Generals Bell or Campbell be in the advance of General Jackson, they will turn back as above directed." At six o'clock on the night of the 31st the following later order was dispatched by courier to Jackson:

Six Miles from Montevallo, *March* 31, 1865, 6 p.m.
Brigadier-General W. H. Jackson, Cavalry Division:

General—Since the dispatch of 2 p.m. of this date, per Lieutenant Glass, the lieutenant-general commanding directs me to say that the enemy are moving right on down the railroad with their wagon-train and artillery. He directs that you follow down after them, taking the road behind them from Montevallo. He further directs me to say that he does not wish you to bring on a general engagement, as he thinks their force is much stronger than yours; and an engagement should be avoided unless you find the balance of our forces in supporting distance of you.

The courier carrying this dispatch to Jackson was captured early on April 1st near Randolph, by Upton's division, and upon his person were also found the two following dispatches:

Centerville, *April* 1, 1865, 2 a.m.

General—I opened the enclosed despatch from General Jackson, to ascertain his position, etc. Sent couriers last night at 11.30 to Chalmers and Mason. From reports received, and from this despatch, enemy's cavalry, or a portion of it, have crossed the Cahaba, and General Jackson will attack them at daylight. I shall remain here for further orders and developments, and at daylight will take one side of the river or the other. Have sent to General Jackson to know the position of his artillery. If the couriers can be relied on, the enemy is between him and the battery. Have the dismounted men intrenched on this side (east) of the river, and, if the enemy are as represented, will move the battery here, cross it over, and move on the nearest road to Selma, as directed. The courier can explain General Jackson's position and that of the battery. From his statement the battery is in rear of General Jackson, on Tuscaloosa road, and the enemy between his force and his artillery. Have heard nothing of General Armstrong, but sent orders to General Chalmers to move to or between enemy and Selma. Will despatch you all information as soon as received.

Respectfully,   Charles W. Anderson, Aide-de-Camp

[Subenclosure]

March 31, 1865, 8:45 p.m.
James Hill, Sr.:

Major—I find the enemy encamped on Huntsville and Tuscaloosa road at White's, three miles from point where Huntsville road comes into Tuscaloosa road and six miles from this place. Their strength not yet ascertained. I am closing around them with the view of attacking, or, if they move to-night, will drive into them. I am placing a force between them and Tuscaloosa. Have also directed Colonel Cox, who is in charge of artillery and train, some fifteen miles from here, that in case I do not gain their front and they advance on Tuscaloosa, to fall back before them, impeding their progress; to notify Colonel Hardcastle, commanding post, to have everything in readiness to meet them; and to tear up planks on the bridge and remove them, nothing preventing. All appears bright, and I expect success.   Respectfully,

W. H. JACKSON, Brigadier-General

From these dispatches Wilson learned that Forrest, with a small portion of his command, was immediately in his front; that Jackson, with his strong division and all the wagons and artillery *en route* from Tuscaloosa toward Centerville, was encamped the night before at Hill's plantation, three miles from Scottsville. Forrest had ordered, and naturally expected, that Jackson would fall in behind Wilson, and when he and Chalmers from the front should attack and check him this division from the rear would join in the fray and destroy the Union forces. Wilson now knew from this intercepted courier that this part of the plan must fail. In addition to this he was informed that Chalmers, with the other division of Forrest's corps, had arrived at Marion, Alabama, and had been ordered to cross the Cahaba and hasten to join Forrest north of Selma. These dispatches also contained information that a small force of dismounted Confederates had been stationed at Centerville, with orders to hold the bridge over the Cahaba at that place at all hazards, and in no event to let it fall into the hands of the Federals.

With this invaluable information in hand, Wilson proceeded to make his dispositions to insure the discomfiture of his adversary. Jackson must be cut off from all hope of closing down upon his rear. To this end, McCook, with LaGrange's entire brigade, was ordered to move rapidly to Centerville, attack the small force left there by Forrest, overwhelm them, seize the bridge, leave a garrison to command it, cross the Cahaba, and develop Jackson's force. If he should be so fortunate as to be able to communicate with Croxton, they were to unite, attack Jackson, beat him if they could, and then rejoin the corps by the Centerville road to Selma.

McCook was successful in capturing the Centerville bridge, but failed to find Croxton. He found Jackson, however, and decided not to risk an engagement with this commander, but retreated across the Cahaba and burned the bridge, leaving Jackson upon the west shore of this stream, and preventing him from joining with Forrest in the fighting which occurred in the next forty-eight hours. General Wilson says in his official report: "Having thus taken care of the right flank, and anticipating Forrest in his intention to play his old game of getting upon the rear of his opponent, I gave directions to Long and Upton to allow him no rest and push him towards Selma with the utmost spirit and rapidity."

On March 31st, at 6 P.M., having sent the dispatches just detailed to Jackson, Forrest also sent a courier to Chalmers, urging him to push forward across the Cahaba with all possible celerity to Ebenezer Church and place his men in position, where he would join him in front of the advancing Federal column. Nothing more brilliant could have been conceived than the plan mapped out by Forrest in this crisis for the destruction of Wilson. He at the head of Crossland's brigade, Roddey's division, a detail of two hundred men from Armstrong's brigade, and the state troops under Dan Adams in front of Wilson's advance would offer resistance at every available position from Randolph on toward Selma. Jackson, unknown to Wilson, was to follow with his strong division immediately in the rear of the Federal column. Chalmers was coming, with plenty of time at his disposal, to join his division to the troops that Forrest had immediately under him at that date, and thus reinforced he would be able to check the Federal advance. While thus engaged, Jackson would attack from the rear and flank as Forrest and Chalmers would assail from the front. Had this plan come to its fulfillment, one of the greatest cavalry battles of the war would have been fought upon this ground.

On the afternoon of March 31st, while Crossland, Dan Adams, and Roddey were being driven southward before the division of Upton, Forrest had arrived on the ground and was moving from Centerville toward Montevallo with his staff, the escort company of seventy-five men, and two hundred of Armstrong's command. The route along which they were traveling came into the road over which the Confederates had just retreated and along which the pursuing Federals were then moving. Having approached to within less than one hundred yards of the Federals, who were in considerable disorder, having lost their formation in the pursuit of the flying Confederates, and seeing that his presence had not been observed, Forrest, boldly at the head of his staff and escort, ordered his men to draw their six-shooters, and in columns of fours they charged directly into the road, riding along with the Federal cavalry.

This sudden and unexpected attack, its boldness, together with the severe work of the repeating pistols in the hands of these picked men, threw the Federal cavalry at this point into great confusion and drove them in a stampede from the scene.[4] Having captured a number of prisoners, General Forrest learned that Wilson's command had passed down the road and was between him and Selma. With this information he left the main road, and after a swift detour of eight or nine miles passed around the Federal column, and reached his command about ten o'clock that night in the vicinity of Randolph and in the path of the enemy.

As the divisions of Upton and Long advanced toward Selma early on the morning of April 1st, they encountered small detachments of the Confederates and drove them back with slight effort until they reached a point several miles north of Plantersville known as Ebenezer Church. Here Forrest was greatly chagrined to receive a message from Chalmers informing him that he had met with such obstacles in his route that he could not reach Plantersville in time to unite with him on that day. Forrest was furious with rage upon receipt of this dispatch. He sent an urgent dispatch to his lieutenant that Wilson was pressing down upon him with great vigor and overwhelming force, and that he would admit of no excuse in not uniting with him at Plantersville, or between that place and Selma, before he should be driven into the works of that city. Forrest insisted that General Chalmers had not moved his division with the alacrity and swiftness which the emergency demanded, and which had characterized him on other occasions. He, with Starke's brigade, was marching eastward by one route, while Armstrong, who commanded the other brigade of his division, was some five miles farther northward, traveling by a parallel road.

A messenger from Forrest to Chalmers passed through Armstrong's command, and this officer read the dispatch and forwarded it immedi-

---

[4] Manuscript notes of Captain J. N. Taylor of Forrest's escort, in possession of the author.

ately to General Chalmers. He informed Chalmers that under the circumstances he would not wait to receive orders from his immediate superior, but would march to Forrest on his own responsibility, and urged his division commander also to press on toward Plantersville to the rescue of their chief. He added that he could then hear firing in that direction, and would march rapidly toward it. Armstrong, who had the soldierly habit of always arriving in time, swept forward with great rapidity and reached Forrest just at dark on the night of the 1st of April.

Realizing the desperate situation of his command at this juncture, and the necessity for holding the advance of the Federals in check until Chalmers could reach Plantersville and be in supporting distance, Forrest had selected a naturally strong position at the crossing of Bogler's Creek, had thrown up layouts of rails and logs, and had placed the small force and the artillery at his command in the best possible position for defense. Here Roddey's division, Crossland's brigade, and several hundred militia under General Dan Adams were thrown into line of battle. Forrest, with his escort and the two hundred men of Armstrong's brigade, took position immediately with the artillery commanding the road approaching from the north. To his left Crossland's three hundred Kentuckians were posted, while on the extreme right a detachment of state troops under Adams was placed. The entire Confederate force on the field did not number 2000 men.

To assail this force General Wilson had on the ground and in action Upton's division, 3900 strong, Long's division of 5127, and two full batteries of artillery. It is claimed in the reports, as well as in the *Life of General George H. Thomas,* that Forrest had a much larger force than this present; but after a most careful inquiry I am convinced that he did not have a larger number on the field than above given. The Federal commander claimed that Armstrong, with his brigade, took part in this engagement, but General Armstrong informed the writer personally that he did not effect a junction with Forrest until the latter arrived that night at Plantersville. He says that General Wilson got the idea that he was present from the fact that there was with Forrest in the engagement at Bogler's Creek a detail of two hundred men from his brigade. This detail was made from the various regiments of his command on account of their having the most serviceable horses, and it accompanied Forrest as a reinforcement to his escort.

At four o'clock in the afternoon the Federals appeared, with Long's division in front. As soon as the skirmishers opened fire Long reinforced his advance guard, which was composed of a battalion of the Seventy-second Indiana, by the remainder of that regiment, which was dismounted and formed on the left of the road going south. Pushing these forward, Wilson and Long ordered a rash saber charge by four companies of the Seventeenth Indiana. As soon as Forrest saw these gallant troopers riding down upon him with sabers in air he placed himself in line with his escort and Crossland's Kentuckians. He ordered his men to reserve the fire of their rifles until the enemy had arrived within one hundred yards of their position. They were then to draw their revolvers and with one in each hand to ride in among and along with their assailants and use their weapons at close quarters.

As the Federals came near, the horse of one of the front platoon became unmanageable, ran away ahead of his line, bolted through the Confederates, and struck the wheel of one of the guns with such velocity that it knocked the wheel from the spindle, dismounted the gun, killed the horse, and threw his rider to the ground, where he was immediately killed by being knocked in the head with a gun stick by one of the artillerists. As the main body of the charging column swept into the Confederate line, Forrest and his escort, and two companies of Crossland's Kentuckians, under Captain H. A. Tyler, rode in among them, and the desperate character of the encounter which occurred may well be imagined. It was one of the most terrific hand-to-hand conflicts which occurred between cavalry soldiers during the war. It was a test between the saber in the hands of as brave a lot of men as ever rode horses and the six-shooter in the hands of experts that were just as desperately brave.

Forrest was most viciously assailed. His conspicuous presence made him the object of direct attack by a brave young officer, Captain Taylor of the Seventeenth Indiana, who with five or six others of the Union troopers were killed in this attempt to slay the Confederate general. In this fierce onslaught the Federals lost twelve killed and forty wounded.[5] On the Confederate side, General Forrest and Captain Boone, commanding the escort, and about a dozen of the

---

[5] *Official Records,* vol. xlix, part i, p. 406.

troopers were wounded, but none fatally.

From two officers of the escort who took part in this thrilling encounter and witnessed Forrest's struggle with Captain Taylor and his men, the following description is taken:

Lieutenant George L. Cowan says:

As the Federals dashed forward in their charge upon our line, they evidently recognized General Forrest's headquarters flag, near which he himself was, with his escort gathered about him. He told us to draw our six-shooters and stand our ground, no matter how many rode into us. As they came on, we fired with our rifles one volley, and then drew both of our pistols and rode forward to meet them. . . . Fortunately for the escort the Federals were using the sabre while we had our six-shooters, and this accounts for the difference in the losses on both sides. I saw General Forrest surrounded by six Federals at one time, and they were all slashing at him. One of them struck one of his pistols and knocked it from his hand. Private Phil Dodd was fortunately near and spurred his horse to the general's rescue, and shot the Federal soldier who was so close upon him, thus enabling General Forrest to draw his other pistol, with which he killed another of the group, who was still persistent in his attack upon our commander. General Forrest and Captain Boone, of the escort, were both wounded. Although the Federals rode through and over us, those that survived were beaten back, and we did not leave the field until we saw their main column advancing later.[6]

Captain J. N. Taylor says:

Early on April 1st the fighting began, and we were at it practically the entire day. The odds were heavily against us, but Forrest told us we must hold them back until he could concentrate the troops near Selma. He was at the front all the time. On one occasion, in a particularly important moment of the day, the general called for some volunteers to make a desperate charge, offering to lead them himself. Sergeant Parks said: "General, if you are going into this charge the escort will leave, but if you will stay where you are we will do whatever you tell us." The general said, "All right, boys," and we accomplished the task set out for us. While we were doing this a new position was selected just at Bogler's Creek. We had scarcely reached this line of battle when a cloud of dust was seen up the road, and a heavy column of Federals at full gallop with drawn sabres glistening in the sunlight came towards us. Captain Boone was in command of the escort, and in obedience to orders we rode forward along the

[6] Manuscript notes of Lieutenant G. L. Cowan, in possession of the author.

side of the road to meet them and joined in a gallop alongside of them. The conflict was now terrible. Every one of us, the general, staff, and escort, were surrounded by the Federals, and it seemed as if it was a fight every man for himself.[7]

Just as this fight was commencing, Upton's division, with Alexander's brigade in the lead, advanced upon the flank and practically in the rear of the Confederates. Striking the militia, these, without offering any resistance, ran from the field in great disorder, compelling the entire Confederate line to retreat precipitately, losing three guns and two hundred prisoners. A desperate running fight was continued to Plantersville, nineteen miles from Selma. After crossing Bogler's Creek, Lieutenant Cowan of the escort was placed in command of the rear guard and was desperately engaged in a running fight until near sundown. Forrest was sorely pressed, but Cowan and the escort and the rear guard gathered about him and thus kept off the pursuers until he was safe.

The rear guard of the Confederates camped at Plantersville on the night of the 1st of April, while the Federal advance under Winslow bivouacked in front of that place, nineteen miles from Selma. The fighting throughout the day had been almost constant. The Confederates had been driven twenty-four miles since morning.

At daylight on the 2nd the Federals advanced toward Selma, Long's division in front, closely followed by Upton. General Long was directed as he approached the city to cross to the Summerfield road without exposing his men, and to develop his line as soon as he should arrive in front of the works. General Upton was directed to move on the Range Line road, sending a portion of his troops across to the Burnsville road.

Lieutenant Rendlebrock, with a battalion of the Fourth United States Cavalry, was instructed to continue parallel with the railroad, and to destroy the stations, bridges, and trestlework as far as Burnsville. Without material opposition the Union forces were in sight of Selma and in line of battle about four o'clock in the afternoon.

Forrest had arrived in Selma early on the morning of April 2nd. He immediately reported to General Taylor, who was the departmental commander over him, and received his final instructions from

[7] Manuscript notes of Captain J. N. Taylor, in possession of the author.

this officer, who, as the place was being invested later on in the afternoon, escaped by train toward Demopolis.

Of Forrest, in this crisis, General Richard Taylor says: "Forrest fought as if the world depended on his arm. He appeared, horse and rider covered with blood, and announced the enemy at his heels, and that I must move at once to escape capture. I felt anxious for him, but he said he was unhurt and would cut his way through, as most of his men had done, whom he had ordered to meet him west of the Cahaba. My engine started toward Meridian and barely escaped."[8]

Being thus placed in command of all the forces in Selma, Forrest bent his energies to make the best possible defense of that place. It was fortified with a single line of works, which surrounded the town in horseshoe shape and terminated upon the bank of the Alabama River above and below the city. Within this outer crescent there was a second line, as yet unfinished and untenable. The most intense excitement prevailed among all classes. Everyone who could escape had fled to the country, and although Forrest in such emergencies was merciless in forcing all able-bodied male citizens into the ranks, he found he could not muster men enough to man the works.

It is said of him that early on the morning of the 2nd he had issued an order that every male citizen, no matter what his calling or position, "must go into the works or into the river." It was no time for men to hold back, as the cause needed every musket that could be made available. Relying chiefly upon Armstrong's brigade, which numbered 1432[9] men, he stationed these to hold the left of the Confederate position. So long was the line which they had to cover that there was an interval of from six to ten feet between the men as they stood behind the works. Roddey's men were placed on the extreme Confederate right, while the militia filled in the center between these two commands. Rearward of the militia Forrest was stationed with his escort and the Kentuckians.

Upon approaching Selma on the afternoon of the 2nd of April, General Wilson, with his division commanders, made a careful reconnaissance of the breastworks, and was pleased to discover that the sketch of the fortifications which an English engineer who had been

[8] *Destruction and Reconstruction,* by Lieutenant General Richard Taylor.
[9] War Office Records.

employed in the construction of these defenses had given him was suprisingly accurate. In order to be safe from any advance of Jackson or Chalmers upon his right and rear, Long posted one regiment in this direction to protect the led horses and the pack train, and formed the rest of his division, about 4500 strong, across the Summerfield road. His line of battle was entirely concealed from the Confederates by a low intervening ridge. His front line contained 1500 men, and the remainder of his troops followed in close column and in supporting distance. Upton's division was also carried rapidly into position, all dismounted except Alexander's brigade.

As Long was advancing to the attack, he was informed that the regiment left in the rear had been assailed by the advance of Chalmers's division. Appreciating that if he halted with his portion of the line at this juncture the assault might fail, with utter disregard of the prearranged plan and with great boldness, Long in person led a desperate charge of his gallant troops upon that portion of the Confederate works defended by Armstrong. With well-attested courage and stubbornness Armstrong stood his ground, for the brunt of the Federal attack fell upon his position.

General Boynton says: "In less time than it takes to tell it, over three hundred of Long's men were killed and wounded. Long himself was stricken down, together with two of his three brigade commanders and four colonels."[10] At the same time Upton moved forward with his division, and struck that part of the Confederate line which was guarded by the militia. These troops again fled the field, leaving a gap through which the Union soldiers swarmed. Forrest, seeing these men give way, rushed into the break in his line and endeavored to stem the tide of disaster until Roddey could be moved over to unite with Armstrong. In overwhelming and irresistible force the Federals swept him back, however, before the new alignment could be made, forcing Armstrong and Roddey to withdraw their troops, with considerable loss, to a second or interior line. Here again further resistance was made, until Wilson's force had not only vigorously assailed their second position from the front, but had overlapped them on the flank and was well in their rear.

Seeing further resistance now hopeless, Forrest ordered the dismounted men to secure their horses and escape as best they could.

[10] *Life of General George H. Thomas.*

Armstrong, still holding his men together, and conspicuous for his personal daring and cool head, covered the stampede into and through the city, and was by all odds the hero of the day. Forrest, with his escort and a considerable number of men from various detachments who rallied about him, escaped on the road toward Burnsville; not, however, without collision with the enemy, as he was moving northward now upon the road upon which Wilson's troops had advanced. He was again compelled to fight his way through, and it was here his last personal encounter of the war took place, in which he slew a Federal cavalryman who with rashness had endeavored to cut him down.

This was the thirtieth enemy that the personal prowess of General Forrest had placed *hors de combat* in hand-to-hand encounter since his first engagement at Sacramento in 1861. He closed his fighting career at Selma, having had twenty-nine horses shot from under him during the war.[r]

Armstrong, also hurrying out of Selma with his sturdy fighters around him, found the Federals formed across his path. Without hesitation he placed himself at the head of his men and cut his way through with little loss. A considerable number of the Confederates, being unable to escape, concealed themselves in the houses of citizens, a good many of them remaining hid away until the Federals left Selma, when they came out of their hiding places and escaped.

It was now pitch dark, and as Forrest and his escort were marching along their attention was attracted by the screams of women coming from the direction of a residence a short distance from the highway. He ordered a detachment to proceed at a gallop and to investigate the cause of the disturbance. As the Confederates surrounded the house, then in possession of the pillagers, several men wearing the Federal uniform ran out and endeavored to escape, but were all killed or captured.[11]

General Wilson had not been unmindful of his obligations as a commander to protect the lives and property of the citizens of the section through which his troops were marching. He had issued orders intended to prevent this disgraceful practice, but without the desired result, as the following "Special Field Order" will show:

[11] Manuscripts of Lieutenant George L. Cowan, in possession of the author.

[Special Field Orders, No. 20]

HEADQUARTERS CAVALRY CORPS
MILITARY DIVISION OF THE MISSISSIPPI
Colonel Harrison's House, *April* 11, 1865

The attention of division commanders is called to orders heretofore published in regard to pillaging. The evil has increased to such an extent as to call for the most prompt and decided measures, and all officers and men are enjoined to aid in suppressing a practice dishonorable and unbecoming a Christian soldiery. Hereafter no enlisted man, servant, or employé belonging to the cavalry corps will be allowed to enter a house under any pretence whatever, except under the direction of a commissioned officer, and then only for the purpose of obtaining provisions or information. Any violation of this order may be punished by death, or any other punishment that division commanders may direct. Commanding officers are ordered to use every possible effort to arrest pillagers and robbers, and provost marshals will punish with the utmost severity. It is not the intention of this order to prevent the troops from taking provisions or forage. Every pound of provisions or forage will be taken from the inhabitants of the country passed over by the troops before a single man or animal of the command shall suffer; but all such supplies must be taken in a proper manner. This order to be read to every regiment of the command every day until it is thoroughly understood.

By command of Brevet Major-General WILSON:

E. B. BEAUMONT,
Major and Assistant Adjutant-General

As the advance guard of the escort moved along the narrow road in the darkness they came unexpectedly upon a Federal outpost near the residence of Mr. M. Godwin, and the pickets, supposing the troops approaching from the direction of Selma belonged to Wilson's command, did not realize that Forrest's men were upon them until the latter had made them prisoners. Lieutenant George L. Cowan, at this time in command of Forrest's escort, having learned from the captured troopers that they belonged to a scouting detachment from the Fourth United States Regulars, which was then encamped upon the premises of Mr. Godwin, determined to attempt their capture. As General Forrest started forward with the detail who were to make the attack, Lieutenant Cowan, Acting Lieutenant John Eaton, and the private soldiers as well protested against this unnecessary exposure on the part of the general, and persuaded him to remain with the horse-holders.

As they approached the premises cautiously, a number of the Federals were seen about their campfires in the horse lot, a short distance from the dwelling house. Lieutenant Cowan dispatched several of his men to surround the residence, while a second detachment was sent on a detour to approach the horse lot from a different direction from the main body of the Confederates, which, having waited until the details had time to reach the positions designated, now advanced with a rush upon the regulars. They did not, however, reach the fence around the enclosure before the Federals, by this time aroused, fired a volley at their assailants. Lieutenant Cowan was wounded by this fire. In the brief and sanguinary encounter which ensued, this squad of hard-fighting cavalrymen sustained their well-earned reputation for desperate courage by resisting to the last the onslaught of Forrest's men.

Finally, those who survived, realizing that they were about to be surrounded, as the second detachment of Confederates now opened upon them from another direction, leaped over the fence and made their escape. Two of those who escaped were captured on the following morning by the Confederates several miles from the scene of the encounter. Mr. M. Godwin, who was at the time of this attack at the house of a friend, says: "I went home with Dr. Mixson, and about daylight two Union soldiers came from my house bareheaded and with no shoes on. They took Dr. Mixson's shoes from him and started away, when two Confederate soldiers came along and captured them."[12]

When the firing began at the horse lot two officers and an orderly, who had ensconced themselves in Mr. Godwin's residence, ran out in the hope of escaping, but in the attempt were shot. One of the officers was instantly killed; the other was mortally wounded, and died on the following day.

In the Federal official reports of this campaign it is stated that "Forrest, retreating from Selma, came across a party of Federals asleep in a neighboring field, and charged on them, and, refusing to listen to their cries for surrender, killed or wounded the entire party, numbering twenty-five men."[13]

[12] Sworn statement of Mr. M. Godwin, in possession of the author.
[13] *Official Records,* vol. xlix, part i, p. 406.

In the *Life of General George H. Thomas*,[14] in referring to this incident, this statement occurs: "Forrest fell upon the party with the ferocity of a wild Indian, and killed every man of it."

Such exaggerated and false statements are in line with the equally unjust and untruthful charges of inhuman and unsoldierly conduct made against General Forrest at Fort Pillow. He took no part whatever in this attack, but remained with the horse-holders, who were four hundred yards from the scene. The firing had ceased before he came upon the premises.

It is the testimony of the Confederate officers who took part in this affair that the Union troops resisted to the last, and it is well known that the Fourth Regulars were among the most desperate fighters in the National army.

Lieutenant George L. Cowan, residing (in 1898) in Franklin, Tennessee, in response to a letter from the author, states: "In this attack the Federals fired the first shot, the scar from which I bear to this day. They made a strong fight, and at one time drove us back, when a timely charge in their rear by a small squad detached from our right saved us the victory. Not a single man was killed after he surrendered, and any statements to this effect are wholly untrue."

Early on the morning of April 3rd Forrest and his escort arrived at Plantersville, where he captured the Federal hospital and a considerable number of wounded in charge of Dr. McGraw of General Wilson's staff. The consideration invariably shown by the Confederate leader for the Union troops, wounded or unwounded, who fell into his hands was shown here, and is attested by General Wilson in an order dated April 8, 1865: "Out of the stock . . . select twenty-five horses to be turned over to the Confederate surgeons to replace those taken from them. General Forrest allowed our surgeons to retain their horses, and this is a reciprocal act of courtesy."[15]

From Plantersville Forrest proceeded to Marion, Alabama, where he arrived on the morning of the 4th and found here Jackson's division, Starke's brigade of Chalmers's division, and the entire train and artillery.

Meanwhile General Wilson had turned eastward toward Montgomery, which without resistance fell into his hands. From thence he proceeded by rapid marches to Columbus, West Point, and finally to Ma-

---

[14] By Donn Piatt and H. V. Boynton, p. 614.
[15] *Official Records,* vol. xlix, part ii, p. 272.

con, Georgia, where he arrived in May, to find that the armies of Lee and Johnston had surrendered and that the war was over. On the 13th of April he had notified General Thomas from Montgomery that there was no force to resist him, and that supplies were sufficiently abundant to subsist his command. He was under the impression that Forrest would follow him.

This the Confederate commander did not do. He realized that it would be a needless sacrifice of his men to pursue and harass the rear of Wilson's column with nothing to be gained. Moreover, his duties were confined to the department over which he was in command, and when Wilson left the State of Alabama he entered another of the Confederate departments. Forrest, after his defeat at Selma, had determined to concentrate his scattered forces in the vicinity of Marion, where he remained for about ten days, and on the 15th of April he established his headquarters at Gainesville, in that state.

General Lee had surrendered the Army of Northern Virginia at Appomattox on the 9th of April, and rumors of this great disaster had already reached the ears of the troops in Forrest's department, causing consternation and great depression among the men, who, however, still remained loyal to their colors. As late as the 25th of April, Forrest issued an address to his soldiers, in which he stated that he did not believe General Lee had surrendered and urged them to remain true to the cause they had espoused. He says:

It is the duty of every man to stand firm at his post and true to his colors. Your past services, your gallant and heroic conduct on many victorious fields, forbid the thought that you will ever ground your arms except with honor. Duty to your country, to yourselves, and the gallant dead who have fallen in this great struggle for liberty and independence demand that every man should continue to do his whole duty. With undiminished confidence in your courage and fortitude, and knowing you will not disregard the claims of honor, patriotism, and manhood, and those of the women and children of the country, so long defended by your strong arms and willing hearts, your commander announces his determination to stand by you, stay with you, and lead you to the end. A few more days will determine the truth or falsity of all the reports now in circulation. In the meantime let those who are now absent from their commands, for the purpose of mounting themselves or otherwise, return without delay. Be firm and unwavering, discharge promptly and faithfully every duty devolving upon you. Preserve untarnished the reputation you have so nobly won, and leave results to Him who in wisdom controls and governs all things.

Five days later he was notified by General Richard Taylor that he had entered into an agreement with General Canby of the United States Army for the cessation of hostilities, and on the 6th of May an official circular was issued to the troops announcing the surrender of Lee's army on the 9th of April and, later, that of General Johnston.

About this time it was reported to General Thomas that Forrest did not intend to surrender, no matter what other commanders might do; that he would lead his command across the Mississippi to Texas and Mexico, marching by way of Memphis, which city he proposed to capture. Thomas attached such credence to this rumor that on the 2nd of May he telegraphed to General Hatch, at Eastport, Mississippi, as follows: "Send under a flag of truce a summons to Forrest to surrender upon the terms given by General Grant to Generals Lee and Johnston. Inform him of the rumors which have reached you, and that you are prepared for him, and if he attempts such a reckless and bloodthirsty adventure he will be treated thereafter as an outlaw, and the States of Mississippi and Alabama will be so destroyed that they will not recover for fifty years."

Thomas evidently did not understand the character of Forrest, who had no intention of sacrificing the life of a single man after he had been ordered by his superior officer to disband his troops. It was his purpose to be as earnest and faithful in the effort to restore kindly feeling between the divided sections, and to reconcile his soldiers and friends among the noncombatants of the South to the failure of the struggle to establish an independent confederation of the slaveholding states, as he had been indefatigable and loyal to the cause now lost forever.

It required all of Forrest's tact and influence with his troops to persuade them to the submission which he accepted. It is narrated in the *History of the Seventh Tennessee Cavalry*,[16] one of the commands disbanded at Gainesville, that when the determination of the commander was made known to the men they were overwhelmed with amazement and grief. They gathered in groups to talk over the situation, while some of them wept like children. Many said they would never surrender as long as they had their guns and horses; they proposed to General Forrest to lead them to the Trans-Mississippi and

[16] By J. P. Young.

to continue the struggle for independence; "but General Forrest said no, what could not be accomplished here could never be done in the thinly settled West."

They finally realized, under the calm and convincing reasoning of their leader, the hopelessness of the fight, and with grim determination turned their faces homeward to meet an uncertain future. "The old bullet-torn flag, whose blue cross had been triumphantly borne aloft for years at the cost of so much blood and valor, they would never part with. On the eve of surrender, as the shadows of night fell, the men reverently gathered around the staff in front of regimental headquarters, and, cutting the silk into fragments, each soldier carried away with him a bit of the coveted treasure. The flag had been the gift of a young lady of Aberdeen, Mississippi, made from her bridal-dress, and had never for an instant been abandoned by the men of the Seventh Tennessee Cavalry after it was committed to their guardianship."

On the 9th of May, 1865, General Forrest took his farewell of these gallant men, in an address probably not excelled in the literature of the Civil War.

[Circular]

HEADQUARTERS FORREST'S CAVALRY CORPS
GAINESVILLE, Alabama, *May* 9, 1865

SOLDIERS—By an agreement made between Lieutenant-General Taylor, commanding the Department of Alabama, Mississippi, and East Louisiana, and Major-General Canby, commanding United States forces, the troops of this department have been surrendered. I do not think it proper or necessary at this time to refer to causes which have reduced us to this extremity, nor is it now a matter of material consequence as to how such results were brought about. That we are beaten is a self-evident fact, and any further resistance on our part would be justly regarded as the very height of folly and rashness. The armies of Generals Lee and Johnson having surrendered, you are the last of all the troops of the Confederate States Army east of the Mississippi River to lay down your arms. The cause for which you have so long and manfully struggled, and for which you have braved dangers, endured privations and sufferings, and made so many sacrifices, is to-day hopeless. The government which we sought to establish and perpetuate is at an end. Reason dictates and humanity demands that no more blood be shed. Fully realizing and feeling that such is the case, it is your duty and mine to lay down our arms, submit to the "powers that be," and to aid in restoring peace and establishing law and order throughout the land. The terms upon which you were surrendered are favorable, and should be satisfactory and acceptable to all. They manifest a spirit of magnanimity and liberality on the part of the Federal author-ities which should be met on our part by a faithful compliance with all the stipulations and conditions therein expressed. As your commander, I sincerely hope that every officer and soldier of my command will cheer-fully obey the orders given, and carry out in good faith all the terms of the cartel.

Those who neglect the terms and refuse to be paroled may assuredly expect when arrested to be sent North and imprisoned. Let those who are absent from their commands, from whatever cause, report at once to this place, or to Jackson, Mississippi, or, if too remote from either, to the nearest United States post or garrison, for parole. Civil war, such as you have just passed through, naturally engenders feelings of animosity, hatred, and revenge. It is our duty to divest ourselves of all such feelings, and, so far as it is in our power to do so, to cultivate friendly feelings towards those with whom we have so long contested and heretofore so widely but honestly differed. Neighborhood feuds, personal animosities, and private differences should be blotted out, and when you return home a manly, straightforward course of conduct will secure the respect even of your enemies. Whatever your responsibilities may be to government, to society, or to individuals, meet them like men. The attempt made to establish a separate and inde-pendent confederation has failed, but the consciousness of having done your duty faithfully and to the end will in some measure repay for the hardships you have undergone. In bidding you farewell, rest assured that you carry with you my best wishes for your future welfare and happiness. Without in any way referring to the merits of the cause in which we have been engaged, your courage and determination, as exhibited on many hard-fought fields, has elicited the respect and admiration of friend and foe. And I now cheerfully and gratefully acknowledge my indebtedness to the officers and men of my command, whose zeal, fidelity, and unflinching bravery have been the great source of my past success in arms. I have never on the field of battle sent you where I was unwilling to go myself, nor would I now advise you to a course which I felt myself unwilling to pursue. You have been good soldiers, you can be good citizens. Obey the laws, preserve your honor, and the government to which you have surrendered can afford to be and will be magnanimous.

N. B. FORREST, Lieutenant-General

Admirers and partisans of General Forrest bemoan the fact that his last campaign was not attended with the brilliant success which characterized his almost unbroken series of victories. It should be borne in mind that the fight against General Wilson was made under circumstances which placed the Confederate leader at great disadvantage. His command was greatly inferior in numbers to that of his able adversary, and much of it was composed of a material upon which he could not with confidence rely. General Grant in his *Memoirs,* in commenting upon the relative strength and efficiency of these contending forces, says: "Wilson moved out with full twelve thousand men, well equipped and well armed. He was an energetic officer and accomplished his work rapidly. Forrest was in his front, but with neither his old-time army nor his old-time prestige. He now had principally conscripts. His conscripts were usually old men and boys. He had a few thousand regular cavalry left, but not enough to even retard materially the progress of Wilson's cavalry."

TWENTY-TWO

After the War

G ENERAL FORREST remained at Gainesville for several days after the troops had surrendered, giving his personal attention to their disbandment and departure. He missed no opportunity to impress upon them not only the propriety but the necessity of going directly to their homes and abandoning all idea of further resistance to the Federal government. He then started by rail for his own home near Memphis. In journeying toward Jackson, Mississippi, the cars were greatly overcrowed with soldiers and refugees making their way homeward. The railroads were in such wretched condition that progress was not only slow but dangerous.

The late Congressman C. B. Kilgore happened to be a passenger in the same coach with General Forrest. On one occasion, although they were moving slowly, the rails spread, and the train came to a halt with the wheels off the track. He says that Forrest naturally took command and gave directions about everything. "He ordered every one of us out of the cars, and soon had us at work with levers placed in position to lift the trucks and coach so that the displaced rails could be pushed back in proper line. Our first effort was not successful, and some one said to Forrest: 'General, there are still some men in the car, and if they would get out we could lift it more readily.' To think that his first command to vacate the cars had not been obeyed was enough to kindle the ire of this irascible ruler of men, and springing on to the steps and platform he shouted out: 'If you damned rascals don't get out of here and help get this car on the track I will throw every one of you through the windows.' " Mr. Kilgore says: "At this the laggards in rapid fashion tumbled out at the other end of the coach, with Forrest following. He soon had them swinging on the lever, and in a few minutes the car was in the air, the trucks adjusted to the rails, and we

545

were again on our way. It seemed under all conditions he was the man for the occasion."[1]

Arriving at his plantation, citizen Forrest applied himself most diligently to the work of saving what he could from the wreck and ruin his property had suffered. A number of his old slaves (some of whom he had himself made free)[2] proved their affection and devotion to him by returning to work again upon the old plantation. Within a few weeks after the surrender, an incident occurred which shows how fully he had accepted the terms of his surrender. Admiral Semmes had been arrested in Mobile and taken to New Orleans for imprisonment and trial. It was claimed that this was a violation of the terms of surrender which Admiral Semmes had accepted. It so happened that General Dabney H. Maury was a passenger upon the steamer that conveyed the admiral from Mobile to New Orleans. As he was walking up and down the deck, Semmes, who was in charge of an officer and a guard of marines, said to him: "General, they have arrested me; they are going to disregard the paroles of all of us." This greatly excited the apprehensions of Maury in regard to Forrest, for the reason that he had noticed the Northern papers had indicated him as a proper object of Federal vengeance.

With this in mind, General Maury, who was affectionately attached to Forrest, hurried to Memphis in order to urge him to leave the country. Forrest was not in Memphis at the time, and Maury was told that he was on his plantation at work. He immediately called on Colonel Sam Tate and informed him of Semmes's arrest and imprisonment in disregard of his parole, telling him that he apprehended Forrest would suffer a similar annoyance. Colonel Tate asked Maury to write Forrest at once what had occurred, and to say to him that a letter of credit would be forwarded to him which would enable him to leave the country and remain in Europe until it was safe to return.

General Maury left Memphis on the following day, and did not for some time know of Forrest's action in the matter. Colonel Tate informed him later that Forrest had returned the letter of credit, thanking his generous friends for their thoughtfulness. His acknowledgment closed as follows: "This is my country. I am hard at work upon my

[1] Manuscripts of Judge C. B. Kilgore, in possession of the author.
[2] The distinguished author, Mr. George W. Cable, who was a Confederate soldier, was at one time detailed as secretary to General Forrest, and drew up the papers of manumission which he issued to his slaves.

plantation, and carefully observing the obligations of my parole. If the Federal government does not regard it they will be sorry. I shall not go away."

Forrest immediately repaired to Memphis and called in person upon the Federal commander there, stating that he had come to report and to find out what the government was going to do with him. He said: "I understand that Admiral Semmes's parole has been disregarded, and that I am to be arrested." The commanding officer assured him that there was no thought of any such action.

General Basil W. Duke, who came to know Forrest well after the war, writes in his Civil War sketches[3] that Forrest "took much interest in politics at this time, and, so far as a man in his situation could do, tried to influence the course of political events."

He was a delegate to the first Democratic presidential convention which assembled after the war, that which nominated Seymour. I witnessed an incident on our way to New York which very well illustrated his capacity to intimidate men not supposed to be subject to such influences. A number of us, from Tennessee and Kentucky, were, of course, in the same coach. When the train reached some town, the name of which I have forgotten, it stopped before pulling up at the depot at a water tank a short distance below.

The train conductor, who had been a Federal soldier, and was a very fine, manly young fellow with whom we had all fraternized readily, came to me at this point and said that he apprehended some trouble when we reached the depot. He had just been informed, he said, that a crowd, having learned that Forrest was on the train, had collected there, and that the town bully, a very truculent fellow, was loudly proclaiming his intention to take him off the train and thrash him. The conductor did not believe that the crowd was disposed to back the bully in such attempt, but thought it had assembled merely out of curiosity. But he was apprehensive that in the excitement some of them, who had formed no such previous intention, might render him assistance, and then, as we would certainly stand by Forrest, a serious riot might occur.

"Now," he said, "if anything of the kind happens, I'm going to side with you men and give you all the help I can. I don't like this sort of thing, and moreover it's my duty to protect my passengers so far as I can. But let's have no trouble if it can be avoided. I want you, therefore, to advise General Forrest to remain in the coach—where, if it comes to a fight, we

[3] Published in *Home and Farm*, 1906.

can make the best showing, anyhow—and not go out on the platform, no matter what that fellow says or does."

The conductor said further that he believed the man would seek a quarrel, inasmuch as he was a noted fighter and had never met his match.

I immediately communicated the information to Forrest, and advised that he act as the conductor suggested. He received the news very calmly, being too much accustomed to affairs of that kind to become excited, and agreed to the program as indicated. But when the train stopped at the depot, the bully immediately sprang upon the platform and entered our coach. He was a very powerful man in appearance, larger than Forrest, and I believe meant to execute his threat up to the time that he caught sight of the party he was looking for. As he entered the door he called out loudly: "Where's that d——d butcher, Forrest? I want him."

I never in my life witnessed such an instantaneous and marvelous transformation in anyone's appearance as then occurred with Forrest. He bounded from his seat, his form erect and dilated, his face the color of heated bronze, and his eyes flaming, blazing. He strode rapidly down the aisle toward the approaching champion, his gait and manner evincing perfect, invincible determination. "I am Forrest," he said. "What do you want?"

The bully gave one look. His purpose evaporated and, when Forrest had gotten within three or four feet of him, he turned and rushed out of the coach faster than he had entered. Forrest followed him into the midst of the crowd outside, vainly shouting to him to stop, and several of us followed Forrest. But the man whose prowess that crowd had gathered to witness had no thought of holding his ground. He darted into and down the street with quarter-horse speed, losing his hat in his hurry, and vanished around a corner. Then the humor of the thing struck Forrest, and he burst into a great shout of laughter. In a few moments the entire crowd joined in his merriment and seemed to be in complete sympathy with him, many of them pressing forward to shake hands with him. When the train, five minutes later, pulled out, Forrest was standing on the platform receiving the cheers and plaudits of the multitude and gracefully waving his thanks to his new friends and admirers.

Forrest attracted a great deal of attention at the Democratic convention of 1868, not only from the delegates, but from the large crowd assembled to witness its deliberations. Having had no practice as a speaker, and unfamiliar with parliamentary methods, he took little part, of course, in its more public proceedings; but his counsel, as one who knew the sentiment of the Southern people and perfectly possessed their confidence, was sought and heeded by the Democratic leaders. There was, also, a very lively curiosity entertained by people generally to see one whose career in the Civil War had been so remarkable and the remembrance of which was yet recent.

For the two or three years immediately following the close of the war Forrest continued to give his personal attention to the working of his plantations, and as soon as these were again made productive and placed in such condition that they could be carried on successfully without his personal supervision, he engaged in the larger enterprise of constructing a railroad from Selma, Alabama, to the Mississippi River. To this undertaking he devoted his entire energies for a period of about three years. The right of way was secured, securities issued, contracts made, and the work was being pushed with rapidity and success when, as a result of the great financial crisis which swept over the United States at that period, this, with hundreds of other undertakings of a public nature, was swept away in the general wreck and ruin.

While engaged in the construction of this road Forrest became a party to a controversy with one of his contractors, an honorable and courageous man by the name of Shepherd. From reports Forrest had received he had been led to believe that this contractor had not complied satisfactorily with the requirements of his work, and when they met, without waiting for any explanation, Forrest, who at the time happened to be in bad humor, spoke abusively to his employee. This gentleman, stung by the injustice of the attack upon him, resented it so bitterly that he challenged Forrest to mortal combat. In the heat and violence of the moment Forrest accepted the challenge, selecting his favorite weapon, "navy sixes," at a distance of ten paces, to fire at the word, and advance and continue firing until one or the other was killed.

The details of this affair were obtained from Mr. Charles E. Waller, a reliable citizen of Greensboro, Alabama, who was a contractor on the road at the same time and was well acquainted with both parties to the quarrel. While a great admirer of Forrest, and still devoted to his memory, Mr. Waller says that the general was exceedingly overbearing and unnecessarily severe in his denunciation of Colonel Shepherd.

The duel was to take place at sunrise the next morning. Forrest spent the night with Mr. Waller, occupying the same room with this gentleman. "I noticed that Forrest was restless throughout the night, for with the knowledge of the impending duel I was unable to sleep. About daylight I looked across the room and saw the general sitting upon the side of his bed, and inquired of him why he was restless. He replied: 'I haven't slept for thinking about the trouble with Shepherd. I feel sure I can kill him, and if I do I will never forgive myself. I am convinced that he was right in resenting the way I talked to him. I am in the wrong, and I do not feel satisfied about it.' " Mr. Waller replied: "General Forrest, your courage has never been questioned. I have no reputation of being a brave man, but under the circumstances I should feel it to be my duty to apologize to Colonel Shepherd and openly tell him that I was in the wrong." The general said: "You are right; I will do it."

They immediately got up, dressed themselves, and he and Forrest went directly to Shepherd's quarters, where they found him surrounded by a group of friends. Forrest walked directly to him, offered his hand, and said: "Colonel, I am in the wrong in this affair and I have come to say so." Colonel Shepherd expressed himself as being very glad that General Forrest had taken this view of it, and with this the matter ended.

In 1871–72, General Forrest was summoned before the committee of Congress appointed to inquire into the condition of affairs in the late insurrectionary states[4] in regard to the formation of the Ku-Klux organization. The committee stated that perhaps Generals Forrest and John B. Gordon knew more about the formation of this secret society than any others. Forrest testified that while he did not take an active part in the organization of the Ku-Klux, he knew that it was an association of citizens in his state (Tennessee) for self-protection. There was a great, widespread, and deep feeling of insecurity felt by those who had sympathized with the South in the war, as a result of Governor Brownlow's calling out the militia and his proclamation, which they had interpreted as a license for the state troops, without fear of punishment, to commit any kind of depredation against those lately in arms against the Union. Forrest stated that he had advised against all manner of violence on the part of the Southern people, and when the Loyal Leagues, for fear of the Ku-Klux, began to disband, he

[4] Reports of Committees, House of Representatives, Second Session, Forty-second Congress, pp. 7–449.

urged the disbanding of the other society.

The impression which Forrest made on this committee may be inferred from their report: "The statements of these gentlemen (Forrest and Gordon) are full and explicit. . . . The evidence fully sustains them, and it is only necessary to turn to the official documents of Tennessee to show that all Forrest said about the alarm which prevailed during the administration of Governor Brownlow was strictly true. No State was ever reduced to such humiliation and degradation as that unhappy commonwealth during the years Brownlow ruled over her."

After the failure of his railroad enterprises, Forrest returned to his plantation and continued at work not only to support those immediately dependent upon him, and to whom he was bound by natural ties, but to give largely of his greatly diminished income to the support of the wounded and helpless soldiers of his command, and the widows and orphans of others who had fallen while fighting under his flag. To the day of his death he continued to share his income with these helpless people, and after he was dead his noble wife carried out his wishes in this direction until she had practically given away in charity the entire fortune the general had left.

On September 21, 1876, he attended a reunion of the Seventh Tennessee Cavalry, in one of the companies of which he had volunteered as a private soldier in June of 1861. In a moving address to his old comrades in arms, he concluded by saying, "Soldiers, I was afraid that I could not be with you to-day, but I could not bear the thought of not meeting with you, and I will always try to meet with you in the future. I hope that you will continue to meet from year to year, and bring your wives and children with you, and let them and the children who may come after them enjoy with you the pleasure of your reunions."

Forrest never made a promise to the men who had followed his fortunes through the war which he did not if possible fulfill, but this engagement to meet with them again was canceled by the decree of fate.

General Wheeler, who saw Forrest about this time, says: "It so happened that I had not seen General Forrest for several years . . . and I could but notice the startling change which had come over him. He was greatly emaciated, as a result of an exhausting diarrhoea from which he was hopelessly suffering, and the pale, thin face seemed to bring out in bolder relief than I had ever observed before the magnificent forehead and head. Every line or suggestion of harshness had disappeared, and he seemed to possess in these last days the gentleness of expression, the voice and manner of a woman."[5]

Although he had scarcely passed the meridian of life, the tremendous expenditure of energy which he had made in the four years of terribly earnest warfare such as he had carried on had at last told upon the constitution even of this man of iron. In the intensity of his devotion to the cause of the South he had violated the first of nature's laws—the preservation of self. In battle, on the march, or in the camp he had permitted to mind or body only the minimum of rest. He was now demonstrating the truth of the axiom that he who disregards the laws of nature curtails his own existence.

General John T. Morgan,[6] who had been acting for some years as the legal adviser of General Forrest in the many perplexing suits which were developed as a result of the financial crisis and the discontinuance of his railroad enterprise, says that Forrest at this time called upon him and ordered the discontinuance of all litigation with which he was connected. In the course of the conversation with General Morgan he said: "General, I am broken in health and in spirit, and have not long to live. My life has been a battle from the start. It was a fight to achieve a livelihood for those dependent upon me in my younger days, and an independence for myself when I grew up to manhood, as well as in the terrible turmoil of the Civil War. I have seen too much of violence, and I want to close my days at peace with all the world, as I am now at peace with my Maker." He told General Morgan that he had for some time been attached to the Cumberland Presbyterian Church, and that he intended to live a peaceful and a better life for the remainder of his days. Although assured by his distinguished attorney that the suits were favorable to his interests, he persisted in their abandonment, saying he would not leave his only son a heritage of contention.

Early in the summer of 1877, his faithful friend, Major Charles W. Anderson, was asked to visit him at Hurricane Springs, in middle Tennessee, where Forrest was spending the hot months in the hope that the waters would prove beneficial to his health. Major Anderson was

[5] Personal communication to the author.
[6] Personal communication from United States Senator Morgan.

quick to observe a softness of expression and a mildness of manner which he had not noticed in the trying times of war, and he must have shown something of surprise at this in his expression, for Forrest, as if reading his thought, said: "Major, I am not the same man you were with so long and knew so well. I hope I am a better man now than then. I have been and am trying to lead another kind of life. Mary has been praying for me night and day for all these years, and I feel now that through her prayers my life has been spared and I have passed safely through so many dangers."

Although he received the tenderest and most watchful care, this could not stay the dread disease which was destroying his life. In the early autumn he returned without improvement to his home in Memphis, where he died on October 29, 1877, at the early age of fifty-six.

His death created a profound impression throughout the country, and called forth universal expressions of sympathy and respect. Many of those against whom he had fought in battle, uniting with the South, paid respectful tribute to his memory. The ex-President of the Confederacy and some of the surviving members of the Confederate cabinet, and thousands upon thousands of high and low degree, followed the funeral cortege to Elmwood Cemetery, where, with imposing ceremony and glowing tribute, the body of this great soldier was returned to the dust from which it had sprung.

Well might one write upon the shaft that will stand in everlasting vigil upon his ashes as a fitting epitaph the lines of Lord Wolseley, commander in chief of the British army: "Forrest had fought like a knight-errant for the cause he believed to be that of justice and right. No man who drew the sword for his country in that fratricidal struggle deserves better of her; and as long as the chivalrous deeds of her sons find poets to describe them and fair women to sing of them, the name of this gallant general will be remembered with affection and sincere admiration. A man with such a record needs no ancestry."

TWENTY-THREE

Forrest the Man and the Soldier

THE career of Nathan Bedford Forrest will stand a chapter apart in the annals of our country, a story as unique as his personality was picturesque. In the obscurity of his origin, the success of his struggle against poverty, and the splendor of his achievements in war, it will be difficult to match it in all the pages of history. The son of a blacksmith, his childhood, youth, and early manhood spent amid the wild scenes of the American frontier, he was reared to such hard labor in the struggle for existence that even the scantiest opportunities for an education were denied him.

One of the strongest arguments in favor of the assertion that Forrest never enjoyed the advantages of even a country school is the fact that he who possessed such a remarkable intellect and quick grasp of mind was woefully incapable of correct spelling. This is evident in the interesting specimen of his writing shown in the chapter which deals with the capture of Colonel Streight. In spelling words he was, as Major Anderson says, "governed by sound, and his spelling, like his fighting, was the shortest way to the end." In spelling "headquarters" he did not appreciate the necessity of the letter "a" in "head." He spelled "her" with an "i," and although the note to Emma Sansom was written in pencil, the dot above the "i" is exactly in the right place and is still distinct. He was perfectly conscious of his shortcomings in this direction, and to Major Ellis he once expressed his disinclination to write by saying, "I never see a pen but what I think of a snake."

Despite the lack of a school education, contact with businessmen and constant reading of newspapers (for he kept himself thoroughly versed in the records of the day) gave him an excellent idea of the use of words and the construction of phrases. When, after dictating a dispatch, it was read over for correction, he would instantly detect a grammatical error or the awkward construction of a phrase, and would say to Major Strange or Anderson, as the unsatisfactory paragraph was concluded, "That won't do, it hasn't the right pitch." He would then change the diction, and always shaped it into a forcible expression. There were, however, a few words learned in his boyhood days of which he could not rid himself. He always said "betwixt" and "fetch" for the words "between" and "bring." "Tell Bell to move up and fetch all he's got" was the famous note at Brice's Crossroads. He used the word "mout" for "might," and "fit" for "fought." After Forrest became famous, these idiosyncrasies were repeated and exaggerated until the idea prevailed in the minds of many that he was more awkward and boorish in his speech as well as manner than he really was. He keenly felt the want of education, and once remarked: "No one knows the embarrassment I labor under when thrown in the company of educated persons."[1]

Dr. J. B. Cowan says: "The general was an excellent reader, had a large fund of general information and a remarkable knowledge of men. The real development of his mental powers was far in advance of the world about him." It was this practical education and common-sense training which made him always master of his environment. He was not only great in strategy and tactics, and in dealing with matters connected with his military career, but he possessed a remarkable genius for mathematics, a subject in which he had absolutely no training. He could with surprising facility solve the most difficult problems in algebra, geometry, and trigonometry, only requiring that the theorem or rule be carefully read aloud to him.

Colonel D. C. Kelley says: "Forrest was a fine conversationalist; his voice was soft and pleasant, his eyes twinkled as he spoke, giving an attractive expression to his face. He seemed to know men intuitively, and would have been great in any department of life. As in war, he would have met every emergency with daring skill, and every obstacle with dauntless energy. In politics few men would have equalled him in controlling the masses by shrewd common-sense methods, or in grasping great issues. He was an impressive speaker, and on several occasions I have heard him deliver an address in most effective manner."

Away from the pressing duties of the field or camp, Forrest was ever ready to enter into the spirit of the company in which he found himself, and would enjoy a good laugh even at his own expense. He

[1] Manuscripts of Major Charles W. Anderson.

often brought a smile to the many friends gathered around him in telling of the incident at Cowan's Station, when he was being hotly pursued through that village by the Federals, and a fiery Southern dame, not knowing that she was addressing the great General Forrest, shook her fist at him and upbraided him as a coward for not turning about to fight the Yankees. The last words he heard her say as he passed on the roadside were: "Why don't you turn and fight, you cowardly rascal? If old Forrest were here, he'd make you fight."

A specimen of his aptness in repartee is given by Dr. John O. Scott, now residing in Sherman, Texas, who was present at a dinner at Marion, Alabama, near the close of the war, at which Forrest was the guest of honor. There was at the table a loquacious widow, who at one moment interrupted the general conversation to ask Forrest why his beard was still black while his hair was turning gray. With great politeness he answered that he could not give a satisfactory explanation, unless it was that he "might have used his brain a little more than he did his jaw." That the curiosity of the widow (whose hair still refused to take on a shade of gray) was satisfied with the explanation was evident from the silence that settled down upon her. In physique, carriage, and expression, Forrest possessed a striking personality. He was six feet two inches in height, with broad shoulders, full chest, long arms, a powerful muscular development, and an average weight of 180 pounds.

Mr. Bryan McAllister, a partisan of the Union side, who at the time in which he wrote (May, 1865) could not conceal the bitterness of his animosity, wrote of him: "Forrest was a man of fine appearance, having piercing eyes, carefully trimmed mustache and chin-whiskers, dark as night, with finely cut features and iron-gray hair. His form was lithe, plainly indicating great physical power and activity. He was neatly dressed in citizen's clothes of some gray mixture, the only indication of military service being the usual number of staff buttons on his vest. I should have marked him as a prominent man had I seen him on Broadway. When I was told that he was the 'Forrest of Fort Pillow' I devoted my whole attention to him."

Colonel Adair, of Atlanta, Georgia, for many years a neighbor and an intimate personal friend of Forrest, says: "He was more than six feet high, well proportioned, with hands tapering like those of a woman, small feet and very high instep, exceedingly graceful in his movements, a swarthy complexion, and a look of the eye that indicated absolute fear of nothing. He was naturally left-handed, but by practice became ambidextrous."

Major Anderson says:

Few men were neater in personal appearance or in his surroundings than General Forrest. He abhorred dirt and disorder. To have papers scattered about the floor, or ashes on the hearth, brought a reproof from him, not always in words, for he would frequently take the broom himself and never stop until things were neat and clean. His habits were strictly temperate. In the two and a half years I served with him I never knew him to take liquor but twice, and then only immediately after being wounded —once at Tunnel Hill, Georgia, and on another occasion at Old Town Creek, in Mississippi. He did not know whiskey from brandy, but called everything liquor. He was often invited to take a drink, but always declined, and would at times, in refusing the invitation, remark with humorous suggestion and a mild reproof to his aides, "My staff does all my drinking." He never used tobacco in any way, and while he would occasionally swear at my pipe, he never failed to get me a good pouch of tobacco if it came his way.

His strict morality was evident in every particular, with this one exception of swearing, and to this weakness he never gave way unless in the presence of great excitement. During these paroxysms of excitement or rage he had one very noticeable physical peculiarity. His complexion, which was naturally sallow, changed completely in color. The capillaries became so greatly engorged with blood that the skin of the face and neck took on almost a scarlet hue. The blood vessels of the eye took on the same congestion, giving him an expression of savageness which could not be misunderstood. Everything that was suggestive of kindly feeling or tenderness seemed to vanish from his nature as thoroughly as if his heart had never throbbed with human sympathy. His voice, naturally soft, became harsh, husky, and metallic in tone, and loud enough to be heard above the roar of cannon, the crackling of small arms, or the wild yells of his men. It was noticeable that in these moments of excitation the acuteness of his perception was increased. Nothing seemed to escape his glance, and each emergency or change, no matter how rapidly the scene shifted, was met with promptness and almost invariably with success.

Without the least affectation of piety, Forrest was by nature deeply reverent and religious, despite his terrible temper and violent language. In later years he heartily repented of these grievous faults, and won at last his greatest triumph in becoming victorious over himself. Obscene or vulgar words were entirely foreign to his conversation, and such was his detestation of these expressions that he would not under any circumstances permit a smutty story to be told or a vulgar expression used in his presence. In the family relation Forrest lived with the manly consistency which his strong character would indicate.

Colonel Kelley says:

His devotion to his wife was deep and sincere. She was a quiet, refined, Christian woman, and could control him with a word even when his temper was at the highest. He had absolute confidence in the piety of his mother and wife, and was himself a thorough believer in Christianity, and was as fully persuaded of the efficacy of prayer in times of danger or in battle as Napoleon was a believer in fate. Throughout the war he always gave me the fullest opportunities for preaching in camp, courteously entertaining at his mess-table all preachers whom I might choose to invite. He was always present at such service when it was practicable. While we were messmates there was always family prayer in his tent at night, conducted alternately by the chaplain and myself.

On one of our expeditions a chaplain of the Federal army was overtaken and captured. When he learned that he was to be taken to Forrest's headquarters, every feature showed the deepest anxiety and depression. As he approached, General Forrest bade him to be seated while he was attending to other matters. A little later supper was announced, and the chaplain was requested to share our meal with us. When all were seated, Forrest turned to him reverentially and said: "Parson, will you please ask the blessing?" The minister could not conceal his surprise, which was evident from the manner in which he looked at Forrest before being assured that he was in earnest. He gave expression to the gratitude he felt at being thus considerately treated. He had evidently expected to be killed by the fierce fighter. The next morning Forrest gave him an escort through our lines, telling him that he had no war to make on non-combatants, and humorously remarked to him as he bade him good-bye: "Parson, I would keep you here to preach for me if you were not needed so much more by the sinners on the other side."

Dr. J. B. Cowan says:

In those days we never started on an expedition but what the men were drawn up in line, and the chaplain, while the heads of all were uncovered, evoked God's blessing on our cause. Nothing called down [Forrest's] ire quicker or brought surer punishment than for a man to disturb religious service in any part of the camp.

One side of General Forrest's nature was as gentle and tender as a woman's; the other, when he was aroused, was desperate and thoroughly destructive. In quiet moments he was confiding, gentle, kind, and considerate. When not aroused there was no man on earth more tender than he. It was when the battle was over that the kinder and gentler part of his nature came out. He would come to my hospital, help me with the wounded, go about them with kind words of encouragement, and aid me in caring for them as tenderly as a mother. I have known him to give his clothing and personal effects away on many occasions to the needy wounded. He would say to me: "Doctor, do all you can for those poor fellows." I have seen the tears running down his cheeks as he was speaking to some unfortunate soldier who had not long to live.

Colonel C. R. Barteau, now a practicing attorney in Memphis, Tennessee, writes me: "I have thought that one feature of General Forrest's character deserves special mention—to wit, his idea of morality. During the war, when the protection of the weak depended so largely upon the military arm, the violation by any soldier in his command of the strict rules he established, if reported to him, was promptly punished. In the presence of his wife he was as tractable and loving as a child, though fierce in battle and among men when aroused, yet as a guardian of female virtue and the sanctity of dependent homes and unprotected families he stood in striking contrast with others of the service."

Major Powhatan Ellis says: "On one occasion, while approaching his tent, I heard him in tones of great anger using the most bitter denunciatory language to an officer who, although as brave a man as served in the war, and a warm personal friend of Forrest, had been guilty of immoral conduct of which Forrest had just heard. He denounced him in the severest language I think I ever heard, dismissed him from his command on the spot, saying, 'I will not have any man about me who will be guilty of such conduct to a woman.' "

The natural simplicity and tenderness of this stern warrior were shown in his fondness for little children. Two days after the capture of Colonel Streight and his command, he stayed all night at the home of a personal friend of the writer of this book, who was greatly surprised to find that Forrest took no interest in talking about military matters, nor of his recent successful campaign, but spent most of the time during the evening carrying his host's little two-year-old boy about in his arms and playing with the child, seemingly indifferent to the older members of the household. On the following day, when about to continue his journey on horseback, he asked that he might be permitted to carry the child a short distance on the road. Placing a pillow on the pommel of the saddle, he rode away with his little comrade, requesting the father to accompany him in order to bring the boy back.

It has been said of Forrest that he "was born a soldier as men are born poets."[2] The truth of this assertion is evident in the fact that, without education or the knowledge of what others had done, he showed from the outset of his career an extraordinary capacity for war. A private soldier in the ranks in June, 1861, against obstacles which seemed almost insurmountable he fought his way to a lieutenant generalship, the highest rank but one accorded to its soldiers by the Confederacy. While he "seemed to go by his horses' leaps from promotion to promotion,"[3] it is a sad comment upon the intelligence of the authorities under whom he served that they were slow to appreciate and profit by his wonderful ability.

In fact, it was not until the Civil War was over, and men in quiet moments took time to reflect upon his unsurpassed record in the army, that he was awarded the place to which his genius entitled him. At the funeral of General Forrest, Governor James D. Porter of Tennessee rode in the same carriage with the ex-President of the Southern Confederacy. In a letter to the author, Governor Porter states:

As we were driving to the cemetery, Mr. Davis spoke in the highest terms of Forrest's ability as a soldier. I remarked: "History has accorded to General Forrest the first place as a cavalry leader in the war between the States, and has named him as one of the half-dozen great soldiers of the country." Mr. Davis replied with great earnestness: "I agree with you. The trouble was that the generals commanding in the Southwest never appreciated Forrest until it was too late. Their judgment was that he was a bold and enterprising partisan raider and rider. I was misled by them, and I never knew how to measure him until I read his reports of his campaign across the Tennessee River in 1864. This induced a study of his earlier reports, and after that I was prepared to adopt what you are pleased to name as the judgment of history." In reply I said: "I cannot comprehend

[2] General Dabney H. Maury.
[3] Mr. George W. Cable.

such lack of appreciation after he fought the battle at Brice's Crossroads in June of 1864. That battle was not a cavalry raid nor an accident. It was the conception of a man endowed with a genius for war." Mr. Davis replied to this: "That campaign was not understood at Richmond. The impression made upon those in authority was that Forrest had made another success- ful raid, but I saw it all after it was too late.

The Scriptural adage that "A prophet is not without honor, save in his own country" was never more directly applicable than in the case of Forrest, for it was among those against whom he was battling with all the energy of his nature that he was first measured in the fullness of his ability. No higher compliment could have been paid to any gen- eral of the Confederacy than that accorded to him by the famous commander of the Army of the Tennessee, General William T. Sher- man, who early in 1864 deemed the death of Forrest so essential to the success of the Union cause that, as he wrote then, ten thousand lives and a limitless expenditure of means were as naught to its ac- complishment. To him, the unlettered soldier stood as the chief source of his anxiety, the most dreaded obstacle to his success in the great strategic game he was playing with the immortal Johnston from Dalton to Atlanta. He knew full well that he had the South by the throat, and the burden of his dispatches and his official correspondence was: "Keep Forrest away from me, and I will attend to Johnston and cut the Con- federacy in two."

Several years after the war, in a conversation with General Frank C. Armstrong, whose intimate relations as a lieutenant of Forrest were known to him, General Sherman said: "After all, I think Forrest was the most remarkable man our Civil War produced on either side. To my mind he was the most remarkable in many ways. In the first place, he was uneducated, while Jackson and Sheridan and other brilliant leaders were soldiers by profession. He had never read a mili- tary book in his life, knew nothing about tactics, could not even drill a company, but he had a genius for strategy which was original, and to me incomprehensible. There was no theory or art of war by which I could calculate with any degree of certainty what Forrest was up to. He seemed always to know what I was doing or intended to do, while I am free to confess I could never tell or form any satisfactory idea of what he was trying to accomplish."[4]

[4] Personal communication from General Frank C. Armstrong.

It is a remarkable coincidence that Sherman's famous antagonist, General Joseph E. Johnston, deemed by many the greatest strategist and the ablest general on the Confederate side, reached the same conclusion as to the proper place to be accorded to Forrest among the soldiers of the world.

Dr. George Ben Johnston, of Richmond, Virginia, informed the writer that a few months before the death of his uncle, General Joseph E. Johnston, he called, while passing through Washington, to pay him a brief visit. Without being announced, he went immediately to the library, where he knew his relative spent most of his leisure moments, and as he greeted him he noticed in his hand a history of Tamerlane. This volume naturally suggested the subject of great leaders in war, and in the course of the conversation Dr. Johnston asked the general who he considered the greatest soldier of our own war. He says that without a moment's hesitation his uncle replied: "Forrest, who, had he had the advantages of a thorough military education and training, would have been the great central figure of the Civil War." He went on at some length to point out those features of Forrest's career which justified this conclusion. Dr. Johnston says: "I recollect, moreover, that he spoke most affectionately and lovingly of the personality of the general."[5]

This estimate of Forrest by Johnston is corroborated by General Dabney H. Maury, who, in that charming book, *Recollections of a Virginian,* says: "Several years after the war the Legislature of Virginia had ordered the portrait of General Johnston to be painted for the Capitol. I was requested to attend the sittings with General Johnston on one or two occasions, in order to converse with him while the artist was at work. In the course of our conversation he spoke with a great deal of animation upon the great soldiers of the world and of their campaigns. Reverting to our own war, he discussed the ability and campaigns of Lee, Jackson, Forrest, and others, and, according to Lee and Jackson the full measure of their fame, he pronounced General Forrest the greatest soldier the Civil War produced."

In a conversation with General Maury, General Beauregard once remarked: "Forrest's capacity for war seemed only to be limited by the opportunities for its display."

[5] Personal communication, in possession of the author.

General Wolseley, commander in chief of the British army, wrote of him:

Forrest had no knowledge of military science nor of military history to teach him how he should act, what objective he should aim at, and what plans he should make to secure it. He was entirely ignorant of what other generals in previous wars had done under very similar circumstances. What he lacked in book lore was to a large extent compensated for by the soundness of his judgment upon all occasions, and by his power of thinking and reasoning with great rapidity under fire, and under all circumstances of surrounding peril or of great mental or bodily fatigue. Panic found no resting-place in that calm brain of his, and no danger, no risk, appalled that dauntless spirit. Inspired with true military instincts, he was verily nature's soldier. It would be difficult in all history to find a more varied career than his, a man who, from the greatest poverty, without any learning, and by sheer force of character alone became the great fighting leader of fighting men, a man in whom an extraordinary military instinct and sound common-sense supplied to a very large extent his unfortunate want of military education. His military career teaches us that the genius which makes men great soldiers is not to be measured by any competitive examination in the science or art of war. "In war," Napoleon said, "men are nothing; a man is everything." It will be difficult to find a stronger corroboration of this maxim than is to be found in the history of General Forrest's operations.

With all this endowment by nature for the career of a soldier, he could not have achieved such results had there not been combined with this natural ability a spirit of devotion to the cause he had espoused, to which all else was a secondary consideration. To the success of the effort to establish the Southern Confederacy he subordinated his fortune, his boundless ambition, and freely offered his life. When the Confederacy was unable to furnish him with necessary supplies and arms, his private fortune was frequently called into requisition. The arms and equipment for his original battalion were thus secured, and on a single expedition into west Tennessee he spent some $20,000 of his personal funds in the purchase of supplies needed for the Confederacy. When the war ended, carrying with it great financial loss to him, that which was left he never ceased to share with the widows and orphans of those who had fallen in defence of his battle flag, or the soldiers who were disabled and survived, until he left himself and his family practically bankrupt.

This earnest devotion of the elder brother carried every able-bodied male member of his mother's family into the field, while his only child, then a mere lad, was permitted to quit college in order to serve with his father in active duty until the war was over. In one battle, in which his boy was injured and carried to the rear, the father, as soon as it was possible, went to see how dangerously his son was hurt. Upon being assured that the wound was not serious, he ordered him to mount his horse and to continue in the fight, which command the plucky lad was only too willing to obey.

General Forrest possessed not only a mind of unusual power, but one capable of reasoning calmly and rapidly, no matter how serious or perplexing the problems which presented themselves. Even in moments of extreme peril, so rapid was the process by which his brain registered and analyzed every detail of the picture which flashed through it that any action which the emergency demanded followed as logically and as quickly as the roar of the thunder follows the lightning's flash. The ordinary mind can deal with reasonable certainty and success with the things that are expected, but to cope successfully with the unexpected is the crucial test of extraordinary ability. In war, and especially upon the battlefield, it is the unexpected which most often happens, and in these great emergencies the mind is too often dazed by the rapid and kaleidoscopic changes which are occurring, or temporarily stunned by the shock of an unlooked-for stroke. It is on such occasions that he who hesitates is lost, and as in nature

> Everything that grows
> Holds in perfection but a single moment,

so in the crises of human affairs a single moment of time holds success or failure as the opportunity it brings is or is not grasped. Whether his life alone was in the balance or whether the safety of his command was involved, this wonderful presence of mind did not fail.

When the attempt upon his life was made at Hernando, and again at Columbia, in 1863, even after he had received a severe and painful wound from a pistol of large caliber, his conduct was marked with as much deliberation and coolness as if nothing important was transpiring. In a larger sense this great gift of nature was exhibited at the battle of Parker's Crossroads in 1862, and had Forrest made no other campaign than this expedition into west Tennessee, and had fought no other battle, it would have stamped him as a commander of extraordinary capacity. Considering all the conditions which prevailed, the extrication of his command with insignificant loss, his retreat to the Tennessee River only a few hours away, and the safe passage of his troops, wagons, and artillery, with a victorious army at his heels and a fleet of gunboats patrolling the mighty stream which in the dead of winter he was compelled to cross, was an unequalled achievement.

In all his military operations, to his quick grasp of the best strategic or tactical maneuver Forrest added a native cunning which stood him well in many of his ventures. This is evident in the constant exaggeration of the strength of his command. In the west Tennessee expedition, in 1862, with a small brigade of new levies, the first thing he did when well in the country occupied by the enemy was to arrest a number of Union sympathizers and place them under guard within the limits of his camp. Having carried a number of kettle and bass drums, he caused these to be beaten at all hours of the day and night, and had his troops march on foot in sight of the prisoners, who were informed that it was Cheatham's division of infantry passing by. When the men on foot had disappeared behind some dense wood or hill which intervened, they were made to return by another route, mount their horses, and again file by as cavalry over the road along which they had just paraded. These captives were then permitted to escape and, as Forrest intended, made their way rapidly to the headquarters of the nearest Federal commander and informed him of the great strength of the Confederate force, the soldiers of which made no secret of their intention permanently to occupy and hold that section of the country.

The presence of Cheatham's division of infantry is repeatedly mentioned in the official dispatches of the Union commanders at this date, and Forrest's cavalry was reported several times larger than the number of troops he actually commanded. The object of the expedition was not only to capture what supplies and prisoners he might come upon during the fortnight he was to remain in that section, but to cause the withdrawal from the immediate front of the Confederate army of as many of the enemy as possible. While Forrest did not have more than 3000 soldiers in this little army of invasion, it caused General Grant to detach, in order to drive him across the Tennessee, between 25,000 and 30,000 men.

In the capture of Murfreesboro in 1862, of Streight's command in

1863, of Athens, Alabama, in 1864, and in many other instances, he repeated this practice.

General John T. Morgan relates that when, early in the war, with a new regiment thoroughly drilled and equipped, he was ordered to report to General Forrest, the latter was greatly pleased as well as surprised to observe the perfection of this regiment in drilling to the sound of the bugle. Forrest asked him if he could in this way cause his men to pass in a circle around any given point. The order was given and the movement was satisfactorily accomplished, at which the general expressed great satisfaction, saying: "I will often have need of this maneuver, as it will be necessary from time to time for me to show more men than I actually have on the field."[6]

The strategy and tactics which seemed intuitive with Forrest were demonstrated in a brilliant manner at Murfreesboro in July of 1862. To reach this place he marched one hundred miles, crossing the Tennessee River and three formidable mountains—namely, Walden's Ridge, Lookout, and the Cumberland. So guarded and rapid was his approach that at daylight on the 13th of July, before his presence was suspected by the enemy, his men were riding into their camps. Discovering the Federals in three separate positions, he quickly interposed a sufficient number of his troops between their central column and the two outlying bodies to hold these at bay. With the remainder of his force, in overwhelming numbers he assaulted and carried the central position, capturing the commanding general as well as all the Union troops engaged at this point. He then turned his entire attention to their right wing, which he also overwhelmed and caused to surrender. The other detachment, together with the battery of artillery, he captured by diplomacy and sheer bluff.

It was Forrest's tactical maneuver at Thompson's Station which carried his own battery and his troops to such an advantageous position that he enfiladed the Federal guns and drove them from the field, following this by a rapid movement to the flank and rear, and by a desperate assault which caused the surrender to him of the entire command.

At Okolona, in the open prairies, where every man in either army was in plain view, he won the opening dash by taking instant advantage of an error in tactics on the part of the Federal commander. Before it

[6] Manuscripts of Senator Morgan, in possession of the author.

could be corrected the charge was sounded, and at full speed he rode with his troopers at his heels toward the spot he wished to strike, and overthrew his adversary. Speaking of this, he remarked: "I saw Grierson make a 'bad move,'[7] and then I rode right over him."

There were few examples of strategy more brilliant in conception and successful in execution than that by which Forrest defeated the expedition under Generals A. J. Smith and J. A. Mower in the latter part of August, 1864. He found himself powerless to offer successful resistance to this army of invasion, which had reached the vicinity of Oxford, Mississippi. Leaving Chalmers to make as vigorous a show of resistance as possible in front of Smith, selecting two thousand of his best-mounted men, he rode around Smith's army at night and, without his absence or the movement being suspected, swept to the Federal rear with lightning rapidity, and on the 21st of August, at daybreak, rode boldly into the heart of Memphis, then heavily garrisoned, carrying alarm and consternation to the heart of the Federal commander in this stronghold. The result of this operation was a rapid withdrawal of Smith's entire army, which was reconcentrated about Memphis, from which point they did not again venture for the invasion of Forrest's territory.

In all probability no strategic move suggested during the war would have proved more beneficial to the cause of the South than that in which General Forrest proposed to close the Mississippi and the Tennessee rivers to navigation in 1864. His west Tennessee expedition in December, 1862, had closed railroad communication and traffic between the northwestern states and the armies which were scattered along the Mississippi and in front of Mobile. Even Grant acknowledged that from this time on he would have to rely upon the river alone for his supplies.

Nearly two years later, Colonel George E. Waring, Jr., while serving in this district, wrote: "Union City was at the crossing of two railroads, one pointing towards Mobile and one towards Memphis, but neither leading anywhere. There was a tradition that trains had run upon each, but many bridges had to be rebuilt to make the short line to Columbus passable, and the rest was ruin, for Forrest had been there with his cavalry."[8] If these streams were closed, then no route was left

---

[7] An expression used in the game of checkers, in which he excelled.

[8] *Whip and Spur*, by George E. Waring, Jr., formerly colonel of the Fourth Missouri Cavalry, U.S.V.

to the Union armies in this portion of the South but the long and perilous voyage by sea. In the light of what Forrest accomplished on the Tennessee River in November of 1864, there can be little doubt that he would have succeeded in this larger enterprise had he been backed even by the slender resources of the Confederacy.

The only hope of success for the Confederacy was in the Fabian policy of prolonging the war by interfering with the supplies of the armies of the Union in the field and fighting as few pitched battles as possible. No less a personage than General Grant expressed in his *Memoirs* that it was possible for the Confederacy to have won had this policy been adopted and adhered to.

Some of the notable features in Forrest's method of warfare were the reckless courage in the attack; the almost invariable movement on the flank and rear, so demoralizing to an enemy, and especially so when made, as he usually did it, under cover, which concealed the strength of the flanking forces; the quick dismounting of his men to fight under cover of every object which offered protection; the use of his artillery, which he often carried along with the troops in line and always placed close to the enemy; and, finally, the fierce and relentless pursuit when his antagonist yielded.

His system of fighting was distinctly aggressive, and when possible he always took the offensive. He realized the value of boldness, even when akin to rashness, and when possible he attacked notwithstanding his disparity of numbers. He knew that the excitement of a forward movement inspired even the timid with courage, while to stand in the open to receive a charge was a severe test of the bravest men. When the enemy was about to charge, or was moving upon him, his rule was to make a counterattack before they reached him. Although, as was very often the case in his encounters, his troops were fewer in number than those he was assailing, he rarely failed to disconcert his antagonist by feigned attacks and a show of force at various points. Concentrating rapidly, he would then lead in person the fierce onslaught, and at the striking point would have the greater strength.

General Basil W. Duke tells of being present at an interview between Forrest and General John H. Morgan,[9] the great romantic figure in the Confederate cavalry service in the Army of Tennessee, when they were comparing notes of their respective expeditions made about the same

[9] General Duke was called "Morgan's right-hand man."

date in the summer of 1862, the one into middle Tennessee and the other into Kentucky. He reports:

Each seemed far more concerned to learn what the other had done and how he did it than to relate his own performances; and it was interesting to note the brevity with which they answered each other's questions and the eagerness with which they asked them. It was upon this occasion that Forrest used an expression which has been very often quoted. I was a good deal amused by it at the time, because of the terse way in which he rendered in the vernacular a proposition which General Beauregard had a few months previously clothed in very sonorous and academic terms.

Some of my readers may perhaps remember the letter which Beauregard wrote to Bragg shortly after the former relinquished and the latter assumed command of the army at Tupelo. Along with other excellent counsel, General Beauregard advised his successor to "be careful always to move by interior lines and strike the fragments of your enemy's forces with the masses of your own." This maxim was certainly not less worthy of suggestion because Napoleon had previously commended it as comprising nearly all of the gospel of strategy. It was new, however, to the majority of the Confederate soldiers, and they read Beauregard's letter with profound admiration. I do not know, therefore, whether my surprise or amusement was the greater when I heard Forrest, in this conversation with Morgan, unconsciously paraphrase it in his own curt and peculiar way.

Morgan wanted particularly to know about his fight at Murfreesboro, where Forrest had accomplished a marked success, capturing the garrison and stores and carrying off everything, although the surrounding country was filled with Federal forces. Morgan asked how it was done.

"Oh," said Forrest, "I just took the short cut and got there first with the most men."

Forrest's aggressiveness did not stop with the active personal direction of his troops in the field. The moral of his teaching and example was never to miss a chance to strike the enemy. He said to his soldiers: "Whenever you meet the enemy, no matter how few there are of you or how many of them, show fight. If you run away they will pursue and probably catch you. If you show fight, they will think there are more of you, and will not push you half so hard."[10] On every occasion Forrest practiced what he preached. With scant regard for his own life, he set an example of desperate courage which justified the statement of General Stephen A. Hurlbut before the congressional

[10] Manuscripts of Mr. W. G. Wilkins, in possession of the author.

committee, that "Forrest is desperate. He will lead his men farther than any one I know."

Whether in the thickest of the battle, where hundreds or thousands were rushing at each other in deadly combat, or on the lonely highway where he came face to face with a single adversary, or in the reconnaissance by day or night, when alone or attended by a single member of his staff he would ride into the enemy's lines and even into their camps, he was with pistol or saber ever ready to assert his physical prowess. It is known that he placed *hors de combat* thirty Federal officers or soldiers fighting hand-to-hand.

General Richard Taylor, in his entertaining book *Destruction and Reconstruction,* says: "I doubt if any commander since the days of the lion-hearted Richard killed as many enemies with his own hand as Forrest."

Mr. George W. Cable has said that his gravest military fault was that he could not keep out of the thickest of the fight. It was one of his favorite maxims that "War means fighting, and fighting means killing." It was not his idea that campaigns could be conducted and battles won without loss. A soldier's duty was to put himself where he could do the most harm to his enemy, and the first duty of a commanding officer was so to direct, control, and influence the soldiers who must do the fighting that he could get the most out of them. It will, I think, be conceded that no commander on either side in our war, or in any war, ever got more fighting, marching, or work out of the men and officers under him than did General Forrest.

With the men he led, strict discipline was not exercised, yet under the wonderful influence of one who inspired the timid with courage and the brave with the spirit of emulation, they fought with the steadiness of trained veterans. The Civil War does not afford an exhibition of more steady, persistent fighting against great odds than that shown by Forrest's command at Brice's Crossroads. Hour after hour, from ten in the morning until nearly five in the afternoon, almost without cessation of firing, they stood up against twice their number of Federal troops thoroughly well armed and equipped, and finally drove them from the field in wild disorder. It is probable that not a regiment of his command on that field could have made a correct tactical movement on foot in action, and, beyond the formation of fours and the evolution into line for the charge, the cavalry manual was practically obsolete.

The impression has prevailed that the men who composed Forrest's command were in the main wild and desperate characters. Such was not the case. A large proportion of them were thoroughly well-behaved citizens—farmers, mechanics, clerks, and the sons of the wealthy and educated. They were naturally not braver than other soldiers of the Confederacy, but they caught the inspiration of courage from their leader. Every soldier under him knew it was expected that he would fight to the death if it became necessary, and he knew, moreover, that Forrest had no respect or mercy for a coward. It was his order to his officers to shoot any man who flickered, and he emphasized this order by his own conduct. There was no false sentiment in the mind of Forrest connected with war. There was an end to be achieved—the independence of the Southern Confederation. To that consummation everything must be subordinated.

To his mind the killing of one of his own soldiers now and then, as an example of what a coward might expect, was a proper means to the end. At Murfreesboro, in 1864, he shot the color-bearer of one of the infantry regiments which stampeded, and thus succeeded in rallying the men to their duty. At Brentwood he did not hesitate to do the same thing in the effort to check some panic-stricken Confederates. In the fight near West Point, General Chalmers relates how Forrest leaped from his horse and seized one of his troops who was running to the rear, and thrashed him soundly with a stick, forcing him to go back in line.

He was always at the front, and close enough for the naked eye to see what his opponents were doing. He never carried field glasses and rarely used those of his staff. As the opposing lines were approaching, he took his place at the skirmish line almost always on his horse. He practiced this from the first days of the war to the last, and his custom was followed more and more by other officers as their experience increased. General Chalmers states that as the battle at Franklin, in 1864, was about to begin, there were with Forrest five general officers upon the skirmish line at one point on the day of that fatal engagement. At no time would he remain far in the rear to give orders, but with rare exceptions led his men in action and relied upon his staff to deliver messages to his subordinate commanders. He would change from point to point, wherever he found the line hardest pressed, and none about him ever found it necessary to ask where the general could be found, but rode straight to that part of the field where the firing was heaviest.

The fact that Forrest was so often wounded, and that he had twenty-nine horses shot, some of these being several times struck before they fell, bears witness that his method of warfare was dangerous business, but whether or not it was a grave military fault is a question for discussion. Nothing so inspires that most important factor in battle, the private soldier, with such determination to conquer and with such disregard for his own life as to be led into action by a commander who is willing to take the same risk that his soldiers take, and who stays with them in the thickest of the fray.

Upon the Union side, Sheridan more nearly resembled Forrest in this particular than any other of the opposing generals, and there was no fighter of cavalry in the Federal army who could compare with him in the enthusiasm his presence aroused or in the ability to bring out the best fighting qualities of his troops. Mr. Charles A. Dana, in his interesting memoirs, says in effect that when he asked Sheridan if he thought it was best for him thus to expose himself so frequently and with such seeming disregard for his personal safety, the great cavalry-man replied that he thought it was, since his men believed in him and would fight better because he was always with them at the front.

Notwithstanding Forrest's eagerness to have a personal hand in the fray, it would be unjust to his ability as a general to conclude that he at any time lost sight of the obligations he owed as a commander to the troops that were with him on the field. In his heavier battles, where success depended upon the proper direction of his various commands, he remained close in the rear, moving from point to point behind his lines where he thought his presence was most needed.

It was in the smaller fights, where the men he commanded were immediately about him, that he led and took part in these desperate hand-to-hand encounters. Thus at Bogler's Creek all the fighting done was by not more than five hundred troops, who were immediately about General Forrest. In the various desperate encounters in the pursuit of William Sooy Smith from West Point toward Memphis, where much fighting of this character was done by the general, there were at no time over one thousand Southern troops immediately engaged. There were fewer at Sacramento, Monterey, and other smaller and hard-fought hand-to-hand melees. At Chickamauga, Brice's Crossroads, Harrisburg, and other battles where a large number of troops were engaged and had to be looked after, he took no part in the fighting because he knew he was more needed in the general direction of affairs.

The value of the flank movement seemed to have occurred to Forrest in the very first action in which he was engaged. His tactics were to throw out skirmishers dismounted, who would engage the enemy from the front and attract their attention. He would then maneuver his troops in such a way as to keep his adversary in constant expectation of an attack. Meanwhile, having picked out a certain proportion of his troops (and for this he usually selected the more daring and reckless of his men), they would sweep around and under cover of timber or some intervening rise of ground to gain the rear and flank of his opposing forces. The moment he saw any suggestion of alarm or confusion in their ranks, or as soon as the firing from his flanking column in their attack was heard, he would charge in the front with every soldier in his command. He did not weaken his fighting strength by holding a proportion in reserve. The most instructive illustration of his employment of the flank attack was in the action at Brice's Crossroads, and it is probable that the small force of less than three hundred men, detached five miles from the battlefield for an attack on the flank and rear, saved the day for him in that desperately fought engagement. Their appearance at the critical moment caused the detachment of a strong body of troops from the main line, and at this juncture Forrest made his final and successful attack.

Very early in the war Forrest had learned that men on horseback could do slight execution with firearms as compared to those dismounted and taking advantage of all possible means for protection and steadiness of aim, and he adopted this method of fighting, using his horses chiefly for transporting his troops.

In 1856, General Dabney H. Maury, then an officer of minor grade in the regular army, so favorably impressed the Secretary of War with a system of tactics for mounted infantry which he had evolved that the method was adopted and demonstrated practically with one or two regiments of troops on duty with the hostile Indians on the plains. Of this Forrest, of course, knew nothing, and, while not novel, it was original with him. It may justly be claimed that he established this important feature of warfare as a part of military science.

In fighting his men dismounted, he would not always conform to the rule of having every fourth man act as horse-holder. At times a single trooper would hold his own and seven other horses, and in certain extreme cases the entire command was made to dismount and hitch their horses to fences or trees, thus carrying every man into action. On one of these occasions, when some of his officers who were drilled in the cavalry manual suggested to him the danger of leaving the animals unprotected, he remarked: "It won't make any difference this time. I need the men to whip the enemy, and if they do not whip them they'll have no need for horses." It is stated in the records that Forrest at one time proposed to press into service old men beyond, and boys well under, the conscription age, to be carried along with the troops to act as horse-holders, while the able-bodied men went into the fight.

In fighting his artillery, when occasion demanded he used them as if they were shotguns, charging right up to the opposing lines, pouring in their double-shotted contents at short range. While this, as Colonel Kelley says, would seem madness in an ordinary commander, the practice was vindicated by the splendid results he won.

Stonewall Jackson said: "Always mystify, mislead, and surprise the enemy if possible. When you strike and overcome him, never give up the pursuit as long as your men have strength to follow; for an army routed, if hotly pursued, becomes panic-stricken, and can then be destroyed by half its number."

No man demonstrated the truth of this axiom in war more successfully than General Forrest. His fierce and untiring two-day pursuit of Sturgis from the battlefield of Brice's Crossroads has scarcely a parallel in history, while that of William Sooy Smith from West Point toward Memphis, and of Streight in the famous raid of 1863, are brilliant illustrations of the value of this method of warfare. On the other hand, in covering the retreat of Hood from Tennessee, Forrest demonstrated that in defensive methods he was equally as successful as in attack.

General Forrest was keenly appreciative of the necessity of giving his personal attention to the smallest details connected with his military operations in order to achieve success. He was not content to accept reports from even his most trusted and faithful subordinates, but he made careful inspection of his artillery, the harness, and the condition of the animals as well as the men, and held his officers strictly accountable for keeping his command supplied with ammunition, forage, and rations. Nothing seemed to escape his careful scrutiny. When on the march, which usually began at daylight, he would take his place by the roadside and observe regiment after regiment as they passed before him. He would then mount his horse and ride through the column from rear to front. If it were raining and he saw a cartridge box exposed to the weather, the delinquent need expect no mercy from the commander. If in crossing a stream a soldier permitted his ammunition to get wet, he might consider himself fortunate to escape with a reprimand.

His quick eye readily detected a lame or tender-footed animal, or one that did not seem to be well fed or properly cared for. A veteran of Forrest's command informed the writer that on one occasion the general ordered him to leave the ranks, remarking: "Why do you let your horse's back get sore? Take your saddle off and let me see what's the matter." The animal's back was found to be chafed. Forrest reprimanded him, and dismounted to give him a practical lesson in the manner of rolling the blanket so that the pressure would be taken from the abraded surface. As he rode away, the general remarked: "You must never again let me see you riding a horse with a sore back; there is no need of it." A few days later the general recognized the same trooper, and also noticed that he had not fixed the blanket as he had been instructed, and, narrating the circumstance, the trooper said: "I did not get off so easily that time. The general gave me hell, but it taught me a lesson I never forgot."

The axiom that "an army, like a snake, must travel on its belly" seemed a part of his military faith. His mind seemed as busy with the problems of the commissary and the quartermaster as with the active operations on the field. In all of the numerous incursions which Forrest made within the Union lines, the country was scoured in every direction for supplies. Every pound of lead, powder, leather, and other articles which were scarce in the Confederacy was gathered up and sent south. Late in the war, he even went so far as to strip the wagon wheels of their tires, and in this way took out with him enough iron to shoe the horses of his command. He not only sent out details to collect deserters and to aid the officers in conscripting, but one of their chief duties was to gather up cattle, horses, mules, and hogs to be taken away. In retreating, he would often fight day after day and incur great risks in order to protect his supplies.

In the west Tennessee expedition of 1863, when escape in all other directions was barred by strong detachments of the enemy sent to capture him, rather than desert his wagon train he passed within sight of the church steeples of Memphis and its garrison of several thousand Federals with a drove of cattle and hogs, and brought the entire convoy safely to his rendezvous in Mississippi. After the overwhelming defeat of Hood at Nashville, he so successfully held back the Federals that he not only saved the wagon train and artillery, and crossed the Tennessee, bringing the animals back for the remaining wagons, but, more than this, brought safe to Duck River a drove of hogs and cattle which he had gathered up in the neighborhood of Murfreesboro—and this in the dead of winter, which made progress exceedingly difficult.

The precautions he took for the comfort and safety of his men were fully appreciated, and formed one of the strong bonds of attachment between the soldiers and their commander. When they bivouacked for the night in proximity to the enemy, he never rested until he saw in person that the pickets were properly posted, and that experienced and reliable men were detailed for important duties. His men felt the most implicit reliance in this watchful care of themselves. A lieutenant of the escort said: "We had that confidence in him which I imagine the Old Guard had in Napoleon. On one occasion, while we were supposed to be in a very dangerous position, with the enemy all about us, we were ordered to go into camp for the night. There were some new recruits with us, who, seeing the older members of the command preparing to lie down and go to sleep, said: 'You don't expect to lie down and go to sleep with the enemy all around you, do you?' The answer was: 'Of course we do; General Forrest told us to do it.' "

A strong point in the military make-up of Forrest was the careful study he made of the officers and men immediately about him, and upon whom he was forced to depend for the delivery and execution of his instructions. He observed them closely in camp, on the march, in action, and his clear judgment enabled him soon to distinguish those upon whom he could depend in the hour of need, and also to determine to what special kind of duty each was best adapted. A subordinate wrote him on one occasion that a certain outpost was such a tempting point for illicit traffic with the enemy that every officer who had been placed there had yielded to the temptation and become corrupt and worse than useless from a military point of view. He suggested to the general that a certain officer, to whom Forrest was much attached, be sent to the post, and who, on account of a recent severe wound, was at that time not fit for duty in the field. Forrest's reply stated that "the officer you mention is one of my best and bravest soldiers, but when money is in question he will not do to tie to."

Forrest's ingenuity seemed capable of surmounting each obstacle as it presented itself. In crossing streams where there were no ferries or bridges, if the water were sufficiently deep to wet the caissons, he would have the ammunition chests emptied and the charges carried over by the men on horseback, each man holding his burden well above the water as his horse floundered across. If the water were deep enough to swim the animals, and thus render it dangerous to attempt this method of transportation, he would construct a raft, or use any dugouts or skiffs or small boats of any description that could be obtained, in or upon which the powder and ammunition were floated over.

On a number of occasions, when by careful measurement it was determined that this method could be safely employed, he would have a floor or layer of rails placed upon the top of the bed of an empty wagon, and upon this temporary platform the ammunition would be placed and carried over dry. Double teams of horses or mules, which had been made to swim to the opposite bank, would then be hitched to one end of a stout rope, the other end of which was attached to the tongue and double trees of the wagon, and in this novel manner it would be drawn across. The artillery would in like manner be dragged along the bottom of the stream, at times completely out of sight until it appeared at the opposite bank. The crossing of Black Creek and other streams in this manner enabled him to overtake Colonel Streight in the memorable raid of 1863.

In the rapid march upon Memphis, in 1864, when he caused the withdrawal of Smith's army from Mississippi, the object of his expedition became threatened with defeat by the sudden and unexpected rise in two streams which it became necessary for him to cross. It was here that he constructed the half-pontoon and half-suspension bridges, using grapevines as cables, supporting these by cypress logs and driftwood, which he floated in the middle of the stream between the cables. These watercourses he crossed in an incredibly short period of time, which, had he stopped to construct upright bridges or to build boats, would have delayed him for at least twenty-four hours and placed his command in great danger. His practice of taking advantage of islands with narrow sloughs of water between them and the mainland, in order to conceal his troops from passing gunboats, and as places of refuge when the enemy were in close pursuit, is an example of the natural shrewdness which he possessed and is worthy of imitation.

In view of what Forrest accomplished, it may well be surmised that had his genius for war been reinforced by a proper education and a systematic military training, he would have won a still higher place among the great soldiers of the world.

Notes

a. It may not be generally known that at this period Major General H. W. Halleck, commander in chief of the department in which General Grant was operating, discussed the propriety of removing him from command; and that General George B. McClellan, general in chief of the armies of the United States, was prepared to approve the action of Halleck. Had it not been for the irretrievable blunder of permitting the surrender of the army at Fort Donelson, the escape of this garrison added to the failure at Belmont and Fort Henry would have deprived Grant of the great popularity which this victory gave him, and would have encouraged Halleck and McClellan to depose him from command.

The following dispatches from the *Official Records* corroborate this statement:

St. Louis, *February,* 1862

To Brigadier-General Buell, Louisville, Kentucky—Without the aid of Hunter, I should have failed before Fort Donelson. Honor to him. We came within an ace of being defeated. If the fragments which I sent down had not reached there on Saturday, we should have gone in. A retreat at one time seemed almost inevitable.

H. W. Halleck.

Headquarters, St. Louis, *February* 19, 1862

Major General H. W. Halleck to Major General McClellan—Brigadier-General Charles F. Smith, by his coolness and bravery at Fort Donelson, when the battle was against us, turned the tide and carried the enemy's outworks. Make him a major-general. You can't get a better one. Honor him for his victory and the whole world will applaud.

St. Louis, *March* 3, 1862

Major General H. W. Halleck to Major General George B. McClellan, Washington, D.C.—I have no communication from Grant for more than a week. He left his command without my authority and went to Nashville. His army seems to be as much demoralized by the victory of Fort Donelson as was that of the Potomac by the defeat of Bull Run. It is hard to censure a successful general immediately after a victory, but I think he richly deserves it. I can get no returns—no information of any kind. Satisfied with his victory, he sits down and enjoys it without any regard to the future. I am worn out and tired with this neglect and inefficiency. C. F. Smith is almost the only officer equal to the emergency.—*Official Records,* vol. vii, pp. 623, 637, 679.

WASHINGTON, *March* 3, 1862, 6 P.M.

MAJOR GENERAL H. W. HALLECK, St. Louis—Your despatch of last evening received. The future success of our cause demands that proceedings such as Grant's should at once be checked. Generals must observe discipline as well as private soldiers. Do not hesitate to arrest him at once if the good of the service requires it, and place C. F. Smith in command. You are at liberty to regard this as a positive order if it will smooth your way.

I appreciate the difficulties you have to encounter, and will be glad to relieve you from trouble as far as possible.

GEORGE B. McCLELLAN,
Major-General, Commanding U.S. Army

Approved

ST. LOUIS, March 4th

To MAJOR GENERAL GEORGE B. McCLELLAN, Washington—A rumor has just reached me that, since the taking of Fort Donelson, General Grant has resumed his former bad habits. If so, it will account for his neglect of my often repeated orders. I do not deem it advisable to arrest him at present, but have placed General Smith in command of the expedition up the Tennessee. I think Smith will restore order and discipline.

H. W. HALLECK.

ADJUTANT GENERAL'S OFFICE, WASHINGTON, *March* 10, 1862

MAJOR GENERAL H. W. HALLECK, U.S.A., Commanding Department of the Mississippi, St. Louis, Missouri—It has been reported that soon after the battle of Fort Donelson Brigadier-General Grant left his command without leave. By direction of the President, the Secretary of War desires you to ascertain and report whether General Grant left his command at any time without proper authority, and, if so, how long; whether he has made to you proper reports and returns of his force; whether he has committed any acts which were unauthorized or not in accordance with military subordination or property, and, if so, what?

L. THOMAS, Adjutant-General

Official Records, vol. ii, pp. 680, 682, 683

On March 4th, General Grant received the following despatch from General H. W. Halleck:

MAJOR-GENERAL U. S. GRANT, Fort Henry—You will place Major-General C. F. Smith in command of the expedition, and remain yourself at Fort Henry. Why do you not obey my orders, to report the strength and position of your men?

Your going to Nashville without authority, and when your presence with your troops was of the utmost importance, was a matter of very serious complaint at Washington, so much so that I was advised to arrest you on your return.

General Grant, in his *Memoirs,* says that "less than two weeks after the victory at Donelson the two leading generals in the army were in correspondence as to what disposal should be made of me, and in less than three weeks I was virtually in arrest and without a command." And later (p. 370): "I was ignored (by Halleck) as much as if I had been at the most distant point of territory within my jurisdiction. Although in command of all the troops engaged at

Shiloh, I was not permitted to see one of the reports of General Buell or his subordinates in that battle."

"General Halleck evidently deemed General C. F. Smith a much better officer for the command of all the forces in the military district than I was. It is probable that the general opinion was that Smith's long services in the army and distinguished deeds rendered him the more proper person for such command. Indeed, I was rather inclined to this opinion myself at that time, and would have served as faithfully under General Smith as he had done under me."

Later on, General Grant, as shown in his *Memoirs,* explained satisfactorily the various criticisms of his chief (vol. i, pp. 326, 328), but those would not have sufficed to have saved him had not the Northern people at large upheld him by reason of the capture of the army at Fort Donelson. This unnecessary surrender made General Grant's great career possible. It made Shiloh a disaster when the Confederates should have crushed and captured the national army. If anyone doubts this, let him read the *Official Records,* especially the report by General D. C. Buell, the second in command there.

b. Dr. Smith, on January 1, 1897, made the following sworn statement:

"I am seventy-eight years of age, and have resided in Dover, Tennessee, since 1853. My occupation had been practising medicine up to a few years ago, when I retired. I was born and reared on a farm one mile from Dover, near the ford of Lick Creek, on the Dover and Clarksville road. My father and I have owned this farm and this ford, now known as 'Smith's Ford,' for over seventy-five years. From my earliest boyhood I have been familiar with this road and creek. On the night of the 15th of February, 1862, about eleven o'clock, I was required by my fellow-townsman, J. E. Rice, to go with him to the room of General J. B. Floyd. I accompanied him to Floyd, finding him in his private quarters, with his aides. As soon as I reached General Floyd he placed before me a map of the battle-ground of Fort Donelson, which had been drawn by General Buckner. Finding that I understood the map and was familiar with the ground, roads, and creeks, General Floyd requested me to go out· on the Clarksville road and investigate and examine the ford of Lick Creek. He requested me specially to ascertain the depth of the water in said ford, whether or not it was possible to cross it on horseback, and to report as soon as practicable to him at the residence of Mr. Rice, in Dover, where he went to hold a council of war. I went to said ford, examined carefully, and found the water just high enough to reach the saddle-skirts on a horse of medium size. It was easily fordable. There were no Federals in that locality, and I returned by way of the big road to the city, and found Generals Floyd, Pillow, Buckner, and Colonel Forrest holding a conference at the house of Mr. Rice, and made my report, assuring him that the road was open and that the creek could be crossed. This was about midnight. General Pillow declared in my hearing that the army could get out and that the attempt should be then made. General Buckner entertained the opposite opinion, saying that an effort to take the army out then would bring on a night engagement, which would result in the loss of three-fourths of their command, and that no commander had the right to sacrifice his men in a hopeless encounter. Colonel Forrest expressed a desire to make an attempt to carry the army out, saying he would look after the rear. About two hours later Forrest went out and crossed at the ford of Lick Creek, on the Dover and Clarksville road above mentioned. I went with him, and was separated from the troops at the main ford. I crossed at the

Hay ford, about three hundred yards above the Dover and Clarksville road. *The water where I crossed was not exceeding eighteen inches deep, and there were no Federals nearer that point at that time than Bufford's place, which is about one mile from the main ford where Forrest crossed."*

c. Colonel Daniel R. Russell, of the Twentieth Mississippi Regiment, testified: "My son made his escape with Adjutant Couper and Lieutenant Conway after they were ordered to stack arms. They waded the slough, which my son says was about breast-high to him, and then they marched, without encountering the enemy, to the railroad, reaching it at Columbia, Tennessee. Williford made his escape after the boat left." (*Official Records,* vol. vii, p. 416.)

General Gideon J. Pillow reported the sworn testimony of Captain Hinson, Dr. Moore, Captain Newberry, and Lieutenant Hollister, all of whom testify that the enemy had not reinvested our position or army on the night of the 15th of February, as was then supposed, and never did reinvest, and that the army was surrendered under a delusion, and that it could have marched out on the night of the 15th or morning of the 16th of February without any obstacle or opposition. (*Official Records,* vol. vii, p. 325.)

Brigadier General Bushrod Johnson, who escaped after the surrender, said: "It is proper to state that many of the men and officers commenced to leave Fort Donelson as soon as they heard of the proposed surrender, and hundreds of them have no doubt made their way to their homes and to the army. I have not learned that a single one who attempted to escape met with any obstacle." (*Ibid.,* p. 364.)

Captain B. G. Bidwell writes from Weatherford, Texas, in 1899: "I escaped from Fort Donelson early Sunday morning by crossing the Cumberland River in a skiff with Captain Frank Duffy, of the Thirty-fifth Tennessee. When we crossed we could have been seen by the Federal troops, but they had not then come into Dover." (*Ibid.*)

Lieutenant Colonel Milton A. Haynes says: "On Saturday night Captain Bidwell and one private of artillery, Lieutenant Burt, and about forty men, and all the horses of Captain Porter's light battery and Colonel Forrest's regiment of cavalry, and many stragglers from various corps made good their retreat without meeting any obstruction from the enemy."

In further proof that the reinvestment had not been effected by Grant's right wing, the following evidence from two well-known residents of Dover, Tennessee, is given.

Mr. G. W. Bufford swears: "I am seventy-one years of age, was born and have lived most of my life in what is known as the Bufford place, which was known during the war as Rollins's or Bufford's place, where I now live, one mile south of Dover. I was living in said town of Dover in February, 1862. My mother lived at that time on the said Bufford farm. I knew all the ground between the Bufford place and Lick Creek ford, where Forrest and his army crossed as they went out of Dover on the morning of February 16th. I stayed at said Rollins's or Bufford place, where my mother lived, on Saturday night, February 15, 1862 (after the battle), and went over the territory embraced between said town, said ford, and said Bufford place next morning after Forrest went out. There were no Federal troops between said points Sunday morning early. I went to said ford on Saturday evening before, and there were no Federal soldiers nearer said ford than the said Bufford place." (Date of affidavit, January 4, 1898.)

Mr. Ed Walter swears: "I am fifty years of age, and resided with my father's family in Dover, Tennessee, in 1862. As a matter of safety, the family, I going with them, moved out of town to a place on the Dover and Clarksville road, near the ford of Lick Creek, where General Forrest and his soldiers crossed on the morning of February 16th. I passed over said road from Dover to Lick Creek early Sunday morning, Forrest having escaped over said road the previous night. I advised several Confederate soldiers to go out, as the way was open and there were no Federals in sight. I saw Confederates crossing Lick Creek, and aided some to cross as late as ten o'clock Sunday morning. The Federal forces came into Dover by way of Fort Henry road and Wynn's Ferry road, which intersects the Dover and Charlotte road one-half mile south of town. In company with my brother, now dead, I passed over the territory between the Dover and Clarksville road and the Dover and Charlotte road, and I know there were no Federal soldiers between said roads." (Date of affidavit, February 18, 1898.)

d. "Johnston was now relieved of the command, and Hood superseded him. For my own part, I think that Johnston's tactics were right. Anything that could have prolonged the war a year beyond the time that it did finally close would probably have exhausted the North to such an extent that they might then have abandoned the contest and agreed to a separation.

"Johnston's policy was the best one that could have been pursued by the whole South—protract the war, which was all that was necessary to enable them to gain recognition in the end. The North was already growing weary, as the South evidently was also, but with this difference: in the North the people governed, and could stop hostilities whenever they chose to stop supplies. The South was a military camp, controlled absolutely by the government, with soldiers to back it, and the war could have been protracted, no matter to what extent the discontent reached, up to the point of open mutiny of the soldiers themselves."—*Memoirs of U. S. Grant,* vol. ii, pp. 167, 345.

e. There were in all twenty-seven regiments of Confederate infantry at Fort Donelson. (*Official Records,* vol. vii.) In sixteen of these the number present is specifically stated, namely:

Second Kentucky	600	Thirtieth Tennessee (page 377,	
Eighth Kentucky	312	Head's Regiment)	450
First Mississippi	331	Thirty-second Tennessee (page	
Third Mississippi	546	351)	555
Fourteenth Mississippi	650	Forty-first Tennessee	575
Twentieth Mississippi (page 380)	500	Forty-second Tennessee (page	
Twenty-sixth Mississippi	443	371, Quarles's Regiment)	498
Third Tennessee	750	Forty-ninth Tennessee (page 392)	300
Eighteenth Tennessee (page 351)	685	Seventh Texas	360
Twenty-sixth Tennessee	410		
		Total officers and men	7965

The following regiments are named, and the strength of the brigades is given in the official reports:

Heiman's brigade: Tenth, Fifty-third (Abernathy's), and Forty-eighth Tennessee (Voorhies's), and Twenty-seventh Alabama (Hughes's)—in all 1600. Drake's brigade: Fourth Mississippi, Fifteenth Arkansas, two companies of the

Twenty-sixth Alabama, and Browder's fragment, 60 strong—total Drake's brigade, 100. (*Official Records,* vol. vii, pp. 366, 367.)

This gives a total of 10,565 officers and men for twenty-two regiments. The two companies of the Twenty-sixth Alabama and Browder's Battalion are included.

Of the foregoing, the average number per regiment is 480.

It is stated that Abernathy's, Voorhies's and Hughes's regiments were decimated by an epidemic of measles, and did not exceed 200 men each for duty. (*Official Records,* vol. vii, p. 290.)

The strength of the Fiftieth, Fifty-first, Fifty-sixth, and Thirty-sixth Virginia, and Fiftieth Tennessee regiments is not given. General Pillow states (*Official Records,* vol. vii, p. 290) that the four Virginia regiments did not exceed 350 each. It will be a liberal estimate to allow these four regiments the average 480, as determined above, making a total of 2400. Estimating Colme's unattached battalion at 200, we have a grand total of 13,165 officers and men of the infantry.

The Forrest Battalion	800
Gantt's demi-battalion	300
Milton's, Williams's, Wilcox's, and Hewitt's companies—each 60	240
Total cavalry under Forrest	1340

In addition to the water and fort batteries of Maury, Dixon, and Culbertson, *manned by the infantry,* and so counted, there were the field batteries of Graves, Porter, Jackson, Maney, Gúy, and Green—estimated at 50 each, or a total of 300 artillerists. The grand total is, therefore:

Infantry	13,165
Cavalry	1,340
Artillery	300
Total	14,805

f. Captain Gurley's gallant conduct in this campaign attracted the attention of General Forrest. He not only mentioned him in his report, as deserving great credit, but, as a token of appreciation for meritorious services on two occasions, he presented him with a fine horse and a pair of pistols.

A few months prior this same officer, in a skirmish near Huntsville, in northern Alabama, mortally wounded and captured General Robert L. McCook. The report of this occurrence given in the official records reflects unjustly upon the reputation of Captain Gurley as a man and soldier. The facts connected with it are here correctly given:

With his own and a part of Hambrick's company, of Russell's regiment, sixty men in all, he had been dispatched for special duty upon the enemy's communication in northern Alabama. Having heard that a drove of beef cattle was coming on the Limestone road from Athens, Alabama, to Winchester, Tennessee, he marched to intercept and capture them. Having reached the highway, he halted his command, leaving them in charge of Captain Hambrick while he rode forward in order to reconnoiter. Having gone about a mile, just as he reached the top of a hill he discovered a body of Union cavalry very near and coming toward him. He immediately fired at them, and started to run towards his command. Seeing him pursued, his troops formed in line and concealed themselves in the woods near the side of the road. In order to decoy his pursuers into the trap, Gurley passed by his men and when the head of the Union column came opposite to the Confederate ambush they were stampeded by a volley fired into them at close range. Gurley immediately turned his horse and ordered his command to charge in among them. The Federals fled down the road in great disorder, with the Confederates in hot pursuit. The road was exceedingly dry and dusty, and as Gurley, at the head of his men, dashed on, he saw dimly through the cloud of dust that had been raised by the flying troopers a school wagon drawn by two horses at a runaway pace and making desperate efforts to keep up with the Union cavalry which had passed them in the rout.

Gurley says: "As I was coming upon them, I made out the driver and two other men sitting in the wagon—one an officer in full uniform and the other in his shirt-sleeves. I shouted to them to halt and surrender, but still the horses dashed down the road in the trail of their cavalry. As they did not halt I fired at them, as did several others of my command, who were well up with myself. Selecting the officer in uniform, Captain Brooke, as an important personage, I had fired at him three times, when at this moment the carriage or school-wagon ran under a peach-tree that knocked off the entire top of the vehicle, and not until then did the driver stop his horses, and I rode up beside the party. The officer in uniform remarked 'This man is shot,' referring to the one in his shirt-sleeves, at whom I had not directed my aim. I noticed then that he had on the uniform pants of the Federal army. I asked the driver why he had not stopped his horse when ordered. The wounded man said that he could not stop them. I did not know then who the wounded person was, nor did I ask, for I passed immediately to the front, leaving them with some of my men. Some little distance farther down the road the cavalry, which we were still pursuing, came up with a column of infantry, and, turning about with this infantry, they drove us off through the woods. Later in the evening when I reached our rendezvous the officer at whom I had fired, Captain Hunter Brooke, was in the camp a prisoner, and then informed me that the man who had been wounded in the carriage was General Robert L. McCook."

It has been stated that General McCook was ill at the time, and was riding in an ambulance. The vehicle was a school wagon or light carriage, much used in that section of the country before the war. It had steps and a door of entrance from behind, and the seats were parallel along each side. General McCook was not undressed, but simply had his coat off, and, as the weather was intensely hot, this was no indication of invalidism. He was sitting upright as the wagon sped along, and Captain Gurley could not have known that he was suffering from any indisposition. In fact, he fired at the other officer for the reason that he was trying to shoot the one whose uniform gave him an appearance of importance.

According to the report of Colonel Van Derveer (*Official Records,* vol. xvi, part i, p. 841), the Federal troops were so enraged at the shooting of General McCook that "many of the soldiers spread themselves over the country and burned all the property of rebels in the vicinity, and shot a rebel lieutenant who was on furlough," etc. A year after this occurrence Captain Gurley was captured and tried by a Federal court-martial for the murder of McCook and sentenced to be hanged. The Confederate government intervened and prevented the execution under threat of retaliation, and after that he was treated as a prisoner of war. When peace was declared he was again arrested, placed in irons, and carried to Nashville, Tennessee, and imprisoned, and later on was taken to Huntsville,

Alabama, and there kept in jail for many months. He was ultimately liberated, and has since been honored with a high official position by his own people. Beloved and respected by all in the community where he has spent a long and useful life, his record is unsullied.

The death of General McCook was much to be regretted, but under the circumstances Captain Gurley did no more than his duty as a soldier.

g. The foregoing account is taken from the manuscript of Mrs. Johnson, in possession of the author. Miss Emma Sansom married Mr. C. B. Johnson, of Company I, Tenth Alabama regiment, October 29, 1864. They moved to Texas in 1876, where her husband died in 1887, leaving her with seven children—five boys and two girls. If they inherit the courage of their mother the world should be the better for their coming. The Legislature of Alabama in 1899 voted her, as a token of "admiration and gratitude," a gift of 640 acres of land, commemorative of her heroic action. The note of thanks written by General Forrest in lead pencil on the stained leaf of an old pocket memorandum or account book was presented to the writer by Mrs. Johnson, and is doubly treasured by him as coming from such a woman and written by such a man.

h. The First brigade, commanded by Colonel J. J. Neely, comprised the Seventh (Colonel W. L. Duckworth), Twelfth (Lieutenant Colonel J. U. Green), Fourteenth (Colonel J. J. Neely), and Fifteenth (Colonel F. M. Stewart) Tennessee regiments.

The Second brigade, commanded by Colonel Robert McCulloch, comprised the Second Missouri (Lieutenant Colonel R. A. McCulloch), Willis's Texas battalion (Lieutenant Colonel Leo Willis), First Mississippi Partisans (Major J. M. Parks), Fifth Mississippi Cavalry (Major W. B. Peery), Nineteenth Mississippi battalion (Lieutenant Colonel W. L. Duff), Eighteenth Mississippi battalion (Lieutenant Colonel A. H. Chalmers), and McDonald's battalion—Forrest's old regiment—(Lieutenant Colonel J. M. Crews).

The Third brigade, commanded by Colonel A. P. Thompson, comprised the Third (Lieutenant Colonel G. A. C. Holt), Seventh (Colonel Ed. Crossland), Eighth (Colonel H. B. Lyon), and Twelfth (Faulkner's) Kentucky regiments, and Jeffrey Forrest's regiment (Lieutenant Colonel D. M. Wisdom).

The Fourth brigade, commanded by General T. H. Bell, comprised the Second (Colonel C. R. Barteau), Sixteenth (Colonel A. N. Wilson), and Twentieth (R. M. Russell) Tennessee regiments.

Neely's and McCulloch's brigades were formed into one division, which was placed under Brigadier General James R. Chalmers, while Thompson's and Bell's were organized into another division under General A. Buford.

i. General Shepley was en route from New Orleans to St. Louis on the steamer *Olive Branch.* As this boat approached Fort Pillow she had on board two full batteries of the Seventeenth Corps and a detachment of artillerists. He says that as the boat was approaching, and before it was in sight of Fort Pillow, "some women hailed it from the shore and said that the rebels had attacked Fort Pillow and captured two boats on the river, and would take us if we went on."

The captain of the *Olive Branch* refused to go farther, and turned about to go back to Memphis. General Shepley compelled him to stop, hailed a small steamer approaching from below, and ordered it alongside. "I ordered the captain of this boat to cast off the coal barges he had in tow and take me on board with a section of battery to go to Fort Pillow. While he was trying to disencumber his boat of the coal barges, another boat (the *Cheek*), better fitted for the purpose, hove in sight. Finding that I could get her ready quicker than the other, I had her brought alongside and went aboard myself with Captain Thornton, the ranking officer of the batteries. Before we could get the guns on board, a steamer with troops hove in sight, coming down the river from Fort Pillow. We could not distinguish at first whether they were Union or rebel soldiers. When she approached we saw United States infantry soldiers on board that had just passed the fort. She hailed the *Olive Branch:* 'All right up there; you can go by. The gunboat is lying off the fort.' This steamer was the *Liberty.* We then proceeded up the river in the *Olive Branch.* Near Fort Pillow some stragglers or guerillas fired from the shore with musketry, aiming at the pilot-house. I was then in the pilot-house, and as we kept on I observed that one of the other two boats which followed us at some distance was compelled to put back. The *Olive Branch* kept on, to report to the gunboat at the station. An officer came off from the gunboat in a smaller boat and said he did not want any boat to stop; ordered us to go to Cairo and tell Captain —— to send him immediately four hundred rounds of ammunition. *There was no firing at the fort at this time. The Union flag was flying, and after we had passed the fort we could see a flag of truce outside the fortifications. No signal of any kind was made to the boat from the fort or from the shore. No intimation was given us from the gunboat, which had the right to order a steamer of this description, other than the order to proceed to Cairo and send down the ammunition."* (Italics not in original.)

j. The fate of Major Bradford, although he escaped even a wound in the capture of Fort Pillow, was eventually as tragic as it was unwarrantable. He had been one of the most "active loyal Tennesseans" in the enlistment of the citizens of this section of his native state in the Union army. As the vast majority of the citizens here were Southern sympathizers, a very bitter feeling toward him was the result. A great many of the soldiers in Forrest's command felt that they had a personal grievance against this man, and it is not a matter of great surprise that opportunity was taken to wreak private revenge upon him at this time. Indeed, it is proof of the control that Forrest had over his men that he was not shot even after the surrender at Fort Pillow. Just after the capture of this fort, when the prisoners were being moved away, Major Bradford was placed under the charge of Colonel Robert McCulloch, and he requested to be permitted to superintend the burial of his brother, who had been killed in the action. He gave his parole of honor that he would report again to the Confederates in their camp that night as soon as his brother was interred. (This statement is made in *Campaigns of General N. B. Forrest;* and in a letter to the author from Colonel Robert McCulloch, written in 1898, he states that the account given in these *Campaigns* is correct.) Suffice it to say that Major Bradford did not report to his captors. Instead of returning, he escaped in the darkness, and was recaptured in citizen's clothes on the day after the battle, near Covington, by one of Colonel W. L. Duckworth's scouts. He was brought into the camp and delivered to this officer. (Manuscripts from Colonel W. L. Duckworth, in 1898 in possession of the author.) On the 14th of April, Colonel Duckworth sent him with other prisoners to the headquarters of Brigadier General Chalmers at Brownsville. On the following day Major Bradford was with other prisoners sent under guard by General Chalmers in the direction of Jackson, Tennessee, to the headquarters of General Forrest. Colonel Duckworth writes that "when they were about three miles from Brownsville the guards took Bradford a short distance from the road into a thicket of woods and shot him." There is nothing in the records to show that the men who murdered Major Bradford were ever brought to trial for this unwarrantable act.

k. On April 18th a subcommittee was appointed to take "testimony in regard to the massacre at Fort Pillow." The spirit which impelled these bitter partisans is in evidence in the opening lines of their report: "Although your committee were instructed to inquire only in reference to the attack, capture, and massacre at Fort Pillow, they have deemed it proper to take some testimony in reference to the operations of Forrest and his command immediately preceding and subsequent to that horrible transaction. (*Rebellion Record,* vol. viii, doc. i, p. 1.)

This committee reported in substance:

"1. That Forrest, in violation of the rules governing civilized warfare, had taken advantage of the existence of a truce to place a portion of his command in a position favorable for assault, which position he could not have obtained but for the prevalence of the truce.

"2. That after the fort had been carried by storm, an indiscriminate slaughter, which spared 'neither age nor sex, white nor black, soldier nor civilian,' was carried on.

"3. That after the fighting had ceased, several of the wounded of the garrison were intentionally burned to death in the barracks and tents which were destroyed by fire.

"4. That the 'rebels buried some of the living with the dead.'"

It concludes the report by saying: "Many other instances of equally atrocious cruelty might be enumerated, but your committee feel compelled to refrain from giving here more of the heart-sickening details!"

In regard to the charge of a violation of the flag of truce by Forrest, it has already been shown by the official report of Brigadier General Shepley of the Union army that while the truce was in force a steamer loaded with Federal soldiers was approaching Fort Pillow, where a battle was pending, and when the Federal garrison was in need of succor and looking for relief; and that General Shepley, on another steamer, with artillery on board, was also steaming toward the fort, intent on going to the rescue of the beleaguered garrison. This officer says: "*No signal of any kind was made to the boat from the fort or from the shore.*"

The charge that at this time Forrest advanced his forces to a more favorable position for assault is refuted in the official reports of the very committee which framed it. The following is taken from their report:

"The gunboat *New Era,* Captain Marshall, took part in the conflict, shelling the enemy as opportunity offered. Signals had been agreed upon by which the officers in the fort could indicate where the guns of the boat would be most effective. There being but one gunboat there, no permanent impression appears to have been produced upon the enemy, for *as they were shelled out of one ravine they would make their appearance in another. They would thus appear and retire as the gunboat moved from one point to another. About one o'clock the fire on both sides slackened somewhat, and the gunboat moved out in the river to coal, clean its guns,*" etc. (*Rebellion Record,* vol. viii. Italics not in original.)

Here is a distinct admission that before 1 P.M., and nearly three hours prior to the truce, the Confederates had full possession of the ravines above as well as below the fort.

The charge of an indiscriminate massacre after the fort was taken, which spared neither age nor sex, white nor black, soldier nor civilian, is equally false with the charge of violation of the truce. In the first place, the Union official reports show there were no women or children in the fort when it was assaulted, and that such of the civilians as desired to go to a place of safety had the opportunity to leave. Those who remained voluntarily took up arms and fought with the garrison. Captain Marshall, of the gunboat, testifies: *"I came along up, and the women and children, some sick negroes, and boys were standing around a great barge. I told them to get into the barge if they wished to save themselves, and I would take them out of danger. They went in, and I towed them up and landed them above Cold Creek ravine, where the rebel sharp-shooters commenced firing at them. I told them to go up to a house. The trees and bushes around them there probably prevented them from being hit. On knowing that they were fired at, I kept a steady fire up to about one o'clock."* The evidence shows that only one of these women was shot.

Dr. C. Fitch, who was surgeon of the Fort Pillow garrison at this time, says: "Early in the morning all of the women and all of the non-combatants were ordered on to some barges, and were towed by a gunboat up the river to an island before any one was hurt." (*Southern Historical Society Papers,* vol. vii, p. 439.)

While it is true that the proportion of killed and wounded of the troops of the garrison engaged was unusually large, it must be borne in mind that the circumstances connected with the assault and capture of Fort Pillow were unusual, and in arriving at a just conclusion as to the cause of the great loss of life every feature of the battle should be carefully considered.

The Federal reports show that they had suffered very great loss in the preliminary engagement before the fort was stormed. Lieutenant M. J. Leaming, adjutant of the Thirteenth Tennessee, swore that Major Booth, the commanding officer, was killed about 9 A.M; that his adjutant fell about the same time. (*Rebellion Record,* vol. viii, p. 23.) He states also that about 8 A.M. two companies of his regiment were compelled to retire into the fort, after considerable loss, in which Lieutenant Barr was killed. "We suffered pretty severely in the loss of commissioned officers *by the unerring aim of the rebel sharp-shooters."* (*Official Records,* vol. xxxii, part i, p. 559.) Lieutenant Van Horn states that at this time Lieutenant John D. Hill was also killed in front of the works. About 11 A.M., Leaming further says, the Union troops failed to destroy the barracks as ordered: "After severe loss on our part in the attempt to execute the order, our men were compelled to retire"; and "from these barracks the enemy kept up a murderous fire on our men despite all our efforts to dislodge them." Finally, where the assault is described in his affidavit, he says, as the Confederates began to climb to the parapet out of the ditch, "in the meantime nearly all the officers had been killed, especially of the colored troops, and there was no one hardly to guide the men. *I do not think the men who broke had a commissioned officer over them."*

In addition to this great loss before the works were gained, when the Confederates swarmed into the fort the slaughter must have been very much greater. The front rank of the assailants leaped right in among the defenders and, placing their guns or pistols practically touching their bodies, inflicted wounds almost of necessity instantly fatal. In this front line there were about six hundred of

Forrest's men, and it is safe to estimate the garrison at not over five hundred at the time the Confederates appeared on the parapet. Six hundred guns and pistols at this close range, in the hands of such experts with firearms as these men were, must have inflicted an exceedingly heavy loss upon the five hundred of the garrison before they broke and fled. As the survivors turned to run, and were in the act of running away, six hundred more guns and pistols opened upon them from the parapet.

Of the original 570 Union troops who were on duty when the battle opened, fully 250 never reached the bluff. When the Federal commander saw the works were lost, as Forrest's men passed the ditch and were clambering upon the parapet, had he lowered his colors, waved a white flag, his troops thrown down their guns and shouted a "surrender," very many lives which were lost then and there would have been saved. But Major Bradford, as his superior, General Hurlbut, stated, was inexperienced, and had agreed, in case the fort was successfully assaulted, to retreat beneath the bluff, as shown by the Federal reports, and *this was his fatal error*. Of those among the garrison who leaped over the bluff, about 275 carried their guns with them.

The conduct of Major Bradford with the garrison points conclusively to the understanding to which Captain Marshall testifies, for as they jumped over the bluff they all ran south along the bank toward the steamboat landing in order to get out of the way of the canister which Marshall, from his gunboat, had agreed to fire into the Confederates as they came in sight. Bradford and his officers and men evidently were not aware of the presence on the face of the bluff, either above or below the fort, of the two heavy detachments of sharpshooters; for as they were rushing pell-mell to give the *New Era* a wide berth for her fire, they ran very near to Captain Anderson's detachment, which now arose from its place of concealment and emptied two hundred muskets into the Union troops, killing and wounding many, and also, unfortunately, shooting some of those already wounded.

Still hoping for escape, the survivors rushed northward along the face of the bluff, only to meet another volley from Colonel Barteau's detachment, which turned them back again; and now the troops who had carried the fort and were lining the top of the bank had had time to reload their guns, and joined in the fusillade. In this crisis, hemmed in on all sides, with escape or succor hopeless, many of those yet unhurt, having thrown down their guns or swords, raised their hands and ran toward the Confederates, begging for their lives. Had there been no exceptions to this conduct a much larger number would have been spared, but a volume of sworn testimony in the writer's possession shows positively that some of the Federal troops continued to resist by firing back at the Confederates.

The desperate character of the resistance made by the Union troops is shown in the report of Major General Hurlbut, made three days after the battle to General McPherson: *"It is unquestionably true that the colored troops fought desperately, and nearly all of them are now killed or wounded."* (*Official Records,* vol. xxxii, part i, p. 554. Italics are not in original.)

Lieutenant Van Horn, who was in the fight, states that the demand for unconditional surrender was returned with a decided refusal. The fight was renewed and raged with fury for some time, when another flag of truce was sent in and another demand for surrender was made. *"They assured us at the same time that they would treat us as prisoners of war.* Another refusal was returned, when they again charged, and succeeded in carrying the works. *There never was a surrender of the fort, both officers and men claiming they would never surrender or ask for quarter."* (*Official Records*, vol. xxxii, part i, p. 570. Italics not in original.)

Forrest's consideration for the wounded at Fort Pillow is fully attested in the official instructions under which Major Anderson proceeded on the morning after the battle to the scene of the fight. "Burn all the houses at the fort, except the one used as a hospital. Leave the Federal surgeon, and such of the wounded as cannot travel or be moved, and parole them; also the prisoners; and leave with them a nurse or two, or slightly wounded men, sufficient to wait upon them. Leave with the wounded five or six days' supply of provisions, and any medicine they may need." (*Official Records*, vol. xxxii, part ii, p. 664.)

Even so bitter a partisan as General Sherman, speaking of this affair in his *Memoirs*, says: "I was told by hundreds of our men, who were at various times prisoners in Forrest's possession, that he was usually very kind to them."

As to the charge that wounded soldiers of the garrison were permitted to be burned in the conflagration which consumed the barracks, shanties, and tents in and about the fort, and that in one or two instances these unfortunate men were pinioned with nails and thus tortured to death, it is so absurd as scarcely to call for notice. Were it true, it could not in any manner reflect upon the character or reputation of General Forrest, who rode away immediately after the fight, and never returned to the scene of the battle. These occurrences were supposed to have taken place on the day following the fight. If any such horrible acts were committed (and no mind capable of reasoning without prejudice can study the testimony and believe they were), they could only have been perpetrated during the night of the 12th and on the morning of the 13th of April, before nine o'clock. After this hour the place was in possession of the Federal officers, under a truce in caring for the wounded. The evidence is undeniable that no Confederates were at Fort Pillow during the night.

At six o'clock on the morning after the fight a small detachment, to look after the wounded and gather up any property which might have been overlooked in the hurried departure at nightfall of the 12th, as well as to secure information, was sent by order of General Chalmers from his camp, about two miles back from the river, to the fort. As these men arrived at the riverbank Captain Ferguson was approaching from the direction of Memphis with his gunboat, the *Silver Cloud*. These, he reports, he shelled away, and then effected a landing and arranged a truce with Captain Anderson of Forrest's staff, who arrived later in the forenoon. Lieutenant Leaming, who was wounded and lying in one of the barrack buildings, corroborates this, as do other officers. The Confederate officer in command of this scouting party, seeing he was to be driven away by the gunboat, proceeded to set fire to the houses and tents, rather than to leave them standing, to be used again by the enemy. During the night several of the badly wounded had died, and their bodies in some of the buildings were consumed in the conflagration.

One of the Union soldiers, J. W. Shelton (white), swears that he was wounded, and in a house with other wounded, and that the Confederates did not burn the house he and the others were in. (*Official Records*, vol. viii, p. 31.) John Pennell (white Federal) swears that he and an officer of artillery were also wounded, and lying in one of the tents; that the Confederates came and told them to get out of the tent, "as they were going to burn it, and wanted to know whether we could walk. I said I could not. They helped me out, and made me walk some, but carried the officer out." They were removed to one of the houses, and later, when this was about to catch fire, they were again prevented from being burned by the warning of an officer. A number of the Federals were also assisting in removing the wounded. Lieutenant Leaming testifies that he was in one of the burning buildings, and was carried out, and "I think others got the rest out."

The committee were diligent in the effort to prove that Lieutenant Akerstrom was burned to death, yet John F. Ray of Akerstrom's regiment (Thirteenth Tennessee) swears that Lieutenant Akerstrom was shot by his side, the ball entering through the forehead, and, as he thought, was killed.

It will, moreover, be recalled that one row of the barracks was burned by the garrison about nine o'clock in the morning of the fight after a desperate struggle in and around these houses, in which a number of Federals and Confederates were killed, and no doubt their charred remains were found among the ruins. Finally, if any of the wounded were buried alive, it must have been done while they were simulating death for fear of being shown no quarter, or because they became so profoundly stupefied from the liquor they had taken as to deceive the burying squad, which, as already shown, *were all soldiers of the garrison.*

It is worthy of comment that of the seventy-eight witnesses who testified in relation to the capture of Fort Pillow, eighteen were not in sight or sound of this place on the day the battle occurred; and yet some of these persons gave most graphic descriptions and detailed accounts of the harrowing scenes. The purpose of the committee is evident in their use of such evidence, and coincides with the view that their report was a "war measure," justified by them for the purpose for which it was intended.

There is further proof that the Federal authorities did not believe that a massacre really took place. On April 15th, General Grant dispatched to Sherman: "If our men have been murdered after capture, retaliation must be resorted to promptly." (*Official Records,* vol. xxxii, part iii, p. 336.)

Secretary of War Stanton, on the day following, directed General Sherman as follows: "You will please direct a competent officer to investigate and report minutely, and as early as possible, the facts in relation to the alleged butchery of our troops at Fort Pillow." As no retaliation was ever made, there is in the fact of this investigation, directed by Stanton and Grant, an admission that no massacre occurred.

The writer of this history has come in personal contact with many of Forrest's officers and men since the war, and these, without exception, made a positive denial under oath of the story of the massacre which the report of the subcommittee of Congress asserted had taken place.

General James R. Chalmers, member of the United States Congress since the war, a lawyer of Memphis, Tennessee, was second in command to General Forrest in this engagement. He swears that the charge of a massacre is absolutely false; that those of the garrison who were sober enough to realize the hopelessness of their situation after the fort was stormed, surrendered, and thus escaped being killed or wounded; that General Forrest rushed into the fort as quickly as he could ride from the position he occupied at the time of the assault, and while the firing was going on beneath the bluff, and after the surrender of most of the whites and some sixty Negroes had taken place, he gave orders to stop the firing, which was done immediately. One Confederate within his observation, who disregarded this order, he personally arrested and placed under guard for the offence.

Some of the Federals, mostly Negroes, who in fright or desperation broke through the Confederates in the effort to escape, were pursued and shot, as were those who attempted to escape by swimming down the river. Some of these were killed and some few succeeded in getting away. He further testifies, "the Federal flag was not lowered and no surrender of the garrison was ever made. As the Federals rushed down the bluff they carried their guns with them, and many of them turned and fired as they retreated, and continued to fire from beneath the bluff, and these were the only men shot after the flag was hauled down."

Brigadier General Tyree H. Bell, now a prominent citizen of Fresno, California, was in command of the right wing of the assaulting column and was among the first to reach the interior of the fort. He states, under oath: "The bugle sounded, and our command moved at once to the assault and scaled the walls of the fort, each man with his gun and navy-six loaded, the garrison firing continuously as they went over. *Our troops never fired a gun until they landed inside the fort. The firing lasted not exceeding three minutes, and there was no more firing from either side.* I went over the parapet with my men, and the first thing I noticed after the firing ceased was three or four vessels of whiskey with tin cups attached."

General Bell further testifies that he had these vessels overturned to prevent his troops from getting at the liquor, and that General Forrest galloped to the fort almost immediately after the Confederates had gained an entrance and ordered the firing to cease. *"The captured prisoners were then detailed to bury their dead.* Between sunset and dark we moved out with our command and the prisoners, and camped about fifteen miles back in the country. The drunken condition of the garrison and the failure of Colonel (Major) Bradford to surrender, thus necessitating the assault, were the causes of the fatality. [In some recruiting papers in the author's possession, taken at Fort Pillow, this officer signs his name W. F. Bradford, Colonel.] The statements in relation to the alleged 'cruelty and barbarism' practised by Forrest's command are a tissue of lies from end to end."

Colonel Robert McCulloch, who commanded the left wing of the Confederates, now living at Clark's Fork, near Booneville, Missouri, and at this date Major General of the Missouri Division of United Confederate Veterans, swears that there was no massacre at Fort Pillow, and that nothing occurred during or after the engagement which, with due regard for fairness and the truth of history, could be construed into a massacre. "Not a gun was fired, nor a prisoner or non-combatant shot, to my knowledge or belief, after the surrender was made. I do solemnly swear that I was a member of the command of General N. B. Forrest, and was present at, and took part in, the capture of Fort Pillow, on April 12, 1864. That the testimony of certain witnesses made before the sub-committee of the United States Congress soon after the battle in 1864, stating that a massacre of the garrison took place after the fort was captured, is false. The presence of open whiskey barrels within the fort, together with the conduct of the troops after the Confederates had carried the works, showed plainly that a large proportion of the garrison were under the influence of liquor at the time of the assault. The Federal flag flying over the fort was not lowered until after the garrison had fled for refuge under the bluff immediately behind the works, and no surrender was made by any officer of the garrison. As the Federal soldiers rushed for the bluff they carried their guns with them, and many of them turned and fired at us as they retreated, and some continued to fire from the crowd below the bank."

Colonel C. R. Barteau, one of Forrest's most gallant and trusted subordinates, at present (1899) practicing law in Memphis, Tennessee, commanded the Second Tennessee in Bell's brigade, and went over the works with his soldiers. It was from his troops that the detail of about two hundred men was made to take position below the bank near Cold Creek ravine. In his affidavit he statees that a number of the Federals, after others had surrendered, continued to fight beneath the bluff until they were shot down. "They were in a frenzy of excitement or drunken delirium. Some even, who had thrown down their arms, took them up again and continued firing. Some of my own men had to take down the flag. [Private John Doak Carr, who died in 1897, at Hartsville, Tennessee.] The Federals did not do it, nor at any time make a surrender. During the truce they openly defied us from the breastworks to come and take the fort. All was done that could be done by General Forrest and his subordinates to save unnecessary loss of life and protect all who surrendered as soldiers in good faith. General Forrest deprecated the great slaughter that had taken place, and I heard him tell the prisoners it was the fault of their officers. The prisoners were placed in my charge, to be taken to Tupelo. Almost without exception they blamed their officers for the great loss of life. They told me that they had been led to believe that if they surrendered they would be killed by Forrest, and they were surprised and gratified at their humane treatment. On the route south, to relieve their fatigue, I had my men dismount at times and let the prisoners ride."

Major Charles W. Anderson was at the time of the fight Captain and Acting Adjutant General of. the command. He now resides at Florence, in Rutherford County, Tennessee, and is President of the Confederate Veterans of that state. As he took such a prominent part in the encounter which occurred beneath the bluff, his affidavit is given in full:

"I, Charles W. Anderson, of Florence, Rutherford County and State of Tennessee, do solemnly swear that I was at the time Captain of Cavalry and Acting Adjutant-General on the staff of General N. B. Forrest, and was the only member of the staff with him at the capture of Fort Pillow, April 12, 1864. Before the assault on the works I was temporarily placed in command of three companies of dismounted men from McCulloch's brigade, and ordered to take position on the face of the bluff just below the fort, and prevent the landing of steamers (then approaching) during truce.

"When Forrest's last and imperative demand for immediate surrender was refused, the general in person ordered me to 'hold my position on the bluff, prevent any escape of the garrison by water, to pour rifle-balls into the open ports of the *New Era* when she went into action, and to *fight everything blue betwixt wind and water until yonder flag comes down.*'

"When driven from the works, the garrison retreated towards the river, with guns in hand, and firing back, and as soon as in view we opened fire on them, and continued it rapidly until the Federal flag came down, when firing was stopped at once, the detachment ordered back to their regiment, and in less than two minutes after the flag came down I joined the general inside of the works.

"To the best of my knowledge and belief it did not exceed twenty minutes from the time our bugles sounded for the assault until the fort was in our possession and firing had ceased on every part of the ground.

"I further swear that six cases of rifle ammunition were found on the face of the bluff, in the immediate rear of the fort, with tops removed and ready for immediate distribution and use; also that about two hundred and seventy-five serviceable rifles and carbines were gathered up between the water's edge and the brow of the bluff, where they had been thrown down by the garrison when they found the gunboat *New Era* had deserted them and escape impossible. As my command did the most destructive as well as the very last firing done at Fort Pillow, the testimony of certain witnesses made before a sub-committee of the United States Congress, that a massacre of the garrison took place after capture, is false, and I further swear that to the best of my knowledge and belief the heavy loss in killed and wounded during their retreat was alone due to the incapacity of their commander, the drunken condition of the men, and the fatal agreement with and promise of Captain Marshall of the *New Era* to protect and succor them when driven from the works.

"CHARLES W. ANDERSON

"State of Tennessee, ⎱
County of Rutherford ⎰

"Personally appeared before me, W. H. Hindman, Notary Public of Rutherford County and State of Tennessee, Charles W. Anderson, of said County and State, who makes oath to the facts set forth in the above statement this February 23, 1898.

"W. H. HINDMAN,
"Notary Public of Rutherford County"

HEADQUARTERS FORREST'S CAVALRY
l.   Tupelo, Mississippi, *June* 28, 1864

SOLDIERS—After a long and laborious campaign, the major-general commanding deems it an appropriate occasion to address you a few words of recapitulation, acknowledgment, and congratulation. About the 15th of February last the campaign which so gloriously terminated at Tishomingo Creek was inaugurated. Major-General Sherman, with a large and well appointed army, undertook to penetrate the central counties of Alabama and Mississippi. His object was avowedly to capture Selma and Mobile, and to desolate that productive region of country from which the granaries of a large section of the Confederacy were supplied. Generals Smith and Grierson had their duties assigned them, and were to act a conspicuous part in the work of spoliation and piracy. With a large co-operating cavalry force, thoroughly armed and equipped, they were to descend through northern Mississippi, carrying fire and sword with them. On they came like a blighting sirocco. At West Point you met them. There you threw yourselves across the rich prairies, a living bulwark, to stay the desolating tide. Compared with the enemy, you were but few in numbers, but every man became a hero, for all seemed impressed with the importance of the momentous struggle. You proved yourselves equal to the expectations of the country. You met the proud and exultant enemy. The result is known to the world; you drove him howling back in ignominy and shame, broken and demoralized. Sherman's campaign was thus brought to an abrupt conclusion, and Mississippi and Alabama saved. The victory was a glorious one, and with heartfelt pride the general commanding acknowledges your unexampled gallantry. This great work was accomplished by Colonel Bell's brigade, commanded by Colonel Barteau, Colonel McCulloch's and Colonel Forrest's brigades. But great as was this victory, it is not without its alloy. The laurel is closely entwined with the cypress, and the lustre of a brilliant triumph is darkened by the blood with which it was purchased. It was here that Colonel Barksdale gave up his life, a willing sacrifice, upon the altar of his country. He fell in front of the battle, gallantly discharging his duty. He sleeps, but his name is imperishable. Here, too, fell the noble brother of the general commanding, Colonel Jeffrey E. Forrest. He was a brave and chivalrous spirit, ever foremost in the fight. He fell in the flower of his youth and usefulness, but his dying gaze was proudly turned upon the victorious field which his own valor had aided in winning. Peace to the ashes of these gallant young heroes.

After a short repose you were called to a new theatre of action. By long and rapid marches, which you endured without murmur or complaint, you found yourselves upon the waters of the Ohio, sweeping the enemy before you wherever you met him, capturing hundreds of prisoners, valuable and needed stores in the quartermaster's and ordnance departments, while securing for yourselves a character for endurance, valor, and efficiency which might well excite the envy of the most famous legions in military history. At Fort Pillow you exhibited the same conspicuous gallantry. In the face of a murderous fire from two gunboats and six pieces of artillery on the fort, you stormed the works and either killed or captured the entire garrison, a motley herd of negroes, traitors, and Yankees. This noble work was accomplished by parts of Chalmers's and Buford's divisions, composed of Bell's and McCulloch's brigades, commanded by Brigadier-General Chalmers; and for his gallantry on this and other occasions General Chalmers deserves the enduring gratitude of his countrymen. For the exhibitions of high soldiery bearing on these fields you have earned from your country and its government the most grateful and well-deserved plaudits. Congress has voted you complimentary resolutions of thanks and tendered you a nation's homage.

But the crowning glory of your great deeds has yet to be named. Tishomingo Creek is the brightest leaf in your chaplet of laurel. General Grierson, not satisfied with his test of your prowess, united with General Sturgis, at the head of one of the best-appointed forces ever equipped by the Yankee nation— complete in infantry, cavalry, artillery, and supply-trains. They came forth with threats of vengeance towards you and your commander for the bloody victory of Fort Pillow, made a massacre only by dastardly Yankee reporters. Again you responded bravely to your general's call. You met the enemy and defeated him. Victory was never more glorious, disaster never more crushing and signal. From a proud and defiant foe, *en route* to the heart of your country, with declarations both by negro and white troops of "no quarter to Forrest or his men," he became an enemy beaten, defeated, routed, destroyed. You drove the boasted minions of despotism in confused flight from the battle-field. Seventeen guns, 250 wagons, 3000 stands of arms, 2000 prisoners, and killed and wounded 2000 more are the proud trophies which adorn your triumphant banners. The remainder is still wandering in the bushes and bottoms, forever lost to the enemy. There were not over three thousand of you who achieved this victory over ten thousand of the enemy. Had you never before raised an arm in your country's cause, this terrible overthrow of her brutal foe would entitle you to her deepest gratitude. Again your general expresses his pride and admiration of your gallantry and wonderful achievements. You stand before the world an unconquerable band of heroes. Whether dismounted, and fighting shoulder to shoulder like infantry veterans, or hurling your irresistible squadrons on the flying foe, you evinced the same courageous bravery.

Soldiers! amid your rejoicing do not forget the gallant dead upon these fields of glory. Many a noble comrade has fallen, a costly sacrifice to his country's independence. The most you can do is to cherish their memory and strive to make the future as glorious as you and they have made the past.

To Brigadier-General Buford, commanding division, my obligations are especially due. His gallantry and activity on the fields were ever conspicuous, and for the energy displayed in pursuing the enemy he deserves much of his government. He has abundant cause to be proud of his brigade commanders, Colonels Lyon and Bell, who displayed great gallantry during the day. Colonel E. W. Rucker was prompt in the discharge of every duty. His brigade displayed conspicuous steadiness during the fight. Colonel W. A. Johnson, commanding brigade from General Roddey's command, merits notice for his coolness and bravery on this occasion, and for the valuable services rendered by his troops. Nor can the general commanding forget to mention the efficient aid rendered by the artillery, commanded by Captain John W. Morton. He moved rapidly over the roughest ground and was always in action at the right time, and his well-directed fire dealt destruction in the masses of the enemy. The general commanding also takes pleasure in noticing the intelligent alacrity with which Major C. W. Anderson, Captain W. H. Brand, Lieutenants Otey, Donelson, Titus, and Galloway, of my staff, conveyed orders to all parts of the field. They were ever near my person, and were prompt in the discharge of every duty. Soldiers! you have done much, but there is still work for you to do. By prompt obedience to orders and patient endurance you will be enabled to repeat these great achievements. The enemy is again preparing to break through the living wall erected by your bosoms and big hearts. In the name and recollections of ruined homes, desolated fields, and the bleaching bones of your martyred comrades, you are appealed to again. The smoke of your burning homesteads, the screams of your insulted women, and the cries of starving children will again nerve your strong arms with strength. Your fathers of '76 had much to fight for, but how little and unimportant was their cause compared with yours. They fought not against annihilation, but simply to be independent of a foreign yet a constitutional and free government. You are struggling against the most odious of all tyranny, for existence itself, for your property, your homes, your wives and children, against your own enslavement, against emancipation, confiscation, and subjugation, with all their attendant horrors.

In conclusion, your commanding general congratulates you on the brilliant prospects which everywhere pervade our cause. The independence of the Confederate States is a fixed, accomplished, immutable fact. The ray of peace is glimmering like bright sunshine around the dark clouds. Be true to yourselves and your country a little while longer and you will soon be enabled to return to your desolate homes, there to collect together once more your scattered household gods.

By order of Major-General N. B. Forrest.

C. W. ANDERSON, Assistant Adjutant-General.

(*Official Records*, Series I, vol. xxxix, p. 228.)

m. In the desperate fighting of the 13th, 14th, and 15th during the battle at Harrisburg, the Confederate loss was extremely heavy. In Crossland's brigade this officer was wounded, and Colonel Harrison and Lieutenant Colonels Cage, Nelson, and Sherrill were killed, and Faulkner twice wounded. Crossland says: "The action of the 14th was the most severe and destructive ever encountered by the troops of this brigade, who were veterans in the service. Their loss was unprecedented. Nobly each man did his duty, not one failing to respond. There were no laggards or cowards; every man was keenly alive to the interest he had personally in the contest."

Crossland reports that he had 800 men on the field. Deducting the horse-holders, 600 troops of this brigade went into action, of which number 276, or 46 per cent, were killed or wounded. Only 30 were reported missing.

The loss in Crossland's brigade was not often surpassed during the war, and then only in those long continuous engagements which occupied one or more days; but in no battle of the war which lasted no longer than an hour and a half (the time the troops were engaged at Harrisburg) was there such great loss.

Of the remnant of General Morgan's Kentucky cavalry, 80 in number, who arrived upon the field just before the engagement, under the command of Captain Campbell, 5 were killed, 19 wounded, and 2 missing, or 30 per cent. Mabry went into the charge with 750 men and left 33 per cent upon the field in killed and wounded. Bell's brigade lost 47 killed, 353 wounded, and none missing. Four of his field officers—Colonel Isham Harrison, Lieutenant Colonel John B. Cage, Lieutenant Thomas M. Nelson, and Major Robert C. McKay—were killed.

General Forrest, in closing his report of this sanguinary affair, pays an eloquent and touching tribute to those who perished there: "The battle of Harrisburg will furnish the historian a bloody record, but it will also stamp with immortality the gallant dead and the living heroes it has made. Prominent among the former are the names of Colonel Isham Harrison, Lieutenant-Colonel Thomas M. Nelson, Lieutenant-Colonel John B. Gage, Lieutenant-Colonel L. J. Sherrill, and Major Robert C. McKay will shine in fadeless splendor. They were lion-hearted officers. It was a sad blow that struck down these gallant spirits. In unselfish devotion to the cause and high courage they leave no superiors among men. Their noble natures and ardent patriotism, it is to be hoped, will find in the soldier's grave that peace for which their country has thus far struggled in vain, and for the achievement of which they have sacrificed their lives. Future generations will never weary of hanging garlands upon their graves."

n. Forrest's command, only a portion of which accompanied him on this expedition, was constituted as follows:

Chalmers's Division—McCulloch's Brigade, Colonel Robert McCulloch commanding: Second Missouri Cavalry, Lieutenant Colonel R. A. McCulloch; Willis's Texas Battalion, Lieutenant Colonel Leo Willis; Seventh Mississippi Cavalry (formerly First Mississippi Partisans), Lieutenant Colonel Samuel M. Hyams; Fifth Mississippi Cavalry, Major William Gaston Henderson; Eighth Mississippi Cavalry, Colonel William L. Duff; Eighteenth Mississippi Cavalry, Colonel Alexander H. Chalmers. Rucker's Brigade (formerly Neely's), Colonel Edward W. Rucker commanding: Forrest's (old) Regiment, Lieutenant Colonel D. C. Kelley; Seventh Tennessee, Colonel W. L. Duckworth; Fourteenth Tennessee, Colonel J. J. Neely; Fifteenth Tennessee, Colonel F. M. Stewart; Twelfth Tennessee, Lieutenant Colonel J. U. Green.

Buford's Division—Lyon's Brigade, Brigadier General H. B. Lyon commanding: Third Kentucky Cavalry, Colonel G. A. C. Holt; Seventh Kentucky, Colonel Ed. Crossland; Eighth Kentucky, Lieutenant Colonel A. R. Shacklett; Twelfth Kentucky (Faulkner's), Colonel W. W. Faulkner. Bell's Brigade, Colonel T. H. Bell commanding; Second Tennessee, Colonel C. R. Barteau; Nineteenth Tennessee, Colonel J. F. Newsom; Twentieth Tennessee, Colonel R. M. Russell; Twenty-first Tennessee (formerly Sixteenth), Colonel A. N. Wilson.

o. In justice to the memory of the gallant Cheatham it should be stated that, as shown by the following letter from Governor Harris, the order which General Hood sent him was not delivered by the staff-officer to whom it was entrusted until too late for General Cheatham to have executed it as directed:

Governor James D. Porter:

DEAR SIR—General Hood, on the march to Franklin, spoke to me in the presence of Major [Lieutenant Colonel A. P.] Mason [Assistant Adjutant General, Army of Tennessee] of the failure of General Cheatham to make the night attack at Spring Hill, and censured him in severe terms for his disobedience of orders. Soon after this, being alone with Major Mason, the latter remarked that "General Cheatham was not to blame about the matter last night. I did not send him the order." I asked if he had communicated the fact to General Hood. He answered that he had not. I replied that "it is due General Cheatham that this explanation should be made." Thereupon Major Mason joined General Hood and gave him the information. Afterwards General Hood said to me that he had done injustice to General Cheatham, and requested me to inform him that he held him blameless for the failure at Spring Hill; and on the day following the battle of Franklin I was informed by General Hood that he had addressed a note to General Cheatham assuring him that he did not censure him with the failure to attack.

Very respectfully,

ISHAM G. HARRIS

MEMPHIS, Tennessee, *May* 20, 1877

(*Battles and Leaders of the Civil War,* vol. iv, p. 432)

p. Bearing upon the same theme, he wrote the following:

HEADQUARTERS FORREST'S CAVALRY CORPS
WEST POINT, Mississippi, *March* 18, 1865.

Colonel E. Surget, Assistant Adjutant-General:

COLONEL—I have the honor to state that a few days since I directed Brigadier-General Wright to order out of west Tennessee a number of officers purporting to have authorities to raise troops between the ages of eighteen and forty-five years. In reply I received from General Wright a letter, an extract from which I respectfully enclose. I, of course, was not aware that Colonel ——, or any one else, held authority from the lieutenant-general commanding to raise new commands in west Tennessee, and from a conversation had with him am not yet satisfied that they have such orders from department headquarters. In regard to Colonel ——, I desire to say that he was a friend and fellow-townsman of mine before the war, a lawyer, and an out-and-out war man. He raised a regiment, fell out with General Bragg at Shiloh, got out of his command, and has done nothing since. He has been ostensibly engaged since 1862 in raising a regiment. He has not succeeded, nor do I believe, even under the most favorable circumstances, he ever will succeed. I hope, therefore, that all such officers may be ordered to report to department headquarters, that the authorities given them may be revoked, and they be put in the service. Colonel —— is a stout, able man, has played around long enough, and it is due to himself, his family, and the country that he should go into the army, and into the ranks if he can do no better. I herewith enclose a letter to the honorable Secretary of War, which I hope the lieutenant-general commanding will endorse and forward. If men engaged in raising commands were ordered into the ranks, and all squads and unattached companies not regularly in the service were outlawed, we would get ten men to fill up our old commands where we now get one. Those we could not run down and catch, the Federals would drive out to us. At any rate, we would rid ourselves of the odium attached to their paternity, and would not by the people be held responsible for their acts of lawlessness and crime. I do not for a moment question the motives of the honorable Secretary of War or the lieutenant-general commanding in giving these authorities, for every one is naturally desirous of increasing our strength, and willing to do almost anything to accomplish that end. It is not the authority itself, but the abuse of it, which is complained of, and in giving them the benefit of my experience and observation as to practical results, I hope I shall not be deemed officious, or as assuming to myself superior judgment in such matters; but I speak truly when I say that whenever a paper of the kind is presented to me I can but regard it as an exemption from duty for the war, a license to plunder, and a nest-egg of desertion, all of which is chargeable, not to the measures adopted to increase the strength of our army, but to the men, who not only fail to make good their representations and promises in raising additional troops for the army, but are actually creating uncontrollable currents of desertion, which are rapidly depleting commands already in the field.

I am, Colonel, very respectfully, your obedient servant,

N. B. FORREST

q. General Forrest made no official report of the campaign in Alabama in 1865. I have been unable to obtain a roster of his entire command at this time. In November, 1898, in answer to an inquiry on this subject addressed to the War Department at Washington, I received the following: "A report of Chalmers's division, Forrest's Cavalry, dated at Pickensville, Alabama, March 24, 1865, shows the following effective total:

Escort	64
Armstrong's brigade	1432
Adams's brigade	1077
Starke's brigade	1013
Hudson's battery	62
Total	3648

"As Chalmers's escort, Adams's and Starke's brigades, and Hudson's battery took no part whatever in the fighting with Wilson's column, it would leave only Armstrong's men with Forrest in this campaign. A report of Ross's brigade, Jackson's division, dated March 25, 1865, shows present an effective total of 328. There is no available official report of Bell's brigade, of Jackson's division, except one dated May 23, 1865, which shows present an effective total of 984. This would make Jackson's division number an effective total of less than 1500, none of whom, however, took part with Forrest in contesting Wilson's advance in front of Selma."

r. In the engagement at Sacramento, Kentucky, in 1861, Forrest was unhorsed in a running hand-to-hand fight. His horse went down after colliding with that of a Union officer with whom he was engaged in personal combat, but it is not known whether the general's horse was killed or wounded. At the first battle of Fort Donelson he had two horses killed under him, and one of these received seven bullet wounds before it fell. The second horse was wounded, but not seriously enough to compel Forrest to dismount. Later in the action a cannonball passed through the belly of the animal, just behind Forrest's leg, killing the horse instantly. On Tuesday, April 8, 1862, at Monterey, on the retreat from Shiloh, his horse was mortally shot in the charge which he led, and in which he was severely wounded in the hip. The animal lived long enough to bear his rider safely out of this great danger, and then fell to the earth from loss of blood. At Munfordville, Kentucky, during the Perryville campaign, Forrest was again unhorsed, he having his shoulder dislocated by the accident. In the second engagement at Dover, in 1863, Forrest had two horses killed under him. At Thompson's Station, Roderick, one of his famous war horses, was killed; and in the pursuit of Streight, in April and May of that same year, he had three horses shot. At Chickamauga, Highlander was killed, and at Rossville, the day after the battle of Chickamauga, his horse was shot through the neck while he was leading the charge with a detachment of Armstrong's brigade. The blood spurted out, and Forrest, realizing that the horse would bleed to death before he could complete the attack unless the hemorrhage was stopped, leaned forward and thrust his finger into the wound, thus controlling the hemorrhage. The animal bore his rider safely through the fight, when, his rider dismounting, the hemorrhage recurred and the horse soon expired. At Okolona, Mississippi, the horse he was riding was several times wounded and fell dead. A second horse was killed here, and Forrest continued the fight and pursuit on King Philip, a large dapple-gray animal, as sluggish as a dray horse until he heard firing, and then he was all excitement. King Philip was wounded at Okolona, and several times after that, but survived and was with Forrest at the surrender in 1865. At Fort Pillow two horses were killed under Forrest and a third wounded. At Plantersville his horse was wounded, but not mortally. At Selma, Alabama, another horse was shot.

INDEX

603